Social Work in Juvenile and Criminal Justice Settings

Third Edition

Social Work in Juvenile and Criminal Justice Settings

Edited by

ALBERT R. ROBERTS, PH.D., D.A.B.F.E., D.A.A.E.T.S.

Diplomate, American Board of Forensic Examiners
Diplomate, American Academy of Experts in Traumatic Stress
Professor of Criminal Justice and Social Work
Administration of Justice and Interdisciplinary Criminal Justice Programs
Director, Certificate Program in Crisis Management and Criminal Justice
Rutgers-the State University of New Jersey
Livingston College Campus, Piscataway, New Jersey

and

DAVID W. SPRINGER, PH.D.

University Distinguished Teaching Professor
Associate Dean of Academic Affairs
School of Social Work
Joint appointment as Professor of Psychology
Senior Faculty Research Associate
Interdisciplinary Center for Criminology and Criminal Justice Research
University of Texas at Austin

With a Foreword by

Barbara W. White, PH.D.

Dean and Centennial Professor in Leadership
School of Social Work
University of Texas at Austin
Past President, National Association of Social Workers
Past President, Council on Social Work Education

CHARLES C THOMAS • PUBLISHER, LTD.
Springfield • Illinois • U.S.A.

Published and Distributed Throughout the World by

CHARLES C THOMAS • PUBLISHER, LTD.
2600 South First Street
Springfield, Illinois 62704

© 2007 by CHARLES C THOMAS • PUBLISHER, LTD.

ISBN 0-398-07676-6

Library of Congress Catalog Card Number: 2006045645

With THOMAS BOOKS *careful attention is given to all details of manufacturing
and design. It is the Publisher's desire to present books that are satisfactory as to their
physical qualities and artistic possibilities and appropriate for their particular use.*
THOMAS BOOKS *will be true to those laws of quality that assure a good name
and good will.*

Printed in the United States of America
UB-R-3

Library of Congress Cataloging-in-Publication Data

Social work in juvenile and criminal justice settings / edited by Albert R. Roberts and
David W. Springer. -- 3rd ed.
    p. cm.
Includes bibliographical references and indexed.
ISBN 0-398-07676-6 (pbk.)
   1. Social work with criminals--United States. 2. Social work with juvenile
delinquents--United States. I. Roberts, Albert, R. II. Springer, David W.

HV7428.S5745 2007
364.3--dc22   2006045645

Contributors

ALBERT S. ALISSI, D.S.W., M.S.L.
Professor
School of Social Work
University of Connecticut
West Hartford, Connecticut

G. FREDERICK ALLEN, PH.D.
Professor
Central Michigan University
Department of Sociology and Social Work
Mt. Pleasant, Michigan

ARLENE BOWERS ANDREWS, PH.D.
Professor of Social Work and Director
Institute for Families in Society
University of South Carolina
Columbia, South Carolina

MIGDALIA BAERGA, L.C.S.W.
Mental Health Administrator
Administrative Office of the U.S. Courts
Office of Probation and Pretrial Services
Washington, DC

LESSIE BASS, D.S.W.
Associate Professor
School of Social Work
East Carolina University
Greenville, North Carolina

JENNIFER BECKER, M.S.W.
Doctoral Student
School of Social Work
Florida International University

PATRICIA BROWNELL, PH.D.
Associate Professor
Graduate School of Social Service
Fordham University of Lincoln Center
New York, New York

MICHAEL CLARK, M.S.W.
Director, Center for Strength-Based Strategies
Former Senior Juvenile Court Officer
30th Judicial Circuit Court–Family Division
Ingham County, Michigan

ELAINE P. CONGRESS, D.S.W.
Professor and Associate Dean
Fordham University
Graduate School of Social Service
New York, New York

GLORIA CUNNINGHAM, PH.D.
(Deceased)
Professor Emeriti
School of Social Work
Loyola University of Chicago
Chicago, Illinois

CATHERINE N. DULMUS, PH.D.
Associate Professor and Director
Social Work Research Center
School of Social Work
State University of New York at Buffalo

SOPHIA F. DZIEGIELEWSKI, PH.D.
Professor and Director
School of Social Work
University of Cincinnati
Cincinnati, Ohio

RICHARD FELDMAN, L.C.S.W.
Senior United States Probation Officer
Baltimore, Maryland

SUSAN HOFFMAN FISHMAN, M.S.W.
Executive Director
Women in Crisis
Hartford, Connecticut

SHELDON R. GELMAN, Ph.D.
Professor and Dorothy and David I.
*   Schachne Dean*
Associate Vice President for
*   Academic Affairs*
Wurzweiler School of Social Work
Yeshiva University
New York, New York

JAMES A. HALL, Ph.D.
Professor
School of Social Work
The University of Iowa
Iowa City, Iowa

MARION HUNSINGER, L.B.S.W.
Social Worker
Mental Health Unit
Kansas State Penitentiary
Lansing, Kansas

ANDRÉ IVANOFF, Ph.D.
Professor
School of Social Work
Columbia University
New York, New York

MARY S. JACKSON, Ph.D.
Professor
School of Social Work and
*   Criminal Justice*
East Carolina University
Greenville, North Carolina

SHERRY JACKSON, M.S.W.
Ph.D. Candidate
Florida State University
College of Social Work
Tallahassee, Florida

JEFFREY M. JENSON, Ph.D.
Bridge Professor of Children,
*   Youth, and Families*
Graduate School of Social Work
University of Denver
Denver, Colorado

H. WAYNE JOHNSON, M.S.W.
Emeritus Professor
School of Social Work
University of Iowa
Iowa City, Iowa

DENISE JOHNSTON, M.D.
Director, Center for Children of
*   Incarcerated Parents*
Eagle Rock, California

JOHNNY M. JONES, Ph.D.
Assistant Professor
College of Social Work
University of South Carolina
Columbia, South Carolina

KAREN S. KNOX, Ph.D.
Associate Professor and Director of
*   Field Placements*
School of Social Work
Texas State University – San Marcos
San Marcos, Texas

ELIZABETH S. MARSAL, Ph.D.
Assistant Professor
School of Social Work and Criminal Justice
East Carolina University
Greenville, North Carolina

C. AARON McNEECE, Ph.D.
Dean and Walter W. Hudson
Professor of Social Work
Florida State University
Tallahassee, Florida

KEVA M. MILLER, L.C.S.W.
Doctoral Student and Adjunct Professor
Graduate School of Social Service
Fordham University at Lincoln Center
New York, New York

CAROLYN NEEDLEMAN, Ph.D.
Professor
Graduate School of Social Work and
*   Social Research*
Bryn Mawr College
Bryn Mawr, Pennsylvania

JOAN PETERSILIA, PH.D.
Professor of Criminology and Criminal Justice
College of Social Ecology
University of California at Irvine
Irvine, California

CARRIE J. PETRUCCI, PH.D.
Assistant Professor
California State University, Los Angeles
School of Social Work
Los Angeles, California

DANIEL POLLACK, M.S.W., JD
Professor
Wurzweiler School of Social Work
Yeshiva University
New York, New York

CATHRYN C. POTTER, PH.D.
Associate Professor and Director of Research
Graduate School of Social Work
University of Denver
Denver, Colorado

MARTHA L. RAIMON, JD
Senior Associate
Center for the Study of Social Policy
Washington, DC

FRANK B. RAYMOND III, PH.D.
Dean and Professor Emeritus
College of Social Work
University of South Carolina
Columbia, South Carolina

ALBERT R. ROBERTS, PH.D., DABFE
Professor of Criminal Justice and Social Work
Faculty of Arts and Sciences
Rutgers – The State University of New Jersey
New Brunswick and Piscataway, New Jersey

BEVERLY J. ROBERTS, M.ED.
Director, Mainstreaming Medical Care
  Program
The Arc of New Jersey
North Brunswick, New Jersey

ERIK ROSKES, M.D.
Director
Forensic Treatment and Correctional Services
School of Medicine
Springfield Hospital Center
Sykesville, Maryland

BUSHRA SABRI, M.S.W.
Doctoral Student
School of Social Work
The University of Iowa
Iowa City, Iowa

DAVID SHOWALTER, L.M.S.W.
Former Associate Director
Mental Health Unit
Kansas State Penitentiary
Lansing, Kansas

RISDON N. SLATE, PH.D.
Chair of the Sociology and Criminology
Department and Professor of Criminology
Florida Southern College
Lakeland, Florida

NANCY J. SMYTH, PH.D.
Dean
School of Social Work
State University of New York at Buffalo
Buffalo, New York

DAVID W. SPRINGER, PH.D.
Associate Dean for Academic Affairs
University Distinguished Teaching Professor
The University of Texas at Austin
  School of Social Work
Austin, Texas

MARCIA SWARTZ, M.S.W.
Metropolitan Health Department
Nashville, Tennessee

BARBARA THOMLISON, PH.D.
Professor, Director of Institute for Children
  and Families at Risk
School of Social Work
Florida International University
Miami, Florida

HARVEY TREGER, M.S.W.
(Deceased)
Professor Emeritus
School of Social Work
University of Illinois at Chicago

STEPHEN J. TRIPODI, M.S.S.W.
Doctoral Student
The University of Texas at Austin School of
   Social Work
Austin, Texas

EDGAR TYSON, Ph.D.
Assistant Professor
College of Social Work
Florida State University
Tallahassee, Florida

KENNETH R. YEAGER, Ph.D.
Director, Outpatient Clinic and
Director of Quality Assurance
Department of Psychiatry, Ohio State
   University Medical Center

Foreword

In recent years there has been a surge of interest and evidence-based studies on social work practice in forensic settings, such as juvenile offender assessment and treatment programs, victim assistance and domestic violence intervention programs, and adult correctional rehabilitation and re-entry programs. This timely and thoroughly up-to-date third edition of a classic book provides valuable summaries of key issues, trends, program developments, and research findings on the most effective policies and programs in forensic settings. This book is timely because the number of men and women under some form of correctional supervision in the United States and Canada has reached epidemic numbers – approximately 7.5 million alleged and convicted offenders. There are also several million victims of violent crimes without access to woefully needed crisis intervention, trauma recovery services, cognitive-behavioral treatment, victim assistance, legal advocacy, victim compensation, case management, and other social services. In addition, as more and more inmates max out or are released on parole, they have to be better prepared for the transition to the community, including obtaining full-time employment, becoming involved with a local church and faith-based programs, building social relationships, coping with everyday stresses, reuniting with families, and gaining access to urgently needed social services. **This groundbreaking book provides the necessary blueprints and guidelines for best practices with crime victims as well as juvenile and adult offenders in institutional, community-based, diversion, and aftercare programs.**

Almost ten years ago, Charles C Thomas published the second edition of Social Work in Juvenile and Criminal Justice Settings, which became an essential guide for all forensic social work administrators and practitioners. As the number of incarcerated juvenile and adult offenders reached unprecedented proportions, it became clear that an updated edition of this work was critically needed. The result is practically a new book with half the book consisting of 16 brand new chapters, and the other chapters thoroughly updated. Professors Albert R. Roberts and David W. Springer called upon 50 of the most diligent and respected forensic social work scholars to contribute original chapters on the current state-of-the-art of evidence-based forensic social work. As a result, this third edition surpasses the two earlier editions in scope and content. This is the first all-inclusive, authoritative, exceptionally well-written volume on social policies and social work practices in both juvenile justice and criminal justice settings.

In Professors Roberts and Springer's overview chapter they eloquently document social work's mission toward respecting human dignity, accepting individual differences and believing in each individual's self-worth and potential for positive change. In response to the examination of forces and factors that enhance or inhibit creative solutions, the authors state:

We wrote chapters one and two, and compiled and edited the other 30 chapters, in full support of the social work profession's 107 years of dedication to serving oppressed, vulnerable, at-risk, and devalued groups. During the past century, the most neglected and devalued groups have been victims of violent crimes and criminal offenders. In the past two decades, professional social workers have made growing progress in advocating for and obtaining critically needed social services for juvenile offenders, adult offenders, and victims of violent crimes. However, the case, class, and legislative advocacy efforts of forensic social workers (also known as correctional social workers) have increased and decreased in cycles over the past century. Specialized training and standards for forensic social work practice are critically needed. Therefore, we highly recommend that our professional organizations, including NASW, CSWE, NAFSW, and SSWR, form a task force to draft forensic social work educational standards, and lobby for federal and state legislation that mandates a minimum of an MSW, DSW, or Ph.D. in social work and five years post-master's experience, plus 90 hours of specialized training in forensic assessments and treatment protocols in order to be a forensic social work or correctional social work supervisor. (Roberts & Springer, p. 18)

I commend the two editors, the 50 esteemed chapter authors, and the readers of their important work. When you read this book, you can rapidly focus on a neglected and sometimes forgotten group of vulnerable and oppressed individuals – juvenile and adult offenders – who desperately need our help, guidance, and support. As social workers, we dedicate our professional careers to helping vulnerable and oppressed individuals and groups. A major part of our social work mission is advocating for vulnerable clients, groups, and communities at the individual, group, community, and legislative levels. Professors Roberts and Springer, and their esteemed author team document the challenges, insights, experiences, and best practices of forensic social workers in beginning to meet the critical needs of vulnerable and at-risk populations. Furthermore, Professors Roberts and Springer express the hope that this third edition will stimulate debate and discussion. They are being humble. I firmly believe it is destined to be one of the foundations on which further forensic research and practices will be based in the important years ahead. **This book is a landmark achievement**.

BARBARA W. WHITE, Ph.D.
Dean and Centennial Professor in Leadership
School of Social Work;
University of Texas at Austin
Past President, National Association of Social Workers
Past President, Council on Social Work Education
Austin, Texas
July 26, 2006

Foreword to the Second Edition

The system established to deal with crime and justice in the United States is huge and complex, consumes billions of dollars annually, and affects millions of individuals and families. A look at the size and makeup of the correctional population provides one indicator of the nature and magnitude of the criminal justice problem. At mid year 1995, more than 1.5 million adults were confined in prisons and jails. The majority of persons were poor and a substantial number, in some states as many as 60 percent, were African Americans. Most were young and parents of dependent children and many were convicted on drug charges. Most new admissions to the system during the year were for nonviolent, economic-related crimes. More than five million adults were under correctional supervision with some groups affected more negatively than others. One out of every three African American males between the ages of 20 and 24 was under some form of correctional supervision, up from one out of every four only five years earlier.

The large and rapidly increasing correctional system population can be traced to several key factors. Foremost among these is the absence of public policies and programs that address major social problems, i.e., poverty, unemployment and the absence of work in many communities, hopelessness and despair, and the lack of opportunities for success that are the root causes of most illegal activity. Other factors include a willingness to use punishment as a means of addressing drug addiction and drug-related crime, politicians' perceptions that they must be seen as the toughest on crime in order to be elected to office, and the enactment of new laws that call for harsher punishment and longer sentences. No less important is the philosophical orientation toward the poor and racial minorities held by many persons in power. The lack of compassion for the poor and the willingness to label and define entire communities as the "underclass" and "endangered species" help create an atmosphere of fear of these groups. They also support the mindset that some groups are dispensable, undeserving, and beyond help and need to be separated from the rest of society.

If we continue to move along the same path established by the enactment of punitive social welfare reform measures and tough criminal justice legislation, the future can be expected to bring more of the poor and other disadvantaged groups into the criminal justice system and the custody of the state. It is not possible, however, to process all of the poor through the criminal justice system, nor is it wise or economically sound to label and stigmatize entire groups of people for life, or to lock up more and more people for longer periods of time. Research studies and policy impact analysis indicate that more prisons and harsher punishments do not prevent crime, lower recidivism, reduce fear of crime, or restore crime victims. Ongoing punishment and humiliation of the most vulnerable populations of society are likely to lead not only to widespread rebellion in prisons and jails could be better spent on meeting other social needs such as education for children and health services for the elderly.

The promotion of safe communities and the well-being of children and families command a different orientation and vision at the highest levels of public policy making. The problem of crime and the administration of justice, however, is not just a matter of enforcing laws but also one of providing programs and services that meet common human needs, address human behavior problems and improve social and economic conditions. Social workers and other human service professional are needed as active and willing partners in shaping and directing a different kind of criminal justice system. Envisioned is a system wherein justice and fairness, social and behavioral understandings, empirical research, practical realities, and ethical standards are as important as political considerations.

Meaningful social work partnerships depend heavily on professional endorsement of criminal justice as an important area of social work advocacy and practice and the educational preparation of social workers for practice in criminal justice settings. During the latter half of the twentieth century, however, social workers and established social services organizations have overlooked the needs of individuals and families involved in the criminal justice system. Social workers have had minimal involvement in providing social services for prisoners or their families, in advocating for changes in the criminal justice system, and in establishing correctional family programs. Only about one dozen schools of social work prepare students to work in criminal justice and social work degrees are not required to provide social services in most prisons, jails, courts, and community programs.

Social Work in Juvenile and Criminal Justice Settings is an excellent resource for helping social workers understand why the social work profession and other social and behavioral scientists should be involved in criminal justice and the history and reasons for periods of both intense interest and limited or noninvolvement in the past. The primary thrust of this inspirational and very timely volume is that justice social workers, juvenile justice specialists, correctional counselors, and victim advocates have important roles in criminal justice and can be effective in rehabilitation and restoration.

This pathfinding and extraordinarily comprehensive work critically examines the most salient issues, policies and program developments related to helping both persons who commit crime and victims of crime. Dr. Roberts and the other contributing authors give the reader insight into traditional and newly emerging areas of criminal justice practice and concerns and provide many illustrations of how to implement reform legislation and develop quality services. Family programs in prison, services for battered women, police social work, and wilderness programs for juveniles are among the featured topics. The chapters are well written and instructive and highly appropriate for use as both a major text for courses focused on social services in criminal justice and as assigned readings in more general social policy or social work practice courses. This is clearly the best single source on social work in criminal justice settings as well as a valuable resource for the many professionals who have responsibility for formulating and carrying out the mandates of the criminal justice system.

CREASIE FINNEY HAIRSTON, PH.D.
Dean and Professor
Jane Addams College of Social Work
University of Illinois at Chicago Circle
Chicago, Illinois

Foreword to the First Edition

Social Work as a profession is a twentieth century development, but it has a long legacy in private philanthropy and religious movements. The "Good Samaritan" (Luke 10: 30–37) was only one example during ancient times of compassion for less fortunate people that can be traced from primitive man to the present day. The monasteries provided services to children and minor offenders through the Middle Ages. Welfare programs began in England on a small scale after Henry VIII closed the monasteries in 1636 to 1639. Concern for the welfare of children and minor offenders was included in the Elizabethan Poor Law of 1601, which made use of the "bridewells" begun in 1557 to house debtors, dependent children, and others who needed governmental care. In 1648, concern for children in trouble was shown by the establishment of a home for wandering children in Paris by St. Vincent de Paul and the establishment of a church-affiliated institution in Milan to house boys with behavior problems. Pope Clement XI established the Hospice di San Michele (House of St. Michael) in 1704, in Rome, to care for children now referred to as "delinquent". That institution still stands and is still used for its original purpose. While there had been places for detention, including rooms in the ancient temples, there were jails and private prisons from the twelfth through the eighteenth centuries, prior to the beginning of prisons as they are known today.

The first prison was introduced at Simsbury, Connecticut, in 1773, when an old copper mine was converted into an institution for detaining "criminals"; George Washington used it as a military prison. In 1787, the Quakers started the Philadelphia Society for Alleviating the Miseries of the Public Prisons. The goal of the Society was to improve the sad plight of convicts by advocating that imprisonment in solitary confinement be substituted for the death penalty and physical torture. As a result, the "penitentiary movement" began with the Walnut Street Jail in 1790. The name of the Philadelphia Society was changed to the Pennsylvania Prison Society in 1887.

John Howard (1726–1790) and Elizabeth Gurney Fry (1780–1845) initiated lay visiting in England's jails and prisons that marked the beginning of private social work in prisons. Fry was known for lending material aid to individual prisoners, while John Howard was most concerned with improving the overall prison condition. The Correctional Association of New York was formed in 1844. The Prisoners' Aid Association of Maryland was formalized in 1869, but its beginnings went back to 1829, when the rector of St. Paul's Church in downtown Baltimore provided food and other assistance to men leaving the penitentiary. The Massachusetts Correctional Association was established in 1889 as the John Howard Society. The first John Howard Society had been established in England in 1866. Since that time, there have been prisoners' aid societies functioning around the world that handle all probation and parole functions in many countries.

A group of Quakers opened a halfway house for women in New York City in the

1880s, which continues today as the Isaac T. Hopper House and now houses the American Correctional Association for Women. Settlement houses began to appear in London in the 1880s. The first settlement house in the United States was the "Neighborhood Guild" in New York City in 1887, an outgrowth of the London Movement founded in Toynbee Hall. The most significant and influential settlement house was Hull House, founded in 1889 by Jane Addams and Ellen Gates Starr. Addams and Starr rented a house built by Charles G. Hull at 800 South Halsted Street in Chicago. Although it was geographically replaced in January, 1961, by the University of Illinois at Chicago Circle, the original Hull House still remains as a museum, and in 1967 it was designated a national landmark. The present Jane Addams School of Social Work is a part of the University of Illinois.

Social work had its beginnings as a profession around 1904. Charles Booth participated in the Charity Organization Movement, studied social condition in London from 1886 to 1903, and his Life and Labour of the People of London, published in 1904, became a monumental contribution of the time, and others in England and America followed its tradition in social work. With Paul Kellogg, Charles Booth's most ambitious work was the Pittsburgh Survey in 1909 to 1914, financed by the Russell Sage Foundation. Summer training courses for charity workers were begun by the New York Charity Organization Society in 1898. By 1904, the first School of Social Work was established at Columbia University as a one-year program, then called the New York School of Philanthropy. As of 1919, the 15 Schools of Social Work had organized into the Association of Training Schools for Professional Social Work, including nine programs operating within university auspices and six independent schools. Adoption of a minimum curriculum had taken place by 1932. In 1935, the American Association of Schools of Social Work ruled that only those schools connected with universities could be accredited. By 1940, the Association required graduate-level education as part of all social workers' professional development. Social work had emerged as an accepted profession.

From the beginning, the field of corrections had been an anathema to professional social work. Problems of the poor, family services, child protective services, philanthropy, and general social welfare became the primary concern of social work. Some writers, such as Warner, Queen, and Harper, in 1935, date the beginning professional social work back to 1893, when settlement workers were trying to gain recognition just to be on the program of the National Conference of Charities and Correction. This group subsequently gained recognition and "blundered" into the emerging professionalism of social work.

Correctional work had always been part of philanthropy and preprofessional social work. As social work became recognized as a profession, however, the field of corrections was excluded from its purview as being beyond its concern. While professional social workers did work with families, settlement houses, low-income families, and the new child guidance clinics begun in Philadelphia in 1897, and worked with predelinquents and delinquents in that context, they were moving away from the criminal offender. In 1917, Mary Richmond's Social Diagnosis (published by the Russell Sage Foundation) established the guidelines and the norms for professional social work. It was aimed at, "those processes which developed personality through adjustments consciously effected, individual by individual, between men and their social environment." Among the dicta were that caseworkers worked with individual "cases," not large groups and – most damaging to corrections – the doctrine of "self-determination," which cannot function in an authoritative setting. The "constructive use of authority" was seen as withdrawing services when the individual became ineligible for any reason.

Professional social work had moved out of corrections. Attention continued in family problems and social welfare concerns, but the emphasis began to focus toward mental health. In 1921, the American Association of Social Workers was founded to provide an organizational base for professional social workers. In 1922, the Commonwealth Fund created scholarships for professional "Social Workers" to become assistants to psychiatrists in the mental health field, and this funding continued through 1928. With the coming of the Great Depression, social work was inundated with income maintenance problems, but continued its other functions in private Family Welfare Associations, the Child Welfare League of America, the National Federation of Settlements, and other private organizations, while governmental concerns primarily focused on poverty and income maintenance as a result of the Depression. In the meantime, social work remained away from corrections because of (1) the large caseloads, (2) the doctrine of self-determination that prevented them from working in an authoritative setting, (3) the definition of "authority" as a withholding of services, rather than as an authoritative person or agency, and (4) the belief that social work techniques should remain the same, regardless of the clientele and the circumstances of the host agency, which is an oversimplification in the correctional setting.

In 1945, Dr. Kenneth Pray, Director (frequently called Dean) of the School of Social Work at the University of Pennsylvania, was a major speaker at the annual meeting of the American Association of Social Workers in Chicago, where he had been elected president. His speech was revolutionary. Dean Kenneth Pray contended that professional social workers could and should work in corrections. All that was needed was an extra step in the early confrontations to "sell" or motivate" the client into wanting to help "reform" himself. The response was vitriolic. Traditional social workers engaged Dean Pray intensely and almost viciously. Some of the debate can be read in the issues of the Social Service Review after that 1945 meeting and several years afterward. His papers were subsequently published posthumously as Kenneth Pray; Social Work in a Revolutionary Age and Other Papers by the University of Pennsylvania Press in 1949. The debate continued for years.

In 1959, the famous thirteen-volume Curriculum Study was made under Werner W. .Boehm in order to consolidate the social work curriculum. Volume V on Education for Social Workers in the Correctional Field was done by Elliot Studt, who concluded that, "no separate specialty seems required in order to prepare social workers to take their place in correctional service." The last sentence was that, "professional education should elect and prepare students for early leadership responsibility." Even this writer entered the fray with an article on "The University Curriculum in Corrections" that appeared in the September, 1959, issue of Federal Probation. The article presented two possible curricula, one for corrections and another for social workers interested in corrections. The Council on Social Work Education had a five-year Corrections Project (1959–1964) financed by The Ford Foundation. Throughout its deliberations, the debate involved whether additional information should be added to the curriculum for corrections or whether it should not. Those in favor of adding new information referred to the problems resulting from Mary Richmond's Social Diagnosis in 1917. The project reached the same conclusions that Elliot Studt had made in the curriculum study, that no separate or additional information was needed.

An outgrowth of that project, however, was the Arden House Conference on Manpower and Training for Corrections, held June 24 to 26, 1964, at Harriman, New York, involving over 60 national organizations. Outgrowths from this conference included the Correctional Rehabilitation Study Act of 1965, the Prisoner's Rehabilitation Act of 1965, and Joint Commission on Correctional Manpower and Training, which was funded by The Ford Foundation, 1966 to 1969. The social work profession continued to maintain that no new information was needed to serve social workers working in corrections. This history of social work practice in corrections has been one of bouncing back and forth between expressing inability to work in an authoritative setting, to having state legislative committees demanding that the M.S.W. (master's degree in social work) be the basic requirement for the correctional position, particularly in probation. The push for the M.S.W. requirement was successful in several states, such as New York, Michigan, Wisconsin, Minnesota, and others. Some long-term probation officers were surprised when the M.S.W. probation workers in New York discharged persons who had violated probaion as "not eligible for probation," rather than recommending that the judge revoke probation and send them to the institution, as had been their custom. But the social work concept of "constructive use of authority" is based on ineligibility for service, rather than further punishment. Such conceptual misunderstandings have occurred between social workers in corrections and some correctional personnel and administrators with backgrounds in other areas.

This is the first book of major importance that covers professional social work in the field of corrections. It covers all the fields in which social work functions in just about the amount proportionate to their functioning in practice. The reentry of social work was first in the juvenile area, particularly in the court and the community, followed by adult probation. Parole took a little longer, as did medium and minimum security institutions for adults. The maximum security prison has been the last to experience this reentry. This book reflects this progression in its text and in its format. More than the first half of the book is devoted to social workers in the juvenile field, the point of reentry. Probation, parole, and court settings are discussed next. Finally, the maximum security prison is discussed as well, although there are more restrictive settings in some stronger maximum security institutions in which some of the examples used could not have taken place – the setting of the writers of this chapter was the Mental Health Unit of the Kansas State Penitentiary, rather than the maximum security unit. This fits into the scheme and reflects the progression of social work back into the correctional field as it actually did happen. The other three chapters in the prison section involved volunteers and family relations. In summary, then, this book reflects almost exactly the way social work came back into corrections and discusses the problems of working with authority, the problem of client self-determination, the problem of caseloads, and the problem of specialization in social work, as it relates to the entire field of corrections. Ellen Handler's excellent article (published in *Criminology: An Interdisciplinary Journal*, August, 1975) focuses on corrections and social work being "an uneasy partnership." This is only one example of the thorough breadth of literature that characterizess the support for this book.

Dean Kenneth Pray would have been proud to see this book after his being embroiled in turmoil and debate following his revolutionary speech in Chicago in 1945 when he said that social work could and should work in the field of corrections. As a participant in and a follower of the field of corrections and welcoming the assistance of any legitimate profession for many years of turbulent and frenzied efforts to stay even with the challenge, this writer is also proud of this book. It has been, in fact, "an uneasy partnership," but it should not have been. There are still many professionals working in practices based in the behavioral sciences who have difficulty in working with authority and want to "help the client help himself" and have other troubles in working with offenders. Even so, the number of people who can work comfortably in corrections is increasing — even in maximum security prisons — which are a rewarding observation after these many years of frustration. It is a gross disservice to the client for a professional to wait for the client to become "motivated" so he can "help him help himself" when that client is so "beat down" and angry that he will never achieve that kind of motivation. There are some who consider this kind of aloofness as downright immoral in a "helping" profession. There are now professional social workers who can talk about "agressive casework," "hard-to-reach groups," "reaching out," and motivating people "to help themselves." While this book is important to help social workers understand corrections, it is far more important that all correctional administrators and practitioners read it to gain an understanding about what the new professional social worker has to offer and how he or she functions. This book is the most significant contribution in many years to the mutually rewarding understanding of the alliance between professional social work and corrections.

VERNON FOX
Professor
School of Criminology
Florida State University
Tallahassee, Florida

Acknowledgments

Most important, we particularly thank close to half of our diligent author team for writing new original chapters according to our guidelines, and the other half of the team for thoroughly updating their chapters for this new edition. With half the chapters being brand new, this third edition becomes comprehensive, timely and up-to-date.

We are extremely grateful to Michael Thomas, President of Charles C Thomas Publisher, for motivating us to compile and edit a third edition because of the important changes to the field in the nine years since the second edition was published. Special thanks to the diligent editorial and production team under Michael Thomas' leadership, including Claire Slagle. A special acknowledgment is extended to Harris Chaiklin for incisive and useful editorial suggestions on Chapters 1 and 2. The systematic support throughout the editing and camera-ready copy preparation process for this book by Hollee Ganner, Diana Villarreal, and Kathleen Kelleher of The University of Texas at Austin is sincerely appreciated. The cover and other illustrations by Carole S. Roberts add a new dimension to the third edition so we applaud Carole for her creative contribution. David Springer would like to thank his wife Sarah for her steadfast support and encouragement. Al Roberts would like to thank his wife Beverly for wise counsel.

ALBERT R. ROBERTS. PH.D.
Kendall Park, New Jersey

DAVID W. SPRINGER, PH.D.
Austin, Texas

Contents

Social Work in Juvenile and Criminal Justice Settings

Section I

Evolving Trends, Policies, and Practices

Chapter 1

The Emergence and Current Developments in Forensic Social Work

Albert R. Roberts, David W. Springer, and Patricia Brownell

INTRODUCTION

Forensic social work assessment and treatment with crime victims, juvenile offenders, and convicted felons has been viewed by some as the weakest link of social work practice, and by others as a way to provide much needed services to large groups of poor, vulnerable, and neglected clients. There has been a growing concern in recent years regarding the increasing number of offenders and victims in urgent need of mental health treatment and social services; some of whom are at high risk of future violence if they do not receive the evidence-based interventions they urgently need. Social workers and other human service and health care professionals spend large parts of their careers helping vulnerable and at-risk populations. Thus, forensic social work seems to be a challenging and ideal way to advocate for social justice while facilitating assessments and improved psychosocial functioning among a large and vulnerable group of clients.

There are five trends that have emerged underscoring the critical need for forensic social work. (1) Prison sentences in the United States are much longer than in most other countries, and there are a disproportionate number of people of color currently incarcerated in federal and state prisons. (2) A significant percentage of juvenile and adult offenders (between 40% and 70%) have a mental health disorder. (3) According to the federal Office for Victims of Crime (OVC) (2005), in 2004, there were 24 million youths and adults ages 12 and over who were victims of crimes. In this same year, over 16 million services were provided thru federal- and state-funded victim service and victim-witness assistance agencies, and almost half (47.3%) of these victims were domestic violence victims. (4) According to the Bureau of Justice Statistics (2005) at the end of 2004, more than seven million adult offenders were under some form of correctional supervision including adult correctional institutions, juvenile correctional facilities, jails, detention centers, probation and parole agencies, or community diversion programs. The largest group of almost five million persons (4,916,480) were under the supervision of probation or parole agencies. (5) There has been a slow but steady growth in the number of forensic social work courses and continuing education workshops. The focus and content areas of these workshops and courses include the following:

- Child custody evaluations and assessments to determine whether parental rights of persons who are mentally ill, convicted felons, and/or abusive parents should be terminated;
- Risk assessments of offenders who are mentally ill and substance-abusing (i.e., MICA-mentally ill chemically addicted, also known as dual disorders), with special attention to their risk of future violence and repeat criminality;
- Assessment and treatment of juvenile and adult mentally ill offenders in the criminal justice system and forensic mental health units to help in treatment planning as well as planning for a safe discharge or parole date;

- preparation of presentence reports for juvenile court and criminal court judges;
- Assessment of dangerousness and likelihood of recidivism among convicted sex offenders;
- Crisis assessment, crisis intervention, and trauma treatment protocols and strategies with victims of violent crimes;
- Domestic violence policies and intervention strategies with battered women and their children;
- Batterers psychoeducational and group treatment protocols and intervention strategies;
- Assessment and treatment with suicide-prone juvenile and adult offenders;
- Motivational interviewing and other strength based treatment strategies with substance abusing clients;
- Multisystemic treatment for juvenile offenders and their families;
- Restorative justice policies and practices;
- Treatment engagement and retention among substance-abusing offenders; and
- Applying the Stages-of-Change and Transtheoretical Models to clinical treatment with criminal offenders.

A major challenge facing the future of forensic social workers is treatment engagement and retention of juvenile and criminal offenders receiving clinical treatment. Concern regarding challenges in attracting and retaining substance-abusing clients in treatment, for example, has led researchers to focus on motivation as a construct that may contribute to an enhanced understanding of treatment engagement and retention (Battjes, Gordon, O'Grady, Kinlock, & Carswell, 2003; Battjes, Onken, & Delany, 1999). Secondary analysis of two large national effectiveness studies found a positive relationship between adolescents' length of substance abuse treatment and their outcome (Hubbard et al., 1985; Sells & Simpson, 1979). Hubbard et al. (1985) also found that client motivation is a major factor in determining length of treatment involvement and, thereby, treatment success. More recently, Battjes et al. (2003) investigated factors that predict motivation among youth admitted to an adolescent outpatient substance abuse treatment program; findings revealed that factors involving various negative consequences of substance use emerged as important predictors of motivation, whereas severity of substance use did not.

Despite these advances, new research is needed to identify factors that impact retention and therapeutic engagement, with the need especially for research that examines the relationship between client outcomes and elements of the therapeutic process – namely, the treatment environment, client needs, and delivery of services (Battjes et al., 2003; Simpson, Joe, Rowan-Szal, & Greener, 1997). Additional concepts, such as those representing a client's stage of change and motivation (DeLeon, Melnick, Kressel, & Jainchill, 1994; Simpson & Joe, 1993) should also be integrated into a more comprehensive analytic model (Simpson et al., 1997). The importance of motivation and retention is underscored by the findings of a study by Lawendowski (1998) at the University of Mexico's Center on Alcoholism, Substance Abuse, and Addiction, which found that 50 percent of adolescent clients did not return after initial treatment and 70 percent terminated treatment prematurely. Additionally, Simpson et al. (1997) found that pretreatment motivation was a significant predictor of session attendance during early treatment among adult opioid addicts.

One theoretical framework relevant to motivation for engagement and retention in substance abuse treatment is the Transtheoretical Model (TTM). This model grew in response to dissatisfaction with simple behavioral models and the search for a more comprehensive approach to describe complex processes of human behavior change. Since its development, this model has been used extensively with practitioners, clinicians, and researchers in the field of addictions and drug use. The stages-of-change model is the most frequently applied construct of the TTM model, and it offers the most research concerning the validity of TTM constructs (cf. Prochaska, Norcross, Fowler, Follick, & Abrams, 1992; Prochaska, Velicer et al., 1994; Velicer, Norman, Fava, & Prochaska, 1999).

This model conceptualizes five stages-of-change that integrate processes and principles of change from a number of major theories (Prochaska & Norcross, 1999). The first stage is Precontemplation, in which there is no intention or motivation to change. People in this stage generally have no awareness of the problem or have greatly underestimated the seriousness of the problem. The second stage is Contemplation, in which there is awareness of a problem and a desire to overcome it, but no commitment to take the actions necessary to accomplish change. The third stage, Preparation, involves a decision to take action sometime in the near future, but a specific plan for accomplishing this goal is not present or has not yet been implemented. The fourth stage is Action, in which the individual makes changes in behavior and/or lifestyle and sustains those from one day to six months. The final stage, Maintenance, involves those activities necessary to maintain change and avoid relapse.

Progression through these stages is not expected to be linear and reversion to earlier stages is expected. Most clients move through the stages-of-change in a spiral pattern. Indeed, in one study (Prochaska & DiClemente, 1984), approximately 15 percent of smokers who relapsed went back to the precontemplation stage, and 85 percent went back to the precontemplation or contemplation stage. Preliminary data suggest that this framework is useful in providing services to minority clients (Longshore, Grills, & Annon, 1999), preventing alcohol exposed pregnancy after a jail term (Mullen, Velasquez, von Sternberg, Cummins, & Green, 2005), and guiding treatment with substance-abusing juvenile offenders (Springer, Rivaux, Bohman, & Yeung, in press), to name just a few.

Springer, Rivaux, Bohman, and Yeung (in press) examined factors that predict, and interventions that maximize, substance abuse treatment retention in three modalities among high-risk Anglo, Mexican American, and African American juvenile offenders. The study sample includes youth (N=211) who were discharged from probation supervision and who received substance abuse services through a CSAT-funded federal demonstration project. Among the juveniles in this sample, 56 (18%) were female and 255 (82%) were male. Approximately half (n=163, 52.4%) were Mexican American, one-quarter (n=88, 28.3%) were African American, and the remainder were Anglo (n=50, 28.3%). The key predictors examined included the stage-of-change (i.e., precontemplation, contemplation, preparation) in which a juvenile fell, various dimensions captured by the Comprehensive Addiction Severity Index for Adolescents, and other intervention status (probation, case management, and mental health treatment). The research questions were addressed using survival analysis statistical models that treated time from entry into substance abuse treatment to exit from substance abuse treatment as the outcomes. Among key findings were that females were 73 percent more

likely to leave day treatment relative to males; for each additional family problem ever experienced, Mexican American adolescents were 15 percent more likely to leave residential treatment compared to African American adolescents; and African American and Mexican American adolescents in the contemplation stage-of-change were 50 percent less likely to leave day treatment compared to Anglo adolescents.

While studies such as this speak to the progress that has been made in recent years, little research has been conducted that examines factors that predict treatment retention and engagement for substance-abusing female and minority offenders (Longshore, Grills, Annon, & Grady, 1998). The results from the Springer et al. (in press) study suggest that continued research is needed to explore the extent to which various treatment components – such as family therapy or motivational interviewing – contribute to substance abuse treatment engagement and retention among African American and Mexican American clients across the stages-of-change continuum.

Motivational interviewing is one well-known clinical application of the stages-of-change model that aims to move clients through the precontemplation and contemplation stages into the preparation and action stages. One other innovative intervention that has been used to enhance treatment readiness among offenders is called node-link mapping (Pitre, Dansereau, Newbern, & Simpson, 1998; Simpson, Chatham, & Joe, 1993; Simpson, Dansereau, & Joe, 1997). Simpson and colleagues have developed a series of treatment readiness interventions as part of the NIDA-supported CETOP (Cognitive Enhancements for the Treatment of Probationers) Project. These interventions are designed specifically for use with offenders early in the treatment process (precontemplation or contemplation), and can be used in groups of up to 35 participants.

Essentially, node-link mapping is a visualization tool, in which elements of ideas, feelings, actions, or knowledge contained within "nodes" (circles, squares) are connected to each other by "links" (lines) that are named to specify relationships between the nodes (Dees, Dansereau, & Simpson, 1997; Pitre, Dansereau, & Simpson, 1997). These maps are usually drawn by practitioners in collaboration with their clients during group or individual sessions.

Node-link mapping has produced modest positive effects across studies. Mapping appears to increase counseling efficiency, help clients focus their attention, facilitate the development of the therapeutic relationship, and increase counseling efficiency (cf. Czuchry, Dansereau, Dees, & Simpson, 1995; Dansereau, Joe, & Simpson, 1995; Pitre, Dansereau, & Simpson, 1997). Mapping has been found effective in outpatient methadone clinics (Dansereau, Joe, & Simpson, 1993) and in a residential criminal justice treatment settings that uses a modified therapeutic community approach with large-group sessions (Pitre, Dansereau, Newbern, & Simpson, 1998). More specifically, an examination by client subgroups indicates that the following types of individuals benefit the most strongly from mapping-enhanced counseling: clients with attention difficulties (Czuchry, Dansereau, Dees, & Simpson, 1995; Dansereau, Joe, & Simpson, 1995); cocaine-using opioid addicts (Joe, Dansereau, & Simpson, 1994); African American and Mexican American clients (Dansereau, Joe, Dees, & Simpson, 1996); and clients who do not have a high school degree or GED certificate (Pitre, Dansereau, & Joe, 1996) (cited in Pitro, Dansereau, & Simpson, 1997).

Treatment Readiness Manuals are available through Lighthouse Institute, which is a part of the Chestnut Health Systems, for a charge of $15 to $20 per manual (see more information at http://www.chestnut.org). The manuals are also available for downloading from the website of the Institute of Behavioral Research (IBR) of the Texas Christian University (TCU) (http://www.ibr.tcu.edu), where Simpson and his colleagues are based.

Using the stages-of-change model to proactively apply stage-matched interventions (such as motivational interviewing and node-link mapping) with criminal offenders brings with it the potential to increase treatment engagement, retention, and outcomes. Exploring this in research, and subsequently applying it in practice, is important to the future of forensic social work if we are to enhance the effectiveness of clinical interventions with offenders.

Social workers such as Michael Clark (see Chapter 25) also embolden the future of forensic social work. For those reading this introduction who might be considering entering the field of forensic social work, or for those already in the field who long for a sense of renewed energy to advocate for and empower their clients, we'd like to highlight the career of an exemplary forensic social worker – Michael D. Clark, who is the Director of the Center for Strength-Based Strategies. When Professor Roberts and Professor Springer approached Mr. Clark about contributing to this book, he was asked to share his story about how his career had evolved. Accordingly, his biographical narrative below is exactly that – a narrative – written in the first-person.

Michael D. Clark, MSW, LMSW, Director, Center for Strength-Based Strategies

It is humbling to be asked to describe my career as a forensic social worker. However, it would be a mistake to begin by speaking of my career path without first acknowledging two groups of people who have absolutely changed how I practice forensic social work. The first group involves mandated clients with whom I have been fortunate to meet and to have worked. The second group consists of authors and researchers who have brought their research into my world through publications. I am so thankful for the written word as these texts caused profound shifts in my social work practice. Allow me to describe my career path and the positions I've held by addressing these two groups.

The Mandated Clients

I must begin by mentioning the one probationer that died while under my probation supervision. Shot and killed in broad daylight, a homicide statistic listed on police blotters in Lansing, Michigan, during the 1980s. A life ended because of some capricious drug dispute. I'm sure he's all but forgotten now save those family members and friends who loved him, and oddly enough, me. I believe he would have been approaching his forties this year. As I think of how many serious cases "age out" of trouble, odds are he would have found his way out of the system by now, probably married with children and working a job or having started a small business in our community. But he's not – he didn't get the chance to "age out." It's a form of healing to write this exemplar as it allows one more chance to speak of this boy. I wish he had lived to know this kind of accolade. Surely many more died and I read their obituaries in the local papers but their deaths came after dismissal from my caseload. Their printed names and pictures would begin a shadowy malaise that often lasted for days. The University doesn't prepare you for the deaths. Nothing could I suppose. Sometimes I wonder if you pick the field of forensic social work or if somehow "it" picks you. Don't come into this field to help. Come into this field to *help people live.*

Even though I seemed to have worked mostly with males, it is two adolescent girls that I remember distinctly. One was a juvenile delinquent who had also suffered sexual victimization. She sat in a courtroom and suffered through endless retelling of her past abuse. First the prosecutor, then the defense attorney, then the police officer, then a psychologist, all recounting the horrors she had experienced in dispassionate and dehumanizing detail – and all seemingly justified in the pursuit of the "right" treatment plan. The scenario reminded me of the adage, "The road to hell is paved with good intentions." As the litany of her ill-treatment was recounted, her body language changed, growing increasingly angry until tears ran from her cheeks. Suddenly, she stood up with such force that her chair catapulted backwards. When she reached full height, she screamed, "YOU CAN ALL JUST SHUT UP! You stupid people could never know that *I am more than the worst thing that has ever happened to me!*" In the stunned silence that followed, I had come "up close and personal" with resiliency-in that instant resiliency had moved from classroom concept to the actual and tangible. As a forensic social worker, my fear was that the juvenile "system" was stymied in a learning curve that was far behind her and wasn't keeping pace.

The other female was a young adult who had successfully completed drug court programming. She had been brought in front of a focus group – a panel of professionals convened by the Department of Justice to investigate and compile "sanctions and incentives" that might aid drug court programming. She was asked by a panel member, "So many participants don't graduate from drug court programs, yet you did. You stayed with this year long program and finished successfully. Could you tell us: What sanction, in your view, helped to keep you 'on board' and in compliance with your drug court program?" The girl immediately threw her head back and laughed. It was through this belly-laughter that she replied, "No *SANCTION* helped me. I mean, c'mon, get real! Whenever I broke program rules and used drugs, I knew I was going to get caught by a urinalysis screen, so I would just go on the run until they caught me!" A stunned silence passed over this focus group as well. The Chair found his voice and stumbled to ask, "Well, ah, then, could you tell us what *did* work?" To this question, the girl immediately looked down at the floor. Silence ensued until tears began to stream down her cheeks. Finally, she looked up and said, "Because the staff never gave up. No matter how many times I got locked up, they never gave up. How can you run from that? I couldn't run from their love." I remember looking into myself and thinking, "*We're asking these kids the wrong questions.*"

Another courtroom drama brought still more hushed silence that engendered change. An adolescent boy committed to a juvenile drug court program had relapsed (again) as his urinalysis drug screen had tested positive for street drugs. He was back in the courtroom and was being pelted by professionals in the courtroom with a litany of his failures and faults. Detention was authorized (again). The mother rose in anger and yelled at the professionals assembled, "WHAT'S THE MATTER WITH YOU PEOPLE? You're the ones who should know better. *Do you really think you can punish my son into sobriety?*" As the saying goes, "the silence was deafening." The judge eventually found his voice to hush this mother and weakly tried to recover the collective pride of the drug court professionals assembled in the courtroom. Too late though, as the mother's indictment of the program's approach stood firm like the walls of Jericho – for this drug court program, designed to engender sobriety through therapeutic means and motivational incentives had experienced a form of negative "drift" – a slow receding lapse back to a sole focus on sanctions and punishment.

These epiphanies and "wake up calls" have not always occurred in courtrooms. As a newly-minted juvenile court officer, I remember visiting a juvenile residential facility with another officer to check up on a court ward under probation supervision. In an open campus setting, he was not in his "cottage" day room when we arrived, which sent the staff member scurrying to find him. It was believed he had "just left the building" and the staff member invited us along to walk the campus to find him – noting that he couldn't have gone far. As we threaded our way through a parking lot adjacent to the cottage, we quickly came upon him in a startling scene. Here was the boy, having opened a gas cap on a parked pick up truck, bent over "huffing" gasoline fumes for a noxious "high." Although my anger at this "violation" peaked immediately, I witnessed an almost unconscious split-second reaction by this residential staff member – one that I will never forget. He immediately gathered up the boy in his strong arms, wrapping him in almost a fatherly hug. As he kept the boy in this embrace he repeated, "*I'm not going to let you kill yourself Johnny. We're going to love you son. Love you 'till you can love yourself.*" The boy did not grapple or wrestle but allowed himself to be held. The staff member continued in almost a chant-like fashion, "*You are loved son. You are loved. You are loved.*" This time the silence that ensued was all mine. This unconditional love had been exhibited so quickly, I knew it came from a place beyond "treatment," beyond technique or theory. At that moment I realized that a great portion of forensic social work was an "inside job" that consisted not only of imparting discipline but also extending compassion for those that hurt – a deeply-held concern that emanates from within. How shortsighted to believe forensic practice all comes from knowledge and the building of requisite skills.

Flash forward to the present and my most recent client experience is one that has lingered for months. It occurred while serving as a Strengths consultant to a court program that sought better partnerships with parents. With the promise of anonymity, I interviewed a mother of a delinquent son and asked her what she thought of this staffing group. Her reply? "*I may not be as educated as some of these court workers, but from the way I see it, they do a whole lot of tellin' but very little askin'!*" I can't get her words out of my head. I may be in danger of oversimplification, but I feel her answer represents the absolute crux of what ails our field.

What about this field of forensic social work? I began my social work career at Michigan State University in East Lansing, Michigan at the height of the punishment decade in the early 1980's. In my senior year at Michigan State I was fortunate to be assigned to the Family Division of the Circuit Court for my field placement. When the practicum concluded I was hired by this court and took my oath as court officer immediately after graduation. I was overjoyed to be "in" but *what was I in for?* As a rookie juvenile probation officer, I was quickly "pounced" on by older probation agents who ridiculed my "social work" penchant for creating a helping alliance with probationers. I was angry that they would use the term "social work" to describe ineffective or indulging practice. Their advice was harsh, "You're not friends with *these people*. You come on hard – you can't save the world, these aren't friendships." My answer was one of "quiet defiance." I realized that I could not turn my back on my social work training as well as my own inner beliefs as to the type of helping relationship I should try to establish. Regardless of the jeers and the teasing, my approach has never changed. I held firm to my social work tenets and began to see success. Compliance seemed a good staring point, but what of behavior change? I soon noticed a complete absence of any tactical curiosity regarding positive behavior change. Why was the offender always blamed for lack of success?

The Researchers And Authors

I experienced the impact of this second group when I returned to Michigan State University for a Master of Social Work degree in 1990. I returned for graduate training in the hopes that I would be able to find and detail offender problems and pathologies with more sophistication and specificity. What I found was the exact opposite. I found the Strengths Perspective[1] and Solution-Focused Brief Therapy.[2] I was struck by the fundamental difference found in eliciting, amplifying and reinforcing someone's strengths and resources. Finding these positive approaches became the single greatest event in my career. After so much training in how offenders "fall down," my passions were ignited as I had discovered the science of "getting up." I have dedicated my professional life to bringing a Strengths Perspective into forensic work and encouraging methods that move the offender from the role of passive recipient to that of active participant.

Embracing a Strengths Perspective in a criminal justice world has been fraught with frustration. Criminal justice is a field that is unbalanced as it entertains only problems, failures, and flaws. Compliance is king while behavior change is often left wanting – viewed as something best left to others ("treatment"). I began to find inroads for using a Strength-based approach with my probation caseload and soon published articles detailing the application within juvenile delinquency.[3,4] I loved writing as it gave me a chance to put voice to all that I was learning – and in an odd sort of way, gave me a chance to apologize.

Practicing from a Strengths Perspective soon made me aware of the dangers of inflicting iatrogenic harm or harm committed in the act of helping. I felt the burden of all of the past assessment and probation plans that I had developed. Believing that I was "helping" and doing all that I had been taught, I know now I stole hope from those who could least afford it. It's an insidious injury we can impose on marginalized offenders. I can't tell you how many juvenile offenders and family members I brought into my office to develop a court report/probation plan. The harm began as I reviewed only what was wrong, broken, missing, and flawed. Strengths, past successes, indigenous resources,

1. Saleebey, Dennis. (ed.) (1992). *The Strengths Perspective in Social Work Practice.* New York: Longman.
2. Berg, Insoo Kim, & Miller, Scott. (1992). *Working with the Problem Drinker: A Solution-Focused Approach.* New York: W. W. Norton.
3. Clark, Michael D. (Spring 1985). "The Problem with Problem Solving: A Critical Review." *Journal for Juvenile Justice and Detention Serivces.*
4. Clark, Michael D. (June 1988). "Strength-Based Practice: The ABCs of Working with Adolescents Who Don't Want to Work with You." *Federal Probation Quarterly.*

or aspirations were ignored. As I would walk them to the lobby door, I realize now that by my sole focus on deficits, the problems for the family had *grown* during the office visit and their sense that they could overcome these problems had *shrunk*. This was the exact opposite of what I intended, yet sadly it was the maddening result of deficit-based work in the juvenile field. The redemption I had found with a strength-based practice became as empowering for me as it proved to be for my offenders.

I made progress in my probation department, and believe I influenced it for the better as well. I found a small group of like-minded practitioners and increased my skills. After a full year of advocacy, I was able to convince our court management to change a deficit-based family history form to one that was balanced between both problems and strengths. The old form was so bad; I often have groups review the old deficits form in my trainings as a good example of "what not to do." To gain more experience, I moved into a child welfare position and spent five years performing abuse and neglect casework. I was eventually appointed a Senior Juvenile Court Officer which included the duties of a Judicial Referee (Magistrate), holding preliminary hearings for our Judges in both delinquency and child welfare cases. My publications led to conducting workshops and that spiraled into a complete career change. I was taking so much time off that I had to choose between consulting and training and my work at the court. I left the court and formed the Center for Strength-Based Strategies, a research and technical assistance organization that seeks to import strength-based and outcome-informed practices for work with mandated clients. Our Center champions direct practice and is actively engaged in training staffing groups in the "how to's" for one-on-one efforts with challenging clients.

Another book that changed my thinking was *Motivational Interviewing.*[5] I challenge you to a "dare." I dare you to read the first five chapters of the first edition of *Motivational Interviewing* and be able to resist a fundamental change in your practice. Go on, read it – take the dare! I don't care if you read one page further past chapter five, for the change will have already occurred. I do not believe it is possible to read these first five chapters and not change how you approach recalcitrant offenders. I found formal training in this approach and then moved my practice to another level, completing a train-the-trainer session to be named a "MINT" member (Motivational Interviewing Network of Trainers). I now am engaged in training probation officers in

motivational interviewing across the country. Several states are engaged in training all (!) of their supervising probation and parole officers in motivational approaches. Initiatives such as these lend an enthusiasm to forensic social work that becomes altogether contagious.

I would advise all forensic social workers to never stop reading. You may be besieged by assigned reading lists while in school but when you graduate, remember that graduation represents a starting bell, not a finish line. Continue to read and you'll continue to grow. And by all means, pick up the phone and call the authors that stretch your thinking and excite your passions. You'll be surprised at how they will receive you and readily discuss their work. That was how I "met" Professor Al Roberts, one of the editors of this volume – I read a challenging treatise he had published and called him! He has remained a friend and mentor since that first phone call many years ago. As noted by Nelson Mandela in his inaugural speech when elected Prime Minister of South Africa, "Your playing small doesn't serve the world. There's nothing enlightened about shrinking...". So don't shrink, move towards those that capture your attention and ignite your enthusiasm.

To my disbelief, I was recently mailed a congratulatory letter from my airline that I had flown over a million air miles – all moving from one consulting job and training program to another. These multiple trips have allowed me to meet so many committed professionals and find them working in such innovative programs – certainly no one could witness what I have seen and remain pessimistic about the future of forensic social work. As hard as constant travel can be, the benefit is coming in contact with programs that often leaves me awe-struck!

Why do I continue in forensic social work? Because as encouraging and inspiring as these mandated programs can be, I have also seen the "dark side;" the side of forensic work that occurs when probation staff won't shake an offered hand from a probationer ("What do you think you're doing? I don't shake hands with offenders!"). It exists wherever disrespectful and heavy-handed treatment of offenders becomes demeaning and unethical. I've been in the field too long and I'm no Pollyanna. I'm not talking about taking an out-of-control offender into custody for stabilization or bringing a probationer back before the judge for violations of probation orders. What I'm speaking about are abuses of power that occur everyday in this field as a matter of course. And worse, many look away when these abuses occur – or actively join in with derisive laughter.

---

5. Miller, William R., & Rollnick, Stephen. (1991). *Motivational Interviewing: Preparing People for Change.* New York: Guilford Press.

What can be done? Out of many options, I use the "power of the pen" and call attention to how this behavior undermines hoped-for behavior change. My latest article is the first of a two-part series that will be published by the American Probation and Parole Associations' *Perspectives* Journal. The first article, *Motivational Interviewing for Probation Staff: Entering the Business of Behavior Change*, has recently been accepted for publication (Winter, 2006). In this article, I outline research that demonstrates how overly-directive approaches actually incur greater resistance (!) while I track our field's growing interest in motivational strategies. It examines how probation staff have found ways to navigate the conflicting duties of having to supervise and lend consequences to a probationer while simultaneously setting up a helping alliance with this same person. It's being negotiated and developed in progressive probation departments – small cells of staff that are springing up all across our field.

The two most recent books that have peaked my interest are the *Heart and Soul of Change*[6] and a following treatise, *The Heroic Client.*[7] These two books have challenged a majority of what I've learned or thought I knew about "treatment" and have challenged my assumptions about where change originates. Want to lay waste to many, long-held sacred beliefs in the fields of social work and psychology? Pick up these two texts and give them a read. Your view of randomized clinical trials (RCT's) and research that trumpets the latest and greatest treatment approaches ("battle of the brands") will be altered. These two books should include a "warning label" that your social work practice may change 180°. These researchers find that the true "engine to change" is the client – not our favored treatment models. Two of these researchers have banded together and have established the Institute for the Study of Therapeutic Change (ISTC) in Chicago, Illinois. I am proud to have been recently named an "associate" to this Center, bringing a forensic agenda into this arena of client-directed, outcome-informed practice. You can find multiple resources regarding this new research at www.talkingcure.com.

These meta-analytic studies give rise to an encouraging horizon. I believe the justice field is poised to begin what might be construed as the "age of the responsivity." Three decades of trying to understand the offender from our perspective gives way to possibly a much more useful view – viewing motivation *from the offender's perspective.* I see a renaissance occurring in corrections that is truly being fueled by the basic tenets of social work practice; respect, listening, and starting where the client is. I apologize if you may have been looking for something sexier or full of intrigue, but it's social work's core concepts that represent all that corrections has seemingly bypassed or ignored. In the effort to move beyond compliance to behavior change, it will be forensic social work that will lead this movement into the next decade – and beyond.

Indeed, Mr. Clark's career trajectory intersects with many of the topics covered in this book. We have made significant advances since what could be defined as the beginning of forensic social work – the opening of the first juvenile court in 1899 in Cook County, Illinois, and the first organization to assist abused women – the Chicago Protective Agency (for women and children) established in 1885 (Roberts, 1996). Jane Addams and Julia Lathrop, founders of the Settlement movement and strong advocates for the legislation that led to the first juvenile court, were leaders among the Progressive era reformers who built a foundation for the significant reforms in juvenile justice, domestic violence, and victim assistance programs and services during the past 107 years. During these years and the key historical periods they represent, we see declines, and flourishing periods for major policy shifts in social workers' involvement and responsiveness to both criminal offenders and their innocent victims.

Forensic social workers have knowledge and skills on diagnostic and risk assessments, the nature of human development and behavioral dysfunctions, juvenile and adult laws, juvenile and criminal court procedures and structure, crisis intervention and trauma treatment protocols, the strengths perspective and solution-focused therapy, and mental health treatments for criminal offenders as well as violent crime victims. Forensic social work has also been defined generically as "the practice specialty in social work that focuses on the law and educating law professionals about social welfare issues and social workers about the legal aspects of their objectives" (Barker, 1995, p.140). This definition incorporates

---

6. Hubble, Mark, Duncan, Barry, & Miller, Scott. (1999). *The Heart and Soul of Change: What Works in Therapy.* Washington, DC: American Psychological Association.
7. Duncan, Barry, Miller, Scott, & Sparks, Jacqueline. (2004). *The Heroic Client: A Revolutionary Way to Improve Effectiveness through Client-Directed, Outcome-Informed Therapy.* San Francisco: Jossey-Bass.

the practice of social work in family violence and the courts, juvenile delinquency and adult corrections, and law enforcement (Gibelman, 1995). Building on the above definitions, we operationally define *forensic social work* as: policies, practices, legal issues and remedies, and social work roles with juvenile and adult offenders as well as victims of crimes.

During colonial times and up to the first part of the 1800s, youths labeled as rowdy and out-of-control were either sent home for a court-observed whipping, assigned tasks as farmer's helpers, or placed in deplorable rat-infested prisons with hardened adult offenders. The turning point was 1825 with the opening of a separate institution for juvenile offenders in New York City – "the New York House of Refuge . . . . Similar juvenile facilities opened in1826 and 1828 in Boston, and Philadelphia respectively" (Roberts, 2004a; p. 130–131). By the mid-1800's, social work had become identified with corrections and other forms of social welfare institutions, including the "child-saving movement" whereby juvenile institutions and making juvenile delinquents indentured servants and apprentices for farmers and shop owners, also referred to as "parent surrogates" took place (Roberts, 2004a). By the late 1800s, many social reformers were involved with prisons, juvenile delinquency, and reformatories (Gibelman, 1995). Prior to the birth of the social work profession in 1898, the Conference of Boards of Public Charities was renamed the National Conference of Charities and Corrections in 1879 (Alexander, 1995; Katz, 1997).

In 1898, the first social work training school was established as an annual summer course for agency workers by the New York Charity Organization Society (Alexander, 1995). Social workers of that time, whether associated with the charity organization movement or the settlement house movement, were viewed as social reformers whose primary concerns were with serving the poor, beggars and disadvantaged, and social outcasts.

Reconsidering and Reframing Forensic Social Work as a Field of Practice

If we conceptualized and reframed social work in corrections and probation, forensic mental health, substance abuse, family and criminal courts, domestic violence and child abuse/neglect, juvenile justice, crime victims including the elderly, and police social

work, it would become clear that many in our profession are engaged in forensic social work. However, the profession does not acknowledge the large number of MSW field placements with social work clients who have been either victims of violent crimes or juvenile or adult offenders (Gibelman, 1995). The late Professor Margaret Gibelman was one of a small group of social work scholars who understood this and devoted an entire chapter to social work and the criminal justice system in the first edition of *What Social Workers Do*, published by NASW Press (Gibelman, 1995).

What is most promising for forensic social work are the three comprehensive volumes that were recently published and in which the latest social policies, social services, and social work practice roles with crime victims and offenders are documented. These books include original chapters by the leading forensic social workers in the United States. These are *Juvenile Justice Sourcebook: Past, Present and Future* (Roberts, 2004a), which includes chapters by 10 leading forensic social workers; *Oxford's Social Workers Desk Reference* (Roberts & Greene, 2002), with 12 original chapters in the forensic social work section by 16 experts in the field. *Substance Abuse Treatment for Criminal Offenders: An Evidence-Based Guide for Practitioners* (Springer, McNeece, & Arnold, 2003) is one of the first books to focus on evidence-based practice with this population.

Applying our definition of forensic social work, we identified 38 articles in the journal *Social Work* and during the 12-year period (1993-2005) that are germane to the growing field of forensic social work. Of these, six articles focused directly on the forensic population, including mothers in prison (Beckerman, 1994; Singer, Bussey, Song, & Lunghofer, 1995); pregnancy outcome during imprisonment (Siefert & Pimlott, 2001); court ordered treatment as opposed to voluntary treatment (O'Hare, 1996; Regehr & Antle, 1997; Rittner & Dozier, 2000; De Jong & Berg, 2001); the relationship between social work values and the corrections environment (Severson, 1994); therapeutic jurisprudence (Madden & Wayne, 2003); issues involved in working with forensic clients (Solomon & Draine, 1995); and multidisciplinary mitigation teams (Guin, Noble, & Merrill, 2003).

In addition, we identified seven articles on juvenile delinquency, which included female gang members (Molidor, 1996); group work with youths on probation (Goodman, Getzel, & Ford, 1996); environmental and developmental influences on youth violence (Fraser, 1996); the impact of community violence on children and youth (Guterman & Cameron, 1997); youth crime, public policy, and the juvenile justice system (Jenson & Howard, 1998); adolescent substance abusers (Ellis, O'Hara, & Sowers, 2000); and delinquent behavior in incarcerated youths (Van Dorn & Williams, 2003). One article was published on sexual harassment law (Gould, 2000) as well as one prison memoir (Sternbach, 2000). Seven articles were published on domestic violence (Bennett, 1995; Davis, Hagen, & Early, 1994; Forte & Franks, 1996; Mills, 1996; Stosny, 1994; Danis, 2003; Levin & Mills, 2003). An additional five articles were published on violence and victims (Umbriet, 1993; Barnes & Ephross, 1994; Newhill, 1995; Van Soest & Bryant, 1995; and Burman & Allen-Meares, 1994).

Another two articles focused on prostitutes (Weiner, 1996) and sexually abused children (Gellert, Berkowitz, Gellert, & Durfee, 1993). Finally, three articles focused on substance abuse, including substance-abusing women (Goldberg, 1995) and mothers whose substance abuse may bring them into contact with the child welfare system (Carten, 1996; Azzi-Lessing & Olsen, 1996).

Applying our definition of forensic social work, we also identified 29 articles in *Research on Social Work Practice* during the most recent six-year period (1999-2005). Of these, there were several that coalesced around social work with troubled youth and juvenile delinquents, including school violence (Whitfield, 1999), antisocial behavior in a runaway shelter (Nuget, Bruley, & Allen, 1998 & 1999), reintegration services for adjudicated delinquents (Ryan, Davis, & Yang, 2001), mental health and substance abuse problems for detained youth (Jenson & Potter, 2003), risk prediction among juvenile offenders (Krysik & LeCroy, 2002), short-term outcomes for runaway youth (Thompson, Pollio, Constantine, Reid, & Nebbitt, 2002), delinquency programs for youth (Wilson, Lipsey, & Soydan, 2003), wrap-around services to reduce juvenile recidivism (Carney & Buttell, 2003), and interventions for adolescent aggression (Martsch, 2005).

Additionally, we found one article on victim-offender mediation and reoffense (Nugent, Umbreit, Wiinamaki, & Paddock, 2001), one on substance-abusing women with children (Sowers, Ellis, Washington, & Currant, 2002), two that focused on PTSD among inmates (Kubiak, 2004; Valentine & Smith, 2001), four articles on court-ordered batterers (Buttell, 2001; Buttel & Pike, 2003; Buttell & Carney, 2004; Carney & Buttell, 2004), and two more on batterer intervention programs (Buttell & Carney, 2005; Tutty, Bidgood, Rothery, & Bidgood, 2001).

There were several articles in RSWP that coalesced around forensic social work with children, including child welfare and the courts (Ellet & Steib, 2005); assessment and outcome measure for child welfare and juvenile offenders (Glisson, Hemmelgarn, & Post, 2002); child maltreatment and the justice system (Sedlak et al., 2005); nonvoluntary child protective services clients (Yatchmenoff, 2005); child-abuse training and police recruits (Patterson, 2004); abuse and neglect investigations (Harder, 2005; Walton, 2001); and sex offender risk classification (Gentry, Dulmus, & Perez, 2005).

Under the able leadership of Associate Editor Rosemary Sarri, the latest edition of the *Encyclopedia of Social Work* (Edwards, 1995) was significantly expanded to include many articles related to forensic social work with victims and offenders. The 19th edition of the *Encyclopedia of Social Work* includes 31 articles on a number of forensic related topics. This includes sections on adult corrections (McNeece); adult courts (Isenstadt); adult protective services (Austin); child abuse and neglect overviews (Wells) and direct practice (Brissett-Chapman); child sex abuse overview (Conte) and direct practice (Berliner); community-based corrections (Butts); criminal behavior overview (Sarri); criminal justice – class, race, and gender issues (Iglehart), and social work roles (Miller); domestic violence (Davis) and legal issues (Saunders); elder abuse (Tatara); family views in correctional programs (Hairston); female criminal offenders (Gabel & Johnston); health care – jails and prisons (Rowan); homicide (Morales); juvenile and family courts (Ezell) and juvenile corrections (Barton); legal issues – confidentiality and privileged communications (Gothard) and low income and dependent people (Moore); police social work (Treger); probation and parole (Allen); rehabilitation of criminal offenders (Gendreau); sentencing of criminal offenders (Mauer); sexual assault (Byington) and harassment (Singer); substance abuse: legal issues (Burke); victim services and victim/witness assistance programs (Roberts); violence overview (Fraser); and victims of torture and trauma (Chester).

In *Social Work Almanac* (Ginsberg, 1995), substantial space is given to a discussion of corrections and juvenile delinquency. As Ginsberg notes, "among the social issues of increasing concern in the United States are crime and delinquency and the societal approaches for dealing with them" (p. 90). The *Encyclopedia of Social Work Supplement* (Edwards, 1997) includes three updates on forensic social work-related topics: domestic violence and gay men and lesbians (Carlson & Maciol); legal issues and recent developments in confidentiality and privilege (Polowy & Gorenberg); and prostitution (Weiner).

It is certainly evident based on this content analysis of *Social Work* and other NASW publications, including the *Encyclopedia of Social Work*, that NASW seems to recognize the importance of social work involvement with forensic-related issues. This is in spite of the acknowledgment that forensic social work has not yet received the attention it deserves within the profession.

History of Social Work and Corrections

As noted, preprofessional social work was sufficiently identified with corrections that the National Conference of Charities and Corrections was founded in 1879. Jane Addams, founder of Hull House, served as its first woman president (Solomon, 1994). A brief historical overview of social welfare and social work demonstrates how much professional social work was identified with corrections and what we now define as forensic social work from its inception. For this overview, the authors use a modified version of the existing historical framework developed by Day (2006). Roberts and Brownell (1999) offer a more extensive overview of the evolution of forensic social work in American social welfare history for those readers with special interest in this topic.

Post-Civil War and Recovery, and Progressive Era (1865–1925)

While social Darwinism was embraced as the dominant social philosophy of the charity organization movement, other social trends – including the settlement house movement – promoted progressive change (Day, 2006). The first juvenile court in the United States started in 1899 in Illinois as part of the circuit court of Chicago, through efforts initiated by the Chicago Women's Club (Popple & Leighninger, 1996). The Juvenile Psychopathic Institute was founded by Dr. William Healy, through the advocacy efforts of Hull House resident Julia Lathrop, to diagnose offenders brought before the Juvenile Court. The Institute began the practice of delinquency research and psycho social assessment of children by a professional team (Popple & Leighninger, 1996).

Between 1915 and 1920, Women's Bureaus within police departments were established. All of the police women served in social work advocacy roles (particularly with juveniles). By 1919, Chicago had 29 police social workers; by 1920, there were police social workers in all the major urban areas (Roberts, 1997b).

Great Depression and Social Security for Americans (1925–1949)

While the 1929 stock market crash did not bring immediate and widespread devastation to the American economy, it damaged public confidence and brought to the surface a conern about the role of government in ensuring the social welfare of citizens (Day, 2006). While the charity organization and settlement house workers had successfully advocated for widow's pensions and old age assistance at the state and county levels, the federal government was not seen as responsible for social insurance and assistance. Private charity and local government was seen as the primary means of addressing poverty and deprivation until the widespread economic dislocations of the 1930s brought a realization that systems and not individual failings can cause poverty on a wide scale.

The Great Depression and the New Deal brought an influx of social workers into public life and government work. Harry Hopkins, a prominent New York social worker associated with the Charity Organization Movement, was appointed first by President Hoover and then FDR to implement a program of emergency assistance and public works programs, including the WPA Youth Forestry Camps and the Civilian Conservation Corps, forerunners of modern day youth delinquency prevention programs. One of the earliest wilderness programs for juvenile offenders was established in the early 1930s in the Los Angeles County Forestry Department (Roberts, 2004a).

According to Roberts (2004a), "by the 1930's and 1940's, large numbers of psychiatric social workers had been hired to work in teams with psychiatrists to treat emotionally disturbed children, pre-delinquents and delinquents" (p. 131). This represented the beginning of interagency collaboration between the juvenile courts and child guidance clinics management. In addition, individualized treatment programs were started in corrections. Casework with offenders, especially youthful offenders, drew social workers into forensic work as treatment specialists.

Civil and Welfare Rights in the New Reform Era (1945–1970)

The emerging critical need for social workers to work in the field of corrections was underscored by University of Pennsylvania social work Dean Kenneth Pray (1945). Police social work expanded as interest in juvenile delinquency increased due to the widespread proliferation of youth gangs. By the late 1950s, the number of child guidance clinics had grown to over 600 nationally; these included social workers who served as court liaisons (Roberts, 1998c).

In 1959, a set of 13 volumes on the social work curriculum was published by the Council on Social Work Education (CSWE). Among them was volume V: Curriculum for Teaching Correctional Social Work by Studt (1959). This led to the development of correctional social work courses at major schools of social work.

During the 1940s, 50s, and early 60s, great strides were made in developing community-based councils and programs for delinquency prevention. Model programs such as NYC Mobilization for Youth, developed by social work professor Richard Cloward, the Midcity Program (Boston), and youth service bureaus proliferated (Roberts, 1998b). The continued concern about juvenile delinquency spurred innovative program initiatives such as juvenile diversion, youth service bureaus, detached street workers (social workers doing group work and community organizing). President Johnson's Task Force Report on Juvenile Delinquency and Youth Crime in 1967 recommended "dramatic policy innovations (such as decriminalization) of status offenders, the diversion of juveniles from official court processing" (McNeece, 1998, p. 22). In 1967, *In re Gault* decision by the U. S. Supreme Court ruled that due process must be observed in juvenile delinquency proceedings. This landmark legal decision solidified due process protection for juveniles at the adjudication stage (Alexander, 1995).

The role of social workers in probation increased dramatically by the mid-1960s. Probation departments were established in all 50 states and over 2,300 counties nationwide. Social worker Milton Rector, Executive Director of the National Council on Crime and Delinquency (NCCD), directed a national study of probation and recommended that all new probation officers and supervisors should be required to have a M.S.W. and two years' casework experience (Roberts, 2004).

Retreat from the Welfare State and the New Federalism (1970–1992)

Social welfare programs shrank during the 1970s and 1980s, as the country experienced a conservative retrenchment, especially during the Reagan era (Day, 2006). However, there continued to be advancements in services and programs for juvenile offenders as well as victim services. In 1972, community-based alternatives (e.g., a network of group homes) and education programs for juvenile delinquents were established by the Massachusetts Youth Services Department after it closed several juvenile reformatories (Alexander, 1995). By 1980, the closing of juvenile correctional institutions and the expansion of community-based group homes had extended to other states, such as Pennsylvania, Illinois, and Utah.

The Juvenile Justice and Delinquency Prevention Act of 1974 was the first major policy legislation with a major funding appropriation that resulted in a new federal office – the Office of Juvenile Justice and Delinquency Prevention (OJJDP) (see Chapter 5 by C. Aaron McNeece and associates). The first director of OJJDP was social worker Ira Schwartz (now Provost, Temple University in Philadelphia). Schwartz and his staff implemented the far reaching legislation that provided federal funding to many states to deinstitutionalize status offenders, remove juveniles from adult jails and lock-ups, establish runaway youth shelters and counseling programs, and improve delinquency prevention programs. Social workers, through their respective state governors' juvenile justice commissions and/or state criminal justice planning agencies, were able to advocate for important system changes, particularly the deinstitutionalizing of runaways, truants, and incorrigible youths.

The Child Abuse Prevention and Treatment Act of 1974 provided funding for demonstration programs to test prevention, intervention, and treatment strategies for child abuse and neglect, and resulted in the establishment of the National Center on Child Abuse and Neglect (Alexander, 1995). In 1978, the Act was extended and funded new adoption initiatives. This child abuse federal funding initiative resulted in the development of interdisciplinary hospital-based child abuse assessment and treatment teams, usually with medical social workers as the coordinators or team leaders.

The women's movement focused attention on domestic violence and victims' rights issues and programs. The Law Enforcement Assistance Act (LEAA), which passed in 1974, provided state block grants for local funding of police social work, as well as domestic violence and victim assistance programs. Model demonstration projects included the first shelter for battered women, which opened in St. Paul, Minnesota, and the first two police-based victim assistance programs, which were in Ft. Lauderdale and Indianapolis (Roberts, 1996). The civil rights movement and concerns about links between racism and imprisonment gave rise to a renewed focus on prison conditions and reform. In 1976, in a class action suit, the U.S. District Court of Alabama ruled that conditions of confinement in the Alabama penal system constituted cruel and unusual punishment when they bore "no reasonable relationship to legitimate institutional goals" (Alexander, 1995, p. 2644).

By the mid-1980s, a major policy shift resulted in the provision of woefully needed social services and crisis intervention for crime victims and fewer rehabilitation programs for convicted felons. The crime victims movement was bolstered significantly with the passage of the landmark Victims Of Crime Act (VOCA) of 1984 in which the many millions of dollars in funding came from federal criminal penalties and fines.

Decade of the 1990s (1990–1999)

Between 1984 and 1997, $2 billion was allocated throughout the nation to aid domestic violence, rape, child sexual assault, and other violent crime victims. There are currently close to 10,000 victim/witness assistance, victim service, domestic violence, and sexual assault treatment programs nationwide. These programs have a total average staff of seven full-time workers, of which 32 percent or approximately 22,400 are professional social workers (Roberts, 1997d). We predicted that the growth phase for forensic social workers would continue during the 1990s in victim assistance and domestic violence programs, and they did as a result of the $3.3 billion of funds through VAWA II (Roberts, 2002). As the prison census escalates (Ginsberg, 1995), social workers in community corrections continues to expand. Community-based courts, such as the Midtown Manhattan Community Court, which began in New York City in the early 1990s (Brownell, 1997), incorporate social work services into the overall program design. The specialized domestic violence courts which started to emerge in 1999 and 2000 in major cities throughout the United States also bodes well for the growing number of social workers working with domestic violence victims, batterers, and probationers (Keilitz, 2002).

Alternatives to incarceration programs for misdemeanor level crimes, as well as nonviolent felony level crimes related to IV drug use – highly associated with contemporary public health crises such as HIV and AIDS, and Hepatitis C – include social workers as case managers, addiction treatment specialists, crisis counselors, and family service specialists. The new welfare reform legislation has opened up additional opportunities for social workers in welfare-to-work programs with recipients of Temporary Assistance for Needy Families (TANF) for whom domestic violence and substance abuse present barriers to employment (Brownell, 1998).

Current Status of Forensic Social Work

Opportunities exist for professional social workers at the Legal Aid Society and work in family courts with abused and neglected children, as well as juvenile offenders with mental health and addictions problems. Victim service programs for crime victims and domestic violence survivors employ professional social workers to work with victims as well as perpetrators of family crimes.

The emergence of specialized courts, such as drug courts and domestic violence courts, has resulted in an increasing presence of social workers in the courts. Schools of Social Work have developed inter-disciplinary programs with law schools, as well as joint degree programs in social work and the law.

The increase of women in prison due to some states' "get-tough" drug laws, and increased recognition of the plight of the forensic mentally ill, require the services of professional social workers for counseling and to serve as the link between child welfare, substance abuse, health and mental health systems on one hand, and the correctional system on the other. Other social and pubic health problems with which forensic social workers are engaged include the alarming surge of hepatitis C, HIV and AIDS, cancer, cardiovascular diseases, diabetes, as well as tuberculosis, among the county and city jail and state prison populations, and the increasing recognition of a forensic MICA and developmentally disabled inmate population.

A Look to the Future

Our vision for the future is that all vulnerable and at-risk clients will have the opportunity to be helped by forensic social work advocates, clinicians, and policy-makers. Forensic work is complex and involves an understanding of systems: intrapsychic, interpersonal, familial, and societal. Case management is an important model with the highly vulnerable offender populations (Rothman, 2002), one of the many services in which social workers excel. The primary functions of case management include intake assessment, formulating personal objectives and service goals, treatment planning, linking with informal and formal support groups, resource identification, matching clients to agencies and concrete services, monitoring, outcome evaluation, and termination. Forensic social workers often focus on providing the full range and continuum of concrete services and clinical interventions to their clients.

One of the major opportunities for forensic social workers and educators is to orient and inform legislators, juvenile and adult correctional administrators, corrections professionals, and students about the latest model offender treatment and prevention programs as well as the latest research documenting the effectiveness of these programs in reducing recidivism (Roberts, 2004a). At the present time, too many legislators, correctional administrators, and practitioners are unaware of the latest research documenting the most effective interventions. As indicated by Mc-

Neece and Jackson (2004), the current emphasis in a number of states on punitive treatment and contracting out to private correctional companies who only care about making money by providing the lowest costing services are unjust, ineffective, and inhumane. A number of promising, humane, and effective rehabilitation programs are available in different parts of the United States. In recent works, Roberts (2004a) and Springer (2004) documented over 10 different evidence-based offender treatment models that are effective based on longitudinal research. These evidence-based interventions include: Probation-monitored restitution and work placement, establishing offender treatment goals and targets for change, motivational interviewing and solution-focused treatment, structured wilderness education programs, occupational trades training and job placement, multisystemic therapy, problem-solving skills training, brief strategic family therapy, cognitive-behavioral approaches such as anger management and behavioral contracting, community day treatment and aftercare by case managers, and graduated community-based sanctions (Roberts, 2004a; Springer, 2004).

The tension between social control and social support is an ongoing and necessary one with which the profession must continue to struggle. Issues of poverty, gender, race, ethnicity, disabilities, domestic violence, mental illness, and pregnant and parenting substance abusers intersect with forensic social work (see Chapter 14 by McNeece, Tyson, and Jackson; Chapter 26 by Ivanoff, Smyth, and Dulmus; and Chapter 27 by Brownell, Miller, and Raymon). For decades, there has been a debate among social workers as to whether or not we should help involuntary clients. A growing group of dedicated forensic social workers have navigated, advocated for, and overcome obstacles for their clients in the criminal justice system. Social workers in forensic settings do their best to adjust to the constraints of courts and correctional settings, while advocating for offenders and victims to realize their full potential.

We wrote this chapter in full support of the social work profession's 107 years of dedication to serving oppressed, vulnerable, at-risk, and devalued groups. During the past century, the most neglected and devalued groups have been victims of violent crimes and criminal offenders. In the past two decades, professional social workers have made growing progress in advocating for and obtaining critically needed social services for juvenile offenders, adult offenders, and victims of violent crimes. However, the case, class, and legislative advocacy efforts of forensic social workers (also known as justice or correctional social workers) have increased and decreased in cycles over the past century. We highly recommend that the National Association of Forensic Social Work (NAFSW), the Society of Social Work and Research (SSWR), the National Association of Social Workers (NASW), and the Council on Social Work Education (CSWE) form a taskforce to draft and lobby for federal and state legislation that mandates a minimum of an M.S.W., D.S.W., or Ph.D. in social work and five years post-master's experience, plus 90 hours of training in forensic assessments, expert testimony and crisis intervention, before being allowed to conduct child abuse and neglect or battered women risk assessments, or testify in homicide, child custody, sexual assault, and domestic violence cases.

As professional social workers who abide by our code of ethics, we respect human dignity, accept individual differences, and are nonjudgmental. No other human service professional is bound by a unique and comprehensive code of ethics that accepts all individuals as they are, no matter what mistakes they have made or crimes they have committed. Being nonjudgmental means that we firmly believe in the individual's self-worth and potential for positive change, whether she is a battered woman suffering from PTSD who murdered her husband or a mentally retarded juvenile offender or a person suffering from mental illness and drug addiction. We look to the support of our professional organizations – Society of Social Work and Research (SSWR), the National Association of Forensic Social Work (NAFSW), the Council on Social Work Education (CSWE), and the National Association of Social Workers (NASW) in recognizing the far-reaching potential of forensic social work.

REFERENCES

Alexander, C. A. (1995). Distinctive dates in social welfare history. In *Encyclopedia of social work* (19th ed., pp. 2631–2647). Washington, D.C.: NASW Press.

Allen, G. F. (1995). Probation and parole. In R. L. Edwards (Ed.), *Encyclopedia of social work* (19th ed., pp. 1910–1916). Washington, D. C.: NASW Press.

Austin, C. D. (1995). Adult protective services. In R. L. Edwards (Ed.), *Encyclopedia of social work* (19th ed., pp. 89–95). Washington, D.C.: NASW Press.

Azzi-Lessing, L., & Olsen, L. J. (1996). Substance abuse affecting families in the child welfare system: New challenges, new alliances. *Social Work, 41*, 15–23.

Barnes, A., & Ephross, P. H. (1994). The impact of hate violence on victims: Emotional and behavioral responses to attacks. *Social Work, 39*, 247–251.

Barker, R. L. (1995). *The social work dictionary*. Washington, D.C.: NASW Press.

Barton. W. H. (1995). Juvenile corrections. In R. L. Edwards (Ed.), *Encyclopedia of social work* (19th ed., pp. 1563–77. Washington, D.C.: NASW Press.

Beckerman, A. (1994). Mothers in prison: Meeting the prerequisite conditions for permanency planning. *Social Work, 39*, 9–14.

Bennett, L. W. (1995). Substance abuse and the domestic assault of women. *Social Work, 40*, 760–771.

Berliner, L. (1995). Child sexual abuse: Direct practice. In R. L. Edwards (Ed.), *Encyclopedia of social work* (19th ed., pp. 408–417). Washington, D.C.: NASW Press.

Battjes, R. J., Gordon, M. S., O'Grady, K. E., Kinlock, T. W., & Carswell, M. A. (2003). Factors that predict adolescent motivation for substance abuse treatment. *Journal of Substance Abuse Treatment, 24*(3), 221–232.

Battjes, R. J., Onken, L. S., & Delany, P. J. (1999). Drug abuse treatment entry and engagement: Report of a meeting on treatment readiness. *Journal of Clinical Psychology, 55*, 643–657.

Brisset-Chapman, S. (1995). Child abuse and neglect: Direct practice. In R. L. Edwards (Ed.), *Encyclopedia of social work* (19th ed., pp. 353–366). Washington, D.C.: NASW Press.

Brownell, P. (1998). Women, welfare, work, and domestic violence. In A. R. Roberts (Ed.), *Battered women and their families: intervention strategies and treatment programs* (2nd ed., pp. 291–312). New York: Springer.

Brownell, P. (1997). Female offenders in the criminal justice system: Policy and program development. In A. R. Roberts (Ed.), *Social work in juvenile and criminal justice settings* (2nd ed., pp. 325–349). Springfield, Illinois: Charles C Thomas.

Bureau of Justice Statistics (2005). *Probation and parole in the United States, 2004*. NCJ 210676, Washington, D.C.: U.S. Department of Justice, U.S. Government Printing Office.

Burke, A. C. (1995). Substance abuse: Legal issues. In R. L. Edwards (Ed.), *Encyclopedia of social work* (19th ed., pp. 2347–2357). Washington, D.C.: NASW Press.

Burman, S., & Allen-Meares, P. (1994). Neglected victims of murder: Children's witness of parental homicide. *Social Work, 39*, 28–34.

Buttell, F. P. (2001). Moral development among court-ordered batterers: Evaluating the impact of treatment. *Research on Social Work Practice, 11*(1), 93–107.

Buttell, F. P. & Carney, M. M. (2004). A multidimensional assessment of a batterer treatment program: An alert to a problem? *Research on Social Work Practice, 14*(2), 93–101.

Buttell, F. P., & Carney, M. M. (2005). Do batterer intervention programs serve African American and Caucasian batterers equally well? An investigation of a 26-week program. *Research on Social Work Practice, 15*(1), 19–28.

Buttell, F. P., & Pike, C. K. (2003). Investigating the differential effectiveness of a batterer treatment program on outcomes for African American and Caucasian batterers. *Research on Social Work Practice, 13*(6), 675–692.

Butts, J. A. (1995). Community-based corrections. In R. L. Edwards (Ed.), *Encyclopedia of social work* (19th ed., pp, 549–555). Washington, D.C.: NASW Press.

Byington, D. B. (1995). Sexual assault. In R. L. Edwards (Ed.), *Encyclopedia of social work* (19th ed., pp. 2136–2141). Washington, D.C.: NASW Press.

Carlson, B. E. & Maciol, K. (1997). Domestic violence: Gay men and lesbians. In R. L. Edwards (Ed.), *Encyclopedia of social work* (19th ed., pp. 101–111). Washington, D.C.: NASW Press.

Carney, M. M., & Buttel, F. P. (2003). Reducing juvenile recidivism: Evaluating the wraparound services model. *Research on Social Work Practice, 13*(5), 551–568.

Carney, M. M., & Buttell, F. P. (2004). A multidimensional evaluation of a treatment program for female batterers: A pilot study. *Research on Social Work Practice, 14*(4), 249–258.

Carten, A. J. (1996). Mothers in recovery: Rebuilding families in the aftermath of addiction. *Social Work, 41,* 214–223.

Chester, B. (1995). Victims of torture and trauma. In R. L. Edwards (Ed.), *Encyclopedia of social work* (19th ed., pp. 2445–2452). Washington, D.C.: NASW Press.

Conte, J. R. (1995). Child sexual abuse overview. In R. L. Edwards (Ed.), *Encyclopedia of social work* (19th ed., pp. 402–408). Washington, D.C.: NASW Press.

Czuchry, M., Dansereau, D. F., Dees, S. M., & Simpson, D. D. (1995). The use of node-link mapping in drug abuse counseling: The role of attentional factors. *Journal of Psychoactive Drugs, 27,* 161–166.

Danis, F. S. (2003). The criminalization of domestic violence: What social workers need to know. *Social Work, 48*(2), 237–246.

Dansereau, D. F., Joe, G. W., & Simpson, D. D. (1995). Attentional difficulties and the effectiveness of a visual representation strategy for counseling drug-addicted clients. *International Journal of the Addictions, 30,* 371–386.

Dansereau, D. F., Joe, G. W., Dees, S. M., & Simpson, D. D. (1996). Ethnicity and the effects of mapping-enhanced drug abuse counseling. *Addictive Behaviors, 21,* 363–376.

Dansereau, D. F., Joe, G. W., & Simpson, D. D. (1993). Node-link mapping: A visual representation strategy for enhancing drug abuse counseling. *Journal of Counseling Psychology, 40,* 385–395.

Day, P. J. (2006). *A new history of social welfare* (5th ed.). Boston: Allyn & Bacon.

Davis, L. V. (1995). Domestic violence. In R. L. Edwards (Ed.), *Encyclopedia of social work* (19th ed., pp. 780–789). Washington, D.C.: NASW Press.

Davis, L. V., Hagen, J. L., & Early, T. J. (1994). Social services for battered women: Are they adequate, accessible and appropriate? *Social Work, 39,* 695–704.

Dees, S. M., Dansereau, D. F., & Simpson, D. D. (1997). Mapping-enhanced drug abuse counseling: Urinalysis results in the first year of methadone treatment. *Journal of Substance Abuse Treatment, 14,* 45–54.

De Jong, P., & Berg, I. K. (2001). Co-constructing cooperation with mandated clients. *Social Work, 46*(4), 361–374.

DeLeon, G., Melnick, G., Kressel, D., & Jainchill, N. (1994). circumstances, motivation, readiness, and suitability (The CMRS Scales): Predicting retention in therapeutic community treatment. *American Journal of Drug and Alcohol Abuse, 20,* 495–515.

Edwards, R. L. (Ed.) (1995). *Encyclopedia of social work* (19th ed.). Washington, D.C.: NASW Press.

Edwards, R. L. (Ed.) (1997). *Encyclopedia of social work supplement 1997.* Washington, D.C.: NASW Press.

Ellet, A. J., & Steib, S. D. (2005). Child welfare and the courts: A statewide study with implication for professional development, practice, and change. *Research on Social Work Practice, 15*(5), 339–352.

Ellis, R. A., O'Hara, M., & Sowers, K. M. (2000). Profile-based intervention: Developing gender-sensitive treatment for adolescent substance abusers. *Research on Social Work Practice, 10*(3), 327–347.

Enos, R., & Southern, S. (1996). *Correctional case management.* Cincinnati, OH: Andersen Publishing Company.

Ezell, M. (1995). Juvenile and family courts. In R. L. Edwards (Ed.), *Encyclopedia of social work* (19th ed., pp. 1553–1562). Washington, D.C.: NASW Press.

Forte, J. A., Frank, D. D., Forte, J. A., & Rigsby, D. (1996). Asymmetrical role taking: Comparing battered and non-battered women. *Social Work, 41,* 59–73.

Fraser, M. W. (1995). Violence overview. In R. L. Edwards (Ed.), *Encyclopedia of social work* (19th ed., pp. 2453–2460). Washington, D.C.: NASW Press.

Fraser, M. W. (1996). Aggressive behavior in childhood and early adolescence: An ecological-developmental perspective on youth violence. *Social Work, 41,* 347–361.

Gabel, K., & Johnston, D. (1995). Female criminal offenders. In R. L. Edwards (Ed.), *Encyclopedia of social work* (2nd ed., pp. 1013–1027). Washington, D.C.: NASW Press.

Gentry, A. L., Dulmus, C. N., & Theriot, M. T. (2005). Comparing sex offender risk classification using the Static-99 and LSI-R Assessment Instruments. *Research on Social Work Practice, 15*(6), 557–563.

Gellert, G. A., Berkowitz, C. D., Gellert, M. J., & Durfee, M. J. (1993). Testing the sexually abused child for the hiv-antibody: Issues for social workers. *Social Work, 38,* 389–394.

Gendreau, P. (1995). Rehabilitation of criminal offenders. In R. L. Edwards (Ed.), *Encyclopedia of social work* (19th ed., pp. 2034–2039). Washington, D.C.: NASW Press.

Gibelman, M. (1995). *What social workers do.* Washington, D.C.: NASW Press.

Ginsberg, L. (1995). *The social work almanac.* Washington, D.C.: NASW Press.

Glisson, C., Hemmelgarn, A. L., & Post, J. A. (2002). The short-form assessment for children: An assessment and outcome measure for child welfare and juvenile justice. *Research on Social Work Practice, 12*(1), 82–106.

Goldberg, M. E. (1995). Substance-abusing women: False stereotypes and real needs. S*ocial Work, 40,* 789–798.

Goodman, H., Wetzel, G. J., & Ford, W. (1996). Group work with high-risk youth on probation. *Social Work, 41,* 375–381.

Gothard, S. (1995). Legal issues: Confidentiality and privileged communication. In R. L. Edwards (Ed.), *Encyclopedia of social work* (19th ed., pp. 1579–1584). Washington, D.C.: NASW Press.

Gould, K. H. (2000). Beyond Jones v. Clinton: Sexual harassment law and social work. *Social Work, 45*(3), 237–248.

Guin, C. C., Noble, D. N., & Merril, S. T. (2003). From misery to mission: Forensic social workers on multidisciplinary mitigation teams. *Social Work, 48*(3), 362–371.

Guterman, N. B., & Cameron, M. (1997). Assessing the impact of community violence on children and youths. *Social Work, 42,* 495–505.

Hairston, C. F. (1995). Family views in correctional programs. In R. L. Edwards (Ed.), *Encyclopedia of social work* (19th ed., pp. 991–996). Washington, D. C.: NASW Press.

Harder, J. (2005). Prevention of child abuse and neglect: An evaluation of a home visitation parent aide program using recidivism data. *Research on Social Work Practice, 15*(4), 246–256.

Hemphill, J. F., & Howell, A. J. (2000). Adolescent offenders and stages of change. *Psychological Assessment, 12*(4), 371–381.

Hubbard, R. L., Cavanaugh, E. R., Craddock, S. G., & Rachel, J. V. (1985). Characteristics, behaviors and outcomes for youth in the TOPS. In G. M. Beschner and A. S Friedman (Eds.), *Treatment services for adolescent substance abusers.* (Treatment Research Monograph Series, HHS Publication [ADM]) (pp. 84–1286). Rockville, MD: National Institute on Drug Abuse.

Iglehart, A. P. (1995). Criminal justice: Class, race, and gender issues. In R. L. Edwards (Ed.), *Encyclopedia of social work* (19th ed., pp. 647–653). Washington, D.C.: NASW Press.

Isenstadt, P. M. (1995). Adult courts. In R. L. Edwards (Ed.), *Encyclopedia of social work* (19th ed., pp. 68–74). Washington, D.C.: NASW Press.

Ivanoff, A. & Smythe, N. J. (1997). Preparing social workers for practice in correctional Institutions. In A. R. Roberts (Ed.), *Social work in juvenile and criminal justice settings* (2nd ed., pp. 309–324). Springfield, IL: Charles C Thomas.

Jenson, J. M., & Howard, M. O. (1998). Youth crime, public policy, and practice in the juvenile justice system: Recent trends and needed reforms. *Research on Social Work Practice, 43*(4), 324–334.

Joe, G. W., Dansereau, D. F., & Simpson, D. D. (1994). Node-link mapping for counseling cocaine users in methadone treatment. *Journal of Substance Abuse, 6,* 393–406.

Keilitz, S. (2002). Specialized domestic violence courts. In A. R. Roberts (Ed.), *Handbook of domestic violence intervention strategies.* New York, N.Y.: Oxford University Press.

Krysik, J., & LeCroy, C. W. (2002). The empirical validation of an instrument to predict risk of recidivism among juvenile offenders. R*esearch on Social Work Practice, 12*(1), 71–81.

Kubiak, S. P. (2004). The effects of PTSD on treatment adherence, drug relapse, and criminal recidivism in a sample of incarcerated men and women. Research on Social Work Practice, 14(6), 417–423.

Lawendowski, L. A. (1998). A motivational intervention for adolescent smokers. *Preventive Medicine, 27,* A39–A46.

Levin, A., & Mills, L. G. (2003). Fighting for child custody when domestic violence is at issue: Survey of state laws. *Social Work, 48*(4), 463–470.

Longshore, D., Grills, C., & Annon, K. (1999). Effects of a culturally congruent intervention on cognitive factors related to drug-use recovery. *Substance Use & Misuse, 34*(9), 1223–1241.

Longshore, D., Grills, C., Annon, K., &Grady, R. (1998). Promoting recovery from drug abuse: An Africentric intervention. *Journal of Black Studies, 28,* 319–333.

Madden, R. G., & Wayne, R. H. (2003). Social work and the law: A therapeutic jurisprudence perspective. *Social Work, 48*(3), 338–347.

Martsch, M. D. (2005). A comparison of two group interventions for adolescent aggression: High process versus low process. *Research on Social Work Practice, 15*(1), 8–18.

Mauer, M. (1995). Sentencing of criminal offenders. In R. L. Edwards (Ed.), *Encyclopedia of social work* (19th ed., pp. 2123–2129). Washington, D.C.: NASW Press.

McNeece, C. A. (1995). Adult corrections. In R. L. Edwards (Ed.), *Encyclopedia of social work* (19th ed., pp. 60–68). Washington, D.C.: NASW Press.

McNeece, C. A., & Jackson, S. (2004). Juvenile justice policy: Current trends and 21st century issues. In A. R. Roberts (Ed.), *Juvenile Justice Sourcebook: Past, Present and Future* (pp. 41–68). New York, N.Y.: Oxford University Press.

Miller, J. G. (1995). Criminal justice: Social work roles. In R. L. Edwards (Ed.), *Encyclopedia of social work* (19th ed., pp. 653–659). Washington, D. C.: NASW Press.

Mills, L. (1996). Empowering battered women transnationally: The case for post modern interventions. *Social Work, 41*, 261–268.

Molidor, C. E. (1996). Female gang members: A profile of aggression and victimization. *Social Work, 41*, 251–257.

Moore, E. (1995). Legal issues: Low-income and dependent people. In R. L. Edwards (Ed.), *Encyclopedia of social work* (19th ed., pp. 1584–1590). Washington, D.C.: NASW Press.

Morales, A. (1995). Homicide. In R. L. Edwards (Ed.), *Encyclopedia of social work* (19th ed., pp. 1347–1358). Washington, D.C.: NASW Press.

Mullen, P. D., Velasquez, M. M., von Sternberg, K., Cummins, A. G., & Green, D. (April 2005). *Efficacy of a dual behavior focus, transtheoretical model-based motivational intervention with transition assistance to present an alcohol-exposed pregnancy (AEP) after a jail term.* 26th Annual Meeting and Scientific Sessions for the Society of Behavioral Medicine. Boston, MA.

Newhill, C. E. (1995). Client violence toward social workers: A practice and policy concern for the 1990's. *Social Work, 40*, 631–636.

Nugent, W. R., Bruley, C., & Allen, P. (1998). The effects of aggression replacement training on antisocial behavior in a runaway shelter. *Research on Social Work Practice, 8*(6), 637–656.

Nugent, W. R., Bruley, C., & Allen, P. (1999). The effects of aggression replacement training on male and female antisocial behavior in a runaway shelter. *Research on Social Work Practice, 9*(4), 466–482.

Nugent, W. R., Umbreit, M. S., Wiinamaki, L., & Paddock, J. (2001). Participation in victim-offender mediation and reoffense: Successful Replications? *Research on Social Work Practice, 11*(1), 5–23.

Nugent, W. R., Williams, M., & Umbreit, M. S. (2004). Participation in victim-offender mediation and the prevalence of subsequent delinquent behavior. *Research on Social Work Practice, 14*(6), 408–416.

Office for Victims of Crime (2005). *Report to the nation 2005.* Washington, D.C.: Office for Victims of Crime, U.S. Government Printing Office.

O'Hare, T. (1996). Court-ordered versus voluntary clients: Problem differences and readiness for change. *Social Work, 41*, 417–422.

Patterson, G. T. (2004). Evaluating the effects of child abuse training on the attitudes, knowledge, and skills of police recruits. *Research on Social Work Practice, 14*(4), 273–280.

Pitre, U., Dansereau, D. F., Newbern, D., & Simpson. D. D. (1998). Residential drug abuse treatment for probationers: Use of node-link mapping to enhance participation and progress. *Journal of Substance Abuse Treatment, 15*(6), 535–543.

Pitre, U., Dansereau, D. F., & Simpson, D. D. (1997). The role of node-link maps in enhancing counseling efficiency. *Journal of Addictive Diseases, 16*, 39–49.

Polowy, C. I., & Gorenberg, C. (1997). Legal issues: recent developments in confidentiality and privilege. In R. L. Edwards (Ed.), *Encyclopedia of social work supplement 1997* (pp. 179–190). Washington, D.C.: NASW Press.

Popple, P. R., & Leighninger, L. L. (1996). *Social work, social welfare, and American society* (3rd ed.). Needham Heights, MA: Allyn & Bacon.

Pray, K. (1945). The place of social casework in the treatment of delinquency. *The Social Service Review, 19*, 244.

Prochaska, J. O., & Norcross, J. C. (1999). *Systems of psychotherapy: A transtheoretical analysis* (4th ed.). Pacific Grove, CA: Brooks/Cole.

Prochaska, J. O., Norcross, J. C., Fowler, J. L., Follick, M. J., & Abrams, D. B. (1992). Attendance and outcome in a work site weight control program: Processes and stages of change as process and predictor variables. *Addictive Behaviors, 17*(1), 35–45.

Prochaska, J. O., Velicer, W. F., Rossi, J. S., Goldstein, M. G., Marcus, B. H., Rakowski, W., Fiore, C., Harlow, L., & Redding, C. A. (1994). Stages of change and decisional balance for twelve problem behaviors. *Health Psychology, 13*, 39–46.

Prochaska, J. O., & DiClemente, C. C. (1984). *The transtheoretical approach: Crossing the traditional boundaries of therapy.* Homewood, IL: Dow Jones-Irwin.

Regehr, C., & Antle, B. (1997). Coercive influences: Informed consent in court-ordered social work practice. *Social Work, 42*, 300–306.

Reisch, M., & Gambrill, E. (Eds.) (1997). *Social work in the 21st century.* Thousand Oaks, California: Pine Forge Press.

Risler, E. A., Sutphen, R., & Shields, J. (2000). Preliminary validation of the juvenile first offender risk assessment index. *Research on Social Work Practice, 10*(1), 111–126.

Rittner, B. & Dozier, C. D. (2000). Effects of court-ordered substance abuse treatment in child protective services cases. *Social Work, 45*(2), 131–140.

Roberts, A. R. (1995). Victim services and victim/witness assistance programs. In R. L. Edwards (Ed.), *Encyclopedia of social work* (19th ed., pp. 2440–2444). Washington, D.C.: NASW Press.

Roberts, A. R. (1997b). The history and role of social work in law enforcement. In A. R. Roberts (Ed.), *Social work in juvenile and criminal justice settings* (2nd ed., pp. 105–15). Springfield, IL: Charles C Thomas.

Roberts, A. R. (1997c). Police social work: Bridging the past to the present. In A. R. Roberts (Ed.), *Social work in juvenile and criminal justice settings* (2nd ed., pp. 126–132). Springfield, IL: Charles C Thomas.

Roberts, A. R. (1997d). The role of the social worker in victims/witness assistance programs. In A. R. Roberts, *Social work in juvenile and criminal justice settings* (2nd ed., pp. 150–159). Springfield, IL: Charles C Thomas.

Roberts, A. R. (1998a). *Juvenile justice: Policies, programs, and services* (2nd ed.). Chicago: Nelson-Hall Inc.

Roberts, A. R. (1998b). Community strategies with juvenile offenders. In A. R. Roberts (Ed.), *Juvenile justice: Policies, programs and services* (2nd ed., pp. 126–134). Chicago: Nelson-Hall, Inc.

Roberts, A. R. (2004a). *Juvenile justice sourcebook: Past, present and future.* New York: Oxford University Press.

Roberts, A. R. (2004b). The emergence of the juvenile court and probation services. In A. R. Roberts (Ed.), *Juvenile justice sourcebook: Past, present and future* (pp. 163–182). New York: Oxford University Press.

Roberts, A. R., & Brownell (1999). A century of forensic social work. Social Work. 44(4):359–369.

Roberts, A. R., & Greene, G. (Eds.). (2002). *Social workers' desk reference.* New York: Oxford University Press.

Rowan, J. R. (1995). Health care: Jails and prisons. In R. L. Edwards (Ed.), *Encyclopedia of social work* (19th ed., pp. 1177–1185). Washington, D.C.: NASW Press.

Ryan, J. P., Davis, R. K., & Yang, H. (2001). Reintegration services and the likelihood of adult imprisonment: A longitudinal study of adjudicated delinquents. *Research on Social Work Practice, 11*(3), 321–337.

Sarri, R. C. (1995). Criminal behavior overview. In R. L. Edwards (Ed.), *Encyclopedia of social work* (19th ed., pp. 637–646). Washington, D.C.: NASW Press.

Saunders, D. G. (1995). Domestic violence: Legal issues. In R. L. Edwards (Ed.), *Encyclopedia of social work* (19th ed., pp. 789–795). Washington, D.C.: NASW Press.

Saunders, D. N. (1995). Substance abuse: Federal, state, and local policies. In R. L. Edwards (Ed.), *Encyclopedia of social work* (19th ed., pp. 2338–2347). Washington, D.C.: NASW Press.

Sedlak, A. J., Doueck, H. J., Lyons, P. L., Wells, S. J., Schultz, D., & Gragg, F. (2005). Child maltreatment and the justice system: Predictors of court involvement. *Research on Social Work Practice, 15*(5), 389–403.

Seifert, K. & Pimlott, S. (2001). Improving pregnancy outcome during imprisonment: A model residential care program. *Social Work, 46*(2), 125–134.

Segal, E. A., & Brzuzy, S. (1998). *Social welfare policy, programs, and practice.* Itasca, IL: F. E. Peacock Press.

Sells, S. B., & Simpson, D. D. (1979). Evaluation of treatment outcome for youths in the Drug Abuse Reporting Program (DARP): A follow-up study. In G. M. Beschner (Ed.), *Youth drug abuse: Problems, issues and treatments* (pp. 571–628). Lexington, MA: Lexington Books.

Severson, M. (1994). Adapting social work values to the corrections environment. *Social Work, 39*, 451–456.

Simpson, D. D., Chatham, L. R., & Joe, G. W. (1993). Cognitive enhancements to treatment in DATAR: Drug abuse treatment for AIDS risk-reduction. In J. Inciardi, F. Tims, & B. Fletcher (Eds.), *Innovative approaches to the treatment of drug abuse: Program models and strategies* (pp. 161–177). Wesport, CT: Greenwood Press.

Simpson, D. D., Dansereau, D. F., & Joe, G. W. (1997). The DATAR project: Cognitive and behavioral enhancements to community-based treatments. In F. M. Tims, J. A. Inciardi, B. W. Fletcher, & A. M. Horton, Jr. (Eds.), *The effectiveness of innovative approaches in the treatment of drug abuse* (pp. 182–203). Westport, CT: Greenwood Press.

Simpson, D. D., Joe, G. W., Rowan-Szal, G., & Greener, J. (1997). Client engagement and change during drug abuse treatment. *Journal of Substance Abuse, 7*, 117–134.

Simpson, D. D., & Joe, G. W. (1993). Motivation as a predictor of early dropout from drug abuse treatment. *Psychotherapy, 30*, 357–367.

Singer, T. L. (1995). Sexual harassment. In R. L. Edwards (Ed.), *Encyclopedia of social work* (19th ed., pp. 2148–2156). Washington, D.C.: NASW Press.

Singer, M. I., Bussey, J., Song, L., & Lunghofer, L. (1995). The psychosocial issues of women serving time in jail. *Social Work, 40*, 103–113.

Smythe, N. J. (1995). Substance abuse: Direct practice. In R. L. Edwards (Ed.), *Encyclopedia of social work* (19th ed., pp. 2328–2338). Washington, D.C.: NASW Press.

Solomon, B. (1994). *The empowerment tradition in American social work: A history.* New York: Columbia University Press.

Solomon, P. & Draine, J. (1995). Issues in serving the forensic client. *Social Work, 40*, 25–33.

Sowers, K. M., Ellis, R. A., Washington, T. A., Currant, M. (2002). Optimizing treatment effects for substance-abusing women with children: An evaluation of the Susan B. Anthony Center. *Research on Social Work Practice. 12*(1), 143–158.

Springer, D. W. (2004). Evidence-based treatment of juvenile delinquents with externalizing disorders. In A. R. Roberts (Ed.). *Juvenile justice sourcebook: Past, present and future.* (pp. 365–380). New York: Oxford University Press.

Springer, D. W., Rivaux, S. L., Bohman, T., & Yeung, A. (in press). Predicting retention in three substance abuse treatment modalities among Anglo, African American and Mexican American juvenile offenders. *Journal of Social Service Research.*

Springer, D. W., McNeece, C. A., & Arnold, E. M. (2003). *Substance abuse treatment for criminal offenders: An evidence-based guide for practitioners.* Washington, D.C.: American Psychological Association.

Sternbach, J. (2000). Lessons learned about working with men: A prison memoir. *Social Work, 45*(5), 413–423.

Stosny, S. (1994). Shadows of the heart: a dramatic video for the treatment resistant batterer. *Social Work, 39,* 686–694.

Studt, E. (Ed.) (1959). Education for social workers in the correctional field. Volume V in the *Social Work Education Study.* New York: Council on Social Work Education.

Tatara, T. (1995). Elder abuse. In R. L. Edwards (Ed.), *Encyclopedia of social work* (19th ed., (pp. 834–842). Washington, D.C.: NASW Press.

Thompson, S. J., Constantine, J., Reid, D., & Nebbitt, V. (2002). Short-term outcomes for youth receiving runaway and homeless shelter services. *Research on Social Work Practice, 12*(5), 589–603.

Treger, H. (1995). Police social work. In R. L. Edwards (Ed.), *Encyclopedia of social work* (19th ed., pp. 1843–1848). Washington, D.C.: NASW Press.

Tutty, L. M., Bidgood, B. A., Rothery, M. A., & Bidgood, P. (2001). An evaluation of men's batterer treatment groups. *Research on Social Work Practice, 11*(6), 645–670.

Umbreit, M. S. (1993). Crime victims and offenders in mediation: an emerging area of social work practice. *Social Work, 38,* 69–73.

Valentine, P. V., & Smith, T. E. (2001). Evaluating incident reduction therapy with female inmates: A randomized controlled clinical trial. *Research on Social Work Practice, 11*(1), 40–52.

Van Dorn, R. A., & Williams, J. H. (2003). Correlates associated with escalation of delinquent behavior in incarcerated youths. *Social Work, 48*(4), 523–531.

Van Soest, D., & Bryant, S. (1995). Violence reconceptualized for social work: the urban dilemma. *Social Work, 40,* 549–557.

Velicer. W. F., Norman, G. J., Fava, J. L., & Prochaska, J. O. (1999). Testing 40 predictions from the transtheoretical model. *Addictive Behaviors, 24*(4), 455–469.

Walton, E. (2001). Combining abuse and neglect investigations with intensive family preservation services: An innovative approach to protecting children. *Research on Social Work Practice, 11*(6), 627–644.

Weiner, A. (1996). Understanding the social needs of street-walking prostitutes. *Social Work, 41,* 97–105.

Wells, S. J. (1995). Child abuse and neglect overview. In R. L. Edwards (Ed.), *Encyclopedia of social work* (19th ed., pp. 346–353). Washington, D.C.: NASW Press.

Whitfield, G. W. (1999). Validating school social work: An evaluation of a cognitive-behavioral approach to reduce school violence. *Research on Social Work Practice, 9*(4), 399–426.

Wilson, S. J., Lipsey, M. W., & Soydan, H. (2003). Are mainstream programs for juvenile delinquency less effective with minority youth than majority youth? *Research on Social Work Practice, 13*(1), 326.

Witkin, S. L. (1998). Greetings. *Social Work, 43,* 101103.

Yatchmenoff, D. K. (2005). Measuring client engagement from the client's perspective in non-voluntary child protective services. *Research on Social Work Practice, 15*(2), 84–96.

Chapter 2

An Introduction to Forensic Social Work Perspectives

Albert R. Roberts and David W. Springer

INTRODUCTION

Forensic social workers are woefully needed in the twenty-first century due to the 24 million vulnerable crime victims aged 12 and over, and the 7.5 million adult offenders in the United States and Canada. As forensic social workers, also known as justice or correctional social workers, most of us firmly believe that both offenders and victims have the potential for change provided that each client is given equal opportunities for case, legal, and system advocacy, crisis risk assessment and intervention, cognitive-behavioral treatment, family counseling, group therapy, addictions treatment, trauma recovery services, victim assistance, case management and other social services, vocational rehabilitation and aftercare. In this book, we explore the development of federal, state, and local policies and practices in juvenile and criminal justice settings as a crucial step in meeting the concrete social service and mental health needs of juvenile and adult offenders, their families, and their victims.

The overriding goal of forensic and justice social work is to improve the quality of life and deliver mental health and social services to victims and offenders. We aim to create an environmental milieu and therapeutic programs in which individuals, groups, and communities can flourish, and the pain and suffering inherent in violent communities can be substantially reduced. The scope of forensic social work includes a wide range of evidence-based assessment and treatment methods with crime victims as well as juvenile and adult offenders. Mental health, criminal justice, and other human service professionals have been concerned in recent years about the growing number of offenders and victims in urgent need of mental health care and social services,

many of whom are at increased risk of future violence and retraumatization if they do not receive the evidence-based interventions they so urgently need. As a result, forensic social workers are critically needed to conduct danger assessments, psychosocial assessments, and social work treatment for large groups of victims and offenders. The following summaries encapsulate the focus of each of the six sections and 31 chapters in this book.

Section 1 of the book, comprised of Chapters 1 to 6, provides an introduction to forensic social work trends, policies, and practices and lays the overarching conceptual framework for the rest of the book.

In Chapter 1, Albert R. Roberts, David W. Springer, and Patricia Brownell provide a retrospective and futuristic introduction and overview of key trends, issues, policies, program developments, and events in forensic social work. We also address curriculum-related issues for social work education, and provide an overview for this book. Next, in the current Chapter 2, the volume coeditors delineate and summarize the focus of each of the 31 chapters comprising this book.

In Chapter 3, Sheldon R. Gelman and Daniel Pollack examine a somewhat disconnected set of issues in a systematic and macro way so as to identify the context in which correctional policies develop and operate. They draw on a range of correctional, social work, and legal literature as well as judicial decisions and media reports to illustrate factors that determine policies in the correctional field. Conflicting value premises underlying correctional policies, societal perceptions regarding the threat of criminal behavior, and economic and political considerations play key roles in the development of correctional policies. The intent of correctional policies is mixed, reflecting both "rehabilitative" and "just desserts" elements.

While a given perspective may become dominant at a given time in history, elements of the other perspective are always present. As the factors identified above shift over time, demands for reform are heard, different policies are developed, and resources available for correctional activities are modified.

In Chapter 4, Harvey Treger and G. Frederick Allen underscore the need to understand and use two major concepts – interprofessional cooperation and social change. These types of systematic efforts can result in improving direct practice, planning, management, and evaluation. When interprofessional relationships such as the ones examined in Chapter 4 are developed, the results are a sharing of resources, increased referrals, and the ripple effect of other agencies seeking involvement in the new service. Social work's leadership in the initiation of collaborative programs has the potential of significantly affecting public policy and program developments in the justice system.

In Chapter 5, H. Wayne Johnson, James A. Hall, and Bushra Sabri explore the community context of crime and delinquency and the community responses to this social problem that is collectively termed criminal justice. The authors consider the communities in which crime and delinquency occur and in which the criminal justice system operates – both rural and urban. They report that crime rates are generally higher in cities than in the country, and that crime victimization rates are higher in cities than in suburbs and in suburbs than in rural areas. The phenomenon of deviancy is examined in relation to these factors, considering both the nature and extent of rural and city criminality and their comparison. The three key criminal justice subsystems are explored – law enforcement, judicial, and correctional – with consideration given to both juvenile and adult offenders. Within corrections, both community-based services and institutions are discussed and analyzed, and the social worker's role in metropolitan and rural criminal justice is examined.

In Chapter 6, Elaine P. Congress examines ethical practices as it relates to forensic social work. This chapter explores the role of ethics in the social work and legal professions in general, and more specifically the role of ethics and law in social work practice. Similarities and differences between law and social work ethics, as well as social workers and attorneys, are addressed. The ETHIC model, developed by Professor Congress, is presented as an aid to help in understanding and resolving ethical and legal conflicts. The chapter concludes with guidelines to help social work practitioners and educators navigate when standards are in conflict in forensic social work practice.

In Chapter 7, the late Gloria Cunningham points out that psychotherapy and other types of individual counseling for offenders has been devalued on the basis of the conclusions of effectiveness studies. She also cautions that it is inappropriate to assume the goal of treatment is the modification of the offender's personality. Professor Cunningham questions both the accuracy of effectiveness studies and the need to define treatment in such narrow terms. The probation officer's role is reexamined in view of evolving methods of social work intervention. In contrast to traditional psychodynamic approaches, Professor Cunningham identifies the target of change as being the offender, as well as the offender's spouse, family system, and/or community. She views the probation officer's role as advocate and broker of services in addition to being a therapist, counselor, and teacher.

Section 2 of the book, comprised of Chapters 8 to 11, focuses on crisis intervention components and strategies, and police-based social work. This section begins with two case illustrations of violent crime victims seeking help, and the ways in which the seven-stage crisis intervention protocol results in goal setting and goal attainment, discovering new coping skills, implementing an action plan, crisis stabilization and resolution, and reduction in psychological trauma symptoms. Crisis intervention programs provide valuable assistance to crime victims as well as offenders presenting with suicide ideation, major depression, substance abuse problems, personal or family-related acute crisis episodes, psychological trauma, and life-threatening medical conditions. Thus, Chapter 8 examines each sequential stage of crisis intervention and provides the reader with basic structure, process, and techniques in order to facilitate an active and directive stance while displaying a nonjudgmental, hopeful, patient, normalizing, and positive attitude. The next three chapters focus on the past, present, and future of police social work and law-enforcement based victim service and victim assistance programs. These chapters underscore the importance of rapid 24-hour on-call response from specially trained police-social work teams. Most noteworthy in these coordinated collaborations is the mutual respect and appreciation gained when clinical social workers work side-by-side with caring police officers in volatile, unstable, and potentially dangerous situations when the stability of children and families hang in the balance. Exposure to child maltreatment and domestic violence is a prevalent problem often hidden behind closed doors. Many years of experience among police-social work teams has demonstrated positive outcomes and prevention of life-threatening injuries and PTSD as a result of the teams early intervention activities.

Section 3 of the book, comprised of Chapters 12 to 16, examines the assessment and treatment of juvenile delinquents, juvenile justice policy developments, and the role of the social worker in juvenile justice settings. After increasing for a number of years, and contributing to the spread of "get tough," punitive legislation, juvenile crime peaked in 1994 and then began declining. Despite overall declines in juvenile arrests and even in violent arrests, arrests in some categories have recently increased. Two areas of concern are simple assaults and drug violations. As Professors McNeece, Tyson, and Jackson point out in their chapter, in the early years of the twenty-first century, following more than a decade of rapidly spreading get-tough policies that increasingly placed juveniles in largely ineffective and potentially dangerous environments such as boot camps, adult prisons, and large, overcrowded facilities, a few communities are beginning to return to the rehabilitation-focused roots of the juvenile justice ideal. In large measure, this movement toward evidence-based juvenile offender assessment, treatment, and rehabilitation is the focus of this section.

In Chapter 12, Cathryn C. Potter and Jeffrey M. Jenson examine the prevalence of mental health and substance abuse among youth in the juvenile justice system, consider screening and assessment needs in juvenile justice programs, and review screening and diagnostic instruments aimed at identifying mental health and substance abuse problems. Professors Potter and Jenson also discuss a practice model for assessment and identify complex assessment issues, including the quality of instruments, the role of assessors, and the difficulties of disentangling symptoms across problem domains.

In Chapter 13, Stephen J. Tripodi and David W. Springer address the mental health and substance abuse treatment of juvenile delinquents. The number of drug-related juvenile offenses continues to rise, and is a pressing problem for the juvenile justice system. Tripodi and Springer discuss the role and effectiveness of juvenile assessment centers and juvenile addiction receiving facilities, therapeutic communities, case management, boot camps, alcoholics anonymous, urine drug testing, multisystemic therapy, outpatient family-based interventions (focusing specifically on structural-strategic family therapy and brief strategic family therapy), and problem-solving skills training.

In Chapter 14, C. Aaron McNeece, Edgar Tyson, and Sherry Jackson focus on trends and issues related to juvenile justice policy, including diversion and de-institutionalization programs, jail removal programs, mediation, restorative justice, acupuncture, boot camps, drug treatment, privatization, delinquency prevention programs, and due process. Permeating all of these issues is the broad question of whether the juvenile court should retain jurisdiction with certain types of cases, or refer them to mental health or other social service systems for appropriate treatment. Professors McNeece, Tyson, and Jackson also explore critical issues such as racial/gender disparities and children in jails and prisons.

In Chapter 15, Carolyn Needleman points out that interpreting the practice problems faced by social workers in juvenile justice requires an understanding of the conflicting philosophies built into the system itself. This chapter reviews the rehabilitative ideals with which the juvenile court was founded and outlines three major sources of ideologically-based dissatisfaction with the court as an institution: Constitutionalist concerns about the lack of due process for the accused, retributive justice concerns about lack of deserved punishment of the offender, and humanitarian concerns about the gap that lack of resources has opened between the juvenile court's intentions and its reality. Each of these three critical perspectives has had an impact on the court's development in recent years. Each, however, implies a different kind of reform. As a result, some of the patterns of change in juvenile justice have been inconsistent and even contradictory.

In Chapter 16, Elizabeth S. Marsal, Lessie Bass, and Mary S. Jackson present a nurturing practice model of working with gang members in juvenile settings. This chapter provides forensic social workers with another approach (the NPM) that can be used to work effectively with incarcerated gang members and other at risk adolescents and their families. The chapter focuses on the importance of breaking through communication barriers between youths and adults. Parenting strategies that empower parents, as well as youths, in discovering and sustaining positive communication skills and nonviolent relationships are explored. The hope is that such strategies will eliminate violence, while empowering gang members to remove themselves from violent situations.

Section 4 of the book, comprised of Chapters 17 to 21, coalesces around victim assistance, child maltreatment, domestic violence, crisis intervention, and trauma care. Sadly, most justice-oriented policies and services had been ignored for violent crime victims until the mid-1980s. The most promising boost in federal and state funding which led to the establishment of several thousand prosecutor-based victim/witness assistance programs, domestic violence programs, and sexual assault programs came about as a direct result of the landmark Victims of Crime Act (VOCA) signed into law by President Ronald Reagan in 1984 and implemented starting in 1985. The far-reaching results was the establishment of the new federal Office on Victims of Crime (OVC) through which state-wide and county victim/witness assistance offices, domestic violence shelters and treatment programs, and sexual assault intervention programs were funded throughout the nation. Then, a major boost to federal funding of victim assistance and domestic violence programs became a reality with the passage of the Violence Against Women Act (VAWA I) in 1994, and VAWA II in October, 2000. More specifically, VAWA II funding resulted in a $3.3 billion allocation for the years 2000–2005 to fund police-based domestic violence STOP grants, state-wide domestic violence coalitions and task forces, domestic violence shelters, transitional housing for battered women, the 24-hour national domestic violence hotline and sexual assault treatment programs. As this book went to press, VAWA III was signed into law by President Bush and resulted in an allocation of $3.9 billion for the years 2006–2010 for the continued expansion of domestic violence and sexual assault coalitions, policy reforms, programs, and services.

In Chapter 17, Jennifer Becker and Barbara Thomlison examine assessment and intervention in child sexual abuse. The authors define issues, trends, and the incidence of child sexual abuse, and review the process of disclosure and impact of child sexual

abuse. The roles of the criminal justice system and child protection services are discussed, with a focus on empirically-based forensic assessment and intervention strategies. This includes a discussion of forensic interviewing protocols and standardized scales, multidisciplinary teams and child advocacy centers, court involvement and victim advocacy, and involving the nonoffending parent in treatment. Becker and Thomlison point out that frontline providers – particularly forensic specialists, child protection workers, and clinicians – should be provided adequate education and training to competently perform investigations, assessments, and evidence-based interventions as they emerge. We must continue to close the gap between research and practice.

In Chapter 18, Albert R. Roberts and Beverly Schenkman Roberts focus on the recent prevalence estimates, early warning signs or red flags, assessment issues, and intervention strategies with battered women. They begin their chapter with two brief case vignettes. The first illustrates how a 24-year-old college graduate quickly and permanently broke up with her abusive boyfriend, and how her sleep disturbances and nightmares continued even though the batterer was out of her life. The second case illustrates the years of suffering and physical batterings, and turning point for a 29-year-old school teacher with two young children who was a devout Roman Catholic. This former battered woman describes how she left her husband, a medical doctor, only after the urging of her priest and a support group sponsored by Catholic Charities. Next, the authors document the facts that millions of women are battered each year with specific statistics such as every nine seconds a woman is assaulted or battered by her spouse, boyfriend, or former intimate partner. Methods of assessing safety concerns and dangerousness are discussed next. The last section of this chapter examines practical intervention strategies and survival guidelines for battered women and their children.

In Chapter 19, Arlene Bowers Andrews provides an overview of the basic knowledge that a social worker needs with regard to victimization and survivor services and directs the reader to additional resources for skills development. Topics covered include magnitude of the problem, a conceptual framework for social work action, evolving standards for effective practice, and resources for further study. The author adopts a broad use of the term *survivor*, used to refer to any person who has lived through a victimizing experience because it reflects the intrinsic strength and power of the person who is forced to adapt after a victimizing experience. The focus in the chapter is social work responses to survivors of crime, which includes acts that could result in criminal charges against an offender, whether a conviction, diversion, or dismissal of charges is the outcome. People are also victimized through noncriminal events such as disaster, accidents, disease, or population exploitation, but the human intent in a criminal act creates a psychological and social context that precipitates particular psychosocial effects in the survivor. The social worker's role is to prevent and address these effects.

In Chapter 20, Sophia F. Dziegielewski and Marcia Swartz begin their chapter with a detailed case illustration of the dynamics of woman battering. The next section examines the characteristics of the abuser and the abused woman, followed by a discussion of legal remedies. The authors then focus on five different roles for social workers in domestic violence cases. The first role is to provide psychosocial information on the victim to the deputy prosecutor. The second is to provide education and training to police and other criminal justice professionals. Third, the social worker can be the supportive and trusting mental health professional helping the victim through the trauma and ordeal of testifying in court. The fourth critical role is client advocate in addressing the judge before sentencing and working with family members to facilitate social support. Finally, the fifth role involves serving as an expert witness for battered women.

In Chapter 21, Albert R. Roberts first compares the similarities and differences between victim service programs and prosecutor-based victim/witness assistance programs. He then examines the organizational structure, staffing patterns, goals, and purposes of prosecutor-based victim/witness assistance programs. Discussions include the different functions of these programs including court case trial notification for witnesses, transportation services to and from court for victims and witnesses, court advocacy, court-provided child care, assistance with victim compensation applications, crisis intervention services, and notification of an offender's pending parole, work furlough, and/or release dates.

Section 5 of this book, comprised of Chapters 22 to 25, explores probation, parole, and court settings.

According to the U.S. Bureau of Justice Statistics [BJS] (2005), during 2004, the total federal, state, and local adult correctional population – incarcerated or in the community – grew substantially to reach nearly the seven million mark. About 3.2 percent of the U.S. adult population, or 1 in every 31 adults, were incarcerated or on probation or parole at year end 2004. Four states had an increase of 10 percent or more in their probation population in 2004; Kentucky (15%), Mississippi (12%), New Mexico (11%), and New Jersey (10%). The adult probation population decreased in 21 states. However, Washington state was the only state with a double-digit decrease (down 27%). A total of 10 states saw double-digit increases in their parole population in 2004, led by Nebraska (24%). Nine states had a decrease in their parole population. Nevada, down 13 percent, was the only state with a decrease of more than 10 percent.

In Chapter 22, Carrie J. Petrucci examines the basic tenets of therapeutic jurisprudence, reviews current social science and legal research that has explored therapeutic jurisprudence in social work and criminal justice, and discusses common themes across therapeutic jurisprudence and social work. Essentially, therapeutic jurisprudence considers how the law impacts people's health and well-being. Accordingly, the aim of the chapter is to familiarize social work students, policy-makers, and practitioners with therapeutic jurisprudence, the opportunities and debates that it presents, and how it can be utilized to improve social work and legal practice. In many respects, this chapter lays the groundwork for the remaining chapters in this section.

In Chapter 23, Frank B. Raymond, III and Johnny M. Jones focus on administrative functions and explain how these functions can be optimally carried out in the day-to-day work of the administrator – the Chief Probation Officer. The authors discuss the effectiveness of social work education in preparing graduate students for management positions in probation and parole departments, and they acquaint the reader with a contingency perspective on management theory. The usefulness of the five functions of management (planning, organizing, staffing, directing and leading, and controlling) are illustrated through a detailed case illustration of a social work administrator's application of these management fundamentals.

In Chapter 24, Risdon N. Slate, Erik Roskes, Richard Feldman, and Migdalia Baerga examine the extent to which the criminal justice system is equipped to meet the special needs of persons with mental illness who are incarcerated or on custodial-supervised release in the community. As part of this discussion, they explore the criminalization of the mentally ill, the role of probation officers in working with mentally ill offenders, and approaches such as mental health courts and assertive community treatment (ACT). The authors envision a collaborative partnership, where the roles of the probation officer and of the clinical providers are complementary, each contributing to the "whole picture" rather than competing with each other.

Resistance and lack of cooperation often come with the territory in working with juveniles. In Chapter 25, Michael D. Clark encourages probation staff to use motivational interviewing as a way to increase readiness for change with mandated offenders.

Section 6 of the book, comprised of Chapters 26 to 31, focuses on adult corrections in institutional and community-based settings. Approximately 6.6 million people were on probation, in jail or prison, or on parole in the United States at the beginning of this century. We know that the rates of mental health and substance use disorders are typically much higher among incarcerated adults than the corresponding rates among general community populations. Accordingly, this section examines a range of important issues in adult corrections, including the special needs of female offenders and their families, jail mental health services, the treatment of PTSD in inmates, and the restorative justice movement.

In Chapter 26, Andre Ivanoff, Nancy J. Smyth, and Catherine N. Dulmus focus on the institutional environment in correctional settings and the social worker's role in this environment. The authors then discuss specific areas of training appropriate for preparing for a career as a correctional professional. The importance of motivational interviewing and therapeutic engagement are explored. The impact of race, gender, as well as ethical conflicts are thoroughly discussed.

In Chapter 27, Patricia Brownell, Keva M. Miller, and Matha L. Raimon focus on female offenders in the criminal justice system, examining issues such as domestic violence, substance abuse, and entitlements for female offenders' families. Emphasis is placed on re-entry as it relates to reconnecting with children,

other family members, and successful re-integration into the community. Moreover, suggestions concerning issues that forensic social workers should consider when in search of evidence-based interventions are provided. These include direct service provision, collaborative efforts with interdisciplinary teams, and advocacy on behalf of female offenders and their families.

In Chapter 28, David Showalter and Marian Hunsinger describe the role and function of social workers in a maximum security penitentiary. These two forensic social workers have worked with a number of offenders with special needs, including the physically handicapped, persons with mental retardation, chronically ill, and elderly offenders. Special consideration is given to the knowledge and skills necessary to prepare a professional to work in a prison. Social work roles and skills such as advocacy, mobilization of resources, and familiarity with minority needs and cultural barriers are stressed as being especially useful in a prison setting.

In Chapter 29, Denise Johnston addresses correctional social work with parents involved in the criminal justice system and their children. The author begins with an overview of parental crime and arrest. She goes on to address parents under correctional supervision and in jails, the impact this has on the children of these parents, and the tasks of the social worker in the jail. Imprisoned parents are also discussed, including their characteristics, parent-child programs in prisons, the social workers tasks with imprisoned parents, parental identity and empowerment, and maintaining the parent-child relationship. Dr. Johnston then explores parental re-entry, parental recidivism, and parent-child reunification. She ends the chapter by sharing a list of six recommendations developed by The Center for Children of Incarcerated Parents (of which Dr. Johnston is the Director) for human services providers in correctional settings.

In Chapter 30, Susan Hoffman Fishman and Albert S. Alissi present a case illustration of an innovative volunteer service agency – Women in Crisis. The authors demonstrate the effectiveness of this model program in meeting the needs of family members at times of crisis and in strengthening the family as a stable source of help to the offender. This practical program is based on the following two underlying premises: the use of trained volunteers as service providers, and advocacy and client empowerment as a role of the volunteer.

In Chapter 31, Joan Petersilia explores the salient question, *what programs work in prisoner reentry?* In doing so, Petersilia explores principles versus program outcomes from the Canadian and U.S. literature, and then critically examines limitations of the research base that has studied the effectiveness of prison reentry programs. She sees three problems with using the current evidence to answer the important question, "what works in reentry?" The first is that are few rigorous evaluations upon which to base any generalizable knowledge. Second, virtually all of these evaluations use recidivism as the sole outcome criteria. Third, the author draws from her own experience, which suggest that the results from the academic "what works" literature does not feel right to correctional practitioners. The author envisions a system where, start to finish, practitioners and researchers work side-by-side to create corrections programs that are both substantively and administratively effective.

Chapter **3**

Correctional Policies: Evolving Trends

Sheldon R. Gelman and Daniel Pollack
with the assistance of Malca Fink

The American Civil Liberties Union filed an appeal on behalf of Michael Purcell, a University of Alaska-Anchorage student and former prisoner who was denied entry into the school's social work program due solely to his past criminal convictions. The ACLU attorneys say the school's denial of entry to a model student constitutes a violation of Purcell's right to rehabilitation under the Alaska Constitution.

Admissions to the program is based on the successful completion of course requirements and the professional judgment of the faculty. The professional judgment standard includes consideration of whether an applicant is fit for social work practice. Purcell, a 37-year-old student, attended the university since he was released from prison on furlough in 2002.

When attempting to discuss correctional policy, one is immediately confronted by a dilemma arising from two distinct yet interrelated sets of issues. The first issue involves the question, "What is policy?" while the second centers on whether there is something that can be identified as correctional policy. The first issue can be readily addressed through a definitional exercise in which various authors' perspectives on policy are set out (e.g., Jansson, 2003; Flynn, 1996; Schwartz, April, 2000; DiNitto, 1991; Dobelstein, 1996; Tropman, 1989; Moroney, 1998; Morris, 1979; Gilbert & Specht, 1974; Gil, 1973; Kahn, 1973; Rein, 1970). One or several formulations can then be selected that encompass the range of activities that are identified as policy. The second issue is more problematic, in that there appears to be no single policy that guides the field of corrections.

SOCIAL POLICY

Basically, every industrialized society, as part of its organizational structure, attempts to meet the needs of its constituents through a system of formal principles. These principles, laws, or policies attempt to create some degree of order so that the society and its members can reach or achieve their full potential. A society's policies are designed to assist with meeting social needs, alleviate social problems, create an environment in which individuals and the society can grow, and provide a measure of safety to its members. According to Gil (1973), social policies deal with the quality of life in a society, the circumstances of living of individuals and groups, and the nature of intrasocietal human relationships. Kahn describes policy as "the explicit or implicit core of principles, or the continuing line of decisions and constraints, behind specific programs, legislation, administrative practices, or priorities" (Kahn, 1973, 8). Some writers see policy as a process in which problems or needs are identified, choices made, and strategies developed, while others view policy as the outcome or product of this process. According to Moroney (1990), policy choices are shaped by values which are reflective of attitudes and beliefs. Generally, the evolution of policy involves a goal or series of goals that are developed in response to an identified or anticipated problem (Jansson, 2003). Policy is both process and outcome and can be viewed not only as potential solutions to perceived social problems but also as a cause or perpetuating factor in social problems.

CORRECTIONAL POLICY

As indicated, there appears to be no single policy but a variety of policies developed and implemented at various levels in the field of corrections. Correctional policy has been and is developed by many groups and agencies that function in a semiautonomous fashion in various governmental and political jurisdictions. The policies formulated are usually arrived at through political compromise and are more often than not contradictory in terms of direction and focus (DiNitto, 1991). For example:

> Faced with overcrowding in the courts and jails caused by the collision of increased arrests and a shrinking budget, [New York City's Mayor] Giuliani ordered the reopening of a jail that had just been closed to save money. . . . The action highlighted . . . the struggle to reconcile two aims that were pillars of his campaign last year: slash the city's budget while also improving the quality of life in the city by getting tough even with minor criminals. (Fritsch, 1994, B1)

The direction of policies is determined by formal and informal negotiations among various interest groups. The position taken by any interest group is determined by its particular value orientation. Policy is, in the end, a reflection of the values of the public as voiced through its political representatives and implemented or executed through various professional functionaries (Dobelstein, 1996). Therefore, while it is possible to discuss correctional policies in some detail, any effort to identify a single correctional policy or to assess the effectiveness of policies or policy outcomes in the field of corrections is more problematic. Complicating matters further is the difficulty of identifying a policy as either "correctional" or normative public policy. For instance, recent policy changes in curfews for minors, violent mentally ill homeless persons, mentally ill parolees and those infected with the HIV virus invoke issues of civil rights, not just correctional policy.

Additionally, since the development of policy is conceptually and administratively distinct from the implementation process (Dobelstein, 1996), understanding the impact and effect of correctional policies is far from easy (Levine, Musheno, & Palumbo, 1980). Implementation of correctional policy, like policies in other areas, is subject to a range of discretionary actions that color the outcome or impact of policies. Although reference throughout this chapter will be made to the criminal justice "system," we do not want to give the impression that a unitary, easily identifiable system actually exists. The word "system" is used in its broadest sense, referring to a range of activities occurring in the criminal justice field.

Given this background we now can attempt to rationally discuss a somewhat disconnected set of issues in a way that attempts to explain the context in which correctional policies develop and operate. In order to gain a comprehensive understanding of correctional policy, a systematic approach that identifies issues and outcomes is indicated. The approach must define the nature of the problem that requires the development of a correctional response, underlying value premises and theoretical approaches to the problems, goals and objectives, historical responses to the problem, cost, related policies impacting on the correctional field, and intended and unintended effects. Special attention to resources and the issue of "rights" within the correctional field must also be examined.

THE NATURE OF THE PROBLEM

Every society has been confronted with the problem of individuals who violate or are perceived as violating the norms of that society. As a result, all societies have developed policies to deal with norm-violating behavior. Death, physical maiming, ostracism, and incarceration have been utilized as policy choices aimed at curbing norm-violating behavior. Similarly, penitence and rehabilitation (treatment) have also been selected as appropriate policy responses to be applied to law violators. History illustrates that society responses in terms of policy development tend to be cyclical, with preference given to different forms of intervention at different times. Harsh, if not cruel and inhumane, sanctions and punishments have been balanced or replaced with more humanitarian and rehabilitative measures and vice versa.

Theorists have long debated the cause of criminal activities, i.e., norm-violating behavior, and the type of response that is needed in order to protect and maintain a functioning society. The cause of law-violating behavior has been viewed as either a defect within the individual (genetic or biological) and/or caused by an oppressive or unjust society. Neither perspective in terms of cause or response has won out over the other perspective on a permanent basis. No consensus has ever been reached as to which form of intervention is most effective in eliminating, deterring, or limiting rule violation or in creating a just and harmonious society. Dissatisfaction with one or the other perspective is based on perceptions regarding the effectiveness of the intervention in reducing or eliminating criminal activities. Unfortunately, a key element in the development of correctional policies is the reality of societal perceptions relating to the threat or fear of crime, not whether interventions are effective.

UNDERLYING VALUE PREMISES

The perception of crime, the perceived threat or fear of crime, and the belief, often unsupported by data, that current efforts to curb crime are ineffective rather than an actual increase in crime appears sufficient to create a demand for correctional reform. Shifts in correctional policy occur in response to the fear of the public at large and general dissatisfaction with existing practices. These phenomena in part account for the fact that the nation's prison population now exceeds two million prisoners. (BJS, 2005)

Policies in the correctional field deal with the perceived rights and responsibilities of society towards and on behalf of its members. Implicit in all correctional policy is the need to protect society and its members from potential lawbreakers. Maintenance of the social order and the preservation of the public peace, health, and safety are of prime concern. Lawbreakers, with the possible exception of some who claim political motivation and justification, are viewed as deviating from accepted societal norms and values. Such deviation is perceived as a threat to the established order and therefore requires the development of a variety of institutions that act as a means of social control. Societal institutions, whether they be legislative decrees or physical structures, serve as a stabilizing factor in societies undergoing change (Ponsioen, 1969). They provide an ordered and continuous framework for realizing group values and are the most important vehicle through which the sanctions of society are brought to bear upon the individual (Merrill, 1961).

It has long been recognized that the criminal justice system is faced with the often conflicting objectives of protecting society and rehabilitating the offender (Netherland, 1987). One way of looking at these conflicting objectives is to contrast what has become known as the "just dessert" (Von Hirsch, 1976; Dershowitz, 1976) or "justice model" (Fogel, 1975) approach to that of the "rehabilitative ideal" (Allan, 1959). The "just desserts" perspective holds that criminal justice activities should not be concerned with rehabilitation, the remaking or remolding of the individual to better fit the norms of society, but should focus on exacting from each offender "deserved" punishment that is proportional to the offense that has been committed against society or its members (Duffee, 1980).

The moralist approach to criminal justice is one in which the system is seen as upholding the morals and value of society. The system is viewed as having a deterrent force towards lawbreaking. Individuals are encouraged to adhere to societal mandates to avoid retributive sanctions. Punishment is viewed as a major element of the criminal justice system. The threat and application of punishment is viewed as necessary to preserve order. According to Packer, "When the threat of punishment is removed or reduced, either through legislative repeal . . . or through the inaction of enforcement authorities, conduct that has previously been repressed . . . tends to increase" (Packer, 1964, 118). Individuals who violate the law are viewed as deserving punishment, and society is best served by delivering punishment and deterring potential lawbreakers. Sentencing offenders is based on their past behavior and actions and the nature of the offense.

The above approach can be contrasted to the "rehabilitative ideal" or "social welfare" perspective. The social welfare perspective favors the notion of rehabilitation and views retribution and punishment as having little impact on criminal behavior. According to Duffee, the overriding characteristics of those who assume the social welfare perspective is the "insistence that the criminal justice system must be evaluated in terms of its ability to improve the conditions as well as the behavior of people against whom it directly intervenes" (Duffee, 1980, p. 8). While the emphasis within the welfare perspective is on the offender and the treatment or handling of the offender, it is also related to society as a whole and to its welfare. The primary cause of criminal behavior is viewed as rooted in the political and economic system rather than within the individuals themselves.

Rehabilitation must take place on two fronts: rehabilitation of the individual who has committed crimes against society, and rehabilitation of society to eliminate the necessity of an individual engaging in criminal activity. It has been frequently asserted that the welfare of society is and can only be protected through humane treatment and appropriate rehabilitative activities. According to Hussey (1979), "When an offender has been convicted of a criminal act the welfare of society and of the offender are of concern and that both could be served best if the sanction received by the offender could be informed by a study of that particular offender's needs. Indeed, it was believed that the criminal justice response should be tailored to the unique offender. In a phrase, the system adopted the positivist's position and treated the offender, not the offense" (p. 41).

Integral to the "rehabilitative ideal" are the presentence investigation and the discretionary use of probation and parole, which can be used to individualize interventions and help rehabilitate the offender with the overall goal of improving functioning within society.

While attitudes toward adult offenders has shifted toward long-term incarceration, juveniles who were previously viewed more leniently are now being viewed as miniature adults, subject to more severe penalties. In a poll of 250 juvenile court judges, the *National Law Journal* found that most judges would like to see juveniles treated more like adults. To that end, an overwhelming 91 percent of the judges favor extending their power to supervise and incarcerate the most serious youthful offenders past the age of majority, provided they get more resources and options to do the job. Consistent with that preference, they believe the vast majority of delinquents who appear before them can be rehabilitated. At the same time, many judge favor the death penalty for murderers as young as 14 (Sherman. 1994, 1)

Other "get-tough" measures endorsed by the judges include:

- 93 percent favor fingerprinting
- 85 percent want juvenile records open to adult law enforcement authorities
- 68 percent favor open court trials if the juvenile is charged with a felony.

Interestingly, 86 percent of the judges acknowledge that the social service agencies their juveniles are referred to do not have sufficient resources to respond effectively.

GOALS AND OBJECTIVES

There are two fundamental premises that underlay all correctional policy. The first relates to a concern for the safety and protection of the community, the second with a concern for the individual offender. These concerns or policy premises can be combined to yield four general policy objectives with respect to corrections:

1. *Restraint*, in which corrections provides a holding action for the offender. Incarceration and punishment are used as a means of retribution, thus protecting society.
2. *Reform*, in which there is a low emphasis on the offender and a high emphasis on the community. This perspective has a deterrent focus and aims for conformity with dominant societal beliefs and values.
3. *Rehabilitation*, wherein correctional efforts are directed toward changing the pathology of the offender and bringing about conformity to societal norms.
4. *Reintegration*, in which there is a high level of concern for both the offender and the community with attempts being made to enhance opportunities for community interaction and involvement. (Duffee, 1975)

Similarly, four traditional objectives can be identified that have been associated with correctional activities:

1. *Incapacitation*, the prevention of those crimes that would have been committed during the period of incarceration;
2. *Deterrence* of future criminal actions by the convicted offender or by others in the community by way of example;
3. *Retribution*, or punishment proportional to the seriousness of the committed offense; and
4. *Rehabilitation*, in which the offender not the offense, is the primary focus of intervention. (Netherland, 1987)

Since neither the Duffee policy orientations nor the traditional objectives of corrections exist in pure form, the actual operation of correctional activities generally reflect a mixture of these often competing orientations which vary over time. The objective of the criminal justice system is therefore not singular in nature. "The plethora of objectives served by the system makes it difficult to talk about anyone of them as if it were the overriding objective" (Hussey, 1979, p. 36). In spite of these mixed objectives, it appears that the rehabilitative emphasis reached its modern-day peak during the late 1960s and early 1970s. It was during this period that an emphasis on individual rights, civil liberties, due process, deinstitutionalization, educational opportunities, community alternatives, and various treatment and counseling modalities developed. The uses of punishment and incarceration were viewed by many with disdain (Mitford, 1973; Clark, 1970; Menninger, 1969). Today, the tide has once again turned, with forces advocating incarceration and the death penalty gaining ground.

THE SCOPE OF THE PROBLEM

The validity of statistics relating to criminal activity has long been the subject of debate. Counting and perceptions are subjective enterprises and vary according to the "counter" (e.g., FBI National Crime Survey) and the purposes for which statistics are being collected. Nevertheless, everyone is a potential perpetrator or victim of criminal activity, a reality that brings us all into contact with the criminal justice system. The problem of lawbreaking affects us all. We pay either directly, as a victim of crime, or indirectly, as a taxpayer. Perceptions, rather than actual number of crimes or criminals, determine the nature of correctional responses. While serious violent crime levels have in the United Stated declined since 1993, the number of arrests for drug abuse has increased. The number of adults convicted of felonies in state courts has been increasing and over half the increase in the prison population since 1995 is due to an increase in convictions for violent offenses (BJS, 2005).

At the end of 2004, 2,135,901 prisoners were held in local jails and state and federal prisons. This was an increase of 26 percent over 2003. The number of women under the jurisdiction of state or federal prison authorities increased 4 percent from 2003, reaching 104,848. This number is almost three times higher than the number that Snell reported (2000) in his 1994 study. A number of social problems are causing the increase in the female prison population: unwanted pregnancies, homelessness, single motherhood,

AIDS/HIV, drugs, poverty, and poor education. As the numbers of female offenders increases, prison and jail administrators are reporting a need for specialized facilities and programming, new classification systems, and health and mental health services tailored especially for women. With most females serving relatively short sentences, the incarceration environment must emphasize parole aspects as well as long-term institutional concerns.

NEW CRIMES, NEW CORRECTIONS

With the apparent rise in criminal activity and growing prison populations has come an increased demand by the public at large and by politicians in particular for correctional reform. Support for long-term rehabilitative efforts has given way to an increasing emphasis on shock reform, or confinement and punishment. In the early 1980s, primarily as a response to prison overcrowding, the idea of boot camps was inaugurated. The thought was that first-time, nonviolent offenders could be salvaged if put into a rigorous, disciplined, military-style environment. Some states opted for boot camps as a rehabilitation alternative. Others cited reasons of decreased cost or recidivism reduction. Reports do not show any significant decrease in recidivism or cost per inmate associated with this type of correctional environment (Osler, 1991).

The belief in "just desserts" has again come into prominence, pushing rehabilitative and social welfare efforts aside. Dissatisfaction with the "rehabilitative ideal" can in part be traced to the perception of an increase in crime, a growing fear among citizens, difficulties with predicting future behavior-dangerousness (Underwood, 1979), and to the utilization of social science research in correctional policy-making. Politicians and the public at large, faced with growing unemployment, inflation, and crime want results – a reduction in criminal activity and safety for the public. If rehabilitative efforts have little or no impact and if prediction is so difficult, then more effective or at least more satisfying forms of intervention have to be found. Short-range solutions, regardless of cost, that appear as different than those that have gone on before are needed to soothe the public ire.

The move away from rehabilitative activities has been accompanied by a shift in sentencing procedures.

The shift to determinate sentencing is designed to bring about uniformity in the sentences that are imposed on offenders and limit the discretionary power of judges who had permitted the imposition of individualized, customized sentences (Hussey & Lagoy, 1981). Objection to indeterminate sentences centered in part on the widely disparate periods of imprisonment meted out within and among various jurisdictions and claims of racial and socioeconomic bias. Uniformity, equality, fairness, and certainty in the sentences imposed is the desired outcome. However, it is most difficult for individualized justice and equal justice to exist simultaneously (Levine, Musheno, & Palumbo, 1980). In other words, "rehabilitation" and "just desserts" may be mutually exclusive premises on which to operate a criminal justice system.

DRUGS

The shift in attitude toward crime is partly a function of the shift in the types and manner of crimes being committed. Since the mid-1980s, there has been a rise in the use of crack cocaine and methamphetamines and an attendant increase in crime (Inciardi, Lockwood, & Pottieger, 1993; Williams, 1992). The increase in crime triggered an intensified debate between those advocating for more prisons and those emphasizing more treatment availability (Reno, 1993).

The correlation between drug use and crime has been the subject of concern for policy-makers and researchers (Inciardi, Lockwood, & Quinlan, 1993; Inciardi, Horowitz, & Pottieger, 1993; Chaiken & Chaiken, 1990; Huizinga, Menard, & Elliot, 1989). Roth (1994) recently reported on the connection between violence and drug and alcohol. Key findings included that:

> Research has uncovered strong correlations between violence and psychoactive substances, including alcohol and illegal drugs, but the underlying relationships differ by type of drug. Of all psychoactive substances, alcohol is the only one whose consumption has been shown to commonly increase aggression. After large doses of amphetamines, cocaine, LSD, and PCP, certain individuals may experience violent outbursts, probably because of preexisting psychosis. Research is needed on the pharmacological effects of crack, which enters the brain more directly than cocaine used in other forms.
>
> Illegal drugs and violence are linked primarily through drug marketing: disputes among rival distributors,

arguments and robberies involving buyers and sellers, property crimes committed to raise drug money and, more speculatively, social and economic interactions between the illegal markets and the surrounding communities. (Roth, 1994, 1)

Critics remind us that, in any application of drug policy, civil rights must be protected, that there are severe limits to the effectiveness of law enforcement, and enforcement practices can increase the appearance of the drugs-crime relationship well beyond the framework of psychopharmacology, economic demand, and subcultural roles. Drug laws and policy should focus on demand reduction at least equal to supply reduction. Drug law enforcement must never be an excuse for a retreat on hard-won legal and civil rights, and drug law and policy must rest on a strong public base (McBride & McCoy, 1993, p. 274).

AIDS

Drug abuse is also a partial explanation for the dramatic increase in the numbers of prisoners afflicted with HIV/AIDS. The National Institute of Justice reported that 5,000 active AIDS cases have been recorded in prison since 1981. This trend is expected to continue to rise rapidly. Inmates have a higher-than-average risk of HIV/AIDS infection due to drug use, homosexual behavior, and needle-sharing. Concern among correctional systems has shifted significantly from short-term "crisis" matter such as fear of casual transmission to "long-haul" issues such as housing, programming, and medical care for prisoners with HIV disease. Resolving these issues is often complicated by political, legal, and cost considerations (Hammet & Moini, 1990, 1).

FIREARMS

Another concern is the number of violent crimes committed by firearms. Roth estimates that 60 percent of murder victims in 1989 were killed with firearms. He cites National Center for Health Statistics which indicate that "82% of all murder victims aged 15 to 19, and 76% of victims aged 20 to 24, were killed with guns. For black males aged 15 to 19, the firearm murder rate was 105.3 per 100,000; for comparable white males the rate was 9.7 per 100,000" (Roth, 1994, 1).

The teenage homicide has also been rising at a particularly alarming rate. The homicide of adolescents ages 15 to 19 rose 154 percent from the years 1985 to 1991. Almost the entire increase was due to guns (Butterfield, 1994). To combat their alarming statistics, state legislatures have been introducing gun control bills at a record pace. In 1994, the National Council of State Legislatures estimated the number at more than 2,000 (Butterfield, 1994).

SEX OFFENDERS

In the past year, there has been a flood of bills introduced in state legislators to deal more aggressively with sex offenders. Tougher sentencing and more stringent parole guidelines are being enacted rapidly. Features of these new laws include longer incarceration if the victim is a minor, indefinite parole suspension, offender registration with local law enforcement agencies, and notification of nearby residents of the neighborhood into which the offender moves.

Among the special provisions some states have enacted are the following:

- extra supervision during the first six to 12 months after release.
- a requirement to register as a sex offender, not just as a felon
- a prohibition against contact with specific persons, especially minors. There may also be a prohibition against living with a family member who was an incest victim of the offender.
- a requirement that the offender continues to attend group or individual therapy. The type of therapy should be consistent with the treatment being used where the sex offender was incarcerated.
- approval by a panel of mental health professionals prior to going on parole or terminating from parole. This may mean that a minimum score is achieved on a battery of psychological and personality tests, or a penile personality exam.

MENTALLY ILL

Another confounding phenomena that requires the attention of policymakers is the increasing number of individuals suffering from mental illnesses who are incarcerated. Individuals suffering from mental illness comprise anywhere from 10 percent (Adams, 1988) to 25 percent (Cecire, 1992) of the inmate population. Their presence can in part be attributed to the policy of deinstitutionalizing the mentally ill and their placement in the community without appropriate supportive services. Individuals in need of such services often find themselves in the correctional system. Jail is often the only resource available for them, and the special needs of this population presents major management problems (Rock & Landsberg, 2002). Additionally, the lack of appropriate or sufficient treatment resources often results in recidivism and/or public outrage when confronted by individuals unable to meet societal expectations.

CORRECTIONAL EFFECTIVENESS

One of the perennial problems in the field of corrections, both adult and youth, is the lack of systematic outcome data regarding interventions which work. While numerous descriptive studies exist, it has been difficult if not impossible to draw comparisons between programs and to generalize findings in a way that would inform policy makers and correctional officials.

In an effort to overcome these difficulties, a group known as the Campbell Collaboration was formed in February, 2000 (Petrosino, Boruch, et al., 2003). The Campbell Collaboration's mission is to prepare, maintain, and promote access to systematic reviews of high quality evaluation research on the efforts of social and educational polices and practice in the criminal justice and other areas.

The Campbell Collaboration's Crime and Justice Group, an international network of individuals, "will facilitate the preparation, updating, and accessibility of rigorous reviews of experimental and quasi-experimental evaluations in criminal justice" (p. 43). The Collaboration's Social Psychological, Educational and Criminological Trials Register (C2-SPECTR) created an electronic register of more than 700 studies related to social and educational intervention. Studies are reviewed utilizing a "systematic review" first developed by the Cochrane collaboration process which enables comparisons to be drawn between and among quantitative and qualitative studies.

The goal is to create a working database of research on the effects of interventions designed to reduce crime delinquency, which could improve the management and operation of the criminal justice system.

SHIFTING POLICY PERSPECTIVES

As crime has increased and prisons have become overcrowded, legislators have been compelled to act upon their ideologies. Discretion that had previously been left to judges has been revoked. In its place lawmakers have focused on legislative involvement in areas such as mandatory arrest for domestic violence, mandatory suspension of licenses for driving while intoxicated, probation and parole restrictions, minimum and mandatory sentencing, and transferring certain juvenile cases to criminal courts. With prisons in more than 40 states under court order (Koren, 1993), overcrowding is frequently ranked by legislators, corrections officials, and criminal justice researchers as among their priority problems (Welsh, 1993; Gettinger, 1984).

Although the emphasis in correctional policy in the 1990s appears to have shifted once again toward the "just desserts" premise, the existence of mixed-policy objectives continues. References to rehabilitation, with its concern for civil rights, due process, and individualized treatment, continue to dominate much of the professional social work (NASW, 1994) and correctional literature, while the media and legislative task forces increasingly are calling for a "hard-line" approach to deal with criminal activity. For example, the 1994 NASW Policy Statement on the Criminal Justice System asserts that:

> the focus of politicians and the media on crime and the criminalization of many activities has masked the social problems that lie behind the growing crime rate. The emphasis on public fear has served as a rationale for diverting resources from programs that address those problems toward the construction of prisons and the expansion of police power. (NASW, 1994, 50)

Successful efforts to combat crime are believed to be dependent on society's ability and willingness to eliminate poverty and discrimination, overcome the alienation of young peoples, develop and administer just laws, and create rational and coherent law enforcement, courts, and correctional systems. Community-based treatment is the treatment of choice for the overwhelming majority of offenders, with institutions being used only for those who present a dear and present danger to society.

While these policy recommendations are systems oriented and have received support from professional correctional personnel, they, like the social work proposals, do not coincide with current public concerns or present pressures in the correctional field. Along with a "get-tough" attitude is the recognition that prisons may not be punitive, and in fact, must be as humane as possible. For example, Title II of the Americans With Disabilities Act (ADA) requires that correctional and justice agencies provide "equal access" for disabled persons to its programs, services, and activities. For a person to be considered disabled there must be documentation of a physical or mental impairment that substantially limits a major life activity such as seeing, hearing, walking, or learning. Interestingly, there are no national statistics of the number of disabled persons in the justice and correctional systems. Other highlights of the act include the need to have written policies and procedures that address ADA compliance efforts, availability of assistive devices such as books in Braille, sign language interpreters, books on tape, and TTD telephones for the deaf.

The push for longer prison sentences and construction of additional prison beds is not unique to any one state. The rise in state prison populations is attributable to three major factors: (1) the implementation in many states of some type of mandatory sentencing policy, (2) determinate sentencing legislation, and (3) reduction in the number of paroles granted to inmates – all are indicative of dissatisfaction with past correctional activities.

CONFIDENTIALITY AND INFORMATION SHARING

Society's preoccupation with privacy and confidentiality has impacted the corrections field as well. Recent technological developments have made sharing information much easier but have also raised concerns that information will be made available to people or agencies that do not have a legitimate need for it. As long as certain safeguards are used, however, there is no reason correction agencies should not take advantage of the new information system

(Pollack, 1991). When correction agencies properly share information, their clients are the beneficiaries and rehabilitation prospects are enhanced.

In the 1960s and 1970s, people were usually served exclusively by one agency. In the 1980s, they were served by several government agencies that did not effectively share information. For example, a parolee with a mental health problem who needed food stamps would have three different case managers, none of whom could legally obtain the client's files from their sister agencies.

In the 1990s, a necessary change has begun to take place. People are still being served by many government agencies, but now there is a movement toward having one agency as the primary case manager. For instance, a case manager in the Department of Corrections trying to obtain mental health services for a parolee in aftercare will be able to do so much more easily because the appropriate information is shared between the Department of Corrections and the Department of Mental Health. Without this information sharing, the case manager winds up working by intuition alone.

Every state has passed legislation regarding the maintenance of personal information systems. These laws address a system's nature and purpose, identify the other government agencies and organizations that can access it, establish procedures to ensure its safety from unauthorized use, regulate how proper access and disclosure can be attained, and direct ways in which disputes concerning the system's operation can be resolved. In addition, criminal and civil sanctions have been developed to guard against intentional improper use or disclosure of personal information.

To feel comfortable that confidentiality statutes are being reworked without jeopardizing individuals' rights to privacy, there is a need to ascertain exactly what kinds of information can be shared under specific circumstances and what safeguards should exist to ensure that information sharing does not deteriorate into purposeless, unchecked data exchange. With the proper safeguards in place, greater information sharing is of benefit, not harm, to individual clients. This is not a question of the public's right to know weighed against an individual's right to personal privacy. Rather, it is the responsible sharing of information between two or more government agencies so that government can work better on the individual's behalf.

FUNDING

Correctional resources, i.e., funds made available for correctional activities, are closely linked to the goals and objectives to be achieved at any given period in our history. As noted previously, the development of correctional goals and objectives is part of a political process and are quite divergent in expected impact and outcome. Political considerations also have an economic dimension, with total resources available being limited. When resources are directed or in vested in certain types of programs to achieve a specific set of goals, those resources are not available for other purposes. When incarceration or custody become paramount in the minds of politicians and the public, resources for treatment services and community-based options are unavailable or limited. Resources devoted to custodial purposes divert already limited resources away from rehabilitative and/or less restrictive alternatives.

From a historical perspective, it is interesting to note that the rate of incarceration is directly related to social, political, and economic circumstances of the country. Incarcerated populations increase during periods of economic hardship and diminish in times of economic growth, often associated with a wartime economy (Farber, 1968; Abt, 1980). When unemployment is high, demands on the correctional enterprise increase. It is estimated that a 1 percent rise in unemployment results in a 4 percent jump in the rate of imprisonment (Lieber, 1981).

PROTECTING RIGHTS

During the last three decades, a great deal of interest in the issue of "rights" has evolved. A series of activist judicial decisions was handed down affirming the rights of various groups (i.e., racial minorities, the mentally retarded, juveniles, and the physically handicapped) who believed that as citizens they were entitled to standing and to protection from discriminatory actions. Included among the groups requiring protection were prisoners, parolees, and probationers. The courts were called upon to assure that governmental agencies (i.e., the police and correctional authorities) acted according to law and did not exceed their delegated authority by broaching, what has come to be known as the individual's "fundamental rights." These rights, in addition to the right to due process and equal protection, have been expanded to include the right:

1. To have equal educational opportunity;
2. To be free from inappropriate educational classification, labeling, and placement;
3. To receive community services and treatment in the least restrictive environment;
4. To be free from peonage and involuntary servitude;
5. To be free from restrictive zoning practices;
6. To have free access to buildings and transportation systems;
7. To be free from unconstitutional commitment practices;
8. To procreate; and
9. To have equal access to adequate medical services (Gelman, 1981).

Support for judicial decrees is most often heard from inmates, citizen groups, and correctional personnel who want to limit the discretionary power of administration and who supported the notion of rehabilitation. Opposition to these "liberal" reforms comes from those who believe in "justice" or "just desserts" and view these changes as leaving the public at large in a vulnerable position. Prisoners are perceived as having more rights and protections than the potential victims of their criminal behavior.

In more recent years, as previously discussed, there has emerged a countertrend that seeks to assure the safety of the public and the security of correctional institutions. This is to be achieved in part by reestablishing "order" and again applying the notion of "just desserts." This hard-line approach is apparent in the limitations on how much process is due inmates eligible for parole, the move to determinate sentencing, the abolition of parole, and limitations on the immunity of parole board members.

CONCLUSION

We have attempted in the foregoing presentation to identify factors that determine policy in the correctional field. Conflicting if not mutually exclusive value premises regarding the role and function of correctional activities, coupled with economic and political considerations, play crucial roles. The intent

of correctional policies is mixed, reflecting both "rehabilitative" and "just desserts" elements. At different times in history, one or the other perspective becomes dominate. While one perspective may be dominate for a period of time, the other perspective maintains its presence through the support of various constituencies. Over time, fears subside, positions moderate, and concerns shift. Society becomes more liberal or conservative with its resources. Abuses are corrected and new problems are identified requiring new protections associated with the rights of individuals and society. Always, efforts are being made to maintain a dynamic balance.

REFERENCES

Adalist-Estrin, A., & Mustin, J. (2002). Responding to children and families of prisoners: A community guide. *Family and Corrections Network*, www.fcnetwork.org.

Adams, R. D. (1988). *Exemplary country mental health programs: The diversion of people with mental illness from jails and in-jail mental health services.* Washington, D.C.: National Association of Counties.

Allen, F. A. (1959). Criminal justice, legal values and the rehabilitative ideal. *Journal of the Criminal Law Criminology and Police Science, 50,* 226–232.

Bureau of Justice Statistics. (1998). *Correctional populations in the United States, 1990.* Washington, D.C.

Bureau of Justice Statistics (2005). *Prison statistic.* Washington, D.C.

Butterfield, F. (October 14, 1994). Teen-age homicide rate has soared. *New York Times,* A22, Col. 1.

Cecire, R. (1992). *Jail-based mental health services in New York City Department of Correction facilities.* New York: New York City Department of Health.

Chaiken, J., & Chaiken, M. (1990). Drugs and predatory crime. In M. Tonry & J. Q. Wilson (Eds.), *Drugs and crime* (pp. 203–239). Chicago: University of Chicago Press.

Dershowitz, A. M. (1976). *Fair and certain punishment.* New York: McGraw-Hill.

DiNitto, D. M. (2005). *Social welfare: Politics and public policy.* Boston: Allyn and Bacon.

Dobelstein, A. W. (1996). *Social welfare: Policy and analysis.* Chicago: Nelson-Hall.

Duffee, D. (1975). *Correctional policy and prison organization.* New York: Sage.

Duffee, D. (1980). *Explaining criminal justice: Community theory and criminal justice reform.* Cambridge, MA: Oelgeschlager, Gunn & Hain.

Farber, B. (1968). *Mental retardation: Its social context and social consequences.* Boston: Houghton-Mifflin.

Federal Bureau of Prisons. (December 29, 1980). *Monday morning highlights.*

Fingerhut, L. (1993). *Firearm mortality among children, youth and young adults 1–34 years of age: Trends and current status: United States, 1985–90.* Washington, D.C.: U.S.Department of Health and Human Services, National Center for Health Statistics.

Flynn, J. P. (1996). *Social agency policy.* Chicago: Nelson-Hall.

Fogel, D. (1975). *We are the living proof: The justice model for corrections.* Cincinnati, OH: W. H. Anderson.

Fritsch, J. (1994, September 3). Mayor orders jail reopened in Brooklyn. *New York Times.*

Gelman, S. R. (July, 1981). Who should administer social services? *Social Work, 26*(4), 327–332.

General Accounting Office. (December 10, 1980). *Women in prison: Inequitable treatment requires action.* Report #GGOD-81-6.

Gettinger, S. (1984). *Assessing criminal justice needs* (Research in brief). Washington, D.C.: C.S. Department of Justice. National Institute of Justice.

Gil, D. G. (1973). *Unraveling social policy.* Cambridge, MA: Schenkman.

Gilbert, N., & Specht, H. (1974). *Dimensions of social welfare policy.* Englewood Cliffs, NJ: Prentice-Hall.

Hammett, T., & Moini, S. (1990). *Update on AIDS in prisons and jails.* Washington, D.C.: U.S. Department of Justice.

Hindelang, M. J., Gottfredson, M. R., & Flanagan, T. J. (1981). *Sourcebook of criminal justice statistics–1980.* Washington, D.C.: U.S. Dept. of Justice. Bureau of Justice Statistics.

Hirsch, A., Dietrich, S., Landau, R., Schneider, P., Ackelsberg, I., Bernstein-Baker, J., & Hohenstein, J. (2002). *Every door closed: Barriers facing parents with criminal records.* Philadelphia: CLASP and Community Legal Services, Inc. of Philadelphia.

Huizinga, D., S. Menard, & D. Elliot. (1989). Delinquency and drug use: Temporal and developmental patterns. *Justice Quarterly, 6,* 419–455.

Hussey, F., & Lagoy, S. P. (1981). The impact of determinate sentencing structures. *Criminal Law Bulletin, 17*(3), 197–225.

Hussey, F. (1979). Just desserts and determinate sentencing: Impact on rehabilitation. *The Prison Journal, 29*(2), 36–47.

Inciardi, J., Horowitz, R., & Pottieger, A. (1993). *Street kids, street drug, street crime.* Belmont, CA: Wadsworth.

Inciardi, J., Lockwood, D., & Pottieger, A. (1993). *Women and crack-cocaine.* New York: Macmillan.

Inciardi, J., Lockwood, D., & Quinlan, J. (1993). Drug use in prison: Patterns, processes and implications for treatment. *Journal of Drug Issues, 23,* 119–129.

Jansson, B. S. (2003). *Becoming an effective policy advocate* (4th ed.). Pacific Grove, CA: Brooks/Cole/Thomson.

Jeffries, J. M., Menghraj, S., & Hairston, C. F. (2001) *Serving incarcerated and ex-offender fathers and their families: A review of the field.* New York: Vera Institute of Justice.

Jucovy, L. A. *Mentoring children of prisoners in Philadelphia.* Public/Private Ventures, June 2003, http://www.ppv.org/content/reports/amachi.html.

Krauss, C. (November 13, 1994). No crystal ball needed on crime. *New York Times.*

Kahn, A.J. (1973). *Social policy and social services.* New York: Random House.

Koren, E. (1993). Status report: State prisons and the courts – January 1, 1993. *Journal of the National Prison Project, 8*(1), 3–11.

Law Enforcement Assistance Agency. (1978). *Census of jails: Preliminary report – February, 1978.*

Levine, P., Musheno, M., & Palumbo, D. (1980). *Criminal justice: A public policy approach.* New York: Harcourt Brace Jovanovich.

Lieber, J. (March 8, 1981). The American prison: A tinderbox. *New York Times Magazine,* 26–61.

Martinson, R. (Spring, 1974). What works? Questions and answers about prison reform. *The Public Interest, 35,* 22–54.

McBride, D., & McCoy, C. (1993). The drugs-crime relationship: An analytical framework. *The Prison Journal, 73,* 257–278.

Menninger, K. (1969). *The crime of punishment.* New York: Viking.

Merrill, F. (1961). *An introduction to sociology society and culture.* Englewood Cliffs, NJ: Prentice-Hall.

Miltford, J. (1973). *Kind and unusual punishment: The prison business.* New York: Knopf.

Moroney, R. M. (1998). *Shared responsibility: Families and social policy.* New York: Aldine.

Morris, R. (1979). *Social Policy and the American welfare state: An introduction to policy analysis.* New York: Harper & Row.

National Association of Social Workers. (2003). *Social work speaks.* Washington, D.C.: Author.

National Center on Fathers and Families (NCOFF). (2001). *Constructing and coping with incarceration and re-entry: Perspectives from the field.*

Netherland, W. (1987). Corrections system: Adult. In *Encyclopedia of Social Work* (18th ed.). Silver Spring, MD: National Association of Social Workers, 351–360.

New York Times. (October 28, 1994). U.S. prison population crosses 1 million mark, A1.

Osler, M. (March, 1991). Shock incarceration: Hard realities and real possibilities. *Federal Probation,* 34–42.

Packer, H. (1968). *The limits of the criminal sanction.* Stanford, CA: Stanford University Press.

Palmer, T. (1975). Martinson revisited. *Journal of Research in Crime and Delinquency*, 133–152.

Petrosino, A., Boruch, R. F., Farrington, D. P., Sherman, L. W., & Weisburd, D. (2003). Toward evidenced-based criminology and criminal systematic reviews, the Campbell Collaborative and the Crime and Justice Group. *Interventional Journal of Comparative Criminology*, *3*(1), 42–61.

Pollack, D. (June, 1991). Sharing information without forsaking personal privacy. *Corrections Today*, 30–32.

Ponsioen, J. A. (1969). *The analysis of social change reconsidered*. Paris: Mouton.

Rein, R. M. (1970). *Social policy*. New York: Random House.

Reno, J. (May 7, 1993). *Testimony at Congressional drug summit*. Washington, D.C.

Rock, M., & Landsberg, G. (1994). The mentally ill in the criminal justice system: Issues and strategies for change. *Criminal Justice in the Americans, 7*(3), 14–17.

Roth, J. (1994). *Firearms and violence*. Washington, D.C.: U.S. Department of Justice.

Roth, J. (1994). *Psychoactive substances and violence*. Washington, D.C.: U.S. Department of Justice.

Schwartz, J. (2000). *Juvenile justice and public policy*. New York: Lexington Books.

Snell, T. (2000). *Women in prison*. Washington, D.C.: U.S. Department of Justice, Bureau of Justice Statistics.

Sherman, R. (August 8, 1994). Juvenile judges say: Time to get tough. *The National Law Journal, 1*, 24–25.

Studt, E. (1977). Crime and delinquency: Institutions. *Encyclopedia of Social Work*. Washington, D.C.: National Association of Social Workers, 208–213.

Tropman, J. E. (1989). *American values and social welfare: Cultural contractions in the welfare state*. Englewood Cliffs. NJ: Prentice-Hall.

Travis, J., Solomon, A., & Waul, M. From prison to home: The dimensions and consequences of prisoner re-entry. The Urban Institute, June, 2001, www.urban.org.

Underwood, B. (June, 1979). Law and the crystal ball: Predicting behavior with statistical inference and individualized judgment. *Yale Law Journal, 88*(7), 1408–1448.

U.S. Department of Justice, Bureau of Justice Statistics. (September, 1992). *Justice expenditure and employment, 1990*. Bulletin NCJ–135777.

Von Hirsch, A. (1976). *Doing justice*. New York: Hill & Wang.

Welsh, W. (1993). Ideologies and incarceration: Legislator attitudes toward jail overcrowding. *The Prison Journal, 73*(1), 46–71.

Williams, T. (1992). *Crack house: Notes from the end of the line*. Reading, MA: Addison-Wesley.

Chapter 4

Social Work in the Justice System: An Overview

Harvey Treger and G. Frederick Allen

The profession of social work began with its commitment to providing basic necessities to the poor, underprivileged and disadvantaged members of society. In the mid-1940s social work broadened its scope. Kenneth Pray, director of the Pennsylvania School of Social Work, argued for social work's increased visibility in social action (Pray, 1945a). One promising area that needed social service intervention was corrections.

At this point, the courts were fully committed to modify its response to offenders by adopting the concept of rehabilitation.[1] Social work as a profession gradually became noticeable as the major provider of correctional services to offenders. This gradual process of including social work services in the criminal justice system was not easy. In addition to the usual inertia to change there was the contradiction between the involuntary nature of the service delivery in corrections and other values espoused by social workers, such as the client's right to self-determination, advocacy for the client versus support for the correctional agency, and the general idea of providing services to the unmotivated client in an authoritative setting.

Social work's first appearance in the criminal justice system came about at the close of the nineteenth century when the first juvenile court law as enacted in Illinois. This new juvenile court law brought under one jurisdiction all cases involving delinquent, neglected and dependent children. Later, the rehabilitation approach to juveniles was legally extended to adults, mainly through probation and parole. By this time, social work was able to accumulate a body of

knowledge and skills specifically concerned with the modification of the social functioning of offenders, and therefore a profession with a significant potential to contribute to correctional services.

Social work's contribution to the understanding of behavior dovetailed into the basic elements of the criminal justice program: pre-sentence investigation and supervision. The court needed workers who had knowledge of human behavior and the environment as well as intervention skills. Thus, by the 1960s the visibility and presence of social work blossomed as the rehabilitation of offenders became the central concept of correctional intervention. Working to change violative behavior of offenders, social work carved out a niche by fulfilling this useful social function. As a result, correctional agencies such as probation and parole recruited professionally trained social workers to conduct investigations and provide supervision of offenders. Judges relied on social work professionals to provide information about the offender, such as criminal history, individual development, biography of family relations, school history, military history, and present financial status, attitude, and motivation. The social worker's assessments of the offender's individual and environmental situation assisted the court in determining individualized sentences of probation or incarceration.[2] One federal judge in the Northern District of Illinois frequently reminded troublesome offenders that he was placing them in the care of a probation officer who was also a professional social worker and who could provide social and psychological services.

---

1. Beginning with John Augustus, known as the father of probation, between 1841 and 1858.
2. Much of the personal characteristics of the offender is slowly being removed or discounted under new fixed sentencing such as the Federal Sentencing Guideline System that began in 1987.

However, by the 1970s, the concept of rehabilitation fell into disrepute. Although social work programs in the justice system undoubtedly made many worthwhile services available to juveniles and adults, disillusionment with treatment intervention for the offender became widespread. Criticism of the system became abundant. Later, Norman Carlson, then director of the Bureau of Prisons, responded to some of the criticisms as follows:

> Many times the agency is criticized because people don't understand that the Bureau is responsible for running a safe and humane prison, not punishing or rehabilitating convicts. We have to divorce ourselves from the notion that we can change human behavior, that we have the power to change inmates. We don't. All we can do is provide opportunities for inmates who want to change. (Earley, 1984, p. A19)

This suggests an emphasis on the influence of environment on behavior. However, reports on prison environment indicate that the prison system failed to provide these opportunities. As the concept of rehabilitation faded, so did social work in the justice system. As Cressey stated: "When the rehabilitative ideal disappeared, humanitarianism in prisons disappeared with it (Cullen & Gilbert, 1982, page xx). Much of the rehabilitation in community corrections was replaced by risk management through interventions that related more to the community than the individual, such as house arrest, electronic monitoring, intensive supervision, fines, restitution, and community service.

After a decade of adding prisons, developing fixed sentencing structures that resulted in more punitive sanctions, we have not seen a substantial reduction in crime. In addressing members of the law enforcement community, President Clinton in 1994 said that in the last three decades, violent crimes have increased by 300 percent. Over the last three years, almost a third of Americans have either themselves or had someone in their families victimized by crime. According to the U.S. Bureau of Justice Statistics, the number of Americans in federal and state prisons crossed the one million mark on June 30, 1994. This represents a threefold increase in U.S. prison population since 1980. Our reliance on incarceration has given us an international reputation of becoming a punitive society in dealing with offenders. According to Black (1991), "By a widening margin, the United States remains the world's biggest user of prisons as other countries are relying more on alternative sentences. . . ." In 1992–1993, the United States had 1.3 million prisoners behind bars. This represents 519 of every 100,000 people. This figure greatly exceeds the rates in Western Europe and most Asian countries. Mauer (1994) suggests that the gap between the United States and other countries is widening.

As we ponder what to do, new findings of previous social service systems evaluations that were discarded in the 1970s as ineffective are now presenting some hope. The findings are shedding new light on past social service intervention in the justice system – particularly, what treatment intervention works and what does not work. The new findings demonstrate the effectiveness of social service systems (Gendreau & Andrews, 1990; Gendreau & Ross, 1979; Halleck & Witte, 1977). Once again, the criminal justice system may be turning toward social workers and their unique approaches and orientation to keeping offenders in some sort of defined relationship to the community and returning them to law-abiding status. Can the social work profession redefine its scope and respond to the challenges facing social service intervention in the justice system as we approach the year 2000?

REDEFINING THE SCOPE OF SOCIAL WORK IN THE JUSTICE SYSTEM

Social work must redefine its scope to be effective in the current criminal justice system environment. Part of this redefinition involves coming to grips with individualization and the courts. For example, are offenders in general "bad" and therefore should they be punished? Or, are offenders in general "sick" and therefore should they be treated, or are they both?

A country's response to crime is a reflection of the country's basic explanation as to why some people turn to crime while others do not. Historically, the academic, professional, and ideological explanations were based on two distinct approaches: the classical or pro-punishment approach, and the positivist or pro-treatment approach. The classical, or pro-punishment, approach is based on punishment as a means of preventing crime. The positivist, or pro-treatment, approach acknowledges that the source of criminal behavior is determined by factors largely outside the control of the offender, and therefore the offender should be treated as a means of preventing crime. Social workers at large have supported the pro-treatment logic, since this is consistent with social work's association with sociology6 and psychology. Social work's commitment to humanitarian principles have underscored that offenders should expect treatment from the justice system. This is particularly relevant to mentally ill offenders who are incarcerated, and their numbers are increasing.[3]

In practice, sentencing judges have used the assistance of probation and parole officers who have had social work training. These officers prepare presentencing reports (social histories) which aid the judge in an appropriate sentence. In 1987, when the federal sentencing guidelines became effective to correct the unwarranted disparity of different sentences for like crimes, a tremendous amount of power was transferred from the judiciary to the executive branch. In other words, instead of the sentence being decided by the judge, the prosecutor has now been given the authority to implicitly incorporate sentencing into the charges. Under a fixed-sentence arrangement, sentencing now becomes a function of the prosecutor's charging mechanism. The importance of meaningful psychosocial information from probation officer's reports to the court under fixed sentencing is reduced.

There is some consensus in criminal justice that the cause of crime in society can be traced to a variety of sociological factors. Sociological theories hold that the individual is a product of the prevailing environment today (Schmalleger, 1995, p. 102). Whatever environmental factors are operating in a specific case, the justice system is now being held responsible for addressing risk to society at large. Since social workers are a part of the justice system, social workers must resolve the issue of where their primary obligation will lie. To whom is the social worker in the justice system obligated, the offender or the community? The issue should be resolved as follows: Social workers in the justice system must be obligated to both the offender and the justice system with priority to society.

All professions must function within the law; to do otherwise would not support lawful behavior. Treger noted that social work practice with the offender should be guided by the view that:

Law violative behavior may be destructive in its outcome: It places the social worker in the position of an accomplice; it does not protect the community; and it defeats the goal of developing more socially responsible behavior. Further, a person may benefit from coming to grips with the consequences of their behavior. (Treger, 1989, p. 483)

Therefore, social work professionals in the justice system must advocate what suggests a more effective policy direction to control crime. On the surface, this may appear to be a conflict with the basic value orientation of social workers. Years ago, Charlotte Towle argued that:

It is clear that we must accept and maintain our identity as representatives of the law and at the same time extend to the individual help which may become desirable to him because he feels our kindly purpose, our understanding, and our respect for him as a person who has an identity other than that of the offender. (Pray, 1945b, p. 244)

Since social workers at times advocate for their clients, some social workers see their advocacy role extending to offenders. This is consistent with their early relief giving work with the poor, disadvantaged, and underprivileged. However, in order for social workers to be effective in the revised correctional agenda, i.e., an agenda that rejects the nonutility of punishment in favor of rehabilitation, they must adjust social work values to this new environment (Jansson, 1986). Social workers in host organizations often experience conflict between their career goals and professional values. They may be asked to carry out policies that they believe dehumanize clients. The ethical challenge to social workers is to weigh the needs of the justice system against those of the offender. The social worker should take on the challenge by participating in legislative action to mold social policy to create a balance between the justice system and the offender. Thus, the social worker can help the justice system provide more effective services to offenders, their families, and their communities and, at the same time, increase their own credibility as professionals by participating in the process of public policy development.

---

3. Some have noted (e.g., Burkhead, Carter, & Smith, 1990) that people with psychiatric disorders, especially schizophrenia, are more likely today than ever to wind up in prison. One Chicago study (Kagan, 1990) found that among 728 inmates admitted to Cook County jail, almost 6.4 percent were manifesting some form of psychosis.

THE REVISED AGENDA

The revised agenda will promote three interventions: criminal justice conditions, offender risk, and correctional treatment. Conditions are specific parameters of the justice system such as fines, restitutions, community service, and mandatory rehabilitation programs. These parameters are usually imposed by order of the court. In the case of incarcerated offenders, prison officials are forced to abide by the specific limits of the sentences. In the case of community supervision of offenders, the social worker will likewise be forced to abide by the specific limits of the sentence. The social worker will generally not be able to negotiate or input this intervention.

The revised agenda will also present the offender-risk intervention that predicts the amount of potential harm that an offender may place on society. This may be presented in a formal or informal risk-prediction instrument. Once the risk is defined, it is expected that the correctional intervention will operate within the parameters of this risk statement. So, for those offenders who are out of control and who may present substantial risk to society, the treatment apparatus must first seek to control these offenders. Once controlled and stabilized, these offenders may then be amenable to counseling and psychological intervention. The social worker's role in offender risk intervention may be in program evaluation, since the present risk-prediction instruments, such as recidivism, are crude and inaccurate measures of some correctional interventions.

The correctional treatment intervention is where the social worker will be most visible and have the most opportunities to influence the new agenda. Although most correctional settings may lean toward offender-risk intervention, it is expected that correctional treatment will be provided to the offender population that diagnostically is in need of correctional treatment and may benefit from this intervention. Social service will not be provided for all offenders simply on the assumption that their offender status alone justifies treatment.

Whether correctional treatment should be provided directly by criminal justice personnel working in a treatment capacity or by private or public agencies in the community is an area where there is little empirical knowledge. This is an area deserving of study and evaluation to guide future public policy.

JUVENILES

According to the FBI's 1992 *Uniform Crime Reports*, juveniles commit one out of eight, or 13 percent, of all violent crimes, including homicide, rape, robbery, and aggravated assault, in the United States. This 13 percent figure has remained essentially unchanged since 1985.

While the concept of rehabilitation for adults has been seriously questioned, the basic belief in rehabilitation for juveniles remains intact: youthful offenders are still children who, with proper intervention, discipline, and guidance, can develop into productive citizens. However, this concept is changing. Alarmed by the rising tide of gang and youth violence, many Americans want to "get tough" with young criminals by prosecuting them as adults and subjecting them to stiff prison sentences. What role can social work play in this process? Social workers with their social science skills, particularly in research, can demonstrate to society that it is a relatively small number of violent youths who have influenced the public mind toward this punitive response. Society can be shown that some juveniles may benefit from timely, appropriate and purposeful interventions that are enforceable and progressive. The social worker can reveal that intervention on a timely basis could rescue these offenders from the more punitive, reactive criminal justice system. The reactive criminal justice system does not facilitate youthful offenders from recognizing the consequences of their behavior, and, in fact, may actually encourage more serious law violations.

Social work can make its presence known in the juvenile justice system as juvenile probation officers, community workers, treatment specialists, and researchers to demonstrate that serious and violent juvenile problems are multifaceted, requiring a comprehensive, interdisciplinary approach.

SOCIAL WORK'S RETURN TO THE JUSTICE SYSTEM

How can social workers adjust and enhance their credibility in the criminal justice system? Social workers can assume an enabling function in the justice system by first surveying their own experiences and identifying inefficiencies, inadequate communication, and other difficulties that impede high-quality services. When colleagues in the criminal justice community see social workers as addressing those kinds of practice problems, they are more likely to perceive social workers as "team players" who make logistic contributions to the host organization (Rosenberg & Weissman, 1981). Social work units can also increase their credibility by advocating employee assistance programs such as counseling, alcoholic treatment, referral and stress management services to assist staff in criminal justice organizations with their personal problems so their productivity can be increased.

REAFFIRMATION OF THE SOCIAL WORKER IN THE JUSTICE SYSTEM

After a decade of a very expensive response to crime, it is possible to make some definitive statement about effective reduction of recidivism. Andrews (1994) summarizes these conclusions as follows:

1. Punishing offenders without providing correctional treatment services does not work.
2. Providing correctional treatment services to offenders that are inconsistent with the principles of risk to the community and the needs of the offender does not work.
3. What works is the delivery of clinically and psychologically appropriate correctional treatment services to offenders under a variety of setting conditions that may be established by the criminal sanction.
4. The delivery of appropriate correctional treatment service to offenders is dependent upon assessments that are sensitive to community risk and the needs of the offender.

In a study by the Administrative Office of the United States Courts (Wooten et al., 1988), it was found that most contacts with offenders took place in the probation office rather than in the field and that offenders classified as presenting high risks were seen only slightly more often than those classified as low-risk offenders. Approximately one-third of the low-risk offenders, usually white collar offenders, were seen more than once per month. If social work is to be effective in the justice system, social workers need to be trained to work with high-risk offenders. These are offenders who will not respond voluntarily and who

certainly will not respond to traditional counseling by a social service provider. Servicing these offenders has to be perceived on a continuum where the social worker has an array of programs and interventions. Approaching a high-risk offender with only a traditional counseling background, education, and skills will not be sufficient in the revised agenda. A Rand Foundation study (Petersilla, 1985) found that traditional probation services have not been successful with high-risk felony offenders. This is an area where new technologies need to be developed.

Provision of social work services should have an evaluative component. The evaluative component must be realistic or the intervention will provide negative results. Consider the treatment of a chronic drug user. Although early Department of Justice "zero tolerance" mandated that the correctional worker should proceed to sanction all offenders who are tested positive for illicit drugs, the correctional officer's sanction should be tempered with new knowledge of the extent of the drug problem. Chronic abusers may have to be placed in a brief period of custody for detoxification. Following release, unless considerable changes take place in their environment, frequent relapses can be expected. Obviously, a goal of "zero tolerance" presents an inescapable failure for the therapeutic intervention approach with this kind of individual.

It is important that appropriate interventions be offered in a timely fashion to the right offender. There are now abundant studies that demonstrate correctional treatment can work if an individualized community-focused approach to correctional intervention is used.

COOPERATION

Early efforts to engage social workers to work in police districts (Treger, 1975, 1981) provide some classic experience underscoring the idea of interagency cooperation. Interagency cooperation in criminal justice can be accomplished. A review of some early efforts reveals that both the police and social workers were apprehensive about working together. The police-social work project showed that achieving successful interdisciplinary cooperation is a dynamic process that requires a very sensitive, knowledgeable, and experienced approach. Below are some suggested guidelines to be followed in achieving this goal:

1. Recognition and definition of a realistic achievable goal with specific emphasis on the benefits for each profession.
2. Role definition of each profession; special emphasis should be given to clarify and point out the uniqueness as well as the similarities of each discipline to enable a careful, logical, and operative recognition of the boundaries between them.
3. Working toward a mutual commitment to achieve positive attitudes, removing myths, and establishing a contract of goodwill.
4. Identification and a beginning toward resolution of critical areas, e.g., communication, coordination, and decision making.
5. Understanding and coping with the process of social change, i.e., the "chain reaction" and the disequilibrium of established community services that result from introducing programs of interprofessional cooperation (Treger, 1981).

One of the discoveries of the social service project in working with law enforcement was that there was a lack of experience working together. Consequently, the participants developed negative biases and perceptions about each other. Social workers and police lacked knowledge and understanding of each other's professional subculture and system of organized services. They also lacked clarity about the problems of central concern for each of the professions, their values, ethics, and methods as well as the attitudes of diverse client groups regarding their contact with each of the professions in different communities (Bartlett, 1961). As a result, both professions did not know how they could work together and be useful to each other and the community. By working together, the police and social workers learned from each other about their systems, perceptions of each other and the community, and areas where cooperation could be beneficial to all concerned. Similar relationships and service arrangements could be developed between other professionals both within and outside the justice system. As a result, energies can be freed up for investment in the provision of comprehensive, integrated services instead of being consumed in interrelationship problems and fragmentation.

The police-social work project experience also showed that community situations and predicaments are frequently complex and interlocking. They require input from many professionals and systems working cooperatively as a team to maximize their impact on the problem. In this way, each profession may add to its knowledge and service as well as provide new alternatives to its clients. The expansion of social work services in the justice system thus requires cooperation with other professions and systems.

Interprofessional and intersystem efforts are not without risks, as differing orientations, values, and professional needs for status and control in decision-making areas can be conflicting. The issue of "turf" in interprofessional cooperation is a real one. The potential for one party to be swallowed up or taken over by the other exists. We are basically dealing with differences and the discomfort over differences. Sensitive areas such as these require personal and professional security, flexibility, and the capacity for mediation and change. The resolution of these issues will either inhibit or develop cooperative efforts. Working with other professions may provide social work with a vehicle for growth. Social work has a tradition of interprofessional teamwork and the coordination of services with medicine, nursing, psychiatry, psychology, education, law, architecture, and the military. Much can be drawn from this body of knowledge and experience and used in current practice and education for social work in the justice system. Social work has enabled other professions to improve its services. By the same token, other professions may also enable social work. Our new relationships with law enforcement, others in the justice system, community, and various departments in the university can further build upon and enhance social work's established competencies, develop new models for interprofessional and intersystem cooperation, and lead the way to further knowledge building and theory for professional practice and education in the justice system. The bottom line is, "Can we establish a true interdependent relationship that will result in improved services to people?" The Family Assistance Coalition Team, or FACT (Northern Medina County), is an example of linking residents with needed services:

> A man came into the police station and told an officer that he was missing some money, which he believed was stolen by his son's friend. He also shared suspicions that his son was using drugs and said he and his wife disagreed on whether to involve authorities.

"Traditionally, the police would take a theft-of-money report and do an investigation," said Beyer. "In this case, the officer realized that the money was not as important as the way the family was working."

The family needed help because of domestic disputes, drug and alcohol abuse and relationship problems between the child and his parents.

After the man signed a waiver allowing police to share information with appropriate agencies, Northland Counseling contacted the husband and wife. Referrals to a drug and alcohol program also are anticipated. The theft report was put on hold while the family addresses the underlying problems. (Sheldon, 1994, p. 1B)

However, before cooperation between professions, disciplines, or systems begin, there must be a need, a desire and capacity for change, systems that will permit openness and the interchange of ideas. As a result of cooperation, social change can occur.

CURRICULUM FOR SOCIAL WORK IN THE JUSTICE SYSTEM

The university will have a unique role in preparing social work students to fill the needs of the field in contemporary society. Schools of social work must take leadership positions that will contribute to the inclusion of diversity content in the university curriculum.

Social workers entering the field of criminal justice should have knowledge of legal aspects and organizational systems unique to social work practice in the justice system as well as knowledge, skills, and values generic to all social work. The field requires a social worker capable of developing new services where patterns have not yet been defined and where the contribution of social work is not yet readily accepted. Social workers need to be skilled in designing and implementing as well as delivering and critically evaluating services. The curriculum requires a holistic approach to social work, including knowledge of the subculture of other human service professions, the process of cooperation, and of achieving social change. The practice wisdom gained from experiences in innovative justice system programs should be captured and used as ideas for ongoing research and development in social work education and social work practice in the justice system.

Objectives. The general objectives for education in social work in the justice system should be to offer students the opportunity for classroom and field learning experiences to prepare for professional social work practice in the justice system. Specific objectives should include the following:

1. Knowledge base for direct practice with clients and for the planning, administration, and management of social services in the justice system.
2. The opportunity to develop skills in the justice system through use of internships to gain direct "hands-on" practice experiences in planning, administration, and knowledge building.
3. Skills in interprofessional cooperation and managing change.
4. Experience in interdisciplinary study and opportunities for working with a range of professionals in the justice system as well as the dynamics of group process.
5. Orientation to public policy, program development, the process of advocacy, the concept of change and evaluation skills need to be learned to prepare personnel for work in the criminal justice system.

The university as a community and system has an established structure that has been very resistant and slow to change. The implications for creating cooperative relationships between professions and disciplines to begin the development of a new educational model for social work in the justice system would affect the major academic areas: teaching, research, and community service.

While the university is not a public policymaking agency, it does provide an environment in which alternative solutions can be proposed and evaluated. The urban university can fulfill its public service role by providing leadership in the development of innovative ideas and effective programs as well as prepare its graduates for the realities of professional practice. Further, the community, by showing its particular needs and resources, will challenge and stimulate the university to apply and develop its knowledge in new and creative ways. When education involves itself with contemporary problems, issues, and concerns, it may become more effective in improving the conditions of life in our society.

During this time of resource scarcity, it is necessary to try out innovative ideas that may induce multiple social and educational benefits. Indeed, cooperation between the university and community can result in more efficient use of available resources and have a greater impact on urban problems than each could achieve by working alone. It is likely that with closer relationships between universities and communities, a cycle for innovation and service will be put into motion – a shuttle from theory to practice will be initiated. Social work can play a key role in these new arrangements by bringing new groups of people together and coordinating their special contributions to resolve community issues.

If social work is to become relevant to the justice system, it must reconceptualize the field of practice and narrow the gap between education and the needs in the field. A mutually useful relationship between educational institutions and the community may provide a cost-effective model for stimulating the kind of interchange and development that provides multiple benefits to a number of systems.

In conclusion, while social work and the justice system have had a long and somewhat tenuous association, the future seems to point to a new partnership that focuses on the individuals in their environment stressing a range of alternatives. For example, coalition of police and social service agencies working together to divert people into social service rather than criminal justice. This approach is both progressive and necessary if cities are going to address the causes of crime without exceeding their budgets, which would only serve to compound the crime problem. Police officers are usually the first to come face-to-face in disputes; therefore, they are in the best position to assess potential problems and to channel offenders toward help. The partnership of police and social workers can provide needed services to offenders and victims in such areas as counseling, drug or alcohol rehabilitation, or sources of housing and food. It is becoming obvious that incarceration in lieu of appropriate services to offenders and their families will not solve the crime problem. In fact, there is ample evidence that this approach could make matters worse.

The crime bill (Violent Crime Control and Law Enforcement Act of 1994) provisions of stricter sentencing, more police on the streets, and boot camps for juvenile offenders are very expensive strategies that need to be subjected to scientific analysis to validate their effectiveness. Social work can make a significant contribution to designing the evaluative model. In the past, research has made strong contributions to our criminal justice policies. If policies are developed

in response to the public outrage over the issue of crime, there is always the tendency for policy over-reaction. Research guided by social work's one hundred years of experience could help shape the way the criminal justice policymakers and practitioners think about crime, particularly in identifying contributing factors, evaluating alternatives, and developing reasonable, sensible, and achievable objectives. State, regional, and national conferences with legislators attending need to be placed on the revised agenda so those in social work practice can pass on their experience and be part of public policy planning and the legislative process.

REFERENCES

Andrews, D. A., & Bonta, J. (1993). *The psychology of criminal behavior.* Cincinnati, OH: Anderson.

Bartlett, H. (1961). *Analyzing social work practice by field.* National Association of Social Workers: New York.

Black, C. (1991). Paying the high cost of being the world's No. 1 jailer. *Boston Globe,* Jan. 13, at 67.

Burkhead, M., Carter, J., & Smith J. (1990). N.C. program assists mentally ill. *Corrections Today, 52,* 88–92.

Carter, R. (1972). The diversion of offenders. *Federal Probation, 36,* 35.

Clinton, W. J. (1994). Remarks made by the president on February 15, 1994 to members of the law enforcement community, Ohio Peace Officer Training Academy, London, Ohio.

Cullen, T., & Gilbert, K. (1982). *Reaffirming rehabilitation.* Quoted in foreword by Donald R. Cressey, p. xx. Cincinnati, OH: Anderson.

Earley, P. (1984). Chief of prisons bureau, a former guard, stress value of staff training. Quoted in *Washington Post,* March 15, at A19.

Feifer, G. (1978). Slave to his friends. *London Telegraph,* Sunday Magazine Section, April 16, 1978, p. 30.

Gendreau, P., & Ross, R. (1987). Revivication of rehabilitation: Evidence from the 1980s. *Justice Quarterly, 4,* 349–408.

Gendreau, P., & Ross, R. (1979). Effective correctional treatment: Bibliography for cynics. *Crime and Delinquency, 25,* 463–489.

Gendreau, P., & Andrews, D. (1990). Tertiary prevention: What the meta-analysis of the offender treatment literature tells us about "what works." *Canadian Journal of Criminology, 32,* 173–184.

Halleck, S., & Witte, A. (1977). Is rehabilitation dead? *Crime and Delinquency, 24,* 372–382.

Inkles, A. (1965). What is sociology? *Models of Society in Sociological Analysis.* Englewood Cliffs, NJ: Prentice-Hall.

Jansson, B., & Simmons, J. (1986). The survival of social work units in host organizations. *Social Work*, September–October, 339–343.

Kagan, D. (1990). Landmark Chicago study documents rate of mental illness among jail inmates. *Corrections Today, 52,* 166–169.

Mauer, M. (1994). *American behind bars: The international use of incarceration, 1992–1993.* The Sentencing Project, Washington, D.C.

Morris, N. (1974). *The future of imprisonment.* Chicago: University of Chicago Press.

Petersilla, J. et al. (1985). *Granting felons probation: Public risks and alternatives.* Santa Monica, CA.

Pray, K. (1945a). Social work and social action. In the *Proceedings of the National Conference of Social Work: Selected papers from the Seventy-Second Annual Meeting.* New York: Columbia Press, pp. 349–359.

Pray, K. (1945b). The place of social casework in the treatment of delinquency. (Discussion by Charlotte Towle.) *The Social Service Review, 19,* 244.

Schmalleger, F. (1995). *Criminal justice today: An introductory text for the 21st century* (3rd ed.). Englewood Cliffs, NJ: Regents/Prentice-Hall.

Senna, J. (1975). Social workers in public defender programs. *Social Work* (2;0) 271–276.

Sheldon, S. (1994). A policeman is a friend in need; Brunswick shifts from cuffs to counseling. *The Plain Dealer.* Plain Dealer Publishing Co., September 11, 1994, at p. 1B.

Speedy Trial Act of 1974, Administrative Office of the U.S. Courts: Washington, D.C., 1979.

Studt, E. (1965). *A conceptual approach to teaching materials: Illustrations from the field of corrections.* New York: Council on Social Work Education.

Studt, E. (Ed.). (1959). *Education for social workers in the correctional field,* Volume V the Social Work Curriculum Study. New York: Council on Social Work Education.

Treger, H., Collier, J., & Henninger, C. (1972). Deferred prosecution: Community treatment alternative for the non-violent adult misdemeanant. *Illinois Bar Journal, 60,* 922–931.

Treger, H. & Associates. (1975). *The Police-Social Work Team.* Springfield, IL: Charles C Thomas, Publisher.

Treger, H. (1981). Police-social work cooperation: Problems and issues. *Social Casework, 62.*

Treger, H. (1989). *Encyclopedia of police science.* New York: Garland.

Wooten, H., Reynolds, S., Maher, T., & Meierhoefer, B. (1988). *The supervision of federal offenders.* Washington, D.C.: Probation Division of the Administrative Office of the U.S. Courts.

Chapter **5**

Rural and Urban Criminal Justice

H. Wayne Johnson, James A. Hall, and Bushra Sabri

INTRODUCTION

The exploration of criminal justice settings and social work is vast and complex with many dimensions to consider. One major dimension is the context of both the behavior that is defined by the community/society as deviant and the organized societal responses to this social problem that are collectively termed criminal justice. Although it is possible to study social welfare settings in criminal justice without dealing with the community context, such consideration is unwise because the community plays such a profound part in social problems such as crime and in social policies and programs directed to these conditions.

In this chapter, we consider the communities in which crime and delinquency occur and in which the criminal justice system operates – both rural and urban. First, these concepts, urban and rural, are discussed and defined for this chapter. Then the phenomenon of deviancy will be examined in relation to these variables, considering both the nature and extent of rural and city criminality and their comparison. Next the three criminal justice subsystems will be explored: law enforcement, judicial, and correctional. Included are considerations of programs for both juvenile and adult offenders. Within corrections,both community-based services and institutions are discussed and analyzed. Further, the social work role in metropolitan and rural criminal justice is examined. Finally recent trends and future possibilities are discussed, followed by a summary and conclusion.

URBAN AND RURAL AS CONCEPTS

To understand this dimension it is useful to divide communities into rural and urban areas and this necessitates the defining of terms. The U.S. Bureau of the Census classifies urban areas into *urbanized areas* and *urban clusters*. Urban areas consist of core blocks with population density of at least 1000 people per square mile and surrounding blocks with population density of 500 people per square mile. Under certain conditions, less densely populated areas may be part of urban areas and clusters. The area outside of urbanized areas and clusters are known as rural (U.S. Census Bureau, 2002).

There are compelling reasons to utilize, for our purposes, the 50,000 population figure as the dividing line between urban and rural, in spite of the lower figure generally used. In significant respects, many communities of several thousand people are generally more rural than urban and should be thought of as such.

The federal Office of Management and Budget (OMB) divides geographic areas into metropolitan and nonmetropolitan. Counties that meet one of these criteria—one city with 50,000 inhabitants, an urbanized area with 50,000 inhabitants or a total metropolitan population of 100,000—fall under metropolitan counties. Counties that fall outside these criteria are categorized as nonmetropolitan counties (Legal Services Corporation, 2003).

Several things should be kept in mind in this distinction. Communities, like people, are unique and have their own individual characteristics and, therefore, while generalizing upon them is essential, it is also hazardous. There is always the possibility of overgeneralization. Some communities with a 30,000 population may be more urban in important ways than many others double or triple that size. Similarly, there are cities that technically are urban that in actuality are quite rural sociologically and in other respects.

Furthermore, *rural* encompasses both farm and non-farm communities, with the latter being a large majority currently. To equate rural with farm is inaccurate; most rural dwellers live in towns and small hamlets. By the same token, there is a world of difference between cities of 50,000, and 500,000, or 5 million, all technically urban. Suburbanization is just one of many further considerations in this picture.

CRIME AND DELINQUENCY: RURAL AND URBAN

Before examining criminal justice services found in the two groups of communities, it should be worthwhile to review the major types of crime and delinquency found in each. There is an image of the rural community as crime-free. Social problems in general are seen as aspects of urban life and nonmetropolitan areas are thought of as pure, clean, unpolluted, and untainted. This idyllic picture is less fact than fancy, however, because rural communities experience essentially the same social problems found in the cities, including behavior proscribed by law (Johnson, 1993). Research, however, shows that speeding or traffic violations are one of the major crime issues for rural residents (Payne, Berg, & Sun, 2005; Ball, 2001). Another issue is family violence that has not been a focus of attention when compared with urban family violence. Though there are low violent crime rates in rural areas, violence against women seems to be high. It has been estimated that almost one in every five women in rural areas are victims of domestic violence (Payne, Berg, & Sun, 2005; Van Hightower et al., 2000; Websdale & Johnson, 1998). Drug use in rural areas is also a major crime concern. According to a *New York Times* article (Butterfield, 2002), the Federal Bureau of Investigation estimated 10.5 percent increase in drug arrest rates in rural areas in comparison to a decline to 11.2 in cities above 250,000 residents. Highest use of methamphetamine takes place among eighth, tenth and twelfth graders in rural areas (Payne, Berg, & Sun, 2005).

Although crime rates are generally decreasing, drug crime arrests have increased the prison population in recent years. For instance, in 1980, only 19,000 state prisoners were drug offenders. By 2000, the number increased to 251,000 (Cole, Smith, 2005). The period 1990–1999 witnessed a tremendous increase (60.9 %) in the federal prison population due to drug crime arrests (Beck, Harrison, 2001). According to Federal Bureau of Prisons statistics, drug offenses comprised the highest percentage (53.4%) of the total types of offenses in the prisons (Federal Bureau of Prisons, 2005).

The National Institute of Justice reports more details about drug arrests in their Arrestee Drug Abuse Monitoring (ADAM) Program Report (Sourcebook of Criminal Justice Statistics, 2003). Among 43 sites in the United States, the percentage of adult male arrestees who tested positive for any kind of drug (cocaine, marijuana, methamphetamine, opiates, and phencyclidine) ranged from 42 percent in Woodbury, Iowa to 86 percent in Chicago. Marijuana was the most commonly used drug, followed by cocaine. Marijuana-positive arrestees were highest in Oklahoma, and cocaine-positive arrestees were highest in Chicago (Sourcebook of Criminal Justice Statistics, 2003).

Crime rates are generally higher in cities than in the country, and according to the Uniform Crime Report (2005) for 1995 to 2002, crime victimization rates are higher in cities than in suburbs and in suburbs than in rural areas. A statistical indicator was developed by the U.S. Department of Justice in 1981 termed "Households Touched by Crime." In 1992, it found that 28 percent of urban households, 21 percent of suburban and 17 percent of rural experienced crime that year (Rand, 1993).

The Federal Bureau of Investigation's (FBI) *Uniform Crime Reports* for 2002 includes the following crime rate information (see Table 5-1) showing quite clearly that the rate is higher in urban contexts than rural, but also that there is a substantial amount of crime in nonmetropolitan areas as well in cities. Breakdowns are included for each of the eight so-called index offenses for which detailed information is compiled by the FBI (Federal Bureau of Investigation, 2005).

Arson rates were added to these offenses in 1979. Though arson is considered a property crime, it is not included in the property crime total. There was a 6.8 percent decrease in the arson rate for the year 2004, when compared to 2003 (Federal Bureau of Investigation, 2005). When examining the changes to the Crime Index Total from 1992 until 2002, the rates for all three areas – cities, suburban counties and rural counties – have dropped significantly (see Figure 5-1). In 2002, the crime rates for rural and suburban areas

Table 5-1
CRIME RATE BY AREA, 2002 (RATE PER 100,000 INHABITANTS)

Offenses	Total United States	Metropolitan Area	Other Cities	Rural Area
Crime Index Total	11,877	10,202	4,524	659

Modified Crime Index total
    Violent
    Property
	
	1,426
	10,451
		
		1,262
		8,939
			
			91
			926
				
				73
				585

Murder	16	14	1	1
Forcible rape	95	78	9	8
Robbery	421	401	14	6
Aggravated assault	894	769	67	58
Burglary	2,152	1,778	181	193
Larceny-theft	7,053	6,008	699	347
Motor vehicle theft	1,247	1,154	47	46
Arson*	32	36	27	17

* Arson rates for metropolitan areas were calculated for cities with populations above 10,000. Arson rates for other cities and rural areas were based on counties in the original data source.

Adapted from Statistical Abstract of the U.S., 2004–05, U.S. Federal Bureau of Investigation, p. 187, *Crime in the United States, 2002*, Department of Justice, Federal Bureau of Investigation.

was almost equivalent but these rates were about half of the rate for cities. Nationwide, from 1993 to 2002, crime trends show that the personal crime victimization rates in rural, suburban, and urban areas declined from 53.7 in 1993 to 23.7 in 2002. Property crime rates in all areas also decreased from 322.1 in 1993 to 159 in 2002 (Bureau of Justice Statistics (BJS), 2005a). Only 13 percent of households were affected by property crimes in 2003 as compared to 21 percent in 1994 (Klaus, 2004). Additionally, the trends from 1993–2002 also suggest proportionately more crimes in the cities (Bureau of Justice Statistics, 2005b).

Data on rural and urban arrests reported by the FBI for 2002 are seen in Table 5-2. These data suggest that more crime occurs in large cities than in small cities or rural areas. From 1995–2002, arrest trends show higher number of arrests in the cities than suburban or rural counties. Additionally, the trend data from 1993–2002 also suggests that there are proportionately more violent and property crimes in cities (Bureau of Justice Statistics, 2005a, b).

Table 5-3 provides a comparison of the breakdown of offenses known to police in 1992 and 2002 and cleared by arrest as related to communities grouped by size from largest to smallest. It is seen in this table that, although many more known offenses led to the highest number of arrests in cities when compared to suburban and rural counties, the rate of these clearances were highest in rural and suburban counties in the year 2002.

Table 5-4, comparing rural and urban arrests by gender in the year 2002, shows that arrests are mostly of males, even more overwhelmingly in rural counties than in suburban areas and in suburbs than in cities.

Based on the National Crime Victimization Survey (NCVS), Table 5-5 reports crime victimization or households experiencing crime by residence. Again, the city, suburb, rural pattern is fairly pronounced with higher rates of household victimization in urban areas (Klaus, 2004). Nationwide, violent crime rates declined to 33.4 percent from 1993–2003. Property

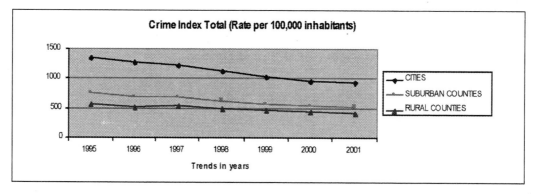

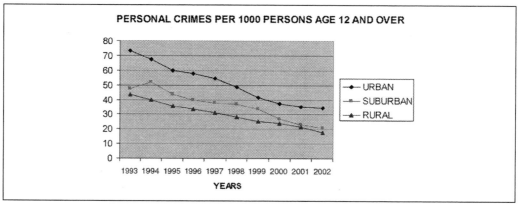

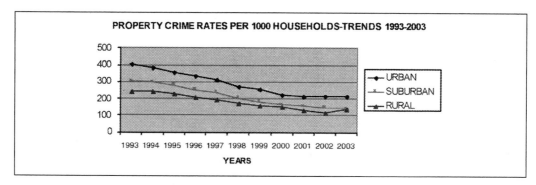

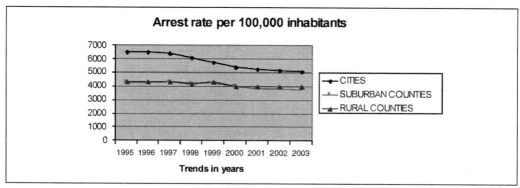

Figure 5-1. Crime Index Total Rates from 1992 to 2002.

Table 5-2
ARRESTS BY AREA, 2002 (FREQUENCIES)

Offense Charged	City	Suburban Areas	Rural Country
Total	7,367,845	3,628,725	882,727
Murder and non-negligent manslaughter	7,467	2,660	886
Forcible Rape	14,515	6,893	2,171
Robbery	66,834	20,577	2,014
Aggravated assault	260,392	110,807	23,887
Burglary	151,343	72,415	20,873
Larceny-Theft	716,186	293,756	33,227
Motor Vehicle theft	85,662	29,520	6,473
Arson	8,372	4,894	1,069

Adapted from *Sourcebook of Criminal Justice Statistics, 2002.* pp. 260, 278, 287.

crime rates were down to 23 percent from 1993–2004 (Bureau of Justice Statistics, 2005a).

As with adult criminality, juvenile delinquency in a given year sometimes increases more in rural than in urban communities. However, the higher rates of delinquency traditionally are in cities, and this continues to be the trend most years. Data about juvenile offenders in Table 5-6 are very similar to the data for adults in Table 5-3. The pattern that emerges from these data is higher numbers and rates of delinquency in urban than in semi-urban areas and in semi-urban than rural.

Property offenses, as compared to crimes against the person or violent acts, predominate in both rural and urban areas. Theft in various forms is among the most common illegal acts in both kinds of communities. The nature of the acts differs, however, as does what is stolen. In farming areas at the present time, it is fairly common to find theft of livestock, grain, and farm supplies/equipment occurring. Cities, rural nonfarm, and farm areas all experience burglary/breaking and entering of homes, outbuildings, business places, and other facilities.

There is some evidence that rural areas have proportionately as much crime as urban centers, although they do not have as much reported crime. Two of the reasons that have been advanced for the nonreporting of rural deviance are that rural communities are strongly independent and intolerant of proactive law enforcement strategies except in unusual circumstances. Second, in rural areas there is reliance on social control agencies other than the police to handle minor transgressions (Karr, 1978). Weisheit and Donnermeyer (2000) also postulated that, in comparison to urban residents, rural residents tend to rely more on informal social control agencies. Their reliance on informal social control networks may be affecting the number of reports for minor offenses. On the other hand, Newman (1978) found no differences in attitudes toward the police or the courts between rural and urban persons and that these attitudes did not appear to affect the likelihood of reporting. Some authors, however, point toward a difference between rural and urban residents' attitudes towards law enforcement agencies. In a study of small-town residents, it was found that people expected that police officers be more personal in their approach, blurring the lines of their traditional professional roles. The authors posited that the emphasis of small-town and rural law enforcement is on crime prevention and service activities, as opposed to urban law enforcement officers who emphasize crime control through arrests (Payne, Berg, & Sun, 2005).

Table 5-3
OFFENSES KNOWN TO POLICE AND CLEARED BY ARREST, 1992 AND 2002

Offense Charged	Total[1]	Total City[2]	Cities						Counties	
			Group I[3]	Group II[4]	Group III[5]	Group IV[6]	Group V[7]	Group VI[8]	Suburban Counties[9]	Rural Counties[10]
Total Offense										
1992	13,644,292	11,129,801	4,388,956	1,605,099	1,651,115	1,354,617	1,200,248	1,019,766	1,968,541	545,952
2002	10,121,721	7,966,962	2,746,733	1,320,491	1,187,713	965,387	929,803	816,835	1,636,611	518,148
Cleared by Arrest										
1992	21.4%		18.8%	21.4%	22.0%	23.7%	25.9%	24.1%		
2002	20.0%	19.7%	16.8%	18.6%	20.4%	21.7%	23.9%	22.9%	20.8%	23.2%

Key for Population size by Category

Note Number	Category Sizes	1992 Population	1992 Numbers of Units	2002 Numbers of Units	2002 Population
1		235,810,000	13,246 agencies	12,862 agencies	240,070,262
2		160,465,000	9,301 cities	9,130 cities	159,128,836
3	250,000 and over	46,186,000	63 cities	65 cities	40,220,526
4	100,000 to	19,456,000	130 cities	158 cities	23,822,400
5	249,999	24,230,000	350 cities	381 cities	26,328,053
6	50,000 to 99,999	23,595,000	678 cities	682 cities	23,803,053
7	25,000 to 49,999	24,890,000	1,577 cities	1,555 cities	24,675,220
8	10,000 to 24,999	22,109,000	6,503 cities	6,289 cities	20,279,224
9	under 10,000	49,330,000	1,313 agencies	1,279 agencies	54,106,364
10		26,015,000	2,632 agencies	2,453 agencies	26,835,062

Adapted from Sourcebook of Criminal Justice Statistics, *Crime in the United States, 1993* – p. 450, *2002* – p. 223, 224.

Table 5-4
ARRESTS BY GENDER AND AREA, 2002 (PERCENTAGES)

Offense Charged	City		Suburban Area		Rural Counties	
	Percent Male	Percent Female	Percent Male	Percent Female	Percent Male	Percent Female
TOTAL	76.7	23.3	76.9	23.1	78.7	21.3
Murder and nonnegligent manslaughter	90.1	9.9	86.1	13.9	87.6	12.4
Forcible rape	98.6	1.4	98.8	1.2	98.7	1.3
Robbery	89.6	10.4	89.4	10.6	90.6	9.4
Aggravated assault	79.2	20.8	80.8	19.2	82.9	17.1
Burglary	86.3	13.7	87.6	12.4	88.9	11.1
Larceny-theft	62.3	37.7	63.1	36.9	72.5	27.5
Motor vehicle theft	83.3	16.7	83.7	16.3	84.0	16.0
Arson	84.6	15.4	86.6	13.4	85.2	14.8

Adapted from Sourcebook of Criminal Justice Statistics, *Crime in the United States,* 2002

CRIMINAL JUSTICE SETTINGS

In responding to the problems of crime and delinquency, society has developed a criminal justice system (actually more a nonsystem of not always well-interconnected parts) encompassing three subsystems of measures aimed at controlling or changing behavior: law enforcement, judicial, and correctional. While the social control features of these provisions are rather conspicuous, they differ only in degree from the social control aspects of many other social welfare instruments generally. All three subsystems have problems and limitations, varying some with size of community, but also characteristic of all regardless of size.

Law Enforcement Subsystem

As far as law enforcement is concerned, municipal police are the major consideration in urban centers.

Rural areas are served by county sheriffs units and towns by marshals, or other persons, with these two working together and supplementing each other. Beyond these, there are various state and federal officials. State police are important in both urban and rural environments, dealing with traffic control, public safety, emergencies, and other activities.

A principal difference between urban and rural law enforcement has to do with distance and time. Typically, an urban officer is only a very few minutes from a cover car to help in the event of a problem as compared to the nearest deputy sheriff's car, which may be 45 minutes or more away. This makes the job of the rural law enforcement person a lonely one and may place the officer in a position of feeling especially isolated and vulnerable with few supportive resources (Haafke, 1994). Besides feeling isolated, they may feel obliged to fulfill different kinds of expectations of the rural and suburban residents. They are required to be more generalist in approach and

Table 5-5
HOUSEHOLDS EXPERIENCING CRIME BY RESIDENCE, 2002

Percent of Household Experiencing:	Place of Residence		
	Urban (%)	Suburban (%)	Rural (%)
**Any NCVS crime	19.1	13.3	10.9
*Personal crimes	34.4	20.6	17.6
Crimes of violence	33.1	20.0	17.5
Rape	2.2	0.7	0.6
Robbery	4.3	1.8	0.7
Assault	26.7	17.6	16.2
Aggravated	6.5	3.5	3.3
Simple	20.2	14.1	12.9
Purse snatching/pocket picking	1.2	0.6	0.2
*Property crimes	215.3	145.3	118.3
Household burglary	40.5	22.4	22.6
Motor vehicle theft	17.1	7.5	2.2
Theft	157.7	115.4	93.5

**Any NCVS crime excludes murder and vandalism.
*Personal crime rate estimates are based on numbers per1000 persons age 12 or older.
*Property crime rate estimates are based on numbers per1000 households.
Source:
1. Klaus (2004). *Crime in the nation's households, 2002* Bureau of Justice Statistics Bulletin.
2. US Department of Justice, Bureau of Justice Statistics, *Criminal Victimization in the United States, 2002, Statistical Tables,* Tables 52–53.

to provide services in a personal, nonpublic manner (Cole, Smith, 2004; Payne, Berg, & Sun, 2005). Police in rural areas also find it difficult to practice community-oriented policing or a neighborhood approach because rural people prefer to stay in open surroundings far away from their neighbors. For some rural communities, there are cultural problems such as emphasis on informal social controls affecting reporting of crime, reluctance to seek outside assistance and mistrust of the government affecting utilization of services. For some, the economic barriers may affect affordability of services (Weisheit & Donnermeyer, 2000).

Another difference between law enforcement in rural and urban areas has to do with the relatively higher degree of specialization found in city forces as compared to the diversity of tasks performed by rural officers. Metropolitan police officers also often have to be almost "all things to all people" but not to the extent that this characterizes rural law enforcement activity. In addition, the urban police system tends to be more bureaucratized as is true of larger, more complex organizations generally.

Traditionally, urban law enforcement is more sophisticated than rural technically and in training. In the 1970s, the Law Enforcement Assistance Administration (LEAA) was described as helping departments modernize in communities of all sizes, especially with regard to hardware. However, LEAA was abolished in 1982 in part due to criticism that it granted too large a portion of federal crime funds to police hardware. Later, the Victims of Crime Act (1984) recommended developing training programs for law enforcement officers and states began receiving funds under VOCA in 1985 (Young, 2001). Though present-day rural law enforcement organizations run a wide range of sophistication, it has been found that the smaller tax base results in limited funding for adequate police staffing and training in rural areas (Drug Enforcement Administration, 1999; Logan, Walker, & Leukefeld, 2001; Weisheit, Falcone, &

Table 5-6
POLICE DISPOSITION OF JUVENILE OFFENDERS TAKEN INTO CUSTODY, 2002

	Total[1]*	Total City[2]	Cities						Counties	
			Group I[3]	Group II[4]	Group III[5]	Group IV[6]	Group V[7]	Group VI[8]	Suburban Counties[9]	Rural Counties[10]
Number	732,282	611,897	122,767	81,488	111,816	94,913	105,574	95,379	86,648	33,737
Percent		83.6%	16.8%	11.1%	15.3%	13.0%	14.4%	13.0%	11.8%	4.6%

* Includes all offenses except traffic and neglect cases.
[1] 6,073 agencies; population 130,229,927
[2] 4,577 cities; population 92,489,061
[3] 32 cities; 250,000 and over, population 23,601,703
[4] 88 cities; 100,000 to 249,999; population 13,193,782
[5] 235 cities, 50,000 to 99,999; population 16,120,073
[6] 405 cities, 25,000 to 49,999; population 14,310,637
[7] 896 cities, 10,000 to 24,999; population 14,336,965
[8] 2,921 cities, under 10,000; population 10,925,901
[9] 568 agencies; population 25,198,464
[10] 928 agencies; population 12,542,402

Adapted from Uniform Crime Reports 2002.

Wells, 1994). Researchers at Eastern Kentucky University's Justice and Safety Center studied law enforcement technology in small and rural agencies. The study found that rural law enforcement agencies around the nation are lagging behind their urban counterparts in the use of new technologies. A majority of the respondents said that the barriers to obtaining new technologies were financial and budget constraints (National Institute of Justice, 2004).

An example of a problem experienced by a significant number of law enforcement officers across communities of all sizes is suicide. The National Association of Social Workers *NASW News* (1994, p. 9) reports a Columbia University study of the high rate of police suicide in the New York City Police Department. The latter study concluded that this suicide rate is four or five times higher than that of the general population. There were 57 suicides of New York City police officers from 1985 to mid-1994 with the officers' guns involved in all but four. The researcher, Andre Ivanoff, indicated that the police resist showing weakness or discussing problems or feelings. Problems such as drug and alcohol use and depression were seen by the officers who were surveyed as the basic reason for suicide, not the stress inherent in police work (NASW, 1994). While this study is based

in the largest metropolitan center in the nation, it is not unique to cities. The authors are familiar with police suicides in tiny hamlets of a few hundred people, the opposite end of the population scale in the Midwest and in sparsely populated western states. More recently, Robert Douglas, head of the National Police Suicide Foundation estimated that there were 484 suicide cases among police officers in 2003. John Violanti, a professor at the University of Buffalo, estimated the suicide rate for police officers to be 17 per 100,000 (Mental Health Weekly, 2005, p. 8). Research evidence shows that suicide among police officers is related to the violent nature of police work, the stress of their role as police officers, and the easy access to firearms (Violanti, 1996).

Judicial Subsystem

There are parallels between the rural-urban similarities/dissimilarities in law enforcement and those in the judicial realm. Here, too, rural adjudication has often been rather unsophisticated in the past and may continue to be in some communities today. Some of the factors in this are the fact that the rural prosecuting attorney is more likely to be only part-time in this role and also maintaining a private law practice concurrently. Being unable to devote oneself totally and exclusively to being a district or county attorney may detract from performance of the role. By the same token, fewer rural attorneys develop substantial practice expertise as criminal or trial lawyers serving defendants.

For defendants who are poor, three systems of criminal defense have evolved: public defenders, counsel assigned by courts from a list of available attorneys, and contract systems in which, for example, a bar association or a law firm contracts to provide services. Many counties use a mixture of methods of providing counsel to indigent defendants in the United States (Cole & Smith, 2004). Out of the most populous counties in the United States in 1999, a public defender system operated in 90 counties, a counsel system in 89 counties and a contract system in 42 counties. The majority of the caseload in these counties was handled by the public defense system (Bureau of Justice Statistics, 2001). However, excess caseloads among public defenders are often sent to assigned counsel in counties with adequate resources (Cole & Smith, 2004). Assigned counsel systems have been dominant in rural areas and continue to be widely used in these areas, as well as in small cities (Cole & Smith, 2004; Johnson, 1993).

In some cases, a person charged with committing an offense retains an attorney with a reputation in criminal law from an urban center at considerable distance. Similarly, a state attorney general may send someone from that office to a local county in any part of the state to lead or assist with a case and its prosecution. While there are proportionately and numerically fewer criminal hearings and trials in rural courts, an individual case of a bizarre murder, for example, may receive as much publicity in the media as one occurring in a metropolitan center. Some rural trials even end up receiving attention nationally.

Judges in a city may serve for years in one building, whereas in a nonmetropolitan environment the judge may "ride a circuit" covering a number of county courthouses or other facilities. With respect to adjudication of juveniles, it has been estimated that about half of the rural juvenile courts have part-time judges who preside in other courts as well. For both adult and juvenile offenders the judge, magistrate or other hearing official who is partially or entirely working in rural areas may gain greater perspective on broader geographic factors but have to sacrifice

the deeper knowledge of one individual community that his/her counterpart may have in the city.

Corrections Subsystem

The most important of the three subsystems generally for social work is corrections. One significant exception to this statement is the juvenile court, which, because it is a court, belongs under the judicial group. But, because of the extensive involvement of counseling and probation attached to many juvenile courts, it actually is a hybrid entity bridging the judicial and correctional subsystems.

Juvenile Court

The juvenile court was urban in its Chicago and Denver origins at the turn of the century in 1899, and most separate courts exclusively hearing juvenile cases are still today located in urban settings. Regardless of community size, however, the cases of young offenders are usually handled by a court acting on its juvenile jurisdiction and authority.

Often this is a person sitting as a juvenile judge on only a part-time basis, hearing nonjuvenile cases a greater share of the time. This arrangement particularly characterizes rural communities. Another practice allows one or more judges or referees in mostly rural counties to specialize in juvenile cases by traveling to multiple counties in the course of a week or several weeks. It has been contended (Levin & Sarri, 1974) that juvenile court judges should hear enough such cases to develop expertise in this practice. Depending upon how a system is organized, this is possible even in rural areas.

Detention

One important aspect of corrections is temporary detention of persons: (1) being held by the police during investigations; (2) awaiting hearings or trials; (3) following a commitment or sentence by a court to a longer-term institution, awaiting transportation and admission to that facility; and (4) in the case of mainly adults, incarceration locally for generally short penalties (sentences) often up to one year or even longer. In the instance of youth, this is a juvenile detention facility and for adults it is jail, either municipal or county.

Most counties have jails, and these are among the oldest and frequently most neglected correctional institutions. Paradoxically, the closest-to-home facilities (except for municipal lockups) are often overlooked in the interest in and concern about the more publicized state prisons and institutions. There are immense liabilities in county jails generally, given their age, decrepit crumbling conditions, poor sanitation, inadequate staffing, and virtual dearth of any meaningful programming for inmates. This picture is characteristic of both rural and urban jails, the major difference being simply one of size. Here and there around the country in all sizes of communities there are newer, generally better facilities, some of which are freestanding jails and others part of law enforcement centers, justice buildings, or other more modern structures. The solution for most rural counties and many small cities may lie in regionalization in which two or more counties share a facility.

A serious problem in this nation is the lack of specialized detention facilities for juveniles, the result being that often youngsters are held in jails. All too frequently there are destructive results for young people. Most separate juvenile detention facilities are in cities, just as is true of independent juvenile courts. The majority of rural counties do not have positive routine arrangements for detaining juveniles. A solution for nonmetropolitan areas is regional detention facilities serving multiple counties. Regional jails are a parallel version for adults. These should be centrally located in a geographical area small enough so that all sections are accessible within reasonable driving time, yet sufficiently large to contain a population base warranting a jail or detention facility constituting an efficient operation.

There is a question as to whether a single detention facility can be utilized for both juveniles and adults. This happens often in the case of traditional jails and should be prohibited because of what happens all too often to younger persons: homosexual rape, assault, suicide, and generalized contagion in an environment with often older, more sophisticated, and hardened offenders. There has been federal pressure on states to cease jailing juveniles generally and to cease doing so with adults.

Regional facilities in rural areas could be designed and operated to handle both age groups while maintaining their total separation, visually, auditorily, and in absolutely all respects. At the same time, economies can result (e.g., a single kitchen preparing food for both groups and centralized medical and social services and so forth). There has been some movement in the United States toward regional facilities for adults, juveniles, or both.

A caveat is necessary relative to erecting new correctional facilities, jails, juvenile detention centers, and especially prisons. Experience demonstrates that, if available, they will be used and filled. All too often these are overused, and many people are institutionalized for short or long periods of time who do not actually require such structure and security. This is true in both urban and rural environments. Present day proponents of juvenile detention reform argue that juvenile detention may exacerbate the problems of juvenile offenders in most cases. The results of a San Francisco study of 1500 nondetained juveniles in an alternative-to-detention program revealed that the recidivism rates among the program participants were lowered by 26 percent when compared with similar detained juveniles (Center for Policy Alternatives, 2005).

Probation

Another traditional correctional program, this one community-based, is probation, both adult and juvenile. Probation agencies and services are found in both rural and urban areas, but, again, they differ because of the population density. Often officers in rural environments serve two or more counties, whereas a probation worker in a large city may be assigned to only one portion of the single community. This means that the rural probation officer may spend an inordinate amount of time traveling to see only a few clients. It also means he or she may not work out of an "office" in the usual sense much of the time, doing more home visits and meeting clients in municipal or county facilities, schools, and other arrangements. Structurally, many juvenile probation officers are county employees, while often those working with adults are state agents, although there are numerous variations in such patterns around the country. Nationwide surveys of juvenile probation reveal that the median caseload for probation officers was greatest in urban areas, followed by suburban and then rural areas (Office of Juvenile Justice and Delinquency Prevention [OJJDP], 1996). Whereas the president's commission recommended caseloads of 35 and other organizations have suggested 50, recent figures show probation load averages nationally double to triple these standards. Nationally, there was a 44 percent increase in the number of cases placed on probation during the period 1990–1999 (Puzzanchera, 2003). Today, urban probation caseloads can be as high as 300 (Cole & Smith, 2004).

Institutions

Long-term correctional institutions include training schools and variations thereof for juveniles, and camps, reformatories, prisons, and prerelease centers for adults. In all of these, a common pattern is incarcerating mainly urban offenders in institutions frequently, if not usually, located in rural settings. Many problems result.

Years ago when legislatures established public state institutions for offenders, the mentally ill, the mentally retarded, and other special groups, these facilities were typically placed in out-of-sight, out-of-mind rural areas. From the point of view of contemporary modern America, they were often not well situated in central locations close to population centers. But in a horse-and-buggy era, the location often made sense; for example, in Iowa, a rural state, there are four state mental hospitals, each centrally located in the four quarters of the state. But none of these and none of the correctional facilities are in or adjacent to today's largest cities. Often state institutions were originally designed in conjunction with a farm. More recently, the farms have sometimes been sold or have ceased operations and clientele are less likely to work on the farm.

Problems of urbanites being incarcerated in rural institutions are numerous and are exemplified by the notorious Attica, New York prison eruption of 1971. Distance for visitors is an obstacle, yet visits from interested supportive family members is important, as is maintenance of family ties. Remembering that many offenders are poor and/or from financially poor families, the great distances become a serious financial burden whether the costs are bus fare, driving, or some other mode of transportation. Time is a consideration also, including loss of income resulting from time away from work.

In September, 2005, Hurricane Katrina posed many issues for prisoners in the flooded areas along the Gulf coast. First, they had to be transferred to different facilities in the state. For instance, around 8,400 prisoners from south Louisiana were transferred to 39 facilities around the state (Wereschagin, 2005). Second, some of these prisoners lost their families. Also, some prisoners were abandoned in floodwaters by the prison staff (Human Rights News, 2005). Additionally, some accounts told of evacuee prisoners being physically abused by the staff at one of the rural facilities (Rohde & Drew, 2005; Weinstein, 2005).

Because such institutions are in rural environments, people employed to staff them in most nonprofessional levels such as guards, correctional officers, or youth workers tend to be from the immediate farm and small-town vicinity. Typically, these are white, working class/middle class people employed to work with a population heavy in racial and ethnic minorities and the poor, and they have the greatest amount of direct contact with the incarcerees. For institutions to attempt to employ more blacks and other minorities is extremely difficult generally because so few such persons reside in the rural and small community area from which most employees are customarily drawn.

It has been observed that there is little communication between rural staff and urban residents in a juvenile training school setting and that the communication that does exist tends to be directive toward the residents. This directiveness is an easy way for staff to deal with situations, but it creates hostility and prevents change on the part of the residents (Towley, 1994).

Another problem is attracting and retaining experienced professionals to positions in rural institutions (Towley, 1994). While this may be slightly easier currently with the back-to-the-country movement and in some places rural growth, generally it is difficult to recruit physicians, psychologists, psychiatrists, social workers, and other professionals to institutions in rural environments. Part of this is probably resistance to the idea of working in a correctional institutional context, but some of it is due to the rural setting which may be perceived by prospective employees as lacking cultural opportunities and professional stimulation.

The growing number of institutions or units termed security medical facilities or some such designation present special issues (Clemens, 1994). These vary in purpose but usually are for the diagnosis and treatment of mentally ill offenders and/or evaluation of persons for courts, institutions, and parole authorities. Sometimes mental and physical health activities are combined in a single facility. Because of these particular functions, they require more specialized personnel (e.g., psychiatric and medical) than the usual prison. These forensic hospitals may be less in vogue now than they were a few years or decades ago, at least partly because of the current pressures faced by the entire criminal justice apparatus, especially court overloads and prison crowding. In a study of people engaged in corrections mental health policy, 81 percent were concerned with inmates' accessibility to services. Mental health treatment for repeat offenders was a concern for 78 percent of the respondents (Commission on the Status of Mental Health of Iowa's Corrections Population, 2001). Now the issue is just sheer numbers of beds because the increase in overall numbers of prisoners exceeds the capacities of prisons. For example, at present in Oakdale, the number of prisoners is 839 whereas the capacity is for 528 (Iowa Department of Corrections, 2005). The Iowa Department of Corrections Annual Report, 2000, predicted that the number of inmates with mental health-related problems was likely to increase from 1,424 inmates in 2000 to about 2,280 inmates in 2010 – an increase of 60 percent (Commission on the Status of Mental Health of Iowa's Corrections Population, 2001). To accommodate this increase in prisoner population will require a large investment of resources. However, it is more difficult now to transfer prison inmates into psychiatric hospitals because of due process issues. The whole emphasis on rights and due process has impacted on this picture. In some states the inmates/patients who have made pleas of not guilty by reason of insanity are being sent back to court as soon as they stabilize. In the present scenario, there have been more mentally ill inmates in jails and prisons than in the state hospitals (BJS, 1999; Cole & Smith, 2004). A study by the University of Iowa estimated that in Iowa, one in six prisoners, or about 1,400 prison inmates, has a psychiatric diagnosis (Petroski, 2002). However, a *New York Times* article in 2003 stated that Iowa had only three psychiatrists for more than 8,000 inmates (Butterfield, 2003). Lack of adequate care facilities can make them further vulnerable to problems like psychological distress (Cole & Smith, 2004).

Some of these facilities are now seeing more third-offense persons convicted of operating a vehicle while intoxicated with the national movement to be more severe with drunken drivers. There are also more offenders with dual diagnoses. Sexual predator laws are another contributor to and complication of populations in these forensic hospitals and a question is where to keep such persons (Clemens, 1994). With the deinstitutionalization nationally of state mental hospitals, some people who cannot function in the community end up in prison as *boarders*. Prisons increasingly become state homes for the socially maladaptive (Clemens, 1994).

The security medical facilities are the kind of program that may be located within the vicinity of a university, at least partially because of the professional personnel needs as well as for other reasons. Universities, too, run the gamut with regard to urban and rural settings. College and university environments not only bring together professionals, they also afford an opportunity to utilize students in a variety of ways – residents, interns, and practicum and field experience students from a variety of fields including social work. Furthermore, it is not uncommon for criminal justice programs to employ persons, part-time or full-time, who may simultaneously be students.

Parole

The last traditional correctional service is parole for adults, often termed aftercare for youth, who have been institutionalized. Much of what has been noted previously relative to probation also characterizes parole. Parole officers are more likely to be state employees than county or local, and parole tends to be more uniform within a state relative to its administration. With both probation and parole, urban agencies often have such large caseloads that most of the time is spent just attempting to fit clients as a group into the agency mainstream. Rural officers/workers, on the other hand, may handle their smaller loads in a more individualized, personal way with more procurement of services and more mediation. The other side of this is that the rural worker may be assigned such an expansive territory that a great deal of time is consumed in travel.

Boot Camps

An interesting and controversial development, particularly since the late 1980s, has been boot camps or "shock incarceration," especially for youthful first-time offenders. This is an intermediate punishment between probation and longer-term incarceration in prison. The rationale for this approach includes the ideas that: (1) short intensive confinement can be productive; (2) a military-style setting can contribute to physical conditioning and self-discipline that was otherwise lacking in inmates' lives; (3) there is value in the education, job training, drug treatment, and counseling provided; and (4) it is less costly financially (Austin, Jones, & Bolyard, 1993). Often a stay in a boot camp is followed by a period under probation or parole supervision.

Until the 1990s, most boot camps focused on state prison populations. In 1993, there were 28 state systems running 43 boot camp programs (Austin et al., 1993). The number of boot camps declined after the mid-1990s, and by the year 2000, nearly one-third of the state prison boot camps had closed – only 51 camps remained. There was also more than a 30 percent decrease in the average daily population of the state boot camps (Camp & Camp 2001).

Now this approach is being used with county and municipal jail populations. The research on the latter programs has tended to focus on those in larger communities and jails, although the boot camp idea is used elsewhere and could be applicable in smaller settings as well. In fact, most such programs are of modest size, according to Austin et al. (1993). Their research considered counties ranging from only 95,000 population to one with over a million. Research shows that the military component of boot camp programs is not effective in reducing criminal behavior of the offenders (Wilson, MacKenzie, & Mitchell, 2005). Recently, the Federal Bureau of Prisons proposed to abolish boot camps in California, Texas, and Pennsylvania on the premise that boot camps are ineffective in preventing released offenders from returning to crime (St. Gerard, 2005).

The Austin et al. (1993) survey stresses the importance of setting realistic goals for boot camps in relation to such program objectives as: (1) relief of jail overcrowding, (2) rehabilitation, and (3) improving community relations and jail operations. The reduction of crowding goal will be attained only if the program admits only or mostly inmates who are slated to be incarcerated 90 days or more, given the fact that most inmates have only short stays in jail. Rehabilitation expectations should be modest in view of the short duration of the program (e.g., 90 days) as compared to the cumulative negative experiences prior to the offense. The greatest benefit in boot camps may emanate from improved jail conditions associated with the creation of an "efficient inmate work force," a "safe housing environment," and staff training that enhances "direct but supportive" activity with inmates (Austin et al., 1993). And community work projects can greatly improve the jail's community relations.

With the exception of boot camps, which are relatively new, thus far we have examined traditional correctional services, both community-based field services and institutions, with regard to their rural/urban similarity and dissimilarity attributes. There is a danger of overstating the dissimilarities, especially in terms of stressing the image of rural areas as totally lacking services. Elsewhere, one of the authors (Johnson, 1980) has suggested that, rather than a simple dearth of resources in rural environments, more accurately what exists is a difference in the nature of services, in how they are delivered. Of course, many of the differences are ones of degree. Everything considered, urban and rural criminal justice are much more alike than unalike.

COMMUNITY-BASED ALTERNATIVES

We turn our attention now away from the traditional criminal justice programs to those newer alternatives that are community-based. Only a few will be considered in the interest of space limitations. At the outset, it should be noted that innovation has occurred and is taking place currently in both metropolitan and rural communities in spite of the fact that criminal justice generally is a conservative, slow-to-change field. It should also be recognized that these newer developments are, or at least could be, alternatives to incarceration.

In recent years, considerable attention has been given to *diversion* of accused or convicted juveniles and adults from the usual channel of procedures and practices that all too often in the past have led to negative labeling, destructive consequences, and high recidivism. The major unofficial diverters traditionally, without using the term, have been the police, but now as diversion has begun to be structured and institutionalized, special projects have appeared such as the teen courts that handle about 100,000 youth per year. On the other hand, the proportion of youth diverted from formal processing has decreased from 50 percent of the referrals in 1990 to 43 percent in 1999. Other evidence, however, supports diversion programs as the most cost-effective interventions for juvenile delinquents (Steven & March, 2005). An evaluation of the Detention Diversion Advocacy Project (DDAP) in San Francisco showed that it reduced the likelihood of recidivism among the project participants (Sheldon, 1999). In many programs, diversion comes much later in the process than with the police. In one county of 96,000 population, including a city with 60,000, a separate diversion project operative from 1978 to 1985 provided diversion for juveniles early, at the time of a "preliminary inquiry," which is similar to an arraignment for adults. At this hearing, the judge referred the youth to the diversion unit (Liggett, 1994). Many cases, however, do not even come to the formal case processing. They are diverted to other services. In other communities, both rural and urban, diversion comes later. In 1985, this project was terminated by bringing the worker into the juvenile court/probation office where she did most of the intakes and recommended to the county attorney whether cases should be processed formally or informally. If the latter, the worker handled the case through informal (unofficial) probation. If the youth successfully completed this program there was no record (Liggett, 1994). Therefore, the present system in this small city/county retained the diversion concept without the separate structure. Recent studies show nationally that 45 percent of all cases filed are disposed of at the intake hearing without court decision or formal processing by the judge (Cole & Smith, 2004).

Pretrial and related services are another group of community-based programs. The first project in the nation to be awarded the "Exemplary Program" designation by LEAA was a community-based correctional endeavor in Des Moines, Iowa, a city of 193,000 in a county of 327,000, the largest community in a rural state. The exemplary projects program (National Institute of Justice, 1981) was a systematic method of identifying outstanding criminal justice programs throughout the country, verifying their achievements, and publicizing them widely toward the goal of replication. To be eligible for consideration, projects must have demonstrated goal achievement, replicability, measurability, efficiency, and accessibility. The four components of the Des Moines program, "pre-trial release screening; a pre-trial community supervision effort; a county-administered probation unit; and a community-centered corrections facility" (National Institute of Law Enforcement 1973), operated from a single administrative unit. It was fairly simple in design, relatively low in cost, and effective.

Very much related to the community-centered correctional facility are *partial confinement* (Von Hirsch, 1976) and *work release* (Cole, 1992, pp. 649-650). These programs are most likely in municipal or county jails or other local residential facilities. Such provisions are found in large and small communities. The idea is to incarcerate offenders at certain times (e.g., nights and/or weekends) and permit them to obtain or continue employment concurrently. A number of advantages are inherent in this kind of arrangement, several of which are economic. There is reduced need for basic assistance or welfare for the family of an offender who is employed. Similarly, the work release or partial incarceration person may be charged for his/her public "board and room," thus relieving the taxpayer. There are other potential gains as well, and all can benefit the rural and urban communities offering such services.

Intensive supervision on probation is another recent development arising from the need to more closely monitor the activities of offenders presenting greater risk of recidivism. While probation itself is an old established correctional service found in communities of diverse population density, the newer idea is, with smaller and selected caseloads, to provide greater service and supervision. Barton and Butts (1990) discuss this approach with juveniles, and other researchers have noted its utility for adult offenders. Intensive supervision is more expensive than traditional probation but still less costly than institutionalization.

Related to intensive probation, and sometimes an integral part of it, is *house arrest* as analyzed by Petersilia (1988) and others. With this sanction the offender is ordered or sentenced to remain on his/her premises with specified exceptions such as employment or school. Some corrections clients being handled this way are monitored using electronic devices attached to the ankles or wrists coupled with telephonic technology. Through such mechanisms, it is possible to monitor the location of the person and supervise him/her in other ways. The equipment is expensive but less costly than imprisonment. It is used in rural areas as well as urban (Rath, Arola, Richter, & Zahnow, 1991). The active electronic monitoring, or "continuously signaling device," constantly monitors the offender's presence at the particular location by actively sending signals to the device attached to the offender. An alternative method for verifying the offenders' presence is the programmed contact device, or the "passive device," through which the offender verifies his presence through answering periodic calls from a probation officer. Despite its popularity, there is criticism of this system of monitoring. Some believe that this type of monitoring is an infringement on privacy, while others point out periodic technical problems with the devices. Also, this system may be insufficient for controlling the offender in cases like assaults and abuse (Bartollas, 2006; Cole & Smith, 2004). Finally, most states require adults to bear the cost of the monitoring device which makes this option difficult for persons with low income, although these devices are provided to juveniles usually without cost to the youth or family (Gibson, 2005).

Another community-based program that is regaining popularity is the sanction of *restitution*, related both to the growing concern with crime victims as well as the recognition that repayment by offenders to persons who have suffered loss at the hands of the perpetrator can have significant restorative value for both the offender and the victim. By its very nature, restitution lends itself almost equally well to both rural and urban contexts. In fact, it is found in both, whether administered by courts, probation/parole, or some other arrangement.

Community service is another sanction being used in some places in several variations. Offenders are required, in this plan, to do stipulated amounts of work in nonprofit organizations, such as charities or government. As with any program, this one is no panacea and there are problems to be resolved, but its potential is considerable in both urban and nonmetropolitan areas. Its benefits for the public may be doubly significant in rural communities when townspeople perhaps more directly observe and experience offenders constructively occupied repairing or maintaining public buildings, facilities, and grounds or working with "charity" organizations. To the extent that this produces more positive public attitudes toward offenders (improved offender attitudes

are reciprocal in these dynamics), the potential payoff for everyone concerned is substantial (Cole & Smith, 2004; Harris, 1979;). Still, it is the most underused sanction in the country (Tonry, 1997). A study of 13,219 offenders receiving community-based sanction found that the assignment to community service as an alternative to jail had the lowest rearrest rates for high and medium-risk offenders (Martin, 2003). The criticism by some, however, is either that assignment to community service takes jobs from law-abiding citizens or that it is too mild punishment for upper class and white-collar criminals (Cole & Smith, 2004).

One of the authors has been involved with senior college students in social work who staffed a community service project in a university community. Among the latters' duties were screening, training, and supervising the activities of sophomore-level student volunteers in the same program, recruiting new community agencies to participate in the program, providing liaison to participating agencies, and overall monitoring. Activities included interviewing, data collection, record keeping, case management, and working with resources. In another corrections setting (a security medical facility), a graduate practicum social work student interested in supervision, administration, and teaching provided supervision and instruction for an undergraduate field experience student functioning as a generalist. All of this involving the author's participation has occurred in small cities. This is significant when one realizes how many of the colleges and universities with Council on Social Work Education (CSWE) accredited undergraduate programs (448 in 2005) are in smaller communities (CSWE, 2005). The same thing is true of 172 graduate schools. The point is that the potential for innovative impacting on criminal justice is considerable if fully exploited.

Group homes for juveniles and *halfway houses* for young and adult offenders exist in various patterns in urban and rural areas. Some are in lieu of institutionalization in more secure facilities. Others serve to smooth the transition from institutions back into the community and others serve still additional purposes. There is a common phenomenon when the establishment of group homes and halfway houses is proposed: neighborhood opposition. This is seen in communities of all sizes and kinds. Some of the expressed fears are reduction of property values, danger due to the presence or bad example of offenders, and similar notions. Interestingly, however, when there is a proposal to close or reduce in scope a state institution such as a prison in a rural community, there is as much or more opposition. In some towns, an institution is literally the largest employer in the community and the major "industry." To lose it can be quite damaging economically to the local community.

In recent years, there have been a number of developments having to do with *runaway* youth, often taking the form of *shelters* for short-term care. This population is relevant for juvenile justice to the extent that running away is defined as delinquency, albeit a status offense. Such acts are being substantially redefined nationally to decriminalize. This does not completely solve the problem, however, of the needs of youth on the run. A directory of shelters (National Directory, 1993) suggests that they are present in all sections of the U.S., more so in urban centers but even in quite small communities. Research evidence shows that the majority of youth have a positive perception of the shelters (Administration of Children & Families, 1995). According to National Runaway Switchboard Statistics for 2004, 58 percent of the youth were already on the street – this included runaways, throwaways, and homeless – and 11 percent were contemplating running away. Shelters were found to be the means of survival for only 9 percent of the youth on the street (National Runaway Switchboard, 2004). Regarding runaway youth, most states have an official designation for runaways as a status offense which makes them eligible for services. For example, Arizona could classify a runaway youth as an adjudicated incorrigible (i.e., not a delinquent) and then provide services. States like Iowa have no such law and youth need to have another legal charge in order to receive any type of service (Gibson, 2005).

The same thing is true of *shelters* for persons experiencing *spouse abuse* and family violence. These even newer facilities are distributed unevenly in various parts of the nation but are found in communities ranging widely in size. Rural towns would have trouble maintaining such a facility because it is usually important that the location remains unidentified and unknown, and this is difficult to do in a nonmetropolitan community. Directories of spouse shelters reflect largely urban locations. While the general approach in child abuse is to help parents rather than punish, the act of abuse is itself illegal and hence can and sometimes does become a matter for criminal justice.

Rape crisis programs are another recent innovation. Although rape occurs in all regions, it may be more difficult to establish relevant social services in rural areas because of the community's propensity to ignore or deny some of its problems such as this one. Now it is increasingly well established that so-called "date rape" and acquaintance rape are common. They occur without respect to community size and nature. The issue of providing protection to dating violence victims is addressed in the Violence Against Women Act of 2005 (Morris, 2005). Part of the rural social worker's challenge is to sensitize the community to its own needs and enable it to take constructive action (Davenport, 1978).

Across the United States, services are provided to victims by an estimated 1,315 rape crisis centers. Some research shows that the services provided by these centers can reduce the amount of time victims show posttraumatic stress symptoms following rape (Morris, 2005). The Violence Against Women Act of 1994 established Center for Disease Control's Rape Prevention and Education programs for different areas within the United States. In 2002, the program funded training of 280,000 professionals including social workers in the area of rape prevention and education. It also provided funding to 36 state sexual assault coalitions, more than 1,000 rape crisis centers, and 140 other nonprofit and faith-based organizations (CDC, 2004).

THE SOCIAL WORK ROLE IN URBAN AND RURAL CRIMINAL JUSTICE

The function of the social worker in criminal justice is essentially the same as that in other major fields of service: applying the helping or problem-solving process with offenders. The involuntary nature of the clientele makes some significant differences, but the principal activities are basically the same. These generally are conceptualized as study (often called investigation in criminal justice), assessment, formulating a plan of action, implementation of the plan, intervention or action, and evaluation.

Common social work roles in criminal justice are probation/parole officer, juvenile court officers, forensic social workers, institutional counselor or social worker, pre-trial worker, police social worker, or one of the other newer, more specialized roles such as those having to do partially or entirely with restitution or community service. Social workers' roles have expanded to further include "diversionary programs, support for convicts' reintegration into their communities, social services for families of criminals as well as advocacy for victims of crimes" (DuBois & Miley, 2005; Johnson, 1998). Many of these social work roles are examined in more detail in subsequent chapters. Although most social workers in criminal justice provide direct service to individuals, families, and/or small groups (casework and group work in traditional terminology), others can be found in administration at various levels including state director of corrections, and in research, teaching, and other aspects. Less directly involved with corrections, perhaps, but still related to the criminal justice spectrum are some of the more specialized roles like substance abuse counseling, work with persons convicted of sexual abuse, family violence interventions, and others. Any or all of this may be part of the activities for a probation or parole officer or an institutional counselor, but it also is carried out in settings focusing specifically on these areas.

The literature on rural social work stresses the need for a generalist worker in nonmetropolitan areas (Johnson, 1980). This is true in rural corrections also. Such a professional is one skilled in the major methods, who is able to provide direct service, engage in some program development, and operate with self-help activities. He or she is very much attuned to the nature of the community, its customs, and its traditional service network, often involving law enforcement persons, clergy, school officials, clubs and lodges, and others and to the existent "natural helpers." This is a worker who can function autonomously without much supervision or professional stimulation.

In contrast to the rural generalist, there is more specialization (and formalization) in urban settings. This does not necessarily mean that such programs are therefore better or more effective, however. Actually, upon examination, criminal justice is seen to be largely a hodgepodge nonsystem rather than a well-organized and smoothly integrated social mechanism. This is true when considering the urban or rural situations separately or both together.

Many social workers from noncriminal justice settings encounter offenders in the course of their practice, just as many offenders experience social workers in and out of criminal justice. Therefore, it is important that most social service professionals be able to deal comfortably and competently with this client group.

TRENDS AND THE FUTURE

As far as crime and delinquency are concerned, the trend over the years from 1993–2003 shows a decrease in personal and property crimes in rural, suburban, and urban areas. Relative to each other, per capita urban crime rates, both personal and property, are consistently much higher than rural or suburban rates. The rates for suburban and rural areas have converged for the most part, with rates always lower than the urban crime rates.

Although there are offenses characteristic of each kind of community, most types of offenses are now found in central cities, suburbs, and rural areas. Traditional criminal justice provisions are present in both rural and urban areas and innovative programs exist in communities of various size. Not surprisingly, more community-based measures are established in cities, but the latter certainly have no monopoly on these. Some promising programs are present in sparsely populated areas. There is every indication that these developments will continue in at least the near future, although shrinking funds, both federal and state, may negatively impact on the picture, rural and urban.

Crime continues to be in the national spotlight. Public opinion polls show that it is one of the major concerns of most people. However, in a 2005 survey, crime was a serious issue for only 2 percent of Americans as compared with 29 percent in 2004 and 54 percent in 2003 (Carroll, 2005). Crime is often a primary issue in the presidential and other campaigns with each party and the competing candidates trying to appear tougher on crime. Candidates for office seem to believe, with good reason apparently, that their job is not to educate the public about crime, which they could do, but to reflect the public's apprehension and anger. This emotionality and irrationality is not helped by the media that so sensationalizes crime, whereas it too could play a large role educating the public and informing objectively.

Much of what happens in the future with respect to criminal and juvenile justice depends on federal and state legislation and law enforcement, especially at the local level. If, for example, there were to be significant decriminalization in such areas as drug offenses or further decriminalization relative to public drunkenness or different treatment of the drunk driver, this could have far-ranging consequences for all three criminal justice subsystems. But at this writing such changes appear unlikely to occur in the near future. More likely is further movement in the direction of "getting tough" with offenders unless there is some societal awakening to the extreme costs (e.g., financial, civil liberties) of this approach, its destructiveness, and its meager positive results.

Another variable in future trends is the success of the helping professions such as social work in developing more effective approaches for working with and changing the attitudes and behaviors of involuntary clients. Corrections is one of the most difficult and challenging fields for all of the human services, and this situation seems unlikely to change substantially.

SUMMARY AND CONCLUSION

In this chapter, we have considered the concepts urban and rural as related to crime and delinquency. The three subsystems of criminal justice and a variety of settings, both traditional and nontraditional, have been examined as these are found in rural and urban areas. Community-based alternatives to institutions have been included. The social work role in both metropolitan and rural criminal justice was explored.

While some distinctiveness has been noted in urban and rural crime problems and criminal justice programs, it has been seen that these differences are easily exaggerated. There appears to be convergence taking place between large and small communities with regard to deviancy and criminal justice. Stereotyped and inaccurate notions of communities in general and of their problems such as crime and their social welfare services like corrections require balancing and reason. Programs, whether in the law enforcement, judicial, or correctional realm, are more likely to be of maximum benefit if properly understood in their rural and urban environmental contexts. Most program ideas can be adapted to communities of various sizes and characteristics.

There are no panaceas for crime and delinquency, urban or rural. But all sizes and kinds of communities have or could have programs useful in dealing with deviancy. Each community's problems of criminality need to be considered individually since these may vary in nature and extent from place to place and require different interventions. Enough is known about delinquency and crime causation to conclude that, in general, probably most communities and regions would benefit from giving attention to the facts that nationally these problems are largely a matter of: (1) older adolescents and young adults; (2) people from racial and ethnic minority groups made up of societally disadvantaged people who experience discrimination and second-class citizenship; (3) poor people who increasingly seem to constitute an underclass; and (4) persons manifesting mental or emotional disorder, intellectual limitations, addiction, character defect, illiteracy, educational failure, or some combination of these characteristics. Beyond these general traits, each community needs to examine its own crime problem and to design programs accordingly.

Of course, there are offenders who do not fit this picture (e.g., the well-educated, middle or upper class, white-collar offender). And these must be programmed for as well. But they are not the majority in virtually any community (at least of those apprehended) and do not warrant attraction of most of the attention and resources.

A real need in all communities is for prevention. Based on what is already known about the nature of the "client" groups cited above, it seems clear that any or all of the following could be useful in reducing crime and delinquency: (1) decently-paying jobs for all people of all ages needing and wanting them; (2) adequate systems for income maintenance, housing and health, nutrition and education; (3) equality of opportunity without regard to such factors as age, class, race, nationality and ethnic characteristics, and elimination of prejudice and discrimination; (4) access to quality treatment programs for addictions, mental and personality disorders and limitations; and (5) neighborhoods that are sensitive to and make provisions for human needs in such areas as education, religion, and recreation/leisure and in doing so acknowledge the importance to the human of enrichment, opportunity, variety, and challenge. Crime prevention and reduction has its national context, but much can be and is accomplished at the local or community level. This is the challenge for the future.

REFERENCES

Administration of Children & Families. (1995). *Youth with runaway, throwaway and homeless experience, prevalence, drug use, and other at-risk behaviors.* Washington, D.C.: U.S. Department of Health & Human Services.

Austin, J., Jones, M., & Bolyard, M. (1993). *The growing use of jail boot camps: The current state of the art.* Washington, D.C.: U.S. Department of Justice.

Ball, C. (2001). Rural perceptions of crime. *Journal of Contemporary Criminal Justice, 17*(1), 37–48.

Bartollas, C. (2006). *Juvenile delinquency* (7th ed.). Boston: Allyn and Bacon.

Barton, W. H., & Butts, J. A. (1990). Intensive supervision programs for juvenile delinquents. *Crime and Delinquency, 36*(2), 238–256.

Beck, A. J., & Harrison, P. M. (2001). *Prisoners in 2000.* Bureau of Justice Statistics, U.S. Department of Justice, Washington, D.C.

Bureau of Justice Statistics. (1999). *Special report,* July.

Bureau of Justice Statistics. (2001). *Indigent defense statistics.* Summary findings. Retrieved October 11, 2005 from http://www.ojp.usdoj.gov/bjs/id.htm#caseload.

Bureau of Justice Statistics. (2005a). *Victimization rates by type of crime and locality of residence.* Table 53. Property crimes – 1993–2002

Bureau of Justice Statistics. (2005b). Victimization rates for persons age 12 and over by type of crime and locality of residence of victims. *Criminal Victimization in the United States.* Table 52, Personal Crimes 1993–2002.

Butterfield, F. (2002). As drug use drops in big cities, small towns confront upsurge. *The New York Times,* February 11.

Camp, C. G., & Camp, G. M. (2001). *The 2000 corrections yearbook,* Adult Corrections. Middletown, Connecticut: Criminal Justice Institute.

Carroll, J. (2005). American public opinion about crime in the United States. *The Gallup Organization.* Retrieved September 12th 2005 from http://www.gallup.com/poll/content/default.aspx?ci=15247.

Center for Disease Control and Prevention. (2004). CDCs rape prevention and education grant program – Preventing sexual violence in the United States. Department of Health and Human Services.

Center for Policy Alternatives. (2005). Juvenile detention reform. Retrieved from http:www.stateaction.org/issue/issue.cfm/issue/JuvenileDetentionReform.xml.

Clemens, C. (Nov. 7, 1994). Personal communication. Oakdale, Iowa.

Cole, G. F. (1992). *The American system of criminal justice* (4th ed.). Belmont, CA: Wadsworth.

Cole, G.F., & Smith, C.E. (2004). T*he American system of criminal justice.* Belmont, CA: Wadsworth/Thomson.

Commission on the Status of Mental Health of Iowa's Corrections Population. (2001). Good public mental health policy is a good public safety policy. Community Corrections Improvement Association, Cedar Rapids (prepared by State Public Policy Group). Retrieved September 30, 2005 from http://www.iowacbc.org/articles/mentalhealthreport.pdf.

Council on Social Work Education. (2005). *Social Work Education Report, 5*(33), p. 23, Alexandria, VA.

Davenport III, J. (1978). *Rape crisis service in rural areas* (a videotape). Lexington, KY: University of Kentucky, Appalachian Education Satellite Program.

Drug Enforcement Administration. (1999). *Crisis in Middle America: Report of the national conference on drugs, crime and violence in mid-sized communities.* Washington, D.C: U.S. Department of Justice.

DuBois, B., & Miley, K. K. (2005). *Social work: An empowering profession* (5th ed.). Boston: Allyn and Bacon.

Federal Bureau of Investigation. (2005). *Preliminary crime statistics for 2004.* Retrieved 18th Aug, 2005 from http://www.fbi.gov/pressrel/pressrel05/preliminary060605.htm

Federal Bureau of Prisons. (2005). *Types of offenses.* Retrieved October 9, 2005 from http://www.bop.gov/about/index.jsp.

Gibson, J. (September 21, 2005). Personal communication. Iowa City, Iowa.

Haafke, R. L. (August 13, 1994). Personal communication. Sioux City, Iowa.

Harris, M. K. (1979). *Community service by offenders.* Washington, D.C.: U.S. Department of Justice, National Institute of Corrections.

Human Rights News. (2005). *New Orleans: Prisoners abandoned to floodwaters.* September, 22. Retrieved October 10, 2005 from http://hrw.org/english/docs/2005/09/22/usdom11773.htm.

Iowa Department of Corrections. (2005) Statistics. Retrieved September 24th from http://docia.a-t-g.com/DailyStats.asp.

Johnson, H. W. (1998). Crime and juvenile justice. In H. W. Johnson, *The social services: An introduction* (pp. 211–234). Itasca, IL: F. E. Peacock.

Johnson, H. W. (1993). Rural crime and corrections. In L. H. Ginsberg (Ed.), *Social work in rural communities* (pp. 208–217). Alexandria, VA: Council of Social Work Education.

Johnson, H. W. (Ed.). (1980). *Rural human services.* Itasca, IL: F. E. Peacock.

Karr, J. T. (1978). *Rise of proactive police strategies – An alternative approach to bureaucratic rationalization and rural-urban crime differentials.* Unpublished doctoral dissertation, University of Kansas, Lawrence, Kansas.

Klaus, P.A. (2004). *Crime and the nation's households, 2003.* Bureau of Justice Statistics Bulletin, October.

Legal Services Corporation. (2003). *A report on rural issues and delivery and the LSC-sponsored symposium.* Retrieved September 10, 2005 from http://www.lri.lsc.gov/pdf/03/RIDS_rprt042403.pdf.

Levin, M. M., & Sarri, R. C. (1974). *Juvenile delinquency: A study of juvenile codes in the U.S.* Ann Arbor, MI: University of Michigan, National Assessment of Juvenile Corrections.

Liggett, J. (November 7, 1994). Personal communication. Iowa City, Iowa.

Logan, T. K., Walker, R., & Leukefeld, C. G. (2001). Rural, urban influenced and urban differences among domestic violence arrestees. *Journal of Interpersonal Violence, 16*(3), 266–283.

Martin, G. (2003). The effectiveness of community-based sanctions in reducing recidivism. *Corrections Today, 65*(1).

Mental Health Weekly (2005). *Suicide rates higher among police officers.* A Manisses Communications Group Publication.

Morris, J. (2005). Written testimony on the Violence against Women Act on behalf of the National Coalition against Domestic Violence as presented to Senator Arlen Specter, Chairman, United States Senate Committee on the Judiciary on July 19, 2005. N.C.A.D.V. Retrieved October, 9, 2005 from http://www.ncadv.org/files/NCADVSenateTestimonyS1197.pdf.

NASW News. (1994). N.Y.P.D. suicide studied. Washington, D.C.: *National Association of Social Workers, 39*(10), p. 9.

National Directory of Children, Youth and Families Services 1993-94: *The Professional Reference* (9th ed.) (1993). Longmont, CO: Marion L. Peterson Publishers.

National Institute of Law Enforcement and Criminal Justice. (1973). *Community based corrections in Des Moines.* Washington, D.C.: U.S. Department of Justice, Law Enforcement Assistance Administration.

National Institute of Justice. (1981). *Exemplary projects.* Washington, D.C.: U.S. Government Printing Office.

National Institute of Justice. (2004). *Law enforcement technology – Are small and rural agencies equipped and trained?* U.S. Department of Justice, Office of Justice Programs.

National Runaway Switchboard Statistics. (2004). Retrieved September 15, 2005 from http://www.nrscrisisline.org/2004stat.asp.

Newman, J. H. (1978). *Differential reporting rates of criminal victimization.* Unpublished doctoral dissertation, Washington State University, Pullman, WA.

OJJDP-Juvenile Justice Bulletin. (1996). *Juvenile probation: The workhorse of the juvenile justice system.* Washington, D.C.: U.S. Department of Justice.

Payne, B. K., Berg, B. L., & Sun, I. Y. (2005). Policing in small town America: Dogs, drunks, disorder, and dysfunction. *Journal of Criminal Justice, 33*(1), 31–41.

Petersilia, J. (1988). *House arrest.* Washington, D.C.: U.S. Department of Justice.

Petroski, W. (2002). *Torment, tumult persist for prisoners.* Retrieved September 6, 2005 from http://namiscc.org/News/2002/IowaPrison.htm.

Puzzanchera, C. M.(2003). *Juvenile delinquency probation caseload 1990–1999 factsheet.* Retrieved September 14, 2005, from http://ojjdp.ncjrs.org/ojstatbb/publications/StatBB.asp.

Rand, M. R. (1993). Crime and the nation's households 1992. Washington, D.C.: U.S. Department of Justice.

Rath, Q. C., Arola, T., Richter, B., & Zahnow, S. (1991). Small town corrections – A rural perspective. *Corrections Today, 53*(2), 228–230.

Rohde, D., & Drew, C. (2005). Storm and crisis: The inmates; prisoners evacuated after hurricanes allege abuse. *The New York Times,* October 2.

Sheldon, R.G. (1999). Detention diversion advocacy: An evaluation. OJJDP, *Juvenile Justice Bulletin,* September.

Sourcebook of Criminal Justice Statistics. (2003). *Drug use by adult male arrestees in 43 U.S. cities and counties by type of drug, 2000–2003.* Table 4.30. Retrieved October 9, 2005 from http://www.albany.edu/sourcebook/wk1/t430.wk1.

Steven, P., & March, R. (2005). *Criminal Justice Policy Review, 16*(1), 59.

St. Gerard (2005). Federal prisons to eliminate boot camps. *Corrections Today, 67*(2), p. 13.

Tonry, M. (1997) *Intermediate sanctions in sentencing guidelines.* Washington, D.C.: U.S. Department of Justice, Office of Justice Programs, National Institute of Justice.

Towley, J. F. (November 4, 1994). Personal communication. Waterloo, Iowa.

United States Census Bureau (2002). *Census 2000 urban and rural classification.* U.S. Census Bureau. Retrieved September 30, 2005 from http://www.census.gov/geo/www/ua/ua_2k.html.

Van Hightower, N. R., Gorton, J., & De Moss, C. L. (2000). Predictive models of domestic violence and fear of intimate partners among migrant and seasonal farm worker women. *Journal of Family Violence, 15*(2), 137–154.

Violanti, J. M. (1996). *Violence turned inward: Police suicide in the workplace.*

Von Hirsch, A. (1976). *Doing justice.* New York: Hill and Wang.

Websdale, N., & Johnson, B. (1998). An ethno statistical comparison of the forms and levels of woman battering in urban and rural areas of Kentucky. *Criminal Justice Review, 23*, 161–196.

Weinstein, H. (2005). *Evacuated inmates at one prison allege abuse by guards.* October 2. Retrieved October 9, 2005 from http://www.latimes.com/news/nationworld/nation/

la-na-prisons2oct02,1,7420887.story?coll=la-headlines-nation.

Weisheit, R. A., & Donnermeyer, J. F. (2000). Change and continuity in crime in rural America. In G. LaFree (Ed.), *Criminal justice*, 1. The nature of crime: Continuity and change (pp. 309–357). Washington, D.C.: National Institute of Justice.

Weisheit, R., Falcone, D., & Wells, L. (1994). *Rural crime and rural policing*. Washington, D.C.: U.S. Department of Justice.

Wereschagin, M. (2005). Pittsburgh attorneys off to Gulf coast. *Pittsburgh Tribune Review*, September, 21. Retrieved October 9, 2005 from http://www.pittsburghlive.com/x/tribune-review/trib/pmupdate/s_376297.html.

Wilson, D. B., MacKenzie, D. L., & Mitchell, F. N. (2005). *Effects of correctional boot camps on offending*. A Campbell Collaboration Systematic Review available at http://www.aic.gov.au/campbellcj/reviews/titles.html

Young, M. (2001). Victim rights and services, National Organization for Victim Assistance.

Chapter 6

Ethical Practice in Forensic Social Work

Elaine P. Congress

INTRODUCTION

The growing cultural diversity among social work clients and their families has been documented by Professor Elaine P. Congress and Professor Winnie W. Kung (2005). Based on the U.S. Census report of 2000, Congress and Kung estimate ". . . that by the year 2050 almost half (49.9%) of the population will be non-Caucasian. In large metropolitan areas such as New York City the majority of the population now already come from various countries in Asia, South and Central America, and the Caribbean, and as much as 36% of its residents are foreign born . . . In the most recent Code of Ethics social workers are advised to understand and respect cultural differences among clients and to demonstrate competence in working with people from different cultures" (Congress & Kung, 2005, p. 3). The new immigrants are usually poor, vulnerable, oppressed, and victimized by urban crime. As will be discussed in the case illustrations in this chapter, ethical issues of confidentiality, legal and fiduciary responsibilities, boundaries, and self-determination are even more challenging to culturally diverse families.

Social work and law as professions are based upon ethical standards delineated in their respective codes of ethics. Social workers frequently work collaboratively with lawyers and social work ethics and the law usually coincide. However, at times law and ethics collide rather than coincide, with consequences for both professions. Social workers who work in forensic settings have an ethical duty to be responsive to the ethical principles of the social work

profession. This chapter will first explore the role of ethics in the professions in general and then more specifically the role of ethics and law in social work practice. Similarities and differences between law and social work ethics, as well as social workers and lawyers will be addressed. The ETHIC model (Congress, 1999 and 2002) can help in understanding and resolving ethical and legal conflicts. The chapter will conclude with guidelines to help social work practitioners and educators navigate when standards are in conflict in forensic social work practice.

The chapter will focus on ethical practice in forensic social work. Forensic social work has been defined as "the application of social work to questions and issues relating to law and legal systems. This specialty of our profession goes far beyond clinics and psychiatric hospitals for criminal defendants being evaluated and treated on issues of competency and responsibility. A broader definition includes social work practice which in any way is related to legal issues and litigation, both criminal and civil. Child custody issues, involving separation, divorce, neglect, termination of parental rights, the implications of child and spouse abuse, juvenile and adult justice services, corrections, and mandated treatment all fall under this definition" (www.nofsw.org).

LITERATURE REVIEW

Forensic social work has been understudied and even the term underused (Roberts & Brownell, 1999), although the importance of integrating legal

---

* An earlier version of this paper was presented at the National Organization of Forensic Social Work (NOFSW) Conference on April 19, 2005 in New Orleans, Louisiana.

issues into social work education has been noted (Kopels & Gustavsson, 1996). A review of recent social work literature indicated only six articles that focused on challenges in social worker and lawyer collaboration (Forgey & Colarrosi, 2003; Maidenberg & Golick, 2001; Pierce, Gleason, & Milller, 2001; Bassuk & Lessem, 2001; Green, Glenwick, & Schiano, 1999; Johnson & Cahn, 1995). Yet ethical conflicts for the social worker in a legal setting frequently arise, especially in the area of child abuse (Forgey & Colarrosi, 2003; Greene, Glenwick, & Schiaffino, 1999). While several earlier articles (Russell, 1988; van Wormer, 1992) focused on role conflict between social workers and lawyers, none relate to the ethical practice of social workers in forensic social work settings, the primary focus of this chapter.

CODES OF ETHICS

Since the time of Hippocrates, ethics have played a role in guiding professional practice. Among early codes of ethics were those adopted by physicians and attorneys. More recently among the helping professions, codes of ethics have been adopted by psychologists, psychiatrists, marriage and family therapists, counselors, and social workers (Dickson & Congress, 2000). Codes of ethics exist to guide professionals in resolving ethical dilemmas, provide protection to the public from unscrupulous practitioners, ensure self-regulation rather than government regulation, offer consistent standards for professional behavior, and protect professionals from litigation (Congress, 1999).

Codes of ethics combine broad aspirations with specific rules of conduct. The NASW Code of Ethics statement that "Social workers should promote the general welfare of society from local to global levels, and the development of people, their communities, and their environments..." (NASW Standard 6.01) is an example of the former, while the mandate "Social workers should under no circumstances engage in sexual activities or sexual contact with current clients, whether such contact is consensual or forced (NASW Standard 1.09) is an example of the latter. While a social worker's failure to promote the general welfare of society on a global level is probably a violation of the Code which will not be subject to sanctions, sexual contact with a current client is more likely a violation that will result in sanctions. Such violations are enforced by professional associations, and penalties range from admonishment to suspension of practice to expulsion from the profession. There may be legal ramifications for ethical violations as well, including proceedings in criminal courts, civil actions for malpractice, or damages resulting from specific harms.

HISTORY OF NASW CODE OF ETHICS

Although the social work profession has been value based since it began over a hundred years ago, the first professional Code of Ethics was not developed until 1920, by Mary Richmond. A chapter of the American Association of Social Work (the organization that preceded NASW) in Toledo, Ohio, is credited with developing the first organizational Code of Ethics (Lowenberg, Dolgoff, & Harrington, 2000).

Five years after the 1955 formation of the National Association of Social Workers as the primary professional organization for social workers, a Code for the National Association of Social Workers was developed. This 1960 NASW Code of Ethics was one page in length and consisted of fourteen abstract and idealistic statements that described social workers' responsibility to the profession. The Code was revised in 1967, 1979, 1990, 1993, and 1996 and amended in 1999.

The current Code was approved by the National Association of Social Workers Delegate Assembly in 1996 after much study and input from social workers around the country. In sharp contrast to earlier codes, this Code had 28 pages and 156 provisions. While a criticism of the former Codes had been that the Code applied primarily to individual practitioners, the new code included a focus on social work practice with groups and families, as well as the ethical responsibilities of supervisors, administrators, educators, trainers, and researchers. Timely topics of concern to social workers included limits to confidentiality, technology, sexual harassment, managed care, cultural competency, and dual relationships – especially of a sexual nature. Of particular relevance to this discussion of law and ethics was the new section on interdisciplinary colloboration and the increased focus on exceptions to confidentiality in the 1999 revision.

The NASW Code of Ethics offers general principles by which to guide ethical behavior, yet by definition all situations cannot be included (Reamer, 1998). The Code is not "meant to provide a set of rules that prescribe how social workers should act in all situations" and states that applications of the Code must always consider the context in which practice occurs (NASW, 1999, pp. 2–3). In contrast to other countries, however, the NASW Code of Ethics is much more detailed and specific (Congress & Kim, 2005; Congress & McAuliffe, in press).

Similarities and Differences between Law and Ethics, Lawyers and Social Workers

While both laws and professional ethics often have similar goals and underlying value perspectives, laws are seen as more enforceable. In contrast, ethical codes vary among professions and are primarily enforceable among each profession's members.

Social workers and lawyers are professionals and maintain a fiduciary responsibility toward their clients. It is most important given the greater knowledge of the professional and the vulnerability of the client that both professionals behave in a trustworthy manner toward their clients. Despite both professions having similar fiduciary responsibility to their clients, there are significant differences in role and function that may be challenging for social workers and lawyers in interdisciplinary settings.

Social workers in the child welfare field frequently work collaboratively with lawyers. Public and private agencies may retain attorneys to represent the agency in hearings involving termination of parental rights. Furthermore, the child, birth parents, and adoptive parents are represented by attorneys in court proceedings. Social workers usually conduct psychosocial studies and make recommendations to the attorneys about what would be in the best interests of the child.

In an early article (Stein, 1991), four areas were identified as particularly challenging in interdisciplinary work with lawyers: (1) Definition of client, (2) task delineations, (3) differences in terms of recording, and (4) confidentiality responsibilities.

The greatest conflict between social worker and attorney often emerges in defining who is the client. The ethical issue for the lawyer appears clearer. The lawyer can only represent one party, either the birth parent, the foster care agency, the child, or the adoptive agency. In court proceedings, this leads lawyers to assume an adversarial role in only presenting evidence which would be helpful to the party they are representing and suppressing evidence that would be detrimental. Social workers, however, adopt more of a mediation role, that is trying to reconcile conflicting positions. While the NASW Code of Ethics states that social workers should promote the best interests of their clients, the definition of client is not defined. In a child welfare agency, a social worker may find herself trying to balance the conflicting demands of an agency advocating for the return of children to their birth parents, a birth mother who seems uncertain about resuming care of her children, and a child who wants to continue to remain with his foster parents. Yet often social workers question who is the client. In the child welfare field is the client – the birth parent, the foster parent, the adoptive parent, or the child? For lawyers, defining who the client might be is much easier. A lawyer would be assigned to represent the interests of one party, either the birth parent, the child, or the foster care agency.

This example illustrates some of the differences in how social workers and lawyers define their roles:

Mrs. Brown had been arrested for selling drugs, but the charges were finally dropped because of insufficient evidence. Jill, a social worker in a child welfare agency, was assigned to make a psychosocial assessment of this family. When she contacted the school the Brown children attended, she learned that the children were often sent to school dirty and without breakfast. Would placement of the children, however, support the dignity and worth of the mother? Since an important role for Mrs. Brown might be that of parent, what would be the effect of placing her children?

Social workers struggle with the social work value of promoting autonomy and self-determination. Should the social worker promote the mother's self-determination? What if the children, as many children do, want to exercise their self determination by staying with their parent? The new Code states that "social workers' responsibility to promote self-determination is limited when in their professional judgment a client's actions or potential actions pose a serious, foreseeable and imminent threat to themselves or others" (NASW, 1999, p. 7). This provision may lead to ethical dilemmas for the child welfare practitioner. Are the children at risk? Is the mother taking or selling drugs? Are the dirty clothes and no breakfast the result of oversleeping one day or symptomatic of a more serious problem?

A lawyer assigned this client would define his/her role as advocating for the client's legal rights to continue as parent. Promoting the legal rights and interests of the client would be paramount and there would be less attention to looking at the total family situation. In contrast, as guided by social work education, the social worker would approach this situation looking at the total situation, the needs and strengths of all family members without focusing on the legal rights of one individual person in this family.

Task delineation is the second challenging area in interdisciplinary work with social workers and lawyers. There may be disagreement between charges in a petition and future recommendations. Problems may emerge when each profession strays from its area of competence. For example, a classic publication in the child welfare field notes that judges and lawyers may make psychosocial assessments and social workers may assume the lawyer's role by withholding evidence for fear that it will be misconstrued (Goldstein, Freud, Solnit, & Goldstein, 1986). Clear understanding of role differences is essential for ethical social workers in the child welfare field. Social workers may rely primarily on inferential recording, i.e., as in the example, Mrs. R. was not motivated to follow a case plan (Stein, 1991), while attorneys, on the other hand, want specific descriptive facts such as what did the parent do or not do. Lawyers and social workers sometimes do not confer about the case until immediately before the court date. Sometimes it is impossible for the social worker to reconstruct specific facts that leads to conflict between the lawyers and social workers with the latter feeling inadequate. This points to the need for social workers who are involved in child welfare cases to be especially cognizant of maintaining good factual records to improve their communication with attorneys before court appearances. Also it should be noted that a good inferential assessment should be based on facts. For example, the social worker should not report that a client is unmotivated unless there are specific facts that can be used to substantiate this.

Finally, differences in confidentiality responsibilities often produce conflicts between attorneys and social workers. In all 50 states, social workers are mandated child abuse reporters while attorneys are not. This often produces ethical challenges for the social worker especially when the social worker works for a legal agency, as this example suggests:

Susan, a social worker with Legal Aid who was representing the birth mother in a pending termination of parental rights hearing for Tony, interviewed the mother prior to the hearing. She noted that when eight-year-old Tony's birth mother came to the agency with another child who was still in her care, this five-year-old child, Ben, had bruises on his arms which the mother attributed to falling off his bike. Susan wanted to report this suspected abuse to the child abuse central registry but was told by the attorney not to as this report might be damaging for the impending court case. Susan was very concerned because she knew she was a mandated child abuse reporter and she wanted to promote the best interests of her many clients, including Tony and Ben, while the lawyer only seemed to be concerned about Mrs. Smith's legal interests.

Within the legal agency, Susan can talk with the attorneys to increase their understanding of a familial approach to child welfare. If Ben is abused, Tony may also become abused, which ultimately may have negative consequences for the lawyer's primary client. Before accepting employment in a legal agency, it is important for the social worker to learn about the policies of the agency in situations regarding child abuse. Then the social worker can make an informed decision about whether she wants to work at an agency where legal ethics seem to override social work ethics.

Ethical Dilemmas in Social Work Practice

Social workers in forensic social work are faced with making decisions which may have significant consequences for their client's lives and well-being, ranging from allocation of resources and access to programs to removals of children from their homes; recommendations of probation or parole revocation; and counseling clients around such weighty issues as abortion, divorce, and the termination of life. At the same time, these activities have important ramifications for the social worker, exposing the worker to potential legal actions and liability.

Not uncommonly, the social worker in choosing a course of action is faced with choices between two or more competing ethical principles, such as client self-determination and client protection, or maintaining client confidentiality and a need to disclose certain information, where guidance from ethics and values is confusing or conflicting. In resolving difficult ethical dilemmas, the social worker must be cognizant of both social work ethics and laws that are applicable to the situation.

Under most circumstances, legal standards and social work ethics coincide. However, at times they do not. The NASW Code of Ethics notes that, "Instances may arise when social workers' ethical obligations conflict with agency policies or relevant laws or regulations. When such conflicts occur, social workers must make a responsible effort to resolve the conflict in a manner that is consistent with the values, principles, and standards expressed in this Code. If a reasonable resolution of the conflict does not appear possible, social workers should seek proper consultation before making a decision" (NASW, 1999, p. 3). Social workers have been advised to attempt to advise these conflicts "through consultation, mediation, lobbying, and other forms of social action" (Reamer, 2002, p. 66).

It is interesting to note how the 1996 Code was revised in 1999. In the most recent revision, section 1.07(c) that speaks to maintaining confidentiality unless disclosure is necessary to prevent serious, foreseeable, and imminent harm to a client, omitted the phrase, "when laws or regulations require disclosure without a client's consent." This change came about because of the profession's ethical concern about unethical laws that undermine our social justice value system, as for example laws limiting the rights of gay people or undocumented immigrants. The current provision in the Code suggests that it is not ethical to violate confidentiality in order to follow a law or regulation that would undermine the rights of a specific population.

Social work has a long tradition of promoting social justice and engaging in civil disobedience to promote the rights of vulnerable populations. One illustration is social workers' participation in the civil rights demonstrations of the 1960s. The Code of Ethics should protect social workers who engage in this behavior, not label their behavior as unethical.

The American Psychiatric Association acknowledges this problem in their Principles of Medical Ethics:

It would seem self-evident that a psychiatrist who is a law-breaker might be ethically unsuited to practice his/her profession. When such illegal activities bear directly upon his/her practice, this would obviously be the case. However, in other instances, illegal activities such as those concerning the right to protest social injustices might not bear on either the image of the psychiatrist or the ability of the specific psychiatrist to treat his/her patient ethically and well. While no committee or board could offer prior assurances that any illegal activity would not be considered unethical, it is conceivable that an individual could violate a law without being guilty of professionally unethical behavior. (American Psychiatric Association, 1992, Section 3.1)

Law and Ethics in Social Work: A Paradigm

It is useful in this analysis to consider law and ethics as independent entities, with different sources and different enforcement mechanisms, although the two often overlap. A paradigm about the relationship of law and ethics considers four possible combinations: professional conduct which is both ethical and legal; conduct both unethical and illegal; conduct which is unethical yet legal; and finally, professional conduct which is ethical yet illegal (Dickson & Congress, 2000) These four possibilities are depicted in Table 6-1.

In the first cell, professional conduct that is both legal and ethical, which is found most often, is considered acceptable social work practice, and presents few problems. Two examples are as follows: Social workers may legally and ethically disclose confidential information based on the client's valid informed consent (NASW standard 1.07(b)) and social workers should legally and ethically provide services based on an informed consent, and where the client

Table 6-1

Cell I
Conduct which is:
    Ethical and
    Legal
	Cell II
	Conduct which is:
	    Unethical and yet
	    Legal

Cell III
Conduct which is:
    Ethical and yet
    Illegal
	Cell IV
	Conduct which is:
	    Unethical and
	    Illegal

lacks capacity to give consent, seek permission from the appropriate third party (NASW standard 1.03).

The forth cell appears equally unproblematic, especially in light of the revised NASW Code of Ethics which contains a number of clear proscriptions. For example, NASW standard 1.11 provides:

> Social workers should not sexually harass clients. Sexual harassment includes sexual advances, sexual solicitation, requests for sexual favors, and other verbal or physical conduct of a sexual nature.

Standard 1.03 states:

> Social workers should provide services to clients only in the context of a professional relationship based, when appropriate, on valid informed consent. Social workers should use clear and understandable language to inform clients of the purpose of the services, risks related to the services, . . . reasonable alternatives, clients' right to refuse or withdraw consent, and the time frame covered by the consent.

Both provisions closely approximate the existing laws of sexual harassment and informed consent. While these areas are generally not problematic, it is the other two cells that may present some problems for the social worker who is aware of both the ethical prescriptions and legal requirements. Conduct which is legal yet unethical.

Some of the prescriptions found in the social work code of ethics do not have a corresponding legal provision. For example, in most states, it is not legally mandated to discuss the limits of confidentiality, although this is sound ethical practice (NASW section 1.07(e)). Similarly, while it is true at law that agreements to maintain confidentiality in couple, family, marital, or group counseling are often unenforceable, there is usually no law requiring that the social worker apprise these individuals of this fact, although it is an ethical prescription that "Social workers should inform participants in family, couples, or group counseling that social workers cannot guarantee that all participants will honor such agreements" (NASW section 1.07(f)). It is clearly unethical for a social worker to engage in sexual activities or sexual contact with a current or former client (NASW section 109(a): (Social workers should under no circumstances engage in sexual activities or sexual contact with current clients, whether such contact is consensual or forced), with former clients, with client's relatives or others in a close personal relationship to the client, or to provide

clinical services to individuals with whom the social worker has had a past sexual relationship (NASW section 1.09 (b), (c), (d)). However in most states, there is no corresponding legal prohibition of sexual relationships with consenting competent adults, especially those involved with past clients or their relatives. The social worker violating these ethical prescriptions and causing harm to the client, however, could be subject to a malpractice action.

There may be times when a course of conduct is preferable, even though it violates some ethical provision. In the absence of any legal penalty, it may be desirable to gather enough information about a potential child abuse situation so that a report may be made, despite the ethical prescription that social workers should inform clients about disclosure of confidential information and the potential consequences before the disclosure is made. Similarly, while a social worker is to respect and promote the right of clients to self-determination (NASW Standard 1.02), a social worker believing that a minor has made a decision to have an abortion because of peer pressure or pressure from a boyfriend might violate this prescription and decide to discuss the issue with the minor's parents. The conduct of the social worker would be legal, unethical, and defensible. A social worker learning of a client's past criminal act might decide that it should be reported despite promises of confidentiality, even if there is no law requiring this report. Conduct which is ethical yet illegal.

Finally, there may be instances where the action by the social worker is ethically permissible, yet illegal. Under Code of Ethics standard 6.04:

> Social workers should engage in social and political action that seeks to ensure that all people have equal access to the resources, employment, services, and opportunities they require to meet their basic human needs . . .", should "advocate for changes in policy and legislation to improve social conditions", and should "act to prevent and eliminate exploitation and discrimination."

Accomplishing these ethical requisites may involve the social worker in protests and civil disobedience which are in violation of the law — conduct which is ethical yet illegal. A social worker who believes that a client who is HIV positive and will not practice safeguards to prevent the spread of the virus could decide to violate confidentiality and take steps to prevent harm to another. While in some states this is a permitted exception to confidentiality statutes, in many others it is a clear violation of HIV/AIDS confidentiality statutes and can be severely punished at law. The actions by the worker would be clearly illegal and yet ethical. Because AIDS is such a stigmatized disease and also such a challenging issue in forensic social work, maintaining confidentiality in working with people with AIDS is especially important (Poindexter, 2005). Finally, a social worker who refuses to honor a subpoena and disclose information which a client wishes to keep confidential is in violation of the law, yet there may be sound ethical reasons for refusing to disclose the sought after information. The social worker in this situation could be held in contempt of court, fined, or even imprisoned, yet be acting ethically. One positive example of this is in the Jaffe v. Redmond case, when a social worker steadfastly refused to reveal records in spite of a court order, and the social worker's decision was eventually upheld by the U.S. Supreme Court (Albert, 2000).

The ETHIC Model for Navigating Conflicting Standards

How social workers resolve ethical dilemmas has been a subject of some concern to the profession. Social workers are often guided by two main principles. The first, beneficence (or positive obligations), speaks to providing good, while the second principle, nonmaleficence (or negative obligations), relates to causing no harm (Reamer, 1995). Both principles affect ethical decision making. Those who favor beneficence would most likely take a proactive stance that might involve placing children in order for them to have a better life. Nonmaleficence would promote causing no harm by taking the least intervention. Social workers acting from a nonmaleficence perspective might decide to take no action and wait for further results.

Most social workers use a combination of absolute (deontological) and consequential (teleological) thinking. One can argue that the values of the social work profession are absolute in nature, but often social workers use consequential arguments to decide complex ethical dilemmas. Many social workers do not use a philosophical approach at all but base their decisions on practice wisdom (Walden, Wolock, & Demone, 1990) or the Code of Ethics (Congress, 1992). A more recent Australian study conducted by

McAuliffe (1999) found that social workers, although relatively familiar with the Code of Ethics, did not consider using it as a resource to assist decision making when confronted with an ethical dilemma.

A review of social work literature shows that several models of ethical decision making have been proposed. An early model, developed by Lewis (1984), incorporated both deontological and teleological thinking but proposes that the deontological approach should prevail, while an early model, developed by Pine (1987), focused on ethical decision making in child welfare. Adapting a philosophical approach, Reamer (1995) proposes a deontological system based on Rawls' theory of justice and Gewirth's rank ordering of conflicting duties. The following year, Conrad and Joseph (1996) presented at a NASW Conference on a process model that uses the Code of Ethics in resolving ethical dilemmas. More recently, Lowenberg, Dolgoff, and Harrington (2000) have applied a hierarchical model ranking different social work values to help social workers arrive at the most ethical decision.

Social workers have frequently raised concerns about the use of the Code to resolve difficult ethical dilemmas. The NASW Code, like other Codes, is most helpful with clear-cut good and bad ethical issues but is less helpful with the more ambiguous situations that social workers often encounter (Lowenberg, Dolgoff, & Harrington, 2000). Social workers frequently make speedy decisions without much deliberation (Walden, Wolock, & Demone, 1990). This may be related to limited time in which to make decisions, as well as perceived organizational constraints.

Developed to help social workers make ethical decisions as quickly and as effectively as possible, the ETHIC model (Congress, 1999) includes consideration of social work values, the Code of Ethics, and the social work context. Modified to help social workers facing ethical dilemmas when law and ethics collide (Cell III of the ethics and law paradigm) the model consists of the following five steps:

E: Examine Relevant Personal, Societal, Agency, Client and Professional Values

Personal, societal, agency, client, and professional values all influence ethical decision making. The social worker who relies only on professional values is not likely to have a full range of experience on which to base decisions. For example, self-determination is a very important social work value, but how does this interface with a client with a strong personal value of family determination? Should the social worker encourage an adolescent to attend a distant college or heed the adolescent's personal value that he should stay close to his family?

In interdisciplinary settings social workers need to be aware of differing professional values of social workers and lawyers. For example, social workers may afford clients more self-determination and choice, while attorneys often offer more advice and direction to clients. A discrepancy between agency and professional values can also produce dilemmas for the social worker. This may be especially challenging for the social worker who works in a legal setting when values in terms of self determination, confidentiality and client definition may differ. An example of this conflict is evident in the previous example of the social worker employed by Legal Aid who was prevented from reporting suspected child abuse.

T: Think About What Ethical Standards, Laws, Case Decisions, and Regulations Apply and Theorize About Existing Conflicts

Social workers must first identify the relevant ethical standards in the NASW Code of Ethics. Social workers need to be cognizant of relevant federal, state, and local laws which may impact on the ethical dilemmas they encounter.

Social work ethics is different from, but often parallels, legal regulations. The 1996 Code of Ethics included the provision that social workers could violate confidentiality "when laws and regulations require disclosure without a client's consent" (NASW, 1996, p. 6). This suggests that social work ethics and the law would often coincide (Cell I in the ethics and law paradigm). The 1999 Delegate Assembly, after lengthy, heated debate, removed this provision because of concern when laws may seem in contradiction to social work values. Current laws in regard to reporting of sexual orientation for adoptive couples, as well as Proposition 187 in California that requires reporting of immigrant status, also can be seen as legal, but unethical. These laws seem contrary to social work ethical standards in regard to social justice and anti-discrimination (NASW News, Oct. 1999, p. 10).

The social worker needs to be aware of when laws and ethics practice may conflict as in Cell III of the ethics and law paradigm discussed previously. Historical examples include Jim Crow laws in the South and discriminatory welfare regulations. The Code encourages social workers to "engage in social and political action that seeks to ensure that all people have equal access to resources, employment, services, and opportunities" (NASW, 1996, p. 27). This may lead social workers to illegal behaviors like sit-downs and demonstrations that indicate a conflict between law and social work ethics.

H: Hypothesize About Possible Consequences of Different Decisions

This step makes use of teleological reasoning to resolve ethical dilemmas. If protecting confidentiality is a concern, the social worker should think about different scenarios, one in which confidentiality is maintained and the other in which confidentiality is violated. The social worker can list pros and cons about maintaining confidentiality versus breaking confidentiality.

This step may be especially helpful in instances when confidentiality law differs from ethical standards. For example, many states have very clear laws about maintaining confidentiality around HIV status, but social workers with ethical standards about protecting the safety of others may be led to violate confidentiality. Analyzing possible results in terms of all clients may help the social worker decide which is the preferred alternative for the specific incident.

I: Identify Who Will Benefit and Who Will Be Harmed in View of Social Work's Commitment to the Most Vulnerable

Often social workers must decide between two bad alternatives, rather than one that is clearly right and clearly wrong (Keith-Lucas, 1977). This step may elicit very convincing reasons for or against different courses of action.

Social work has had a lengthy tradition of concern for the most vulnerable in our society. While maintaining a fiduciary professional responsibility is important for both social workers and lawyers, the attention to the most vulnerable has been seen as distinguishing social work from the other professions

(Lewis, 1972). The current Code proposes that "social workers should act to expand choice and opportunity for all persons, with special regard for vulnerable, disadvantaged, oppressed, and exploited persons and groups" (NASW, 1999, p. 27). Therefore, this step is most important for social workers in resolving an ethical dilemma.

C: Consult with Supervisor, as Well as Social Work and Legal Colleagues About the Most Ethical Choice

Because making an ethical decision alone can be so challenging, talking to others who can suggest alternatives or present new information is essential. A social worker who has a supervisor should use this person as a first resource in ethical decision making. With current cutbacks, more experienced social workers and even beginning workers may have minimal supervision.

Social workers are encouraged to bring questions about ethical dilemmas to other colleagues for consultation. If the issue involves a conflict between social work ethics and law, the social worker should discuss personal and agency liability issues with a staff attorney.

Ethical dilemmas can be presented as part of a case conference. Sometimes social workers can help the agency develop an ethics committee. This may be especially useful in a multidiscipline agency in which the social worker works with other professionals with differing values and ethics. Differences between social workers and doctors (Roberts, 1985), public school educators (Congress & Lynn, 1994) and attorneys (Stein, 1981) have been noted (Congress, 1999). When social workers participate in ethics committees, however, their decisions about ethical dilemmas are often respected by other members (Joseph & Conrad, 1989).

Mental Health Example Using ETHIC Model

Using the ETHIC model may help social workers resolve ethical dilemmas. Both social work and lawyers stress the importance of maintaining confidentiality with clients, but this example illustrates differences between the profession that may occur:

Carmen, a bilingual social worker, has seen Cecilia, a 34-year-old Mexican woman, for individual therapy in a mental health clinic. When Cecilia was hospitalized last year with a diagnosis of chronic undifferentiated schizophrenia, her five-year-old child, Juan, was placed in foster care.

Carmen received a call from the attorney with a public child welfare agency that had placed Cecilia's child informing her that the lawyer was preparing for a court hearing about continuation of foster care. The attorney indicated that he wanted to know the following information:

1. What was Cecilia's immigration status?
2. What relatives and friends did she have in the city?
3. What behavior led up to Cecilia's hospitalization? Was she abusive to her son?
4. Has Cecilia come regularly for treatment?
5. What has been discussed during these treatment sessions?
6. Does Cecilia have delusions about her child?
7. What antipsychotic medication is Cecilia taking?
8. How long will Cecilia remain in treatment?
9. Does Carmen think that Juan will be at risk if he is returned to Cecilia's care?

The attorney indicated that he would be subpoenaing the records for the pending termination of parental rights case.

As a first step in the ETHIC model, Carmen examined the values of her client, her professional values and also thought about the values of the lawyer who had called her. She knew that Cecilia really wanted to have her child returned. She also knew that Carmen came from a cultural background where confidentiality was viewed differently than in the NASW Code of Ethics (Congress, 2005). She looked at the values of the lawyer who saw his professional responsibility as advocating for the public child welfare agency. Also she thought about her own professional value in terms of maintaining confidentiality.

Carmen knew she should be very careful in terms of sharing information over the telephone. Often in interdisciplinary collaboration, if a member has a Dr. before the name or an Esq after the name, social workers may feel intimidated and share more information than they should. Information about clients should never be shared unless there is a release of information form completed by the client. Blanket release forms are often inadequate and a comprehensive release form should include the name of the client to whom the information is to be released, the nature of the information to be released, and the time limit for the release of information (Wilson, 1978). Assuming that there is an acceptable release on file, Carmen should be careful about releasing information on the phone as the identity of the caller can not be verified. A better strategy is to take the caller's number and call back to verify the identity.

As a second step of the ETHIC model, Carmen knew that she should think about what ethical standards, as well as laws, applied. She reviewed the 18 provisions in the Code of Ethics that applied to maintaining confidentiality. She also examined the state statutes on confidentiality in mental health settings.

Should Carmen convey all the information she has been requested to share? The question about Cecilia's immigration status is highly confidential information, especially in an era in which there is renewed emphasis on identifying and deporting undocumented immigrants. Carmen's professional responsibility is to her client. Ethically she may choose not to report on her client's immigration status to any public agency. Carmen should be concerned about what use the attorney may make of this information, especially as this information does not seem related to the issue at hand.

Some of the above questions are informational, i.e., "What antipsychotic medication is Cecilia taking?", while others involve assessment, "Does Cecilia still have delusion about her child?" or prediction, "Does Carmen think that Juan will be a risk if he is returned to his mother?" Assuming that Carmen has a release in the folder, she can feel safest about sharing informational questions. If Carmen answers assessment questions, she must be sure that they are based on facts. Also using the strengths perspective and client advocacy model, it is often best to frame responses in a positive way. For example, "Cecilia was seen three times for individual therapy" rather than "Cecilia missed most of her therapy appointments, coming only three times." Prediction questions are the most difficult and it is best to avoid answering them if possible. Even the most skilled practitioners have difficulty predicting future violence (Rosenthal, 1993). Social workers would do well to avoid making damaging generalizations, as

one experienced social worker noted early in her career. This social worker once described a client as "the craziest client I've ever seen." Four years later, this statement reappeared when her exact words were quoted in a child welfare termination of parental rights hearing.

The best practice for a social worker receiving a call from a professional in another agency is to discuss this with the client. This affords the client the greatest respect for her autonomy and supports the Code of Ethics provision that "social workers should inform clients, to the extent possible, about the disclosure of confidential information and the potential consequences, when feasible before the disclosure is made. This applies whether social workers disclose confidential information on the basis of a legal requirement or client consent" (NASW, 1999, p. 10).

In the previous case example, a conflict of interest exists between Carmen and the attorney of the child welfare agency. Carmen's primary client is Cecilia, while the attorney is representing the child welfare agency. Carmen should be clear that she maintains confidentiality for her client. Yet Carmen is a mandated child abuse reporter, and if she learns that Cecilia is abusing Juan during a weekend visit, she is required to report it. This may challenge the trusting relationship that her client has developed with her.

In order to apply the third step of the ETHIC model, hypothesize about possible consequences of different decisions, Carmen reviewed different scenarios. If she maintained confidentiality, she might be subpoenaed.

How should she handle the subpoena? Often social workers become very anxious upon receipt of a subpoena and fearful that they must submit all confidential information. The NASW General Counsel has offered the following suggestions in responding to a subpoena:

1. The social worker should read carefully the subpoena, including the date for response, the action required, and the court and attorney issuing it.
2. The client should receive a copy of the subpoena and provide written consent to its release. If the client does not want to have the information released, now that communication to social workers is considered privileged communication (Greenhouse, 1996) the information can be kept confidential.
3. If the information is privileged or procedurally incorrect, the social worker can object by filing written

objections, requesting a protective order, or filing a motion to rescind or change the subpoena.

4. The social worker should consult with the agency attorney about the best way to handle the subpoena. (Palowy & Gilbertson, 1997)

If she did release the information, her client might not trust her again. There was also the possibility that this information might end up with federal Immigration Naturalization Service department and lead to her client's deportation.

Applying the fourth step of this model, Carmen was also very concerned about who would benefit and who would be harmed. She recognized that Cecilia, her client who was an undocumented immigrant and had been diagnosed with a serious mental illness, was especially vulnerable and might be harmed if she was to release the information to the lawyer.

As a final step, Carmen consulted with other social work colleagues and her supervisor, all of whom spoke to her about the ethical issue of maintaining confidentiality. She also was able to talk with the staff attorney who confirmed that she had a legal duty to maintain confidentiality. He was also helpful in talking with the child welfare attorney about what information could be shared with the public child welfare agency.

In using the five-step ETHIC model, Carmen was able to gain greater understanding about issues related to the case and resolve the ethical dilemma around confidentiality and the request for extensive information.

SUMMARY AND IMPLICATIONS FOR SOCIAL WORK PRACTICE AND EDUCATION

The NASW Code acknowledges that, "instances may arise when a social worker's ethical obligations conflict with agency policies or relevant laws or regulations" (NASW, 1999, p. 3). When this happens social workers are urged to "make a reasonable effort to resolve the conflict in a manner that is consistent with the values, principles and standards in the Code of Ethics" (NASW, 1999. p. 3). The Code itself does not offer any specific solution for resolving this dilemma. While there has been growing literature on social work ethics, there is little to guide the social worker in addressing ethical practice and dilemmas in forensic social work.

The following guidelines are presented to help social work practitioners and educators in this area:

1. Teach students about laws, case decisions, and regulations relevant to their client populations.
2. Recognize and teach students about differences in orientations between lawyers and social workers.
3. Encourage practitioners and students to consult more frequently with staff lawyers in multidiscipline settings.
4. Teach students skills to use in interdisciplinary consultation and collaboration.
5. Learn to identify areas in which laws and ethical standards may differ and move toward resolution.
6. Increase skills in mediating professional differences.
7. Use a model of ethical decision making in understanding and resolving professional dilemmas.

Applying these guidelines will help social work students and practitioners promote ethical practice in forensic social work practice.

REFERENCES

Albert, R. (2000). *Law and social work practice* (2nd ed.). New York: Springer.

Bassuk, K., & Lessem, J. (2001). Collaboration of social workers and attorneys in geriatric community based organization. *Journal of Gerontological Social Work 34*(3), 93–108.

Congress, E. (1999). Social work values and ethics: Identifying and resolving professional dilemmas. Belmont, CA: Wadsworth.

Congress, E. (2005). Ethical issues and future directions. In E. Congress & M. Gonzalez, *Multicultural perspectives in working with families* (2nd ed.), pp. 442–452. New York: Springer.

Congress, E., & Kim, W. (2005). *A comparision of the Korean social work Code of Ethics and the NASW Code of Ethics.* Presentation at the Asian Pacific Social Work Conference, Seoul, Korea, September 23.

Congress, E. & McAuliffe, D. (in press). Professional ethics: Social work codes in Australia and the United States. *International Social Work.*

Congress, E., & Lynn, M. (1994). Group work programs in public schools: Ethical dilemmas and cultural diversity. *Social Work in Education, 16*(2), 107–114.

Conrad, A., & Joseph, V. (November 1996). *A model for ethical problem solving: A process for resolving questions and quandaries.* Presentation at the Annual NASW Conference, Cleveland, OH.

Dickson, D., & Congress, E. (2000). *When social work ethics and the law collide: Identifying and navigating conflicting standards.* Paper Presentation, Annual Program Meeting, Council on Social Work Education, New York, February 28.

Lowenberg, F, Dolgoff, R., & Harrington, D. (2000). *Ethical decisions in social work practice.* Itasca, Il. Peacock.

Forgey, M., & Colarossi, L. (2003). Interdisciplinary social work and law: A model domestic violence curriculum. *Journal of Social Work Education, 39*(3), 459–476.

Goldstein, J., Freud, A., Solnik, A., & Goldstein, S. (1986). *In the best interests of the child.* New York: The Free Press.

Greenhouse, L. (1996, June 14). Justices recognize confidential privilege between therapist and patient. *The New York Times.* (http://www.nytimes.com.96/14/6/front/scotus/privilege-html).

Greene, L., Glenwick, D., & Schiaffino, K. (1999). Mental health and legal professionals' perceptions of child abuse. *Journal of Family Social Work, 3*(4), 25–38.

Johnson, P., & Cahn, K. (1995). Improving child welfare practice through improvements in attorney-social worker relationships. *Child Welfare, 74*(2), 383–394.

Joseph, V., & Conrad, A. (1989). Social work influence on interdisciplinary decision making in health care settings. *Health and Social Work, 14*(1), 22–30.

Keith-Lucas, A. (1977). Ethics in social work . In *Encyclopedia of social work* (17th ed., pp. 350–355). Washington, D.C.: NASW.

Lewis, H. (1972). Morality and the politics of practice. *Social Casework, 5*(3), 404–417.

Lewis, H. (1984). Ethical assessment. *Social Casework, 65*(4), 203–211.

Lowenberg, F., & Dolgoff, R. (1995). *Ethical decisions in social work practice* (5th ed.). Itasca, IL: Peacock.

Lowenberg, F., Dolgoff, R., & Harrington, D. (2000). *Ethical decisions in social work practice* (6th ed.). Itasca, IL: Peacock.

Maidenberg, M., & Golick, T. (2001). Developing or enhancing interdisciplinary programs: A model for teaching collaboration. *Professional Development, 4*(2), 15–24.

McAuliffe, D. (1999). Clutching at codes: Resources that influence social work decisions in cases of ethical conflict. *Professional Ethics, 7*(3/4): 9–24.

National Association of Social Workers. (1996). *Code of ethics.* Washington, D.C.: NASW.

National Association of Social Workers (1999). *Code of ethics.* Washington, D.C.: NASW.

Pierce, C., Gleason, W., & Miller, M. (2001). Social work and law: A model for implementing social services in a law office. *Journal of Gerontological Social Work, 34*(3), 61–71.

Pine, B. (1987). Strategies for more ethical decision making in child welfare practice. *Child Welfare, 66*(4), 315–326.

Poindexter, C. (2005). Working with HIV-affected culturally diverse families. In E. Congress & M. Gonzalez. *Multicultural perspectives in working with families* (2nd ed., pp. 311–338). New York: Springer.

Reamer, F. (1995). *Social work values and ethics.* New York: Columbia University Press.

Reamer, F. (1998). *Ethical standards in social work: A critical review of the NASW Code of Ethics.* Silver Springs, MD: NASW Press.

Reamer, F. (2002). Ethical issues in social work. In A. Roberts & G. Greene, Eds., *Social work desk reference* (pp. 65–69). New York: Oxford University Press.

Roberts, C. (1989). Conflicting professional values in social work and medicine. *Health and Social Work, 14*(3), 211–218.

Roberts, A., & Brownell, P. (1999). A century of forensic social work: Bridging the past to the present. *Social Work, 44*(4), 359–369.

Russel, R.(1988). Role perceptions of attorneys and caseworkers in child abuse cases in juvenile court. *Child Welfare, 67*(3), 205–216.

Stein, T. (1991). *Child welfare and the law.* New York: Longman.

Vandecreek, L., Knapp, S., & Herzog, C. (1988). Privileged communication for social workers. *Social Casework, 69,* 28–34.

Von Wormer, K. (1992). No wonder social workers feel uncomfortable in court. *Child and Adolescent Social Work Journal, 9*(2), 117–129.

Walden, T., Wolock, I., & Demone, H. (1990). Ethical decision making in human services. *Families in Society, 71*(2), 67–75.

Chapter 7

Social Work and Criminal Justice: New Dimensions in Practice[1]

Gloria Cunningham

At a workshop several years ago a respected colleague with over 40 years of practice in the field of juvenile justice confided to the rest of the participants that among the benefits of becoming a senior citizen was knowing what "new" approaches were worth getting excited about and which were simply old ideas being rediscovered by a new generation. There is, indeed, a depressing regularity about the cyclical quality of alternating philosophies of rehabilitation and control in criminal justice as succeeding generations of helping professionals become disenchanted with one approach or another having failed to take into consideration the inherent vulnerability of any argument concerning something as poorly understood as human behavior. In frustration we are inclined to look for someone or something to blame for our failure to predict with accuracy how thousands of unique individuals in unique environments will respond to our helping effort. Sometimes we blame the clients and declare them "untreatable." We blame our theoretical forebearers: Freud, Skinner, or Mary Richmond or our methodologies. Most often we blame one another for not having all the right answers, and our professional name-calling makes us vulnerable to attacks by others, especially in the light of the escalating competition for dwindling funding resources. Frequently concern for the client and the community get lost in the midst of these polemical discussions and everyone is the loser. It would be a genuine mark of professional maturity if criminal justice practitioners could acknowledge openly what we know to be the truth; that people can be helped in a variety of ways, that no one approach will work with everyone, nor will any one approach work with the same person every time.

For some time now direct counseling efforts have been the methodological scapegoats in criminal justice for their failure to deliver what they promised 20 or 30 years ago in terms of altering the course of criminal careers. There is no question that social workers and other mental health practitioners naively promised too much, but the claims that casework is a "dead-end" as far as criminal justice is concerned or that psychotherapy in general is "ineffective" can be challenged. Some of the points made in this article are: First, that arguments about effectiveness are sometimes political and not accurate reflections of the services being offered; second, that some of the problems we experienced in applying counseling techniques to criminal justice clients were the result of narrow and unselective application of treatment models which did not take into consideration the profound treatment significance of many of the routine interventions of probation officers; and finally to make the point that counseling approaches with individuals and families have not remained static but have evolved in ways which make them more relevant to a wider range of clientele. There is much in these contemporary approaches to social treatment that is consistent with evolving views of community-based corrections.

HOW EFFECTIVE ARE EFFECTIVENESS STUDIES?

Most of the claims for the ineffectiveness of psychotherapy and one-to-one counseling originated in Esynick's studies published in 1959 and 1965. Esynick's

---

1. From *Federal Probation.* 1980 *44*(1), 64–69. Reprinted with permission of the publisher.

pronouncements about the ineffectiveness of conventional psychotherapy have assumed the status of the graven tablets of Moses in spite of the fact that Esynick has been challenged on the basis of his methodology, his scholarship and his conclusions. For example, Esynick's first report was based on only four studies of psychotherapy when 30 were available, many of which indicated effectiveness (Meltzoff & Kornreich, 1970, p. 973). By 1964 there had been at least 70 controlled studies on the effects of psychotherapy, but again Esynick's 1965 conclusions were based on a small unrepresentative example of the available evidence. Meltzoff and Kornreich comment, "the widespread myth that controlled, evaluative studies have not been done has been passed along to those of us who relied upon Esynick's reviews but did not ourselves examine the literature in depth. It had become almost customary for researchers and reviewers alike to introduce their papers with the erroneous observation that few studies on the effectiveness of psychotherapy exist" (Meltzoff & Kornreich, 1970, p. 74).

Meltzoff and Kornreich conducted their own review of 101 studies on the effectiveness of psychotherapy. They concluded on the basis of their review that the weight of experimental evidence is sufficient to enable them to reject the null hypothesis that psychotherapy is ineffective. Far more often than not, psychotherapy of a wide variety of types and with a broad range of disorders has been demonstrated under controlled conditions to be accompanied by positive changes in adjustment that significantly exceed those that can be accounted for by the passage of time alone. In addition they found that the more carefully controlled the study, that is, the more sophisticated the research methodology, the more likely the study was to demonstrate the effectiveness of psychotherapy (Meltzoff & Kornreich, 1970, p. 100).

It is important at this point to make clear that this is not an argument for psychotherapy or intensive treatment of all criminal justice clients, nor is it a denial of the fact that treatment often is ineffective and even destructive. The point is being made that the polemical discussions about what approach to helping works or does not work are often waged without any serious consideration into the validity of the arguments or the actual relevance of the method to the clients involved. Academic careers are often

built on the basis of such publicized debates. Academic institutions and other service organizations are frequently dependent financially on the grant research money, and the eventual findings of the research are often immaterial. The politics of funding are such that the funding resources are much more anxious to make money available to constituencies with more clout than helping professionals have, and to claim that a particular group "has failed to demonstrate their effectiveness" is a handy excuse, valid or not, to redistribute the funds in other ways. Wilks and Martinson refer to the way in which findings of their study on the effectiveness of incarceration were used to support arguments for mandatory sentencing in spite of their findings that offenders placed on probation almost inevitably perform better relative to recidivism than do those of similar background and criminal history who are placed in prison (Wilks & Martinson, 1976, p. 3).

We are also becoming more aware of the fact that many of the effectiveness studies reflected not so much the ineffectiveness of casework or psychotherapy as it did the ineffectiveness of the research methodology to measure such variables. There are many areas of specialization within research, and researchers trained in survey, evaluation, and other forms of research dealing with aggregate data are often not knowledgeable about some of the special problems involved in conducting research on clinical treatment models.

UNDERSTANDING "REAL TREATMENT"

In the past, "treatment" of the criminal offender tended to be viewed undimensionally with little recognition of the reality that no one model will be equally relevant to all types of correctional clients. In addition, the nature of criminal justice practice is such that we are often involved in long-term relationships with our clients and that unique adaptations of existing models must be made in order to accommodate to this fact and other realities of correctional practice. For example, long-term or intensive clinically oriented treatment may be relevant to a relatively small portion of offenders. It may be most relevant early in our contact with them or at points of crisis, but we know from experience that long-term intensive clinically oriented counseling geared toward personality restructuring is neither relevant nor necessary with the *majority* of our clients. By the same token, although we can derive much that is useful from short-term treatment models, the nature of our extended relationship with probationers and parolees means certain adaptations must be made in short-term treatment models.

An unfortunate side effect of a too narrow view of "treatment" is the fact that probation officers are prevented from recognizing the value of what they do, those tasks that are not included within more traditional definitions of counseling or therapy. Narrow methodological adherence promotes the idea that anything less than long-term, intensive counseling oriented to achieve personality restructuring is second best or "band-aid" help. Because this clinical model was upheld as a sine qua non of professional practice, we do not value the important, significant and highly skilled work we do with people in other ways. We depreciate our high level performance in the difficult tasks of working effectively with a client's environment to promote a more receptive milieu that helps modify destructive behavior. We are led to believe that anything shot-term, reality oriented, or concerned with concrete services and environmental intervention is somehow not "real treatment." It is important to understand that "real treatment" is a status game that professionals play with one another. It has very little to do with actual, significant help to people in need. Real treatment can be understood as any kind of purposeful intervention rendered within the context of an ethically bound professional relationship and directed toward aiding the client in easing some problematic aspect of his or her functioning. The "realness" of the treatment should not be based on the extent to which it adheres to a particular theoretical framework or how much other professionals are impressed by the technique. A more rational basis for evaluation is in terms of the extent to which it is appropriate to the client and the particular case situation. Is it meeting some real need? Is it likely to produce some real change in the situation for the better? Can the client and other people involved make some real use of the help you are offering?

Some of the narrower treatment methodologies assumed that the individual client was inevitably the target of change. Whether or not one talked in terms of short-term or long-term treatments or intensive or nonintensive psychotherapy the basic assumption was the person who needed changing was the client. Practice wisdom tells us that this is not always the case. Sometimes the most realistic target for change is a significant person in the client's environment. Sometimes it is the family system or the larger society which has denied resources and opportunities to the client to fulfill necessary role expectations. Sometimes it is, indeed, the client who must change, but our knowledge of the situation tells us that change can be induced more readily if changes in other systems occur first. The relevance of this point is that the adjustment of the individual can be enhanced by intervention in a variety of ways, and that no one single technique is necessarily more likely than another to produce more positive social functioning. Periodic interviews with a client's wife may be much more effective than long-term intensive interviews with the client himself. Using your clout to relieve a client of a dunning creditor may be more significant than helping the client ventilate his anger and rage over the experience. We are not talking in either/or terms. We are saying that no technique is inherently better than any other technique, or is a more "real" form of treatment, and that the final decision rests on the basis of the professional judgment of the practitioner who bases his decision in turn on an indepth knowledge of the client, his situation, and the interventive alternatives available. Many probation officers have conducted their practice in this way for many years, and for them there is nothing new in such a point of view. What may be new is the acknowledgement that this represents the highest form of professional service, one which involves a myriad assortment of skills, knowledge and expertise.

SOCIAL WORK INSIGHT FOR CRIMINAL JUSTICE

In spite of the scapegoating role social work has assumed in recent years it still has much to offer the criminal justice practitioner and client including the broadened perspective on direct treatment outlined above. Some of these insights represent discoveries of old truths rather than new knowledge. Application of new concepts arising from systems theory has helped social work clarify the significance and implications of its long-term traditional focus on the "person-in-the-environment" and the nature of the interaction between the two, a focus, incidentally, particularly relevant to criminal justice practice. Social workers are also developing techniques of assessment and intervention focused on current functioning and ongoing social interaction rather than on psychosexual and early childhood development. They are redefining their professional activity in terms of the multiple forms of activities they perform with a wide range of clients in many different types of service settings, activities which include but which are in no way limited to direct counseling with individuals around psychological and personality problems. A typical listing of such role behaviors includes professional tasks involving advocacy and brokerage functions in addition to those of therapist, counselor, and teacher.

The role of the advocate is a familiar one to probation officers, and it is likely that the advocate role is assumed more frequently in behalf of a client outside of rather than in the courtroom. Probation officers must frequently act as an advocate with employers, with family and neighbors, with public welfare agencies, or investigative agents, "pleading the cause" for clients who lack the skill, opportunity or the influence to do so for themselves. Advocacy assumes a broad and sophisticated attitude toward assessment or "diagnosis" that recognizes from the outset that some of the options for bringing about change in a situation lie in the environmental systems impinging on the client. It further assumes a complicated array of skills and knowledge in dealing with many different kinds of individuals, groups and organizations in ways that will enhance rather than alienate their interaction with the probationer.

Brokerage functions are also familiar to probation staff and there is one school of thought that suggests that is the only real function probation officers should render, the linking up of the client with community based agencies that can do the therapy, the counseling, the employment placement, and all the other types of services probationers and parolees need. The experienced practitioner knows that this is a very involved and time-consuming function, one which requires much more than developing a list of agency names and telephone numbers which can be handed over to the client. If this is all there was to it

a part-time clerk could do the job. *Effective* brokerage services mean knowing both the client and the community resources very well. It means constant surveillance of these resources to keep up-to-date on policy and personnel changes, shifts in service philosophy, special programs, and how individual staff are going to receive and follow through with the correctional client. It often means a massive education task with community resources to preclude their overt or passive rejection of clients simply on the basis of their being offenders (and therefore psychopaths and therefore untreatable). Effective brokering also requires a sensitive awareness of the particular stresses and strains the client and family may be experiencing relative to a referral to another resource, and the skill to use this understanding to maximize the chances that the referral will "take." Finally, it means sticking with the client to see what does happen and if a first referral falls apart, to hang in there until the need is met in some way. This is a valuable service, indeed, but whether it is the only one that probation officers should offer seems unrealistic given the practice reality.

By using some of the skills mentioned above, the probation officer can greatly increase the probability that the client will receive needed services from those community based resources best equipped to provide them, and this is a most efficient use of everyone's time and money. The reality is, however, that there are many communities lacking the needed resources. If the resources exist they may be poorly run, inadequately staffed or funded, just generally incompetent or reluctant to include offenders in their client group. Even when adequate services exist the client may be unwilling or unable to make the best use of them. In those situations it is not acceptable to just throw up one's hands and give up. Probation officers have the responsibility to do what they can within the limits of their skills and what the client is willing to accept to remedy the situation in some way. If the local family service agency has a three-month waiting list it is unrealistic to ignore the current marital pressures a client is experiencing if the probation officer has the skill to intervene in a situation to prevent it from escalating or to bring about some positive improvement. A timely, short-term intervention by a probation officer who has already developed a trust relationship and who has demonstrated consistent interest and concern may be far more potent than a new relationship with an unknown counselor no matter how skilled that person may be.

In addition we must keep in mind the significance of the probation and parole officer as a "teacher" or educator. Some of our clients come from backgrounds in which they had not had the opportunity to understand the expectations of normal role behavior. It is difficult for a young adult to perform adequately in the role of worker if no one in his family has ever been employed in a well-paying, steady, secure job for a long period of time. It is difficult for individuals who have themselves never experienced a stable family life or mature nonpunitive parenting to know what is required in the establishment of a marital relationship and the rearing of children. It is difficult for any individual to make a transition from an institutional life with its unique set of role behavior and interpersonal transactions to have to learn or relearn different modes of behavior in the free community.

A recent development in criminal justice which has confused practitioners as to their counseling role with clients has been the increasing emphasis on civil rights of offenders and some question as to whether or not we have the right to do anything other than provide control and surveillance. Clearly there are politics involved in that debate also, but as professionals there are certain ethical and value positions that must be explicated. Many of the abuses of clients' rights as far as "treatment" was concerned occurred because helping professionals assumed that all offender clients were psychiatrically disabled patients. It was assumed further that because of their offender status and the presumed threat to the larger community they were a captive clientele and could be subjected voluntarily or not to any effort on the part of helping professionals intended to "make them well" or protect the community. The fact is that being an offender is a legal definition and not a psychiatric diagnosis. The offender group is probably much more like the population as a whole than most people are willing to acknowledge, if self report studies of crime and delinquency are any indication. Our pragmatic experience tells us that those factors that determine when and how a person first becomes labeled as deviant and is processed through the criminal justice system have little or nothing to do with the innate psychological makeup of the individual involved.

But criminal justice clients are human beings and they function in a real and problematic world. They, like all of us, will have ongoing problems in social functioning. They experience the predictable traumas of adolescence, marriage, ill health, aging, and a range of other kinds of crises that occur in the life of most of us. In addition they will have to deal with other types of problems of interaction with their environment because they are probationers or parolees. We have the skills to enhance their ability to cope with these problems more effectively and to help moderate, relieve some of the stresses of the environment by intervening with family, employer, mental health or welfare agencies and other significant institutions as described above. We have the professional training, the experience and the skill to assist clients in more effective problem-solving generally, to direct them to more effective styles of living, and to provide linkages for them with resources in the community that can help them live more satisfying lives. To refuse to offer these services to offender clients in the name of their "civil rights" seems a very perverse, cynical and unrealistic view of the total situation.

We do have to be clear about rights' violations. We do not impose our helping efforts on someone who clearly sees no need, will not benefit or refuses to cooperate in these efforts. We do have a responsibility, however, to interpret to all clients the availability of such services, our skills in helping them to negotiate ordinary and extraordinary developmental or life stage problems, and our conviction, when it exists, that we can make a significant and positive impact on their lives by so doing. We have, in short, the right to "sell" our skills to clients. This does involve the conviction, however, that we do have an important function to perform, that rights will be protected in the process and that the services we have to offer are professional, effective and of real worth.

The message is that we have to develop an accurate perception of what probation and parole services have to offer offenders and their communities, and the skills to document and communicate these perceptions to one another, to clients, to administrators and to funding sources. How we define our services need not be methodologically respectable or "fashionable" as long as we render it responsibly with due recognition of client rights and assume as part of our professional responsibility our ongoing, unbiased and nonpolitical assessment of its effectiveness. It is often suggested that helping professionals avoid evaluations of effectiveness out of fear of having their inadequacies exposed; however, there is evidence to suggest that rational, well-designed studies may turn out to be our ace in the hole.

REFERENCES

Meltzoff, J., & Kornreich, M. (1970). *Research in psychotherapy*. New York: Atherton Press, p. 973.

Wilks, J., & Martinson, R. (1976). Is the treatment of criminal offenders really necessary? *Federal Probation, 40*:1, 3.

Section II

Crisis Intervention and Police-Based Social Work

Chapter **8**

Crisis Intervention with Victims of Violence

Albert R. Roberts and Kenneth R. Yeager

INTRODUCTION

The primary purpose of police-based, mental health, outpatient psychiatric, disaster management crisis response teams is to rapidly respond to aid victims and survivors of violent crimes, domestic violence incidents, and survivors of collective trauma and crisis directly resulting from terrorist attacks, and natural disasters such as floods, hurricanes, earthquakes, and tornadoes. Many thousands of victims of violent crimes are turning to police departments, victim assistance programs, mental health centers, domestic violence shelters, and victim compensation programs for help in coping with the crisis of being victimized. Two case examples of the impact of violent crime on victims are presented. Next, we briefly examine crisis theory and crisis concepts. The main section focuses on Roberts Seven-Stage Crisis Intervention Protocol, as well as Roberts and Yeager's discussion of postvictimization and posttrauma crisis intervention – this includes predisposing factors, safety and security, active listening and reassurance, bolstering inner strengths and resiliency/protective factors, cognitive functioning, and restructuring activities of daily living – mental rehearsal, psychological reframing, bolstering coping skills, and developing an action plan. The final section of this chapter examines what society and governmental agencies are doing to help crime victims in such areas as victim/witness assistance, victim services, victim compensation, police crisis intervention, and domestic violence programs.

During the past 15 years, a dramatic shift in public policy and program development has taken place, resulting in a rapid expansion of theory, research, and legislation to protect victims' rights and provide services for survivors. The significant accomplishments of community leaders, legislators, and victims' rights advocates in America include the lobbying for and passage of thousands of laws and state constitutional amendments protecting the rights of crime victims at the federal and state levels. In addition, much of the federal and state legislation included increased funding appropriations for approximately 18, 000 community crisis response teams, crisis intervention units of community mental health centers, victim service/witness assistance programs, rape crisis, and domestic violence agencies and services during the 1990s and the early twenty-first century (Roberts, 2005).

The following two case examples depict the unpredictable nature of becoming a victim of a violent crime, and the psychologically painful and sometimes fatal outcome of being victimized.

Sam, a 21-year-old automobile parts salesman, was robbed at gunpoint upon returning to his apartment in Yonkers, New York. Sam recalls looking down the barrel of a 9 millimeter semi-automatic gun. The criminal took $169 in cash, several credit cards, and Sam's coat, watch, glasses, and shoes. Sam had nightmares several times each week for about four weeks after the crime. He finally went for counseling at the local mental health center. In addition, the victim advocate at the local victim assistance agency in Westchester County helped Sam complete a victim compensation application so he could be compensated for his monetary and property losses. Victim compensation also eventually reimbursed him for six weeks of mental health counseling.

Julie, a 28-year-old advertising executive, was raped at knifepoint when she returned from work to her apartment in Brooklyn, New York. It was midnight, and Julie had worked late. The lock on the front door to her building was broken, and she was concerned. She then went to the little alcove where all the mailboxes were for the tenants. She unlocked her mailbox, took the mail out, and proceeded to walk toward the steps when someone grabbed her from behind. She recalls that her rapist put a knife to her throat, and told her that if she did not immediately remove her skirt and panties he would cut her clothes off and stab her in the throat. She removed her clothes quickly, and closed her eyes when the rapist penetrated her. She recalled the rapist whispering in her ear that he might be back in a week or two because Julie had a great body just like his sister who he had a lot of sex with before she got married. Julie told the female detective in the sex crimes unit that she was worried that the rapist might have AIDS or another sexually transmitted disease, and she was fearful that he would return.

CRISIS INTERVENTION

Crisis intervention is challenging and is difficult to do well. As the acuity of mental health consumer's increase and the service delivery system buckles under the increasing pressure of those seeking services, it becomes clear that specific and efficacious interventions and guidelines are needed to keep the process flowing. Additionally, there are increasing numbers of persons requiring psychiatric intervention as a result of victimization of crime, cross over between programs that identify detainees with mental illness within the court system and increasing involvement of both law enforcement, and mental health professionals collaborating in providing services such as specialized crisis intervention teams, emergency response and trauma centers, programs that identify detainees with mental disorders and work with diversion staff, community-based providers, and courts to produce a mental health disposition in lieu of incarceration.

There is growing evidence of the risk factors for suicide, including a precipitating event such as multiple stressors (an accumulation of small traumatic events or a single remarkable traumatic event, in most cases trauma responses are identified as major depression, increased substance abuse, deterioration in social or occupational functions, hopelessness, and verbal expressions of suicidal ideation) (Weishaar, 2004), when in fact each of the above diagnosis may be at least in part driven by the individual's response to the traumatic event(s). For some individuals, dealing with ambivalence related to their impression of and response to violence results in simultaneous thoughts of self-harm or thoughts of immediate relief to the symptoms experienced. Frequently the victim seeks satisfaction in response to the subtle nagging frequently unidentified day-to-day response to victimization (Yeager & Roberts, 2003). For some, the thought of suicide mistakenly appears to be an immediate fix to an emotionally painful or acutely embarrassing situation that seems insurmountable. For the chemically dependent individual, suicide may be the easy way out of a cycle of substance dependence and withdrawal (Roberts & Yeager, 2005). The scenarios are endless and diverse as the population served. Therefore it may be helpful to begin with a working definition of crisis:

> **Crisis:** An acute disruption of psychological homeostasis in which one's usual coping mechanisms fail and there exists evidence of distress and functional impairment. The subjective reaction to a stressful life experience that compromises the individual's stability and ability to cope or function. The main cause of a crisis is an intensely stressful, traumatic, or hazardous event, but two other conditions are also necessary: (1) the individuals perception of the event as the cause of considerable upset and/or disruption; and (2) the individual's inability to resolve the disruption by previously used coping mechanisms. Crisis also refers to "an upset in the steady state." It often has five components: A hazardous or traumatic event, a vulnerable state, a precipitating factor, an active crisis state, and the resolution of the crisis. (Roberts, 2002)

The definition of a crisis stated above is particularly applicable to persons in acute crisis because these individuals usually seek help only after they have experienced a hazardous or traumatic event and are in a vulnerable state, have failed to cope and lessen the crisis through customary coping methods, lack family or community social supports, and want outside help. Acute psychological or situational crisis episodes may be viewed in various ways, but the definition we are using emphasizes that a crisis can be a turning point in a person's life.

Crisis intervention generally refers to a counselor, behavioral clinician, or therapist entering into the life situation of an individual or family to alleviate the impact of a crisis episode in order to facilitate and mobilize the resources of those directly affected. Rapid assessment and timely intervention on the part of crisis counselors, social workers, psychologists, or child psychiatrists is of paramount importance (Roberts, 2005).

Crisis intervenors should be active and directive while displaying a nonjudgmental, accepting, hopeful, and positive attitude. Crisis intervenors need to help crisis clients to identify protective factors, inner strengths, psychological hardiness, or resiliency factors which can be utilized for ego bolstering. Effective crisis intervenors are able to gauge the seven stages of crisis intervention, while being flexible and realizing that several stages of intervention may overlap. Crisis intervention should culminate with a restoration of cognitive functioning, crisis resolution, and cognitive mastery (Roberts, 2005).

Figure 8-1. Crisis Model.

TRAUMA INFORMED CARE

As crisis intervention continues to progress and be refined through application of evidence-based practice and the application of best practices, it is important to recognize the need to apply current best-evidence in the area of trauma informed care. This chapter seeks to integrate Roberts' Seven Stage Crisis Intervention Model with current best practice knowledge related to trauma informed care. In today's world, it is paramount that all care providers recognize that the psychological effects of violence and trauma in our society are profoundly disabling, and remarkably underdiagnosed and therefore under-treated. Current research indicates violence and trauma including sexual and or physical abuse are widespread, and present with a growing impact on a variety of social issues. It is now noted that the experience of trauma can in fact create irreversible neurological damage resulting in mild to catastrophic consequences for an individual's physical as well as emotional well-being.

The presence of trauma crosses multiple service systems and requires specialized knowledge, training, and collaborative skills between not only health care disciplines but across mental health, health, nursing, EMT's, and police and fire professionals. An issue that further complicates and confounds the application of trauma informed care is the fact that many health, mental health, and criminal justice interventions services are themselves extending the trauma or retraumatizing the victim. The use of coercive interventions such as seclusion, restraing, force, involuntary medication practice and methods based in control, containment, and protocol override the individual's freedom of choice in a way that leads to unintentional retraumatization in what are already traumatized populations.

Trauma Informed Care is defined as care that is grounded in and directed by a thorough understanding of the neurological, biological, psychological, and social effects of trauma and violence on humans and is informed by knowledge of the prevalence of these experiences in persons who receive mental health services. Trauma Specific Services are defined as promising and evidenced based best practices and services that directly address an individual's traumatic experience and sequalae and that facilitate effective recovery for trauma survivors (NASMHPD, 2004).

Crisis intervention for trauma survivors should be reflective of concepts, policies and procedures that not only provide "safety" and "good care," but also provide a voice and empowerment to the trauma victim. Services to trauma survivors should be flexible, individualized, and culturally competent. The implementation of trauma informed crisis intervention should be grounded in principals that protect and promote respect for the dignity of the victim and are based on evidence-based approaches and best practices. Current evidence suggests the most effective approaches for supporting trauma informed care are provided within well-integrated behavioral health services that reflect the centrality of trauma in the lives and experiences of those victimized.

This chapter integrates the concepts of trauma informed care with Roberts' Seven Stage Crisis Intervention Model utilizing two case exemplars to demonstrate potential approaches for individuals who have experienced traumatic experiences as the victims of crime. The next sections will deal with direct practice application of trauma informed crisis intervention.

APPLICATION OF ROBERTS SEVEN-STAGE MODEL: A TRAUMA INFORMED PERSPECTIVE

In applying Roberts' Seven-Stage Model to the case of Sam, the crisis intervenor plans and conducts a crisis assessment (including lethality measures). Traumatic events and victimization walk hand in hand, few will debate the deleterious effects on the individual's well-being. Conducting a lethality assessment and crisis assessment is essentially walking the fine line between gathering the information needed, and conducting the information in a manner that is not retraumatizing to the patient. Application of trauma informed care within Roberts' Seven-Stage Model provides a uniquely stabilizing process for the client when crisis intervenors apply knowledge related to trauma informed care within assessment of crisis experiences. The skilled clinician will gently probe the symptomotology presented by the patient, while initiating stage two of Roberts' Seven stage Model, by rapidly establishing the patient/victim relationship and rapport (Behrman & Reid, 2005).

Sam indicates he has experienced nightmares several times each week for about four weeks following the crime. When developing the crisis intervention model in a trauma informed manner, the worker carefully frames questions related with the symptoms rather than the experiences initially to determine the relative impact on the patient/victims reaction to re-experiencing the event. If the patient/victim responds in a manner that appears supportive of further investigation the clinician can then move into problem identification (Yeager & Roberts 2003; Roberts, 2000). Note the difference between problem identification vs. experiences with traumatic event the clinician is examining the individual thoughts related to the experience. Functioning on a cognitive level may lead to emotional responses, but this should only be attempted if the patient victim demonstrates the ability to tolerate this line of questioning without experiencing retraumatization. For example:

Clinician: Sam you indicated you are having difficulty experiencing nightmares several times. How has that impacted your day-to day-functioning?
Sam: I have noticed that I'm frequently tired throughout the day, and have some problems concentrating.
Clinician: Is that something you think we can work on together?
Sam: I hadn't really given this any thought. What are my options?

The skilled clinician will aid in the identification of patient/victim's identification of major problems (stage three of Roberts' Seven Stage Model) in a manner that is collaborative in all aspects empowering the client to define the therapeutic alliance and working relationship. In doing so, the client is empowered rather than victimized, with the role of the clinician to provide the needed emotional support while examining issues from a practical manner in order to facilitate recovery (Roberts, 2000).

Once and only once the patient/victim has demonstrated a tolerance to examine potentially emotionally charged issues are they ready for application of stage five of Roberts' Seven Stage Model. Within this stage, the clinician builds on the previously established mechanism for emotional support and may begin by examining trauma-related skill deficits. In most cases, victims of violent crime have diminished capacity for self-soothing; for example, the individual may see a similar crime on the news and become overstimulated, experiencing symptoms of anxiety,

helplessness, and hopelessness. This is based in the victim's recent decreases in levels of self-awareness or ability to separate his/her experiences from those seen around him/her, on the television or in society. An additional factor requiring treatment that frequently emerges is the victim's impaired ability to accurately label his/her responses to environmental stimuli associated with his/her trauma experience. In session Sam related:

Sam: Yesterday was difficult; I saw a piece on the news about a robbery gone bad. In the news story three victims were murdered. I began to shake, my heart was racing, and for a few minutes I just sat on the couch wondering what would have happened if I had reacted differently when I was robbed.
Clinician: Where was this crime?
Sam: It was in St. Louis.
Clinician: You are in Yonkers?
Sam: Yes, but this can happen anywhere.
Clinician: I agree, but I'm more concerned with your reaction. Can we discuss why you think you responded the way that you did?

The stage has now been set to examine the patient/victim's assignment of labels to his experiences, as frequently external stimulus are misidentified, or mislabeled, leading to increased anxiety, depression, startle, and at times psychosis. This can be linked to physical responses within the central nervous system that are common among victims of violent crime. Additionally, as these symptoms are normalized as part of the recovery process, the patient/victim becomes empowered to develop his/her own plan for responding to these symptom experiences (Yeager & Gregoire, 2005).

Roberts' fifth stage dovetails at this point by encouraging the patient/victim to generate and explore alternatives in how he/she is responding to the victimization. Key principals within this area of Roberts' seven stage intervention are understanding and appreciating the impact trauma dynamics have on all relationships, specifically, issues of power, blame, relationship building, and the establishment of trust. In Sam's case, he is reacting to the trigger of the news story. In therapy, Sam can examine his response to the news story. He can examine how he has mislabeled the stimulus, and he can begin to examine the interaction this mislabeling will have on how he progresses forward in his life. Sam indicated that he was not only experiencing difficulties with the television news story, but that he was experiencing difficulties in his work environment, as he found he was reacting in unusual ways "for him" to the instructions of his suppliers. Questioning why certain recommendations or decisions have been made by his customer base and handed down to him, he acknowledged that he had been withdrawing from the people he usually sought out, voicing fear that this would have a negative impact on his business (Roberts, 2005).

In stage six of Roberts Seven Stage Model, Sam began constructing a plan of action. In previous conversations, Sam had acknowledged something remarkable; he stated: "once you've experienced the trauma, it's nearly impossible to stop thinking about it. It's always there in some form or another." This is a key point, as the continuous thought process can be utilized to move Sam forward to resolution of his trauma. It was at this point when Sam completed the application for victim compensation and made contact with victim compensation to submit and process this application. Sam agreed to remain in therapy until he felt he had sufficiently worked through the issues he faced. He developed his support network, began working through similar situation approximations until he was able to function without undue anxiety. The entire process was completed within approximately 18 sessions (Yeager & Gregoire, 2005; Roberts, 2000).

Stage seven of Roberts' Seven Stage Model is Follow-Up. At the end of his treatment, Sam was able to acknowledge that the continuous thoughts of his victimization had in fact decreased. He reported transient thoughts of the event that were neither intrusive or anxiety provoking. Rather the thoughts were more or less matter-of-fact when faced with an environmental trigger. Sam no longer reports vivid dreams, but acknowledges a plan to address with others when and if these occur in the future. Sam is planning to expand his business over the next several months. And feels he will be able to utilize this experience to help him to move forward with his life as planned prior to the robbery (Roberts, 2000).

Case Review Julie

Unfortunately the case of Julie is all too familiar to the crisis response team. Community surveys indicate

that approximately 15 percent of women in the United States have experienced either physical or sexual assault at some point within their lifetime. More often than not, the assailant is known to the victim. More than 300,000 women (0.3%) and over 90,000 men (0.1%) reported being raped in the previous 12 months. One in six women (17%) and one in thirty-three men (3%) reported experiencing an attempted or completed rape at some time in their lives (Elliott, Mok, & Briere, 2004).

Rape usually occurs more than once. Among adults who report being raped, women experienced 2.9 rapes and men experienced 1.2 rapes in the previous year (Tjaden & Thoennes, 2000).

Additionally, the prevalence of physical assault or battering is estimated to be 22.7 percent. (Chrestman, Prins, & Koss, 1996). In addition to the emergence of PTSD, survivors of physical and sexual assault are more likely than nonassaulted women to present with a history of mental health problems, including but not limited to phobias, anxiety, chemical dependency, depression, and somatization. There is also evidence that physical health is adversely affected by criminal victimization. Women with histories of assault are more likely to report problems with chronic pelvic pain, other pain-related disorders, functional gastrointestinal disorders, and premenstrual syndrome. Finally, a history of physical or sexual victimization leads to the emergence or exacerbation of detrimental health behaviors and chronic conditions. It is to be expected that women who have been victims of physical or sexual assaults are frequent utilizers of medical services including emergency departments, outpatient care, various procedures, x-rays, and hospitalizations.

How to Respond to Sexual or Physical Violence

Stage One of Roberts' Seven Stage Model Plan: Conduct a Crisis Assessment

There is a fine balance between gathering crisis assessment information, gathering evidence, and completing both in a manner that does not further traumatize Julie.

When conducting crisis assessment in cases of rape we strongly recommend avoiding loaded terms such as rape, although violence is common, it is not uncommon for the individual to feel alone and frightened.

Being scared to discuss the crime is a common response to victimization. Practitioners of trauma informed care will utilize terms such as "forced or coerced to be sexual with someone when you didn't want to." It is further recommended that the assessment process include an education component teaching the individual that they are not alone, e.g., "Many women have experienced violence in their lives, frequently by someone they know." Application of a matter-of-fact approach can help the victim to feel the provider will not be shocked or put off by the details of their recent traumatic experiences (Roberts, 2000, AMA, 1992).

Stage Two of Roberts' Seven Stage Model: Establishing Rapport and Rapidly Establishing Relationship

In a trauma informed approach to crisis intervention, it is always appropriate to say, "I am very sorry this happened." By focusing on the subjective experience of the victim, the clinician implies neither judgment nor blame. It is always appropriate to acknowledge the victim's discomfort or fear when noticed or it becomes evident throughout the interview (Roberts, 2002).

Finally, in cases such as Julie's, avoid assumptions of understanding the patient's perception of the experience. Each individual's perception of the crime is experienced differently. Professionals who may have experienced similar trauma are particularly at risk for this error. Remembering the experience of trauma is highly individualized, leading to remarkably different trauma responses in persons experiencing similar events, will keep professionals aware of the need for the individual to have their own experience. In doing so, the clinician, healthcare professional, or criminal justice professional communicates personal recognition of the issue as a health care issue and suggests to the victim that she is not alone and that help is available whatever her experience of the trauma may be (Roberts, 2002; Sassetti, 1993).

Stage Three of Roberts' Seven Stage Model: Identify Major Problems

In the case of Julie, in addition to validation of her feelings, it is also important to normalize her response to victimization. This can be provided by providing

information related to the prevalence of violence within her local area, providing information with potential reactions to the crisis and common responses experienced by other survivors of trauma. For example, Julie related:

Julie: I don't know why I can't stop crying. I feel like I'm going Crazy!
Clinician: I don't think there is any thing wrong with crying; it's a natural response.
Julie: I'm not over reacting? I mean it's not like me to not be able to pull myself together.
Clinician: Everyone has to find their own way through a crisis; it seems to me, there isn't any right or wrong way. It's simply your way and I'm alright with that.

It is important for crisis intervenors to understand that traumatic reactions are ways of coping with extreme violence. Victims begin to develop their understanding of the trauma by their experience and the way that it has impacted their life, family, health, and emotional well-being. Providing information in the form of handouts and brochures will assist in helping individuals to inform their experience. This type of "psychoeducational" approach to crisis and trauma serves to normalize the victims' response to trauma and to inform their response. This is a critical aspect of recovery from crisis/trauma and victimization (Yeager & Gregoire, 2005; Roberts, 2005).

Stage Four of Roberts' Seven Stage Crisis Intervention Model: Dealing with Feelings and Emotions

In a crisis intervention process that is trauma informed, the professional is acutely aware that there will be a variety of feelings and emotions that will bubble to the surface. Utilization of active listening skill, combined with ongoing validation and normalization, serve as the foundation to assess the needs, values, feelings, and emotions. Frequently staging the expression of feelings and emotions is appropriate. This can be accomplished by determining the most pressing and collaborating with the victim to prioritize issues to be addressed. As mentioned previously, trauma informed care is a balancing act when completing crisis intervention. Establishing processes for accurate labeling, self-soothing, and self-awareness serve as critical tools for the resolution of lasting emotional issues. Maximizing consumer choice and building on skills and resilient factors are key skills to be developed for the trauma informed crisis intervenor (Roberts, 2005).

Resilience is defined as the process of, or capacity for, successful adaptation in circumstances normally associated with psychological dysfunction and low competence. Resilience refers to individuals who effectively use internal (e.g., temperament) and external resources to overcome life circumstances (Dulmus & Hilarski, 2003). Resilience is not necessarily something that people understand how to access in the time of crisis. Few would argue the emotional toll of the traumatic event; the long term impact of the trauma can be minimized by the skilled clinician. By accessing secure, supportive times, the patient and clinician can begin to explore factors of resilience.

Stage Five of Roberts' Seven Stage Model: Generate and Explore Alternatives

Roberts' Fifth Stage is to generate and explore alternatives. By linking the trauma with secure, supportive ties to family and peers, the work of rebuilding the supportive structure can begin. Protective factors such as peers and family serve as the foundation of an underlying expectation that the world can again be predictable and safe, that others are benign, and that the dangers inherent in the world can be surmounted. Although the experience of trauma clearly calls the aforementioned into question, the reestablishment of internalized perceptions of soothing and protective factors in the form of support networks can influence the overall impact of the trauma experience.

Stage Six of Roberts' Seven Stage Model: Develop and Formulate a Plan of Action

Often, preparing in advance for environmental triggers can help the crime victim to sufficiently navigate the posttrauma experience. Utilization of relaxation or distraction techniques is frequently successful in assisting the individual to address the heightened arousal frequently associated with trauma. It is important to consider the individuals' lifestyle; where they work; circumstances under which they will interact with others; and the types and relative strengths,

weaknesses, and potential for volatility in relationships are all factors for examination. Frequently, physical characteristics of coworkers can without warning trigger reexperiencing of the trauma. Common experiences include coworkers of the same gender or race as the assailant; perceived differences in power can also serve as a trigger for persons who were harmed in situations where power was a key factor in the victimization (Roberts, 2000).

Additionally, give consideration to commonly experienced life events that will not be the same, e.g., the crowded subway, leaving the office when working late, entering dark or poorly lit areas, and taking the late night walk through the parking garage unaccompanied. Finally, give particular planning to medical procedures involving physical contact or restraint, and procedures that may be physically uncomfortable, painful, or perceived as life threatening, as all of these can act as a trigger recapitulating aspects of the assault. Examples of this include breast and gynecological examinations, oral thermometers and/or tongue depressors, restraints used for securing an IV, or palpitation of a specific area of the body (Roberts, 2000; American College of Emergency Physicians, 1999; Chrestman, Hearst-Ikeda, & Wolf, 1996).

A word about antianxiety agents: two cautionary notes should be taken into consideration when considering antianxiety agents. Some individuals may actually feel more anxious or out of control when taking antianxiety agents. For some, the sedating effects of antianxiety agents simulate the depersonalizing state experienced within the trauma event. Second, the use of antianxiety agents must be used with extreme caution in trauma victims as there is a high prevalence of substance dependence within this population. Frequently, individuals become dependent upon the antianxiety agents, creating further issues to be addressed (Roberts, 2005).

Stage Seven of Roberts' Seven Stage Model: Establish Follow-up Plan and Agreement

Despite your best efforts and planning, victims of violent crime may become distressed, anxious, distraught, or even dissociative when faced with a situation that triggers the trauma response. It is important to anticipate what might be helpful for the individual should he/she find this occurring. If the client has learned and practiced specific ways to address the anxiety, he/she should be reminded to utilize these early in the event. If the individual develops symptoms that are progressing toward "out of control," the individual should be encouraged to have a plan for safety and escape. Frequently, lists of trusted contacts and even in extreme events, those who are willing to drop everything to come to the assistance of the individual are important. Follow-up options should be clearly outlined with the individual having a clear understanding of what his/her options are for professional assistance if required (Roberts, 2000).

Evidence-Based Practice, Crisis Intervention, and Trauma Informed Care

Evidence-based practice has been defined as the conscientious, explicit, and judicious use of the best available scientific evidence in professional decision making (Sackett, Richardson, Rosenberg, & Hanes, 1997). More simply defined, it is the use of treatments for which there is sufficiently persuasive evidence to support the effective care and management of individuals utilizing the best evidence in obtaining the desired outcomes (Roberts & Yeager, 2004). The practice of evidence-based forensic social work begins with the formulation of a question to drive the evidence-based approach. This is followed by a comprehensive systematic review of the literature. Next in the process is a rigorous evaluation of the evidence presented.

In the case of crisis intervention and trauma informed care, social workers, clinicians, nurses, and physicians may find they are faced with issues or situations where they are asking what will be the best approach in treating this individual's trauma. There will be times when there is not sufficient evidence to formulate an approach to treatment. In such cases, the treatment team will be required to develop its own evidence-based search to inform the care provided. Within evidence-based practice, it is common practice to divide the question you would like to answer into four parts. The question should consider: the client or problem of interest; the intervention you are considering; inclusion of a comparison group, either implicit or explicit as applied to the population; and the outcome of interest, either positive or negative (Roberts & Yeager, 2005; Gray, 2002; Badenoch & Heneghan, 2002; Mckibbon et al., 2002; Sackett et al., 2000).

In application of evidence-based practice, practitioners do have time to ask specific questions with each case addressed if they are familiar with the process of asking the right question. Social workers will face situations where the questions asked become an important component in developing the most appropriate course of action within a given case.

You begin the four-part question process by addressing the individual problem of interest. How specifically you ask this question will impact not only your ability to find the right answer to the question, but also the applicability of this answer to the individual's unique needs. Your description of the individual is the starting point for the question; therefore it should be as specific as possible. For example, if you are interested in crisis intervention within victims of violent crimes, phrasing your question as "crisis intervention, victims of violent crime" will be more effective than searching *treating emergency room patients who are victims of violent crimes*. On the other hand, if your question is too specific, you will have little luck finding sufficient information to address the question at hand; for example, searching for, *23-year-old, females with anxiety, as a result of violent crime*.

The intervention and comparison portion of the four-part question can address a treatment, diagnostic test, and social intervention or support program. In most cases, the intervention portion of the question should be combined with a comparison component. That is, the intervention is compared with another intervention or "treatment as usual." There are also diagnostic questions; these address a particular diagnostic test, or rating scale. In cases of diagnostic questions, you will want to compare against whatever test is identified as "the gold standard" or in the absence of a gold standard test, the comparison is with a screening instrument that is commonly accepted and has demonstrated high levels of validity and reliability in similar situations. Etiology questions address the intervention. In this case, the comparison can be a risk factor; for example, the comparison can be the presence or absence of a risk factor, the absence or presence of alcohol or drug abuse. Prognosis questions may be either three- or four-part. Three-part questions address the prognosis of patients with a particular illness, such as a first time depressive disorder. A four-part question of prognosis will query if the presence of an individual characteristic or complicating factor may alter the prognosis of the patient. For example, in persons with a recent history of trauma, who are substance dependent but abstinent from all mood-altering substances, are such persons at a greater or less risk for relapse? As crisis intervenors develop skills in the application of evidence-based practice questions, several interventions may be considered, such as the impact of social support programs in combination with medication management and a particular therapeutic approach (Roberts & Yeager 2005).

Evidence-based practice addresses questions about the probabilities of benefit or harm to people rather than answering questions about underlying mechanisms of pathology and cures. It is important to note that evidence-based questions will not answer questions about what is actually occurring with the patient or victim of violent crime. There will be times when application of the evidence-based approach will in the case of crisis intervention and trauma informed care expose gaps in the evidence. In such cases, the individual practitioner is challenged to find the best evidence, and apply this evidence in consideration to the case. This is the challenge facing crisis intervenors in applying a trauma informed approach. There is only an emerging evidence-based foundation. It is the hope of the authors that this brief application model will provide practitioners with a foundation to build upon in the development, establishment, implementation analysis, and measurement of evidence-based practice within areas of trauma informed care and crisis intervention.

CONCLUSION

Today's practitioner is faced with a myriad of crises that are the result of violent crime. Without a doubt there have been significant strides in crisis intervention, brief treatment approaches, and the application of trauma informed care. There remain, however, significant challenges. It is possible that the combined approach of Roberts' seven-stage crisis intervention model and trauma informed approach can lead to more rapid response and stabilization in victims of violent crimes. In this population, there exists a remarkable gap in evidence-based approaches with this population. The practitioner will be challenged to develop, refine, and apply the skills of question formulation, systematic literature searches, application

of practice guidelines, and treatment protocols with this population. The answers are few and far between, and the challenges are great.

This chapter is intended to provide practice guidance to those working in crisis intervention through the application of case exemplars, demonstrating both Roberts' crisis intervention model and a trauma informed approach. It is the hope of the authors that this chapter will inspire professionals to take up the challenges of evidence-based practice within this population. The importance of combining the three approaches can not be underestimated. The systematic application of evidence-based practice combined with practice-based research will inform the literature in the years to come. Through a conscious approach of clinicians to move the knowledge base forward through systematic reviews, program evaluation, outcome studies, randomized controlled studies, survey research, and examination of consumer informed care, we are confident that practitioners, when given the appropriate ammunition to inform their practice, will produce new and compelling evidence that will inform and direct the continued development of effective treatment and intervention approaches in crisis intervention and trauma informed care.

REFERENCES

American Medical Association Council on Scientific Affairs. (1992). Violence against women: Relevance for medical practitioners. *Journal of the American Medical Association, 267,* 3183–3189.

Behrman G., & Reid, W.J., (2005) Post trauma intervention basic tasks. In A.R. Roberts, *Crisis intervention handbook: Assessment, treatment and research* (3rd ed., pp. 291–304). New York: Oxford University Press.

Chrestman, K.R., Hearst-Ikeda, D., & Wolfe, J. (1996). *Identification and management of trauma survivors in the primary care setting.* Unpublished manuscript. Womens Health Sciences Division, National Center for PTSD.

Chrestman, K.R., Prins, A., & Koss M. (1996). Enhancement of primary care treatment for women trauma survivors. National Center for PTSD, *NPC Clinical Quarterly, 6*(4): Fall, 1996.

Dulmus C.N. & Hilarski, C. (2003). When stress constitutes trauma and trauma constitutes crisis: The stress-trauma-crisis continuum. *Brief Treatment and Crisis Intervention, 3*(1), 27–36.

Elliott, D.M., Mok, D.S., & Briere J. (2004). Adult sexual assault: Prevalence, symptomatology, and sex differences in the general population. *Journal of Traumatic Stress, 17*(3):203–11.

National Association of State Mental Health Program Directors (2004). http://www.nasmhpd.org/general_files/position_statement/NASMHPD%20TRAUMA%20Positon%20statementFinal.pdf.

Roberts, A. R. (2000). *Crisis intervention handbook: Assessment, treatment and research* (2nd ed.). New York: Oxford University Press.

Roberts, A. R. (2002). Assessment, crisis intervention and trauma treatment: The integrative ACT intervention model. *Brief Treatment and Crisis Intervention, 2*(1):1–21.

Roberts, A. R. (2005). Bridging the past and present to the future of crisis intervention and crisis management. In A. R. Roberts (ed.). *Crisis intervention handbook: Assessment, treatment and research* (3rd ed., pp. 3–34) New York: Oxford University Press.

Roberts, A. R., Yeager, K.R., & Streiner D.L. (2004). Evidence-based practice with comorbid substance abuse, mental illness and suicidality: Can the evidence be found? *Brief Treatment and Crisis Intervention, 4*(2): 123–136.

Roberts A.R., & Yeager K.R. (2005). Lethality assessment and crisis intervention with persons presenting with suicidal ideation. In A.R. Roberts, *Crisis intervention handbook: Assessment, treatment and research* (3rd ed., pp. 35–63). New York: Oxford University Press.

Sassetti, M.R. (1993). Domestic violence. *Primary Care, 20,* 289–305.

Tjaden, P., Thoennes, N. (2000). Full report of the prevalence, incidence, and consequences of violence against women: Findings from the national violence against women survey. Washington: National Institute of Justice, Report NCJ 183781.

Weishaar, M. E. (2004). A Cognitive-behavioral approach to suicide risk reduction in crisis intervention. In A. R. Roberts & K. Yeager (Eds.), *Evidence-based practice manual: Research and outcome measures in health and human services.* New York: Oxford University Press, pp. 749–757.

Yeager, K.R., Gregoire, T.K., (2005). Crisis intervention application of brief solution-focused therapy in addictions. In A.R. Roberts (Ed.), *Crisis intervention handbook: Assessment, treatment and research* (3rd ed., pp. 556–602). New York: Oxford University Press.

Yeager, K.R., & Roberts, A.R. (2003). Differentiating among stress, acute stress disorder, crisis episodes, trauma and PTSD: Paradigm and treatment goals. *Brief Treatment and Crisis Intervention, 3*(1), 1–26.

Chapter 9

The History and Role of Social Work in Law Enforcement[1]

Albert R. Roberts

The history of police social work is almost exclusively one of policewomen providing social work services and, consequently, is closely intertwined with the emergence of policewomen, many of them having social work backgrounds. In the early 1900s, at a time when policemen were mostly assigned to patrolling the streets and to the other duties traditionally associated with law enforcement, the first police social workers were policewomen who were responsible for providing certain social services, usually to women and juveniles. There is no evidence that policemen were ever assigned to perform social work functions during the first quarter of the twentieth century. At that time, social work was a predominantly female profession, and it is understandable that the first police social workers were women.

Although the police social worker movement had a spirited beginning, accounts of police social work faded from the literature after approximately forty years. By the end of World War II, it seemed to have been almost completely forgotten. Although a new surge of interest is now emerging and several police departments have demonstrated their concern for helping people in need of social and medical services, much remains to be done before even the most enlightened and humanistic police departments can be said to be responding fully to the acute need for social work intervention within their areas off responsibility.

The author's interest in expanding the points of entry into social service delivery systems led to extensive research into the history of police and social work collaboration. The review of the literature presented here was undertaken to discover and synthesize the widely scattered information on the police social work movement and determine what has impeded its development in this country. Briefly, the development of this movement has been hampered by various forms of misconception, resistance, and ignorance, and because the documentation is at best sketchy, an integrated assessment of its history must consist of piecing together many obscure threads in the literature.

The research did not uncover specific evidence that during the first half of this century police departments specifically allocated positions for social workers. However, many of the early policewomen had social work training prior to being hired by the police departments, and they performed police social work roles in their protective work with children and youth. Although there is no clear-cut means of distinguishing between the early policewomen and the first police social workers, the author has determined that the history of police social work is often synonymous with that of women's bureaus in police departments and of policewomen generally. Indeed, the origin of the police social worker movement can be traced to the establishment of women's bureaus in police departments during the first quarter of this century. The establishment of these women's bureaus was, in turn, a direct result of a desire for better protective and preventive social services for women and children.

It is the author's belief that by studying the problems that impeded the police social worker movement from flourishing similar mistakes can be avoided as the social work profession attempts to reestablish these services. This chapter includes a discussion of

1. Adapted from *Social Work*, 1976, *21*(4), 294–299 with the permission of the National Association of Social Workers, Inc.

the origin and growth of the women's bureaus that became the prototypes of police social work, an analysis of the problems leading to the decline of police social work, and finally, several recommendations for planning and developing much needed collaborative efforts between police and social workers.

WOMEN'S BUREAUS AND POLICE SOCIAL WORK

Police departments have traditionally been concerned with, among other things, protective services for women and children, and as a result, they have provided some social services, particularly for juveniles. A crucial step in the gradual evolvement of the police social worker movement was the establishment of Women's Bureaus within police departments during the 1910s and 1920s.

Although the first protective service for young girls was developed as early as 1905 in Portland, Oregon (Pigeon, 1939), the year 1910 is frequently cited as the origin of the policewomen profession in the United States. In September of that year, Mrs. Alice Stebbins Wells was appointed a police officer in Los Angeles. Prior to her employment in police work, Mrs. Wells had made a study of crime and concluded that there was a strong need for women in police service (Graper, 1920). However, she did not acquire her position without the concerted effort and support of many local citizens, a hundred of whom she had persuaded to sign a petition to the mayor requesting that she be put on the police force. Fortunately, Mrs. Wells had been able to keep the knowledge of the petition from both the local press and politicians until its actual presentation, which allowed the mayor and the aldermen to grant her request in an unpressured climate (Darwin, 1914). Only one year after Mrs. Wells had obtained her position on the Los Angeles police force, the position of policewoman became classified under civil service, thus enabling other women to be recruited to work with juveniles.

While these events were taking place in Los Angeles, similar developments occurred in Chicago. Minnie F. Low (1911) reported that a social worker was on duty at the Chicago police station. Many people had been coming to the police station to air their grievances, both real and imagined, and the

social worker was assigned to doing away "with petty, degrading litigation and adjust[ing] the less serious complaints." Because of the social worker's efforts, such litigation was considerably reduced, and this arrangement won favorable comments from the courts. As a result, within two years (in August, 1913) the Chicago Police Department had appointed ten policewomen with social work experience under civil service regulations. By 1919, the number had increased to twenty-nine (Minor, 1919).

Initially, there was strong opposition among policemen in most departments to the hiring of female officers. However, this overt opposition gradually faded, at least on the surface, and the hiring of policewomen spread. By 1915, it was reported by the United States Census Bureau that twenty-five cities employed policewomen who were paid from police appropriations. The largest number of policewomen in any city, a total of twenty-one, was reported in Chicago, while the cities of Baltimore, Pittsburgh, Los Angeles, San Francisco, Minneapolis, Seattle, Portland, St. Paul, Dayton, and Topeka had each hired from two to five policewomen.

At the Conference of Charities and Correction in 1916, Alice Stebbins Wells, who had become the President of the International Association of Policewomen, spoke on the topic of the policewomen movement. She stated that the impetus for women to become policewomen had derived from a desire to care for young people who needed help. Mrs. Wells also remarked that many troubled women who had been able to confide in policewomen may have had difficulty relating to a policeman. "The power of the policewomen to counsel and protect fills a real need," she said, and urged the expansion of recruitment and training of women for this field.

By 1920, the prospect of policewomen serving in social work advocacy roles (particularly dealing with juveniles) seems to have taken hold. In a speech before the National Conference of Social Work, Mina Van Winkle (1920), Director of the Women's Bureau at the Metropolitan Police Department in Washington, D.C., clarified the role of policewomen serving in her Bureau, saying, "Policewomen are aiming to bring about a close relationship between social workers, the public and the police." Van Winkle further described the Women's Bureau as, "a separate unit in the police department with a woman as director responsible to the head of the department and giving entire time to all cases in which women and children are involved as well as to preventive and protective work." Her stated goal was to have a Women's Bureau, directed by a woman, in every large city throughout the country. Van Winkle distinguished four types of responsibilities – protective, preventive, corrective, and general police work – and specified the activities in which the policewomen were involved, as "follow-up work for women and girls, securing employment, improving and changing environment that causes delinquency, voluntary probation, . . . physical and psychopathic examinations, careful investigation of questionable circumstances . . . locating missing girls, assistants in case work for the police, juvenile and criminal courts." She also mentioned other responsibilities for policewomen such as searching for runaway girls, helping policemen secure evidence against prostitutes, and providing temporary boarding where necessary (Van Winkle, 1920).

Between 1915 and 1920, the number of policewomen had increased sufficiently to support an International Association of Policewomen. The original constitution of this Association set forth standards including the following:

> . . . to act as a clearinghouse for compilation and dissemination of information on the work of women police, to aim for high standards of work and to promote preventive and protective service by police departments.

> . . . the use of policewomen chiefly for protective and preventive work, the employment of professionally trained women, the establishment of courses of instruction in universities or schools of social work, and the keeping of proper records. (Pigeon, 1934)

However, the growth of the International Association of Policewomen was limited because the police social worker movement was prevalent only in a few large urban areas such as Washington, D.C., Berkeley, Chicago, Detroit, Cleveland, Indianapolis, New York City, Los Angeles, Seattle, and St. Louis.

In the decades following the inception of a corps of policewomen, there was a steady increase in their numbers. By 1930, for example, there were 509 policewomen in 200 police departments throughout the United States (U.S. Department of Labor, 1931). By 1949, employment statistics of the Women's Bureau of the U.S. Department of Labor indicated that there

were over one thousand policewomen in the United States. Yet, this group comprised less than 1 percent of the total number of police officers in the country. Although the numbers of those early policewomen were small, their work was important and the level of their education remarkably high. This can be illustrated by the Detroit Police Department, which in 1944 had fifty-eight policewomen in its Women's Division. They had all attained a college degree or the equivalent and had two years of practical experience in youth work prior to employment with the Women's Division. Broadly defined, a large part of the work carried out by these educated women could have been classified as social work intervention. Although the policewomen were required to perform patrol work and investigative duties, they were also able to provide early case finding and referral to appropriate social agencies.

Two case examples, from the records of the Women's Division of the Detroit Police Department from the early 1940s will serve as an illustration of the intervention strategy utilized by these policewomen (Connolly, 1944).

The first is a vivid account of a policewoman, Miss Kidder, picking up in her patrol car a young runaway girl, just as she is about to be taken to a hotel by a stranger. Despite some initial lying and subterfuge on the girl's part, Miss Kidder's "kind, expert questioning" back at police headquarters brings out the whole, sad story of a seventeen-year-old girl who, having run away from a drunken father and stepmother in Akron, Ohio, comes to Detroit hoping to live with her aunt, only to find out that the latter has left town. Unable to keep her job in a cheap vaudeville theater, the girl is now penniless, homeless, hungry and cold, and vulnerable to transients and pimps who want to pick her up. At this point, let us turn to the actual dialogue between the policewoman and the girl as it was recorded:

> "Where was he taking you when we picked you up?"
> "He was going to rent a room for me."
> "You mean – for both of you?"
> "No. He said not. He promised. . . ."
> Miss Kidder turned directly to the girl. "Jean, have you had anything to do with men or boys, sexually? If you have, you should be examined for venereal disease."
> "No," was the vehement protest. "I never have.

Never! But go ahead, examine me. I don't mind."

"Good. Now, Jean, we'll have to detain you here at headquarters while you case is investigated. You'll be in a clean, private room. Not with anyone else. And you are *not* being arrested or given a police record. You are just being protected."

"Don't send me home!" the girl begged.

"Your home will be investigated. If it's what you claim it is, you won't have to go back. If you do stay in Detroit, we'll help you get adjusted. Social agencies will find you a clean place to live, a job, some young friends and some fun. You'd like that?"

Tears of relief sprang to the girl's eyes. "Yes," she said huskily.

This case is representative of police social work during the early 1940s, in which timely assistance was provided to juveniles in danger of becoming involved in delinquent acts.

A second case, also from the records of the Detroit Police Department, shows perhaps even more forcefully the critical need for timely intervention on behalf of young and troubled girls.

In Detroit, a girl of eleven, missing from her home for a week, was found by policewomen as a result of dogged day and night searching. This child, Helen, left alone evenings, had wandered downtown to a movie, been picked up by a young procuress of fourteen, lured to her apartment and dressed up to look eighteen. She had been offered to sailors as a V-girl. But though she looked eighteen, the men had decided, from her childish voice, that she must be very young and had let her alone. Her hostess then turned her out. Helen escaped rape almost by a miracle. (Connolly, 1944)

Mrs. Coolidge, lieutenant of the Detroit women's division, was appalled by the fact that the number of rapes was on the increase and that policemen were being assigned the difficult and delicate task of questioning the victims. The lieutenant strongly believed that because of the strain on the young victim of recounting the horrid events, all rape investigations should be handled by policewomen.

Van Winkle (1924) was in the vanguard of those urging collaboration between social work and police work; as early as 1924, she was recommending that social workers enter the police force. She called for employing social work techniques when working with juveniles with the goal of preventing delinquent acts and proposed that educated police social workers be hired to work toward that end. Van Winkle

hoped that this would lead to a reduction in the continuing controversy between police, courts, and probation personnel as to which agency was responsible for reducing the delinquency problem.

Van Winkle further recognized and deplored the tendency of some agencies to be concerned only with their own specific function, without being concerned with the overall service delivery system. She concluded that all agencies were at fault in this regard, stating emphatically that:

Each group is only too prone to see the question of delinquency from its own angle without reference to the problem as a whole, and certainly without reference to society. Let us, therefore, join hands. Police wok is social work, and until you include it in social service we shall continue to pass delinquents from one agency to another, and then from reformatory to jail, workhouse, and prison. Socialized policework is but a further extension of the government's responsibility for public welfare. (Van Winkle, 1924)

As has been seen then, beginning in 1910, women had become an important part of police departments in several urban areas across the United States by providing social service oriented police work, dealing particularly with juveniles and women. The emergence of a corps of well-educated police social workers was, however, fraught with unresolved problems.

The next section of this article will deal with these problems and misconceptions before discussing recommendations for the future.

MISCONCEPTIONS AND PROBLEMS

Throughout the early 1900s, policewomen had to contend with publicized misconceptions of their role. Published accounts of their responsibilities frequently overlooked the social work functions that policewomen carried out. Caricatures of policewomen appeared in the newspapers, which depicted them as tight-lipped, masculine-looking creatures, with "billy" clubs swinging at their sides and a revolver in hand. The adverse treatment in the press reached such proportions that in 1919 the Executive Secretary of the New York Probation and Protective Association, Maude E. Minor, responded by declaring emphatically that policewomen did not police a beat and make arrests as the men did. Policewomen's major responsibilities, as Maude Minor explained them, were in the realm of protective work with juveniles.

In addition, and even more damaging to the police social worker movement than the resistance of the press toward policewomen, was the resistance from male police officers and police administrators. Policemen had difficulty accepting the presence of females within their department. Their antagonism toward the police social workers seems to have stemmed not only from the chauvinistic view that women belonged in the home but also from prejudices against social workers. The powerful, authoritarian role in which policemen perceived themselves was diametrically opposed to the human service casework orientation of most police social workers.

In studying and analyzing the police social worker movement during the first quarter of the twentieth century, it is important to remember that in those years a certain amount of contempt was directed at all women who were pursuing a professional career; therefore, there was even greater disdain for women who chose to enter a traditionally male profession such as policework. Policewomen were continually faced with criticism, i.e., that they were attempting to do a "man's job" by arresting hardened criminals, when in fact, the early policewomen were far more interested in providing social work intervention services than they were in doing patrol work. It comes as no surprise, then, that policewomen's energies were often diverted from working full-time in areas such as protective services to repeatedly defend and explain their true purpose and function.

In addition to the harassment the early policewomen endured from the press and their male coworkers, there were other obstacles that impeded the expansion of the police social worker movement. These were the most significant stumbling blocks: political considerations; lack of interest and support from citizens groups; lack of funds from private organizations and foundations with which to publicize the accomplishments of police social work and expand staff; insufficient support from elected officials for larger appropriations; lack of coordination with and participation in local, state, and national social welfare and police organizations; and limited opportunities for students in schools of social work to take course and field work in the structure and function of police departments.

Political obstacles, especially at the local level, frequently prevented the growth of the police social worker movement; for example, the election of a new mayor or city manager often occasioned the appointment of a new police commissioner, and it was not unusual for such turnovers to result in new policies that restricted the hiring of police social workers and threatened the work of women's bureaus.

The chain of events resulting from new city leadership frequently went like this: direct or indirect pressure caused the director of the women's bureau to resign; internal changes occurred whereby policemen stopped referring appropriate cases to the women's bureau and attempted to handle those cases by themselves; and, as an end product resulting from policemen's lack of knowledge of community resources, the number of referrals to child guidance clinics, traveler's aid, and other social agencies would fall off.

These developments were often, of course, reflections of a lack of police interest in social work objectives. In some cases, policemen had merely been paying lip service to the police social worker movement, and when the support of the police chief began to wane, they were quick to verbalize their opposition to the work of the women's bureau. Also, the stereotyped exaggerations of policewomen that appeared periodically in local newspapers reinforced many policemen's prejudices against the social work responsibilities carried out by female police officers.

In recent years, only limited use has been made of collaboration between social work and law enforcement professionals in the United States. Few areas of the country have utilized the relatively untapped potential of police social workers in providing immediate intervention services to troubled juveniles, adults, the elderly, and families. At the present time such programs are operating in Haywood, California, Honolulu, Hawaii, Lyndhurst and Trenton, New Jersey, Yonkers, New York, Pawtucket, Rhode Island, and several areas throughout the state of Illinois (Carr, 1979, 1982; Michaels & Treger, 1973; Treger, 1972, 1974, 1983). Programs in other locations should also be developed.

In a number of locations across the nation, a more humanistic perspective among police chiefs is becoming apparent. Among the programs that seem to be realistic indicators of police departments' concern about social service objectives are the training of police officers in family crisis and social work intervention and the development of crime-specific rape crisis centers.

RECOMMENDATIONS

The history of police social work lends support to the view that social workers can make a significant contribution to broadening the role of police departments as human service agencies, especially in crisis intervention work with juveniles and their families. Consequently, the question becomes this: What should be the relationship between social workers and law enforcement personnel in the 1980s?

Both types of professionals have expanded their respective functions from what they were in the early 1900s. Social work services are, and should continue to be, provided mostly by social work agencies, and law enforcement functions are properly the province of police departments. However, if police officers are to do their jobs most effectively, it is essential that they gain a basic knowledge of crisis intervention strategies, and awareness of appropriate referral sources in their community, and a sensitivity toward the social problems faced by community residents.

The recommendations put forth here are actually geared to two types of programs. One is aimed at providing training for all police officers to enable them to be more effective in helping the troubled persons they encounter while on patrol. Such skills are particularly important during the evening, weekend, and holiday periods when most social agencies are closed. The problems on which crisis intervention training should focus include child abuse, suicide, alcoholism, violent family quarrels, and juvenile offenses.

Police officers' knowledge and skill need to be broadened beyond just transporting an abused child to the local hospital emergency room. They need training in human relations and mental hygiene, sensitivity training, and to know how to recognize personality disorders. They need training not so that they can take the place of experienced social workers, psychiatrists, and psychologists, but to be able to provide immediate crisis intervention when emergencies arise and the other professionals are not available. Many of the larger police departments already provide some of this training to new recruits. However, there is a need for a more thorough handling of these topics during training sessions and for more standardization to reduce the wide variation that presently exists from one department's training program to the next.

The other area of recommendation encompasses the development of social work teams within police departments. Such teams would be staffed by experienced social workers who are knowledgeable about police procedures, and they would be assigned the following responsibilities: (1) to establish solid working relationships with agencies providing emergency medical, psychiatric, and social work services in the community; (2) to provide the initial diagnostic assessment of clients referred to them by police officers, make appropriate referrals to local agencies, and follow-up to ensure that service was rendered; (3) to provide police officers with in-service training in crisis intervention techniques; and (4) to be on the job twenty-four-hours-a-day to serve as a backup resource for the policemen and policewomen on patrol.

National and statewide training models and research grants should be given high priority and receive the necessary financial support, through federal and private foundation funding. Schools of criminal justice and schools of social work could provide invaluable support by expanding or reallocating their resources – faculty, curriculum, videotape equipment, and computer time – into demonstration, training, and research projects geared toward assembling practice models for social worker-police collaboration.

Without the development of national standards and goals, the mistakes of history may be repeated. The social work profession can learn from past mistakes. A concerted effort must be initiated now so that national leaders in social work practice and police science can provide the unified leadership necessary for building working models of cooperation between police and social workers. Together these recommendations can, in part, provide the initial blueprints for national models of practice.

REFERENCES

Bard, M. & Berkowitz, B (1967). Training police as specialists in family crisis intervention: A community psychology action program. *Community Mental Health Journal, 3*, 315–317.

Bard, M. (1970). *Training police as specialists in family crisis intervention.* Washington, D.C.: U.S. Government Printing Office. Law Enforcement Assistance Administration.

Bard, M. (1969). Family intervention police teams as a community mental health resource. *Journal of Criminal Law, Criminology and Police Science, 60,* 247–250.

Carr, J. J. (1982). Treating family abuse using a police crisis team approach. In M. Roy (Ed), *The abusive partner* (pp. 216–229). New York: Van Nostrand Reinhold.

Carr, J. J. (1979). An administrative retrospective on police crisis teams. *Social Casework 60:*7, 416–422.

Connolly, V. (1944). Job for a lady: Detroit's women police tackle the girl delinquency problem. *Colliers, 113,* 19–20, 48.

Darwin, M. (1914). Police women and their work in America. *Nineteenth Century,* (June) 1370–71.

Graper, E. D. (1920). *Police organization and methods of administration in American cities.* Doctoral dissertation, Columbia University, Faculty of Political Science, New York.

Low, M. F. (1911). Report on joint section meetings. *Proceedings of the Thirty-eighth Annual Session of the National Concerence of Charities and Correction.* Boston, MA.

Michaels, R. A. & Treger, H. (1973). Social work in police departments. *Social Work, 18* (September) 67–75.

Minor, M. E. (1919). The policewoman and the girl problem. *Proceedings of the Forty-sixth Annual Meeting of the National Conference of Social Work.* Atlantic City, NJ.

Pigeon, H. D. (1934). Policewomen. *Social Work Yearbook, 1933.* New York: Russell Sage Foundation.

Pigeon, H. D. (1939). The role of the police in crime prevention. *National Probation Association Yearbook.*

Shimota, K. L. *Police social worker, Eau Claire Police Department: A summary report.* Madison, WI: Wisconsin Division for Family and Youth, mimeographed.

Treger, H. Thomson, D. & Jaeck, G. S. (1974). A police-social work team model. *Crime and Delinquency* (July) 281–290.

Treger, H. (1972). Breakthrough in preventive corrections: A police-social work team model. *Federal Probation, 36,* (December) 53–58.

Treger, H. (1980). Guideposts for community work in police social work diversion. *Federal Probation, 44* (September) 3–8.

United States Census Bureau. (1915). *General Statistics of Cities.* Washington, D.C.: U.S. Government Printing Office.

U.S. Department of Labor. (1931). *Juvenile court statistics.* Publication No. 200. Washington, D.C.: U.S. Government Printing Office.

U.S. Department of Labo, Women's Bureau. (1949). *The outlook for women in police work.* Bulletin No. 231. Washington, D.C.: U.S. Government Printing Office.

Van Winkle, M. (1920). *Standardization of the aims and methods of the work of policewomen.* Proceedings of the national Conference of Social Work at the Forty-seventh Annual Session, New Orleans, La. Chicago, IL: University of Chicago Press.

Van Winkle, M. (1924). *The policewomen.* Proceedings of the Fifty-first Annual Session of the National Conference on Social Work, Toronto, Ont., Chicago, IL: University of Chicago Press.

Wells, A. S. (1916). *The policewoman movement, present status and future needs.* Proceedings of the Forty-third Annual Session of the National Conference off Charities and Correction, Indianapolis, IN. Chicago, IL: Hildman Printing Co.

Chapter 10

Forensic Social Work in Law Enforcement and Victim Service/Witness Assistance Programs: National and Local Perspectives

Karen S. Knox and Albert R. Roberts

CASE EXEMPLAR

Cheryl, her husband, and three small children had recently moved to the Austin area from California. The police department crisis team was called to their home, which was the scene of a domestic violence incident. At the scene, the police arrested the husband and transported him to jail. In the house, several household items were broken and furniture was overturned. The children had awoken and were upset and crying. One of the team members worked with the children while Cheryl related what had occurred to the other crisis team member. She said that she had left her husband several times and been in domestic violence shelters before, but that he always found her and she went back to him, feeling she had no other options. Tonight, he had taken the rifle and threatened to shoot her and himself before the police arrived. She had no family or friends here, and was afraid to stay at the house. Having been through the arrest process before, she knew her husband would make bail and come looking for her.

Cheryl had not received any physical injuries that needed medical attention, but was visibly traumatized by the incident and was shaking and teary. Allowing her to ventilate and deal with her emotional reactions away from the children, the crisis team member waited until she calmed down

and was more composed before initiating any action. This time also provided the children with an opportunity to settle down and not be so scared. The crisis team contacted the local domestic violence shelter and made arrangements to transport her and the children. Gathering what belongings they could take with them, the team and a police car transported the family to the shelter.

While there, the crisis team members coordinated services with the shelter staff, and informed Cheryl of the process to obtain a protective order against her husband. She was reluctant at first, saying she had already tried everything and nothing could stop him, however, she did agree to work with the shelter and victim service staff to follow through on the investigation and legal proceedings.

Cheryl's husband did make bail and returned to the house, where he packed some clothes and left the area. After learning about his actions and not knowing his whereabouts, Cheryl decided to stay at the shelter program that also had transitional housing for women and children after the initial 30-day shelter stay. Cheryl cooperated with the criminal investigation, and filed for a protective order. She received individual and group counseling and the children attended a group as well through the children's program at the shelter. Other supportive services that Cheryl was able to use from the domestic violence program and other local resources, included childcare, transportation (bus pass), job training and placement services, and advocacy during the legal proceedings, filing for victim's compensation benefits, and in obtaining a divorce.

Cheryl's husband was located in California several months later, extradited and tried in court. The prosecutors' office victim witness coordinator assisted Cheryl through the trial and with her court notification and preparation. Having to deal with the criminal proceedings and seeing her husband again brought back fear and memories that were painful. Court accompaniment and crisis intervention services through the victim-witness program helped her with these emotional reactions to ensure that her progress was maintained, and to minimize revictimization through the court system. After her husband was sentenced to prison, Cheryl contacted the crisis team members to update them on her situation and thank them for their help. She related that she had doubts that her life could get better, but was glad she had been in Austin where she got the support and assistance needed for her and her children.

INTRODUCTION

Forensic social work in law enforcement and other criminal justice settings focuses on working with victims and survivors of crime in a variety of areas, including child abuse, sexual assault, family violence, elder abuse, and other crimes against persons (Knox & Roberts, 2002). "Since the 1980's, the growing awareness by the law enforcement and social work professions of the impact of violent crimes on victims, witnesses, and family survivors has resulted in a team approach to provide crisis intervention and victim assistance services. Crime victims are physically, emotionally, and financially damaged by perpetrators of crime. In the aftermath, crime victims and family survivors often have to cope with physical pain, acute stress, psychological trauma, phobias, fear, grief, loss, medical problems and expenses, financial needs, and court proceedings. Many crime victims, witnesses, and family survivors have their first contact through the police department" (Knox & Roberts, p. 669). This is a critical time for intervention, and police social workers have a unique opportunity to provide crisis intervention services (Knox & Roberts, 2002).

A number of cities, counties, and townships throughout the United States have clinical social workers and domestic violence advocates employed by their local police departments. In a number of jurisdictions, there are police-social work teams where specially trained police officers team up with police social workers in responding, investigating, and intervening with domestic violence and other victims of violent crimes. Whether a crime victim in crisis is living in Austin, Texas, or Willmette, Illinois, or New York City, they will have the opportunity for timely crisis intervention from police social work teams. Across the country, social workers are employed by law enforcement agencies to meet the critical concrete and crisis-oriented needs of these crime victims. As police-based victim service programs have gradually increased in a cyclically over the past 25 years, different models of service have emerged to meet the needs of crime victims in urban and rural areas. This chapter provides a brief history during the past two decades, and detailed information on developments during the current decade on police-based civilian domestic violence advocates, police social work programs, prosecutor-based victim/witness assistance, and other types of services for victims/survivors of crime. A review of evidence-based research findings evaluating the availability and effectiveness of victim service programs is presented, along with the practice implications from those research studies (Dziegielewski & Powers, 2005; Johnson, 1997; Roberts, 2005; and Roberts, 1990). A discussion of the types of social work roles and functions in police social work is included, while a case exemplar that illustrates the continuum of service delivery across law enforcement and the court system opened this chapter.

HISTORY OF POLICE SOCIAL WORK

The social work profession has a long history of working with police departments to provide victim services. A crucial step in the gradual evolvement of the police social workers movement was the establishment of Women's Bureaus within police departments during the first half of the 1900s (Roberts, 1997a). The police departments of Los Angeles and Chicago were the first to hire women as police social workers to work with less serious offenses and crimes involving juveniles and women. Law enforcement has traditionally been involved with crimes involving women and children/juveniles, and the focus of most social work services during this early period was on protective and corrective programs for these client populations.

At the Conference on Charities and Corrections in 1916, Alice Stebbins Wells, the first police social worker hired in Los Angeles, spoke about the need for women in police departments to care for young people who needed help, and to counsel and protect the many troubled women who found it easier to confide in policewomen (Roberts, 1997a). In 1920 at the National Conference on Social Work, Mina Van Winkle, Director of the Women's Bureau of the Metropolitan Police Department in Washington, D.C., described the Women's Bureau as a separate unit of the police department that works all cases where children and women are involved, with four types of responsibilities, protective, preventive, corrective, and general police work (Roberts, 1997a). Her goal was to have a Women's Bureau in every major city's police department, and by 1930, there were over 500 policewomen in 200 police departments throughout the U.S. (Roberts, 1997a). There was a steady increase in the police social work movement over the next two decades; however, this growth was found primarily in large urban areas.

Throughout this time period, obstacles such as harassment, sexism, discrimination, and stereotypes of women in law enforcement impacted negatively on this movement. Other problems such as lack of support from politicians, community leaders, and citizens groups; lack of funds for prevention and protective services; and lack of coordination among community, social welfare, and police organizations also contributed to a declining interest in police social work programs by the 1950s (Roberts, 1997b). Although the history of police social work lends support to the view that a team approach by social work and law enforcement can make significant contributions in the area of victim services, it was not until the mid-1970s when the battered women's and rape crisis movements became active that the social work presence was focused again on crime victims. A major boost in funding police social workers came about throughout the 1970s and early 1980s through state and county block grants which were allocated through the federal Law Enforcement Assistance Administration (LEAA). These police social work programs primarily focused on crime prevention activities and interventions on behalf of predelinquents, status offenders, and juvenile delinquents.

Social workers employed in battered women's shelters and rape crisis programs realized that many crime victims were being victimized twice – once, during the actual crime, and then by the criminal justice system, which was designed to protect the rights of the criminal/defendant, not the victim/survivor. The women's movement focused attention on domestic violence and sexual assault, and along with the emerging crime victims' movement resulted in federal legislation and funding to establish victim assistance programs in all states through the Federal Law Enforcement Assistance Administration (LEAA) and the Victims of Crime Act (VOCA) of 1984 (Roberts & Fisher, 1997).

This increased attention and funding brought about the development of more victim services and witness assistance programs (Davis & Henley, 1990). A national survey of such programs in 1985 reported that only 7 percent were police-based; however, by 1990, over 37 percent of law enforcement agencies housed victim service programs (Roberts, 1990; Young, 1990). Between 1984 and 1997, more than $2 billion dollars was allocated to aid victims of domestic violence, sexual assault, child abuse, and other violent crimes, and in 1994, the Federal Violence Against Women Act provided more funding for these programs (Brownell & Roberts, 1999). The Federal Law Enforcement and Crime Control Act of 1994 also allocated billions of dollars to state and city police departments to develop crisis intervention and domestic violence counseling programs. By 1999, there were close to 10,000 victim/witness assistance, victim services, domestic violence, and sexual assault treatment programs nationwide (Brownell & Roberts, 2002).

In October, the Violence Against Women Act of 2000 was signed into law by President Clinton, extending VAWA through 2005, and authorizing funding at $3.3 billion over the five-year period ("Crime victim's rights," 2004). Also in 2000, Congress designated an additional $7.4 million from the Crime Victims Fund to support creating 112 full-time positions for victim assistance specialists in the Federal Bureau of Investigation (FBI), and in 2001, a second earmark was established to support additional victim/witness efforts by the FBI and U.S. Attorneys' Offices (OVC, 2002). By the end of 2002, all 50 states, the District of Columbia, U.S. Virgin Islands, Puerto Rico, and Guam have established crime victim compensation programs (OVC, 2004). In 2003, the Office of Victims of Crime celebrated its 20th anniversary, and Congress made the Office on Violence Against Women (formally the Violence Against Women Office within the Office of Justice Programs) a permanent independent office within the U.S. Department of Justice ("Crime victim's rights," 2004).

TYPES OF PROGRAMS AND SERVICES

At the national level, the Office of Victims of Crime (OVC) is the most significant federal agency for victim assistance, and the OVC is responsible for distributing federal funding to state agencies and other programs that provide victim assistance at the local levels (McCormack, 1997). The OVC website (www.ovc.gov) provides resources and links to other government and victim advocacy organization. The OVC also provides training and resources for professionals and disseminates research and evaluation on victim assistance programs.

Another important victim advocacy organization is the National Organization for Victim Assistance (NOVA), which is a private, nonprofit organization of victim and witness assistance programs and practitioners, criminal justice agencies and professionals, mental health professionals, researchers, former victims and survivors, and others committed to the recognition and implementation of victim rights and services. Founded in 1975, NOVA is the oldest national group of its kind in the worldwide victims' movement, and its mission is to promote rights and services for victims of crime and crisis everywhere (About NOVA, 2005). The organization provides direct services for victims and survivors, training and resources for professionals, research and evaluation, and advocacy on legislative mandates. The NOVA website (www.trynova.org) is a resource for those who want to learn more or join this organization. There are many other victim rights and advocacy organization including:

- *National Center for Victims of Crime (NCVC)* – advocacy and resource center striving to forge a national commitment to help victims of crime rebuild their lives.

- *Safe Horizon* (formerly Victim Services Agency) – direct service, emergency shelter, research, crime prevention and advocacy organization for domestic violence, rape, child abuse, assault victims, victims of school violence, and survivors of homicide. The largest city-wide victim service and victim advocacy not-for-profit agency in the United States with over 700 employees located in all five boroughs of New York City.
- *Crime Victims for a Just Society* – promotes progressive solutions to the issues of crime and violence.
- *Homicide Victim Support Group* – offers emotional help and support for secondary victims of crime at regular meetings.
- *National Sexual Violence Resource Center* – A central clearinghouse for resources, research, help and support. The NSVRC influences policy, practice and research by providing interaction, investigation, and awareness.

At the state level, *victim/witness assistance programs* were established through the Attorney General's Offices to minimize revictimization by the criminal justice system, and to encourage cooperation by victims and witnesses during the court process. The primary objectives of such programs include:

- Informing victims/witnesses of their rights to receive dignified and compassionate treatment by criminal justice professionals;
- Informing victims about compensation and restitution benefits to which they are entitled;
- Providing information to victims/witnesses on the court process and trial notification;
- Providing orientation to court proceedings, court preparation, and accompaniment (Roberts, (1990).

These programs are located in the district attorney or prosecutor's office, and are mandated to provide information and assistance about victim compensation benefits and the legal process, and to notify the victim/survivor about his/her legal rights. An example of a legal right is the *victim impact statement*, which is a way for victims and survivors to confront the defendant and impact sentencing by reading a statement at the trial that describes how the offense affected him/her and their families. Other services include assisting with protective orders in family violence cases, being an advocate with the attorneys and other legal officials in the court system, assisting prosecutors in witness testimony preparation, providing crisis intervention and referrals for other follow-up services in the local community. Other important aspects of being a victim/witness assistance counselor are hearing/trial notification, and arranging transportation, housing, and accompaniment to the court proceedings to provide support.

Victim service programs offer crisis intervention and are located primarily in law enforcement agencies at the federal, state, and local levels, but they are not mandated by federal or state legislation, as are victim/witness assistance programs. Typically, these programs offer a comprehensive range of essential services with the primary objectives of:

- Providing early and timely crisis intervention to crime victims and family survivors;
- Using a team approach with police officers to aid during the investigation and victim/witness statements;
- Providing referrals for emergency assistance and follow-up services through community and social services agencies;
- Assisting with completing victim compensation applications (Roberts, 1990).

Many victim service programs were started in the 1980s through federal grant funding, and some programs are funded internally by the local city/county government. Victim service programs range from large units employing dozens of counselors and social workers to one-person offices, depending on the jurisdiction size of the police department. Some programs have *crisis teams,* which are mobile units that work on-the-scene with police officers, and other programs may be limited to day services with an on-call person for emergencies.

There are quite a range of types of services provided by these programs, which depend on the police chief, law enforcement officers, and other local government officials for support and funding. The most common services are crisis intervention on-the-scene or immediately following the incident, short-term counseling, assistance and referrals for the victim's immediate needs, death notification to family members, advocacy and assistance during the investigative process, and assistance with victim compensation

forms. Depending on the scope of the program, victim services workers may use a team approach with the local domestic violence shelter, rape crisis center, and mental health authorities.

Victims and survivors of crimes are eligible for financial compensation for medical and counseling expenses, lost wages, and other costs incurred as a result of the offense. All states have victim compensation programs that are funded from criminal fines and probation/parole fees. These programs are located in the state's Attorney General's Office, where the application forms are submitted, reviewed, and approved, and where the funds are distributed and administered. In Texas, claims may be approved for benefits up to a total of $50,000. These funds may be paid to the victim/claimant or to service providers on behalf of the victim. Approved claims may be awarded compensation for the following expenses related to the crime:

- medical, hospital, physical therapy or nursing care
- psychiatric care or counseling
- loss of earnings or support
- loss of wages due to participation in, or attendance at, the investigation, prosecutorial and judicial processes, and travel
- care of a child or a dependent
- funeral and burial expenses
- crime scene clean-up
- replacement costs for clothing, bedding, or property seized as evidence or rendered unusable as a result of the investigation
- reasonable attorney fees for assistance in filing the Crime Victims' Compensation application and in obtaining benefits, if the claim is approved
- loss of wages and travel to seek medical treatment
- one time relocation expenses for domestic violence victims or for those sexual assault victims attacked in their own residence

In the case of catastrophic injuries resulting in a total and permanent disability, the victim may be eligible for $75,000 in benefits for:

- making a home or car accessible
- job training and vocational rehabilitation
- training in the use of special appliances
- home health care
- reimbursement of lost wages ("Crime victim services," 2005)

EVIDENCED-BASED RESEARCH FINDINGS

Dziegielewski and Powers (2005) recently documented the ample evidence supportive of the effectiveness of time-limited crisis intervention with victims of violent crimes, community disasters, and other crisis-inducing events. One of the earliest and most influential research projects was a national study of 184 victim service and prosecutor-based and police-based victim/witness assistance programs by Roberts (1990). This study examined the extent, trends, patterns of program development, and type of services offered by these programs. The respondents (n=184) from a sample of 305 programs represented prosecutor's offices, state's attorneys, police departments, nonprofit agencies, hospitals, criminal justice agencies, and the U.S. Attorney's Office. The highest return rate was from prosecutors (58%) with police departments only having a 7 percent return rate (Roberts, 1990). Demographic information was collected to determine when programs began, how many victims were served, staffing patterns, sources of funding, sources of referrals, and educational backgrounds of staff. The highest degree earned by the largest percentage of staff (47.8%, n=259) was a BA/BS, with MSW's comprising the next largest percentage (15.1%, n=82), and BSW's ranking fourth with 10.3 percent (n=56) out of a total of 541 responses (Roberts, 1990).

The four most frequently offered services were explaining the court process (71%), making referrals (69%), providing court escort (65%), and helping with victim compensation applications (64%), which may reflect a sample bias since the majority of respondents were from prosecutor's offices (Roberts, 1990). Other services provided were public education (61%), assistance with employers (60%), providing transportation to court (59%), and crisis intervention (54%); providing child care (38%), emergency money (25%) and repairing locks (12%) were the least offered services (Roberts, 1990). When responding to what changes the programs would make if they had more money, 54% (n=80) of the respondents wanted to hire more staff, 28% (n=29) wanted more office space, and 14% (n=18) wanted to establish a 24-hour crisis intervention program (Roberts, 1990).

The findings showed that programs affiliated with police departments were more likely to provide crisis intervention and home visits than those located in prosecutor's offices, which focused more on court-related activities and assistance. This study was important in identifying and evaluating the development of victim services and victim/witness assistance programs after the tremendous growth of such programs in the 1980s. It gave professionals working in these programs valuable knowledge about the beginning development of this practice field, and what directions they needed to take to meet the future needs of victims and survivors.

A study that examined the prevalence of Post-Traumatic Stress Disorder (PTSD) and victim service utilization by crime victims and family members (n=251) recently involved in the criminal justice system found that about half of the participants evidenced PTSD diagnostic criteria (Freedy, Resnick, Kilpatrick, Dansky, & Tidwell, 1994). Of the 251 participants, 51 percent had been the victim of a direct crime such as physical assault (37.5%), sexual assault (12.5%), robbery (17.2%), and burglary (32.8%). Of the remaining participants, family members (49%), who were indirect victims, suffered from the following crimes, homicide (50.4%), sexual assault (34.1%), physical assault (13%), and burglary/robbery (2.4%) (Freedy et al., 1994).

This telephone survey gathered demographic information about the participants, who had been the victim or family member of a victim in a recent criminal court case during the past year, the crime characteristics, their experiences with the criminal justice system, and their mental health. The relationship between the type of crime and PTSD symptoms was significant with the homicide death of a family member showing the strongest correlation at 71.1 percent suffering from PTSD symptoms, and 59.4 percent of victims of physical assault and 55.2 percent of victims of sexual assault also scored in the clinical range (Freedy et al., 1994). In contrast, the direct and indirect victims of the less violent crimes, burglary (18.6%) and robbery (29.2%), reported fewer PTSD symptoms (Freedy et al., 1994).

The research participants' opinions concerning their needs and access to services indicated that the majority believed the criminal justice system should provide the following services versus the percentage that actually received such services (Freedy et al., 1994):

Table 10-1

Type of Service	Percent think CJS should provide	Percent received the service
Psychological counseling	91.2	39.4
Case status information	98.9	59.7
Personal protection	95.8	44.1
Legal assistance	94.4	58.3
Social service referrals	93.4	43.8
Assistance dealing with the police/courts	98.3	60.4

These findings reflect dissonance between what victims/family survivors want from the criminal justice system, and what they actually received. Furthermore, victims who were involved with the criminal justice system for longer periods of time did not report more access to services (Freedy et al., 1994). Only a majority of the sexual assault victims reported that they had received psychological counseling, and less than a third of all of the participants received any psychological services related to their victimization (Freedy et al. 1994). It appears from these findings that while there was growth in victim service programs in the 1990s, there was also limited access to some needed services.

Another study that examined the psychological impacts and use of professional help by crime victims showed similar results with higher percentages of victims of more serious crimes evidencing symptoms of PTSD than victims of trivial crimes or non-victims (Johnson, 1997). This study gathered data from two telephone interviews conducted with 664 participants from a statewide sample generated from random digit-dialing procedures. The participants responded to an 18-item crime incidence battery, which was a modification of the National Crime Survey. Psychological symptoms were measured using the Brief Symptom Inventory (BSI) developed by Derogatis and Spencer (1982). There were 241 participants who had experienced a violent crime during the previous six months, 476 property crime participants, and 377 nonvictim participants (Johnson, 1997). Six months after the initial contact, the participants were called again to examine their current level of PTSD symptoms and use and helpfulness of health, legal and victim services.

This study found the use of police services to be high (68%), but only 12 percent of crime victims received some type of mental health services, 9 percent needed medical services, and 20 percent used legal services (Johnson, 1997). Two-thirds of the respondents (67%) who called the police rated the quality of service as somewhat helpful or very helpful, 66 percent found the legal services to be helpful, and 92 percent indicated that the mental health services were helpful (Johnson, 1997). However, when the study evaluated whether using mental health services resulted in a decrease of PTSD symptoms, the results showed that use and a favorable assessment of mental health services were associated with an increase in psychological distress, even 6–12 months later (Johnson, 1997). Another interesting finding was that the victims who used legal services 6–12 months after receiving mental health services reported lower levels of psychological distress than those who did not use legal services, which points out the need for continued mental health services and crisis intervention counseling during the court proceedings (Johnson, 1997).

In 1997–1998, the Crime Victims' Institute of the Office of the Attorney General in Texas conducted a baseline study to document the extent and nature of services available to crime victims, and to understand how existing services meet the needs of crime victims in Texas. The study had three phases, with phase one surveying over 1,400 crime victim service providers, phase two surveying over 8,200 crime victims/survivors, and phase three convening six regional focus groups with the assistance of university faculty (OAG, 1998).

In phase one, provider surveys were mailed to district and county attorneys (prosecutors) (n=154), family violence and sexual assault programs (n=121), police departments (n=758), sheriff's offices (n=254), and probation departments (n=122). The highest return rates were from the probation departments (67.2%), the victim assistance programs from the prosecutors' offices (55.2%), and the family violence and sexual assault programs (51.2%); return rates from the police departments (38.7%) and sheriff's offices (46.9%) were the lowest (OAG, 1998). A summary of the key findings highlighted the following categories:

• **Funding:** 86.1 percent of the law enforcement agencies, 87.5 percent of the probation departments, and 57.9 percent of the prosecutors' offices received no funding for crime victim services. All of the family violence and sexual assault programs received partial or full funding from various local, state, and federal sources. Of those programs that received funding, nearly 80 percent reported that the funds were from city/county sources, with the remaining funds coming from the United Way, private donations, state agencies, and the Office of the Governor (federal funds from VOCA and VAWA) (OAG, 1998). Unfortunately, it appears that law enforcement agencies who have the initial contacts with crime victims don't receive the funding needed for staff and salaries, resulting in high turn over rates and burnout of staff, which was also reported in the focus groups in phase three of the research project.

• *Staff:* The Texas legislature mandates that each prosecutors' office designate a victim assistance coordinator, with 98.8 percent indicating that their office did have one; however, the study findings indicated that does not always mean there are sufficient staff to meet victims' needs, particularly in rural areas (OAG, 1998). And, 35 percent of the police departments and sheriffs' offices did not have a designated crime victim liaison, even though they are also mandated to designate a crime victim liaison. Many responded that they relied on the prosecutors' crime victim assistance coordinators, and rural areas reported difficulties in assigning a liaison because of limited staff and a relatively low crime incidence and lack of perceived need (OAG, 1998).

• *Present Services and Usefulness:* Many victims indicated that they were not informed of their constitutional rights as victims with over 30 percent not being informed of court proceedings, and at least 40 percent of the respondents said they were never informed of their right to receive protection from their offenders, about victims compensation, or being informed about sentencing and parole procedures (OAG, 1998). The six most requested services by victims were case information, medical services, spiritual counseling, follow-up services, professional counseling, and education services. Sexual assault victims were most likely to receive professional counseling along with surviving family members of homicide and intoxication manslaughter victims, and the victims revealed that all services were useful, but professional and spiritual counseling were found to be most useful (OAG, 1998). Of service providers of direct crime victim services, only 28.2 percent reported providing crisis intervention and counseling services, 7 percent had spiritual counseling, and 10.5 percent provided family or victim therapy (OAG, 1998).

• *Information Management:* Most victim service providers do not maintain demographic data on the clients they serve, and only 7.6 percent of the respondents said they had automated systems for client data collection. Those respondents did report that automated capabilities improved the quality and quantity of victim information (OAG, 1998). Although case information is the third most requested service, only 22.8 percent of law enforcement agencies provided such information. Most probation departments (76.8%) and prosecutors' offices (90.6%) did provide case information (OAG, 1998). These findings support the previous reported research findings in respect to the lack of availability of needed services but that those services that were utilized were found useful by victims.

A study that examined police officer perceptions and utilization of a domestic violence response team, where social workers and trained volunteers provided crisis intervention at the scene, provides a different perspective on the effectiveness of victim service programs and staff (Corcoran, Stephenson, Perryman, & Allen, 2001). Since crisis teams are housed at law enforcement agencies, it is important that, from the police perspective, those services are seen as positive and contributing. This survey was conducted two years after the implementation of the domestic violence response team (DVRT), and of the 219 participants, 144 (66%) had called out the DVRT to the scene, and 89 (41%) had been on calls to which the DVRT had responded. The majority (55%) had called out the DVRT between 2–10 times, and 173 (79%) thought the DVRT was helpful (Corcoran, et al., 2001).

Those officers who had not called out the DVRT reported the following reasons: 95 (43%) believed the situation was inappropriate for calling out the DVRT, 37 (17%) stated the team had already logged off duty, 14 (6%) reported the DVRT arrival time was too long, and 7 (3%) were unsure of what the DVRT could do (Corcoran et al., 2001). Officer feedback on the DVRT services showed that 61 (28%) of the officers thought the team provided follow-up services to the victim, 135 (62%) said the team helped fill out protective orders, 62 (28%) reported the team transported the victim to a shelter, 101 (46%) said the team explained the criminal justice system and gave referrals, and 68 (31%) reported the team members counseled the victim (Corcoran et al., 2001). Officers were also asked how the DVRT could be more helpful, and 70 (32%) respondents indicated that the team should be available more hours, 42 (19%) thought the team could work calls other than domestic violence, and 47 (22%) said the team should provide continuing education to officers (Corcoran et al., 2001). This study reflects the importance of using a team approach and having the support of law enforcement officers when working together.

Knox and Roberts (2002) conducted a national study of law enforcement agencies from California, Colorado, Indiana, New Jersey, New York, South Carolina, Tennessee, and Texas. Six hundred twenty-eight surveys were mailed to designated victim liaisons in rural towns, mid-sized cities, and large urban areas, who were identified through each state's Attorney General's Office, with only 111 completed surveys returned. Those respondents indicated that 74 percent of police departments provide 24-hour crisis intervention services, with 55 percent responding to requests by patrol officers on the scene and 70 percent providing on-call services. The primary locations for these programs are in police stations (72%) or sheriff's offices (19%) (Knox & Roberts, 2002). This research study focused on three main areas:

• *Social Work Direct Services and Roles:* Respondents indicated that *direct services and counseling roles* begin with the crisis intervention and on-the scene work; however, one-third of the victim service programs also provide short-term counseling services with referral to other community and social service agencies for long-term treatment. Other *mental health services* include conducting mental health assessments (13%) or working with the mental health unit (20%). The majority of these programs have telephone (75%) or letter (52%) *follow-up* with victims and family survivors to inquire about the need for further services or to answer questions about the criminal case (Knox & Roberts, 2002).

The role of *broker* is essential with 90 percent of these programs referring clients to appropriate community and social service agencies. *Basic needs services* are provided through home visits (64%), transportation services (56%), and emergency assistance funds (52%). *Investigative services and roles* include videotaping witness statements (24%), death notification (80%),

hostage negotiation (36%), and debriefing (45%). The role of *educator* is apparent with victim services staff providing training for law enforcement personnel (87%) and community volunteers (68%), and with 72 percent of the programs surveyed involved in public education. *Community level activities* include crisis-response teams with community volunteers (19%) and direct services for natural disasters/accidents (44%). The role of *advocate* is also important with 35 percent of the programs involved at this level of practice. Opportunities for social work student *volunteers* (34%) and *student internships* (16%) are also available with these victim service programs (Knox & Roberts, 2002).

• *Staffing Patterns:* Staffing patterns from this survey range from small, one-person programs (48%) to larger programs with support staff and volunteer components (Knox & Roberts, 2002). These findings are consistent with Roberts' earlier study (1990) which indicated that three-fourths of the programs were staffed by five or fewer full-time employees, and that more than half (53%) relied on volunteers to provide needed services. Approximately 24 percent of the respondents employ social workers with either a BSW or MSW degree and license, compared to only 4 percent with a professional counseling education/license, and 30 percent of the program staff have a bachelor's or master's degree. None of the programs reported having a licensed psychologist, psychiatrist, or nurse/RN on staff (Knox & Roberts, 2002).

• *Theoretical Models:* The primary theoretical model used by the responding victims services programs was crisis intervention (68%), with grief and bereavement therapy used by 23 percent of the programs surveyed; other identified approaches that are used include brief or time-limited treatment (20%), cognitive-behavioral approaches (9%), family therapy (9%), reality and/or rational-emotive (RET) therapy (9%), art/play therapy (5%), and eye-movement desensitization and reprocessing (EMDR) (3%) (Knox & Roberts, 2002). These models reflect the need for short-term treatment and a focus on immediate needs, not past issues or problems requiring long-term treatment.

The most recent statewide survey explored the reasons for use and/or nonuse of victim service programs through a survey of crime victims in the Commonwealth of Pennsylvania (Sims, Yost, & Abbott, 2005). This study consisted of two major components: first was an in-depth inventory of the types of programs currently provided, and second, was the extent to which crime victims made use of those available services and differences between users and non-users. Surveys were mailed to 211 with 79 percent (n=166) respondents. To identify victims of crime who did not use services, a statewide, random telephone survey was conducted to determine whether any household member had experienced any criminal victimization during the previous twelve months. The final sample included 654 crime victims of which only 3 percent reported using any victim service (Sims et al., 2005). To identify victims of crime who did use victim services, participating agencies provided a database of clients served in the 2001–2002 fiscal year. Random samples for each agency were generated, and the programs then contacted individuals to see if they were willing to participate. However, the final sample of crime victim services users was smaller than anticipated with only 206 participants, due to several agencies not cooperating with the researchers (Sims et al., 2005).

Findings of the types of available victim services indicated that 31 percent were victim/witness programs, 28 percent were community-based victim services agencies, 24 percent were domestic abuse centers, and 4 percent were rape crisis centers. On average, respondent agencies reported the following most commonly offered services: court accompaniment (95%), justice support/advocacy (89%), follow-up services (87%), crisis intervention/counseling (86%), community outreach (85%, and crime victims' compensation (81%). Referrals were received from several sources including the police (44%), social service agencies (43%), employees within the justice system (36%), mailings (32%), and medical personnel (24%) (Sims et al., 2005).

Data from the crime victims' surveys (both users and nonusers) were combined in an effort to determine the differences between the two groups. Fewer than 3 percent of crime victims from the telephone survey reported using any victim services, with 43 percent reporting that they were never informed of any available services. Also, only 27 percent of nonusers surveyed knew that crisis intervention services were available, and 40 percent said they did not know what kinds of services were offered by victim service programs. The study reported that nearly half of all nonusers felt that family and friends could give them the help they needed, that they did not need

any help, or that they could solve their own problems (Sims et al., 2005).

Only the type of crime and age were significant predictors of use/nonuse of victim services with those suffering a violent crime being more likely to use services, and as age increased, so did the likelihood that individuals sought the use of victim services. The most obvious reason for not using victim services was a lack of knowledge about such services. These findings mirror previous studies, which indicates that not much has changed since the 1980s. The researchers recommend that victim service providers need to put forth a greater effort in educating the public about their services (Sims et al., 2005).

PRACTICE IMPLICATIONS

Evidence from the research indicates that there are three main practice implications. First, victims service programs must do a better job of educating the public and increasing awareness about their services. The research findings across studies report that victims who don't access services are unaware of and not informed about what services are already available in their communities. Since most victims receive their initial contact with the police, one strategy is to require police officers to hand out brochures or cards that provide information and contact numbers for services. Other ideas are to conduct neighborhood or town hall meetings, do public service announcements on local news and radio shows, and to use other media (newspapers or community fliers) to highlight programs and services.

Second, victim service programs need to focus on those victims who are most likely to need and utilize services. The research findings show that those who experience more traumatic, serious offenses, those who are most vulnerable, and those who have the fewest resources are more likely to access services (Stohr, 2005). This is particularly important for programs that are understaffed so that their efforts are directed at the victims who are most in need and can benefit best from their services.

Third, interagency coordination and cooperation between community victim service providers are necessary to meet the multiple needs of victims. Many community agencies have had to consolidate their programs to continue to provide services in today's competitive economic market for funding. Victim service providers should stress the importance of an interactive approach by law enforcement, social services, local and county government, federal funding, social work professionals and educators, and the criminal justice system. To meet the needs of victims, witnesses, and family survivors, coordination of services is essential in providing a continuity of services along the criminal justice system to minimize the negative impacts and revictimization in the aftermath of violent crime. If experiences with the past obstacles encountered in police social work are to be heeded, then the support and commitment of all the essential providers need to be included in a comprehensive community plan.

In direct practice with victims and survivors, best practices in crisis work means being educated and trained in the most effective treatment models used in crisis intervention, and having knowledge and expertise about specific treatment issues, including sexual assault, domestic violence, and child abuse. Other specialized knowledge about the criminal justice and mental health systems, and other community resources is necessary to be effective on the scene, where you may not have access to a computer or other resource materials to make appropriate referrals. Developing certification and training programs for victim service providers would provide standardization of best practices. Stohr (2005) identifies the following best practices for victim service programs and providers:

- Identifying the multiple needs of clients;
- Focusing services on those who need them most;
- Configuring the programs to fit the most pressing needs;
- Attracting, firing, training, and maintaining skilled and knowledgeable staff;
- Involving clients in their own case and service decisions;
- Providing follow-up or after care services; and
- Building in process and outcome evaluations to enhance service development.

FUTURE TRENDS AND RECOMMENDATIONS

Opportunities to improve and coordinate victim service programs need to be explored at both the local community and statewide levels. The research tells us that there are many strengths and opportunities in victim service programs and police social work, as well as problems and obstacles to receiving services. The research findings from the Texas Crime Victims' Institute's study led to the following recommendations, which were included in the Executive Summary of the Final Report:

- Provide funding for those crime victim services and staff positions required by state law;
- Require law enforcement agencies and prosecutors' offices to report annually their designated crime victim liaison to the Crime Victims' Institute and the Texas Crime Victim Clearinghouse;
- Establish minimum basic service guidelines for criminal justice agencies and receiving state funding;
- Mandate that criminal justice agencies use a standardized form to collect victim information/data that will be developed by the Crime Victims' Institute.
- Develop state-wide certification or set minimum standards for victim services providers;
- Study the feasibility or a state-wide system for victim notification and collection of victim-related information;
- Examine the reasons why certain victims' rights mandated by the state constitution are not being provided;
- Evaluate the needs of minority and ethnic groups and the types of services provided to them; and
- Study the needs of victims of violent juvenile offenders and child victims (OAG, 1998).

Several of these recommendations have been implemented in Texas, one being the certification and training program. Texas State University-San Marcos Department of Criminal Justice, along with the Crime Victims' Institute and many local victim witness programs and professionals, held the first training program three years ago.

Social work practice has a long one hundred year history in law enforcement settings. Its recent re-emergence has pointed out the need for support and commitment from the schools of social work and the major professional associations, such as the National Association of Social Workers (NASW) and the

Council on Social Work Education (CSWE). This renewal of purpose and commitment to working with crime victims, witnesses, and family survivors is needed to meet their needs. Police social workers may have only brief and episodic contact with their clients, but this type of intervention is of an urgent and emergency nature (Roberts, 1997b).

Victim services counselors and social workers need to be trained to work with a wide range of criminal offenses, mental health problems, family violence situations, child abuse and neglect, and drug/alcohol related offenses. Specialized knowledge of the dynamics and behaviors associated with these problem areas is essential and can be provided by social work education programs and continuing education conferences/workshops. Some of these practice areas are offered as electives by social work programs; however, only 10 percent of accredited BSW and MSW programs offer an elective course in criminal justice social work (McNeece & Roberts, 1997). Approximately one-third of the program directors or coordinators of victim services and assistance programs have an MSW degree (Roberts, 1995). These facts point out the need for more emphasis by social work educators to prepare students for this practice field.

The role of social workers in victim services and victim/witness assistance programs is expanding and will continue to receive support from a variety of sources. The problems with prison overcrowding and high recidivism rates has resulted in increased support for mediation, victim impact panels, and restitution services for victims has forced the criminal justice system to implement new approaches to deal with victims' rights and compensation (Gandy, 1997). Therefore, it is important that social workers in victim services be well trained and recognized by their professional schools, educators, and associations.

Social workers can impact at all levels of practice in victim services – at the individual, family, group, community, and macro levels – to improve services and responses by the criminal justice system. Social work researchers and educators can assist community and governmental agencies in conducting studies to evaluate the effectiveness of victim service programs and to determine what content on victims is being taught in social work programs. Social workers must take advantage of such opportunities in the field of victim services that will enable them to provide leadership and direction for police-based social work in the future.

REFERENCES

About NOVA. (2005). Retrieved September 25, 2005, from www.trynova.org.

Brownell, P., & Roberts, A. R. (1999). A century of forensic social work: Bridging the past to the present. *Social Work, 44*(4), 359–370.

Brownell, P., & Roberts, A.R. (2002). A century of social work in criminal justice and correctional settings. *Journal of Offender Rehabilitation, (35)*2, 1–17.

Corcoran, J., Stephenson M., Perryman, D., & Allen, S. (2001). Perceptions and utilization of a police-social work crisis intervention approach to domestic violence. *Families in Society, 82*(4), 393–398.

Crime victims' rights in America: An historical overview. (2004). Office for Victims of Crime, U.S. Department of Justice National Crime Victims Rights Week Resource Guide. Retrieved September 28, 2005, from ://www.boc.ca.gov/40thAnniversaryHistoricalOverview.htm.

Crime victim services: Assisting victims of violent crime. (2005). Retrieved September 25, 2005, from www.oag.state.tx.us/victims/victims.html.

Davis, R., & Henley, M. (1990). Victim service programs. In A. Lurigio, W. Skogan & R. Davis, (Eds.), *Victims of crime: Problems, policies, and programs* (pp. 157–171). Newbury Park, CA: Sage.

Derogatis, L. R., & Spencer, M. S. (1982). *The Brief Symptom Inventory (BSI): Administration, scoring, and procedures manual - 1.* Baltimore: Johns Hopkins University School of Medicine, Clinical Psychometrics Research Unit.

Dzielieweski, S. F., & Powers, J. T. (2005). Designs and procedures for evaluating crisis intervention. In A. R. Roberts (Ed.), *Crisis intervention handbook: Assessment, treatment and research* (pp. 742–773). New York: Oxford University Press.

Freedy, J. R., Resnick, H. S., Kilpatrick, D. G., Dansky, B. S., & Tidwell, R. P. (1994). The psychological adjustment of recent crime victims in the criminal justice system. In M. P. McShane & F. P. Williams, III (Eds.), *Victims of crime and the victimization process* (pp. 94–112). New York: Garland.

Gandy, J. (1997). Social work and victim assistance programs. In A. R. Roberts (Ed.), *Social work in juvenile and criminal justice settings* (2nd ed., pp. 160–178). Springfield, IL: Charles C Thomas.

Johnson, K. W. (1997). Professional help and crime victims. *Social Services Review, 7*(1), 89–109.

Knox, K. S., & Roberts, A R. (2002). Police social work. In G. Greene & A. R. Roberts (Eds.), *Social workers' desk reference* (pp. 668–672). New York: Oxford University Press.

McCormack, R. J. (1997). United states crime victim assistance: History, organization, and evaluation. In M.P. McShane & F.P. Williams, III (Eds.), *Victims of crime and the victimization process* (pp. 197–209). New York: Garland.

McNeece, A., & Roberts, A. (Eds.). (1997). *Policy and practice in the justice system.* Chicago: Nelson-Hall.

Office of the Attorney General, State of Texas, Crime Victims' Institute. (1998). *The impact of crime on victims: A baseline study on program service delivery final report.* Retrieved September 22, 2005, from www.oag.state.tx.us/AG_Publications/ pdfs/cvi_final_part2.pdf.

OVC fact sheet: Victims of crime act crime victims fund. (Jan/2002). Retrieved September 27, 2005, from http://www.ojp.usdoj.gov/ovc/publications/factshts/vocacvf/welcome.html.

OVC fact sheet: What is the office for victims of crimes? (Nov/2004). Retrieved September 27, 2005, from http://www.ojp.usdoj.gov/ovc/publications/factshts/vocacvf/welcome.html.

Roberts, A. R. (1990). *Helping crime victims: Research, policy, and practice.* Newbury Park, CA: Sage.

Roberts, A.R. (1997a). The history and role of social work in law enforcement. In A. Roberts (Ed.), *Social work in juvenile and criminal justice settings* (2nd ed. pp. 105–115). Springfield, IL: Charles C Thomas.

Roberts, A. R. (1997b). Police social work: Bridging the past to the present. In A. Roberts (Ed.), *Social work in juvenile and criminal justice settings* (2nd ed., pp. 126–132). Springfield, IL: Charles C Thomas.

Roberts, A. R. (Ed.). (2005). *Crisis intervention handbook: Assessment, treatment and research* (3rd ed.). New York: Oxford University Press.

Roberts, A.R., & Fisher, P. (1997). Service roles in victim/witness assistance programs. In A. McNeece & A. R. Roberts (Eds.), *Policy and practice in the justice system* (pp. 127–142). Chicago: Nelson-Hall.

Sims, B., Yost, B., & Abbott, C. (2005). Use and nonuse of victim service programs: Implications from a statewide survey of crime victims. *Criminology & Public Policy, 4*(2), 361–384.

Stohr, M. (2005). Victim services programming: If it is efficacious, they will come. *Criminology & Public Policy, 4*(2), 391–397.

Young, M. (1990). Victim assistance in the united states: The end of the beginning. *International Review of Victimology, 1*, 181–199.

Chapter 11

Police Social Work: Bridging the Past to the Present

Albert R. Roberts

Visualize the latest newspaper headlines related to violent carjackings, sniper shootings in a crowded shopping mall, a seventh grader who breaks four school windows because the principal yelled at her, a runaway youth with a drug problem attempting suicide by hanging in a detention cell, a domestic violence-related murder-suicide, a terrorist bombing in a large office building, or a parent who loses his/her job and is evicted and then physically batters his/her four-year-old child. These are the types of unpredictable events in which police-social work teams quickly respond.

In the aftermath of unpredictable crisis-inducing and trauma-inducing events, it is frequently difficult for youths and adults to adapt without timely intervention from law enforcement and mental health professionals. After a potentially life-threatening or highly stressful event, many individuals become vulnerable to experiencing psychological trauma and/or an acute crisis episode. Police, police-social work teams, and emergency room staff are usually the only professionals available 24 hours a day 7 days a week.

Evidence-based studies have documented the fact that the impact of acute crisis reaction can be temporary and quickly stabilized, especially when there is timely assessment, intervention, and follow-up care from police-social work teams. These specially trained police and clinical social workers know how to interact with people in the midst of a crisis reaction. They know how to establish rapport and rapidly conduct a biopsychosocial and lethality assessment. They know how to remain calm, reassuring, and supportive. They know how to respond to feelings in a nonjudgmental and neutral manner, rather than responding to the bizarre or threatening content of a person's statements. They know how to provide early support, ego bolstering, as well as helping the person examine the most realistic possible options and alternative coping skills. They know how to get closure by helping survivors, crime victims, troubled youths, and mentally unstable people to plan and implement a short-term action plan. Thus, recovery from psychological trauma and crisis resolution is optimized, and social functioning is enhanced.

HISTORICAL BACKGROUND

Unlike middle and upper class individuals who will seek help from attorneys, clergymen, marital and family therapists, and family practice physicians, individuals in the lower socioeconomic class tend to seek help from the police in times of crisis. Social work has early roots in working with the poor that dates back to the emergence of the Charity Organization Society (COS) movement in the United States in 1877. Mary Richmond and other social work pioneers conducted investigations to determine an applicant's need for relief, visited families (friendly visitor) in distress to help them to care for their children, and placed abused and neglected children in institutions.

By 1930, there were over five hundred policewomen employed by approximately two hundred police departments in large cities throughout the United States. Most of these policewomen were social workers assigned to police women's bureau or crime prevention units. These early police social workers provided social casework to women and juveniles. In the first half of the 1900s, police social work was synonymous with police women's bureaus working in protective and preventive roles with women and young girls (Roberts, 1983). The female police social workers were involved in searching for runaway girls, locating missing children and youth, helping policemen secure evidence against prostitutes, finding employment for women, serving as volunteer probation officers for juvenile delinquents, determining if persons were mentally ill, and removing children from vice-ridden taverns, abusive homes, and unsanitary environments.

PROBLEMS

Changes in political leadership, misconceptions, sexism, and role strain led to the decline of the police social worker movement in the 1950s. The election of a new mayor or city manager often led to the appointment of a new police chief. As a result, the new chief of police often would establish new sexist policies which restricted the hiring of female police social workers. There was a lot of contempt directed at women pursuing a professional career, especially police work which was viewed as a traditionally male profession. When a new police chief failed to support and fund his police women's bureau, policemen stopped referring appropriate cases and the director of the women's bureau would eventually resign. In addition, local newspapers published caricatures of policewomen "which depicted them as huge, tight-lipped masculine-looking creatures with billyclubs swinging at their sides and a revolver in hand" (Roberts, 1983, p. 98). These stereotyped exaggerations of policewomen reinforced many male police officers' prejudices against the social work roles carried out by female police officers.

RECENT HISTORICAL PERSPECTIVE

During the 1960s, a few police departments in select areas of the country utilized police social workers to provide social services to disturbed youth, adults, the elderly, and families. By the early 1970s, however, specially trained social workers were hired by police departments in both urban and suburban areas throughout the United States. Most of these police social work demonstration projects were funded by the federal Law Enforcement Assistance Administration (LEAA) through state criminal justice

planning agencies (SPAs). The most noteworthy programs were developed in police agencies throughout the states of California, Illinois, New Jersey, New York, Rhode Island, and Washington (Roberts, 1983; Treger, 1983). These police social work programs provided crisis counseling to juveniles and their parents. The police social workers also provided social work intervention to victims of domestic violence and sexual assault. By 1980, with the demise of LEAA, only a small number of police social work programs remained. When the federal seed money dried up, only the few police chiefs most committed to the police social work model continued to fund their respective police social workers. The Community Mental Health Center (CMHC) Act provided capital funding for hundreds of CMHC buildings, staffing, and program developments for a seven-year period. Unlike the LEAA funding which lasted for a few years and then was completely cut off, the CMHC grants were gradually diminished over a seven-year period. This allowed the local sponsoring agency to gradually secure an increasing amount of state, local, and private funding to replace the federal grants before they ended. Third-party payments from clients' health insurance providers also gave a much-needed boost to those mental health centers struggling to survive when federal funds ended.

Funding police social work positions within police departments has been problematic. No state has passed legislation calling for grant appropriations to fund police social workers. No private foundation or corporate sponsor has agreed to underwrite this type of program. No federal agency has provided a continual source of major funding for police social work programs. A promising source of federal funding came from the Victims of Crime Act (VOCA) of 1984 and its reauthorization in 1990 (Roberts, 1990). Six hundred and twenty million dollars had been appropriated between 1984 and 1991 for hundreds of prosecutor-based victim/witness assistance programs and for funding statewide victim compensation programs nationwide (Roberts, 1992). However, as of 1995, only a small yet growing number of police departments have received federal and county general revenue grants for victim assistance programs. By the end of 1995, criminal penalty assessments had surpassed the $1 billion mark. These fines and penalties all go into VOCA grants. The most promising source of grants for community policing is the Federal Law

Enforcement and Crime Control Act of 1994. Between 1995 and the year 2000, several billion dollars will be allocated to state, city, and township police departments. A growing number of police chiefs are developing crisis intervention and domestic violence counseling programs.

DELIVERY OF SERVICES TO CRIME VICTIMS

Fifty to ninety percent of a police officer's time is allocated to gathering information and providing social service referrals. Many individuals in distress call the police for help, particularly at times when social work and family counseling agencies are closed. As a result, law enforcement officers are thrust into situations which usually require social work knowledge and skills. Some officers enjoy talking with people and they derive good feeling from trying to help people. Social workers employed by police departments need to be sensitive to the police officers' interest in helping others (e.g., stranded or lost motorist, lost child). At the same time, police departments are operated in a military and regimental fashion. Patrol officers will follow the orders of a superior officer, but they will resent any orders from a social worker. There is an uneasy balance between the roles of many social workers and the police, and vice versa. There are several common and complementary roles between police and social workers; when these are recognized, cooperative team efforts are facilitated.

THE ROLE AND FUNCTION OF POLICE SOCIAL WORKERS

The role of the police social worker changes and expands based on the view of the social worker and the needs of the clients. Role enhancement among police social workers takes place more in the juvenile and domestic violence units than in other parts of the police department. Because of the life-threatening nature of domestic violence, and the multiple psychological needs of troubled children and youth, social workers employed by police departments are usually assigned to these units. Early casefinding interventions and/or referral to community agencies

are among the primary functions of police social workers. The most important function of police social workers is to provide short-term crisis intervention for children and families as well as filling in the gaps in services.

Crisis intervention involves working directly with troubled children, youths and their families. It also involves working with violent crime victims. A violent crime or car accident with multiple deaths can lead to both emotional trauma and acute crisis in both children and adults. Police departments are rarely prepared to handle such clients. The murder or suicide of a police officer can potentially spark a crisis among many police officers. Police departments are rarely prepared to handle such situations. A battered woman is severely injured by her mate. She and her two children (ages six and eight) are brought to the police department. Police departments are rarely prepared to help the children. In all of the above situations, police social workers are trained to respond in a sensitive and knowledgeable way. Police social workers can provide crisis intervention, grief counseling, concrete services, group counseling, family treatment, play therapy, and/or referral to victim/witness assistance programs, chemical dependency programs, and other appropriate community agencies.

The anxiety level of troubled youths, parents, and crime victims brought to the police department is usually very high. The police department is an unfamiliar and scary place for many people. Crowded and noisy urban police departments in large old buildings increase the anxiety levels of children, families, and the elderly. One of the social worker's functions is to alleviate this anxiety by offering some concerned words or assistance. The social worker usually will explain how the police department operates and what to expect next. He or she can counsel crime victims on how to get their property returned, how to apply for victim compensation, how to obtain emergency financial aid or food coupons, or how best to cope with a crisis situation. The social worker helps clients to mobilize social supports, utilize new coping skills, and develop an action plan.

Police social workers have a tremendous amount of responsibility placed on them. There is no typical day or work-week in terms of their activities. For example, the primary job responsibilities of the police social worker in a police department located in central New Jersey is as follows: Crisis intervention and short-term counseling to troubled youths, groups, and families. In addition, the social worker is a broker of social services referring juveniles and their parents to appropriate community agencies. On one day, the social worker may be counseling a runaway youth and parents of youths addicted to drugs. On another day, the social worker is conducting crisis intervention with a juvenile who shot his older brother in the head by accident, and with parents who are drug addicts and have neglected their children. In another situation, a child's parents are shot to death and the social worker finds caring parents willing to adopt the traumatized child. Referrals come to the police social worker from juvenile detectives, juvenile probation officers, the local juvenile conference committee, and high school guidance counselors. The police social worker is available to intervene in family crisis situations several nights each week. Since about all social work agencies close at 5:00 p.m., the demand for police social workers is especially critical at night.

Police social workers are trained to assist individuals and families with any social and/or emotional problems. Of all the staff in a police department, the social worker is the most knowledgeable of community agencies and social services. Very often, the police social worker functions as the department liaison to the network of community mental health, criminal justice, and social service agencies. With certain cases, the police social worker may determine that the client needs specialized social services or long-term treatment, and accordingly makes a referral. Reasons for referral include marital conflict, depression, anxiety, sexual problems, panic disorder, alcoholism, cocaine or crack addiction, suspected child sexual abuse, school problems (e.g., truancy), woman battering, and/or psychiatric problems.

CONCLUSION

Social work practice in law enforcement settings has a long history. During the 1930s and 1940s, thousands of social workers worked with victims and offenders in the criminal justice system. In the 1970s, with federal funding through the Law Enforcement Assistance Administration (LEAA), a major boost to the development of police social work took place throughout the United States. Unfortunately, with the demise of LEAA in 1981, only a few police social work programs in each state survived. The impact of this demise has been amplified in the post-9/11 world in which we live.

Social work in criminal justice settings must look to the major professional associations–NAFSW, SSWR, and NASW–for renewal of purpose and commitment to advancement of knowledge and skills. NASW has forgotten about the important and unmet social work needs of both crime victims and offenders. There are special qualities and dedication among social workers employed by police departments. Like police officers, fire fighters, and emergency room staff, police social workers have only brief and episodic contact with clients. All too often, intervention is of an urgent and emergency nature. Therefore, it is important for police social workers to be well-trained and recognized by their professional associations if they are to be prepared to meet the challenges of the twenty-first century.

REFERENCES

Berg, B. (1992). *Law enforcement: An introduction to police in society.* Needham Heights, MA: Allyn & Bacon.

Feinman, C. (1986). *Women in the criminal justice system.* New York: Praeger.

Roberts, A. R. (1983). The history and role of social work in law enforcement. In A. R. Roberts (Ed.), *Social work in juvenile and criminal justice settings* (pp. 91–103). Springfield, IL: Charles C Thomas.

Roberts, A. R. (1990). *Helping crime victims.* Newbury Park, CA: Sage.

Roberts, A. R. (1992). Victim/witness assistance programs, *F.B.I. Law Enforcement Bulletin, 61*(12):12–17.

Roberts, A. R. (Ed.). (2996). *Helping battered women: New perspectives and remedies.* New York: Oxford University Press.

Treger, H. (1983). Social work in the justice system: An overview. In A. R. Roberts (Ed.), *Social work in juvenile and criminal justice settings* (pp. 7–17). Springfield, IL: Charles C Thomas.

U.S. Department of Labor. (1931). *Juvenile court statistics.* Publication No. 200. Washington, D.C.: U.S. Government Printing Office.

U.S. Department of Labor, Women's Bureau. (1949). *The outlook for women in police work.* Bulletin No. 231. Washington, D.C.: U.S. Government Printing Office.

Section III

Juvenile Justice Policies and Practices

Assessment of Mental Health and Substance Abuse Treatment Needs in Juvenile Justice

Cathryn C. Potter and Jeffrey M. Jenson

Fernando is sprawled in a seat in the intake office of a juvenile detention center. The latest arrival on a busy Friday night, he waits for his name to be called with a disturbing glare that fades in and out to a vacant stare. Only fifteen years old, Fernando was difficult to subdue after an assault on another juvenile that led to his arrest. His classmates and peers tend to stay away from him, saying he is known to be impulsive, unpredictable, and "good with a knife." Fernando's parents and siblings report that his habit of smoking marijuana and using other drugs only accentuates his unpredictable behavior. Fernando appears glassy-eyed and lethargic following his combative posture of only an hour ago. When called to the intake desk, he struggles to his feet and crosses the room with a sign of disgust and resignation to yet another stay in juvenile detention.

INTRODUCTION

Young people like Fernando point to a common problem in the juvenile justice system: youth who suffer from mental health and substance use problems frequently do not receive the systematic assessment and treatment warranted by their complex problems. Despite advances in knowledge about the concomitant nature of mental health and substance abuse problems, juvenile justice and other major American systems of care have only recently begun to help adolescents like Fernando (Bilchik, 1998; Center for Mental Health Services, 1998; Cocozza, & Skowyra, 2000).

Evidence from studies examining the prevalence of mental health problems and substance abuse among juvenile delinquents indicates that youth in the juvenile justice system experience higher rates of co-occurring problem behaviors than other adolescents (e.g., Aarons, Brown, Rough, Garland, & Wood, 2001; Garland, Hough, McCabe, Yeh, Wood, & Aarons, 2001; Rounds-Bryant, Kristiansen, Fairbank, & Hubbard, 1998; Teplin, 2001a; Ulzen & Hamilton, 1998). However, relatively few studies have investigated the extent, nature, and overlap of these three problems (Potter & Jenson, 2003). Lack of attention to patterns of mental health and substance abuse has also hindered the development of targeted, integrated interventions for young offenders.

In this chapter, we examine the prevalence of mental health and substance abuse among youth in the juvenile justice system, consider screening and assessment needs in juvenile justice programs, and review screening and diagnostic instruments aimed at identifying mental health and substance abuse problems. We also discuss a practice model for assessment and identify complex assessment issues, including the quality of instruments, the role of assessors, and the difficulties of disentangling symptoms across problem domains.

THE SCOPE OF THE PROBLEM: PREVALENCE OF MENTAL HEALTH AND SUBSTANCE ABUSE PROBLEMS IN JUVENILE JUSTICE MENTAL HEALTH

Prevalence of Mental Health Problem Symptoms among Juvenile Delinquents

Efforts to document and understand the prevalence of mental health problems among delinquent youth date back to at least the early 1990s. In one early study, Dembo, William, and Schmeidler (1993) examined 399 youth in a detention setting using the *Symptom Checklist-90-Revised (SCL-90-R)* (Derogatis, 1993). Findings indicated that scores on nine SCL-90-R subscales were significantly higher for male and female delinquents than for a nonpatient normative reference group. Timmons-Mitchell, Brown, Schulz, Webster, Underwood, and Semple (1997) assessed the prevalence of mental health symptoms of 121 male and 52 female delinquents in the Ohio juvenile justice system. Girls reported significantly more mental health problems than boys; 27 percent of boys and 84 percent of girls exceeded at least one clinical problem cut-off score on the *SCL-90-R*. Girls had significantly higher scores than boys on 11 of 12 *SCL-90-R* scales and on overall measures of mental health severity. Gender differences were most pronounced for interpersonal sensitivity, hostility, and depression; girls displayed a significantly greater number of symptoms than boys in each of these problem domains.

Potter and Jenson (2003) used the *Brief Symptom Inventory (BSI)* (Derogatis, 1994), a short version of the *SCL-90-R*, to examine mental health symptoms among 155 youth in detention settings. They found that 41 percent of youth scored in the "warning range" (T-scores greater than 60) on at least one subscale. Approximately a quarter of the sample scored in the warning range on the depression subscale; 21 percent, 17 percent, and 14 percent of youth reached warning levels on psychoticism, anxiety, and paranoid ideation respectively. Potter and Jenson (2001) also used the *SCL-90-R* with 115 boys in a maximum security, forensic setting and found that 63 percent of boys scored in the warning range in at least one area. One-third of youth scored in this range on the anxiety, depression, and psychoticism subscales.

The *Massachusetts Youth Screening Instrument (MAYSI-2)* (Grisso, Barnum, Fletcher, Cauffman, & Peuschold, 2001) has been used in several investigations to estimate mental health problem symptoms in juvenile justice samples. In one study, Grisso and Barnum (2003) found that between eight and 12 percent of boys and 12 and 25 percent of girls exceeded a clinical warning cut-off score on at least one of the five *MAYSI-2* scales. A higher percentage of boys exceeded warning scores on alcohol and drug use (12% vs. 10%) and on angry-irritable (16% vs. 10%), depressed-anxious

(15% vs. 8%), somatic complaints (12% vs. 6%), and suicide ideation (25% vs. 8%) scales.

Dieterich, Jenson, and Potter (2001) used the *MAYSI-2* to assess mental health problem symptoms among 97 youth in two Colorado juvenile detention centers. Twenty-two percent of detainees exceeded the warning range on the alcohol and drug use scale. Twenty-one percent and 19 percent of youth scored at or above the warning cut-off on the suicide ideation and angry-irritable scales, respectively. Thirteen percent of youth exceeded the warning range on the depression scale. Twenty-eight percent of the sample had two or more *MAYSI-2* scales that exceeded the warning score criteria.

In another Colorado study, Jenson and Dieterich (2001) examined *MAYSI-2* scores across four juvenile justice groups that included youth who had been committed to the state division of youth corrections, detained, placed on probation, or diverted from the justice system. Forty-eight percent of committed youth, 26 percent of probationers, 25 percent of youth placed in diversion programs, and 21 percent of detainees had one or more *MAYSI-2* scale scores that exceeded the warning cut-off score.

Taken together, these studies of mental health problem symptoms indicate that a substantial number of youth display immediate mental health problem symptoms. The prevalence of these symptoms is greater among youth in higher security levels of the juvenile justice system and higher for girls than for boys. Among detained youth, estimates of problem symptoms for boys range from 8 to 41 percent; estimates for girls vary from 12 to 84 percent. While variations in instruments and samples have contributed to imprecise prevalence estimates, it is common to find at least a quarter of delinquent youth in the juvenile justice to have elevated scores on a number of mental health problem symptoms. We turn next to a discussion of psychiatric disorders among delinquent youth.

Prevalence of Psychiatric Disorders among Juvenile Delinquents

Timmons-Mitchell et al. (1997) found high rates of mental disorder in a sample of 50 youth in juvenile justice facilities using the *Diagnostic Interview Schedule for Children (DISC)* (Shaffer, Fisher, Piacentini, Schwab-Stone, & Wicks, 1989). Not surprisingly, almost all youth in their study met diagnostic criteria for conduct disorder. In addition, more than 80 percent of boys and 50 percent of girls met criteria for substance abuse disorder; between 50 and 70 percent of youth met criteria for attention-deficit/hyperactivity disorder (ADHD) and mood, anxiety, and sleep disorders. Moreover, both males and females in the Timmons-Mitchell et al. (1997) study averaged just over five diagnoses. Atkins, Pumariega, Rodgers, Montgomery, Nybro, Jeffers, and Sease (1999) used the *DISC* (Shaffer et al., 1989) to examine diagnoses among 75 youth in juvenile justice settings, finding that 72 percent met criteria for at least one diagnosis. Forty-five percent (45%) met criteria for psychosis, 43 percent for any disruptive category, 33 percent for any anxiety category, and 24 percent for any mood category. Atkins et al. found that 72 percent of youth in juvenile justice settings met criteria for at least one diagnosis compared to 86 percent of young people in community mental health services in the same region.

Ulzen and Hamilton (1998) compared the prevalence of psychiatric disorders between 49 incarcerated adolescents and 49 nondelinquents. The *Diagnostic Interview for Children and Adolescents-Revised (DICA-R)* (Welner, Reich, Herjanic, Jung, & Amado, 1987) was used to determine diagnoses. Sixty-nine percent of incarcerated youth and 12 percent of nonincarcerated youth had two or more disorders. Delinquent youth had significantly higher rates of depression (14% vs. 1%), anxiety (31% vs. 14%), attention-deficit, and hyperactivity (27% vs. 2%) than their nondelinquent counterparts.

Teplin (2001b) assessed mental health disorders among 1,800 juvenile detainees in Cook County, Illinois, using the *DISC.* She found that 66 percent of boys and 74 percent of girls met criteria for at least one diagnosis, with girls meeting criteria in significantly greater numbers for affective and anxiety disorders and boys in greater numbers for ADHD and substance disorders. Fifty percent of boys and 47 percent of girls met criteria for at least one substance abuse disorder. Garland et al. (2001) assessed psychiatric disorders among 478 youth in the juvenile justice system in California, using the *DISC-Version IV* (Shaffer, Fisher, Lucas, Dulcan, & Schwab-Stone, 2000). Fifty-two percent (52%) of delinquent youth had at least one disorder. Diagnoses were most common for disruptive disorders; 48 percent of youth

had an attention-deficit/hyperactivity disorder. Nine percent of youth were diagnosed with anxiety disorders and 7 percent received diagnoses of mood disorders. Rates of meeting diagnostic criteria for youth in juvenile justice (52%) were only slightly lower than rates for youth in public mental health programs (61%).

Wasserman, McReynolds, Lucas, Fisher, and Santos (2001) used the *DISC-IV* to evaluate psychiatric disorders in a sample of 281 adjudicated male delinquents. Fifty percent of youth were diagnosed with substance use disorders; 33 percent and 20 percent of youth had disruptive and anxiety disorders, respectively. Ten percent of delinquents received mood disorder diagnoses. Girls received at least one diagnosis significantly more often (69%) than did boys (53%).

Using a stratified random sample of adjudicated delinquents, McCabe, Lansing, Garland, and Hough (2002) examined *DSM-IV* diagnoses using the *DISC-IV* (Shaffer et al., 2000) and the *Composite International Diagnostic Interview-Substance Abuse Module (CIDI-SAM)* (Cottler, Robins, & Helzer, 1989). Sixty-nine percent of girls and 53 percent of boys met criteria for at least one diagnosis on the DISC-IV. Sixteen percent of girls and 5 percent of boys, and 15 percent of girls and 85 of boys, met criteria for any mood or anxiety disorder respectively. Female delinquents were significantly more likely than males to meet diagnostic criteria for at least one diagnosis, and for mood disorder and disruptive disorders. Similarly, girls were more likely than boys to meet criteria for certain "specialty" disorders including major depressive disorder and separation anxiety disorder. There were no gender differences of rates of substance abuse disorders or co-morbidity of mental health and substance abuse disorders.

Summary

This review clearly illustrates that youth in the juvenile justice system have greater problem symptoms and diagnosable disorders than do other youth. Interestingly, rates of mental health problem symptoms tend to be somewhat lower than prevalence estimates that are based on specific diagnostic categories. Problem symptoms are typically in the warning range for between one-quarter and one-half of juvenile detainees, though at least one estimate (Timmons-Mitchell et al., 1997) puts these percentages considerably higher. The prevalence of psychiatric disorders is quite high: studies indicate that between 40 percent and 70 percent of youth in the justice system are experiencing mental health problems that are considerably more acute than short-term symptomatic behavior. Substance abuse, depression, attention-deficit hyperactivity disorder, and antisocial behavior were among the most frequently reported diagnoses. Several studies (Grisso et al., 2001; McCabe et al., 2002; Teplin, 2001b; Timmons-Mitchell et al., 1997; Wassserman et al., 2001) found higher rates of mental health problems among girls than boys.

Substance Abuse

The concomitant nature of adolescent substance use and delinquency has been extensively studied and empirically validated for some years (e.g., Hawkins, Jenson, Catalano, & Lishner, 1988). Substance use among delinquent youth is often assessed using self-report instruments; many self-report measures are developed and administered to fit the needs of specific juvenile justice programs. Standardized screening instruments and comprehensive diagnostic inventories that assess actual levels of drug use are also available.

Evidence from investigations examining risk and protective factors associated with substance use indicate that delinquent youth are at much higher risk for substance abuse than other youth. Studies consistently indicate that delinquent youth have a greater number of risk factors related to substance use than youth who are not involved in the juvenile justice system (Hawkins et al., 1992; Pollard, Hawkins, & Arthur, 1999). And, substance abuse is known to be related to many types of offenses (Snyder & Sickmund, 1999).

Rates of Substance Abuse Among Juvenile Delinquents

Aarons et al. (2001) evaluated substance use disorders among random samples of youth in San Diego County who were referred to the juvenile justice, alcohol and drug, mental health, and child welfare systems. Adolescents referred to school-based services because of emotional disturbance were also assessed. Substance use disorders were evaluated using the *DICA* and were based on subjects' self-reported lifetime alcohol and drug use. Sixty-two percent of youth in the juvenile justice system received

diagnoses for substance use disorders. This rate was second only to youth in the alcohol and drug treatment system; 83 percent of adolescents in this system were diagnosed with substance use disorders. Forty-one percent of youth in the mental health system, 24 percent of students in the school-based sample, and 19 percent of adolescents in the child welfare system had substance use disorders. Aarons et al. (2001) found that alcohol, marijuana, and amphetamine use were most common among delinquent youth. Forty-nine percent of youth in the juvenile justice system were diagnosed with a lifetime substance use disorder.

Dembo and associates (Dembo, Williams, Schmeidler, Wish, Getreu, & Berry, 1991; Dembo, Williams, Fagan, & Schmeidler, 1993a; Dembo, Pacheco, Schmeidler, Fisher, & Cooper, 1997a; Dembo, Schmeidler, Borden, Chin, & Mannig, 1997b) evaluated the prevalence of substance use in a series of reports derived from random samples of juvenile detainees in Florida. Between 60 percent and 75 percent of delinquents in their juvenile justice samples reported lifetime marijuana use. In comparison, between 21 percent and 40 percent of tenth graders reported lifetime marijuana during the years 1991 to 2001 on the annual Monitoring the Future survey of substance use among the nation's youth (Johnston, O'Malley, & Bachman, 2001).

Jenson and Howard (1998) and Howard and Jenson (1999) examined hallucinogen and inhalant use among a sample of 475 probationers. Forty-four percent of probationers used hallucinogens and 34 percent used inhalants in their lifetime. These rates are considerably higher than use reported by the nation's high school youth; 10 and 17 percent of tenth graders reported lifetime hallucinogen and inhalant use on the annual Monitoring the Future survey in 1998 and 1999, respectively (Johnston et al., 2001).

The prevalence of substance use among juvenile delinquents exceeds use found in nondelinquent, community- and school-based samples. Between 70 and 95 percent of delinquents in the justice system report lifetime use of alcohol and/or illicit drugs; approximately 50 percent of youth indicate they have used substances in the past year. Marijuana and alcohol have consistently yielded the highest prevalence rates across all levels of the juvenile justice system.

Prevalence of Substance Abuse Diagnoses among Juvenile Delinquents

Information in the preceding section on mental health diagnoses focused also on substance abuse diagnosis. To summarize, investigations have found that between 50 and 80% of boys and 28 and 50% of girls meet diagnostic criteria for at least one substance abuse disorder (Atkins et al., 1999; McCabe et al., 2002; Teplin et al., 2003; Timmons-Mitchel et al., 1997). Results vary as to whether boys and girls differ significantly in these rates (Atkins et al., 1999; Timmons-Mitchell et al., 1997). We turn now to a discussion of the concomitant nature of substance abuse and mental health problems among delinquent youth.

Prevalence of Co-occurring Problem Symptoms and Disorders among Youth in the Juvenile Justice System

The prevalence and nature of co-occurring mental health and substance abuse disorders has been the subject of fewer investigations, though we do have evidence about the consequences of co-occurring problems. The National Center on Addiction and Substance Abuse (2002) found that recidivism rates are higher for youth with co-occurring mental health and substance abuse problems. Some studies have investigated the presence of one problem set among known members of the others, for example, studying the mental health problems among substance abusing delinquents. Fewer studies have focused on rates of co-occurrence among juvenile justice youth in general, and even fewer focus on the nature of co-occurrence in a complex manner.

Milin, Halikas, Meller, and Morse (1991) found significantly higher rates of ADHD and conduct disorder among juvenile offenders who also abused drugs. Moreover, 39 percent of substance abusers vs. 14 percent of nonsubstance abusers were found to have comorbid mental health diagnoses. Randall, Henggeler, Pickrel, and Brondino (1999) examined criminal and social characteristics of 118 substance-abusing juvenile offenders who met *DSM-III-R* criteria for substance abuse or dependence. Subjects were divided on the basis of externalizing and internalizing psychiatric disorders. Substance-abusing youth with externalizing disorders engaged in higher

rates of delinquent conduct and exhibited less family cohesion than youth with internalizing disorders. Presence of a co-morbid externalizing disorder was associated with higher rates of delinquency, substance use, and out-of-home placement at 16-month follow-up.

Rounds-Bryant and colleagues (1998) examined mental health disorders and crime in a sample of 3,382 adolescents who were treated in drug programs participating in the Drug Abuse Treatment Outcome Study of Adolescents between 1993 and 1995. Six percent of boys and 17 percent of girls met criteria for clinical depression on the *DSM-III-R.* Females were significantly more likely than males to report previous suicide attempts (28% vs. 7%), and more likely to receive mental health treatment (21% vs. 12%). Depression among 99 substance-dependent male delinquents was examined by Riggs, Baker, Mikulich, Young, and Crowley (1995). All subjects had conduct disorder and substance use disorders. Twenty-one percent of boys had a *DSM-III-R* diagnosis of major depressive disorder. Depressed delinquents were significantly more likely to use drugs regularly and had a greater number of non-drug, comorbid diagnoses than nondepressed delinquents.

Neighbors, Kempton, and Forehand (1992) evaluated the co-occurrence of substance abuse with conduct, anxiety, and depression disorders among 111 juvenile detainees. The presence of substance abuse was positively associated with rates of psychiatric disorders. Ninety-six percent of detainees who met criteria for alcohol or marijuana abuse were diagnosed with conduct disorders. Twenty-two and 26 percent of alcohol and marijuana abusers received diagnoses of anxiety and depression, respectively. Conduct, anxiety, and depression disorders were present in 93 percent, 38 percent, and 48 percent of polysubstance abusers. Forty-three percent of alcohol and marijuana abusers and 56 percent of polysubstance abusers received more than one diagnosis.

Abrantes, Hoffmann, and Anton (2005) examined co-occurrence among 252 consecutively admitted juvenile detainees using the *Practical Adolescent Dual Diagnostic Interview (PADDI)* (Estroff & Hoffmann, 2001). Seventy-three percent of youth displayed positive indications of the most prevalent adolescent mental health diagnoses (e.g., major depressive episodes, mania, conduct disorder, and substance dependence), 21 percent of subjects tested positive for one condition, and 52 percent tested positive for multiple conditions. The most frequent co-occurring disorders were conduct disorder and substance abuse. However, substance abuse was less likely to co-occur with a mental health disorder than were mental health disorders to co-occur with each other.

Potter and Jenson (2003) used exploratory k-means cluster analysis to examine the co-occurrence of drug use and mental health problems in the previously described Colorado study. Three distinct patterns of mental health problem symptoms and substance use were found for detained youth. One youth cluster displayed serious mental health problem symptoms. These symptoms co-occurred with high rates of inhalant use and with moderate rates of offending. Youth in this group reported significantly higher levels of problem symptoms on the *BSI* dimensions of interpersonal sensitivity, hostility, phobic anxiety, paranoid ideation, and psychoticism than youth in two other groups. Youth in two other clusters had moderate mental health problems but differed in the severity of substance abuse and delinquent conduct.

Patterns of mental health and substance abuse among the long-term incarcerated group in Potter and Jenson's investigation (2001) differed from the detention sample. Three clusters were found in this sample. However, unlike the detention sample, these clusters did not separate or form on the basis of mental health variables. Rather, it appeared that all youth experienced increased levels of mental health problem symptoms. Substance use was highest among youth in the cluster characterized by involvement in violent crime, gang membership, and drug distribution.

SCREENING AND ASSESSMENT IN JUVENILE JUSTICE

Discussion of the need to identify mental health and substance abuse treatment needs of juvenile delinquents has generally conceptualized screening and assessment as a relatively simple two-stage model. Typically, youth are screened for mental health and/or substance abuse needs at a relatively early point in their juvenile justice experience. Those who score highly on chosen assessment instruments are then assessed more completely with regard to their mental health or substance use disorders (Grisso et al., 2001;

Grisso & Underwood, 2004). Screening is typically envisioned as a brief process focused on triaging youth who are most at risk and in need of immediate intervention.

Most states have developed or are in the process of initiating mental health assessments (Steiner, Cauffman, & Duxbury, 1998). To date, these efforts have been primarily limited to screening processes that identify problem symptoms. Juvenile justice systems may employ brief screening approaches at multiple points in the system. However, these processes are often poorly integrated into system decision making (Trupin & Boesky, 1999.) Screening models include procedures at juvenile probation or detention intake, juvenile or community assessment centers, court-based evaluation clinics, and correctional system diagnostic reception centers (Grisso & Underwood, 2004). In addition, some states have attempted to create mental health and juvenile justice system collaborations that extend from detention to subsequent community treatment (Potter & Jenson, 2003).

Assessment procedures are even less well standardized, but typically include type and nature of mental health and substance abuse diagnosed disorders, consideration of psychosocial issues, and recommendations for treatment (Grisso & Underwood, 2004). Some assessment approaches use standardized diagnostic inventories and/or psychological testing; others take a more individualized, clinical approach.

Assessment Tools

Many instruments are available for screening and assessment purposes (Cauffman, et al., 2002; Goldstein, 2000; Grisso & Underwood, 2004). When choosing an assessment instrument it is important to consider the following questions

- What domains and specific problems does the instrument assess?
- How accurate is the instrument?
- How well does the instrument function as part of a comprehensive screening model?

These questions address important issues related to validity, reliability, and utility that must be answered prior to selection and implementation. Unfortunately, few inventories have been developed or used over extensive periods of time in the juvenile justice system. We review instruments that have been tested and that contain empirical evidence related to assessment below.

Assessment Protocols for Mental Health Problems

Approaches used to assess the prevalence of mental health problems among juvenile delinquents vary considerably in the justice system. In many states, the assessment of mental health problems is accomplished by using a clinical decision-making process in which a trained therapist or practitioner determines whether or not a youth requires mental health intervention. While a valuable tool, clinical judgment in isolation from other procedures may fail to identify youth who display less overt mental health problems. In response to this problem, systematic mental health screening and assessment practices have been introduced in the juvenile justice system.

Screening Inventories. A number of investigations have used the *SCL-90-R* or the *BSI* to assess mental health symptoms (Potter & Jenson, 2003.) The *SCL-90-R* is a 90-item symptom checklist that assesses nine symptom dimensions: somatization, obsessive-compulsive, interpersonal sensitivity, depression, anxiety, hostility, phobic anxiety, paranoid ideation, and psychoticism. The *BSI* is a 53-item instrument that assesses the same nine problem symptom dimensions. Individual items reflect the degree to which subjects have experienced distress during the preceding week on the basis of a five-point response set (0) *not at all*, (1) *a little bit*, (2) *moderately*, (3) *quite a bit*, and (4) *extremely* (Derogatis, 1993, 1994).

Clinical norms for both of these instruments have been established and a clinical cut point has been identified for each subscale at the warning range level. Reliabilities of the subscales range from fair to good for both instruments in samples of adults and adolescents (Boulet & Boss, 1991). The *BSI* has been compared to the *Brief Psychiatric Rating Scale (BPRS)* (Hafkenscheid, 1991, 1993) a clinician-rated instrument that is widely used in Europe. Findings indicate that the BSI dimensions are highly correlated with similar constructs measure by the *BPRS*, indicating that the self-report nature of the instrument is valid (Morlan & Tan, 1998). However, some studies examining convergent and discriminant validity raise concerns about the validity of the subscales (Boulet & Boss, 1991).

Exploratory factor analysis by the authors supports the stability of the nine BSI dimensions (Derogitis, 1994). However, other examinations of structure have found high correlations between the subscales for both instruments (Boulet & Boss, 1991), and factor analyses have not consistently replicated the nine-factor structure (Benishek, Hayes, Bieschke, & Stoffelmayr, 1998). Studies using both adult and adolescent samples indicate that the instruments most likely measure a uni-dimensional construct of general psychological distress (Benishek et al.,1998; Piersma, Boes, & Reaume, 1994). Neither instrument has been tested as a screener against a systematic diagnostic instrument in juvenile justice settings, so it is not clear how the nine dimensions might screen for those who are likely to meet diagnostic criteria.

The *Massachusetts Youth Screening Inventory-2 (MAYSI-2)* (Grisso & Barnum, 2003) is a 52-item measure that assesses mental health problem symptoms and substance use in the past few months preceding a test administration. The *MAYSI-2* contains seven scales including alcohol and drug use, angry-irritable, depressed-anxious, somatic complaints, suicide ideation, thought disturbance (boys only), and traumatic experiences. Individual items are evaluated for the presence or absence of problem symptoms using a dichotomous (yes/no) response set. The *MAYSI-2* was developed specifically for youth in the juvenile justice system. The instrument has not been nationally normed, but clinical cut points have been established.

Grisso et al. (2001) evaluated the psychometric properties of the *MAYSI-2* and found scale alpha coefficient scores ranging from .61 to .86. The authors also found evidence of concurrent validity on the basis of a comparison of *MAYSI-2* scores to the *Millon Adolescent Clinical Inventory* (Millon, 1993) and the *Youth Self Report* (Achenbach & Edelbrock, 1983). The structure of the *MAYSI-2* has been established by exploratory factor analysis (Archer, Stredny, Mason, & Arnau, 2004; Grisso et al., 2001). Correlations between subscales range from .24 to .61. The authors note that the screening instrument may identify more false-positives than might be optimal for use in planning juvenile justice based mental health interventions, and should be followed by a more intensive assessment of mental health needs (Grisso & Barnum, 2003).

Diagnostic Inventories. Relatively few studies have used comprehensive diagnostic instruments to assess mental health disorders among delinquent youth; however, when diagnosis is considered, the *Diagnostic Interview Schedule for Children (DISC-IV)* is commonly used. The *DISC-IV* yields clinically relevant scores across six diagnostic modules including anxiety, disruptive, mood, schizophrenia, substance use, and miscellaneous (e.g., eating, elimination, etc.) disorders. Each module may be administered separately or in combination with other modules. Psychometric properties of the *DISC-IV* are well established (Shaffer et al., 2000). It is also available in voice and computer-aided formats.

The *Diagnostic Interview for Children and Adolescents-Revised (DICA-R)* (Herjanic & Reich, 1982) is a structured inventory that assesses the presence or absence of attention deficit, conduct, substance use, affective, anxiety, phobic, obsessive compulsive, and psychotic disorders (Welner et al., 1987). The *DICA-R* has been widely used in clinical settings with high risk and troubled children and adolescents and its key variables and scales have considerable empirical support. We found only one study that used the *DICA-R* to assess the nature of psychiatric comorbidity in incarcerated juveniles (Ulzen & Hamilton, 1998).

Assessment Protocols for Substance Abuse

Screening Inventories. Substance abuse screening instruments offer juvenile justice practitioners the opportunity to quickly assess the likelihood of a substance abuse problem. Such instruments are short, easy to administer, and provide clinical criteria that identify clients who may benefit from a comprehensive diagnostic evaluation (Martin & Winters, 1998).

Winters (1992) developed the *Personal Experience Screening Questionnaire (PESQ)* to meet the need for a quick adolescent substance abuse screening tool. The *PESQ* is also useful in determining the need for a comprehensive assessment of risk and protective factors associated with substance use. Psychometric properties have been established for an 18-item and a 38-item *PESQ* (Winters, 1992; Winters, Weller, & Meland, 1993b). The *PESQ* is a paper-and-pencil screening tool written at the fourth-grade reading level. The test is scored for problem severity, drug use history, and psychological problems (Winters, 1992).

The *Problem Oriented Screening Instrument for Teenagers (POSIT)* is used to identify risk and protective factors for substance abuse that may require additional assessment (Radhert, 1991). The POSIT is intended to operate as a first screen for substance use problems. Ten functional areas including substance use and abuse, physical health, mental health, family relationships, peers, educational status, vocational status, social skills, leisure and recreation, and aggressive behavior are evaluated. The *POSIT* scoring system is based on expert clinical judgment and has been widely used in juvenile justice settings (e.g., Dembo et al.,1997b).

The *Substance Abuse Subtle Screening Inventory (SASSI)* (Miller, 1990) is an 85-item instrument that evaluates risk and protective factors associated with alcohol and other drug problems. The instrument yields clinically relevant scores for drug and alcohol history. Risberg, Stevens, and Graybill (1995) found that *SASSI* scores corresponded well to subsequent diagnoses of alcohol and drug use disorders among a sample of adolescents referred for residential drug treatment. The updated adolescent version of the *SASSI*, known as the *SASSI-A2*, has been shown to correctly identify 95 percent of youth with diagnosable substance abuse disorders, while correctly classifying 89 percent of those who do not (SASSI Institute, 2001).

Diagnostic Inventories. Diagnostic inventories provide an in-depth examination of actual drug use and of risk and protective factors associated with use. Diagnostic tools are typically used with youth who exceed problem levels on substance abuse screening instruments. We have previously discussed the *DISC-IV* and the *DICA*, both of which have modules focused on substance abuse diagnoses.

The *Personal Experience Inventory (PEI)* is a self-report inventory that measures psychosocial risk factors associated with adolescent drug involvement (Winters, Stinchfield, & Henly, 1993a). The inventory includes five scales that assess personal involvement with drug use, effects of drug use, social benefits of drug use, personal consequences of drug use, and polydrug use. Studies of the *PEI* indicate that the scales are significantly related to *DSM* criteria for substance use disorders and treatment recommendations (Henly & Winters, 1988; Winters et al., 1993a). The *PEI* has also successfully classified high-risk adolescents into outpatient or inpatient treatment referral subgroups (Winters, Anderson, Bengston, Stinchfield, & Latimer, 2000).

The *Adolescent Diagnostic Interview (ADI)* (Winters & Henly, 1993) assesses symptoms of alcohol and drug use disorders as defined by the *DSM-IV*. The *ADI* evaluates a host of risk and protective traits associated with drug use, including psychosocial functioning, mental health problem symptoms, and family relationships. Practitioners working in environments that utilize the *DSM-IV* may find the *ADI* to be particularly helpful in assessing risk and protective factors for drug abuse (Winters, Latimer, & Stinchfield, 1999).

Dennis and colleagues (Dennis, 1999; Dennis, Rourke, & Caddell, 1993) developed the *Global Appraisal of Individual Needs (GAIN)* to assess drug use, and factors associated with drug use, in high-risk adolescents. The instrument is divided into eight areas that include detailed questions about drug use, physical health, mental and emotional health, environmental influences, interpersonal relationships, and legal and vocational status. Administration time for the *GAIN* varies from one to two hours depending on the extent of drug use history.

From Screening to Diagnosis to Treatment: How Strong is the Evidence?

Assessment and diagnostic tools must ultimately yield accurate information for practitioners who aim to treat mental health and substance abuse problems of delinquent youth. Thus, an important issue concerns the ability of an instrument to clearly identify a specific problem area and to discriminate such a problem from other closely related symptoms or behaviors (e.g., identifying and separating depressive symptoms from anxiety or attention deficit problems). We have examined the ability of several assessment issues to clearly identify specific mental health symptoms in several investigations and report these results below.

In one study, Jenson, Potter, and Dieterich (2003) examined the concordance between the *BSI* and the *MAYSI-2* for a sample of 573 male juvenile offenders at community placement, detention, and long-term incarceration stages of juvenile justice processing. Factor and reliability analysis of the subscales of the *MAYSI-2* were similar to those reported by Grisso and colleagues (2003). However, correlations between *MAYSI-2* and *BSI* subscales revealed several *MAYSI-2* subscales to be strongly associated with both

related *and* unrelated BSI subscales. For example, the *MAYSI-2* depressed/anxious and suicidal ideas subscales correlated significantly with *all* subscales of the *BSI* (correlations ranged from .35 to .61). No *BSI* subscales correlated significantly with all *MAYSI-2* subscales, but several correlated with many *MAYSI-2* subscales. There is additional empirical evidence suggesting that the *BSI* may simply be measuring one large mental health symptom construct (Boulet & Boss, 1991). Our findings suggest that the *MAYSI-2* may indeed be doing the same. One exception to this trend is the alcohol/drug use subscale of the *MAYSI-2* which only correlated moderately (r=.303) with the hostility subscale of the *BSI*, and at lower levels with other mental health dimensions.

Authors of the *MAYSI-2* note that the instrument is not designed to correspond to clinical disorders defined by the *DSM-IV* (Grisso et al., 2001). However, a recent study addressed the question of how well the *MAYSI-2* screener accurately predicts later mental health diagnoses (Wasserman, McReynolds, Ko, Katz, Cauffman, Haxton, & Lucas, 2004). The study compared the *MAYSI-2* and Voice *DISC-IV* among 325 New Jersey and South Carolina correctional youth. These analyses considered both questions of individual diagnosis and questions of diagnostic clusters and also focused on positive and negative predictions of diagnoses. Findings indicated that 87 percent of youth scored above at least one cut point on the *MAYSI-2*. While *MAYSI-2* scores did correspond to diagnostic categories in many cases, 29 to 43 percent of youth with specific disorders were not flagged by the corresponding subscale of the *MAYSI-2*. Of particular interest, the suicide ideation subscale correctly identified youth with histories of ideation and/or attempt but was less likely to accurately identify youth with recent attempts and current ideation. Highly comorbid situations also posed difficulties for the *MAYSI-2*.

Assessment tools for substance abuse among delinquent and other youth have generally shown more accurate results than mental health screening tools. Among the substance abuse screeners, the *PEI* has been shown to correctly classify youth into substance abuse diagnostic categories (Henly & Winters, 1988; Winters et al., 1993a). As noted earlier, Risberg et al. (1995) found that *SASSI* scores corresponded well to alcohol and drug use diagnoses for a nonjuvenile justice clinical sample of youth in residential treatment.

Screening and Assessment: Some Thoughts on Best Practices

Careful examination of mental health and substance abuse prevalence and of existing screening and measurement approaches leads to several important conclusions. First, it is clear that youth in the juvenile justice system are more likely than youth in the general population to report problem symptoms and to meet criteria for diagnosis for both mental health and substance use problems. Second, these problems frequently co-occur, though relatively little is known about the patterns of their relatively complex co-occurrence. Third, as noted above, two mental health instruments have been primarily used as a screening function; both appear to lack specificity in distinguishing mental health dimensions from one another. On the other hand, separate screeners for substance use are reasonable well evaluated and have been found to be accurate. Fourth, only one screener – the *MAYSI-2* – has been used extensively to assess *both* mental health and substance abuse screening. These conclusions lead us to assert that, given the state of instrumentation, a simple "screen all, assess few" model is not adequate to the task.

This latter point is of some importance. In general, estimates from screeners are generally thought by their authors to be overestimates of problem symptoms (Grisso & Barnum, 2000). Indeed, one might wish this feature in a screener. That is, it is certainly better to cast a wide net and identify youth who might *possibly* be in need of intervention than it is to miss youth who may later prove to have problems. However, it appears that mental health screeners are actually identifying fewer (or similar) percentages of youth with mental health problem symptoms than are identified using structured diagnostic assessments. Importantly, in one predictive study, the *MAYSI-2* did not correctly identify specific problems (Wasserman et al., 2004). Moreover, one of the weaknesses of existing mental health screeners lies in identifying current suicidal ideation, a critical area for early identification.

The lack of concordance between mental health screeners and diagnostic criteria reveals an underlying conceptual dissonance between the importance of screening to current symptoms or screening to diagnostic criteria. Some investigators have suggested that these two approaches are best used sequentially (Grisso & Underwood, 2004). However, the empirical evidence suggests that the two approaches are overlapping rather than sequential because they often measure similar constructs. This suggests that a two-stage process may not reflect a process in which a less intensive symptom screener will accurately assess the likelihood of an actual diagnostic disorder. Ultimately juvenile justice programs may need to choose an approach that privileges symptoms or diagnoses as important information for screening.

The Consensus Conference: A Model for Screening and Assessment

A recent meeting of juvenile justice assessment experts dubbed the "Consensus Conference" produced recommendations for screening and assessment of mental health needs in the juvenile justice system (Wasserman et al., 2003). Following the RAND Corporation expert consensus guidelines approach (Brook, Chassin, Fink, Solomon, Kosecoff, & Park, 1986), the group asked juvenile justice staff about current and best practices in assessment. Participants in the Consensus Conference then considered information from the survey, a series of scientific presentations, and empirical evidence to propose a model for screening and assessment. Below we describe the model proposed by the conference and suggest ways that it should be extended to incorporate more detail in screening and assessment for substance abuse disorders (see Figure 12-1).

Emergent Risk

The Consensus Conference urges personnel in the juvenile justice system to screen for issues presenting immediate risk for harm within 24 hours of system intake. This early screen for "emergent risk" targets screening for (1) risk of self-harm, (2) risk of harm to others, (3) immediate mental health crises, (4) current medications, (5) recently ingested substances, and (6) recent mental health treatment (Wasserman et al., 2003). Because such screens must take place quickly, it is suggested that emergent risk screening use brief, evidence-based instruments that can be administered by untrained staff. While the mental health screening instruments we have reviewed in this chapter are identified as options, the authors note that no single instrument is adequate to this task. In addition, gathering information about recent mental health treatment and current medications is generally best collected in a brief, standardized interview protocol.

Considering the mental health screening instruments available, none may be precisely appropriate for screening to elements of emergent risk. While the mental health screeners appear to identify global mental health distress, it is unclear whether they are predictive of immediate crisis. Similarly, either the hostility scale of the *BSI* or the angry/irritable scale of the *MAYSI* might serve to identify risk of harm to others, though empirical evidence is still needed to determine how well these scales predict immediate hostile behavior that might pose a danger to others.

Since the existing screeners may be especially weak in identification of suicide ideation, an emergent risk screen should include a strong adolescent suicide screener such as the *Columbia Teen Screen* (Shaffer & Craft, 1999). The *Columbia Teen Screen* is a relatively new 11-item screening instrument that includes items regarding mental health and substance use known to be associated with suicidality. The instrument has been used in a two-stage screening process along with the *DISC* and has exhibited good sensitivity and specificity in "predicting" past known attempts and short-term future attempts (Goldston, 2000; Shaffer & Craft, 1999). For an excellent review of existing suicide assessment instruments see Goldston (2000).

We suggest the addition of two substance abuse screening approaches at this emergent risk stage. First, an instrument such as the *PESQ* (Winters, 1992) or the *SASSI* (Miller, 1990), with demonstrated concordance with diagnostic criteria for substance abuse disorders, should be used at this stage. Second, if there is serious concern about the risks associated with recently ingested substances, an urine analysis should be used as it is the most reliable approach to identifying potential harmful doses of substances. Failing this, a quick, standardized interview focused on recent use of common substances may provide additional reliable information.

Mental Health and Substance Abuse Service Needs

The Consensus Conference attendees suggest that screening mental health problems and identifying needs with an eye to long-term service planning should occur for all youth prior to court disposition.

This constitutes a second-level screen in which the focus must be on obtaining (1) an accurate *diagnosis* of mental health and substance abuse needs, (2) a more complete social history, and (3) an understanding of treatment history. Essentially this recommendation treats standardized diagnostic protocols, such as the *DISC-IV* (Shaffer et al., 2000) and *DICA-R* (Reich, 2000) as screeners, followed by information gathering protocols aimed at individual detail regarding social and treatment circumstances.. Both the *DISC-IV* and *DICA-R* include substance abuse modules. If greater specificity regarding substance use is desired at this stage, use of the *ADI* (Winters & Henley, 1993) may provide both information on diagnostic criteria and a set of scales related to adolescent risk factors for substance use.

Comprehensive Mental Health Assessment

Assessment of a full range of mental health and substance abuse problems should occur after this second screening for those youth identified as meeting diagnostic criteria (Wasserman et al., 2003). This comprehensive assessment is envisioned as being more in the nature of a clinical assessment by a trained clinician. It should include a mental status examination, use information from multiple informants, and focus on co-occurring disorders. Such a comprehensive assessment is considered relevant to treatment planning for any setting in which youth are placed.

Reassessment

The Consensus Conference authors argue also for the reassessment of delinquent youth at subsequent decision points in the juvenile justice system. These points include the point of movement from one level of care to another, the point of system discharge, and at specified follow-up points in the community. These reassessments, which may include second-level screening using diagnostic instruments, can focus on providing continuous information about co-occurring disorders that is relevant to system decisions, such as level of security, parole, and release. We argue that some decision points, especially the move to higher levels of care, following adjudication or failure at a lower level of security, may also be appropriate times to re-assess for emergent risk.

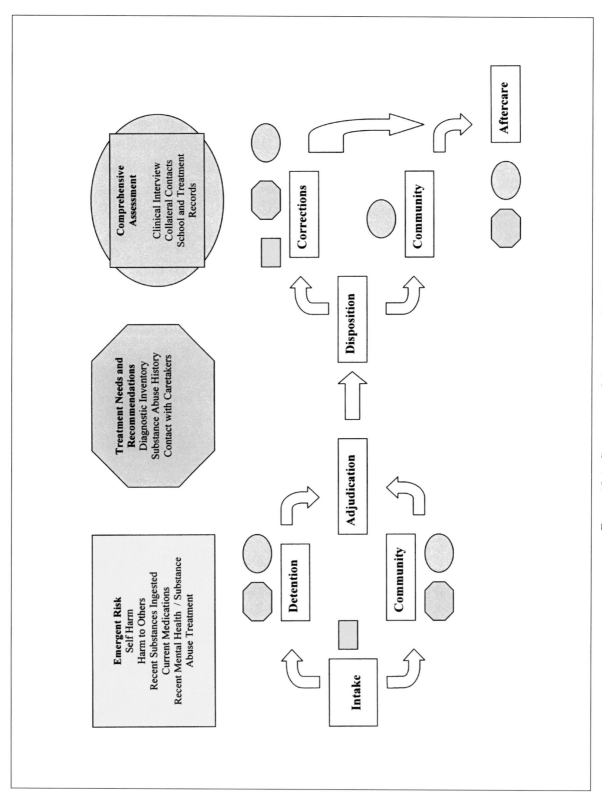

Figure 12-1. Screening and Assessment Model.

Continuity of Care

One final important issue is the need for screening and assessment information to travel with youth as they move through the juvenile justice system. In many juvenile justice systems, medical files are kept separately from court-related documents. Systems seeking to implement a strong assessment system must find a way to incorporate screener and assessment information and reports into standard juvenile justice tracking and reporting mechanisms. This information, especially data related to use of psychotropic medications, is critical to providing continuity of care across juvenile justice settings.

Fernando's Story 1

We introduced readers to Fernando at the beginning of this chapter. To no one's surprise, Fernando was placed in juvenile detention the night of his assault and was later referred to a secure, residential program operated by the state juvenile corrections system. He has completed several screening and assessment inventories since his arrest, including an initial suicide screen and a later inventory to assess his substance use. The instruments used in these assessments were developed by professional staff at each of the juvenile justice facilities; little is known about their ability to accurately identify or predict mental health or substance abuse problems. Fernando's treatment in secure care consists of anger management training and participation in a 12-step substance abuse group five days each week.

As in many juvenile cases, assessment data derived from Fernando's intake and subsequent screening processes were only marginally used to inform his treatment and rehabilitation plan. Like all youth in residential care, Fernando participates in the therapy groups that best match his referral offenses. Fernando continues to be disruptive in treatment and appears to be getting little of the help he really needs.

Fernando's brief story illustrates some of the problems inherent in an inadequate screening and assessment process. Weak and poorly-supported assessment information does little to help practitioners and other professional staff to understand the reasons for Fernando's antisocial behavior.

The lack of an empirically-validated mental health screening tool leaves his subsequent assessment and treatment largely to chance or to what is available in the system at the time he receives his final court disposition. Juvenile justice practitioners do acknowledge his substance abuse problems but the treatment Fernando receives is not specific to his presenting problems or to his history of impulsive behavior or aggression. In short, rather than being carefully matched to a range of possible treatment, Fernando receives only the "business as usual" option in the system that is open to him on his day in court.

Fernando's Story 2

An emergent risk screen done with Fernando the night of his admission to detention revealed several important things. First, Fernando scored very highly on the *Columbia Teen Screen*, indicating high risk for suicidality. This assessment was in concordance with a conversation with his aunt (legal guardian) the next day. She reports two prior suicide attempts and is of the opinion that Fernando's risky behavior is related to depression and suicidal ideation. He has been refusing to see his therapist at the local mental health center. Fernando has antidepressant medication but takes it sporadically. It should not be mixed with alcohol or other drugs. A urine analysis revealed a .09 blood alcohol level and traces of cocaine in Fernando's system, and Fernando reports that he has also taken his medication. Fernando completed the PESQ substance abuse screener during day two of his stay in detention, and reported frequent use of alcohol and marijuana, and moderate use of cocaine.

Because of the results of the emergent risk screen, Fernando is placed on a heightened watch status for his first night in detention. The next morning, his antidepressant medication is obtained from his aunt and a refill prescription is obtained from the mental health center. Fernando completes the second level screen during day two of his detention stay. Results of the voice *DISC-IV* reveal that he meets diagnostic criteria for alcohol substance abuse, major depression, paranoia and conduct disorder.

Fernando meets with the detention mental health clinician who talks with him about the specific results of both the emergent risk screen and the *DISC-IV*. Both the clinician and Fernando agree that a certain level of paranoia is functional in detention settings, but Fernando is able to focus briefly on his own concerns about his easy transition to "white hot" rage. Fernando agrees to take his antidepressant medication, which the clinician agrees should be useful for his depressive symptoms. A mental status exam reveals a lessening of suicidal ideation, and Fernando is taken off of the heightened watch status.

Ultimately, Fernando will be adjudicated for aggravated assault, and given his extensive juvenile justice history will be placed in a high security environment. Screening for emergent risk at the time of the move reveals heightened suicidality for a period of some weeks. While incarcerated , Fernando will see a mental health clinician weekly. He will also engage in three therapeutic groups: one focused on anger management and victim empathy, one focused on depression interruption skills, and one focused on alcohol substance abuse education and recovery. While Fernando's safety and security officers and mental health and substance abuse clinicians recognize that these three problem areas are overlapping, they have not yet tackled the task of designing an integrated intervention.

SUMMARY AND CONCLUSION: SOME THORNY ISSUES

Our discussion has identified several unresolved issues that are directly relevant to the screening and assessment process in juvenile justice. As noted above, these are related to a need for careful conceptualization of the purposes of screening and assessment, the nature of available instruments, and the ability to correctly sequence screening and assessment activities. In addition, we note here a few important domains that are relevant to screening and assessment decisions.

The juvenile justice system is currently struggling with a desire to create risk assessment instruments that are useful in promoting community safety by correctly targeting youth to the appropriate level of security in the system (e.g., Brennan, 2003; Washington State Institute for Public Policy, 2004). While

these instruments are attempting to serve multiple purposes, they are by nature less focused on treatment needs and more focused on security concerns. They often contain items regarding substance use and mental health symptoms, which are typically, though not always, staff-rated. The difficulties in assessing risk in this framework are legion (Gottfredson & Snyder, 2005). Of importance here is the tension in the juvenile justice system between rehabilitation and community safety, and the parallel paths that instrument development takes in this context. Risk assessment instruments are very likely to compete with mental health and substance abuse instruments in the juvenile justice system. To that end, screener and diagnostic assessments that can be completed via voice and computer technology will likely have an edge when it comes to adoption and implementation.

While computer technology and strong standardized instruments can greatly aid the identification of mental health and substance abuse needs, they are no substitute for people who understand critical clinical issues. The juvenile justice system has not traditionally developed roles for strong mental health and substance abuse clinicians, and there can be conflict in worldviews and goals between safety and security officers and intervention staff. Building a culture that supports mental health and substance abuse intervention, risk containment, and personal responsibility for youth requires a melding of professional views. This kind of program development requires strong leadership and a workforce that is trained and educated to work across traditional boundaries.

Program development is also needed. There are a number of published reports on screening and assessment processes; there are far fewer studies, however, of assessment models and subsequent outcomes for youth (Jenson & Potter, 2003; Terry, VanderWaal, McBride, & Van Buren, 2000). Though not the focus of this chapter, solid screening and assessment protocols are only useful if they guide decisions about individual youth and about the programs and systems that contain them.

We have touched on the complexity of co-occurring disorders and identified the lack of understanding of patterns that may exist. Establishing standardized screening and assessment procedures –and providing access to appropriate mental health and substance abuse treatment – is an important step forward. However, we have a long way to go toward the level of understanding that would allow development of evidence-based, integrated treatment approaches for common co-occurring problems. Co-occurring substance abuse and mental health problems present complicated clinical pictures. Youth with these disorders may well be experiencing interactive effects that are not well understood in an interactive way. Those working from differing perspectives may see either consequences of substance use or mental health symptoms, depending on one's perspective. Half of all young offenders in the United States have mental health and substance abuse problems. This is a much-needed area for research, professional education, and program development.

REFERENCES

Aarons, G. A., Brown, S. A., Hough, R. L., Garland, A. F., & Wood, P. A. (2001). Prevalence of adolescent substance use disorders across five sectors of care. *Journal of American Academy of Child and Adolescent Psychiatry, 40,* 419–426.

Abrantes, A. M., Hoffman, N. G., & Anton, R. (2005). Prevalence of co-occurring disorders among juveniles committed to detention centers. *International Journal of Offender Therapy and Comparative Criminology, 49,* 179–193.

Achenbach, T. M., & Edelbrock, C. (1983). *Manual for the Child Behavior Checklist and revised Child Behavior Profile.* Burlington, VT: Department of Psychiatry, University of Vermont.

Archer, R. P., Stredney, R. V., Mason, J. A., & Arnau, R. C. (2004). An examination and replication of the psychometric properties of the Massachusetts Youth Screening Instrument – Second Edition (MAYI-2) among adolescent in detention settings. *Assessment, 11,* 290–301.

Atkins, D. L., Pumariega, A. J., Rogers, K., Montgomery, M.D., Nybro, C., Jeffers, G., & Sease, F. (1999). Mental health and incarcerated youth. I: Prevalence and nature of psychopathology. *Journal of Child and Family Studies, 8,* 193–204.

Benishek, L. A., Hayes, C. M., Bieschke, K. J., & Stoffelmayr, B. E. (1998). Exploratory and confirmatory factor analyses of the Brief Symptom Inventory among substance abusers. *Journal of Substance Abuse, 10,* 103–114.

Bilchik, S. (1998). *Mental health disorders and substance abuse problems among juveniles. Fact Sheet #82.* Washington, D.C.: U.S. Department of Justice, Office of Justice Programs, Office of Juvenile Justice and Delinquency Prevention.

Boulet, J., & Boss, M. W. (1991). Reliability and validity of the Brief Symptom Inventory. *Psychological Assessment, 3,* 433–437.

Brennan, T. (2003). *Youth-COMPAS psychiatrics report.* Traverse City, MI: Northpointe Institute for Public Management.

Brook, R. H., Chassin, M.R., Fink, A., Solomon, D. H., Kosecoff, J., & Park, R. E. (1986). A method for the detailed assessment of the appropriateness of medical technologies. *International Journal of Technology Assessment in Health Care, 2,* 53–63.

Center for Mental Health Services (1998). *1998 inventory of mental health services in juvenile justice facilities, halfway houses, and group homes.* Rockville, MD: U.S. Department of Health and Human Services.

Cocozza, J. J., & Skowyra, K. (2000). Youth with mental health disorders: Issues and emerging responses. *Juvenile Justice Journal, 8,* 1–3.

Cottler, L. B., Robins, L. N., & Helzer, J. E. (1989). The reliability of the CIDI-SAM: A comprehensive substance abuse interview. *British Journal of Addictions, 84,* 801–814.

Dembo, R., Pacheco, K., Schmeidler, J., Fisher, L., & Cooper, S. (1997a). Drug use and delinquent behavior among high-risk youths. *Journal of Adolescent Substance Abuse, 6,* 1–25.

Dembo, R., Schmeidler, J., Borden, P., Chin Sue, C., & Mannig, D. (1997b). Use of the POSIT among arrested youth entering a juvenile assessment center: A replication. *Journal of Child and Adolescent Substance Abuse, 6,* 19–42.

Dembo, R., Williams, L., Fagan, J., & Schmeidler, J. (1993a). The relationships of substance abuse and other delinquency over time in a sample of juvenile detainees. *Criminal Behavior and Mental Health, 3,* 158–179.

Dembo, R., Williams, L., & Schmeidler, J. (1993b). Gender differences in mental health service needs among youths entering a juvenile detention center. *Journal of Prison and Jail Health, 12,* 73–101.

Dembo, R., Williams, L., & Schmeidler, J., Wish, E. D., Getreu, A., & Berry, E. (1991). Juvenile crime and drug abuse: A prospective study of high-risk youth. *Journal of Addictive Diseases, 11,* 5–31.

Dennis, M.L. (1999). *Overview of the global appraisal of individual needs: Summary.* Bloomington, IL: Chestnut Health Systems.

Dennis, M. L., Rourke, K. M., & Caddell, J. M. (1993). *Global appraisal of individual needs: Administration manual.* Research Triangle Park, NC: Research Triangle Institute.

Derogatis, L. R. (1994). *Brief symptom inventory: Administration, scoring and procedures manual.* Minneapolis, MN: National Computer Systems, Inc.

Derogatis, L. R. (1993). *Symptom Checklist Revised: Administration. scoring. And procedures manual.* Minneapolis, MN: National Computer Systems, Inc.

Dieterich, W., Jenson, J. M., & Potter, C. C. (2001). *A point prevalence survey of mental health and substance use symptoms within two Colorado detention centers.* Unpublished manuscript. Graduate School of Social Work, University of Denver. Denver, Colorado.

Estroff, T. W., & Hoffman, N. G. (2001). *PADDI: Practical adolescent dual diagnosis interview.* Smithfield, RI: Evince Clinical Assessments.

Garland, A. F., Hough, R. L., McCabe, K. M., Yeh, M., Wood, P. A., & Aarons, G. A. (2001). Prevalence of psychiatric disorders in youths across five sectors of care. *Journal of the American Academy of Child and Adolescent Psychiatry, 40,* 409–418.

Goldston, D. B. (2000). *Assessment of suicidal risk and behaviors among children and adolescents.* Technical report submitted to NIMH under contract no. 263–MD–9909995.

Gottfredson, D. M., & Snyder, H. N. (2005). *The mathematics of risk classification: Changing data into valid instruments for juvenile courts.* Washington, D.C.: Office of Juvenile Justice and Delinquency Prevention, Office of Justice Programs, U.S. Department of Justice.

Grisso, T., & Barnum, R. (2000). *Massachusetts Youth Screening Instrument – Version 2.* Boston: Department of Psychiatry, University of Massachusetts.

Grisso, T., Barnum, R., Fletcher, K. E., Cauffman, E., & Peuschold, D. (2001). Massachusetts Youth Screening Instrument for mental health needs of juvenile justice youths. *Journal of the American Academy of Child and Adolescent Psychiatry, 40,* 541–548.

Grisso, T., & Underwood, L. (2004). *Screening and assessing mental health and substance use disorders among youth in the juvenile justice system: A resource guide for practitioners.* Technical report submitted to U.S. Department of Justice under award no 199–JR–VX–006.

Hafkenscheid, A. (1991). Psychometric evaluation of a standardized and expanded Brief Psychiatric Rating Scale. *Acta Psychiatria Scandinavia, 84,* 294–300.

Hafkenscheid, A. (1993). Reliability of a standardized and expanded Brief Psychiatric Rating Scale. *Acta Psychiatria Scandinavia, 88,* 305–310.

Hawkins, J. D., Catalano, R. F., & Miller, J. Y. (1992). Risk and protective factors for alcohol and other drug problems in adolescence and early childhood: Implications for substance abuse prevention. *Psychological Bulletin, 112,* 64–105.

Hawkins, J. D., Jenson, J. M., Catalano, R. F., & Lishner, D. L. (1988). Delinquency and drug abuse: Implications for social services. *Social Service Review, 62,* 258–284.

Henly, G. A., & Winters, K. C. (1988). Development of problem severity scales for the assessment of adolescent alcohol and drug abuse. *International Journal of the Addictions, 23,* 65–85.

Herjanic, B., & Reich, W. (1982). Development of a structured psychiatric interview for children: Agreement between child and parent on individual symptoms. *Journal of Abnormal Child Psychology, 10,* 307–324.

Howard, M .O., & Jenson, J. M. (1999). Inhalant use among antisocial youth: Prevalence and characteristics. *Addictive Behaviors, 24,* 59–74.

Jenson, J. M., & Dieterich, W. (2001). *Assessing mental health problem symptoms among youth in the Colorado juvenile justice system: A field test of the Massachusetts Youth Screening Instrument, Version 2.* Unpublished manuscript. Graduate School of Social Work, University of Denver. Denver, Colorado.

Jenson, J. M., & Howard, M. O. (1998). Hallucinogen use among juvenile probationers: Prevalence and characteristics. *Criminal Justice and Behavior, 26,* 357–372.

Jenson, J. M., & Howard, M. O. (Eds.) (1999). *Youth violence: Current research and recent practice innovations.* Washington, D.C.: National Association of Social Workers Press.

Jenson, J. M., & Potter, C. C. (2003). The effects of cross-system collaboration on mental health and substance abuse problems of detained youth. *Research on Social Work Practice, 13,* 588–607.

Jenson, J., Potter, C., & Dieterich, W. (2003). *Mental health problems, substance abuse, and recidivism among delinquent youth: A field test of the Massachusetts Youth Screening Instrument-2.* Seventh Annual Conference of the Society for Social Work and Research. Washington, D.C.

Johnston, L. D., O'Malley, P. M., & Bachman, J. G. (2001). *Drug use, drinking, and smoking: National survey results from high school, college, and young adult populations.* Washington, D.C.: U.S. Government Printing Office.

Martin, C. S., & Winters, K. C. (1998). Diagnosis and assessment of alcohol use disorders among adolescents. *Alcohol Health and Research World, 22,* 95–106.

McCabe, K. M., Lansing, A. E., Garland, A., & Hough, R. (2002). Gender differences in psychopathology, functional impairment, and familial risk factors among adjudicated delinquents. *Journal of the American Academy of Child and Adolescent Psychiatry, 41,* 860–868.

Miller, G. (1990). *The Substance Abuse Subtle Screening Inventory – Adolescent Version.* Bloomington, ID: Substance Abuse Subtle Screening Institute.

Milin, R., Halikas, J. A., Meller, J. E., & Morse, C. (1991). Psychopathology among substance abusing juvenile offenders. *Journal of the American Academy of Child and Adolescent Psychiatry, 30,* 569–574.

Millon, T. M. (1993). *Millon Adolescent Clinical Inventory (MACI) manual.* Minneapolis, MN: National Computer Systems, Inc.

Morlan, K. K., & Tan, W. Y. (1998). Comparison of the Brief Psychiatric Rating Scale and the Brief Symptom Inventory. *Journal of Clinical Psychology, 54,* 885–894.

National Center on Addiction and Substance Abuse at Columbia University (2002). *Justice denied: Substance abuse and Americas' juvenile justice population.* New York: National Center on Addiction and Substance Abuse at Columbia University.

Neighbors, B., Kempton, T., & Forehand, R. (1992). Co-occurrence of substance abuse with conduct, anxiety, and depression disorders in juvenile delinquents. *Addictive Behaviors, 17*, 379–386.

Piersma, H. L., Boes, J. L., & Beaume, W. M. (1994). Unidimensionality of the Brief Symptom Inventory (BSI) in adult and adolescent inpatients. *Journal of Personality Assessment, 63*, 338–344.

Pollard, J.A., Hawkins, J.D., & Arthur, M.W. (1999). Risk and protection: Are both necessary to understand diverse behavioral outcomes in adolescence? *Social Work Research, 23*, 145–158.

Potter, C., & Jenson J. (2001). *Findings from the mental health and substance abuse among committed youth study: Lookout Mountain Youth Services Center 2000.* Unpublished manuscript: Graduate School of Social Work, University of Denver.

Potter, C. C., & Jenson, J. M. (2003). Cluster profiles of multiple problem youth: Mental health problem symptoms, substance use, and delinquent conduct. *Criminal Justice and Behavior, 30*, 1–21.

Radhert, E. (Ed.) (1991). *The Adolescent Assessment/Referral System manual.* (DHHS Publication No. ADM 91-1735). Rockville, MD: National Institute on Drug Abuse.

Randall, J., Henggeler, S. W., Pickrel, S. G., & Brondino, M.J. (1999). Psychiatric comorbidity and the 16-month trajectory of substance-abusing and substance-dependent juvenile offenders. *Journal of the American Academy of Child and Adolescent Psychiatry, 38*, 1118–1124.

Reich, W. (2000). Diagnostic interview for children and adolescents (DICA). *Journal of the American Academy of Child and Adolescent Psychiatry, 39*, 59–65.

Reppucci, N. D., & Redding, R. E. (2000). *Screening instruments for mental illness in juvenile offenders: The MAYSI and the BSI. Juvenile Justice Fact Sheet.* Charlottesville, NC: Institute of Law, Psychiatry, and Public Policy, University of Virginia.

Riggs, P. D., Baker, S., Mikulich, S. K., Young, S. E., & Crowley, T.J. (1995). Depression in substance-dependent delinquents. *Journal of the American Academy of Child and Adolescent Psychiatry, 34*, 764–771.

Risberg, R. A., Stevens, M. J., & Graybill, D. F. (1995). Validating the adolescent form of the Substance Abuse Subtle Screening Inventory. *Journal of Child and Adolescent Substance Abuse, 4*, 25–41.

Rounds-Bryant, J. L., Kristiansen, P. L., Fairbank, J. A., & Hubbard, R. L. (1998). Substance use, mental disorders, abuse and crime: Gender comparisons among a national sample of adolescent drug treatment clients. *Journal of Child and Adolescent Substance Abuse, 7*, 19–34.

SASSI Institute (2001). New adolescent SASSI-A2. *The SASSI Institute Newsletter.* Springville, IA: Author.

Shaffer, D., & Craft, (1999). Methods of adolescent suicide prevention. *Journal of Clinical Psychiatry, 60*, 70–74.

Shaffer, D., Fisher, P., Piacentini, J., Schwab-Stone, M., & Wicks, J. (1989). *Diagnostic Interview Schedule for Children.* New York: Columbia University Press.

Shaffer, D., Fischer, P., & Duclan, M. K. (1996). The NIMH Diagnostic Interview Schedule for children, Version 2.3(DISC 2.3): description, acceptability, prevalence rate and performance in the MECA study. *Journal of the American Academy of Child and Adolescent Psychiatry, 35*, 865–877.

Shaffer, D., Fisher, P., Lucas, C. P., Dulcan, M. K., & Schwab-Stone, M. E. (2000). NIMH Diagnostic Interview Schedule for Children Version IV: Description, differences, from previous versions, and reliability of some common diagnoses. *Journal of the American Academy of Child and Adolescent Psychiatry, 39*, 409–418.

Snyder, H. N., & Sickmund, M. (1999). *Juvenile offenders and victims: 1999 National Report.* Washington D.C.: Office of Juvenile Justice and Delinquency Prevention.

Steiner, H. S., & Cauffman, E. (1998). Juvenile justice, delinquency and psychiatry. *The Child Psychiatrist in the Community, 7*, 653–672.

Steiner, H., Cauffman, E., & Duxbury, E. (1998). Personality traits in juvenile delinquents: Relation to criminal behavior and recidivism. *Journal of the American Academy of Child and Adolescent Psychiatry, 38*, 256–262.

Teplin, L. A. (2001a). *Assessing alcohol, drug, and mental disorders in juvenile detainees. Fact Sheet #2.* Washington, D.C.: U.S. Department of Justice, Office of Justice Programs, Office of Juvenile Justice and Delinquency Prevention.

Teplin, L. A. (2001b). *Psychiatric disorders among juvenile detainees.* Presentation at the annual meeting of the American Society of Criminology. Atlanta, Georgia. November, 2001.

Teplin, L. A., Abram, K. M., McClelland, G. M., Duclan, M., & Mericle, A. A. (2003). Psychiatric disorders in youth in juvenile detention. *Archive of General Psychiatry, 59*, 1133–1143.

Terry, Y. B., Vanderwaal, C. J., McBride, D. C., & Van Buren, H. (2000). Provision of drug treatment services in the juvenile justice system: A system reform. *The Journal of Behavioral Health Services and Research, 27*, 194–214.

Timmons-Mitchell, J., Brown, C., Schulz, S. C., Webster, S. E., Underwood, L. A., & Semple, W. E. (1997). Comparing the mental health needs of female and male incarcerated juvenile delinquents. *Behavioral Sciences and the Law, 15*, 195–202.

Trupin, E., & Boeskym, L. (1999). *Working together for change: Co-occurring mental health and substance use disorders among youth involved in the juvenile justice system. Cross training juvenile justice, mental health, substance abuse.* Delmar, NY: The National GAINS Center.

Ulzen, P. M., & Hamilton, H. (1998). The nature and characteristics of psychiatric comorbidity in incarcerated adolescents. *Canadian Journal of Psychiatry, 43*, 57–63.

U.S. Department of Health and Human Services (2001). *Youth violence: A report of the surgeon general.* Rockville, MD: U.S. Department of Health and Human Services, Centers for Disease Control and Prevention, National Center for Injury Prevention and Control, Substance Abuse and Mental Health Services Administration, Center for Mental Health Services, and National Institutes of Health and Mental Health.

Washington State Institute for Public Policy (2004). *Assessing risk for re-offense: Validating the Washington State Juvenile Court Assessment.* Olympia, WA: Washington State Institute for Public Policy.

Wasserman, G. A., Jensen, P. S., Ko, S. J., Cocozza, J., Trupin, E., Angold, A., Cauffman, E., & Grisso, T. (2002). Mental health assessments in juvenile justice: Report on the Consensus Conference. *Journal of the American Academy of Child and Adolescent Psychiatry, 42,* 752–761.

Wasserman, G. A., McReynolds, L. S., & Ko, S. J. (2001). *Gender differences in psychiatric diagnosis among incarcerated youth.* Presentation at the annual meeting of the American Society of Criminology. Atlanta, Georgia, November, 2001.

Wasserman, G. A., McReynolds, L. S., Ko, S. J., Katz, L. M., Cauffman, E., Haxton, W. & Lucas,. C. P. (2004). Screening for emergent risk and service needs among incarcerated youth: Comparing the MAYSI-2 and Voice DISC-IV. *Journal of the American Academy of child and Adolescent Psychiatry, 43,* 629–639.

Welner, Z., Reich, W., Herjanic, B., Jung, K. G., & Amado, H. (1987). Reliability, validity, and parent-child agreement studies of the Diagnostic Interview Schedule for Children (DICA). *Journal of the American Academy of Child Psychiatry, 26,* 649–653.

Wierson, M., Forehand, R. L., & Frame, C. L. (1992). Epidemiology and the treatment of mental health problems in juvenile delinquents. *Advances in Behavior Residential Theory, 14,* 93–120.

Winters, K. C. (1992). Development of an adolescent alcohol and other drug abuse screening scale: Personal experience screening questionnaire. *Addictive Behaviors, 17,* 479–490.

Winters, K. A., Anderson, N., Bengston, P., Stinchfield, R. D., & Latimer, W. W. (2000). Development of a parent questionnaire for use in assessing adolescent drug abuse. *Journal of Psychoactive Drugs, 32,* 3–13.

Winters, K. A., & Henly, G. A. (1993). *Adolescent Diagnostic Interview Schedule and Manual.* Los Angeles: Western Psychological Services.

Winters, K. A., Latimer, W. W., & Stinchefield, R. D. (1999). DSM-IV criteria for adolescent alcohol and cannabis use disorders. *Journal of Studies on Alcohol, 60,* 337–344.

Winters, K. A., Stinchfield, R. D., & Henly, G. A. (1993a). Further validation of new scales measuring adolescent alcohol and other drug abuse. *Journal of Studies on Alcohol, 54,* 534–541.

Winters, K. A., Weller, C. L., & Meland, J. A. (1993). Extent of drug abuse among juvenile offenders. *Journal of Drug Issues, 23,* 515–524.

LIST OF RELEVANT RESOURCES

1. National Center for Mental Health and Juvenile Justice (http://www.ncmhjj.com/resource_kit/Default.htm). For access to the Tool Kit: Improving Services for Youth with Mental Health and Co-Occurring Substance Use Disorders Involved with the Juvenile Justice System.

2. National Institute of Mental Health (NIMH) Resources for Suicide Researchers (http://www.nimh.nih.gov/suicideresearch/suiresearch.cfm). For easy access to the Goldston (2000) review of suicide assessment measures.

3. U.S. Department of Health and human Services and SAMHSA's National Clearinghouse for Alcohol and Drug Information. (http://www.health.org/default.aspx). For access to information on screening and assessment of substance abuse, including the PEI, PESQ and ADI.

4. The National Youth Screening Assessment Project (http://www.umassmed.edu/nysap). For access and information on the MAYSI-2.

5. Pearson Assessments (http://www.pearsonassessments.com/tests). For access and information on the SCL-90-R and BSI.

6. Center for the Promotion of Mental health and Juvenile Justice, Columbia University (http://www.promotementalhealth.org/atsectionI.htm). For access to a wealth of information on screening and assessment in juvenile justice, including the DISC-IV. The Center will provide the Voice DISC-IV assessment software program, provide training for key personnel, offer ongoing technical support, assist with data interpretation and preparation of reports, and provide guidelines for appropriate mental health referrals.

7. SASSI Institute (http://www.sassi.com/sassi/index.shtml). For information on the Substance Abuse Subtle Screening Inventory (the SASSI).

8. Assessments.com (http://www.assessments.com). For information on the POSIT, and other adolescent measures of functioning.

9. Chestnut Health Services : Lighthouse Institute (http://www.chestnut.org/LI/gain/). For information about the GAIN.

Chapter 13

Mental Health and Substance Abuse Treatment of Juvenile Delinquents

Stephen J. Tripodi and David W. Springer

Marcus

Marcus, a 16-year-old African American male, was recently brought to the Juvenile Assessment Center (JAC) for truancy, possession of marijuana, and possession of a deadly weapon, all direct violations of his already existing probation. The police caught Marcus selling marijuana to other adolescents in a part of town with high crime rates and drug transactions. Marcus was no stranger to the Juvenile Assessment Center staff; this was his fourth time being arrested for possession of marijuana and second time for possession of a deadly weapon. Nine months ago, the last time Marcus was arrested and adjudicated, he was placed on two years probation and instructed to receive outpatient substance abuse treatment based on the results of a substance abuse assessment. Marcus did quite well in outpatient treatment, advancing through the program with relative ease, no relapses, and no confrontations with police. He graduated from the program in five months.

Marcus's father, who was chemically dependent, was arrested for attempted murder ten years ago and Marcus has not seen him since. Marcus considers himself to be very close with his mother and older brother, but sees them very little as the family's TANF eligibility expired a year ago, forcing Marcus's mother to work two jobs that pay minimum wage. Despite Marcus's perception of being close with his mother, however, he often disrespects her by cursing at her and disobeying her rules. Additionally, Marcus has run away from home three times, between the ages of 13 and 15. Marcus shows little remorse for this behavior.

Marcus's older brother recently moved to a nearby city to escape the dangers of the neighborhood. Marcus's IQ is above the normal range and he does well in school when he is present, but Marcus has a history of truancy and negligence towards academic endeavors.

With the help of strong advocacy by the social worker at the Juvenile Assessment Center and the social worker at the outpatient treatment center that treated Marcus, the judge ordered Marcus to residential substance abuse treatment rather than a jail sentence. The two social workers helped convince the judge that Marcus deserved one more chance at treatment. Because Marcus already completed outpatient treatment, the judge sentenced Marcus to residential treatment at the nearby therapeutic community for adolescents. Furthermore, because Marcus's mother and brother did not participate in the family component of the outpatient treatment program, the judge also ordered the family to attend the weekly multifamily groups offered at the residential treatment center.

Marcus was assigned a case manager at the Juvenile Assessment Center who is expected to visit Marcus weekly at the residential treatment services. Moreover, the case manager is expected to link Marcus's family with the necessary resources to increase the chances of posttreatment success.

Rachel

Rachel is a 15-year-old Hispanic female who was recently brought to the JAC for being intoxicated and in possession of pills she was using for recreational purposes. Rachel was with her boyfriend, Bradley, when he was driving intoxicated and pulled over by the police. Bradley was arrested for Driving Under the Influence (DUI) and Rachel was arrested for drug possession.

Because Rachel was severely intoxicated when apprehended by the police, she was taken to the Juvenile Addiction Receiving Facility (JARF) for detoxification. The next morning, when Rachel was sober, she was given a thorough psychosocial assessment.

Rachel is in the tenth grade and has traditionally earned high grades. About three months ago, Rachel met her new boyfriend, Bradley, who is two years older and introduced her to marijuana, acid, prescription medication, and cocaine. Rachel lives with both of her parents. Her father, George, is a construction manager and her mother, Roni, works as an administrative assistant at the local university. Rachel also has an older brother, David, who works for their father and attends the local community college. Rachel's IQ, although still in the normal range, is above average. She has a lot of friends who do not use drugs, but rarely sees them since dating Bradley.

This was Rachel's first offense; accordingly, the judge did not sentence her to residential substance abuse treatment. She did, however, place Rachel on six months probation, and part of the terms of probation was for the family to participate in family-based substance abuse treatment. Furthermore, Rachel was required to submit random urinalyses, as another term of her probation was to remain drug and alcohol free. Rachel and her parents first met with the social worker (family therapist) one week after meeting with the judge.

SCOPE OF THE PROBLEM

Adolescent mental health, substance abuse and juvenile delinquency are interrelated and complex problems that remain prevalent and problematic in the United States. Approximately 70 percent of all twelfth-graders report alcohol use, 38.8 percent report illicit drug use, and 34.3 percent report marijuana use during the past year (Johnston, O'Malley, & Bachman, 2004). According to the Office of Applied Studies (2004), more than 10 percent of all adolescents report using illegal drugs in the past month. More

than 340,000 adolescents state they smoked marijuana in 2004 and 536,000 youths report using marijuana more than 20 days in the past month. The problem is even more severe when considering rates of adolescent alcohol consumption. More than 17 percent of all American adolescents say they drank alcohol within the past month and over 30 percent of 16–17-year-old youth report they currently drink alcohol. Over 20 percent are binge drinkers, meaning they had five or more drinks on the same occasion at least once in the past 30 days (Office of Applied Studies, 2004). Furthermore, among youths 12–17 years old, an estimated 1.3 million need treatment for illicit drug use and an additional 1.5 million youth need treatment for an alcohol problem. Only 113,000 adolescents, however, receive treatment for illicit drug use and only 95,000 receive treatment for alcohol problems.

Rates for illicit drug use are slightly higher for males than females (9.9% vs. 6.1%, respectively), but illicit drug rates for females have increased more than males over the past year. While males are twice as likely to use marijuana, rates of nonmedical use of prescription drugs are higher for females (Office of Applied Studies, 2004). In terms of alcohol and/or drug (AOD) use among various racial/ethnic groups, studies have shown important differences in the prevalence of AOD use (Vega & Gil, 1998), in the risk factors associated with AOD use (Vega & Gil, 1998; Vega, Zimmerman, Gil, Warheit, & Apospori, 1993), and in protective factors that lessen substance use (Vega & Gil, 1998). Broadly speaking, epidemiological studies have found adolescent substance use rates to be highest among Caucasians and lowest among African Americans. More specifically, 11.1 percent of Caucasian adolescents have used illicit drugs, compared with 10.2 percent of Latinos, and 9.3 percent of African Americans.

The FBI (2002) reports over 2.3 million arrests of persons under age 18 in 2001. Juveniles accounted for 17 percent of all arrests, 15 percent of all violent crime arrests, and 21 percent of all property crime arrests. Sixty-nine percent of all adolescent arrestees were between ages 15 and 17, and 72 percent were males. However, between 1992 and 2001, the increase in crime rates was more significant for female adolescents than for males. The number of juvenile arrests involving drug offenses increased by 169 percent from 1990 to 1999 (Stahl, 2003). A disproportionate percentage of juvenile arrests are of minorities; there is an overrepresentation of minorities in the juvenile justice population despite the fact that this overrepresentation does not appear to be due to higher rates of criminal activity (Kaestner, Frank, Marel, & Schmeidler, 1986).

Adolescent Substance Use and Juvenile Delinquency: A Connexus

Research indicates a significant association between adolescent AOD use/abuse and delinquency (Dembo, Pacheco, Schmeidler, Fisher, & Cooper, 1997; Huizinga, Loeber, & Thornberry, 1994; Rossow, Pape, & Wichstrom, 1999). Incarcerated adolescents are three times more likely to have partaken in substance use in the past year than other adolescents, and juvenile offenders are more likely to have substance use problems (Office of Applied Studies, 2003, Molider, Nissen, & Watkins, 2002). In the last decade, the percentage of arrested male youth that tested positive for an illegal drug increased by at least 30 percent (Terry, VanderWaal, McBride, & Buren, 2000). Moreover, delinquent youth are generally more involved in their substance use than nondelinquent substance users, and, among delinquents, juveniles with more intense substance use demonstrate more violent offenses (Sealock, Gottfriedson, & Gallagher, 1997).

Teplin, Abram, McClelland, Duclan, and Mericle (2003) conducted an epidemiological study to examine psychiatric disorders in 1,800 juvenile delinquents in Cook County, Illinois. They found that the most common disorders were substance use disorders and disruptive behavior disorders, such as oppositional defiant disorder and conduct disorder. More specifically, Teplin and her colleagues found that 66 percent of boys and 74 percent of girls met criteria for at least one diagnosis. Girls met criteria in significantly greater numbers for affective and anxiety disorders and boys met more commonly met criteria for externalizing behavior disorders such as ADHD and substance use. Half of boys and girls (50% and 47%, respectively) met criteria for at least one substance abuse disorder. The existing literature also reveals a strong relationship between history of abuse and both current substance use and delinquency. Because of the association between substance abuse and juvenile delinquency, the reduction of AOD use is critical to treating and preventing juvenile delinquency.

LITERATURE REVIEW

Following a number of critical reviews of evaluations, in particular Lipton, Martinson, and Wilks (1975), the accepted wisdom in the field related to substance-abusing juveniles became one of "nothing works." Recent research with this population has been more encouraging.

Lipsey and Wilson (1998) conducted a meta-analysis of experimental or quasi-experimental studies of interventions for serious and violent juvenile delinquents. They reviewed 200 programs, 83 of which involved institutionalized juveniles and 117 involved noninstitutionalized juveniles. McBride et al. (1999, p. 58) summarize the findings of Lipsey and Wilson's meta-analysis.

Among the programs in *noninstitutional* settings, those that demonstrate good evidence of effectiveness include behavioral therapies (family and contingency contracting), intensive case management (including system collaboration and continuing care), multisystemic therapy (MST), restitution programs (parole- and probation-based), and skills training. Program options that require more research to document their effectiveness include 12-step programs (AA, NA), adult mentoring (with behaviorally contingent reinforcement), after-school recreation programs, conflict resolution/violence prevention, intensive probation services (IPS), juvenile versions of TASC, peer mediation, and traditional inpatient/outpatient programs. Program options which do not show evidence of effectiveness include deterrence programs, vocational training or career counseling, and wilderness challenge programs.

In *institutional* settings, evidence of effectiveness has been demonstrated for behavioral programs (cognitive mediation and stress inoculation training), longer-term community residential programs (TCs with cognitive-behavioral approaches), multiple services within residential communities (case management approach), and skills training (aggression replacement training and cognitive restructuring). More research is needed to determine the effectiveness of day treatment centers, as there were too few studies to review. Those programs which have been shown ineffective are juvenile boot camps, short-term residential facilities, and state training schools.

In addition to some of the evidence-based approaches available to treat substance-abusing juvenile delinquents, this literature review will address two interventions that have inadequate or equivocal support in the research, namely juvenile boot camps and Alcoholics Anonymous (AA), given their popularity. Through the case studies of Marcus and Rachel, outpatient family therapy (structural-strategic and brief strategic family therapy [BSFT]) will be discussed. Therapeutic communities, case management, JAC's/JARF's, problem solving skills training, and urine drug screens will be also be reviewed. (This chapter will not provide explicit details on some evidence-based approaches, such as motivational interviewing and Multisystemic Therapy [MST], as these approaches are covered in detail in Chapters 11 and 16, respectively.)

Among the guiding principles in their review of the existing literature on effective programming for substance-abusing adolescents, McBride, Vanderwall, Terry, and Van Buren (1999) asserted that three core elements are needed: (1) intervention must take place early when it has the best chance of reversing or ameliorating problem behaviors; (2) adolescents entering the system must undergo a comprehensive needs assessment in order to tailor interventions to each juvenile's unique needs; and (3) once needs have been identified, adolescents must be provided with a flexible and comprehensive continuum of care that offers the full range of relevant services needed for effective intervention (cited in Dembo, Schmeidler, & Walters, 2004). Juvenile assessment centers, a recent development in juvenile justice, help to meet these elements.

Juvenile Assessment Centers and Juvenile Addiction Receiving Facilities

A Juvenile Assessment Center (JAC) is a centralized intake system where law enforcement can drop off youth charged with truancy, felonies, and misdemeanors generally quickly, usually within ten minutes (Springer, Shader, & McNeece, 1999). The first JAC was developed in Tampa, Florida, where funds were obtained through competition from Drug Abuse Act of 1988 (Byrne Grant) funds. In the mid-1990s, the Center for Substance Abuse Treatment (CSAT) became interested in JACs as an effective approach to intervene with juvenile offenders with substance abuse problems (Dembo, Schmeidler, & Walters, 2004). JACs and community assessment centers (CACs) now exist across many cities and

states in the country, including Kansas, Colorado, and Florida.

The purpose of designing JACs was to help ensure that youths' service needs are addressed in disposition recommendations and to link at-risk or troubled youth and their families with needed services (Dembo, Schmeidler, & Walters, 2004; Springer, Shader, & McNeece, 1999). While the cornerstone of JACs is screening and assessment systems, the Office of Juvenile Justice and Delinquency Prevention (OJJDP) has identified four common elements of the CACs they have funded (Oldenettel & Wordes, 2000, pp. 1–2).

1. Single point of entry: a 24-hour centralized point of intake and assessment for juveniles who have come or are likely to come into contact with the juvenile justice system.
2. Immediate and comprehensive assessments: service providers associated with the JAC make an initial broad-based and, if necessary, a later in-depth assessment of youths' circumstances and treatment needs.
3. Management information systems: needed to manage and monitor youths, help ensure the provision of appropriate treatment services, and avoid duplication of services.
4. Integrated case management services: JAC staff use information obtained from the assessment process and the MIS to develop recommendations to improve access to services, complete follow-ups of referred youths, and periodically reassess youths placed in various services.

Regarding the above criteria, Dembo, Schmeidler, and Walters (2004) clarify that in-depth assessments are often completed following the JAC processing, that MISs vary in their comprehensiveness and sophistication, and that the provision of case management services is often limited to subsets of processed youths, such as those placed in diversion programs.

If a youth is intoxicated or requires nonemergency medical screening or care, he or she is brought directly to the Juvenile Addiction Receiving Facility (JARF), when one is available, which is a complete detoxification unit. JARFs are generally closely associated with the JAC, often in the same building, and if not, at least in the same vicinity. A JARF is typically a traditional detoxification model that provides short-term residential care, consisting of detoxification, stabilization, and substance abuse services (Springer, Shader, & McNeece, 1999).

Dembo and Brown (1994) examined 110 truant juveniles brought to a JAC in Tampa, Florida, and found that it successfully identified multiple-problem, high-risk youth. Of these youth, approximately 96 percent indicated a potential problem in peer relations; 82 percent indicated a potential problem in mental health status; and between 33 and 47 percent had a potential problem in substance abuse, physical health, family relations, and vocational status. Springer, McNeece, and Shader (1999) conducted a study assessing six JACs/JARFs in Florida, and similar to Dembo and Brown, they found that the primary presenting problems of the juveniles presented were peer relations, family relations, mental health, substance abuse, physical health, and school or vocational issues. Many of the staff across the JACs and JARFs appeared stressed because of high caseloads or inadequate work settings. Additionally, they found that a common thread across well-run JACs was an energetic and hard working director with strong interpersonal and mediation skills.

Therapeutic Communities

A therapeutic community is generally a residential treatment environment where the drug user's change in conduct, attitudes, values, and emotions are implemented, monitored, and reinforced on a daily basis (DeLeon, 1986). Therapeutic communities view drug abuse as deviant behavior and believe substance abusers require holistic treatment to engender global change. Treatment is sequenced in phases, and phase advancement requires the client to progress behaviorally, emotionally, and developmentally (Jainchill, Hawke, De Leon, & Yagelka 2000). Proponents of therapeutic communities consider the problem to be the substance abuser him or herself, not the drug(s), and the addiction is a symptom, not the essence of the disorder (Pan, Scarpitti, Inciardi, & Lockwood, 1993).

In the case of work with adolescent substance abusers in therapeutic communities, forms of Positive Peer Culture (PPC) are often used to facilitate group treatment. Positive Peer Culture, developed by Harry Vorrath, was heavily influenced by a peer-oriented treatment model called Guided Group Interaction (GGI). Vorrath and Brendtro (1985) call PPC "a total system for building positive youth subcultures" (p. xx).

PPC is a holistic approach to working with youth in a therapeutic setting. It is not simply a set of techniques, but rather attempts to change the culture in the therapeutic setting. "PPC is designed to 'turn around' a negative youth subculture and mobilize the power of the peer group in a productive manner . . . In contrast to traditional treatment approaches, PPC does not ask whether a person wants to receive help but whether he is willing to give help" (Vorrath & Brendtro, 1985, p. xxi). Proponents of PPC view troubled youth not as rebellious or "bad seeds," but rather as youth that with nurturing have much to contribute. Table 13-1 highlights some of the key aspects and assumptions of a Positive Peer Culture.

According to Obermeir and Henry (1988–1989), adolescents who are successful in therapeutic communities perceive themselves as a member of a group of peers who act as a support network. Rules of the therapeutic community are enforced by the clients themselves, with elder and trusted clients acting as supervisors to the other community members, although staff members generally have more control of enforcing the rules in adolescent therapeutic communities than in traditional adult therapeutic communities. The staff in therapeutic communities consists of recovering substance abusers, licensed substance

Table 13-1
POSITIVE PEER CULTURE

Key Aspects of a Positive Peer Culture
1. Seeks to teach basic values.
2. The peer group has the strongest influence over the values, attitudes, and behaviors of youth.
3. Youth feel positive about themselves when they feel accepted by others and deserving of that acceptance.
4. Youth are experts of their own lives.
5. Youth are resilient.
6. Youth possess strengths that should be recognized by practitioners and tapped throughout the treatment process. Youth are better to help one another when these strengths are tapped.
7. Focus on the here and now.
8. Problems are opportunities.
9. Youth must accept responsibility for their behavior and be held accountable.
10. Both youth and adults must care for and help one another.

abuse counselors, licensed professional counselors, and licensed clinical social workers.

Jainchill et al. (2000) assessed the effectiveness of six residential therapeutic communities for adolescents. While there was a statistically significant difference between treatment completers and treatment dropouts in pretest vs. posttest levels of drug use, it is not possible to rule out selectivity bias and extraneous variables, such as adolescents' motivation levels. Morral, McCaffrey, and Ridgeway (2004) conducted a more rigorous evaluation of a residential therapeutic community for adolescents in Los Angeles, California. Adolescents in the treatment group had significantly better outcomes on all three substance use scales used to measure levels of AOD use. There was not a significant difference between the treatment group and the comparison group in crime outcomes, but adolescents in the treatment group showed greater declines in mean scores over the one-year observation on arrests, property crimes, and violent crimes.

Research on the effectiveness of TCs for adolescents also reveals that the length of stay in treatment is the largest and most consistent predictor of positive outcomes (Catalano, Hawkins, Wells, Miller, & Brewer, 1990/91; De Leon, 1988). Positive outcomes, such as no criminal activity, no use of alcohol or drugs, and employment, are all associated with longer stays in treatment (McBride et al., 1999).

Problem-Solving Skills Training

Problem-solving skills training (PSST) (Spivak & Schure, 1974) is a cognitively-based intervention that has been used to treat aggressive and antisocial youth (Kazdin, 1994). The problem-solving process involves helping clients learn how to produce a variety of potentially effective responses when faced with problem situations. Regardless of the specific problem-solving model used, the primary focus is on addressing the thought process to help adolescents address deficiencies and distortions in their approach to interpersonal situations (Kazdin, 1994). A variety of techniques are used, including didactic teaching, practice, modeling, role-playing, feedback, social reinforcement, and therapeutic games (Kronenberger & Meyer, 2001). The problem-solving approach typically includes five steps for the practitioner and client to address: (1) defining the problem, (2) brainstorming, (3) evaluating

the alternatives, (4) choosing and implementing an alternative, and (5) evaluating the implemented option (Corcoran & Springer, 2005). Several randomized clinical trials (Type 1 and 2 studies) have demonstrated the effectiveness of PSST with impulsive, aggressive, and conduct-disordered children and adolescents (cf. Baer & Nietzel, 1991; Durlak, Furh-man, & Lampman, 1991; Kazdin, 2000; cited in Kazdin, 2002).

Outpatient Family-Based Interventions

While it is a truism that families are critical in a youth's substance abuse treatment, the social worker must be cautious in concluding that family conflict causes a child or adolescent to use drugs, especially considering that all families experience conflict and not all adolescents use substances (Springer, 2005). Working with an individual client without examining the family structure, dynamics, and roles that are influenced by and influence the client's substance use is generally insufficient (McNeece, Springer, & Arnold, 2001). The literature reveals a correlation between adolescent substance use and family system characteristics; specifically that family drug use, family composition, family interaction patterns, and family boundaries all increase the risk of adolescent AOD use (Anderson & Henry, 1994; Denton & Kampfe, 1994).

Joaning, Quinn, Thomas, and Mullen (1992) conducted a study comparing the differences in adolescent substance abuse treatment between family therapy, adolescent group therapy, and family drug education. The findings tentatively revealed that family therapy was more effective in stopping adolescent drug abuse, producing twice the amount of substance-free adolescents than family drug education and three times the amount of adolescent group therapy.

More recently, Austin, Macgowan, and Wagner (2005) conducted a rigorous evaluation of family-based interventions for adolescent substance abuse populations. The purpose of the systematic review was to examine the level of efficacy and effectiveness of the most current family-based treatment approaches. Austin and his colleagues found that Brief Strategic Family Therapy (BSFT) and Multidimensional Family Therapy are the most effective among the family-based interventions, meeting the criteria for *probably efficacious* according to the criteria developed by Chambless and Hollon (1998). In the case of Rachel at the beginning of the chapter, the social worker used BSFT, which is based on structural-strategic family therapy. Accordingly, both BSFT and structural-strategic family therapy are reviewed below. For a review of Multidimensional Family Therapy, please see Liddle (1999) and Ozechowski and Little (2002).

STRUCTURAL-STRATEGIC FAMILY THERAPY. Structural-strategic family therapy is a commonly used family-based intervention with substance-abusing clients. Structural family therapy was developed by Salvador Minuchin and his associates (Minuchin, 1974; Minuchin & Fishman, 1981) at the Philadelphia Child Guidance Clinic, and Jay Haley's work with Cloe Madanes led to the strategic approach (Haley, 1976; Madanes, 1981). Structural-strategic family therapists view the interactive behaviors of family members as forms of communication. When working with a substance-abusing adolescent and his or her family, therapeutic goals are consistently related to drug use, but they also should relate to broader issues, such as family roles and interaction patterns (Springer, McNeece, & Arnold, 2003). A general assumption is that problems are considered to be maintained by dysfunctional family structures and roles. Accordingly, a major goal is to alter the family structure that maintains the substance abusing behavior. We refer readers interested in this approach to several comprehensive sources (cf. Haley, 1976; Minuchin, 1974; Minuchin & Fishman, 1981; Todd & Selekman, 1991).

It is important to note that when working with adolescents, structural-strategic therapists avoid using the terms addict and alcoholic (Springer, McNeece, & Arnold, 2003). Todd and Selekman (1994) believe these labels to be harmful for substance-abusing adolescents, especially early in treatment before the practitioner knows how responsive the juvenile will be to treatment. Studies have demonstrated that adolescents do not accept such identifying labels because of where they are in the developmental process. In general, research indicates that family therapy appears effective in reducing AOD rates with adolescents (Liddle & Dakof, 1995; Stanton & Shadish, 1997; Waldron, 1997), and specifically, structural-strategic modeling has been found effective with drug addicts and

their families (Alexander & Parsons, 1973; Stanton & Todd, 1979; Stanton, Todd, & Colleagues, 1982).

BRIEF STRATEGIC FAMILY THERAPY. BSFT was developed in response to an increase in Hispanic adolescent drug use in the 1970s (Robbins, Szapocznik, Santisteban, Hervis, Mitrani, & Schwartz, 2003), and has since become the primary model used to work with Hispanic families with behavior problem youth, including AOD. BSFT is based on three central constructs: systems, structure/patterns, and strategy. BSFT proponents believe that a family is a system comprised of individuals whose behaviors affect other family members. Structure and patterns refer to the set of repetitive patterns of interactions that are idiosyncratic to a family. A maladaptive family structure contributes to behavior problems such as conduct disorder and AOD use. Strategy is the third central construct on which BSFT is based. Therapists that adhere to BSFT use family interventions that are practical, problem-focused, and deliberate, and they move the family toward desired objectives (Robbins et al., 2003).

Robbins et al. (2003) highlight three key assumptions to BSFT: (1) changing the family is the most effective way of changing an individual; (2) changing an individual and then returning him or her to a detrimental or negative environment does not allow the individual changes to remain in place; and (3) changes in one central or powerful individual can result in changes in the rest of his or her family. Therapy sessions, which involve the entire family, are generally once a week for 8–12 weeks and last between an hour and an hour and a half.

In an experimental study, Santisteban, Coatsworth, and colleagues (2003) randomly assigned 126 Hispanic adolescents with externalizing disorders, including AOD use, and their families to BSFT or a control group. Results revealed that adolescents in BSFT showed significantly greater reductions in conduct disorder and socialized aggression than youth in the control group. Additionally, BSFT appeared to be effective in reducing marijuana use with the same sample, although there were no differences in alcohol consumption.

Case Management

Case management activities originated in early twentieth-century social work practice that provided services to disadvantaged clients. Rothman (2002) defines case management as a service for highly vulnerable client populations to ensure that they receive the help they need within the fragmented American service delivery system. Similarly, Sullivan (2002) asserts that case management is a direct service function that involves skill in assessment, counseling, teaching, modeling, and advocacy that aims to enhance the social functioning of clients. Case management includes at least six primary functions: (1) identification and outreach to people in need of service, (2) assessment of specific needs, (3) planning for service, (4) linkage to service, (5) monitoring and evaluation, and (6) advocacy for the client system. The most common activity for case managers who work with juveniles is coordinating substance abuse services (Jenson, 1997).

Case management with substance-abusing clients has gained considerable attention in the past decade, particularly among populations who have multiple, long-term needs (Springer, McNeece, & Arnold, 2003). While case management appears to be effective with dually-diagnosed youths (those with both a substance use and a mental health disorder) (Evans & Dollard, 1992) and with juvenile delinquents (Enos & Souther, 1996), little is known about its effectiveness in juvenile justice settings (cited in McBride et al., 1999).

Boot Camps

A brief review of boot camps is warranted because of their popularity in the era of treating offenders with retribution and punishment. Today's boot camps can be traced back to the United States' first penitentiaries at the turn of the nineteenth century, which used military-style marches, physical labor, and discipline (Rothman, 1990). Most local and state boot camps (also known as *shock incarceration*) are designed for first offenders and stress discipline, physical conditioning, and strict authoritarian control (McNeece, 1997). Juvenile delinquent bootcamps have grown in popularity over the last several years due to the populace's mentality that these adolescents need more discipline in their lives. The boot camps philosophy is based on breaking down and then building up the juvenile in a quasi-military setting (Parent, 1989).

In general, it appears that despite their popularity among politicians and the media, juvenile boot camps are not cost-effective and do not deliver positive treatment effects for juvenile offenders, when compared to traditional services such as probation or parole (cf. California Youth Authority, 1997; Peters, Thomas, and Zamberlan, 1997; Trulson & Triplett, 1999). Many criminologists believe that boot camps do not make a long-term impact on juveniles because they do not meet the needs of the offenders and that in fact rearrest rates of boot camp graduates are no different than other inmates (MacKenzie, 1994; MacKenzie et al., 2001). Lipsey's (1992) well-known meta-analyses of treatment for juvenile offenders revealed that deterrence programs, such as boot camps, actually had negative treatment effects on delinquent youths.

Alcoholics Anonymous

A brief review of abstinence-based approaches, such as Alcoholics Anonymous (AA), is also essential here, particularly considering the perception that such approaches are a blanket effective modality for substance-abusing adolescents. AA, an abstinence-based, 12-step program, was founded in 1935 by William Wilson and Robert Holbrook Smith. Proponents of AA believe that alcoholism is a disease that cannot be cured; thus, there are recovering alcoholics but not ex-alcoholics.

The surrender steps consist of treatment personnel persuading youth that they cannot control their use of drugs. Youth "surrender" their attempts to control drug use to a higher power. The "higher power" is not always intended to be synonymous with God or any similar deity, and the emphasis is on creating a spiritual defense against drug use. The integrity steps focus on youth's admitting that they have caused harm to others, thus enabling them to accept personal responsibility for conflicts precipitated by tension around drug and alcohol misuse (Brown-Standridge, 1987). Integrity steps allow youth to apologize for difficulties that were caused by their drug and alcohol use. The last three steps in the twelve-step program, serenity steps, are concerned with maintaining a drug-free life-style. While the surrender steps assist chemically dependent youth to cease use, the integrity steps begin the task of rebuilding relationships through apologies, and the serenity steps focus on living a life free of drugs and alcohol.

Research studies assessing the effectiveness of AA groups with adolescents reveal equivocal results. Alford, Koehler, and Leonard (1991) indicate that

AA benefits adolescents who are able to understand and accept AA principles and traditions. However, the lack of a comparison group requires that these results be interpreted with caution and not generalized to all adolescents (Springer, McNeece, & Arnold, 2003). The Chemical Abuse/Addiction Treatment Outcome Registry reveals that adolescents who remained in AA for one-year had better outcomes than adolescents that did not remain in AA for an entire year or did not attend AA at all. Again, these results must not be generalized to all adolescents because of possible differences between the experimental and comparison groups and confounding variables such as motivation levels. Research on the effectiveness of AA usually focuses on middle and upper-class populations with stable lives prior to the onset of a drinking problem (Alexander, 1990), and much of the evidence regarding its effectiveness is based on anecdotal reports (Miller & Hester, 1986).

The effectiveness of AA with adolescents needs to be explored further by professionals and researchers working with substance-abusing adolescents (Springer, McNeece, & Arnold, 2003). In the meantime, the blanket prescription of AA groups for all adolescents who have used or abused alcohol or drugs is not a judicious use of resources, nor is it effective treatment planning (Springer, 2005).

Urine Drug Testing

Urine drug testing in the juvenile justice system is a surveillance method to detect whether offenders are currently using drugs. The offender must provide a urine sample, which is tested to detect for the presence of specific drugs. Two main types of detection are commonly used: immunoassays and chromatography (Timrots, 1992). There are three common purposes for urine drug testing with offenders: (1) as an adjunct to community supervision, (2) as an assessment tool for offenders entering the justice system, and (3) as an assessment of drug use during mandated drug treatment (Timrots, 1992). Results of urine drug tests inform judges of the offender's current drug use when considering sentencing, indicates whether the offender is complying with a mandate to be drug-free, and identifies offenders who need substance abuse treatment.

Given problems with failure to revoke probationary status and a lack of treatment options when someone does has a positive drug screen, Turner, Petersilia, and Deschenes (1994) recommend asking the following questions prior to establishing widespread use of drug testing for those under community supervision:

1. How do probation/parole agencies implement drug testing orders?
2. How many drug dependent offenders have testing conditions revoked?
3. How many offenders are actually tested, with what frequency and results?
4. How does the justice system respond to positive drug tests?
5. Do such tests result in added probation/parole conditions, referrals to treatment programs, or revocation?
6. What impact do Intensive Supervision Probation/Parole (ISP) programs with drug testing have on offender recidivism, as measured by official records of technical violations and new arrests?
7. How do jurisdictions differ on these dimensions? (p. 233).

In the Third District Juvenile Court, Central Probation, Salt Lake City, Utah, an OJJDP-funded project, all juveniles on probation are subject to testing at the discretion of their probation officer. The purpose of the testing is as follows (Crowe & Sydney, 2000):

• To document whether a substance abuse problem exists, and if so, compel the juvenile to participate in treatment; and
• To hold the juvenile accountable for his or her behavior. For the first positive drug test, the probation officer reviews the rules and places the youth under house arrest; for a second positive drug test, the juvenile may be returned to court and possibly detained; and for continuing positive drug tests, the juvenile may be ordered to participate in inpatient drug treatment or long-term residential placement.

Beyond assessing whether an offender is using drugs, it is not clear that drug testing alone appears to serve a useful purpose besides serving as a tool to help monitor offenders with substance abuse problems. The best approach may be to combine random drug testing with drug treatment (Graboski, 1986, as cited in Springer, McNeece, & Arnold, 2003).

CLINICAL AND LEGAL ISSUES

There are three common ethical dilemmas social workers face when working with substance-using juvenile delinquents: (1) advocating for their client to remain on probation to allow the client to complete substance abuse treatment, (2) helping parents find substance abuse treatment for their children without formally adjudicating their son or daughter delinquent, and (3) confidentiality.

First, adolescent probationers sometimes complete their probation guidelines (in terms of length of time on probation) while they are still in substance abuse treatment. For youth in residential treatment, such as therapeutic communities, this usually means that they have the liberty to leave treatment, unless their probation is extended. The substance abuse counselor then has an ethical dilemma to consider; support their client (even if they decide to leave treatment) and help them reduce their chances of recidivism, or advocate to the judge to extend the youth's probation until they complete all stages of treatment.

Regarding the second ethical dilemma, parents with access to few resources sometimes have to decide whether they want their child adjudicated in order for him or her to receive substance abuse treatment. In some counties, formally adjudicating a youth delinquent makes that youth and his or her family eligible for a better treatment package. This is due, in part, because of the expense associated with private treatment facilities. In the case of Rachel presented at the beginning of the chapter, it is plausible that she could finish the terms of her probation in six months and not be subjected to random drug screens. If Rachel starts using drugs again, and her parents think that she needs treatment, they may decide to talk to the judge to discuss their options regarding formal adjudication. Social workers often find themselves working with families making similar decisions. The social worker should first act as a case manager and help the family find treatment (without resorting to adjudication). If the social workers' attempts are unsuccessful (which is too often the case), however, this poses an ethical dilemma.

The third ethical dilemma – that of confidentiality – is a common one faced by social workers treating substance-abusing juvenile offenders. Probation officers or parents often want detailed information about the client's treatment progress. Consider the following two scenarios. In the first, Marcus reports that he has begun using heroin. The social worker must balance her legal mandate to report this probation violation with the therapeutic rapport that she has worked so hard to establish with Marcus, especially given the risk of developing Hepatitis C associated with heroin use. In the second scenario, Marcus tells the social worker that his mother is dealing drugs. The social worker must balance this information against her knowledge that Marcus' father is in prison for murder, and that his mother is his main source of support. In other words, the social worker must decide how to use this information in the context of treatment gains made, and the potential ripple effects associated with revealing this information to the judge.

DESCRIPTION OF INTERVENTION

Marcus

Assessment is the first active phase of treatment (Springer, McNeece, & Arnold, 2003). Without a thorough and complete assessment, the social worker cannot develop a treatment plan that will serve the youth and his or her family. Assessment and diagnosis with substance-abusing juveniles is covered in-depth by Potter and Jenson in Chapter 12; we refer readers to this detailed exposition on assessment of mental health and substance abuse needs for juvenile offenders.

After the judge sentenced Marcus to residential treatment, he had to spend one week in the juvenile county jail due to the therapeutic community being at capacity. Once there was a spot available for Marcus, his probation officer and case manager transported him to his new treatment facility. When Marcus arrived at the therapeutic community, he was introduced to his counselor, Betsy, and his "older brother," an elder community member to act as Marcus's mentor. Later that day, Marcus and Betsy had their first individual session. After explaining the rules of confidentiality, Betsy explained to Marcus that they were going to complete his individualized treatment plan. The four components of the treatment plan were substance abuse, family issues, education, and recreation. Additionally, in this introductory session, Betsy explained to Marcus the expectations of the four stages of the therapeutic community: orientation, phase one, phase two, and community-reentry.

The goal of orientation was to demonstrate to Marcus knowledge of the program philosophy, concepts, and rules that build a foundation of treatment. Betsy told Marcus that she will know he has met this goal when he can recite the rules and philosophy, write his "life story," and complete the standard therapeutic community orientation work book. Additionally, Marcus had to attend six orientation groups and class everyday before advancing to phase one. Furthermore, because families are not able to attend the multifamily therapy groups until the adolescent in on phase one, Marcus's mother and brother attended the family orientation groups once a week to learn the program rules and expectations.

The community coordinator, a resident who acts as leader of the entire community, assigned Marcus to be a house worker for his "job function." During the orientation phase of treatment, Marcus had difficulties following directives from other adolescents. Marcus is a leader among his friends at home and has never had to take orders from other adolescents, so this was a difficult adjustment for him. In the therapeutic community, residents whom staff trust act as supervisors to other residents. After two verbal altercations with his supervisor, Betsy explained to Marcus that he would need to follow directives from his supervisor in order to advance to the next stage of treatment. Although difficult, Marcus followed the treatment slogan, "Act *as if*," which means to act as if you want to comply and follow the rules even when you do not. Three weeks after arrival, Marcus advanced to the next stage of treatment as a result of being able to recite the philosophy and rules of the program, attending six orientation groups and six seminars on substance abuse treatment, receiving adequate weekly reviews regarding his job function, writing a compelling life story, and completing his orientation workbook. Additionally, Marcus's mother and brother followed court orders and attended the orientation family group each of the three weeks.

When Marcus advanced to phase one, he was promoted to work in the kitchen, which is considered more prestigious than working in the house. Instead of simply knowing the rules, concepts, and program philosophy, Marcus was now expected to adhere to them. Additionally, Marcus had to learn to become more accountable and responsible to himself and the

other members in the community in order to advance to the next stage. In large measure, Marcus needed to demonstrate this by an increase in instances of "holding your peers accountable," a major tenet of the therapeutic community. A resident demonstrates that he is "holding his peers accountable" when he "drops meaningful incident slips." When a resident sees another community member commit a violation against the rules, he is expected to write a "ticket" on that resident to let the community know of the violation. Marcus had a very difficult time adjusting to this portion of the treatment program. In Marcus's neighborhood, adolescents do not "dime-out" others, as it is a sign of disrespect and considered disloyal. Betsy and Marcus had several conversations about the importance of living in a safe environment and relating it to the notion of "holding your peers accountable."

Marcus started attending psychotherapeutic process groups such as anger management, grief and loss, gender issues, and intimacy and relationships. Moreover, Marcus began participating in encounter groups, in which the residents confront one another on their maladaptive behavior. Marcus's mother and brother began participating in the multifamily therapy groups every Sunday afternoon.

To help specifically with anger management, which many of her other clients also struggled with, the social worker started an anger management therapy group. The Substance Abuse and Mental Health Services Administration, Center for Substance Abuse Treatment (Reilly & Shopshire, 2002) has issued a 12-week cognitive-behavioral anger management group treatment manual, entitled *Anger Management for Substance Abuse and Mental Health Clients: A Cognitive Behavioral Therapy Manual*, that is available at no cost from the National Clearinghouse on Alcohol and Drug Information (NCADI) (www.samhsa.org). This treatment group is an evidence-based, combined cognitive-behavioral therapy (CBT) approach that employs relaxation, cognitive and communication skills. The approach presents clients with options that draw on these different interventions and then encourages them to develop individualized anger control plans using as many of the techniques as possible. The social worker used this treatment manual to successfully facilitate the anger management group with her clients at the ALC. It is important to note that only a couple of the adolescents in this group had a diagnosis of Conduct Disorder.

Table 13-2
TREATMENT GOALS AND CORRESPONDING INTERVENTIONS FOR MARCUS'S ANGER
MANAGEMENT PLAN

Treatment Goals	Interventions
1. Become aware of intense anger outbursts.	1. Monitor anger using the "Anger Meter." 2. List positive "pay-offs" that Marcus gets from angry outbursts and aggressive actions.
2. Stop violence or the threat of violence (physical and verbal).	1. Explore events that trigger anger and cues to anger. 2. Explore, role-play, and practice alternative coping strategies (e.g., take a timeout, exercise, deep breathing, conflict resolution model, progressive muscle relaxation).
3. Develop self-control over thoughts and actions.	1. Review the Aggression Cycle. 2. Use Ellis' A-B-C-D Model of cognitive restructuring. 3. Model and practice thought stopping.
4. Accept responsibility for own actions.	1. Confront Marcus in group when he does not accept responsibility for his actions, and reward him when he does. 2. Record at least 2 irrational beliefs during the week and how to dispute these beliefs, using Ellis' A-B-C-D Model.
5. Receive support and feedback from others.	1. Use the here-and-now of the group experience to provide feedback to Marcus. 2. Discuss Marcus's progress in family therapy sessions.

Having too many conduct-disordered youths in the same treatment group can actually be counter-therapeutic (Feldman, Caplinger, & Wodarski, 1983).

Marcus's anger management plan reflects many of the interventions used in the 12-week group therapy manual, and consisted of five primary treatment goals along with corresponding interventions. See Table 13-2 for a listing of the treatment goals and sampling of some of the corresponding interventions related to Marcus's anger management plan. Of course, this list of interventions is not exhaustive, and there is some overlap across treatment goals and interventions. For a more detailed example of an anger management plan that includes long-term goals and corresponding short-term objectives and interventions, the reader is referred to Dulmus and Wodarski (2002).

In order to advance to phase two, Marcus had to consistently adhere to the program philosophy, concepts, and rules; consistently "hold his peers accountable" when they broke the rules; participate in meetings, process groups, and encounter groups; consistently complete homework assignments; and regularly identify with positive peers in the community.

Marcus accomplished all phase one expectations after seven weeks, advanced to phase two, and was promoted to supervisor.

Along with continuing to follow the rules, concepts, and philosophy, Marcus was also expected to become an encounter group facilitator while on phase two. Other goals of phase two included increasing personal skills in management of stress and emotionally charged situations and being able to begin to identify the interaction of thoughts, feelings, and behavior. Marcus became much more vocal in the community while on phase two, as he was able to recognize and verbalize other residents' positive and negative behavior. Regarding individual counseling sessions, Marcus was beginning to talk about his feelings concerning his father being in prison for murder and his brother moving out of his neighborhood. Although still not able to make the connection between these feelings and his four arrests, Marcus was able to articulate the need to live crime-free to help his family, particularly his mother, when he got out of treatment.

Marcus started going on passes away from the residential treatment community while on phase two.

The first pass was for three hours, the second pass was six hours, and the third pass was 12 hours. (Community members were not permitted to go on passes for longer than 12 hours while on phase two.) Betsy told Marcus that she expected him to be able to remain drug and alcohol free during these passes, and that he should be cognizant of relapse triggers he would encounter while away from the treatment facility. Marcus shut down emotionally and verbally for three days after his first pass, but Betsy, an experienced social worker, expected this reaction. In the individual session later that week, Marcus explained to Betsy that his sadness was a result of missing his mother. For the first time since entering the TC, Marcus cried. Betsy used this opportunity to discuss the relationship between negative emotions and substance use, and problem-solved with Marcus to generate different alternatives to using substances. Upon arriving back to the treatment center after every subsequent pass, Marcus was able to disclose his emotions in his psychotherapeutic process groups and gradually became cognizant of his relapse triggers. Marcus was also able to discuss his feelings about being away from his mother, and perhaps more importantly, explored how his being arrested four times hurt his mother. Betsy knew Marcus was ready for the reentry phase when he had three consecutive successful 12-hour passes, maintained passing grades in school, succeeded as an older brother to new residents, and accepted responsibility not only for his behavior, but also for the community's overall behavior and functioning.

Marcus was promoted to "chief" of the therapeutic community, the second highest job "function," at the same time that he was promoted to the reentry phase. The chief of the therapeutic community acts as the supervisor for the supervisors. The overall goal of the reentry phase is for the youth to internalize the tools promoted through the treatment process; consistently act a role model by teaching the therapeutic process to younger residents; appropriately handle higher levels of stress on the job, school, and in groups; and pass all classes every week. Betsy was impressed with Marcus's heightened level of personal disclosure in their individual sessions. Eventually, Marcus was able to recognize his anger towards his father's imprisonment, and was able to recognize that he covered up his emotions by drinking and using drugs. Furthermore, Marcus was able to associate the respect he received from his peers in his

neighborhood as "a cover" for the shame he felt regarding his father's circumstances, which Marcus consistently talked about in his individual sessions and groups. Marcus ultimately wrote a letter to his father in an attempt to reconnect and explain his thoughts and feelings regarding his perceived abandonment. Marcus also verbally and tearfully apologized to his mother in the multifamily therapy group one afternoon. He also committed to getting a full-time job and pursuing a high school diploma.

While on the reentry phase, Marcus was able to go on 24-hour passes until he was one-month away from discharge. He was then able to go on 48-hour passes. Betsy gave Marcus the assignment of creating a list of all relapse triggers he confronted while on his passes, as well as what he did (and would continue to do) to avoid a relapse. Furthermore, on these passes, Marcus was expected to develop a positive support network, apply for jobs, and reacquaint himself with teachers from his local high school. Marcus was given a urine drug test after every overnight pass, which he consistently passed. As a result of completing the goals of the reentry phase, including getting a job at a local grocery store, joining a support group at his mother's church, and re-enrolling at his previous public high school, Marcus successfully graduated from the program after being there for six months.

Rachel

Rachel and her family first met with the social worker, Darlene, two weeks after meeting with the judge that sentenced Rachel and her family to family therapy. Darlene told the family they would meet weekly for the first eight to twelve weeks of counseling. After discussing the rules of confidentiality, Darlene explained her choice of using BSFT. According to Gambrill (1999), in evidence-based practice "social workers seek out practice-related research findings regarding important practice decisions and share the results of their search with clients. If they find that there is no evidence that a method they recommend will help a client, they so inform the client and describe their theoretical rationale for their recommendation. Clients are involved as informed participants" (p. 346). Darlene explained to Rachel's family that researchers have found BSFT to be effective with Hispanic juvenile delinquents and explained its primary assumptions.

Darlene, aware that BSFT follows a prescribed process format, spent the first two sessions *joining* with the family – establishing a therapeutic alliance with each family member and the family as a whole (Robbins et al., 2003). Rachel's parents discussed their infuriation with Rachel over the decisions she had been making lately, particularly since meeting her boyfriend, Bradley. Rachel consistently yelled back, "It's not Bradley's fault! I'm 15-years-old and I can make my own decisions! I haven't done anything wrong anyway!" Darlene let the family discuss (reenact) the situation to assess their communicative patterns, and established therapeutic alliances by expressing empathy to each family member. Rachel's brother, David, did not say a word during the first two family sessions.

In keeping with step two in the BSFT sequence, Darlene encouraged Rachel's family to speak with each other about the issues that brought them to therapy (Robbins et al., 2003) in order to allow the social worker to *diagnose* the family by observing their strengths and limitations. Proponents of BSFT believe that the family members communicate with one another as they would if the social worker were absent. Darlene observed Rachel's family discuss Rachel's legal issues for two entire sessions. Darlene noticed that George and Roni, Rachel's parents, rarely talked to each other. Roni appeared much more involved in parenting Rachel. George hinted several times that his job was to work and bring home the money, and he saw his wife's job as tending to the house and keeping the children out of trouble. In fact, on three different occasions, George said to Roni, "That's why you shouldn't work, because Rachel has no supervision." Every time George said this, Roni became very quiet, lethargic, and distant, indicating to Darlene that she may act like this at home after confrontations with George, preventing her from effectively communicating with her daughter. Furthermore, Darlene observed that David only spoke when he was protecting his mother or blaming Rachel for the family going through this turmoil. Darlene sensed that Rachel was acting out her family's problems by doing drugs, getting arrested, and hanging out with a boyfriend that had a history of arrests.

Darlene informed the family of the strengths and weaknesses she observed in the previous two sessions. Regarding the strengths, Darlene pointed out that both parents worked hard at their jobs and took great pride in being employed full-time. All four family members had attended each treatment sessions thus far, which Darlene believed to be a sign that they wanted help and truly cared for Rachel. Furthermore, Darlene mentioned Rachel's ability to earn high grades and David's enrollment at the community college as admirable personal attributes they possessed. Darlene then mentioned the family's problematic relations that she believed were linked to Rachel's problematic behavior, including Roni's tendency to shut down when confronted by George, George's lack of attention to problematic issues at home because of his beliefs that Roni should "deal with it," and the alliance between David and Roni. Perhaps most importantly, Darlene amplified the family's view that Rachel's problems were an individual problem, rather than a symptom of the family's maladaptive patterns. In step five, Darlene and Rachel's family developed their treatment goals using the BSFT change goals in Table 13-3. Darlene then transitioned the counseling sessions to the restructuring stage, which lasted for the remainder of the counseling sessions.

According to Robbins et al. (2003), restructuring involves the implementation of change strategies needed to transform family relations from problematic to effective and mutually supportive. To achieve the goals Darlene and the family developed, Darlene was more problem-focused, direction-oriented, and practical during the restructuring stage. For example, when Darlene observed maladaptive communication interactions, she would often interrupt the conversation and recommend more appropriate ways of interacting. Darlene also attempted to shift family alliances by having David and George or David and Rachel engage in conversations and problem-solving activities. Moreover, Darlene stressed the importance of George and Roni working together on disciplinary decisions and indicated that blaming each other was counterproductive. Most importantly in this stage, the family learned, and ultimately believed, that Rachel's problem behavior – namely her drug use and arrests – were indicators of family turmoil and not just personal hardships for Rachel. After successful cognitive reframing, Darlene indicated that the family only needed to attend once a month for occasional updates and "problem-solving sessions." Darlene told the family that they should document their perceived strengths and limitations over the next

Table 13-3
CHANGE GOALS OF BSFT

Structural Level	*Specific goals*
Family	Increased parental figures' involvement with one another and improved balance of involvement of the parent figures with the child Improved effective parenting, including successful management of children's behavior Improved family cohesiveness, collaboration, and affect and reduced family negativity Improved "appropriate" bonding between children and parents Improved family communication, conflict resolution, and problem-solving skills Correct assignment and effective performance of the roles and responsibilities of the family
Individual adolescent	Reduced behavior problems Improved self-control Reduced associations with antisocial peers Reduced substance abuse Development of pro-social behaviors Bonding to family Good school attendance, conduct, and achievement

Source: Robins, M. S., Szapocznik, J., Santisteban, D. A., Hervis, O. E., Mitrani, V. B., & Schwartz, S. J. (2003). Brief strategic family therapy for Hispanic youth. In A. E. Kazdin & J. R. Weisz (Eds.), *Evidence-based psychotherapies for children and adolescents* (pp. 407–424). New York: Guilford Press. Reprinted with permission from publisher.

month, including whether communication patterns between family members regressed to the way they were before counseling. Furthermore, regarding Rachel, Darlene assigned the family to track her ability to improve her self-control, reduce her associations with problem peers, reduce substance use, and attend school regularly.

SUMMARY AND CONCLUSION

Alcohol and drug use are prevalent among juvenile offenders and many of the risk factors that predict delinquent behavior also predict adolescent drug use. An increasing number of adolescent arrestees are substance-users, and among juvenile delinquents, the more serious and violent offenders use drugs more often. This chapter reviewed a promising institutional-based treatment approach (therapeutic communities) and a promising community-based approach (Brief Strategic Family Therapy) that can be used when working with substance-abusing juvenile delinquents.

When working with youth who have committed crimes, social workers should be sensitive to the risk factors that have the greatest impact on recidivism.

In a study recently conducted by Rivaux, Springer, Bohman, Wagner, and Gil (in press), substance abuse predicted recidivism individually as did older age and being male. These findings highlight the need for a focus on prevention and early intervention services with delinquent behaviors, particularly for substance-abusing youth and for males. This study also found that greater levels of family problems predicted recidivism for Latino youth, while increased levels of psychological problems predicted recidivism for African American youth. Knowledge of these predictors could help social workers in assessments of risk and in targeting interventions in a culturally useful way. For example, such a finding might suggest a greater emphasis on family dynamics when working with Latino youth. The intersection of these various predictors of recidivism also highlights the need for prevention and intervention programs that are responsive to issues of both ethnicity and gender.

We underscore the recommendation made by Mc-Neece, Bullington, Arnold, and Springer (2005) that treatment be linked with a *harm reduction* approach. The harm reduction strategy promotes public health rather than the criminal justice perspective when determining what to do about drug users. Thus, all drug use, whether of "licit" or illicit substances, is seen as potentially problematic. Proponents of this approach assert that the distinctions made between legal and illegal substances are totally artificial and have led to a myopic focus solely on illicit chemicals (McNeece et al., 2005). We should make the receipt of federal funding contingent on the repeal of a number of state laws, including those that prohibit the free distribution of needles and syringes to intravenous drug users.

Traditionally, therapeutic interventions with substance-abusing youth have been driven more by practice wisdom than by scientifically-based outcome studies (evidence-based practice). While we should not abandon our accumulated practice wisdom, to the extent that it is available, practitioners are encouraged to also use evidence-based practice to guide their treatment planning. In short, it is critical that practitioners remain up-to-date on the best practices available, which will be critical in maximizing our effectiveness in treating substance-abusing juvenile delinquents. Given the limited resources that are currently directed to troubled youths, a national commitment to help these youths is warranted if we are to reduce their substance abuse, delinquency, and associated problems (Physician Leadership in National Drug Control Policy, 2002).

REFERENCES

Alexander, B. K. (1990). Alternatives to the war on drugs. *Journal of Drug Issues, 20,* 1–27.

Alexander, J. F., & Parsons, B. V. (1973). Short-term behavioral interventions with delinquents: Impact on family process and recidivism. *Journal of Abnormal Psychology, 81,* 219–225.

Alford, G. S., Koehler, R. A., & Leonard, J. (1991). Alcoholics Anonymous-Narcotics Anonymous model inpatient treatment of chemically dependent adolescents: A two-year outcome study. *Journal of Studies on Alcohol, 52,* 118–126.

Anderson, A. R., & Henry, C. S. (1994). Family systems characteristics and parental behaviors as predictors of adolescent substance use. *Adolescence, 29,* 405–420.

Austin, A. M., Macgowan, M. J., & Wagner, E. F. (2005). Effective family-based interventions for adolescents with substance abuse problems: A systematic review. *Research on Social Work Practice, 15,* 67–83.

Baer, R. A. & Nietzel, M. T. (1991). Cognitive and behavioral treatment of impulsivity in children: A meta-analytic review of the outcome literature. *Journal of Clinical Child Psychology, 20,* 400–412.

California Youth Authority (1997). *LEAD: A boot camp and intensive parole program. Final impact evaluation.* Sacramento, CA: State of California, Department of the Youth Authority.

Catalano, R. F., Hawkins, J. D., Wells, E. A., Miller, J., & Brewer, D. (1990/91). Evaluation of the effectiveness of adolescent drug abuse treatment, assessment of risks for relapse, and promising approaches for relapse prevention. *International Journal of the Addictions, 25,* 1085–1140.

Chambless, D. L., & Hollon, S. D. (1998). Defining empirically supported therapies. *Journal of Consulting and Clinical Psychology, 66,* 7–18.

Corcoran, J., & Springer, D. W. (2005). Treatment of adolescents with disruptive behavior disorders. In J. Corcoran, *Strengths and skills building: A collaborative approach to working with clients* (pp. 131-162). New York, NY: Oxford University Press.

Crowe, A. H., & Sydney, L. (2000, May). Developing a policy for a controlled substance abuse testing of juveniles. *Juvenile Accountability Block Grant (JAIBG) program bulletin* (NCJ Publication 178896). Washington, D.C.: OJJDP.

De Leon, G. (1986). The therapeutic community for substance abuse: Perspective and approach. In D. De Leon & J. T. Zeigenfuss (Eds.), *Therapeutic communities for addictions: Readings in theory, research and practice* (pp. 5–18). Springfield, IL: Charles C Thomas.

De Leon, G. (1988). Legal pressures in therapeutic communities. In C. G. Luekefeld & F. Tims (Eds.), *Compulsory treatment of drug abuse: Research and clinical practice* (pp. 160–177). National Institute on Drug Abuse Research Monograph No. 86 [DHHS Publication # (ADM) 89-1578]. Rockville, MD: U. S Department of Health and Human Services, National Institute on Drug Abuse.

Dembo, R., & Brown, R. (1994). The Hillsborough County juvenile assessment center. *Journal of Child and Adolescent Substance Abuse, 3,* 25–43.

Dembo, R., Pacheco, K., Schmeidler, J., Fisher, L., & Cooper, S. (1997). Drug use and delinquent behavior among high risk youths. *Journal of Child and Adolescent Substance Abuse, 6,* 1–25.

Dembo, R., Schmeidler, J., & Walters, W. (2004). Juvenile assessment centers: An innovative approach to identify and respond to youths with substance abuse and related problems entering the justice system. In A. R. Roberts (Ed.), *Juvenile justice sourcebook: Past, present, and future* (pp. 511–536). New York: Oxford University Press.

Denton, R. E., & Kampfe, C. M. (1994). The relationship between family variables and adolescent substance abuse: A literature review. *Adolescence, 29,* 475–495.

Dulmus, C. N., & Wodarski, J. S. (2002). Parameters of social work treatment plans: Case application of explosive anger. In A. R. Roberts & G. J. Greene (Eds.),

Social Workers' Desk Reference (pp. 314–319). New York: Oxford University Press.

Durlak, J., Fuhrman, T., & Lampman, C. (1991). Effectiveness of cognitive-behavior therapy for maladapting children: a meta-analysis. *Psychological Bulletin,* 110, 204–214.

Enos, R., & Southern, S. (1996). *Correctional case management.* Cincinnati, OH: Anderson.

Evans, M. E., & Dollard, N. (1992). Intensive case management for youth with serious emotional disturbance and chemical abuse. In R. S. Ashery (Ed.), *Progress and Issues in Case Management* (pp. 289–315). NIDA Research Monograph Series (127). Rockville, MD: U.S. Department of Health and Human Service, National Institute on Drug Abuse.

Gambrill, E. (1999). Evidence-based practice: An alternative to authority-based practice. *Families in Society: The Journal of Contemporary Human Services, 80,* 341–350.

Haley, J. (1975). Why a mental health clinic should avoid family therapy. *Journal of Marriage and Family Counseling, 1,* 3–13.

Huizinga, D., Loeber, R., & Thornberry, T. P. (1994). *Urban delinquency and substance abuse: Initial findings.* Washington, D.C.: U.S. Department of Justice.

Jainchill, N., Hawke, J., DeLeon, G., & Yagelka, J. (2000). Adolescents in therapeutic communities: One-year posttreatment outcomes. *Journal of Psychoactive Drugs, 32,* 81–94.

Jenson, J. M. (1997). Juvenile delinquency and drug abuse: Implications for social work practice in the justice system. In C. A. McNeece & A. R. Roberts (Eds.), *Policy and practice in the justice system* (pp. 107–123). Chicago: Nelson-Hall.

Joaning, H., Quinn, W., Thomas, F., & Mullen, R. (1992). Treating adolescent drug abuse: A comparison of family systems therapy, group therapy, and family drug education. *Journal of Marital and Family Therapy, 18,* 345–356.

Johnston, L. D., O'Malley, P. M., Bachman, J. G., & Schulenberg, J. E. (2005). *Monitoring the future national survey results on drug use, 1975–2004. Volume I: Secondary school students* (NIH Publication No. 05-5727). Bethesda, MD: National Institute on Drug Abuse.

Johnston, L. D., O'Malley, P. M., & Bachman, J. G. (2004). *Monitoring the future national survey results on drug use, 1975–2003. Volume I: Secondary school students* (NIH Publication No. 03-5375). Bethesda, MD: National Institute on Drug Abuse.

Kaestner, E., Frank, B., Marel, R., & Schmeidler, J. (1986). Substance abuse among females in New York state: Catching up with the males. *Advances in Alcohol & Substance Abuse, 5,* 29–49.

Kazdin, A. E. (2002). Psychosocial treatments for conduct disorder in children. In P. W. Nathan & J. M. Gorman (Eds.) *A guide to treatments that work* (2nd ed., pp. 57–85). New York: Oxford University Press.

Kazdin, A. E. (2000). *Psychotherapy for children and adolescents. Directions for research and practice.* New York: Oxford University Press.

Liddle, H. A., & Dakof, G. A. (1995). Efficacy of family therapy for drug abuse: Promising but not definitive. *Journal of Marital and Family Therapy, 21,* 511–544.

Lipsey, M. W. (1992). Juvenile delinquency treatment: A meta-analytic inquiry into the variability of effects. In T. D. Cook, H. Cooper, D. S. Corday, H. Hartman, L. V. Hedges, R. J. Light, T. A. Louis & F. Mosteller (Eds.), *Meta-analysis for explanation: A casebook.* New York: Russell Sage Foundation.

Lipsey, M. W., & Wilson, D. B. (1998). Effective intervention for serious juvenile offenders: A synthesis of research. In R. Loever & D. Farrington (Eds.), *Serious and violent juvenile offenders: Risk factors and successful interventions* (pp. 313–344). London: Sage.

MacKenzie, D. L. (1994). Boot camps: A national assessment. *Overcrowded Times, 5*(4), pp. 1, 14–18.

MacKenzie, D. L., Gover, A. R., Armstrong, G. S., Mitchell, O. (2001). A national study comparing the environments of boot camps with traditional facilities for juvenile offenders [On-line]. *National Institute of Juvenile: Research in Brief.* Retrieved June 26, 2006 from http://www.ncjrs.gov/pdffiles1/nij/187680.pdf.

Madanes, C. (1981). *Strategic family therapy.* San Francisco: Jossey-Bass.

McBride, D. C., VanderWaal, C. J., Terry, Y. M., & VanBuren, H. (1999). *Breaking the cycle of drug use among juvenile offenders* [On-line]. Retrieved October 24, 2002, from http://www.ncjrs.org/pdffiles1/179273.pdf.

McNeece, C. A. (1997). Future directions in justice system policy and practice. In C.A. McNeece & A. R. Roberts (Eds.), *Policy and practice in the justice system* (pp. 263–269). Chicago: Nelson-Hall.

McNeece, C. A., Bullington, B., Arnold, E. M., & Springer, D. W. (2005). The war on drugs: Treatment, research, and substance abuse intervention in the twenty-first century. In R. Muraskin & A. R. Roberts (Eds.), *Visions for change: Crime and justice in the twenty-first century* (4th ed.) (pp. 88–120). Upper Saddle River, NJ: Prentice-Hall.

McNeece, C. A., Springer, D. W., & Arnold, E. M. (2001). Treating substance abuse disorders. In J. Ashford, B. D. Sales & W.H. Reid (Eds.), *Treating adult and juvenile offenders with special needs* (pp. 131–169). Washington, D.C.: American Psychological Association.

Miller, W. R., & Hester, R. K. (1986). The effectiveness of alcoholism research: What research reveals. In W. R. Miller & N. Heather (Eds.), *Treating addictive behaviors: Processes of change* (pp. 175–204). New York: Plenum.

Minuchin, S. (1974). *Families and family therapy.* Cambridge,

MA: Harvard University Press.

Minuchin, S., & Fishman, H. C. (1981). *Family therapy techniques.* Cambridge, MA: Harvard University Press.

Molidor, C. E., Nissen, L. B., & Watkins, T. R. (2002). The development of theory and treatment with substance abusing female juvenile delinquents. *Child and Adolescent Social Work Journal, 19*, 209–225.

Morral, A., McCaffrey, D., & Ridgeway, G. (2004). Effectiveness of community-based treatment for substance-abusing adolescents: 12-month outcomes of youths entering phoenix academy or alternative probation dispositions. *Psychology of Addictive Behaviors, 18*, 257–268.

Obermeier, G. E., & Henry, P. B. (1989). Adolescent inpatient treatment. *Journal of Chemical Dependency, 2*, 163–182.

Office of Applied Studies. (2004). *Results from the 2003 National Survey on Drug Use and Health: National findings* (DHHS Publication No. SMA 03-3836, NHSDA Series H-22). Rockville, MD: Substance Abuse and Mental Health Services Administration.

Oldenettel, D., & Wordes, M. (2000). *The community assessment center concept* (Juvenile justice bulletin). Washington, D.C.: U.S. Department of Justice, Office of Justice Programs, Office of Juvenile Justice and Delinquency Prevention.

Pan, H., Scarpitti, F. R., Inciardi, J. A., & Lockwood, D. (1993). Some considerations on therapeutic communities in corrections. In J. A. Inciardi (Ed.), *Drug treatment and criminal justice* (No. 27, pp. 30–43). Newbury Park, CA: Sage.

Parent, D. (1989). *Shock incarceration: An overview of existing programs.* Washington, D.C.: Department of Justice, National Institute of Justice.

Peters, M., Thomas, D., & Zamberlan, C. (1997). *Boot camps for juvenile offenders.* Washington, D.C.: U.S. Department of Justice.

Physician Leadership on National Drug Control Policy. (2002). *Adolescent substance abuse: A public health priority.* Providence, RI: Center for Alcohol and Addiction Studies.

Reilly, P. M., & Shopshire, M. S. (2002). *Anger management for substance abuse and mental health clients: A cognitive behavioral therapy.* Washington DC: U.S. Department of Health and Human Services, Substance Abuse and Mental Health Services Administration.

Rivaux, S. L., Springer, D. W., Bohman, T., Wagner, E. F., & Gil, A. G. (in press). Differences among substance abusing Latino, Anglo, and African-American juvenile offenders in predictors of recidivism and treatment outcome. *Journal of Social Work Practice in the Addictions.*

Robins, M. S., Szapocznik, J., Santisteban, D. A., Hervis, O. E., Mitrani, V. B., & Schwartz, S. J. (2003). Brief strategic family therapy for Hispanic youth. In A. E. Kazdin & J. R. Weisz (Eds.), *Evidence-based psychotherapies for children and adolescents* (pp. 407–424). New York: Guilford Press.

Rossow, I., Pape, H., & Wichstrom, L. (1999). Young, wet, and wild? Association between alcohol intoxication and violent behavior in adolescence. *Addiction, 94*, 1017–1031.

Rothman, J. (2002). An overview of case management. In A. R. Roberts & G. J. Green (Eds.), *Social workers' desk reference* (pp. 467–472). New York: Oxford University Press.

Rothman, J. (1990). *The discovery of the asylum: Social order and disorder in the new republic.* Boston: Little, Brown.

Santisteban, D. A., Coatsworth, D., Perez-Vidal, A., Kurtines, W. M., Schwartz, S. J., & Szapocznik, J. (2003). Efficacy of brief strategic family therapy in modifying adolescent behavior problems and substance use. *Journal of Family Psychology, 17*, 121–131.

Sealock, M. D., Gottfredson, D. C., & Gallagher, C. A. (1997). Drug treatment for juvenile offenders: Some good and bad news. *Journal of Research in Crime and Delinquency, 34*, 210–236.

Springer, D. W. (2005). Treating substance-abusing youth. In C. A. McNeece & D. M. DiNitto (Eds.), *Chemical dependency: A systems approach* (3rd ed., pp. 269–292). Needham Heights, MA: Allyn & Bacon.

Springer, D. W., McNeece, C. A., & Arnold, E. M. (2003). *Substance abuse treatment for criminal offenders: An evidence-based guide for practitioners.* Washington, D.C.: American Psychological Association.

Springer, D. W., Shader, M. A., & McNeece, C. A. (1999). Operation of juvenile assessment centers: Trends and issues. *Journal for Juvenile Justice and Detention Services, 14*, 45–61.

Stanton, M. S., & Shadish, W. R. (1997). Outcome, attrition, and family/marital treatment for drug abuse: A meta-analysis and review of the controlled, comparative studies. *Psychological Bulletin, 122*, 170–191.

Stanton, M. D., & Todd, T. C. (1979). Structural family therapy with drug addicts. In E. Kaufman & P. Kaufmann (Eds.), *The family therapy of drug and alcohol abuse* (pp. 55–69). New York: Gardner Press.

Stanton, M. D., & Todd, T. C., (1982). *The family therapy of drug abuse and addiction.* New York: Guilford Press.

Sullivan, W. P. (2002). Case management with substance-abusing clients. In A. R. Roberts & G. J. Greene (Eds.), *Social workers' desk reference* (pp. 492–496). New York: Oxford University Press.

Teplin, L. A., Abram, K. M., McClelland, G. M., Duclan, M., & Mericle, A. A. (2003). Psychiatric disorders in youth in juvenile detention. *Archive of General Psychiatry, 59*, 1133–1143.

Terry, Y.M., VanderWaal, C.J., & McBride, D.C. (2000). Provision of drug treatment services in the juvenile justice system: A system reform. *Journal of Behavioral Health Services and Research, 27*, 194–214.

Timrots, A. (1992). *Fact sheet: Drug testing in the criminal justice system.* Rockville, MD: Drugs & Crime Data Center and Clearinghouse.

Todd, T.C., & Selekman, M. (1994). A structural-strategic model for treating the adolescent who is abusing alcohol and other drugs. In W. Snyder, T. Ooms (Eds.), *Empowering families, helping adolescents: Family-centered treatment of adolescents with alcohol, drug abuse, and mental health problems* (Publication Series 6, pp. 79–89). Rockville, MD: U.S. Department of Health and Human Services, Center for Substance Abuse Treatment.

Trulson, C. R., & Triplett, R. (1999). School-based juvenile boot camps: Evaluating specialized treatment and rehabilitation (STAR). *Journal for Juvenile Justice and Detention Services, 14*(1), 19–44.

Turner, S., Petersilia, J., & Deschenes, E. P. (1994). The implementation and effectiveness of drug testing in community supervision: Results of an experimental evaluation. In D. L. MacKenzie & C. D. Uchida (Eds.), *Drugs and crime: Evaluating public policy initiatives* (pp. 231–252). Thousand Oaks, CA: Sage.

Vega, W. A., & Gil, A. G. (1998). *Drug use and ethnicity in early adolescents.* New York: Plenum Press.

Vega, W. A., Zimmerman, R. S., Gil, A. G., Warheit, G. J., & Apospori, E. (1993). Acculturation Strain Theory: Its application in explaining drug use behavior among Cuban and other Hispanic youth. In M. R. De La Rosa & J. R. Adrados (Eds.), *Drug abuse among minority youth: Advances in research and methodology.* Rockville, MD: National Institute on Drug Abuse.

Vega, W. A., Zimmerman, R. S., & Warheit, G. J. (1993). Risk factors for early adolescent drug use in 4 ethnic and racial groups. *American Journal of Public Health, 83*, 185–189.

Vorrath, H. H., & Brendtro, L, K. (1985). *Positive peer culture* (2nd ed.). New York: Aldine de Gruyter.

Waldron, H. B., (1997). Adolescent substance abuse and family therapy outcome: A review of randomized trials. *Advances in Clinical Child Psychology, 19*, 199–234.

RESOURCES

1. Office of Juvenile Justice and Delinquency Prevention (OJJDP) (http://ojjdp.ncjrs.org).
2. National Institute on Drug Abuse (NIDA) (http://www.nida.nih.gov).
3. SAMHSA Center for Substance Abuse Prevention (CSAP) (http://www.samhsa/gov/centers/csap/model programs/default.htm).
4. SAMHSA Center for Substance Abuse Treatment (CSAT) (http://www.samhsa.gov/centers/csat/csat.html).

Chapter 14

Juvenile Justice Policy: Trends and Issues

C. Aaron McNeece, Edgar Tyson, and Sherry Jackson

One of the most controversial issues surrounding juvenile justice is the increased use of the adult criminal justice system to deal with our most violent and troubled juvenile offenders. One case that illustrates the potential negative, long-term consequences of this practice is the Lionel Tate case, when he became the youngest American in modern history to be sentenced to life in prison without the possibility of parole. On July 28, 1999, Lionel Tate, a 12-year-old boy, was arrested for brutally beating to death Tiffany Eunick, a six-year old family friend (Smikle, 1999). At the time of the incident, Lionel and Tiffany were allegedly "playing wrestling" in his mother's home while his mother was upstairs in her room taking a nap. While results of the autopsy were never released, it was reported that the young victim in this case suffered a crushed skull, broken ribs, and between 20 (Smikle, 1999) and 30 (Smikle, 2000) additional internal injuries.

As the new millennium began, the Lionel Tate case appeared to resurrect the debate over the use of the adult criminal justice system for juvenile offenders. Some argued that the heinous nature of the act justified an adult trial where Lionel could receive the harshest punishment available for his actions. However, others maintain that for developmental reasons, some juveniles (especially a 12-year-old like Lionel Tate) lack the ability to understand the consequences of their actions and the complex nature of the adult court system (Scott & Steinberg, 2003). Moreover, Lionel appeared to have been further hampered by the fact that he was developmentally delayed for his age. The "adjudicative competence" requirement states that defendants must have the ability to participate in the proceedings against them, and some legal scholars suggest that there is a constitutional basis for

the argument that policy makers and courts should incorporate developmental competence into the procedural architecture of juvenile justice policy (Grisso & Schwartz, 2000).

Adjudicative competence became a particularly relevant issue in the Lionel Tate case because it was discovered that he never received a competency hearing, which ultimately led to his release on appeal (Juvenile Law Center, 2005). Unfortunately, Lionel had already served nearly five years of his original sentence of life in prison. The events that followed Lionel Tate's release are signs that sending him to the adult system merely exacerbated the tragedy of little Tiffany Eunick's death.

Lionel Tate was arrested for giving the police a false identity and possessing a knife at 2 a.m. in the morning on Sept. 7, 2004 while in the company of another young man who had a reputation for being in trouble with the law (Gregory, 2004). According to reports, Tate and his mother had an argument earlier that night. After the argument Tate left the house. He spent 52 days in Broward County Juvenile Detention, had his sentence increased to 15 years probation, and was released with a stern warning from Judge Joel T. Lazarus that another violation would risk a very long prison term (Gregory, 2004).

Tate was then arrested for a third time on May 23, 2005 for armed burglary with battery, armed robbery, and violating probation (CNN, 2005). According to reports, Tate robbed a pizza delivery employee at gun point and assaulted a 12-year-old boy whose house he used to make the call for the pizza. Tate now faces between 10 and 15 years in prison. It is not clear whether the juvenile justice policy that allowed this 12-year-old boy to be treated as an adult instead of receiving the mental health counseling that he obviously needed contributed to his subsequent behavior upon being released in 2004. However, it does suggest that the question should be asked and the issue should be debated.

MAJOR POLICY SHIFTS

Four major shifts in federal juvenile policy have occurred since the l960s (Ohlin, 1983). Community organization models were used in the early 1960s by federal policymakers to foster local responsibility for juvenile misbehavior. Unfortunately, these programs were generally not successful. The second shift in policy came from a number of Presidential commissions studying the problems of crime and violence. In 1967, the first of these commissions recommended dramatic policy innovations such as the decriminalization of status offenses, the diversion of juvenile offenders from official court processing, and the deinstitutionalization of juvenile offenders. The Juvenile Justice and Delinquency Prevention Act of 1974 was the culmination of this policy shift (McNeece, 1980). Although the bill was opposed by both the Nixon and Ford administrations, it passed in the House of Representatives by a vote of 329 to 20, and it received only one negative vote in the Senate. The intent of this bill was to deinstitutionalize status offenders, provide additional funds to communities to improve delinquency prevention programs, establish new mechanisms for dealing with runaway youth, and remove juveniles from adult jails and lock-up facilities (Bartol and Bartol, 1989).

A third major change in juvenile justice policy began in the mid-1970s with a federal shift toward a "law and order" philosophy. Although basically preventive in its approach, the result of the JJDPA legislation soon became more *controlling*. The act was amended in 1977, partly as a response to alleged increases in school violence and vandalism, to allow more flexibility in the deinstitutionalization process. Throughout the late 1970s, an "iron-fisted" punitive approach to nonstatus offenders emerged (Hellum, 1979), and a growing fear of crime pushed the juvenile justice system toward more repressive action (Ohlin, 1983).

The Reagan Administration targeted serious or repetitive juvenile offenders for special attention in 1981, shifting the system even more in the direction of control and punishment. In 1984, the National Ad-

visory Committee for Juvenile Justice and Delinquency Prevention recommended that grants to states for the continued deinstitutionalization of status offenders not be renewed. The Reagan Administration believed that for too long the juvenile justice system had been overly concerned with the protection of juvenile offenders at the expense of society and its victims (Bartol & Bartol, 1989). This new "get tough" approach was evident in the Comprehensive Crime Control Act of 1984.

Since 1992, most states have adopted tougher laws regarding the prosecution of serious, violent, and chronic juvenile offenders. Such laws lower the age at which a juvenile can be transferred to adult court, expand the list of crimes for which a juvenile can be transferred, and make the process for transferring the juvenile easier (Mears, 2000; Office of Juvenile Justice and Delinquency Prevention, 1996; Snyder & Sickmund, 1999).

A final shift occurred on March 1, 2005 when the United States Supreme Court ruled it unconstitutional to execute juvenile defendants (Greenhouse, 2005), which marks a possible reversal from the direction of the last three decades. In a five to four decision (Roper vs. Simmons, 543 U.S. 2005), the U.S. Supreme Court ruled that "a majority of states have rejected the imposition of the death penalty on juvenile offenders under 18, and we now hold this is required by the Eighth Amendment" (Liptak, 2005, p. A14). Justice Kennedy, who wrote the majority opinion, cited three core differences between juveniles and adults as the basis for concluding that juveniles should not be subject to the death penalty: "a lack of maturity and an underdeveloped sense of responsibility; vulnerability to peer pressure; and a personality that is still in formation, making it less supportable to conclude that even an heinous crime committed by a juvenile is evidence of irretrievably depraved character" (Greenhouse, 2005, p. A14).

One immediate implication of the decision was that 72 men on death row for murder they committed while they were 16 or 17 years old will be spared their lives and will now spend the rest of their lives in prison (Greenhouse, 2005). However, for the 22 men who had been executed since the death penalty was reinstated in 1978, who committed crimes when they were juveniles, this ruling came 27 years too late.

Another reason given in Justice Kennedy's opinion as the legal foundation for the shift in the court's position on the death penalty for juveniles was world opinion (Liptak, 2005). It should be noted that the newly appointed Chief Justice of the Supreme Court, John Roberts, found this basis for making legal decisions "very troubling" (Asksam, 2005) and may indicate that this decision is a less than stable one.

DIVERSION AND DEINSTITUTIONALIZATION PROGRAMS

Keeping youth out of the formal juvenile justice process – diversion – and removing juveniles from correctional facilities – deinstitutionalization – have been part of juvenile justice reform efforts since the early 1960s. The overall goal of these efforts is to decriminalize the juvenile justice system. The enthusiastic application of "diversion" programs actually has resulted in the creation of a new semilegal, semiwelfare bureaucracy, which has broadened the effective social control mechanisms of the juvenile justice system without paying much attention to the legal rights of children (Blomberg, 1983; Empey & Stafford, 1991). While many juvenile offenses have been decriminalized and separate dispositional alternatives for status offenders have been created, it is difficult to say that children are being treated much differently than they were before, apart from changes in the labels they now wear. Approximately half of all the juveniles in institutions prior to the passage of the Juvenile Justice and Delinquency Prevention Act of 1974 were status offenders. The implementation of this act resulted in a relatively small reduction in public institutional populations (McNeece, 1980). The number of status offenders in private institutions increased substantially between 1979 and 1989, roughly equivalent to the drop in the number of status offenders in public institutions (Office of Juvenile Justice and Delinquency Prevention, 1991; hereafter OJJDP). The bottom line is that there has been little or no change in the number of juvenile status offenders in custody, despite two decades of "reform." A 1985 review (OJJDP) of more than seventy empirical studies of status-offender deinstitutionalization in nineteen states concluded that "the failure of implementation has occurred both for diversion and deinstitutionalization" at both the local and state levels (p. 2). Even more disturbing was their finding that even where it had "succeeded," deinsti-

tutionalizing status offenders seemed to make little or no difference in the ultimate outcomes for juveniles. Compared to status offenders who were *not* deinstitutionalized, there was little difference in their recidivism rates (OJJDP, 1985).

Most states have at least one loophole that allows the continued incarceration of status offenders; the 1980 amendments to the Juvenile Justice Act permit juveniles who have run away from valid court placements to be charged with contempt of court, a delinquent act (OJJDP, 1985) which may result in the offender being reclassified as a juvenile *delinquent*. Another loophole is the nonlaw violation of probation or aftercare. Once a youth is under court supervision (probation) for even a minor delinquent offense, almost any form of misbehavior, including truancy, missing scheduled therapy sessions, or violating parents' curfews, can be treated as a violation of probation, which is a delinquent offense. Many youth are incarcerated for nonlaw violations of court supervision. For example, in Florida in fiscal year 2003–2004, more than 2,400 of the 8,263 youth were committed to residential facilities with their most serious current offense listed as a nonlaw violation. This had a disproportionate impact on females, with 41 percent of girls incarcerated that year charged with nonlaw probation or aftercare violations (Florida Department of Juvenile Justice, 2005). Official statistics show that the number of juveniles held in public institutions did decrease during the 1970s, but there was a corresponding increase in private correctional facilities, residential treatment programs, and psychiatric units of hospitals serving juvenile offenders. Although confinement to traditional long-term public facilities did decline somewhat, the use of private facilities offset those declines (Lerman, 1980; Sickmund, 2004). A report by OJJDP (1991b) on *Juveniles Taken into Custody* indicated that the trend continued, with declines in the number of status offenders in public facilities offset by increases in the number of such youth in private facilities (p. 6). More aggressive policies are needed to address this trend.

JAIL REMOVAL PROGRAMS

In 1973, Dr. Rosemary Sarri, one of the nation's foremost experts on juvenile justice, testified to the

Senate Subcommittee to Investigate Juvenile Delinquency that:

> An accurate portrait of the extent of juvenile jailing in the United States does not exist. Furthermore, it is difficult to develop one because of the lack of reliable and comparable information from the cities, counties, states and federal government. (BBY, 2003)

In the winter of 1973, Senator Birch Bayh, chair of the subcommittee, introduced the Juvenile Justice and Delinquency Act of 1973, which contained a strong provision on jailing juveniles. Juveniles "shall not be detained or confined in any institutions in which adult persons convicted of a crime or awaiting trial on criminal charges are incarcerated" (U.S. Congress, Senate, 1973b). However, the bill that eventually passed was considerably weakened. A compromise allowed juveniles to be confined in jails so long as they were kept separate from adult prisoners.

In 1980, President Carter signed the reauthorization of the Juvenile Justice and Delinquency Prevention Act into law. This revised act contained an historic amendment mandating the removal of juveniles from adult jails. Only those juveniles who are tried as adults for criminal felonies are allowed to be detained or incarcerated in adult jails. Perhaps the most important impact of this legislation is that states that are out of compliance with its juvenile jail removal mandates can be sued. OJJDP focused attention on rural jails which were often the only place police could detain juveniles. The degree of success varied considerably from state to state. In Colorado, the number of juveniles admitted to adult jails decreased from 6,117 in 1980 to 1,522 in 1984 (Schwartz, 1992). On the other hand, New York and Florida reported a 400 percent increase in jailed juveniles between 1978 and 1983. New York and Florida accounted for an astounding 36 percent of all juveniles in jail on June 30, 1983 (U.S. Dept. of Justice, 1985). Alaska, one of the more successful states, reduced the detention of status offenders in adult jails by 78 percent between 1987 and 1988.

However, the Bureau of Justice Statistics (1991) reported that the percentage of jail inmates who were juveniles rose from 1.3 percent in 1983 to 1.5 percent in 1989. By June 30, 1992, an estimated 0.63 percent of jail inmates were juveniles (BJS, 1993), a dramatic decrease in just three years. In 1990, the National Coalition of State Juvenile Justice Advisory Groups concluded that the jail removal program had been generally successful (OJJDP, 1990). The number of youth under age 18 in adult prisons peaked in 1995, one year after the peak in juvenile arrests, at 5,309. By 2004, that number had been cut by more than half, with 2,477 youth under 18 in state prisons. The same pattern of decline is not evident in the number of youth under age 18 held in local jails, which was 7,800 in 1995 and 7,083 in 2004 (Bureau of Justice Statistics, 2005).

The number of youth under the age of 18 that are held in adult facilities is deceptively low. Not counted in these statistics are youth who were under the age of 18 at the time they committed their offense or entered adult jail or prison but have since turned 18. In fact, most juveniles who enter adult facilities do so at the age of 16 or 17, and within a year or so of entering the facility are no longer counted among "juvenile" inmates, despite being held for offenses committed as minors. The number of prisoners in adult facilities being held for offenses committed as juveniles is significantly higher than the number of juveniles in adult jails and prisons. Amnesty International (1998) estimates that 200,000 juveniles may be incarcerated in adult institutions.

"NEW AGE" JUVENILE JUSTICE: MEDIATION, RESTORATIVE JUSTICE, ACUPUNCTURE, BOOT CAMPS, DRUG TREATMENT, AND PRIVATIZATION

Diversion and deinstitutionalization, whether they have worked or not, are old news. Dozens of new approaches to the problems of juvenile delinquency have been introduced to the juvenile justice system within the past few years. The oldest of these "new" ideas is probably mediation, which has been around since the development of community dispute resolution centers in the 1950s (Ray, 1992). Mediation seems to have had a rebirth within the past decade, and recent evaluations indicate that outcomes are just as desirable as more costly alternatives (Umbreit, Coates, & Kalanj, 1994). In some cases, juveniles are mandated by the court to participate in a mediation program involving the victim(s). In other cases, victims and juvenile offenders are offered an option of mediation as an alternative to formal court processing. Juveniles participating in a mediation program were more likely to pay restitution and less likely to recidivate than those offenders in other programs (Umbreit & Coates, 1993).

Restorative justice is closely linked with mediation. It emphasizes three goals: (1) identifying the obligation created by the juvenile's offense and ensuring that he/she is held responsible for it (accountability), (2) returning the offender to the community competent to interact in a successful prosocial manner (competence), and (3) ensuring that the community is not further injured by the juvenile's future delinquent behavior (public safety) (Ellis & Sowers, 2001).

Boot camps experienced a decade of political popularity as a promising new treatment option, with millions of dollars set aside for such programs in the Violent Crime Control Act of 1994. Boot camps follow much the same regimen. Offenders rise early for drill, rigorous exercise, and obstacle courses. Their routine is characterized by harsh, summary discipline, a rigid dress code, and frequent inspections. Almost all require some drug treatment, education, and psychological counseling. Despite the early enthusiasm for boot camps, recent research indicates that they are no more effective than the more traditional institutional approaches (Zhang, 2001). Additionally, several tragic cases have demonstrated that the confrontational approaches favored in the boot camp model can lead to abuse. Several states are gradually phasing out their juvenile boot camps.

Many studies have indicated that a number of the factors associated with delinquency also are predictive of drug use among adolescents (Hawkins, Catalano, & Miller, 1992). This suggests, of course, that drug abuse intervention and treatment programs are sorely needed in the juvenile justice system. Unfortunately, local governments frequently lack the resources to provide effective substance abuse treatment. In many cases, juvenile justice personnel do not even have the assessment tools needed to determine the severity of drug use among clients they serve (Stone, 1990). Among those programs most often recommended for drug-involved juvenile offenders are: (1) social skills training, (2) family therapy, (3) case management, (4) posttreatment supports such as self-help groups, relapse prevention, and aftercare (Jenson, 1998).

Acupuncture is one of the more recent and more controversial treatment options for drug-involved juvenile offenders. The theory is that acupuncture, generally in the ear, stimulates the production of a beta-endorphin which reduces the client's craving for drugs. It is much more likely to be used with adults or "youthful offenders" than with juveniles, and there is little evidence of its effectiveness, either with juveniles or adults (Springer, McNeece, & Arnold, 2003).

An increasing trend in the justice system, both for juveniles and adults, is the privatization of services. We now have "rent-a-cops" employed by private corporations and homeowners' associations, "rent-a-judges" used in some types of civil disputes and mediation procedures, offenders housed in privately owned jails and prisons, and treatment services for offenders purchased from private corporations (Bowman, Hakim, & Seidenstat, 1992). There is some fear that public accountability for justice system programs may suffer through privatization. Others fear the danger of sacrificing rehabilitation and treatment goals to the overriding concerns of cost-efficiency within a completely privatized system (McNeece, 1995). A recent census revealed that private for-profit companies operated secure juvenile facilities in 23 states and the District of Columbia (Building Blocks for Youth, 2003). During the past decade, the annual growth rate for private youth corrections beds has been 45 percent (National Mental Health Association, 2003). In Florida, about 82 percent of all residential beds for juvenile offenders are provided by private organizations (Florida Department of Juvenile Justice, 2005).

One argument against privatizing services is that it removes those services from public view and oversight. Some critics fear that private companies serving incarcerated youth have no incentive to support prevention services or to reduce recidivism. To do so might erode their potential profit base (National Mental Health Association, 2003). Privatization also increases the clout of private organizations who already have lobbying skills and tremendous influence on state legislators.

DELINQUENCY PREVENTION PROGRAMS

An emerging body of both conceptual and empirical literature exists that suggests community involvement and social justice approaches to prevention programs can be effective (Ginwright & Cammarota, 2002). Therefore, it is promising that policy initiatives continue to encourage community-based prevention programs. The 1992 amendments to the Juvenile

Justice and Delinquency Prevention Act of 1974 (PL 93–415) expanded the funding for delinquency prevention programs. By 1996, more than 230 local governments were awarded grants for "Community Prevention." Common goals for all of these communities included community mobilization, assessment and planning, initiation of prevention efforts, and institutionalization and monitoring of prevention programs (OJJDP, 1996). Whether this represents a paradigm shift in the overall "get-tough" law-enforcement-oriented delinquency policy remains to be seen.

Although generally discredited by recent research, the nation's D.A.R.E. (Drug Abuse Resistance Education) programs seem to remain very popular with schools, law enforcement, and parents. However, recent criticisms have led to an overhaul of the D.A.R.E. curriculum, and many school districts are looking for alternatives (McNeece & DiNitto, 2003). Meanwhile, D.A.R.E. has made substantial changes in its curriculum, hoping that these will produce improvements in outcomes.

In a recent review of what works in prevention that included seven previous reviews of delinquency prevention programs, Nation et al. (2003) identified nine principles or characteristics that have been consistently related to effective prevention efforts. The common characteristics that these programs had were comprehensiveness, variation in teaching methods, sufficient dosage, theoretical underpinnings, promotion of positive relationships, focus on younger juveniles, sociocultural relevance, clear goals and objectives, and well-trained staff. The key is that programs must be matched with the target population on a variety of factors, and the implementation and evaluation of the program must involve well-trained staff.

"JUST DESSERTS" IN JUVENILE JUSTICE

Under a determinate sentencing policy that the state of Washington adopted more than a decade ago, juvenile offenders are sentenced to a specific term of incarceration related to the severity of their offense. This is an attempt to make the punishment fit the crime. This concept obviously is not congruent with the rehabilitative ideal that at one time permeated our juvenile justice system, but some reformers believe it is more equitable and just. Several other states

have followed suit (Ellis & Sowers, 2001; Merlo, 2000; Mears, 2000).

Such changes may also reflect a general sense of frustration and powerlessness in dealing with juvenile offenders. It may also indicate a shift in the public mood away from rehabilitation and toward punishment. This shift is reflected in the policy changes mentioned earlier, with 45 states making changes in their statues to make it easier to place juveniles in the adult criminal justice system (Merlo, 2000). Trends in case dispositions for juvenile offenders throughout the nation also reflect this change in the public mood. The proportion of juvenile cases processed formally increased by 39 percent between 1990 and 1997, then began a gradual decline (OJJDP, 2003). While the proportion of waivers to adult court dropped slightly, the overall number of children placed in the adult criminal justice system exponentially geometrically because of new laws allowing prosecutors to file charges directly in criminal court. One organization (Building Blocks for Youth, 2003) estimates that 85 percent of the decisions to prosecute juveniles as adults are made by prosecutors, not judges. In addition, 82 percent of youth charged in adult court were minority youth. According to Amnesty International (1998), as many as 200,000 youth under age 18 are processed in adult criminal court annually. Of those, 180,000 are from 13 states which set the upper age of juvenile jurisdiction at 15 or 16 years, and the great majority of the others are from states that allow prosecutorial discretion in charging children as adults. At every stage of processing, minority youth are overrepresented and are treated more harshly than nonminority youth (BBY, 2003; Krisberg, 1992a; Snyder & Sickmund, 1999), especially those accused of drug-related offenses. The nation seems to be in no mood to tolerate juvenile crime or to provide significant new funding for treatment or rehabilitation programs. Indeed, punishment seems to be increasingly more severe.

DUE PROCESS

Many believe that Justice Fortas was correct when he proclaimed that prior to the *Kent* decision, juvenile offenders experienced the worst of both worlds: neither adequate due process nor effective rehabilitation (Fondacaro, Slobogin, & Cross, 2005). Since the beginning of the juvenile court movement at the turn of the century, disparities in the legal rights accorded to children and adults have been tolerated. The less rigorous standards applied to juveniles were justified as being in the child's best interest. Children were also believed to have substantially different constitutional rights than adults. Beginning in the mid-1960s, however, a number of Supreme Court decisions strengthened some of the rights of children. *Kent* (1966) extended limited due process guarantees to juveniles. *In re Gault* (1967) provided juveniles with the right to notice of the charges, the right to counsel, the privilege against self-incrimination, and the right to confront and examine witnesses. *In re Winship* (1970) applied the "reasonable doubt" standard to juvenile cases.

Nevertheless, in *McKeiver v. Pennsylvania* (1970), the Supreme Court maintained some different standards for juveniles in rejecting the argument that children were entitled to a jury trial. Proof that the *parens patriae* concept was still alive came in the *Schall v. Martin* (1984) decision, when the court said that "juveniles, unlike adults, are always in some form of custody." Thus, while children still do not have exactly the same constitutional guarantees as adults, the legal system has moved in that direction. Juveniles accused of criminal offenses may not be treated as arbitrarily or capriciously as they were in the first half of this century.

A unanimous decision in *Oklahoma Publishing Co. v. District Court in and for Oklahoma City* (430 U.S. 308) in 1977 allowed the press to use the name and picture of a minor in a juvenile court proceeding in circumstances where members of the press were present during the court proceeding and no objection to their presence was made. The pretrial use of detention for juveniles presenting a serious risk of committing other offenses was upheld by the Supreme Court in *Schall v. Martin*, a New York case (467 U.S. 253) in 1984.

In 1989, the Supreme Court held in *Stanford v. Kentucky* (492 U.S. 361) that the imposition of capital punishment on individuals for murders committed at the age of 16 or 17 years does not constitute cruel and unusual punishment in violation of the Eighth Amendment. Controversy over the execution of juveniles in this country was partly responsible for preventing the United States from ratifying the Convention on the Rights of the Child (Human Rights Watch, 2005).

However, a significant advance in juvenile due process was made in the U.S. Supreme Court's decision to prohibit to executing children who committed a capital offense before the age of 18 (*Roper v. Simmons*, 543 U.S.2005). Prior to this decision, the United States was one of only six countries in the world that permitted the execution of juveniles. Sadly, the United States (and Somalia) has still not ratified the Convention on the Rights of the Child (UNICEF, 2005).

Beginning in the mid-1970s, several states adopted legislation which mandated minimal or determinate sentences for juveniles. Today a majority of the states use explicitly punitive juvenile sentencing strategies. At least 17 states have recently revised their purpose clause or mission statements for juvenile courts to emphasize public safety, punishment, and offender accountability (Torbet & Szymanski, 1998). This has virtually eliminated the differences between juvenile and adult sentencing in those states. It is difficult to believe that the imposition of a mandatory minimum sentence given on the basis of the offense has anything to do with the child's "real needs" or "best interests." The fact that the "the purposes of the juvenile process have become more punitive, its procedures formalistic, adversarial and public, and the consequences of conviction much more harsh" was acknowledged in *In re Javier A.* (1984).

We have corrected a serious deficiency in the juvenile justice system by requiring closer attention to matters of procedural rights, but it will take much more than a mere declaration of those rights by appellate courts before much real change can be expected. For example, insuring that accused juveniles are provided legal counsel will not per se make any significant difference in case outcomes. Several studies have shown that there is no substantial difference in adjudication or disposition decisions when attorneys are assigned to represent juveniles. In fact, some studies show that juveniles who are represented by legal counsel are more likely to receive harsher deposition (McNeece, 1976; Stapleton & Teitlebaum, 1972). The problem is the prevailing attitude concerning procedural rights that still exists in the juvenile justice system. Many attorneys who represent juvenile clients remain convinced that because the juvenile court is really an institution for providing treatment to their clients, they should not aggressively pursue the protection of the legal rights of such clients. After all, the court is still presumed to act "in the best interests of the child."

On the other hand, others (Feld, 2003) believe that *Gault* precipitated a revolution in the juvenile court system that has unintentionally sidetracked its original progressive and rehabilitative ideals and "transformed the juvenile court into a scaled-down, second-class criminal court for young offenders" (p. 16).

In recent years, reforms at the state level have been suggested in at least three different areas. Several states have lowered the age at which youths may be tried as adult offenders for serious offenses, and other states have made it much easier to waive juveniles of any age to adult courts. Some have called for the abolition of the juvenile court altogether, arguing that the U.S. Supreme Court has made the juvenile and adult systems so similar that having separate systems no longer makes sense (Schichor, 1983). Other people have suggested that we abandon therapy or rehabilitation in favor of protecting the public by *punishing* and *confining* dangerous young offenders. Unfortunately, this has become a politically popular position.

One could reasonably assume that the courts might respond to the current conservative backlash regarding juvenile offenders by taking somewhat more punitive actions in processing at least a portion of these clients. We will be looking for those trends in the data described in the following pages.

FUNDING FOR JUVENILE JUSTICE

Budgets present a useful way to analyze policy shifts. We can assume that if decision makers are serious about changes in policy, those changes will be reflected in budgets. The Law Enforcement Assistance Act in 1965 (FL. 89–197) and the Omnibus Crime Control and Safe Streets Act of 1968 (P. L. 90–351) reflect a major policy change in juvenile justice. These two laws provided money and an administrative structure for providing new grants to state and local agencies for law enforcement and related programs. In 1974, the Office of Juvenile Justice and Delinquency Prevention was created within LEAA to coordinate efforts to control delinquency (P. L. 93–415). For the fiscal years 1975 through 1977; 89,125 OJJDP formula grants to state and local agencies were approved (Office of Juvenile Justice and Delinquency Prevention, 1979). In 1977, $47,625,000 was

available through OJJDP for delinquency control and prevention programs.

Budget authority for the Office of Juvenile Justice and Delinquency Prevention was scheduled to increase to $100 million in 1981 and $135 million in 1982 under the proposed Carter budget (Office of Management and Budget, 1981b). The actual expenditure for juvenile justice formula grants in 1980 was $68 million (OMB, 1981b).

However, Congress' dissatisfaction with LEAA resulted in an order to dismantle the agency well before the end of the Carter Administration. While the actual expenditure for all Law Enforcement Administration Programs in 1980 was $444,781,000, the executive budget request for 1982 was only $159,691,000. The few remaining LEAA grants ended in 1982 (OMB, 1981a), and funds that would have been allocated as grants though the Office of Juvenile Justice and Delinquency Prevention were converted to block grants to the states (OMB, 1981c). Until the passage of the Violent Crime Control Act of 1994, few new federal funds were directed specifically at delinquency prevention or treatment programs. With the election of a new, more conservative Congress, federal appropriations for juvenile programs have continued to decline. Since Sept. 11, 2001, Justice Department priorities have favored antiterrorism programs over juvenile delinquency prevention and treatment (OMB, 2005).

Many of the original advocates of the federal cost-sharing approach to crime and delinquency programs now believe that a serious mistake was made in allowing billions of dollars to be spent on criminal and juvenile programs. Some even believe that not only was this money wasted, but also that it might have made matters worse. Wilson (1975) believes that these billions of dollars did not add much to our knowledge about which approaches and programs were most effective, and that rather than testing our theories about rehabilitation and prevention, we were merely "funding our fears."

The bottom line is that it appears federal largesse in juvenile corrections has ended. As one example, the base budget for OJJDP in FY 2002 was $297,379,000, but the President's budget request for FY 2003 only asked for $249,320,000, a decrease of 16 percent (OJJDP, 2003). A large part of this decrease comes from the elimination of the Juvenile Incentive Block Grant Program (OMB, 2003). The President's requested federal budget for the entire Office of Justice

Programs (which includes OJJDP) for FY2006, is only about *one-half* of OJJDP's actual expenditures for 2004 (OMB, 2005). States and localities will continue to bear the bulk of the financial burden for juvenile delinquency prevention and treatment programs. Because federal money was largely responsible for the development of delinquency prevention, there is a fear that states and communities may return to their previous pattern of funding only the more "traditional" juvenile programs, that is, institutions and probation.

OFFICIAL STATISTICS AND TRENDS

After increasing for a number of years, and contributing to the spread of "get tough," punitive legislation, juvenile crime peaked in 1994 and then began declining. In 1994, 2,716,100 juvenile arrests were reported by the FBI (Snyder, 2005). By 2002, that number had dropped to 2,261,000, despite growth in the population of youth. Arrests for violent crimes by juveniles dropped from 150,180 to 92,160, and arrests for property crimes dropped from 748,100 to 481,600. During the same time period, the population of youth age 10–17, the age group generally considered to be "at-risk" of juvenile justice involvement, *increased* by 3,832,900.

Declines were particularly notable in one important offense category, homicide. Juvenile murder arrests peaked in 1993, with 3,790 juvenile murder charges. By 2003, that number had been cut by more than two-thirds, with 1,120 juvenile murder arrests (Snyder, 2005). Arrests for auto theft similarly declined by about two-thirds between 1990 and 2003 (Snyder, 2005).

The number of juvenile arrests per 100,000 persons under the age of 18 dropped from 9,200 in 1994 to 6,778 in 2003, while the number of juveniles arrested for violent offenses per 100,000 dropped from 509 to 276, and the number arrested for property offenses dropped from 1,915 to 1,444.

Despite overall declines in juvenile arrests and even in violent arrests, arrests in some categories have increased. Two areas of concern are simple assaults, which between 1980 and 2003 rose 269 percent for females and 102 percent for males; and drug violations, which rose 51 percent among females and 52 percent among males (Snyder, 2005). However, it

is important to remember when analyzing official crime statistics that it is often impossible to determine whether increases (or decreases) reflect changes in actual behavior, or changes in official response. For example, it has been argued that the widespread adoption of "zero tolerance" policies in schools regarding behavior such as minor fights or threats against peers has resulted in the "criminalization" of behavior that was until recently handled through school-based discipline such as suspension. It is possible that some, or all, of the increases in simple assault and drug arrests reflect the readiness of school officials to have youth arrested for acts that were handled as noncriminal infractions prior to zero-tolerance. Additionally, the increase in arrests for "disorderly conduct" are quite suspect, as this is a common referral reason for youth arrested at school. However, the hypothesis that zero-tolerance policies, rather than changes in actual youth behavior, is responsible for the rise in certain offense categories is difficult to support with data, because prior to zero-tolerance, data on such infractions was not systematically collected. Therefore, information is not available to permit comparisons before and after implementation of zero tolerance policies. However, it is worth noting that in Florida, a state that compiles statistics on school-based referrals, close to one in five juvenile arrests takes place in schools.

Referrals for delinquency offenses do not typically result in placement in juvenile commitment facilities. In fact, based on data from calendar year 2000, 41 percent of cases referred resulted in juvenile justice system probation. The next most common case outcome reported was "release," which accounted for 30 percent of cases referred. Nineteen percent of cases resulted in "other" outcomes, such as diversion options that provide minor sanctions but avoid a delinquency record. Almost 10 percent of juvenile referrals in 2000 resulted in placement in a juvenile residential facility, and .4 percent of cases were waived to adult court.

Although the percentage of total cases waived to adult court is relatively small, waivers still accounted for more than 5,800 case dispositions in 2000. As discussed earlier in this chapter, there are other routes to adult court that account for the majority of juveniles who are prosecuted as adults.

In 1999, the most recent year for which residential commitment data was available at the time of this writing, a one-day population count showed approximately 134,000 youth were held in one of almost 3,000 secure facilities nationwide (Sickmund, 2004). Two-thirds of juvenile facilities were private and one-third were state or county-government operated. However, due to the smaller size of the privately operated facilities, they held only about one-third of the total population of incarcerated juveniles (Sickmund, 2004). In 1999, the states varied tremendously with regard to rates of juvenile incarceration. In fact, states varied from a low of 96 juveniles out of every 100,000 in the population incarcerated (Hawaii) to a high of 632 incarcerated for every 100,000 in the population (South Dakota). Other states with high rates of juveniles incarcerated per 100,000 in the population included Louisiana (580), California (514), and Florida (427). Nationally, in 1999, minority youth accounted for 62 percent of juvenile inmates (Sickmund, 2004).

CHILD MALTREATMENT AND TRAUMA-INFORMED PRACTICE

New research on the prevalence and impact of child maltreatment among troubled youth is also influencing how some practitioners address juvenile offenders. Research has clearly shown that many youth (and most girls) who become deeply involved in the juvenile justice system have histories of physical and/or sexual abuse, and living in troubled families and communities, they often have a dearth of the "protective factors" in their lives that can help buffer children from the impact of trauma. Although PTSD is difficult to assess, one study (Cauffman, Feldman, Waterman, & Steiner, 1998) found that almost half of the girls in one facility suffered from full-blown PTSD. In another study, about one-third of boys in one facility suffered from the disorder (Steiner, Garcia, & Matthews, 1997).

Although the link between abuse and trauma and subsequent mental health and behavioral problems is increasingly well documented, this field of study is a very recent research development that is only beginning to impact juvenile justice policy in a substantive way in a few jurisdictions. Although child abuse has always been a part of the human experience, it was not until the early 1960s that researchers began to seriously investigate the "battered child syndrome" (Zigler & Hall, 1997). Not until 1980 did the Diagnostic and Statistical Manual, the "gold standard" for mental health diagnosis, include Post-Traumatic Stress Disorder (PTSD) as an official diagnosis. Not until several years later did practitioners begin to recognize that children and teens who have experienced abuse and other traumas can develop PTSD. Even more recently, researchers have discovered that abuse and trauma can actually impact neurobiological development in ways that predispose victims to a variety of mental health and behavioral problems, including living in a hypervigilant "fight or flight state," substance abuse, learning problems, and aggression (Perry, 1997). Chronic trauma such as ongoing physical or sexual abuse predisposes its victims to live in a vigilant, defensive, and aggressive state that may help keep them safe in an abusive environment but is maladaptive in other settings.

What does this mean for juvenile justice? Severely delinquent youth, particularly girls, are clearly a highly traumatized population, which calls even further into question the effectiveness of harsh and confrontational disciplinary tactics that may "trigger" traumatic memories and flashbacks in PTSD victims. In fact, even in the absence of harsh approaches, many elements of the incarceration experience, including strip searches, violations of privacy, and the use of handcuffs and other forms of restraint are likely to be especially traumatic for abuse survivors with PTSD.

Individual practitioners and facilities working with delinquent girls are increasingly including some type of treatment for trauma and abuse in their programming. Pennsylvania has developed an innovative program to comprehensively address trauma among delinquent girls. In the programs' first five years of operation, more than 7,000 juvenile justice workers statewide were trained to understand the behavioral impact of trauma and how to minimize provoking traumatic memories.

Additionally, girls in many Pennsylvania institutions are provided with therapeutic group treatment to help resolve PTSD symptoms (Griffin & Bender, 2005). Florida, influenced by Pennsylvania's successes in highlighting the importance of trauma in the rehabilitation of delinquent girls, is experimenting with a trauma-informed approach in several girls' programs, including prevention, detention, and residential treatment facilities (personal communication, September 2005).

Despite promising developments in a few jurisdictions, serious deficiencies and inequities persist in juvenile justice systems throughout the United States. Minority youth remain disproportionately represented among youth formally processed and incarcerated (Hsia, Bridges, & McHale, 2004). Sadly, many facilities continue to be plagued by excessive use of force by staff, harsh and ineffective treatment, inadequate mental health care, and even sexual abuse of youth (American Civil Liberties Union, 2004; Selcraig, 2000).

DISTURBING TRENDS IN OFFENSES AND CASE PROCESSING

Racial Disparities

On the surface it appears that racial disparities are becoming more equitable in case processing decisions in the juvenile justice system in recent years. The rate of increase in formal handling has been more than twice as high for white as for minority youth; the rates of increase in detention and adjudication have been much greater for white than for minority youth; out-of-placements for white youth grew almost five times as the rate for minority youth; and waivers to adult court declined three times as much for minority than white youth. Waivers of minority youth have declined consistently for every category of offense since the mid 1990s. Overall, waivers of minority youth are down 41 percent between 1990 and 2000 (OJJDP, 2003).

This does not mean that things are really getting better for minority youth. The era of punitiveness has been tough on all youth – but particularly African-Americans. Things only look better for minorities in the *juvenile* justice system because so many of them are being processed as adults. The bottom line is that we seem to have decided that minority youth, especially those who are older and commit drug offenses, and not amenable to treatment in the juvenile system (OJJDP, 2003). We treat them as adults. We have come full cycle, as if the juvenile court movement of a century ago had never taken place.

Children in Jails and Prison

Earlier we discussed the "get-tough" legislation passed in 45 states between 1992–1997 (Merlo, 2000; Snyder & Sickmund, 1999). The effect of that legislation was to increase prosecutorial discretion in trying juveniles as adults, lowering the statutory age for referral to the adult court, and to broaden the categories of offenses which go to adult court. True, judges aren't waiving kids as often today. But only 15 percent of those decisions to waive to adult court are made by judges; 85 percent are made by prosecutors or legislative bodies, and 82 percent of kids processed as adults are minority youth (BBY, 2003). The result is that 200,000 children per year are processed in the adult criminal justice system (Amnesty International, 1998).

Females in Juvenile Justice

Approximately 30% of juveniles who are arrested are female. In 2003, approximately 643,000 arrests of girls under 18 were reported (Snyder, 2005). In the 10-year period 1994-2003, the number of girls arrested increased, compared to boys, for most types of offenses (Snyder, 2005) (see Table 14-1).

Girls typically commit less serious offenses than their male counterparts, and the majority of female juvenile offending still consists of status offenses and relatively minor delinquency offenses (OJJDP, 1998). However, in recent years girls have entered the juvenile justice system in increasing numbers and for increasingly serious offenses. Between 1994 and 2003, arrests of boys for felony assault dropped 31 percent, but over the same period dropped just 2 percent for girls, while misdemeanor assaults rose 1 percent for boys and a dramatic 36 percent for girls (Snyder, 2005).

The statistics on girls' offending, and particularly their serious offending, appear alarming. However, there is debate regarding the factors underlying these increases. As noted earlier, zero tolerance policies may explain some of the increase in girls' arrests for misdemeanor assault, as offenses that were once handled as school discipline problems are now handled through arrest. There is also evidence that a much of the increase in official statistics on girls' violent offending is being driven by girls who are abuse victims who are charged with domestic violence when they attempt to defend themselves or strike back during a violent episode. In fact, increases in females entering juvenile justice systems for assaults coincided with the spread of mandatory arrest policies for domestic violence cases, suggesting that reclassification of offenses once handled as family problems are now triggering juvenile arrests.

Table 14-1
PERCENT CHANGE IN JUVENILE ARRESTS,
1994–2003

	Females (%)	*Males (%)*
Aggravated assault	–2	–31
Simple assault	36	1
Burglary	–27	–41
Larceny-theft	–19	–43
Auto theft	–44	–54
Vandalism	–11	–36
Weapons	–22	–42
Drug violations	56	13
Liquor violations	26	–5
DUI	83	25
Disorderly conduct	46	2

Source: Crime in the United States, reproduced in Snyder, 2005.

Some research suggests that female juveniles are treated more harshly than their male counterparts (OJJDP, 1998). For example, a report published by the Florida Department of Juvenile Justice notes that girls committed to secure placement for their first commitment have less serious offense histories than boys given the same sanctions (Florida DJJ, 2001). Another study reported that girls are more likely to be placed in detention and are detained for less serious offenses than boys (OJJDP, 1998).

Media accounts, particularly in the mid-1990s, often suggested a link between women's increasing economic opportunities and the rise in female delinquency. However, research with delinquent girls tells a very different story, namely that delinquent girls generally have backgrounds of victimization, and are more likely than their male counterparts to suffer from a variety of mental health problems. As discussed above, many researchers have noted that girls who become involved in juvenile justice systems generally have been sexually or physically abused, and their offending is often related to the abuse. Chesney-Lind (1997) describes the "criminalization of girls' survival strategies," whereby abused girls run away from home and are arrested for running away or for engaging in crime to survive on the streets. Critics have noted that programming and treatment tactics developed for boys are generically applied to delinquent girls, resulting in a juvenile justice system that fails to address the gender-specific issues associated with their offending (OJJDP, 1998).

The United States Congress recently acknowledged the apparent rise in female juvenile offending and the different issues underlying their delinquency. When the JJDP Act was reauthorized in 1992, it included grant funding to assist states in: ". . . developing and adopting policies to prohibit gender bias in placement and treatment and establishing programs to ensure that female youth have access to the full range of health and mental health services, treatment for physical or sexual assault and abuse, self-defense instruction, education in parenting in general and other training and vocational services" (Title 42, Chapter 72, Subchapter II, Part E, Sec. 5667c). A number of states have received research funding under this provision of the JJDP Act. However, there is much evidence that harsher sanctions as well as treatment more appropriate for boys persist in the processing and rehabilitation of female offenders.

A NEW REFORM MOVEMENT?

In the early years of the twenty-first century, following more than a decade of rapidly spreading get-tough policies that increasingly placed juveniles in largely ineffective and potentially dangerous environments such as boot camps, adult prisons, and large, overcrowded facilities, a few communities are beginning to return to the rehabilitation-focused roots of the juvenile justice ideal. This fledgling movement may have been influenced by the growing body of research showing that such tactics are all ineffective and likely to exacerbate future offending, compared to treatment-oriented approaches. More often than not, reform movements are triggered by high-profile cases of abuse or neglect, or critical reports from outside entities. In recent years there have been many such high-profile cases and critical reports: Nathaniel Abraham, Lionel Tate, Columbine, Jonesboro.

In Missouri, a reform movement was launched in the early 1970s following a federal report critical of one of the state's large training schools. The state revamped its juvenile justice system, creating a system that has remarkably low recidivism rates and has been called a model for the nation. The so-called "Missouri Model" emphasizes small facilities, a homelike living environment, segregation of violent and nonviolent youth, highly trained staff, appropriate therapy with positive peer support, and a "culture of caring" (McGarvey, 2005). Several other state juvenile justice systems, including Louisiana and Georgia, have adopted elements of the Missouri Model, though none have truly replicated it.

Louisiana's reform movement was launched through state legislation and the involvement of the Annie E. Casey foundation in 2003, in the wake of exposes of rampant violence in facilities, lawsuits, and the death of an incarcerated child (Reckdahl, 2005). The state's juvenile justice system has adopted a number of reforms from the Missouri Model, including obtaining "human dignity" training for facility staff from Missouri juvenile justice training coaches.

After a major lawsuit and years of criticism for harsh, violent, neglectful conditions in California Youth Authority facilities, including the widespread practice of placing youth in small cages while they attended counseling sessions and school, the California juvenile justice system announced reform plans. In early 2005, the California Youth Authority issued a statement announcing that "The California Youth Authority is completely broken and can't be fixed." The agency's plan for reform included, in part, development and implementation of a new model based on rehabilitation (Ella Baker Center, 2005).

CONCLUSION

The future direction of juvenile justice policy in America is uncertain. There is a terrible irony in the fact that juvenile violent crime has been decreasing, while state legislatures have been making the juvenile justice system more punitive and adult-like. Part of the explanation undoubtedly lies in the media coverage of events like the tragedies at Columbine and Jonesboro and the notoriety of juvenile offenders such as Lee Boyd Malvo (American Bar Association,

2005; Merlo, 2000). Media coverage and politics have interacted to the detriment of juveniles. "Justice" as a symbolic value is easily dispensed by political leaders. It is cost-free and very popular (Merlo & Benekos, 2000). We still seem to be in a "get tough" period of juvenile justice, but a few states have taken steps to return to a rehabilitative model, and most have abandoned ineffective adult-modeled programs such as boot camps. Recent legislation and budgets indicate that our national leaders are in no mood to expend any effort searching for effective and humane solutions to the problems associated with juvenile crime. However, states and local communities may take the lead. After all, that is how the first national juvenile justice reform movement began.

REFERENCES

American Bar Association. (2005). Lee Boyd Malvo. Obtained 10/2/05 from http://www.abanet.org/crimjust/juvjus/malvo.html.

American Civil Liberties Union. (2004, June). *ACLU urges Hawaii governor to break stalemate over brutal conditions at youth correctional facility.* Obtained 9/29/2005 from http://www.aclu.org/CriminalJustice/CriminalJustice.cfm?ID=15953&c=46.

Amnesty International. (1998). *Betraying the young.* Amnesty International, November.

Asksam (2005). Judge John Roberts confirmation hearings. Retrieved September 30, 2005, from http://www.asksam.com/ebooks/JohnRoberts/confirmation_hearing.asp.

Bartol, C., & Bartol, A. (1989). *Juvenile delinquency: A systems approach.* Englewood Cliffs, NJ: Prentice-Hall.

Blomberg, T. (1983). Diversion's disparate results and unresolved questions: An evaluation perspective. *Journal of Research in Crime and Delinquency, 20,* 24–38.

Bowman, G. W., Hakim, S., & Seidenstat, P. (1992). *Privatizing the United States justice system: Police, adjudication, and correction services from the private sector.* Jefferson, NC: McFarland.

Building Blocks for Youth. (2003). *Transfer to adult court/ Trying kids as adults.* Obtained from www.buildingblocksforyouth.org/issues/transfer/facts_transfer.html 2/04/03.

Bureau of Justice Statistics. (2005). *Prison & jail inmates at midyear 2004.* NCJ 208801.

Cauffman, E, Feldman, S., Waterman, J., & Steiner, H. (1998). Posttraumatic stress disorder among female juvenile offenders. *Journal of the American Academy of Child and Adolescent Psychiatry, 37,* 1209–1216.

Chesney-Lind, M. (1997). *The female offender: Girls, women, and crime.* Thousand Oaks, CA: Sage.

CNN (2005, May 24). Young killer faces armed robbery charge: Lionel Tate on probation in 1999 beating of 6-year-old. Retrieved September, 25, 2005, from http://www.cnn.com2005/LAW/05/24/tate.arrest.

Ella Baker Center for Human Rights. (2005). *Books, not bars.* Obtained from http://www.ellabakercenter.org/page.php?pageid=152 10/5/05.

Ellis, R. A., & Sowers, K. M. (2001). *Juvenile justice practice: A cross-disciplinary approach to intervention.* Brooks/Cole.

Empey, L. T., & Stafford, M. C. (1991). *American delinquency: Its meaning and construction* (3d ed.). Belmont, CA: Wadsworth.

Executive Office of the President, Office of Management and Budget. (1981a). *Budget of the United States government, fiscal year 1982.* Washington, D.C.: U.S. Government Printing Office.

Executive Office of the President, Office of Management and Budget. (1981b). *Budget of the United States government, fiscal year1982, Appendix.* Washington, D.C.: U.S. Government Printing Office.

Executive Office of the President, Office of Management and Budget. (1981c). *Budget of the United States government, fiscal year 1982, budget revisions: Additional details on budget savings.* Washington, D.C.: U.S. Government Printing Office.

Executive Office of the President, Office of Management and Budget. (2005). *FY2006 Budget Priorities, Department of Justice.* Obtained from http://www.whitehouse.gov/omb/budget/fy2006/justice.html 9/25/05.

Feld, B. C. (2003). *Juvenile justice administration.* St. Paul, MN: Thomson/West.

Florida Department of Juvenile Justice. (2001). *2001 Outcome evaluation.* Tallahassee, FL: Florida Department of Juvenile Justice.

Florida Department of Juvenile Justice. (2005). *2004 Outcome Evaluation Report.* Obtained from http://www.nmha.org/children/justjuv/juvenilejustice-privatization.pdf#search='privatization%20of%20juvenile%20corrections' 9/13/05.

Fondacaro, M. R., Slobogin, C., & Cross, T. (2005, August 19). *Reconceptualizing due process in juvenile justice: Contributions from law and social science.* http://ssrn.com/abstract=786666.

Ginwright, S., & Cammarato, J. (2002). New terrain in youth development: The promise of a social justice model. *Social Justice, 29,* 82–59.

Greenhouse, L. (2005, March 2). Supreme court, 5-4, forbids execution in juvenile crime. *New York Times,* A1.

Gregory, D. (2004, November 30). Lionel Tate gets third chance. *Caribbean Today, 15,* p. 4.

Griffin, P. & Bender, V. (2005, June). *Responding to girls. Pennsylvania progress: Juvenile justice achievements in Pennsylvania.* Obtained 9/29/2005 from http://www.pccd.state.pa.us/pccd/lib/pccd/pubs/progress/june2005.pdf.

Grisso, T., & Schwartz, R. G. (Eds.). (2000). *Youth on trial: A developmental perspective on juvenile justice.* Chicago: Univeristy of Chicago Press.

Hawkins, J., Catalano, R., & Miller, J. (1992). Risk and protective factors for alcohol and other drug problems in adolescence and early adulthood: Implications for substance abuse prevention. *Psychological Bulletin 112*(1), 64–105.

Hellum, F. (1979). Juvenile justice: The second revolution. *Crime and Delinquency, 25,* 299–317.

Hsia, H., Bridges, G., & McHale, R. (2004). *OJJDP disproportionate minority confinement: 2002 update.* Obtained 9/29/2005 from http://www.ncjrs.org/pdffiles1/ojjdp/201240.pdf.

Human Rights Watch. (2005). *Children.* Obtained from http://www.hrw.org/doc/?t=usa_children 9/25/05.

Juvenile Justice Law Center (2005). *Appellate court correct to order new trial.* Retrieved September 22, 2005, from http://www.jlc.org/tate.php.

Krisberg, B. (1992a). *Juvenile justice: Improving the quality of care.* Washington, D.C.: National Council on Crime and Delinquency.

Lerman, P. (1980). Trends and issues in the deinstitutionalization of youths in trouble. *Crime and Delinquency, 26,* 28, 1–298.

Liptak, A. (2005, March 2). Another step in reshaping the capital justice system. *New York Times,* A14.

McGarvey, A. (2005, August). A culture of caring. *The American Prospect,* A12-A14.

McNeece, C. A. (1976). *Juvenile courts in the community environment.* Ph.D. dissertation, University of Michigan, May.

McNeece, C. A. (1980). "Justice" in the juvenile court: Some suggestions for reform. *Journal of Humanics,* May, 77–97.

McNeece, C. (1995). Adult corrections. *Encyclopedia of social work.* Washington, D.C.: National Association of Social Workers.

McNeece, C., & DiNitto, D. (2003). *Chemical dependency: A systems approach* (3rd ed.). Needham Heights, MA: Allyn and Bacon.

Mears, D. P. (2000). Assessing the effectiveness of juvenile justice reforms: A closer look at the criteria and the impacts on diverse stakeholders.

Merlo, A. V. (2000). Juvenile justice at the crossroads: Presidential address to the academy of criminal justice sciences. *Justice Quarterly, 17*(4), 639–661.

Merlo, A. V., & Benekos, P. J. (2000). *What's wrong with the criminal justice system: Ideology, politics, and the media.* Cincinnati, OH: Anderson.

National Mental Health Association. (2003). *Privatization and managed care in the juvenile justice system.* Obtained from http://www.nmha.org/children/justjuv/juvenilejustice-privatization.pdf#search='privatization%20of

%20juvenile%20corrections' 9/13/05.

Office of Juvenile Justice and Delinquency Prevention, U.S. Department of Justice. (1991). *Juveniles taken into custody: Fiscal year 1990 report.* Washington, D.C.: U.S. Government Printing Office.

Office of Juvenile Justice and Delinquency Prevention (2003). Personal communication from Daryl Fox, Information Analyst, OJJDP Clearinghouse.

Office of Juvenile Justice and Delinquency Prevention. (2003). Easy Access to Juvenile Court Statistics. Obtained 2/08/03 from http://ojjdp.ncjrs.org/ojstatbb/ ezajcs/asp/ Selection.asp.

Office of Juvenile Justice and Delinquency Prevention (2005). Easy Access to FBI Arrest Statistics. Obtained 9/23/2005 from http://ojjdp.ncjrs.org/ojstatbb/ezaucr/.

Office of Management and Budget. (2003). President's Budget Request, FY 2003. Executive Office of the President.

Office of Juvenile Justice and Delinquency Prevention. (1998). *Guiding principles for promising female programming: An inventory of best practices.* Washington, D.C.: Government Printing Office.

Office of Juvenile Justice and Delinquency Prevention, U.S. Department of Justice. (1996). 1996 report to Congress, Title V. *Incentive grants for local delinquency prevention programs.* Washington, D.C.: U.S. Government Printing Office.

Ohlin, L. (1983). Interview with Lloyd E. Ohlin, June 22, 1979. In J. Laub, *Criminology in the making: An oral history.* Boston: Northeastern University Press.

Perry, B. D. (1997). Incubated in terror: Neurodevelopmental factors in the 'cycle of violence' In J. Osofsky (Ed.), *Children, youth and violence: The search for solutions* (pp. 124–148). New York: Guilford Press.

Porter, L. (2002). Michigan judge rejects early relsease for Nathaniel Abraham. Obtained from http://www.wsws. org/articles/2002/sep2002/abra-s10.shtml on 2/13/03.

Ray, L. (1992). Privatization of justice. *Privatizing the United States justice system: Police, adjudication, and correction services from the private sector.* Jefferson, NC: McFarland.

Reckdahl, K. (2005, August). Bayou betterment. *The American Prospect*, A15-A18.

Schichor, D. (1983). Historical and current trends in American juvenile justice. *Juvenile and Family Court Journal, 34*, 61–75.

Schwartz, I. M. (1992). *Juvenile justice and public policy: Toward a national agenda.* New York: Macmillan.

Scott, E. E., & Steinberg, L. (2003). Blaming youth. *Texas Law Review, 81*, 799–819.

Selcraig, B. (2000, November/December). Camp fear. *Mother Jones.*

Sickmund, M. (2004). OJJDP Juvenile offenders and victims national report series: Juveniles in corrections. Obtained 9/23/2005 from http://www.ncjrs.gov/pdffiles1/

ojjdp/202885.pdf.

Smikle, P. (1999, September 30). Child's death divides Jamaican families. *Caribbean Today, 10,* 21.

Smikle, P. (2000, May 31). Teen's trial may break legal ground. *Caribbean Today, 11,* 7.

Snyder, H. (2005). *OJJDP juvenile justice bulletin: Juvenile arrests 2003.* Obtained 9/22/2005 from http://www.ncjrs. gov/html/ojjdp/209735/contents.html

Snyder, H. N., & Sickmund, M. (1999). *Juvenile offenders and victims: 1999 national report.* Washington, D.C.: Office of Juvenile Justice and Delinquency Prevention.

Springer, D. W., McNeece, C. A., & Arnold, E. M. (2003). *Substance abuse treatment for criminal offenders: An evidence-based guide.* Washington, D.C.: American Psychological Association.

Stapleton, V., & Teitlebaum, L. (1972). *In defense of youth.* New York: Russell Sage.

Steiner, H., Garcia, I., & Matthews, Z. (1997). Posttraumatic stress disorder in incarcerated juvenile delinquents. *Journal of the American Academy of Child and Adolescent Psychiatry, 36*, 357–365.

Stone, K. (1990). Determining the primacy of substance abuse disorders among juvenile offenders. *Alcoholism Treatment Quarterly, 7*, (2), 81–93.

Torbet, P., & Szymanski, L. (1998). *State legislative responses to violent juvenile crime: 1996-1997 update.* Washington, D.C.: Office of Juvenile Justice and Delinquency Prevention.

Umbreit, M. S., & Coates, R. B. (1993). Cross-site analysis of victim-offender mediation in four states. *Crime and Delinquency, 39*, 565–585.

Umbreit, M. S., Coates, R. B., & Kalanj, B. (1994). *Victim meets offender: The impact of restorative justice and mediation.* Monsey, NY: Willow Tree Press.

UNICEF. (2005). The convention on the rights of the child. Obtained from http://www.unicef.org/crc/crc. htm 9/24/05.

United States Congress, Senate. (1973). Hearings before the Senate subcommittee on juvenile delinquency on S.B. 821 Washington, D.C.: U.S. Government Printing Office.

U.S. Department of Justice, Bureau of Justice Statistics. (1993). S*ourcebook of criminal justice statistics, 1992.* Washington, D.C.: U.S. Government Printing Office.

U.S. Department of Justice, Office of Juvenile Justice and Delinquency Prevention. (1985). *Reports of the national juvenile justice assessment centers: The impact of deinstitutionalization on recidivism and secure confinement of status offenders.* Washington, D.C.: U.S. Government Printing Office.

U.S. Department. of Justice, Office of Juvenile Justice and Delinquency Prevention. (1991). *Juveniles taken into custody: Fiscal year 1990 report.* Washington, D.C.: U.S. Government Printing Office.

Wilson, J. Q. (1975). *Thinking about crime.* New York: Basic

Books.

Woolard, J. L., Fondacaro, M. R., & Slobogin, C. (2001). Informing juvenile justice policy: Directions for behavioral research. *Law and Human behavior, 25*(1), 13–24.

Zhang, S. X. (2001). Evaluation of the Los Angeles County juvenile drug treatment boot camp: Executive summary. NCJ Report 187678.

Zigler, E., & Hall, N. (1997). Physical child abuse in America: Past, present, and future. In D. Cichetti & V. Carlson (Eds.), *Child maltreatment: Theory and Research on the causes and consequences of child abuse and neglect* (pp. 38–75). Cambridge, UK: Cambridge Press.

CASES

In re Gault, 387 U.S. 1, 1967.

In re JavierA., 159 Cal., App. 3d 913, 206 Cal Rptr. 386 (1984).

In re Winship (397 U.S. 358, 1970).

Kent v. U.S. (383 U.S. 541, 1966).

Oklahoma Publishing Co. v. District Court in and for Oklahoma City (430 U.S. 308) 1977.

Roper vs. Simmons, 543 U.S.___2005.

Schall v. Martin, (467 U.S. 253) 1984.

Stanford v. Kentucky (492 U.S. 361) 1989.

Chapter 15

Conflictive Philosophies of Juvenile Justice[1]

Carolyn Needleman

Many of the practice problems that social workers presently face in connection with juvenile justice have their roots in the ideological inconsistencies of the juvenile court itself. From its beginnings, juvenile court has differed from other parts of the United States legal system by explicitly combining criminal justice goals with social welfare concerns. As we shall see, the combination has been an uneasy one.

The court's emphasis on social welfare and rehabilitation was largely the contribution of a group of late nineteenth century social reformers, many of them feminists, who have been termed the "child savers" (Platt, 1969). Their ranks included individuals such as Jane Addams, prominent in the development of social work as a profession.

The tradition of juvenile justice the child savers set out to change was harsh indeed (An Historical Overview, 1975). One of the by-products of that era's rapid immigration and extreme urban poverty was a large number of children who lacked the support of family and community; sometimes orphaned and often homeless, they lived by their wits, begging and stealing. When arrested, these children were confined with adult criminals. For serious offenses, they could receive the same penalties as adults, even capital punishment.[2] They often ended up in "Houses of Refuge," where they provided cheap labor for nearby manufacturers. Some were forcibly apprenticed to whaling captains and farmers or sent west to work on ranches. Their natural parents, usually foreign and

impoverished, had a difficult time regaining custody from the state. The child-saving movement sought to improve this pitiable situation by creating a separate juvenile court as a more humane means of dealing with delinquent and dependent children.

Besides compassion, the child savers also reflected a new philosophy of intervention in criminal behavior (Platt, 1969). Challenging the then-prevailing fatalistic view that criminals were born irreversibly depraved, they advanced a more developmental theory of crime: criminal behavior resulted not from biological heritage alone, but also from negative influences in the offender's family life and social environment. Thus for offenders young enough to be still malleable, it made sense to establish a separate court system that would seek not to punish, but to reform the offender.

The child savers successfully translated their ideals into a political movement, supported by allies such as the Educational Commission of Chicago, which saw an opportunity to further the cause of compulsory education and proclaimed,

> We should rightfully have the power to arrest all the little beggars, loafers and vagabonds that infest our city, take them from the streets, and place them in schools where they are compelled to receive education and learn moral principles. (Harpur, 1899)

The fruit of their efforts was the creation of the nation's first official juvenile court in Illinois in 1899, based on a Juvenile Court Act that rapidly became a

---

1. The author would like to thank William W. Vosburgh, Miriam Vosburgh, Milton Speizman, and Martin Needleman for helpful comments on an earlier draft. Correspondence concerning this chapter should be addressed to Carolyn Needleman, Graduate School of Social Work and Social Research, Bryn Mawr College, 300 Airdale Road, Bryn Mawr, PA 19010.
2. However, actual executions of children were apparently rare (Platt, 1969).

model statute for other states. Within the next 20 years, most states set up their own separate courts for children, and by 1932, the United States had over 600 independent juvenile courts (Platt, 1969).

In keeping with their nonpunitive aims, the new juvenile courts followed much more informal procedures than their adult counterparts. Hearings were nonadversarial and organized around the best interests of the child. As Jane Addams remarked enthusiastically, "The child was brought before the judge with no one to prosecute him and no one to defend him – the judge and all concerned were merely trying to find out what could be done on his behalf" (An Historical Overview, 1975). The rationale of the new court was *parens patriae:* the state as a stern but benevolent parent, who would consider the child's entire situation sympathetically and arrive at an individually tailored treatment plan for rehabilitation.

Unfortunately, the new social welfare philosophy meshed poorly with other aspects of the juvenile court retained from the criminal justice system from which it derived. The resulting inconsistencies have given rise to three quite different kinds of criticism.

CONSTITUTIONALIST CRITICISMS

However benignly presented, the court's new philosophy posed some alarming threats to due process for young offenders (Fox, 1970; Platt, 1969; Schur, 1973; Ryerson, 1978; Sosin & Sarri, 1976; Lemert, 1967, 1970). Juvenile court was envisioned as a quite different institution from an adult criminal court, but the consequences of court action could still be just as serious. In fact, because of the practice of indeterminate sentencing for juveniles, a delinquent child could actually be incarcerated for a longer period than an adult convicted of the same crime (Lerman, 1970). In the juvenile court, children faced consequences without the legal protections that they would have been entitled to as adults.

For half a century, evidence was allowed in juvenile court that in other courts would have been considered inadmissible hearsay; transcripts of court hearing were not regularly kept for appeal purposes; the juvenile offender was not represented by legal counsel. The court was not at all limited to the charged offense. Basic civil liberties such as the presumption of innocence, privilege against self-incrimination,

and the right to remain silent were obscured by the court's informality.

Unease about this situation grew, and by the 1960s, it was clear to many that the concept of *parens patriae* has a dark side; by defining juvenile offenders as children in relation to the state as parent, it deprives them of their rights as citizens and grants to the state the arbitrariness allowed to actual parents in dealing with their own children. To constitutionalist critics, the due process disadvantages outweigh any social welfare benefits that might flow from the juvenile court's looseness of procedure and broad discretionary powers. As U.S. Supreme Court Justice Abe Fortas remarked, "Under our Constitution, the condition of being a boy does not justify a kangaroo court" (*In re Gault,* 1967).

RETRIBUTIVE JUSTICE CRITICISMS

A very different theme has been raised by other critics, who fear that the social welfare orientation of the juvenile court may prove damaging to the moral foundations of society (see Hirsch, 1976; van den Haag, 1975; Morris, 1974; Wilson, 1975). According to this argument, a legal system exists primarily to express and implement the social norms of a community. When norms are violated, the court has a duty to respond in a way that satisfies the community's sense of justice and provides moral education to the public. Therefore, when the juvenile court concentrates on the offenders' best interests and fails to punish their transgressions, the legitimacy of criminal law itself suffers. Potential offenders will not be deterred and the community will begin to lose confidence in its legal institutions because proper retribution is absent.

HUMANITARIAN CRITICISMS

A third line of criticism has come from humanitarians, among them a number of social work professionals, who are disturbed by the disparities they see between the juvenile court's social welfare ideology and its daily practice. For instance, consider the ideal of shielding child suspects from association with adult criminals. The stated intent of the court is to release juvenile offenders into their parents' custody pending trial if at all feasible or at least to keep the detained children out of adult jails. But over half of the children referred to court do get detained prior to their court hearings, rather than being immediately released to their parents or other guardians (Empey, 1978). Often there is no place to put them but in adult facilities (National Council on Crime and Delinquency, 1967; Children's Defense Fund, 1976). One investigator estimates that as many as 500,000 children spend time in adult jails each year (Sarri, 1974).

The results can be brutal. For one thing, the conditions in these facilities are typically quite poor. One report estimates that over 80 percent of the jails in which children are held are unfit even for their adult inmates (National Council on Crime and Delinquency, 1967). In addition, there are well documented cases of atrocities committed against the jailed juveniles by both guards and inmates — for instance, a 15-year-old in a maximum security cellblock in Virginia was teargassed for requesting medical help for a fellow prisoner who was a deaf mute and gravely ill; a 17-year-old kicked to death by his jail cellmates in Missouri; a 17-year-old murdered in a Miami jail; a runaway in Iowa, 16 years old, who when left in isolation hanged herself in her cell (Goldfarb, 1976). This grim reality is a far cry from what the founders of juvenile court had in mind.

Humanitarian critics also find disturbing the mechanics of juvenile court hearings. The court is supposed to provide an opportunity for careful deliberation about a child's best interests by a dedicated, well-trained judge who is knowledgeable about helping children in trouble and can use the hearing to guide the offender. But the actual situation is often quite different. A Presidential Commission in 1967 reviewed a doleful list of shortcomings. Most juvenile court judges were not selected for their expertise and training, but rather were elected to office with no special background for the job; only about half of them had college degrees; the average juvenile court hearing lasted less than fifteen minutes; a third of all juvenile court judges lack staff assistance from probation officers who could assemble information about the child's social circumstances; 83 percent of the judges said there was no psychiatric or psychological assistance for the court; where probation officers were available to support the court's efforts at social investigation, their caseloads were unmanageably high (President's Commission, 1967). Others have reported that judges consider juvenile court a low prestige

assignment to be avoided where possible (Rubin, 1976a). Most judges mix their juvenile work with service in other courts if the structure of the justice system in their jurisdiction allows it; a 1973 survey found that among 1,314 juvenile court judges, almost nine out of ten said they spent only half their time or less on juvenile matters (Smith, 1974).

Observing these deficiencies, humanitarian critics feel that juvenile justice has failed to deliver on its promise. While the original social welfare philosophy of the court is the correct one, the system as presently constituted cannot hope to implement it.

CONTRADICTORY REFORM EFFORTS

Because the critics of juvenile court are working from such vastly different perspectives, it is not surprising that their recommendations for reform point in different directions (see Empey, 1979).

Some of the most sweeping changes have been generated by the constitutionalists through a series of landmark Supreme Court decisions. In *Kent v. United States*, the Supreme Court expressed concern about the lack of constitutional guarantees for juveniles and declared that the tradeoff of criminal court's due process in exchange for juvenile court's benevolent treatment had been a poor bargain, exposing juvenile offenders to the "worst of both worlds" (383 U.S. 541, 1966:555–56). The *Gault* decision of the following year (387 U.S. 1, 1967) went further. This case involved a 15-year-old Arizona boy who had received an indeterminate sentence of up to five years in a state institution, for making an obscene phone call to a neighbor; had he been 18 when he made the phone call, the maximum sentence he could have received would have been a 50-dollar fine or a two-month jail sentence. Quite apart from the harshness of the sentence itself, Gerald Gault's experience with juvenile justice was a classic example of arbitrary court practice. In ruling that his Fourteenth Amendment rights had been violated, the Supreme Court affirmed the right of juvenile offenders to be represented by legal counsel, know the specific charges, confront and cross-examine witnesses, and claim privilege against self-incrimination. Adding to these protections, the *Winship* case (397 U.S. 358) in 1970 addressed the process of fact-finding in a juvenile court, ruling that proof of guilt beyond a reasonable doubt is required for juveniles just as it is for adults (*In re Winship*, 1970:365).

These were notable victories, at least on paper. But the Supreme Court left plenty of ambiguity about just how hard it intended to push the juvenile justice system, declaring that due process standards should not be "ruthlessly administered" or allowed to replace "the conception of the kindly judge" (*In re Gault*, 1967:21). Constitutional rights have apparently been slow in coming to the juvenile court in many jurisdictions (Sosin & Sarri, 1976; Sosin, 1978).

Meanwhile, with quite a different goal in mind, retributive justice proponents have moved to make it easier for children charged with serious crimes to be stripped of the shelter of the juvenile court. Juvenile courts have all along had the authority to waive their jurisdiction and transfer particularly serious cases to criminal court, where the juvenile offender is prosecuted as an adult; in general, the application of this option has been restricted to offenders who are at least sixteen years old (National Advisory Commission, 1973a). But recent increases in serious youth crime, particularly in urban areas, have led some jurisdictions to lower the age limit for waiver to adult court – in some cases to as low as thirteen years old. The idea behind the change is to expose the offender to harsher and more certain penalties. Criminal court, organized around values of justice and retribution, is presumably less likely to "coddle" murderers, rapists, and professional thieves just because they happen to be children. Although there is evidence that waiver of juvenile jurisdiction still tends to be used only rarely (Sarri & Hasenfeld, 1976), the lowering of the minimum age standard represents an effort to reform juvenile justice by re-criminalizing delinquency.

And what of the social work humanitarians? Their influence has inspired two other reforms that have little to do with either due process or retribution. The first is a move toward reorganizing the juvenile court into a new kind of institution – "family court." This organizational change, recommended by the National Advisory Commission on Court Standards (1973a), allows a single consolidate court to consider not only juvenile delinquency and status offenses[3] but also a range of family matters including child abuse and neglect, child custody, child support, paternity actions, adoptions, domestic violence, and family conciliation. The aim is to *de*emphasize the criminal dimension of juvenile justice by treating the juvenile offender's behavior as a type of family problem. Only a few states have taken this step (Levin & Sarri, 1974; Ketcham, 1978).

The second kind of humanitarian reform is an increased effort toward diversion in the early stages of court processing (see Cressey & McDermott, 1973; Lemert, 1971; Nejelski, 1976). There is a general feeling that status offenders, charged only with victimless noncriminal acts, are particularly appropriate subjects for diversion. Over half the states have already moved to make diversion status offenders easier by creating special designations for them – PINS (persons in need of supervision) in New York; "601" children in California; UC (unruly child) in Georgia; and CHINS (child in need of supervision) in most of the rest (Empey, 1978; Levin & Sarri, 1974). The complete removal of all status offenders from court jurisdiction into social service agencies or nonjudicial "Youth Service Bureaus" regularly appears as a recommendation in reports by juvenile justice authorities (see President's Commission, 1967; National Task Force, 1977; Institute of Judicial Administration & the American Bar Association, 1977).

Here, then, is the institutional context in which social workers dealing with juvenile offenders must operate – a juvenile justice system that is inconsistent and confusing in its policies, deeply divided in its ideology and goals, characterized by great organizational variation from one jurisdiction to another, and subject to diametrically opposing kinds of reform effort.

REFERENCES

An historical overview of the establishment of the juvenile court system in the United States. (1975). *Landmarks in criminal justice, No. 6.* Haddam, CT: Connecticut Criminal Justice Training Academy.

Children's Defense Fund. (1976). *Children in adult jails.* New York: Washington Research Project, Inc.

Cressey, D. R., & McDermott, R. A. (1973). *Diversion from*

3. "Status offenses" are law violations by juveniles that would not be considered crimes if committed by adults, such as truancy, incorrigibility, and running away from home.

the juvenile justice system. National Assessment of Juvenile Corrections. Ann Arbor, MI: University of Michigan.

Empey, L. T. (1978). *American delinquency: Its meaning and construction.* Homewood, IL: Dorsey Press.

Empey, L. T. (Ed.). (1979). *The future of childhood and juvenile justice.* Charlottesville, VA: University Press of Virginia.

Fox, S. (1970). Juvenile justice reform: An historical perspective. *Stanford Law Review, 22,* 1187–1239.

Goldfarb, R. (1976). *Jails: The ultimate ghetto.* New York: Anchor Books.

Harpur, W. R. (1899). *The report of the Educational Commission of the City of Chicago.* Chicago: Lakeside Press.

Hirsch, A. von. (1976). *Doing justice: The choice of punishments.* Report of the Commission for the Study of Incarceration. New York: Hill and Wang.

Horowitz, D. L. (1977). *The courts and social policy.* Washington, D.C.: The Brookings Institution.

In re Gault. 387 U.S. 1, 18L. Ed. 2d 527, 87 S. Ct. 1428. 1967.

In re Winship. 397 U.S. 358, 25L. Ed. 2d 368, 90 S. Ct. 1068. 1968.

Institute of Judicial Administration and the American Bar Association (IJA/ABA). (1977). *Standards for juvenile justice: A summary and analysis.* Chicago: American Bar Association.

Kent v. United States. 383 U.S. 541, 16L. Ed. 2d i4, 86 S. Ct. 1045. 1966.

Ketcham, O. W. (1978). The development of juvenile justice in the United States. In V. L. Stewart (Ed.), *The changing faces of juvenile justice* (pp. 9–42). New York: New York University Press.

Klein, M. W. (Ed.). (1976). *The juvenile justice system.* Beverly Hills, CA: Sage.

Lemert, E. M. (1967). The juvenile court – quest and realities. President's Commission on Law Enforcement and Administration of Justice, *Juvenile delinquency and youth crime.* Washington, D.C.: Government Printing Office, pp. 91–106.

Lemert, E. M. (1970). *Social action and legal change: Revolution within the juvenile court.* Chicago: Aldine.

Lemert, E. M. (1971). *Instead of court: Diversion in juvenile justice.* Chevy Chase, MD: National Institute of Mental Health, Center for Studies of Crime and Delinquency.

Lerman, P. (1970). Beyond *Gault:* Injustice and the child. In P. Lerman, (Ed.), *Delinquency and social policy* (pp. 236–250). New York: Praeger.

Levin, M. M., & Sarri, R. C. (1974). *Juvenile delinquency: A comparative analysis of legal codes in the United States.* National Assessment of Juvenile Corrections. Ann Arbor: University of Michigan.

Morris, N. (1974). The future of imprisonment: Toward a punitive philosophy. *Michigan Law Review, 72,* 1161–1180.

National Advisory Commission on Criminal Justice Standards and Goals. (1973a). *Courts.* Washington, D.C.: Government Printing Office.

National Council on Crime and Delinquency. Correction in the United States. (1967). In President's Commission on Law Enforcement and Administration of Justice. *Task Force report: Corrections,* Washington, D.C.: Government Printing Office, pp 115–212.

National Task Force to Develop Standards and Goals for Juvenile Justice and Delinquency Prevention. (1977). *Jurisdiction – Status offenses.* Washington, D.C.: National Institute for Juvenile Justice and Delinquency Prevention.

Nejelski, P. (1976). Diversion in the juvenile justice system: The promise and the danger. *Crime and Delinquency, 22*(4), 393–480.

Platt, A. (1969). *The child slavers: The invention of delinquency.* Chicago: University of Chicago Press.

President's Commission on Law Enforcement and Administration of Justice. (1967). *Task Force report: Juvenile delinquency and youth crime.* Washington, D.C.: Government Printing Office.

Rubin, H. T. (1976). The eye of the juvenile court judge: A one-step-up view of the juvenile justice system. In M. W. Klein, (Ed.), *The juvenile justice system* (pp. 133–159). Beverly Hills, CA: Sage.

Ryerson, E. (1978). *The best-laid plans: America's juvenile court experiment.* New York: Hill and Wang.

Sarri, R. C. (1974). *Under lock and key: Juveniles in jails and detention.* National Assessment of Juvenile Corrections. Ann Arbor, MI: University of Michigan.

Sarri, R. C., & Hasenfeld, Y. (Eds.). (1976). *Brought to justice? Juveniles, the courts and the law.* National Assessment of Juvenile Corrections. Ann Arbor, MI: University of Michigan.

Schultz, J. L. (1974). The cycle of juvenile court history. In S. Messinger, et al. (Eds.), *The Aldine crime and justice annual, 1973* (pp. 239–258). Chicago: Aldine.

Schur, E. M. (1973). *Radical non-intervention: Rethinking the delinquency problem.* Englewood Cliffs, NJ: Prentice-Hall.

Smith, D. C. (1974). A profile of juvenile court judges in the United States. *Juvenile Justice, 25,* 27–38.

Sosin, M. (1978). Due process mandates and the operation of juvenile courts. *Journal of Social Service Research, 1,* 321–343.

van den Haag, E. (1975). *Punishing criminals.* New York: Basic Books.

Wilson, J. Q. (1975). *Thinking about crime.* New York: Basic Books.

Chapter 16

Revisiting the Heritage of Forensic Social Work: Applying a Nurturing Practice Model When Working with Gang Members in Juvenile Correctional Facilities

Elizabeth S. Marsal, Lessie Bass, and Mary S. Jackson

Case 1 – Marissa

Marrissa's description of her life as a gang member in a rural eastern North Carolina town offers us a view of a person trapped by negative, life-threatening chronic behaviors in which few incentives or opportunities for change are offered. As is the case generally with gang members, Marrissa's behaviors were rooted in close relationships with gang members, which make them even more difficult to change. Even though Marrissa was weary and wary of the house break-ins, shootings, and other violent gang activities, she was expected by close friends to participate. She, her family members, and her friends were constant prey to acts of reciprocal violence. The nurturing practitioner fully explored with Marrissa the multiple consequences that could come from her effort to change her behaviors and relationships. Such consequences included a loss of companionship and social support with the gang and the challenge of developing renewed companionship with sister, brother, and mother (and the attendant emotional sequelae). The nurturing interventions supported Marissa as she faced the severe challenges of establishing new directions, friendships, and goals. At one point, Marissa bridled at the rules and restrictions of the nurturing practice model. Initially she was nonresponsive and would not cooperate. Over a course of time, the nurturing facilitator explained why rules were important, and why rules were in place at home and in school. As Marissa learned and addressed life developmental needs at each stage of development, the needs felt more natural and common. She began to verbalize life needs with appropriate language and behavior and to experience the meeting of the needs through family interactions. This deliberate and sequenced nurturing exchange, in which rules were made known and explained, severely departed from the customary application of rules and "need-meeting" behavior within the gang. Difficulty in complying with authority and societal rules is a frequent hallmark of gang membership. As Marrissa began to accept the nurturing concepts, principles, beliefs, and interactions, the understanding of what makes gang membership different from family became quite evident.

Case 2 – Tamara

She walked with me, looking up at the stars. "Make a wish Tamara, wish upon a star." She stopped, closed her eyes, and when she opened them we started to walk again. She said she wanted to tell me her wish and I told her that she did not need to do that, but she insisted. Tamara, currently in foster care with her twin sister who is also in the nurturing practice group, wished to be returned to her parents. The parents were inducted gang members for most of their lives. Tamara talked about the parents' "shooting up," interruptions in nights and days of their lives leaving them to question whether mom and daddy would ever change. She wondered, "Why am I here tonight for nurturing, and why are mom and daddy not here?" Why not call them and ask them, I suggested. She seemed pleased to use my cell phone to call her parents. Her mom answered and Tamara questioned her extensively. "Are you high? Have you and daddy been shooting up today? Why are you not here when you know this is what will get the family back together? I'm here, so what was so important that you could not come?" The next week both parents came to the nurturing meeting.

At the next meeting, Tamara's mom shared the following, "I've been pondering my life growing up in a rural town, where gang members try to act like big city gang members. I tried to think through some plans for starting a new life. But the fears get in my way. I wonder how I can avoid the pitfalls of the rural streets and the disaster my life has been for the last seven years [the age of Tamara]. I swore that I would disconnect myself from the gang and gang activities. I am too old and hold the responsibility for two children and a husband. The gang has not sapped my spirit and if I can draw on that, I can manage the hard road ahead of me."

Three weeks later, Tamara's mom continued to attend the group and shared, "Maybe the best thing I've ever done for myself is making the decision to come here. It hasn't been easy, but I didn't expect that it would be. I've gone to lots of educational groups, but this one is like having an AA/NA sponsor yet it's broader that that. I can talk about anything. Patience is something I've been learning about everyday that I am further beyond gang membership. I never realized how much grief and hurt was bottled up inside of me and how that contributed to my violent feelings. Sometimes, it is just too much to talk about it. And in those times, I know that I can take my time. The nurturing facilitator has helped me to enroll in a computer skills class at the community college not far from where I live. My biggest hurt and concern comes from what is going on with my twins. I understand them better as we talk through things in the nurturing meetings. One of the things I've learned from the nurturing facilitator is to take a

deep breath, check out my feelings, check out what my twins need, and think through my options before I act. That's been important because the way I feel right now is just jumbled up guilt, shame (and yes, some anger) at the choices I have made and the consequences that got in the way. When I meet with the group, I am reminded to focus on my objectives. I use them to guide my discussion in the nurturing group and change the ways I have acted in the past. The nurturing group helps me to look at how far I have progressed over the past few weeks. I still feel worried about what's going to happen, but I finally feel in control of my life. Most of all, I have my twins back."

HISTORICAL PERSPECTIVE

Society has become increasingly aware of the presence of gangs and their relationship to criminal actions. The reality of gangs is played out by the media through visual images of gang turf wars, drive by shootings, documentaries, and the commission of crimes. In fact, a large percentage of the increase in violent crime and drug trafficking have been attributed to the existence of gangs (National Institute of Justice, 1999; Oehme, 1997). The 2000 National Youth Gang Survey noted the association between gangs and crime suggesting that as gang membership increases, gang related violence may also increase. In 2000, gang members were responsible for 95 percent of high school violence and 91 percent of the violence in intermediate schools (Egley & Arjunan, 2002). In 1996, 50 percent of gang members were juveniles (i.e., younger than 18) and 50 percent were adults (i.e., 18 and older). In 1999, these numbers were 37 percent and 63 percent, respectively. In 1999, respondents reported that 47 percent of gang members were Hispanic, 31% African American, 13 percent White, 7 percent Asian, and 2 percent "other." In 1999, there were 580 incidents of juvenile gang killings compared to the 819 in 2003. In 2002, there were 75 incidents of gangland killings and a total 115 in 2003 (National Criminal Justice Reference Service, 2005) (http://www.ncjrs.gov/spotlight/gangs/facts.html). Although the characteristics of gang-related activities vary depending on the size of the jurisdiction (ibid.), it is still a major concern as juvenile correctional institutional rates increase.

According to the 1997 Survey of Inmates in State Correctional Facilities, the incarceration rate for juvenile correctional offenders increased by 33 percent from 1991 to 1997. This population made up more than one-fifth of all prisoners incarcerated for violent crimes in U.S. state prisons (Finkelhor & Ormrod, 2001). According to the 2004 Prison Gang Survey, 25.9 percent of males and 6.3 percent of females identified themselves as gang members while being admitted into prison (Knox, 2005). This gang affiliation increases the likelihood of violence and misconduct in our prisons (Gaes, Wallace, Gilman, Klein-Saffran, & Suppa, 2001). The violence perpetrated by gang members does not end once they are released from prison. In fact, 69 percent of law enforcement jurisdictions reported that gang members returning from prison substantially affected their jurisdiction's gang problem (National Institute of Justice, 2003).

One approach to dealing with gangs is suppression efforts that have resulted in the continuous spread of gang activities as gang members migrate to other areas of the country. This migration, as well as the increased commission of crimes, has resulted in the overcrowding of correctional facilities and greater representation of gang members. This incarceration is intended to suppress gang activities, but gang recruitment continues to flourish inside of the prison walls as a means of survival.

Macro-level interventions with a less punitive approach have focused on community collaboration, whereas micro-level approaches have been less popular. Micro-level gang interventions are defined as working with individual gang members and their families to assist them with effecting positive acceptable societal change (Goldstein & Huff, 1991).

OVERVIEW OF THE NURTURING PRACTICE MODEL

The Nurturing Practice Model (NPM) has been effectively utilized and is the focus of this chapter. Nurturing programs have undergone a good deal of investigation and field-testing. The original format was developed with the support of the National Institute of Mental Health (NIMH). The NPM provides a step-by-step, exercise-by-exercise guide. It also includes a rationale for each exercise, as well as the expected outcome of each constraint on the micro-, macro-, and mezzo-level. If properly trained, the NPM can be utilized by most forensic social workers. There are no racial boundaries other than the respect for the dignity and rights of each human being involved in the process, regardless of past or current negative behaviors. The focus of most micro gang level interventionists is upon intervening with the gang member from a deinstitutionalization and decriminalization perspective with the primary focus on prevention. Minimal consideration is given to the family. While families are considered a major risk factor, they are an important aspect when working with gang members and their families (Jackson, Bass, & Sharpe, 2005).

In an effort to experience positive success (rehabilitation) in juvenile correctional facilities, and in order to become successful citizens in the community, children and adolescents need to develop life skills such as effective communication, decision-making, and problem solving (Zastrow & Kirst-Asherman, 2003). These skills help to make them less vulnerable to negative life circumstances and abusive situations (Bavolek, 1984) when they return to the community. As youths develop, they should be encouraged to discuss and label their feelings. The Nurturing Practice Model for children and adolescents and their families help them to recognize their feelings as "normal," and to manage their feelings in a positive framework.

LITERATURE REVIEW

History tells us that there have been good and bad times for infrastructures that hold authority and the responsibility for children and families (Ginsberg, 1998). Roberts and Brownell (1999) note that the 1800's "Revenge-Punishment Confinement"oriented policies were ineffective, and they appear equally ineffective in the twenty-first century (Frindlay, 2004). Roberts and Brownell (1999) have developed a comprehensive perspective "bridging the past to present" in their discussion of forensic social work and its historical emergence. This chapter, utilizing their discussion as the foundation, will provide a promising practice model that is cost-effective and can be used by forensic social workers both practicing in juvenile correctional facilities and in the community. Forensic social workers have been practicing the science of forensics since the early beginnings of social work as a discipline. Roberts and Brownell (1999) suggest that social work founders such as Jane Addams and Julia Lathrop would be very disappointed by the practice environment that is permeated by the current "get tough" rhetoric, harsh and stringent laws, and the seemingly political need to advocate for the punishment of youths. There are numerous definitions of forensic social work. Green et al. (2005) state that forensic social work is practice related to legal issues and litigation in the justice system. Guin et al. (2003) note that the role of the forensic social worker is to bring objectivity and reliable information to the multidisciplinary team that bridges the criminal justice system and the mental health system. Pierce et al. (2001) add that the forensic social worker improves the client's quality of life and assists with the performance of complex tasks and decisions. However, we will rely on the definition as operationalized by Roberts and Brownell (1999), in which forensic social work is defined as "policies, practices, and social work roles with juveniles and adult offenders and victims of crimes" (p. 360). As we focus on the role of forensic social work utilizing a NPM, we will also include in our discussion the need for scientific observation and application to working with adolescents and their families.

The overall aim of this chapter is to provide forensic social workers with another tool (the NPM) that can be used to work effectively with incarcerated gang members and other at-risk adolescents and their families. The chapter will focus on the importance of breaking through communication barriers between youths and adults. Parenting strategies that empower parents, as well as youths, in discovering and sustaining positive communication skills and nonviolent relationships will be explored. The hope is that such strategies eliminate violence while empowering gang members to remove themselves from violent situations.

Local courts around the country order parenting classes for families who need to learn new ways of parenting in the hopes of keeping their families together (Jackson & Knepper, 2003). Court personnel (e.g., judges, juvenile court counselors, attorneys) are aware that parenting skills are crucial prevention and intervention strategies for reducing violent behavior. However, one challenge when working with gang members, especially those that are incarcerated, has been a lack of parental involvement. This lack of parental involvement has been the result of a number of factors, most notably: (1) Forensic social worker responsibility – programs have historically focused on the youth only in treatment process in juvenile correctional facilities, and (2) parental responsibility – parents have been unwilling [or unaware of their need] to take on the responsibility of their parental role, which may have escalated the youth's propensity to become involved in a gang and or violent behaviors.

Historically, forensic social workers in correctional facilities working with gang members have focused on the gang member only with very limited consideration given to the biological family. There is usually attention focused on the surrogate family (gang); however, even that focus has been in an effort to persuade the youth about the importance of complete removal and separation from the gang. In many instances, this tactic has been met with a lack of success. One reason for the lack of success in using this method has been that the separation from gang membership has been approached much like the unsuccessful separation of a Department of Social Services (DSS) worker who separates a youth from a family without properly terminating. Successful family terminations by DSS workers occur when the commitment and efforts of the child welfare worker leads to a nurturing, safe, and understanding family for the court's most vulnerable charges. Full explanation of the separation process to children by the child welfare worker, mental health therapist, clergy, or other helping professionals may be exceedingly important depending on the age of the child. Oftentimes the children have been left out of major decisions which affect their lives. Believing that it is in the children's best interest to be raised in a safe, permanent, and loving family is not enough and must include the commitment to address the emotional bondage that occurs between two people. Children with strong attachments are more likely to trust themselves and the world around them. Strong, nurturing attachment helps a child to attain full intellectual potential, sort out what he or she perceives, think logically, develop a conscience, become self-reliant, cope with life stress and frustration, handle fear and worry, and develop healthy future relationships (Magid, 1987).

According to the Pew Commission on Children in Foster Care, over 500,000 children wake up in a bed other than their own each day in the U.S. (Pew Commission, 2005). These are children who have been so abused or neglected that social workers have had to remove them from their parents. When children are removed, everything that is familiar and important to them is lost. For many, that includes being separated from their brothers and sisters. These children represent a public trust of the highest order, yet all too often the system is unable to provide the nurturing and emotional support necessary for their healthy development (Jacobsen, 2002). Similarly, youths who are gang members are requested to give up their gang membership (that which has created within them a very high self-esteem) and yet the replacement is difficult for them to imagine other than the life of an impoverished (low self-esteem) situation that they left behind them for the gang. Therefore, it is reasonable to suggest the need to apply appropriate separation and permanency procedures when working with gang members (especially younger gang members).

A major consideration should be given to the need to include all significant others in the treatment process. This important strategic intervention is often a missing component in the treatment process with incarcerated youths. However, when applied, it has been a successful intervention tool with substance abusers (Bry et al., 1998; Etz et al., 1998). This intervention method should be utilized with youths who are perceived as gang members and youths who identify themselves as gang members. The forensic social worker may forget that even though the youth may be a gang member, they are still a youthful offender who may be masking their "real" fears. Incarcerated gang members are a captured audience that may profess a lack of interest in the treatment process; however, with persistence, tolerance, common sense, and "old fashioned" social work practice skills, gang members can begin to work on and resolve some of their fears and become productive citizens so that the family gang cycle can be broken. An important factor in breaking this cycle is parental involvement. While parental involvement is inclusive of extended family and church family, the process begins with the biological family, as they are held legally responsible for the behavior of the youth.

Due to the increased violent acts that have been perpetuated by younger offenders, many states have enacted parental liability laws. Today, all states (except New Hampshire and New York) have provisions holding parents civilly responsible for youth crime. Parental liability laws suggest that parents are to be held accountable for the delinquent actions, which

are inclusive of gang behavior, of their children. The category that is used to impose sanctions on parents is referred to as contributing to the delinquency of a minor. As a result, parents can be fined, incarcerated, held in contempt of court, or given community service. In many instances, however, when working with gang members' parents, the issue is not necessarily that parents do not want to participate or assist with improving the youths' behavior; rather, it is that they may feel powerless, helpless, and hopeless to do so. Parents struggle against forces of losing their child to a competing family (gang) as well as the struggle to convince a system (juvenile) that assistance is needed. There also exists the very real struggle that many parents are young parents who have not yet experienced a great deal of success in their own lives.

The literature suggests that many youths join gangs because of the need to fill a gap that is missing in the family of origin. Often parents do not know what this missing gap is and they struggle to "hold on" to their child. However, in many instances, this effort is a losing battle because the parents may not be able to or unwilling to understand how to deal with some of their family dynamics that may be contributing to their child's gang membership.

Youths join gangs as a result of cooperative efforts or coercion. Cooperative efforts are their desires to participate in gang activity because it is a choice that they have made, regardless of the consequences. On the other hand, other youth become gang members because they are fearful of something. That "something" can range from fear of other youths in the community (who are gang members) to fear of life in what they perceive to be a volatile situation engulfed by poverty and low self-esteem. In the general population when children experience fear, it is usually the parent who can comfort them. By contrast, when working with gang members, the discovery has been that many parents feel so helpless that they are unable to assuage their child's fear because they themselves also feel that fear.

One of the major challenges for forensic social workers who work with this client population is the ability to focus on the needs of the family unit (e.g., parents), and not just the youth gang member. Equally important is the realization that family needs may be different in the twenty-first century than they were in the twentieth century for our work with gang members. For example, parents of gang members are younger and appear to be more willing to engage in dialogue to problem solve. Many twenty-first century gang members are products of what was termed "babies having babies" in the twentieth century literature. These babies, who have in turn had babies, are now in many instances parents of gang members. Therefore, the wisdom of nineteenth and early twentieth century parenting is lacking. There is need to "re-parent" the parent, as well as offer parenting strategies that will reduce and or eliminate the fear experienced by both the parent and youth.

Schools prepare youth for successful careers in the United States. Yet there is no institution that has as its primary aim to prepare youngsters to parent. According to American norms, there is an expectation that youths will get an "important" job that they have been properly prepared for and will work to continue to receive training in their professions. Yet, there are no basic requirements for becoming an effective parent, nor are there requirements for continued learning of parenting skills after one has become a parent. Parenting is one of the few jobs that does not require prior knowledge or continuing training. Parents generally learn parenting techniques in their family systems or from persons who participated in raising them. But when there is a situation where children have had children, there has not been that transitional parenting wisdom passed from generation to generation. Thus, there exists the need to have forensic social workers expose young children, adolescents, and adults to a life development model of parenting and re-parenting. The NPM is grounded in systems theory and the psychosocial theory of life development across the life span. The philosophy that drives nurturing parenting emphasizes the importance of raising children in a warm, trusting, and caring household. It is founded on the belief that children who are cared for develop the capacity to trust, care, and respect themselves, other people, and living creatures and their environment.

THE NURTURING PRACTICE MODEL DEFINED

The NPM promotes the philosophy of caring for yourself, family, children, substitute parents, and the community. It is a family-based model that addresses generational and intergenerational issues within the scope of creating new ways of life, new life energies, and a focus on positive life productivity and potential. Educating individuals, families, and communities about nurturing is viewed as the single most important force in the treatment and prevention of violence and abusive behaviors (Bavolek, 1988).

Theoretical Assumptions

Grounded in systems theory, the NPM emphasizes the acknowledgement of synergistic interactions among individuals and that the inner connectedness is weakened or terminated as a result of abuse or other violent acts. Unity of purpose and interrelatedness are two key components of systems theory. Thus, when youths experience conflict in the family, all subsystems are affected. The task of the NPM is to get all subsystems working together to identify goals, objectives, strategies (plans of action), and follow-up methods. The family, the community, the gangs, social services, and juvenile services all are systems. According to systems theory, if we can intervene in one area of a person's life, all of the other areas should be influenced (Greene, 1994). Involving important people in the youth's life (e.g., parents, sibling, substitute parents, social worker, law enforcement officer, minister, probation officer, etc.) is essential to bringing about behavioral change with gang members. This inclusion may involve "negative" and "positive" significant others. For example, when working with youth at risk of joining gangs and those who are gang members, there is need for the forensic social worker to engage both the biological family as well as the gang family. In foster care situations, the foster parents are also included in the process.

Empathy is a principle operating concept of the NPM. Empathy is the single most desirable quality in nurturing youngsters, parents, and other life-related systems. Empathy is the ability to be aware of the needs of others and to value those needs (Bavolek, 2002). When empathy is high among gang-related youngsters and family members, the likelihood of violent behavior and various kinds of abuse is decreased. Empathy and violence are essentially incompatible. The NPM seeks to develop empathy in all stakeholders and players involved in the cessation of gang activities. It is important to understand how children's level of development influences how they respond to their attainment of basic needs and situational problems (Spergel & Grossman, 1997). All families experience healthy and unhealthy interactions. Bavolek (1989) links parenting as it exists on a continuum to the ability of family members to maintain violent or nonviolent behavior. To effect change in the lives of children and their families, strategic interventions must engage the cognitive (knowledge) level and the affective (feeling) level. Youths and adults who feel good about themselves are more likely to promote nurturing interactions with others. Families and community members that feel good about themselves are also more capable of accomplishing their goal than those with low self-worth (Pierre & Mahalik, 2005). The nurturing practice model increases the development of self-esteem and develops positive self-concepts and self-images. Very few youths, including gang members and adults, prefer violent and abusive interactions. Given a choice, families would rather engage in happy, healthy interactions.

STRUCTURE OF THE MODEL

According to Bavolek (1984), research has revealed four parenting and child-rearing constructs most commonly associated with abusive parents. The cognitive and affective education engages the four constructs which represent the internalization of negative learning. The youth gang member has internalized negative learning and existing behaviors reflect the violent negative behavior that is inconsistent with society's expectation. The four constructs incorporated in Bavolek's parenting program include:

1. Lack of Empathy:
   Empathy toward other's needs entails the ability of a person to understand the condition or state of mind of another person without actually experiencing the feelings. Parents often ignore their child that results in the child's basic needs being left unattended. Children who are ignored and whose basic needs are neglected fail to develop a basic sense of trust in self and in others, which results in a profound low sense of self-esteem common to many abused children (Martin, 1976).

2. Inappropriate Parental Expectation of the Child:
   Abusing parents treat their children as adults, and the parents are incapable of understanding the particular stages of development of

their children. The effects of inappropriate parental expectations upon children are debilitating. Martin (1976) suggests that when these expectations are impossible to meet, biologically and/or cognitively [we suggest emotionally as well], children perceive themselves as being worthless and as failures, and as unacceptable and disappointing adults.

3. Valuing Corporal Punishment:
   Studies appear to indicate that abusive parents utilize physical punishment as a unit of behavior designed to punish and correct specific bad conduct or inadequacy on the part of children. According to Steele (1970), in an effort to gain some measure of self-protection and mastery, children identify strongly with the aggressor and develop a pattern of discharging aggression against the outside world in order to manage their own insecurities. Much too often, abused children become abusive parents.

4. Parent-Child Role Reversal:
   The child adopts some of the behaviors traditionally associated with parents. These parents often act like a helpless needy child looking to his/her own child for care and comfort (Steele, 1975). According to Erikson (1950), for children to achieve normal development and a healthy adjustment they need to negotiate the developmental task of each stage of life. Children who experience parent-child reversal do not have that opportunity. Failure to perform any of the developmental tasks hampers development and reinforces feelings of inadequacy. These children have little sense of self and see themselves existing with the sole purpose of meeting the needs of their parents.

The Nurturing Practice Model promotes the intervention process of "undoing" what is not working in the family and "doing" with families what they need in order to replace angry, violent feelings and thoughts (affective and cognitive).

This model is available to help youth, families, communities, neighborhoods, and organizations decrease and change gang activities, and reduce environmental risks that may create a propensity toward gang involvement. This model helps youngsters and families and communities develop life opportunity.

The model helps families and communities engage in healthier, more nurturing ways to live together and interact with each other. Finally, the model offsets the generational perpetuation of dysfunctional and violent behaviors.

Nurturing Practice Model

Biological Families Substitute Families [GANGS]

⇓ ⇑

Institution

⇓ ⇑

Churches . . . Social Services . . .
Juvenile Court . . . Family Court

⇓ ⇑

Community

⇓ ⇑

Churches . . . Social Services . . .
Juvenile Court . . . Family Court

The Nurturing Practice Model is typically administered in the home; however, if there are several families in the community that would benefit from the NPM, then a small group setting is appropriate. Churches, community centers, governmental buildings, private homes, or local restaurants can serve as weekly meeting places. Churches, Department of Social Services (DSS), the local health department, and other organizations/agencies and community leaders are recruited for participation and resources because many incarcerated youths had initial contact with these resources prior to incarceration. The nurturing effort becomes a neighborhood/community effort. Other professionals such as juvenile court counselors, police officers, and school outreach workers are paired with forensic social workers who are trained nurturing facilitators and volunteers in order that they learn as they work with youths and families. The professionals selected are trained prior to the beginning of the nurturing group, or they are assigned to a trained and competent forensic social worker to receive "on-the-job training" as the group evolves. Many of the professionals realize that they have many of the same angry, violent experiences as the "referred" family. Thus, re-training must occur for the professional helper, just as it will occur for the parents (re-parenting) who have violent abusive experiences that they then transfer to their children.

Professionals who counsel the referred families do not enter the nurturing program as participants; they are trained in "train-the-trainer" sessions.

Church leaders and members, community leaders and members, court workers, forensic social workers, child development workers, child and family therapists, psychologists, attorneys for children and families, early interventionists, day care workers, and youth group workers are just some of the people who learn the NPM and become resources to working with incarcerated gang members. The community becomes involved in many ways that include cooking for the families, kitchen server, being a child monitor and being available for child care and one-on-one mentoring. Nurturing behaviors "spread like wild fire" and we recognize that indeed "the village" becomes responsible for permanent lifestyles for children.

The essential elements for successfully implementing nurturing in a juvenile correctional facility include: (1) workers who believe in nurturing or at least are willing and ready for change in the form of an energetic intervention that is focused on the holistic perspective, (2) the belief that gang members are youths who have the same needs and expectations as other youths (those who are not gang members), and (3) the expectation that gang members can change and become positive and productive citizens.

IMPLEMENTATION OF THE NURTURING PRACTICE MODEL

The nurturing program may be formatted to work for all kinds of families. The programmatic formats are developmentally designed to fit families with children from birth to 18. There are special adaptations for parents who are cognitively challenged, for Spanish-speaking families, for African-American families, for teen-aged parents, for foster or adoptive families, and for families recovering from substance abuse.

The sessions are highly structured, and the concepts are taught experientially, through activities that excite the curiosity, empower the self, and are entertaining and pleasurable.

The nurturing components make sense in the day-to-day world of families who are striving for lifetime relationships that work successfully for them. The program is written at the eighth grade reading level and can be interpreted for nonreaders in a dignified manner. Parents and children learn through music and movement, psychodrama and role-playing, discussion, audiovisuals, art, games, sharing food, kangaroo care and infant massage (Kaplan & Bavolek, 1996). The following nurturing skills are taught during the program for parents:

- handle feelings
- communicate needs
- be empathic
- take charge of one's own behavior
- have warm interactions and fun with others
- establish nurturing routines for regular family affairs such as bed and mealtimes
- handle stress and anger
- gain a sense of personal power and positive esteem
- give/receive healthy touch, and
- replace hitting and yelling with more effective discipline techniques (such as redirection, babyproofing, time-out, choices and consequences, problem solving, verbal management, praise, "I-statements" and family rules).

To effectively work with and advocate for incarcerated gang members, the forensic social worker must obtain a comprehensive life history that focuses upon all domains of the gang member's life. These domains have been described by Howell (2003) as risk domains that can predict the youth's vulnerability to gang membership and thus offer an understanding of the individual's rationale and decision to join a gang. These risk domains include family, school, community, peer groups, and individual. Major influential elements within these five domains will impact whether a youth will become a gang member. Youth who are raised in families where gang involvement and activities are being committed by their parents often assume the role of parent because of insufficient parenting skills by the adults in the household. Youth may also assume this role if the family structure is outside of the societal norm and there are generations of unskilled workers in the household. Many gang members struggled in school to succeed as a result of learning disabilities or different learning styles. In addition, they felt caught between their neighborhood and the world outside, as the means for gaining success in each is different. Peer groups also played a major role in the lives of gang members prior to and after joining the gang. Therefore, association with negative adult role models and delinquent youths

contribute to gang membership. Lastly, according to Howell (2003), gang members possess individualized characteristics such as deviant behavior, low self-esteem, low self-control, and substance use.

In addition to the risk factors for gang membership, there are also protective factors that can influence the decision to join or not join a gang. Youth with strong family ties and a sense of belonging are less likely to become a gang member. Unfortunately, many youth who join a gang are from a single parent household where the parent may work two or more jobs in order to provide the daily necessities. Thus, the youth are without adult supervision for extended periods of time. In other situations, the parent is readily available, but does not provide appropriate supervision because they do not know how. Parental skills are lacking as the parents are very young and inexperienced themselves.

To ensure that the forensic social worker understands the risk and protective factors for incarcerated gang members, a comprehensive life history should be completed. A life history is an empirical inquiry into a person's life that explores the domains that have been linked to criminal behavior. Guinn, Noble, and Merrill (2003) proposed a comprehensive life history for death penalty mitigation teams that is also appropriate for gang members. It addresses each of the relevant life domains: family, community, school, peer groups, and individual.

Personality Factors: Coping Strategies: abilities to solve problems, handle stress, and manage anger, feelings of self worth, self confidence, and competence in social relationships; ability to manage life survival tasks (managing money, holding jobs, etc.); spiritual and moral perspectives (how the individual perceives his or her responsibilities and relationships towards others and society).

Social Factors: Age, gender, race, ethnicity, outstanding physical features; geographical environment and stability of life situation; religious beliefs and relationships, community connections, and important friendships; and any public social services received.

Health Factors: Mental orientation to time, place, person, and circumstances; health status (illnesses, injuries, disabilities, or unusual birth circumstances); mental health status, competence, and family history of mental concerns; and medication, substance or alcohol abuse, and other chemical issues.

Family Factors: Family of origin constellation and configuration; situations of trauma, violence, abuse and neglect; out-of-home placement; extended family and outside relationships during childhood and adulthood; present family constellation and configuration; number of marriages, children, divorces; and any traumas and violence.

Education Factors: Grade attainment and age appropriateness of school setting; level of achievement; school progress and attitude toward learning; over or underachievement; social relationships, behavior, and extracurricular activities in school settings; and native intelligence and potential, mental or learning disabilities, and documented level of intellectual functioning.

Economic Factors: Family income and education levels; sources of income, types of employment, and stability of employment; living environment and community demographics; and military experience.

Criminal Factors: History of immediate and extended family interaction with law enforcement; number and types of prior offenses; age at first contact with law enforcement; conduct and progress during incarcerations; understanding of legal processes and ability to participate in defense; and perspective toward the crime (sense of remorse, denial, or defiance). (Guinn, Noble, & Merrill, 2003, p. 3)

The forensic social worker is the logical professional to complete the life history, as the social worker is trained to achieve a holistic perspective utilizing interviewing and therapeutic skills that can assist with uncovering hidden or suppressed information. The comprehensive life history provides the forensic social worker with evidence that can be used to advocate and plan for the eventual release of an incarcerated gang member, as well as identifying those risk factors that contributed to the decision to join a gang. The most important task for the forensic social worker is to develop a trusting relationship with the client; only through that relationship can the most intimate details of the client's life emerge (Guinn, Noble, & Merrill, 2003). Once the forensic social worker has established rapport, completed a comprehensive life history, and understands the factors contributing to gang membership then intervention and prevention strategies can address the risk factors that will contribute to continued involvement in gangs utilizing the micro level NPM.

Changing a gang member's behavior (via rehabilitative process) depends heavily on the worker's ability to assist the youth and his or her family with breaking the cycle of violence. This can occur by assisting him/her with understanding self (self-reflection),

desires, goals, and capabilities. In order to break the cycle, parents and caretakers must be "re-parented." Steele (1970) asserts that abusive parenting behaviors are learned by children during the developmental stages of their childhood in an effort to gain some measure of self-protection and mastery. Children identify strongly with the aggressor and develop patterns of discharging aggression against the outside world in order to manage their own insecurities. These learned patterns of behavior are often duplicated in adult life. Steele and Pollock (1968) have indicated in their clinical work that abusive and neglectful parents have a history of being abused or neglected as children and are simply reenacting the same pattern in rearing their children. The cycle of poor parenting is learned and can be broken.

Re-parenting skills is a hands-on technique whereby parents, along with the youth, meet in group sessions in the institution to discuss different ways of monitoring and providing guidance to their children. Because the youths are also involved in this process it allows them an opportunity to bear witness to the re-parenting. This in turn eliminates the "unknown" factor (the unknown of returning to the family and community after a period of incarceration), thereby reducing the youth's fears associated with returning home. The youth is able to voice his or her thoughts and fears along with the parents. School teachers, social workers, court workers, community members, church members, and law enforcement officers are also involved in the process. In this way, the entire community is working in assisting the family to change the illegitimate outcomes to legitimate ones (Ohlin & Cloward, 1960; Spergel & Grossman, 1997).

Jackson and Knepper (2003) suggest that the Nurturing Practice Model is a useful intervention for gang members and their families. There are six phases of the NPM that can be delineated: oral history, taking responsibility, capitalize on strengths, involvement of significant others, experience success, and evaluation.

1. Oral History Phase: Jackson (2006) maintains that gangs instill within their members the importance of "looking out for each other" and "staying together." Human service systems work hard to instill the very same important principal in families at-risk of separation. Gangs maintain their gang family by "showing their love" of one another as they lash out at anyone who may try to cause dissention among their family. They preserve their family history by

OG's (Original Gangsters) passing it on to younger gang family members. The relating of their history, like all histories, including family histories, secures their roots (heritage) and instills self-esteem within the youth who is seeking meaning to life. One of the primary tenets of the Nurturing Practice Model is the need to be non traditional and flexible and tenacious. An ecological perspective is utilized where all factors are considered and addressed that may impact the youth and the family, which includes all significant others when working with the family (Zastrow & Kirst-Ashman, 2003.) Recall that the comprehensive life history provides a method for conducting an empirical inquiry to determine those factors that contribute to a person's success in the NPM.

2. Taking Responsibility Phase: The NPM emphasizes the need for individuals to take responsibility for their actions (Bass, 1999). Accordingly, gangs and gang activity become the collective responsibility of not only the youth involved in the activity, but the biological family, and the neighborhood (which includes systems such as the gang family, school, court, and law enforcement). Nurturing strategies presume that the initial strategy will be proactive and focus on the family as the beginning point for treatment (Jackson & Knepper, 2003). In situations of gang members, the issue would be which family should the focus begin with: the biological family or the gang family? Like any treatment model, the initial assessment determines the target system.

3. Capitalize on Strengths: The primary goal when working with gang members should be to capitalize on the youth's strengths and assist the youth with refocusing those strengths into legitimate ventures. Family plays a major role in this process of change. Thus, immediate attention should be given to the circumstances of the biological family because there may be a need to strengthen this component first by considering the strengths that the family has and then working with those strengths. Often when youth join gangs, there is a void between them and their biological family; for example, some families may not be able to provide needed structure and guidance. Thus, youths may seek out gangs because they do provide them with structure and guidance. One goal of nurturing would be to provide parental structure that is termed re-parenting (Bass, 1999) so that the biological or the family of origin (legal custody) can begin to fill the gap and reclaim the area

that was missing from the youth's life that led to gang membership.

Jackson and Bass (2003) indicate that a key to the success of nurturing for youth is the worker's ability to see the strengths within the youth and the family. In some instances, this may mean seeing something as simple as their presence in a session as a very strong foundation upon which to build. It is extremely important to discuss the nurturing process with the youth prior to beginning any other processes. Explaining what the goals are and what the expected outcome will be is important information for the youth to know and understand.

4. Involving Significant Others: Involving the community by assisting the parent/caretaker in locating volunteers from the neighborhood and helping the community and church plan activities for the youth is an important step. For forensic workers in institutional settings, this step may appear to be beyond the call of duty. But when working with gang members, "beyond the call of duty" is often required because the gang works 24/7 to recruit and maintain their members. Thus, it is necessary for forensic social workers to have an equally intense strategy. The forensic social worker will find it necessary to collaborate and partner with community social workers and probation officers as they prepare for the youth's community reintegration. Gang members often form partnerships and collaborate within their sets. As they migrate to other areas, they send individuals ahead to assess the boundaries (Klein & Maxson). Thus, it is important for the forensic social worker to act accordingly and make community contacts in preparation for the youth's return to the community. One contact may be with the probation officer to determine if there are any nurturing facilitators in the community so that the youth and family can continue their nurturing strategies with the assistance of a community nurturing facilitator.

Training a nurturing facilitator in the community works well in terms of leaving the product and process as a gift to the neighborhood. Gang researchers often enter a community abstracting data, leaving nothing behind for the community. The Nurturing Practice Model provides the community not only with the desired training, but with trained trainers.

Initially, small steps have to be taken, which means that the youth's mother may be able to manage only one night a week at home, so other alternatives often have to be considered. For example, can the grand-parent stay with the youth until the mom returns home from work? Or, can a mentor work with the youth after school? These are considerations that the forensic social worker will have to sort out while re-maining cognizant about the needs of the youth. If the worker can be successful with just one youth, positive ripple effects are sure to follow.

5. Experience Success: Youths do not want to be criminals. They do not, for the most part, wake up one morning and say: "Okay, today I am going to become a gang member." Becoming a gang member is a slow process. Thus, nurturing youths from gang membership is also a slow process and the worker will experience setbacks. However, if the worker is as persistent as the gang recruiters, the worker will win the youth over because the advantage that the worker has over the gang recruiter is that the youth really does not want to spend time locked up away from his or her family.

Nurturing can be used as a primary prevention technique, as well as an intervention strategy. Utiliz-ing nurturing as an intervention strategy will require the use of more options than if utilized as a primary prevention tool. Intervening with a youth who is a "regular" member requires harder work; however, it can be done. The regular members have undergone an initiation process and can move to the next level of "hardcore" if they remain in the gang for a long period of time. The "hardcore" gang members are usually those members who are older and have been in the gang for a long period of time, and may be repeat offenders. The re-parenting process requires a different level of intensity where the worker may recruit a "gang" of nurturing community leaders, peers, and teachers from the community as partici-pants. We refer to them as volunteers who can work with the "regular" gang members. Thus, the focus of nurturing with gang members is more effective with regular members and the wanna-be members (Jack-son & Knepper, 2003).

This model has been tested and utilized by DSS workers who promote the Nurturing Practice Model as a useful intervention tool (Perry, 2002). The health care system also views it as a comprehensive model that is ethically competent and adequate for the pop-ulation they serve (Garrison, Nobles, & Franzetti, 2000). The NPM is also a very useful tool for work with gang members in juvenile correctional facilities.

The provision of education, training, and counseling provided to the youth and family is paramount.

6. Evaluation Phase: Outcomes are extremely important in working with gang members. The Adult Adolescent Parenting Inventory (AAPI) serves as the primary outcome measure. The AAPI, developed by Bavolek (1984), is a simple 32-item questionnaire that is easy to score. It is used to assess the degree to which attitudes held by adolescents and adults tend to be nurturing or violent and abusive. In each of the four constructs addressed by this practice model, the tool has been validated and norms established with over 2,000 adults and 6,500 adolescents in the U.S.A Spanish version has been validated in Mexico. Attitudes are the interface between affect (feeling) and beliefs, and are known to affect behavior. The AAPI may be used as a follow-up tool to measure continued effectiveness.

This assessment scale is utilized to evaluate and monitor success rates when using the nurturing ap-proach. The Adult Adolescent Inventory (AAPI) may be administered at intervals in the practice model. For example, in the case of a gang member, the AAPI will serve as a useful tool of measurement for anger management over a period of time. The instrument may be utilized to determine parental functioning and effectiveness at later periods in the life of the family. Other nurturing resources may be identified or as-surance that all is going well for the family. The AAPI is not and should not be viewed as the "end all as-sessment tool" but is an indicator of what the family needs are at a particular time. The AAPI is the as-sessment instrument used in nurturing practice to measure outcomes. The AAPI has two components: pretest and posttest that require the client (primary client) to self-report at the beginning of treatment, at the mid-point, and at the end of treatment. The initial field-testing of the Adult Adolescent Parenting In-ventory Scale with adolescents occurred with 2,541 teens enrolled in grades 10, 11, and 12 in high schools located in Utah and Idaho. Since the initial research in 1978, an additional 3,939 nonabused adolescents and 214 abused adolescents throughout the country have participated in developing normative data of the Adult Adolescent Parenting Inventory Scale (Bavolek, 1989). The initial field-testing of the Adult Adolescent Parenting Inventory Scale with 194 adults was con-ducted in 1980 in the Chicago area. Since the initial research with adults, 782 adults with a known history of child abuse and 1,045 adults from the general population around the country have participated in developing normative data for the Adult Adolescent Parenting Inventory Scale (Bavolek & Keene, 1999).

The Adult Adolescent Parenting Inventory Scale achieved content validity by the following method: the construct definitions and the item pool were disseminated to experts from disciplines related to child rearing, parenting education, child abuse, family life, and tested construction for evaluation. The results of the content validation activities indicated 100 percent agreement among the experts relative to the accuracy of the identification and description of the four abusive parenting constructs. The construct validity of the Adult Adolescent Parenting Inventory Scale was determined through the analysis of the data generated from inter-item correlations, item-construct correlation, and factor analyses.

Meza-Lehman (1983) administered the AAPI to 200 Mexican-American and Mexican-born adolescents in Chicago. The purpose of the study was to: (1) assess the parenting attitudes of Mexican-American and Mexican born adolescents, (2) assess parenting differences between males and females, and (3) assess differences between self-responses and subject-perceived maternal and paternal responses. The AAPI was administered to 132 males and 69 females. Results of her study indicated significant differences were found between males and females in all four constructs. Males were significantly more abusive in Empathy and Corporal Punishment ($p < .001$) and in Expectations of Children and Role Reversal ($p < .05$). The findings are consistent with the findings of previously mentioned studies which indicate males tend to express attitudes towards parenting and child rearing that are consistently more abusive than the parenting attitudes of females, regardless of age and race (Bavolek & Keene, 1999).

The Nurturing Quiz and Pretest may be administered prior to the beginning of group sessions. The nurturing quiz is a fun instrument and the pretest assesses the level of violence and anger of the individual. After a positive rapport has been established between the worker and the youth, they can proceed to include the youth's significant others in the change process.

The ultimate success of the Nurturing Practice Model with gang members is a decrease in gang activity and membership, as well as departure from gang life. However, these long-term goals will be preceded by other short-term successes. Forensic social workers utilizing the Nurturing Practice Model should see strengths develop within the youth, family, and community. A success may be as simple as a gang member attending a meeting session, which is the beginning of a foundation upon which to build. As rapport develops between the forensic social worker and the youth, family members and significant others can be included in the change process. It is important to remember that the change process in the youth's life begins when the youth agrees to meet with the worker (Jackson, Bass, & Sharpe, 2003). How the forensic social worker handles the change process form the initial meeting forward will determine whether or not the youth continues to participate and eventually accomplishes the long-term goal of the Nurturing Practice Model, leaving the gang.

ETHICAL CONSIDERATIONS

The primary mission of the social work profession is to enhance human well being . . . and empowerment of people who are vulnerable, oppressed, and living in poverty . . . Fundamental to social work is attention to the environmental forces that create, contribute to, and address problems in living. (NASW, 2005)

The decision to become a gang member is not made overnight, and thus the decision to leave a gang is given comparable forethought. Forensic social workers must be conscious of the difficulty of these decisions and provide the youth with respect and dignity. The youth needs to know that the forensic social worker has empathy for his/her situation and thus treats him/her with dignity and self-worth. The decision to leave a gang can not be mandated or forced upon the youth. Instead the client needs to be given the right of self-determination, which is supported and guided by the forensic social worker. The Nurturing Practice Model provides the forensic social worker with the tools to intervene with the gang member, while operating within the Social Work Code of Ethics. Youth who feel pressured to make a decision regarding their gang activities will abandon their involvement with the Nurturing Practice Model and return to their gang family.

Forensic social workers must have a solid foundation of knowledge regarding the risk factors for gang membership and the commitment and struggles that these youth face on a daily basis. In addition, the worker must understand gang culture and its purpose within the youth's life and society. Although the gang culture may be hard for the worker to understand, the strengths of this culture must be appreciated. Sensitivity to these differences must be demonstrated and sought to successfully intervene using the Nurturing Practice Model.

In addition to the Code of Ethics, forensic social workers are bound by legal obligations to protect the privacy and confidentiality of these youth. Exceptions do apply when disclosure is necessary to prevent serious, foreseeable, and imminent harm. As the forensic social worker builds rapport with the youth more information will be shared, and thus must be protected, unless it violates administrative policies and laws.

IMPLICATIONS FOR PRACTICE

Forensic social workers who work in juvenile correctional settings, regardless of their location, will have to deal with gang members. Depending on the area (urban or rural) will determine whether the numbers will be large or small in terms of their incarceration rates. Although violence perpetuated by gang members (and those perceived to be gang members) is on a decline, gang members committed an average of 373,000 of the 6.6 million violent victimizations between 1998 and 2003 (Harrell, 2005). Those gang members who returned to the community had a negative impact on the youth gang problem (Egley & Arjunan, 2002). Therefore, it is extremely important that forensic social workers in juvenile correctional settings consider treatment tools that will stop the cycle of violence perpetuated by gang members. An effective mechanism is the Nurturing Practice Model which has implications for the need to "go back to the basics" of social work practice while utilizing science to enhance the process.

The AAPI, discussed earlier, can be utilized to assist the courts. Some parents learn that they do not desire to parent, nor do they hold the skills to parent their children. Some parents come to the realization that they need their life energy for themselves and are unable to negotiate their life developmental processes and raise children. Relinquishing their children to

gangs is a challenge at best, and certainly a challenge for the social worker who has the task of breaking the cycle.

Breaking the cycle of violence relies to a great extent on worker effectiveness and the willingness of the juvenile correctional facility to allow the worker to incorporate a Nurturing Practice Model within its treatment regime. Often juvenile correctional facilities seek effective methods of assisting youths and their families under their care, but rely on what we term "computerized treatment planning" where you push a button and presume that all the data is there and the problem resolved. One of the major challenges for forensic social workers working with incarcerated gang members is the need to take a holistic approach and involve all significant others (inclusive of appropriate community agencies) and the need to establish a collaborative partnership with community agencies that can impact the youth's life and decision making (e.g., church, school personnel, social services, etc.).

Collaborative effort as exemplified by a nurturing approach can ensure a successful outcome for the gang member, family, and the neighborhood and force the field of forensic social work to examine critical questions. Have we really dropped the ball with gang members when using a flawed approach where we simply lock them up without providing effective prevention or intervention? Have we dropped the ball by attempting to distinguish treatment programs for youths from treatment programs for gang members? Have we dropped the ball when we have attempted to work only with the specific gang members without any interaction with significant others?

Gang membership and gang activities are individual choices for the youth. However, they are a community concern, and the community should be involved in the process of deterring and reducing gang activities in the neighborhood. There is an urgent need to bombard the literature with research on working with gang members, just as the literature has been flooded with research on violent gang activities. When we focus on intervention strategies that amplify the importance of interacting with youths and their families to change their negative behaviors, we will then be able to make a stronger impact on deterring serious violent behavior by street gang members. Suppressive efforts are not challenging the creative boundaries of gang members, as they are becoming more astute.

The implications for using the NPM with incarcerated gang members are far-reaching. Youth who remain with their families after nurturing interventions will live an emotionally and cognitively balanced life. The parents are more knowledgeable and skillful at effectively intervening in their child's life.

The Nurturing Practice Model provides a micro-level intervention for working with gang members and their families. For a youth to leave the gang, he or she needs the support of his/her family and community, but most importantly, he/she needs to feel needed and loved. This micro-level intervention instills the strength and rationale for making this life-changing decision.

CONCLUSION

The social work profession has traditionally embraced interventions that identify and service at-risk youths and families. During the past century the most neglected and devalued groups have been crime victims and offenders. Social workers have made great strides during the past century advocating for obtaining vital services for these individuals (Roberts, 1990, 1998a, 1998b). The forensic social worker understands the value of micro-level interventions and the relationship between criminal justice and individualized systems such as the family, community, and school. The forensic social worker must adjust to the constraints of the criminal justice system while advocating for offenders and victims (Roberts, 1999).

Problem-free is not the same as being fully prepared. This mistaken assumption has resulted over time in a significant lack of programs and models that contribute to the overall healthy development of youth and their families, especially those youth who are incarcerated. Few families in today's society, and particularly those served by the juvenile justice system, have access to treatment models that promote development by building on strengths, creating opportunities and real life skills, and facilitating mutually beneficial participation in communities (Nixon, 1997). The Nurturing Practice Model asserts that the client's drive for personal growth requires forensic social workers to focus on their strengths and create nurturing environments that support positive and long-term outcomes.

Dreams can come true. Children, adolescents, and adults may purposefully develop in ways that shape their futures for legitimate fortunes to be made in their lives. Juvenile correctional facilities, and the communities that surround them, represent a place where millions of youth (ranging from the very young to the older) prepare themselves for permanent lifestyles for the rest of their lives. Yet, many of these youths (and their families) may not even consider the possibility of positive quality of life (without the gang) if there is not a conscientious effort to work with all of the subsystems. This effort will be laborious, and often trying, but the end result will be worth the struggle. The nurturing model creates and sustains a sense of success, builds self-esteem, and provides a productive replacement for gang membership.

By reparenting the last two generations, we can once again instill the value of family and strengthen the commitment to self, each other, and community. As each individual becomes a stronger parent and community member, society is improved. In turn, the recruitment efforts of gangs are less effective as youth feel committed to and loved by their families and community, and most importantly, to themselves. With each success, youth become stronger and more resistant to gang membership.

The Nurturing Practice Model will affect future generations as parenting skills are once again part of the fabric of the younger generation so that they may pass this knowledge and skill to the next generation. There is an old saying, captured by Hillary Rodham Clinton (1996) in her book, that exemplifies the need for micro-level interventions. Indeed, it takes a village to raise a child. The Nurturing Practice Model provides the forum to do just that by enriching the lives of gang members, families, communities, and society.

REFERENCES

Agnew, R. (2003). An integrated theory of the adolescent peak in offending. *Youth and Society, 34*(2), 263–299.

Bavelok, S. (2002). *Nurturing parenting programs: Creating a better world through nurturing.* Park City, UT: Family Development Resources, Inc.

Bavelok, S. (1984). *Adult-Adolescent Parenting Inventory.* Park City, Utah: Family Development Resources.

Bavoleck, S. J. (1984). *Handbook for: Adult-Adolescent Inventory.* Park City, Utah: Family Development Resources.

Bavelok, S., & Dellinger, J. (1985). *Nurturing program for parents and children birth to five years.* Utah: Family Development Resources.

Bavelok, S., & Keene, R. G. (1999). *Adult-Adolescent Parenting Inventory AAPI-2: Administration and development handbook.* Park City, Utah: Family Development Resources.

Bolton, F. (1983). *When bonding fails,* Vol. 151. Newbury Park, CA: Sage Publications.

Brazelton, T., & Kobayashi, N. (1982). *The growing child in family and society.* Tokyo: University of Tokyo Press.

Brietbach, K. (1993). What is kangaroo care? *Iowa health book: Pediatrics* [Online]. Available: America Online.

Bry, B. H., Catalano, R. F., Kumpfer, J. E., Lochman, J. E., & Szapocznik, J. (1998). Scientific findings from family prevention intervention research. *National Institute of Drug Abus Research Monography 177,* 103–129.

Clinton, H. R. (1996). *It takes a village.* New York: Simon and Schuster.

Egley, A., & Arjunan, M. (2002). *Highlights of the 2000 national youth gang survey.* Washington, D.C.: United States Department of Justice.

Erickson, E. (1950). *Childhood and society.* New York: W. W. Norton

Etz, E. K., Robertson, E. B., & Asbery, R. S. (1998). Drug abuse prevention through family based interventions: Future research. *National Institute of Drug Abuse Research Monograph 177,* 1–11.

Ferketich, S. L., & Mercer, R. T. (1995). Paternal-infant attachment of experienced and inexperienced fathers during infancy. *Nursing Research, 44,* 31–37.

Findlay, M. (2004). The demise of corrections fifteen years on: Any hope for progressive punishment? *Current Issues in Criminal Justice, 16*(1), 57–70.

Finkelhor, D., & Ormrod, R. (2001). *Offenders incarcerated for crimes against juveniles.* Washington, D.C.: United States Department of Justice.

Gaes, G. G., Wallace, E. G., Klein-Saffran, J., & Suppa, S. (2001). *The influence of prison gang affiliation on violence and other prison misconduct.* Washington, D.C.: Federal Bureau of Prisons.

Garrison, Nobles, & Franzetti. (2000). Personal interview. Greenville, NC. 2004.

Ginsberg, L. H. (1998). *Social work in rural communities.* Alexandria, VA: Council on Social Work Education.

Goldstein, A., & Huff, R. (1993). *The gang intervention handbook.* Champaign, IL: Research Press.

Greene, R. R. (1994). *Human behavior theory: A diversity framework.* New York: Aldine de Gruyter.

Guinn, C.C., Noble, D.N., & Merrill, T.S. (2003). From misery to mission: Forensic social worker on multidisciplinary mitigation teams. *Social Work, 48*(3), 363–371.

Harrell, E. (2005). *Violence by gang members, 1993–2003: Bureau of Justice Statistics Crime Data Brief.* Washington, D.C.: United States Department of Justice.

Howell, J. (2003). *Preventing and reducing juvenile delinquency: A comprehensive framework.* Thousand Oaks, CA: Sage.

Jackson, M. S. (2006). *Policing in a diverse society.* Durham, NC: Carolina Academic Press.

Jackson, M. S. (2003). Law enforcement's response to gang activity. In A. R. Roberts (Ed.). *Critical issues.* Belmont, CA: Sage.

Jackson, M. S., Bass, L., & Sharpe E. G. (2005). Working with youth street gangs and their families: Utilizing a nurturing model for social work practice. *Journal of Gang Research, 12*(2), 1–17.

Jackson, M. S., & Knepper, P. (2003). *Delinquency and justice: A cultural perspective.* Boston: Allyn & Bacon.

Kennell, J., & Klaus, M. (1976). *Maternal-infant bonding.* St. Louis, MO: C. V. Mosby.

Lamb, M. E. (1981). *The role of the father in child development.* New York: John Wiley & Sons.

Magid, K. (1987). *High risk.* New York: Bantam.

Martin, H. (1976). The environment of the abused child In H. Martin (Ed.), *The abused child: A multidisciplinary approach to the developmental issues and treatment.* Cambridge: Ballinger.

Mathews, M., & Stevens, J. (1978). *Mother/child father/child relationships.* Washington, D.C.: National Association for the Education of Young Children.

Meza-Lehman, O. (1983). Doctoral dissertation. Loyola University of Chicago, Chicago, IL.

National Institute of Justice. (1999). *1997 National youth gang survey (NCJ 178891).* Washington, D.C.: United States Department of Justice.

Nixon, R. (1997). What is positive youth development. *Child Welfare, 76*(5), 571–575.

Oehme, C. G. (1997). *Gangs, groups and crime: Perceptions and responses of community organizations.* Durham, NC: Carolina Academic Press.

Ohlin, L. E., & Cloward, R. A. (1960). *Delinquency and opportunity: A theory of delinquent gangs.* Glencoe, IL: Free Press.

Pew Commission on Children in Foster Care. (2005). *Ranking of foster care population by state* [Online]. Available: Sprint DSL.

Pierre, C. T., Cleason, W. P., & Miller, M. G. (2001). Social work and law: A model for implementing social services in a law officer. *Journal of Gerontological Social Work, 34*(3), 61–71.

Pierre, M. R., & Mahalik, J. R. (2005). Examining African American self consciousness and black racial identity as predictors of black men's psychological well being. *Cultural Diversity and Ethnic Minority Psychology, 11*(1), 28–40.

Roberts, A. R. (1998). *Battered women and their families: Interventions strategies and treatment approaches* (Vol. 1 in the Springer Series on Family Violence). New York: Springer.

Roberts, A. R. (1998). *Juvenile justice: Policies, programs, and services* (2nd ed.). Belmont, CA: Wadsworth.

Roberts, A. R. (1990). Introduction and overview of victimology and victim services. In A. R. Roberts (Ed.), *Helping crime victims: Research, policy, and practice* (p. 19–35). Newbury Park, CA: Sage.

Roberts, A. R., & Brownell, P. (1999). A century of forensic social work: Bridging the past to the present. *Social Work, 44*(4), 359–369.

Spregel, I. A., & Grossman, S. F. (1997). The little village project: A community approach to the gang problem. *Social Work, 42*(5), 456–471.

Steele, B. (1970). Violence in our society. *The Pharos of Alpha Omega Alpha*, Vol. 33, 42–48.

Steele, B. F., & Pollock, C. B. (1968). A psychiatric study of parents who abuse infants and small children. In R. F. Helfer & C. H. Kempe (Eds.) *The battered child.* Chicago, IL: University Chicago Press.

Stevens, V. (1997). Nurturing touch: A parents gift of love. *Parent Line* [Online]. Available: America Online.

Wright, L. F. (1981). *The effect of anxiety on paternal-infant bonding.* Michigan: University Microfilms International.

Zastrow, C., & Kirst-Asherman, K. K. (2003). *Understanding human behavior and the social environment.* Belmont, CA: Wadsworth.

Section IV

Victim Assistance and Domestic Violence Intervention

Assessment and Intervention in Child Sexual Abuse: A Forensic Social Work Perspective

Jennifer Becker and Barbara Thomlison

In its many forms, interpersonal violence is systemically linked with other significant social problems and public health concerns, including but certainly not limited to poverty, substance abuse, and mental health issues. Community violence, intimate partner violence, child maltreatment, and specifically child sexual abuse present serious challenges to the criminal justice system, child protection services, policymakers, and society at large. Moreover, the impact of interpersonal violence has far-reaching consequences for victims. As the scope of interpersonal violence and child maltreatment is broad and cannot be fully addressed here, this chapter focuses specifically on child sexual abuse, including forensic and clinical assessment and intervention strategies. This chapter is organized as follows: first, definitional issues, trends and incidence of child sexual abuse are presented. The process of disclosure and impact of child sexual abuse are briefly reviewed. The roles of the criminal justice system and child protection services are discussed, with a focus on empirically-based forensic assessment and intervention strategies. Available best practice approaches are identified. Case vignettes are included to highlight definitional constructs and challenges of intervention. At the end of the chapter, an annotated bibliography serves as a resource guide for accessing research and evidence-based practices.

Child sexual abuse may not only result in physical harm but may impact socioemotional, cognitive, and psychological development, and other areas of well-being of children and youth, often extending into adult life long after the actual abuse occurred (IASWR, 2003). A review of the research focused on the identification, correlates, and consequences of child sexual abuse consistently report linkages between the experience of child sexual abuse and poor outcomes in children and adults (Briere & Runtz, 1993; Kendall-Tackett, Williams, & Finkelhor, 1993). Despite an extensive literature on child maltreatment, it is surprisingly difficult to comprehend the full range of influences and effects of child sexual abuse and even more difficult to establish scientific evidence for prevention and effective intervention strategies. What is apparent is that child sexual abuse is multidetermined and multidimensional, resulting from a range of interacting variables at the individual, family, community, and broader environmental levels. This concept is central to the focus of this chapter, as well as to the advancement of practice and systemic interventions in addressing the complex nature of child sexual abuse.

Case Study of Jonathan: Is This a Case of Child Sexual Abuse?

Read the case of Jonathan and then discuss the case from the following questions.

1. Obtain a legal definition of child sexual abuse used in your state, province, or borough. Based on the presenting facts, should this be considered a case of sexual abuse?
2. Discuss whether an abusive condition is present.
3. Discuss whether sexual activities involving a child are present.
4. Identify the behavioral indicators of concern.
5. Describe other contextual factors you would want to consider such as culture, age, gender, and family.

6. What if any actions or intervention is warranted.
7. Discuss whether this case should be further investigated for possible contact sexual abuse in the home.
8. If so, is this a case for a social worker, a police office, or both? Explain your answer.

Exhibit 1: Case Study of Jonathan

Jonathan is a seven-year-old Caucasian male, who is relatively quiet. According to his teacher, he does well in school, but rarely socializes with peers and "prefers to keep to himself." One day in class, Jonathan's teacher noticed that in his "My Family" drawing, Jonathan drew breasts on his mother and a penis on his father. Alarmed by the depiction, his teacher contacted the school social worker, who than contacted Child Protective Services (CPS). The CPS worker interviewed Jonathan at school and asked about the drawing. Jonathan stated, "That's Mommy and Daddy before bedtime." He reported that he sleeps in the same bed with his parents, but gave no indication that he had been touched in any sexual manner. He indicated that both his parents bathe with him sometimes. Upon further investigation, Jonathan's parents reported to authorities that they are often nude "in the privacy of their home." They stated that, because they cannot afford a bigger apartment, they sleep in bed with their son. They stated there "may have been times" they engaged in sexual activity in their bed while Jonathan was sleeping. His parents reported they share household responsibilities, including bathing and dressing Jonathan. Both parents adamantly denied ever touching Jonathan inappropriately.

THE CONTEXT OF DEFINING CHILD SEXUAL ABUSE

Despite significant advances in the study of understanding of human functioning and adaptation there is still limited consensus of an operational definition of child sexual abuse. This is important as definitions affect the knowledge about the etiology of problem behavior and consequently may affect efforts to promote interventions to enhance adaptive functioning. Defining child sexual abuse is a fundamental issue

that remains unresolved and controversial (Haugaard, 2000). In this regard, how one defines child sexual abuse shapes the response of the criminal justice and child protection systems to the identification of cases. Definitions and perceptions of what constitutes child sexual abuse also vary among social science researchers, clinicians, and the general public (Bensley et al., 2004, Finkelhor, 1984). This legal and social contextual variation in definition has a direct impact on the number of officially reported, substantiated cases, and the estimates of the incidence and prevalence of child sexual abuse. Broad, inclusive definitions of sexual abuse are often thought of as advantageous in focusing political and public attention on the extent of the problem of child sexual abuse. However, broad definitions create large errors in the search for predictors because the factors that give rise to various types and degrees of child sexual abuse are different. Narrow definitions identify a smaller but severely at-risk population. Narrow definitions are usually more precise and more likely to identify child sexual abuse within the at-risk population and this tends to make up the referral base for protective services (Giovannoni & Becerra, 1979; Hutchison, 1994; Korbin, 1994; Korbin, Coulton, Lindstrom-Ufuti, & Spilsbury, 2000; Lindsey, 1994).

Determination of whether or not a behavior is sexually abusive is dependent as well on the mandate and goal of the individual constructing the definition. For example, a prosecutor filing charges against a person who has committed a sexual offense requires a clear, specific description of illegal sexual behaviors. On the other hand, a clinician may be more interested in experiences perceived by the individual as sexually abusive in nature, regardless of legal issues. As a result, definitions of child sexual abuse range from specific acts of commission to very broad experiences.

Finkelhor (1994a) identifies child sexual abuse as requiring at least two elements (1) sexual activities involving a child, and (2) an abusive condition. Sexual activities are typically categorized as *contact* sexual abuse (e.g., sexual kissing, touching, fondling, or penetrating child's genitals, vagina, anus, mouth with sexual organ or other object) and *noncontact* sexual abuse (e.g., exhibitionism, voyeurism, child pornography, sexual exploitation, sexual harassment). However, controversies remain over what is considered sexualized behavior and what constitutes an abusive condition. While there is a general consensus among most disciplines and the public that adult intercourse, oral and anal sex with a child under age 12 are considered sexually abusive acts, other behaviors are not as easily identified as sexual in nature, such as when parents bathe or sleep with their children (Bensley et al., 2004).

An abusive condition presents similar dilemmas conceptually. Child protection systems generally define abuse as "any willful act or threatened act that results in any physical, mental, or sexual injury or harm that causes or *is likely* to cause the child's physical, mental or emotional health to be significantly impaired," (Florida Statutes Chapter 39). Others argue the term "abuse" should indicate the measurable presence of harm, as used in scientific research (Rind, Tromonovich & Bauserman, 1998). Rind and colleagues (1998) generated great controversy in the field of child sexual abuse when they purported that sexual contact between an adult and a child that does not result in negative consequences for the victim should not be deemed child sexual abuse. Most researchers and academics argue that child sexual abuse is characterized by the child's inability to consent to the sexual act (Finkelhor, 1984). The child's sexual ignorance, developmental vulnerability, emotional immaturity, fear, or desire to please a person in a caretaking or authoritative role have been cited as limiting the child's ability to provide willful consent. As a result, the issue of consent has become a central focus of what is determined to be sexually abusive, in both legal and clinical contexts. "Abusive conditions exist when: the child's partner has a large enough age or maturational advantage over the child; or the child's partner is in a position of authority or in a caretaking relationship with the child; or the activities are carried out against the child using force or trickery" (Finkelhor, 1994a, p. 33). Constructs of consent have further broadened the definition of a sexually abusive relationship by including age disparity, role of the perpetrator, the child's developmental delays or physical impairments, and the offender's tactics used in gaining the child's compliance.

Definitional ambiguity presents many challenges in research. Investigations into the prevalence, causes, and consequences of child sexual abuse are confounded by the use of varying definitions across studies and often a wide range of inclusion criteria. While broad definitions benefit the researcher in collecting a more powerful sample size, these variations in definitions jeopardize the validity of the investigation and present problems in the comparison of empirical studies. Additionally, the broadening of legal definitions has generated statutory inconsistencies among states. There are many factors to consider in identifying child sexual abuse as suggested by the following case situation. Use the case of Jonathan in Table 17-1 to discuss with other colleagues to determine the complexities and difficulties of assessing whether child sexual abuse has occurred. This case sets the stage for understanding the complex and multiple issues associated with each child sexual abuse situation.

SCOPE OF THE PROBLEM

In the year 2003, over 78,000 children and youth across the United States were verified by child protection agencies as victims of sexual abuse, accounting for approximately 10 percent of substantiated child maltreatment cases (U.S. Department of Health and Human Services [USDHHS], 2005). However, cases substantiated through the child welfare system are not considered an accurate estimate of actual incidence. Moreover, given the lack of physical evidence typically available during the investigation of child sexual abuse, few allegations result in substantiation. Also, sexual abuse cases in some jurisdictions are handled exclusively through law enforcement systems and are not included in child protection substantiation statistics. Perhaps most importantly, the fear, shame, and secrecy involved in the experience of sexual victimization prevent many victims and their families from disclosing the abuse to authorities (Finkelhor, 1984). Children often do not seek assistance due to their young age, developmental circumstances, and dependent status. Since sexual abuse is secretive in nature, it makes it difficult to detect. Parents fear the loss of children if they disclose problems, retribution from perpetrators, and being charged with a crime (Thomlison, 2004). Consequently the sexual abuse may persist and even increase in severity and duration. It is estimated that at least 30 percent and as many as 80 percent of victims do not disclose their sexual abuse experience before adulthood (Alaggia, 2004).

Over the past 20 years, efforts to determine more accurate prevalence rates have been focused on retrospective surveys of adults. Prevalence studies vary widely in their sampling procedures, definitions of abuse, methodology, and instrumentation, resulting in mixed reports of prevalence estimates. In a review of retrospective studies, Finkelhor (1994) found the percentage of adults who reported sexual abuse during childhood in prevalence studies ranged from 2 to 62 percent of females, and 3 to 16 percent of males. Through 1994, the most valid and reliable studies indicated that at least 20 percent of women and 5 to 10 percent of men in the U.S. experienced some form of sexual abuse as children (Finkelhor, 1994a).

More recently, Briere and Elliot (2003) conducted a telephone survey of a nationally representative sample to examine the prevalence of childhood sexual abuse in the general population. The survey included both standardized measures and project-developed questions to detect childhood experiences that were considered sexually abusive. Among a sample of 1,442 randomly selected adults, 32.3 percent of women and 14.2 percent of men reported sexual victimization during childhood (Briere & Elliot, 2003). The mean age of onset of abuse was between 9 and 10 years old. Among the sample population, 46.8 percent experienced intrafamilial sexual abuse and 52.8% experienced oral, anal, or vaginal penetration. Most were victimized by more than one perpetrator, with a mean of two to five incidents of sexual abuse.

In another comprehensive telephone survey of a nationally representative sample of 2,030 children ages 2–17 and their parents, Finkelhor, Ormond, Turner, and Hamby (2005) found that one in 12 children and youth reported some type of sexual victimization (including both contact and noncontact offenses by adults or juveniles) during the study year. Finkelhor and colleagues (2005) estimated the incidence of sexual victimization in the study year as 82 per 1,000, the national equivalent of 5,191,000 child victims during the study year. Among the sample, 32 per 1,000 experienced sexual assault and 22 per 1,000 experienced completed or attempted rape. Sexual victimization, including assault, rape, and harassment, were more common against girls than boys and occurred disproportionately to adolescents in the sample (Finkelhor et al., 2005). Ninety-seven percent (97%) of children and youth in the sample who experienced sexual victimization had also experienced some other type of victimization, such as assault or maltreatment, during the study year.

IMPACT OF CHILD SEXUAL ABUSE

There is no core-symptom model that can be used to explain the impact or long-term sequelae of child sexual abuse. A plethora of symptoms and behaviors have been found to be associated with child sexual abuse, including but certainly not limited to depression, anxiety, general posttraumatic stress, nightmares, fear, avoidance, sexualized behaviors, aggression, somatic complaints, eating disorders, dissociation, and suicidal behaviors (Briere & Runtz, 1993; Kendall-Tackett, Finkelhor &Williams, 1993). In addition to behavioral problems and affective disorders, victims are at increased risk of consequential social problems well into adulthood, including substance abuse, domestic violence, problems with intimate partner relationships, disturbed sexual functioning, and difficulties in the parenting role (DiLillo, 2001; Swanston et al., 2003). "There is virtually no general domain of symptomatology that has not been associated with a history of sexual abuse" (Kendall-Tackett et al., 1993, p. 173). However, establishing a linear connection between the abuse experience and specific outcomes has proven to be elusive (Friedrich, 1998). For the most part, posttraumatic stress symptoms, inappropriate sexual behaviors and sexual concerns are the presenting symptoms most commonly associated with child sexual abuse (Briere & Runtz, 1993; Kendall-Tackett et al., 1993).

Yet in clinical studies, child victims exhibit a wide variation in severity of symptomology, and some present with no observable symptoms at all. Many sexually abused children appear asymptomatic at times, performing normally at school and with peers. Evidence indicates that asymptomatic children may exhibit delayed onset of symptoms, or may experience problems other than those typically associated with sexual abuse (Putnam, 2003).

To explain the wide variation in symptomology, several researchers have proposed alternative theoretical models to studying the impact of child sexual abuse. Finkelhor and Browne (1985) introduced the traumagenic dynamics model of child sexual abuse, which identifies four realms of the sexual abuse experience: traumatic sexualization, stigmatization, shame, and powerlessness. This model has been widely applied to understanding the way sexual abuse affects the child's cognitive processes, self-concept, and orientation to himself/herself and others. Additionally, other researchers in the field (see Cole & Putnam, 1992; Finkelhor, 1995; Finkelhor & Kendall-Tackett, 1997; Trickett & Putnam, 1993) promote the integration of developmental theories into understanding the impact of child sexual abuse. Developmental psychology and developmental psychopathology have been proposed as models to understand the more disruptive, profound impact of child sexual abuse. In their endorsement of studying child maltreatment within the context of development, Wolfe and McGee (1991) state, "This emphasis requires divergent methodologies aimed at detecting developmental differences that appear among maltreated children across the life span, while de-emphasizing unitary explanations for observable symptomology" (p. 258). Hartman and Burgess (1989) describe the potentially profound developmental impact of child sexual abuse:

> Of particular concern is its impact on the victim's sense of right and wrong, their sense of self, their arousal capacities and their inhibition capacities, their awareness or lack of awareness of body states, their sense of personal power, and their self-comforting, self-preserving, and protective behavior (p. 118).

It is asserted that examining the effects of child sexual abuse with consideration to developmental stages and processes may fill in the gaps of knowledge and inform more appropriate and effective assessment and intervention strategies (Cicchetti, 2004; Cole & Putnam, 1992; Trickett & Putnam, 1993).

There is also substantial evidence indicating that sexual victimization increases one's likelihood of being sexually victimized again, during both later childhood and adulthood. In a national random sample of 2,000 children ages 10–16, Boney-McCoy and Finkelhor (1995) found that children who had been previously sexually victimized were at alarmingly increased risk – 11.7 times more likely than those not abused – of being sexually abused again before turning 18. This relationship remained statistically significant when children sexually abused by the same perpetrator were excluded from the analysis (Boney-McCoy & Finkelhor, 1995). In a recent review of empirical literature of sexual revictimization, Classen, Palesh, and Aggarwal (2005) report 35 studies that suggest child sexual abuse as a risk factor for revictimization and four studies that found a causal relationship between child sexual abuse and sexual revictimization.

DISCLOSURE OF CHILD SEXUAL ABUSE

For the most part, child sexual abuse is revealed either by an individual in the child's life or the child victim discloses the abuse. In many cases, the child's behaviors prompt the suspicion of a parent, teacher, counselor, physician, or another adult who initiates intervention. Mandated reporting laws, which require most professionals to report suspicions of child maltreatment to authorities, have contributed to increases in reporting over the past 30 years. However, because there is often little evidence of abuse and children are typically reluctant to openly disclose the details of abuse, very few cases actually come to the attention of authorities. When a child does make a disclosure of sexual abuse, there is a significant likelihood he or she is telling the truth. Empirical evidence indicates that as few as 2 to 8 percent of abuse disclosures are false or erroneous (Oates et al., 2000). It is important to understand the process of disclosure and how to respond appropriately when child sexual abuse is suspected or a child discloses abuse.

Why Don't They Tell?

The disclosure of sexual abuse is an extremely difficult process for children, especially those who are younger and do not possess developmental abilities to effectively identify or verbalize aspects of the abuse experience (Brilleslijper-Kaper, Friedrich & Corwin, 2004). Shame, guilt, and fear of retribution by the offender also seriously impede the child's ability or willingness to disclose (Finkelhor, 1984; Summit, 1983). Sexual abuse, especially that which is prolonged, is often committed by an adult known to and trusted by the child, and the child is heavily influenced by secrecy imposed by the offender. In some cases, the perpetrator makes threats of violence against the child or the family members, convinces the child he or she would not be believed, or blames the child for provoking the abuse. The nature of the secret is central to the victim-offender relationship, and is a powerful impediment to the child's disclosure (Lovett, 2004). The child's fears of the consequences of disclosure are induced by feelings of self-blame and guilt. The child may feel responsible for the abuse or may be concerned that he or she would be at fault for breaking up the family if the abuse were discovered (Brilleslijper et al., 2004).

Disclosure of abuse is often delayed, with a mean of 3 to 18 years between occurrence of abuse and disclosure (Alaggia, 2004). Goodman-Brown, Edelstein, Goodman, Jones, and Gordon, (2003) review several factors that influence the delay of disclosure: (1) developmental factors; (2) gender; (3) relationship to the perpetrator (intrafamilial versus extrafamilial); (4) fear of negative consequences; and (5) perceptions of responsibility. The child's developmental factors including verbal skills, cognitive and emotional development play a role in the child's ability to appreciate the wrongness of the abuse and then openly disclose the experience (Campis, Hebden-Curtis, & Demaso, 1993; Goodman-Brown et al., 2003) Empirical evidence consistently indicates that males are more likely to delay disclosure than females (Goodman-Brown et al., 2003). Male victims often experience shame and fear of stigma (e.g., homosexuality, victim label), which further inhibit their willingness to disclose abuse (Finkelhor, 1984). Research consistently indicates that children who are abused by extrafamilial offenders are more likely to disclose the abuse than children who are abused by a caregiver or family member (Goodman-Brown et al., 2003). Children abused by a family member, someone in a position of authority and trust, may be less inclined to betray the offender or may be fearful of disrupting the family. Goodman-Brown and colleagues (2003) identify the child's fear of consequences to himself/ herself or the family, as well as their attributions of responsibility for the abuse, as additional factors, which influence disclosure. Children who blame themselves or feel responsible for the abuse are less likely to report the abuse.

Supporting Sexual Abuse Allegations

Disclosure is conceptualized as an ongoing process, during which the child gradually constructs a series of revelations, sometimes coupled with recantations or retractions of the abuse (Summit, 1983). Recantation may be related to the child feeling unsupported or not believed by others, family pressure on the child to recant, delays in prosecution of the offender or disruption to the family system (e.g., placement in foster care, financial problems, emotional reactions of family members). Again, it is important to note that very few children fabricate or make erroneous allegations of sexual abuse. Studies indicate that between 4 to 27 percent of child victims recant their allegations during the investigation or prosecution of the offender (London, Bruck, Ceci, & Shuman, 2005). Therefore, when a child discloses sexual abuse, every effort should be made to provide the child with a supportive environment. Early intervention by social workers and other professionals, clinical interventions for the child and family members, as well as ongoing support throughout investigation and prosecution of the offender are critical to the child's adjustment following disclosure.

SYSTEM INTERVENTIONS

The United States Department of Justice states, "No single agency has the training, manpower, resources or legal mandate to intervene effectively in child abuse cases" (United States Department of Justice [USDJ], 1997, p. 1). However, in their efforts to both protect children and prosecute offenders, multiple systems interventions have the potential to retraumatize and revictimize child victims. Research indicates that participating in multiple investigative interviews, undergoing medical examinations, recalling traumatic events in the presence of professionals who are strangers to the child, as well as facing their offenders during court testimony may increase trauma-related symptoms in victims (Berliner & Conte, 1995; Brennan & Brennan, 1988; Goodman et al., 1992; Goodman, Quas, Bulkley, & Shapiro, 1999; Henry, 1997; Tedesco & Schnell, 1987; Whitcomb, 2003). Nevertheless, there is no consensus about how to best protect and accommodate child victims, minimize the iatrogenic impact of legal interventions, while also effectively prosecuting offenders.

In addition, both the criminal justice system and child protection system are overwhelmed by the number of investigation reports, assessments of safety and placement, and referrals for intervention. They are faced also with the challenge of gathering credible statements from children. This is coupled with the lack of physical evidence and corroborating witnesses, where the focus is the child victim's testimony and the prosecution of offenders (Coulborn-Faller &

Henry, 2000; USDJ, 1997). The inclusion of child victims in the legal system is now necessitated in apprehending and prosecuting sex offenders.

Child Protection System Intervention

Child protective services (CPS) are the local authority mandated to receive child abuse reports, investigate and intervene in cases of child sexual abuse when the alleged offender is in a caretaking role of the child, or when the child's parent failed to protect the child from the abuse (USDHHS, 1993). In 1999, 96 percent of all confirmed cases of child sexual abuse involved adult family members of the victims or someone known to or trusted by the child, and 84 percent of substantiated cases occurred in the child victims' homes (USDJ, 2000). Therefore, CPS response is necessitated in the majority of sexual abuse cases. Child protection service workers are specially trained to perform risk assessment for reabuse and are expected to prioritize the child's safety in the home, or make decisions about placing the child with a relative or in foster care (USDHHS, 1993). The goal is to strengthen families' abilities to care for their children (Pence & Wilson, 1994). However, most cases of child sexual abuse result in the child's removal from the home and "The CPS goal of keeping families intact or family reunification may be compromised in sexual abuse cases" (USDHHS, 1993, p. 2).

Criminal Justice System Intervention

Prior to the 1980s, cases of child sexual abuse were usually deferred to the responsibility of child protective services, particularly if the offender was a family member (Pence & Wilson, 1994). In the event that police investigated a case of child sexual abuse, they conducted their investigation separate from that of child protective services, with little to no cooperation or communication with them (Pence & Wilson, 1994). Police officers, as well as attorneys, were untrained and inexperienced in communicating and interacting with children. In fact, prior to the 1980s, children rarely participated in the legal system at all. They were viewed to be emotionally, developmentally, and cognitively unprepared to handle the stressors and demands of providing accurate accounts of crimes and testifying in public (Whitcomb, 2003).

Given that child sexual abuse is a felony offense in every state, police officers and detectives are required to respond to allegations. Since there is rarely physical or medical evidence of abuse, police interviews of the alleged victim, the alleged victim's nonoffending parent/caregiver, family, and friends, as well as the suspect, are monumental in gathering evidence (USDJ, 1997). Officers conducting investigations use guidelines established by the Department of Justice to gather accurate and thorough statements from child victims. "The focal point of the investigation is the child, and the interview with the child is likely to be the single most important part of the investigation" (USDJ, 1997, p. 4). "Although law enforcement agencies espouse their goal of protecting children from abuse, their ultimate goal is arresting offenders. The mandate of law enforcement is not to help families with their problems, but to gather evidence toward prosecution of offenders" (USDHHS, 1993, p. 2).

Prosecution and incarceration of individuals who commit sexual offenses has been prioritized as a strategy in both punishing individuals who commit sexual offenses, as well as ensuring safety in the community. Prosecutors, and their superiors, also have a unique role in decision making about how each case will proceed, including whether depositions, pretrial hearings and trial will necessitate the child victim's involvement. Prosecutors' decisions are influenced by not only the state or federal court system where they are employed, but also the community at large. Although they too may espouse the value of minimizing involvement of children in legal proceedings, their primary goal is to convict offenders.

Intervention Impact and Opportunities for Reform

"Sexually abused children are required to participate in several system interventions simultaneously, with each system having its own demands and expectations" (Henry, 1997, p. 499). What is the impact of a comprehensive response system of intervention on children given the vulnerabilities of child victims of sexual abuse? Research examining iatrogenic effects found that children are often expected to participate in multiple interviews with different professionals, testify in the presence of the offender, and enter into an unfamiliar and intimidating environment in the courthouse. Evaluation of potential physical trauma and collection of physical evidence also require child victims to undergo invasive and often uncomfortable physical examinations. Such experiences have been associated with increased anxiety, trauma-related symptoms, and emotional distress (Goodman et al., 1992; Goodman et al., 1999; Henry, 1997; Whitcomb, 2003).

In an effort to achieve the seemingly contrary goals of protecting children while also prosecuting offenders, experts in the field of sexual abuse have recommended strategies for creating a more "child-friendly" system of interventions. Implementing these reforms requires collaborative efforts between multiple organizations, and the professionals who work within them. Events associated with iatrogenic effects of systems interventions, and collaborative strategies for reducing the frequency and negative impact of these events are outlined below.

Forensic Medical Examinations

Following allegations of child sexual abuse, children are referred to a physician for three primary reasons. First, the parent often seeks reassurance from a doctor of the child's physical integrity (Allard-Dansereau, Hebert, Tremblay, & Bernard-Bonnin, 2001). Second, the child's physical health and well-being are assessed for abnormal anogenital or genital injury, sexually transmitted diseases, and in some cases, pregnancy. Third, medical exams are conducted in attempts to gather physical evidence of abuse. Although very few cases result in physical evidence or substantiation of sexual abuse, examinations which do result in medical findings significantly improve the likelihood of successful prosecution of the offender (Jones et al., 2005). Prior to the 1990s, there was no standard protocol for conducting gynecological or genital examinations on prepubescent children. Sexual assault examinations designed for adults are difficult and uncomfortable to perform on children. The overwhelming increases in reports of child sexual abuse and requests for medical examinations of children have prompted physicians to develop child forensic medical examinations.

In 1991, the American Academy of Pediatrics (AAP) published a forensic examination protocol, which continues to be updated. The AAP recommends that forensic exams be conducted within 72 hours of acute sexual assault or sexual abuse (AAP, 1999). These examinations are designed to not only ease the discomfort experienced by children and fears of parents/caregivers, but also to collect and document physical evidence of sexual abuse. Specialized knowledge and training are required to conduct the examination, as well as attend to the needs and concerns of children and their families. Forensic examinations using advanced medical technologies, including photocolposcopy, videocolposcopy, and computer imaging technology, are currently considered best practice in collecting physical evidence and decreasing stress on the child (Jones et al., 2005). These medical innovations produce enhanced visual images of magnified tissues, which can be closely examined to detect abnormal anogenital and genital trauma. In addition, evidence indicates that use of these technologies demystify, distract, and even comfort the child during the exam, as he or she can observe what is happening on a video screen (Allard-Dansereau et al., 2001). The AAP protocol also includes a psychosocial and behavioral history of the child and detailed documentation.

While many children do not respond negatively to medical examinations, some react with anxiety, fear, anger, and opposition. However, empirical evidence indicates that the physician's behavior toward the child is associated with the child's feelings of fear and anxiety (Allard-Dansereau et al., 2001). Physicians and medical personnel who interact with the child in an empathic, comforting and reassuring manner may reduce the child's distress (Allard-Dansereau et al., 2001). It is important to note that, in cases of child sexual abuse, serious genital injury is not common and very few exams result in substantial physical evidence. Therefore, it is important to weigh the potential risks posed to the child against the potential benefits of the forensic medical examination.

Forensic Investigative Interviews and Joint Investigations

The involvement of children in criminal investigations has raised many concerns. Perhaps the most substantial evidence in the literature illustrates the negative impact of multiple interviews by professionals. Multiple interviews may invoke or exacerbate feelings of shame, guilt, fear, and doubt in the child, creating a traumatic experience secondary to the abuse itself (Brennan & Brennan, 1998). Similarly, Henry (1997) found that the number of investigative interviews was predictive of trauma- and stress-related symptoms. In addition, child testimony has been highly criticized in the criminal justice system, as it is purported that children are suggestible, have limited memories, and will make untrue statements in order to please the interviewer.

Two primary strategies have been proposed to mediate the impact of multiple interviews on child victims, streamline the investigative process, and produce more reliable statements from children during interviews. The two strategies are forensic interview protocols and joint investigations.

FORENSIC INTERVIEWING PROTOCOLS. First, specialized forensic interview protocols (expert consensus guidelines) have been informed and developed by child sexual abuse experts, mental health professionals, and law enforcement. Cross-training of police officers and child protection investigators in specialized forensic interviewing also teaches sexual abuse

investigators how to communicate with children in a developmentally-appropriate and sensitive manner, while optimizing the content of information gathered during the first interview. "If complete information is obtained during the original interview, the need for additional interviews may be reduced, resulting in decreased pressure on the child" (Ghetti, Alexander, & Goodman, 2002, p. 242). Furthermore, the testimony gleaned from forensic interviewing for child victims, as opposed to traditional police interviewing protocol, is designed to enhance the credibility of statements by child victims (USDJ, 1997). Forensic interviewing strategies are designed to help the child feel supported and comfortable, and hence more willing to spontaneously disclose. Empirical investigation indicates that the use of rapport building techniques, empowerment strategies, and open-ended questions and prompts decrease suggestibility and contribute to more reliable information-gathering during the investigative interview (Orbach et al., 2000) (see Table 17-1: Forensic

Table 17-1
FORENSIC INTERVIEWING PROTOCOL

Stage	*Goals*	*Example Statements/Questions*
Preparing the Interview Environment	Remove distracting material from the room; position chairs and recording equipment. Ensure child has taken a bathroom break and eaten prior to bringing child in.	N/A
The Introduction	Acclimate the child to the room and model relaxed, patient tone. Interviewer introduces self, explains professional role and purpose of interview. Provide orienting information.	"Hello, my name is _____. I am a police officer/social worker/detective and part of my job is to talk to kids about things that have happened in their lives." "I can't always remember everything kids say, so I have a video camera/tape recorder here." "I talk with lots of kids about things that have happened in their lives. After we are done talking, I will bring you back to your mom/dad/caregiver, who is waiting right outside.
Legal Competency	Assess child's developmental abilities to distinguish between the truth and a lie. Avoid asking children to define concepts; use examples instead.	"Before we begin, I want to make sure you understand the difference between the truth and a lie. What color is my shirt? My shirt is blue. Is that the truth or a lie. [Wait for response.] Yes, that would be a lie, because my shirt is white. How old are you? You are 8 years old. Would that be the truth or a lie? [Wait for response.] Exactly, that would be the truth because you are 8 years old."

(Cont'd.)

Table 17-1
FORENSIC INTERVIEWING PROTOCOL *(Cont'd.)*

Stage	*Goals*	*Example Statements/Questions*
Establishing Ground Rules	Ensure the child understands that he/she should not answer questions he/she does not understand, or answer about events he/she does not remember. Practice with the child responses such as "I don't know" and "I don't remember."	Discuss with child the importance of telling the truth throughout the interview. "Sometimes kids don't know the answers to all my questions. Or, I ask strange questions they don't really get. If I ask you a question and you don't know the answer, I want you to tell me you don't know. It's ok to say 'I don't know.' Like, 'What's my dog's name?' [Wait for response.] That's right. You don't know my dog's name. Good." "If I ask you something you don't remember, don't make it up. Just say 'I don't remember.'" "Also, if I make a mistake about something, you tell me, make sure you correct me. I am not always right. Like if I say, 'So you are 5 years old, right?' What would you say? [Wait for response.] Exactly, you would say, 'No, you made a mistake. I am 8 years old.'"
Completing Rapport Building with Practice Interview	Building rapport has three primary purposes: (a) Make the child comfortable in the interview setting. (b) Make a preliminary assessment of the child's verbal skills, cognitive and emotional maturity. (c) Convey that the goal of the interview is for the child to talk about his/her life.	Ask questions about child's teacher, family, hobbies, likes and dislikes using open-ended questions such as "Tell me about your teacher." If the child gives short answers, train him/her to talk in detail. Ask the child to describe a recent incident from beginning to end. For example, "Christmas (or another holiday) just passed. Think real hard about everything you did on Christmas and tell me all about your day, from the minute you got up to when you went to bed." Use prompts such as "Then what happened?" or "Tell me more." Younger children may have a more difficult time with one-time events. Ask questions about recurring activities. "Tell me about what you do to get ready for school in the morning." Encourage a reluctant child by stating, "It's ok to talk now." or "This is your special time to talk about your life."
Introducing the Topic	Interviewer prompts a transition to the target topic. Start with the least suggestive prompts that might raise the topic of abuse. Remember that closing the interview without a disclosure of abuse is acceptable.	"Now that I know you a little better, it's time to talk about something else. Tell me why you came here today." "I understand there may be some problems in your family. Tell me what they are." Avoid words such as *hurt*, *bad*, *abuse* or other terms that project adult interpretations of the allegations. Avoid direct questions such as "Did someone touch your private parts?" "I understand that someone has been bothering you."

(Cont'd.)

Table 17-1
FORENSIC INTERVIEWING PROTOCOL *(Cont'd.)*

Stage	*Goals*	*Example Statements/Questions*
The Free Narrative	After the topic is raised, the interviewer asks the child to provide a narrative description of the event. Children's responses to open-ended questions and prompts provide more detail and are more reliable.	"Tell me everything you can about that." "Then what? What else can you tell me?" Give the child permission to talk about target issues such as: Child: "and then he . . ."; Interviewer: "It's ok to say it." If a child becomes upset or quiet, acknowledge the behavior, but do not make extensive comments. "I noticed you stopped talking."
Questioning and Clarification	This phase begins when it is clear the child has finished the free narrative. The goal is to seek and clarify legally relevant information, such as identity of the perpetrator, number of incidents, types of abuse, whether there were witnesses. Avoid probing for unnecessary details.	Use the least suggestive questions possible. "Earlier you said something about the 'yucky movies' you saw. Tell me more about them." Specific nonleading questions are used to gather details such as "You said 'Todd.' Who is Todd?" or "What was Tom wearing?" Clarify contradictions by stating, "You said Mom wasn't home, but she walked in the room. I'm confused; tell me more about that day." Make sure to clarify the child's terminology for body parts. "You said 'tushee'; tell me which body part that is."
Closure	Complete interview with positive reinforcement to child, regardless of the outcome.	"Is there anything else you'd like to tell me about?" "Are there any questions you want to ask me?" Thank the child for coming, but do not specifically ask him/her for disclosures.

Citation: State of Michigan Governor's Task Force on Children's Justice and Family Independence Agency.

Interviewing Protocol). In cases where abuse is suspected or alleged, but more extensive assessment is required, The National Child Advocacy Center (NCAC) promotes a protocol for extended forensic evaluation (see Table 17-2). Several national organizations, including NCAC and the American Prosecutor Research Institute, provide professional training in forensic interviewing.

JOINT INVESTIGATIONS. The second strategy to reduce the number of interviews is through joint investigation, including both child protection and law enforcement professionals. Joint investigations streamline the investigative process, improve the accuracy of investigations, and improve outcomes for child safety (Pence & Wilson, 1994). This strategy requires not only interagency coordination to schedule joint interviews, but also interprofessional collaborative efforts between police officers and child protection workers during the investigation. Historically, the relationship between law enforcement and child protection agencies has been tenuous, at best (Pence & Wilson, 1994). Differences in professional philosophies, mandates, investigative procedures, and beliefs have contributed to problems in their successful collaboration. Cross, Finkelhor, and Ormrod (2005) aptly describe these historical professional role conflicts:

> Child protective services workers worry that police will antagonize families and undertake heavy-handed, punitive interventions, interfering with their attempts to protect children and repair families. Police are concerned that CPS workers will inadvertently interfere with evidence collection and criminal investigation and, thereby, interfere with bringing perpetrators to justice. (p. 225)

Table 17-2
EXTENDED FORENSIC EVALUATION PROTOCOL

The National Children's Advocacy Center (NCAC) extended forensic evaluation model should be implemented when: (1) the child does not disclose sexual abuse, but exhibits behaviors or other indicators that strongly suggest victimization; (2) the extent or nature of abuse is not disclosed during the initial investigative interview; or (3) when information gathered during the initial investigative interview needs clarification. This model was evaluated in a two-year pilot study at 20 NCAC sites across the United States, with the following outcomes: 47 percent of children referred for forensic evaluation ultimately disclosed abuse in a credible manner; court findings further supported 71 percent of those cases. A subsequent multisite study replicated findings of the pilot-study: in 44.5 percent of cases, a credible disclosure was obtained, with 73 percent of cases supported in court. For more details of this model and available training programs, visit the NCAC website at http://www.nationalcac.org/professionals/model/forensic_eval.html.

Evaluation Stage	*Methods/Goals*
Caregiver Interview	*Gather information from nonoffending caregiver pertaining to:* (a) Family history and dynamics (b) Current family composition (c) Names and relationships of any other significant individuals in child's life (d) Child's social and developmental history (e) Care routines (f) Access to sexual information (g) Family names for body parts (h) Nonoffending caregiver's understanding of current allegations or concerns
Rapport Building	*Goals of rapport-building:* (a) Establish the context of evaluation and role of the evaluator (b) Establish a precedent for narrative responses (c) Begin assessing child's developmental status (d) Establish a comfortable relationship with the child
Developmental Assessment	*Goals of developmental assessment:* (a) Determine child's capacity for giving specific, credible accounts of events (b) Begin to learn about the domains that challenge our ability to enter the child's world (e.g., child's affective/expressive capabilities, ways child perceives connections between events, people and places)

Social & Behavioral Assessment	*Social and behavioral assessment accomplished through:*
	(a) Review of behavioral checklists:
	  – Child Sexual Behavior Inventory (Friedrich, 1990)
	  – Child Behavior Checklist (Achenbach, 1988)
	  – Trauma Symptom Checklist for Children (Briere, 1996)
	(b) Developmentally-appropriate in-session activities:
	  – Exploration of child's self-understanding and self-esteem
	  – Assessment of child's perceptions of others in the environment

Focus on Topic of Concern	*Moving into more specific questioning, the evaluator:* (a) Remains neutral (b) Maintains a hypothesis-testing approach (c) Uses open-ended, neutral prompts (d) Uses a variety of means to introduce topic of concern, moving from general to specific

(Cont'd.)

Table 17-2
EXTENDED FORENSIC EVALUATION PROTOCOL *(Cont'd.)*

Evaluation Stage	*Methods/Goals*
Gain More Specific Detail	When children disclose abuse, they may at first provide skeletal descriptions due to anxiety or developmental limitations. See **Forensic Interviewing Protocol** for useful techniques in gathering more specific details that: (a) Increase credibility of the child's disclosure (b) Enhance ability to make the most accurate decisions about protection of the child and prosecution of the offender.
Closure	In the last session, the evaluator includes: (a) Final review and clarification of any abuse disclosures made (b) Summarizes the forensic evaluation experience with the child (c) Discusses any plan for a therapy referral

Published with permission by Connie Carnes, National Children's Advocacy Center.

Coordinated efforts between CPS and law enforcement reduce interprofessional conflict especially when both agencies are committed to the safety and well-being of children. Recent evidence suggests that CPS and law enforcement joint investigations of child abuse may also in fact reduce the number of interviews, improve effectiveness and decision making, as well as gather more accurate information from child witnesses (Coulborn-Faller & Henry, 2000; Cross, et al., 2005; Jones, Cross, Walsh, & Simone, 2005).

MULTIDISCIPLINARY TEAMS (MDTs) AND CHILD ADVOCACY CENTERS (CACs). The concept of joint investigation has been expanded to include the multidisciplinary team (MDT) approach. Similarly to joint investigations, the MDT approach to investigating child sexual abuse relies on the cooperative efforts of child protection workers, police officers, prosecutors, and mental health professionals. With the goal of reducing the number of interviews, utilizing the skills and expertise of multiple professionals in decision-making, increasing the accuracy of investigations, and using agency resources more efficiently, MDTs have been highly recommended by researchers, as well as the U.S. Department of Justice (USDJ, 2000). "MDT approaches are being recognized by an increasing number of professionals as a viable community response to the concern that a system designed to protect children may, in fact, be causing additional harm to child victims" (Kolbo & Strong, 1997, p. 61). Furthermore, the increase of collaboration

and communication between multiple professionals involved is designed to prevent child victims from "falling through the cracks." Currently, at least 36 states have enacted legislation requiring the use of MDTs in cases of child sexual abuse (Jones et al., 2005).

A more comprehensive effort to ameliorate the potential harm of system intervention and improve the investigative process includes the development of Children's Advocacy Centers (CAC). A formalized venue for multidisciplinary team response to child sexual abuse, CACs are community-based, child-friendly facilities where, "law enforcement, child protection, prosecution, mental health, medical and victim advocacy work together, conducting joint forensic interviews and making team decisions about the investigation, treatment, management and prosecution of child abuse cases" (The National Children's Advocacy Center [NCAC], 2005). Child Advocacy Centers (CACs) provide a unique venue to facilitate interorganizational and interprofessional collaboration, with the goals of maintaining open communication, information sharing and case coordination (NCAC, 2005). The CAC model is designed to provide access to therapeutic services and mental health treatment for children and families affected by sexual abuse. Additionally, CACs engage in professional training, public education, and prevention efforts.

Court Involvement and Victim Advocacy

Testifying in the courtroom, especially in the presence of the offender, has also been found to be associated with negative outcomes for child victims (Goodman et al., 1992; Henry, 1997; Oates & Tong, 1987). Child victims often experience fear, shame, anxiety, and trauma-related symptoms both in the anticipation of testifying, as well as during the actual act (Goodman et al., 1999; Henry, 1997). Whether or not the case actually goes to trial, child victims are thrust into an unfamiliar and often intimidating environment in the courtroom. Given the often lengthy timeline of criminal cases, this anxiety may persist throughout the course of the process. On the other hand, some children do not exhibit increased trauma-related symptoms when testifying in the presence of the offender. In fact, it is hypothesized that some children find it empowering and therapeutic to confront their offender and participate in his/her prosecution. There is no guideline for determining how children will react to their participation in court testimony. Therefore, every precaution should be taken to ensure their involvement in the criminal proceedings is as non-threatening and comfortable as possible.

Informed by social scientists, psychologists, and social workers, innovative strategies in the legal system have been proposed to decrease the need for children to testify in live court, including: the use of closed-circuit televised testimony, inclusion of expert witness testimony, and the admittance of child hearsay evidence (Goodman, Quas, Bulkley, & Shapiro, 1999). Proposed procedural reforms also allow for expediting of legal proceedings and the presence of a support person, such as a victim advocate or social worker, in the courtroom while the child testifies. Empirical evidence indicates that children who possess greater knowledge about the legal system and familiarity with the courthouse environment experience fewer symptoms of anxiety and emotional distress (Whitcomb, 2003). In an effort to create a more comfortable environment for child victims and their families, court preparation and support strategies have been implemented through victim advocacy programs. These programs are designed to orient child victims to court processes by touring the courthouse, meeting the judges and attorneys, and supporting them throughout their legal involvement. Victim advocacy programs are typically located within the courthouse and may also provide counseling, claims-assistance, and other court-related services (Jones et al., 2005). Formalized court preparation programs have been instituted in

Canada for over 10 years, and have been found to minimize the iatrogenic impact of court involvement on child victims (Sas, Wolfe, & Gowdey, 1996).

ASSESSMENT AND INTERVENTION

Intervention begins with valid and accurate assessment of the child and family, as well as social and environmental factors. Valid and reliable abuse-specific measures should be used in conjunction with clinical assessment of the child and family system. Evidence indicates that the child victim's nonoffending caregiver plays a critical role in supporting the child's treatment, and creating an environment conducive to healing following abuse. Therefore, it is paramount to assess for these qualities. Unfortunately, the child's caregiver is not always emotionally, cognitively, or financially prepared to handle the stressors associated with learning of their child's abuse.

Assessment

It has been clearly established in the literature that the use of valid and reliable standardized measures provides for more accurate assessment of bio-psychosocial problems and strengths than unguided clinical interviews. In early studies of child sexual abuse, researchers typically utilized diagnostic interview protocols and measures of general psychopathology, such as depression and anxiety. Furthermore, most researchers relied on reports of caregivers and caseworkers to assess emotional and behavioral problems among victims of child sexual abuse. In response to the need for valid and reliable trauma/abuse-specific measures, several empirically-based measures have been developed. Currently, these measures are commonly used in impact and intervention studies, as well as clinical practice.

Clinical assessment should include not only symptoms that may be related to the abuse, but should also focus on the child's preabuse functioning, developmental issues, and current feelings related to the abuse experience and consequences of disclosure. "Abuse-specific (e.g., self-blame, guilt) and abuse-related (e.g., stigmatization, shame) attributions are associated with increased distress and may lead to conditions such as depression, low self-esteem, and impaired socialization that are common in abused children" (Saunders, Berliner, & Hanson, 2004, p. 25). Assessment of the parent/caregiver, parent-child relationship, social system, and other environmental factors should also be included. Family functioning, as well as the parent-child relationship, is critical to the child's adjustment following sexual abuse. Evidence indicates that treatment outcomes are influenced by family cohesion and adaptability, parental support of the child, and parental emotional reaction to the child's abuse (Cohen & Mannarino, 2000). Furthermore, the family may be experiencing a range of social problems that impede their compliance with treatment and appropriate protection of the child victim. Therefore, a thorough family assessment is paramount. The following valid measures should be considered.

Abuse-Specific Measures

1. *Trauma Symptom Checklist for Children* (TSCC). Perhaps the most frequently used, the Trauma Symptom Checklist for Children (TSCC) evaluates children's responses to unspecified traumatic events in a number of different symptom domains (Briere, 1996). The TSCC has been standardized on a large sample of racially and economically diverse children from a variety of urban and suburban environments (Briere, 1996). This 54-item self-report measure, designed for children ages 8 to18, has demonstrated good reliability and validity in detecting trauma-related symptoms (Brier, 1996). It measures presence and severity of symptomology across the following clinical scales: Anxiety, Depression, Anger, Posttraumatic Stress, Dissociation (Overt and Fantasy subscales), and Sexual Concerns (Preoccupation and Distress subscales). For children developmentally incapable of completing the TSCC,

2. The Trauma Symptom Checklist for Young Children (TSCYC) was designed to measure similar symptoms among children as young as three years old (Briere et al., 2001). The TSCYC is a 90-item caretaker-report measure, which includes additional features that assess the caretaker's response style, detecting overreporting and underreporting (Briere et al., 2001) The TSCYC contains the following clinical scales: Posttraumatic Stress-Intrusion, Posttraumatic Stress-Avoidance, Posttraumatic Stress-Arousal, Sexual Concerns, Dissociation, Anxiety, Depression, and Anger/Aggression. Among a sample of 219 ethnically

diverse children (mean age 7.1), this scale demonstrated good reliability, predictive validity, and absence of rater bias (Briere et al., 2001).

3. *Children's Impact of Events Scale-Revised* (CITES-R). The Children's Impact of Events Scale-Revised (CITES-R) is a 78-item standardized interview for children ages 8 to 16 (Wolfe, Gentile, Michienzi, Sas, & Wolfe, 1991). The CITES-R is designed to measure trauma-related symptomology across the following scales: PTSD (Intrusive Thoughts, Avoidance, Sexual Anxiety, and Hyperarousal); Social Reactions (Negative Reactions by Others and Social Support); Attributions (Self-Blame/Guilt, Dangerous World, Empowerment and Vulnerability); and Eroticism (Wolfe et al., 1991; Chaffin & Shultz, 2001). The CITES-R demonstrated good internal consistency and reliability in detecting trauma-related symptoms in children.

4. *Child Sexual Behavior Inventory* (CSBI). Given that sexual behavior problems are often associated with child sexual abuse, the Child Sexual Behavior Inventory (CSBI) has been developed to detect sexual behaviors of concern among children (Friedrich et al., 2001). The CBSI is a 38-item caretaker-report measure that assesses sexualized behaviors and concerns, as well as boundary issues among children ages 2 to 12 years old. The most current version of the CBSI demonstrated satisfactory reliability and predictive validity when 620 sexually abused children were compared with a sample of 1,114 children from normative populations and 577 psychiatric patients (Friedrich et al., 2001). It is important to note that, while sexually abused children demonstrated a significantly higher degree of sexualized behaviors than others in the sample, nonabused children also demonstrated sexualized behaviors. In the absence of sexual abuse, family factors and other behavior problems were found to be associated with sexualized behaviors (Friedrich et al., 2001). Therefore the CBSI, as well as every other measure, cannot be used to *predict* or *substantiate* the presence of sexual abuse. [For a comprehensive list of trauma-related measures, see Strand, Sarmiento, & Pasquale, 2005 or visit the Mental Measurements Yearbook on-line at http://www.unl.edu/buros/bimm/html/subarts.html.]

The Nonoffending Parent

Nonoffending parents or caregivers are perhaps the most valuable resource for children who have experienced sexual abuse. Although it is not uncommon for police, child protection workers, clinicians, and the public to blame parents for their child's abuse experience, nonoffending parents should be supported and included in interventions whenever possible. Some of the earliest studies of child sexual abuse portray mothers as "collusive, denying, and indirectly responsible for the abuse of their children" (Deblinger, 1996, p. 113). Mothers were perceived as unwilling to believe their child's disclosure of sexual abuse and unable to effectively protect and support them. In the late 1980s and early 1990s, however, such theories were discredited with empirical studies. Investigations into whether nonoffending mothers were aware of their child's sexual abuse consistently report that most mothers are totally unaware of the abuse or "felt powerless to stop it" (Bolen, 2001). Furthermore, mothers are often found to be responsible for reporting the sexual abuse of their children. In the past 20 years, at least 13 studies report that between 69 percent and 84 percent of nonoffending parents believed their child's allegations and took action to protect them from further abuse (Elliot & Carnes, 2001).

The response of the nonoffending parent following discovery of their child's sexual abuse is consistently found to be correlated with the child's recovery. Empirical evidence indicates that children of nonoffending parents who respond in a supportive, protective manner demonstrate decreased symptoms of psychopathology, improved social and emotional functioning, and higher self-concept when compared with child victims whose parents are unsupportive or do not believe their child's allegations (Adams-Tucker, 1982; Everson et al., 1989; Morrison & Clavena-Valleroy, 1998). Furthermore, children whose mothers are perceived as unsupportive by child protective services workers are significantly more likely to be placed in out-of-home care (Hunter, Coulter, Runyan, & Everson, 1990). Removal from the nonoffending caregiver has the potential to further isolate the child and foster feelings of guilt and self-blame for the abuse.

It is perhaps not enough to teach nonoffending parents means of supporting their children after sexual abuse, but to also address the impact sexual abuse has had on the parents and the entire family system. Kazdin and Weisz (1998) found that child treatment outcomes are associated with parental support, but also parental mental health, parental marital conflict,

family functioning, family life stressors, and family socioeconomic factors. Research consistently indicates that parents of children who have been sexually abused often experience disruption in family and parental functioning, marital discord, problems with family relationships, decreased satisfaction with their parenting roles, and decreased parenting self-efficacy (Manion et al., 1996). When the offender is the child's father, step-father, or mother's paramour, nonoffending mothers may lose a primary source of financial and emotional support. "Treatment may also be necessary for parents to help them focus on and address the stressors that are sometimes associated with disclosure, such as separation from a partner, moving, the loss of financial resources, the loss of social support from family and friends, and participation in criminal and/or civil legal investigations" (Corcoran, 2004, p. 61). As a result, nonoffending parents often exhibit depression, general emotional distress, and symptoms of secondary traumatic stress (Elliot & Carnes, 2001; Manion et al., 1995). In addition, mothers of children who have been sexually abused may have their own histories of childhood sexual abuse, domestic violence, social isolation, and substance abuse (Deblinger, Hathaway, Lippman, & Steer, 1993). Given their critical role in protecting children from sexual abuse, reporting, supporting, and seeking help, nonoffending parents are valuable resources in intervention strategies. Practitioners should make every concerted effort to promote the nonoffending caregiver's support of the child and participation in both system and clinical interventions.

Case Study of Brittany

Read the case of Brittany and based on the preceding discussion of forensic interviewing discuss the case from the following questions.

1. Why might Brittany's mother react with ambivalence toward the allegations?
2. Review the Forensic Interviewing Protocol and decide what ground rules should be established for this interview.
3. What questions need to be asked in order to make some decision about the alleged sexual abuse?
4. What impact will substantiation of the abuse have on the family system?

5. What can the practitioner do to promote Brittany's mother's support of her daughter?
6. What system interventions are warranted in this case?
7. Which of the abuse specific measures of assessment are helpful in this case?

Exhibit 2: Case Study of Brittany

Brittany is a 15-year-old African American female. She recently disclosed to her best friend that her stepfather has been sexually abusing her since she was 12 years old. Brittany's friend informed a school guidance counselor, who then contacted child protective services. Brittany told the CPS investigator that she was afraid to tell her mother about the abuse because her stepfather said no one would believe her and she would be sent to foster care if she told. Brittany further indicated that she did not want to upset her mother, who had been taking care of her grandmother for years until recently, when her grandmother passed away. During an unannounced visit by the CPS investigator and a police officer, Brittany's mother seemed ambivalent about the allegations and stated that she believed Brittany was angry with her stepfather and "might have exaggerated what happened." Brittany's mother indicated that Brittany "has a problem with lying" and may have provoked her husband because she "dresses like a grown woman." It was noted by investigators that Brittany's stepfather is the sole provider for the family, which includes Brittany's three younger siblings. Brittany's mother has been grieving the loss of her own mother and has limited social support.

Evidence-Based Interventions

CORRELATIONAL STUDIES. Despite the potential benefits of receiving clinical treatment following sexual abuse, many child victims and their families fail to receive services (Demarest-Tingus, Heger, Foy, & Leskin, 1996). Several studies indicate that factors influencing whether or not the child and family enter into treatment include ethnicity, child's age, and the family's access to resources (Demarest-Tingus et al., 1996). Additionally, involvement of CPS and law enforcement has also been found to be significantly related to service delivery. In a study of 511 sexually victimized children, Demarest-Tingus and colleagues (1996) found that 69.3 percent of the sample entered into treatment within six months of reported abuse. They found that Caucasians were significantly more likely than Hispanic and African American children to receive therapeutic services. Children between the ages of 7 and 13 were significantly more likely to enter into treatment than children under age 6 and older than 13. Furthermore, children who experienced more severe, prolonged abuse, as well as children placed in out-of-home care entered into treatment at higher rates than children whose abuse was considered less severe or did not result in removal from the home. Also, in cases when there was involvement of *both* CPS and law enforcement, 96 percent of children received treatment, as compared with 58 percent when there was CPS involvement only. In cases where neither CPS nor law enforcement were involved, none of the children entered into therapy (Demarest-Tingus et al., 1996).

Prior to the 1980s, failure to receive appropriate treatment was in large part due to a lack of resources. However, over the past 20 years, there has been a dramatic increase in clinical programs designed to treat sexually abused children and their families (Mannarino & Cohen, 2001). Intervention research continues to provide insight into the most effective treatment interventions for those affected by child sexual abuse. Furthermore, the development of multidisciplinary teams and child advocacy centers may be contributing to improved rates of entering into therapy for victims of sexual abuse and their families. A recent survey of outcomes of CACs indicates that they have made progress in both referring clients to abuse-specific treatment and providing counseling services in a child-friendly, accessible environment (Newman, Dannenfelser, & Pendelton, 2005).

OUTCOME STUDIES. In recent years, a number of important, well-designed intervention outcome studies have proliferated in the field. "By and large, studies have focused on abuse-specific therapies that have used cognitive-behavioral techniques in conjunction with psychoeducational interventions, coping skills training and family involvement" (Saywitz, Mannarino, Berliner, & Cohen, 2000). Although some child victims demonstrate psychosocial improvements over time without intervention, studies consistently indicate that treatment is significantly related to improvements in behavioral and emotional outcomes (Saywitz et al., 2000). Controlled studies, using randomized assignment to treatment conditions indicate that children who receive cognitive-behavioral therapy with the involvement of the nonoffending parent, demonstrate greater improvements when compared with supportive group therapy (Deblinger, Stauffer, & Steer, 2001) and child-centered therapy (Cohen, Deblinger, Mannarino, & Steer, 2004). Outcomes of cognitive behavioral strategies have also shown to be maintained over time, in one- and two-year follow up assessments (Cohen, Mannarino, & Knudsen, 2005; Deblinger, Steer, & Lippmann, 1999). The manualized cognitive behavioral treatment known as *trauma-focused cognitive behavioral treatment* (TF-CBT) has become widely accepted as the most efficacious appropriate treatment. Due to its results in significantly reducing child trauma-related symptoms and externalizing behaviors, while improving parental efficacy and functioning, TF-CBT for children and their nonoffending parents is currently designated a Model Program by Substance Abuse and Mental Health Services Administration (SAMSHA). [See Table 17-3 Evidence Based Interventions for program descriptions and outcome data.] Clinical training in TF-CBT is available through the American Prevention Society of the Abuse of Children (www.apsac.org) and the Medical University of South Carolina National Crime Victims and Research Center (http://tfcbt.-musc.edu).

At the time of this writing, TF-CBT is considered the most efficacious treatment, which can be applied in variety of settings with different age groups and cultural populations. However, other treatments with a lesser degree of evidence should not necessarily be dismissed. For instance, the National Child Advocacy Center has identified *Forensically Sensitive Therapy* (FST) as a promising practice program, to be used with child sexual abuse victims when criminal and civil court cases are actively pending (NCAC, 2005). The FST model "is designed to help the child begin the healing process while still preserving the integrity of the portion of the case that is built upon the child's statement" (NCAC, 2005). This treatment applies the theoretical framework of Finkelhor and Browne's (1986) traumagenic dynamic model, and employs evidence-based intervention techniques drawing on various treatment models. Currently, the FST model demonstrates promising evidence in

reducing both internalizing and externalizing behaviors in child victims, while maintaining the integrity of the legal case (NCAC, 2005). A standardized treatment manual is currently in development and more rigorous outcomes studies are in progress (see Table 17-3: Evidence Based Interventions, for program description and outcome data). The NCAC also plans to offer in-depth training in the FST model. For more information, visit the NCAC website (http://www.nationalcac.org).

It is very important to note that, in cases of intrafamilial sexual abuse, reunification with the offender should only occur when the offender, nonoffending parent and child victim have undergone abuse-specific treatment and safety planning, to ensure safety of the child. In many cases, it is not appropriate for the child and offender to be reunited or have any contact. It is highly recommended that treatment providers pursuing family reunification following sexual abuse refer and adhere to specific guidelines published by the Association for the Treatment of Sexual Abusers (www.atsa.com).

SUMMARY AND CONCLUSIONS: WHAT DO WE KNOW ABOUT ASSESSMENT AND INTERVENTION OF CHILD SEXUAL ABUSE?

There is no doubt that the amount of research on assessment and intervention of child sexual abuse is both inadequate and insufficient given the magnitude of the problem. However, it is known that the impact of sexual abuse on children can be severe. Increased aggression and externalizing behaviors, compounded by anxiety, depression, and internalizing behaviors are some of impacts on children (Kendall-Tackett et al., 1993). Other reported effects of sexual abuse are age-inappropriate sexual behaviors, low self-esteem, poor academic achievement, somatic complaints, and other behavioral and social difficulties (Friedrich, 1998; Kendall-Tackett et al., 1993). Empirical evidence consistently indicates that the experience of child sexual abuse may produce negative outcomes well into adulthood, including psychopathology, substance abuse, eating disorders, and poor relationship and interpersonal skills (Briere & Runtz, 1993). As well, it is known that there is no syndrome or set of symptoms to clearly identify a sexually abused child

Table 17-3
EVIDENCE-BASED INTERVENTIONS FOR CHILD SEXUAL ABUSE

Intervention and Program Developer(s)	Program Theory and Strategies	Target Population and Setting	Outcomes
Trauma-Focused Cognitive Behavioral Therapy (TF-CBT) **Level of Evidence:** Model Program* Judith Cohen, Ph.D. Professor of Psychiatry Medical Director Center for Traumatic Stress in Children & Adolescents Allegheny General Hospital Toll free for manual 1.877.773.846 SAMHSA Anthony P. Mannarino, Ph.D. Professor of Psychiatry and Chair Department of Psychiatry Center for Traumatic Stress in Children and Adolescents Allegheny General Hospital	Cognitive behavioral interventions, designed to improve adaptive skills and enhance positive cognitions. Treatment focus on enhancing interpersonal trust. Targets symptoms of PTSD, depression and externalizing behaviors, as well as poor self-esteem, mood instability and self-injurious behaviors. Addresses parental distress and encourages increased parental support of child. Intervention manual available	Ages 3 to 18 Male and Female Caucasion, African American, and Hispanic/Latino Rural, Suburban, and Urban	Children who receive TF-CBT treatment demonstrate significant decreases in: (1) Depressive symptoms (2) Externalizing behaviors (3) Feelings of self-blame and shame Caregivers in the TF-CBT groups report: (1) Less severe symptoms of depression (2) Less severe abuse-related distress (3) Improved support of their children (4) Improved parenting practices Both children and caregivers demonstrate maintenance of improvements one year after treatment (Cohen, Deblinger, Mannarino & Steer, 2004; SAMHSA, 2005)
Forensically Sensitive Therapy (FST) Level of Evidence: Promising Practice* Contact Connie Nicholas Carnes Director of Clinical Research and Program Development National Children's Advocacy Center http:www.nationalCAC.org	Designed for child victims to begin the healing process, while preserving the integrity of an active criminal or civil investigation Evidence-based treatment techniques, with inclusion of art and play tools for expression. Focus on establishment of trusting therapeutic relationship, trauma assessment, psychosocial assessment and trauma-focused activities. Empowerment strategies, resiliency enhancement and closure. Intervention manual currently being field tested in 50 sites in 20 states. International sites are included.	Children ages 4 to 17 who have experienced sexual abuse Male and Female Clinical outpatient setting	Children evidence significant decreases in: (1) Internalizing behaviors (2) Externalizing behaviors Promising evidence in reducing behaviors indicative of traumagenic states. Additional research currently being conducted to include larger, diverse sample and measures of trauma symptoms and sexual behaviors.

*Note: For description of a well supported and efficacious program, and promising practice and acceptable program, see Saunders, B. E., Berliner, L., & Hanson, R. F. (Eds.). (2004). *Child Physical and Sexual Abuse: Guidelines for Treatment* (Revised Report: April 26, 2004). Charleston, SC: National Crime Victims Research and Treatment Center.

and therefore, many sexually abused children appear asymptomatic at times, performing normally at school and with peers (Kendall-Tackett et al., 1993).

From the collective findings of these studies, several guidelines for practitioners who work in the field of forensic social work are presented below. All practice interventions related to child sexual abuse must insure the safety of the child and promote healthy child development, either within the family setting or in out-of-home placements if necessary. Investigation and intervention must be designed to involve multiple systems, while also minimizing the impact of multiple interviews by numerous professionals. Interviewing must be developmentally appropriate, culturally sensitive, and should occur in the context of a child-friendly organization. On the basis of the research, optimizing the content of information gathered during the disclosure process includes following a forensic interviewing protocol developed by experts. Collaboration with other professionals is essential. At this time, the multidisciplinary team approach and joint investigations by criminal justice professionals and child protection professionals are best practices.

In clinical practice, the use of abuse-specific standardized assessment measures can identify a range of emotional issues and behaviors for treatment. Across many domains, cognitive-behavioral interventions have emerged as the technique of choice for child, parent-child, and family level change. Although intervention programs, such as the Trauma Focused Cognitive Behavioral Therapy (TF-CBT) and Forensically Sensitive Therapy (FST) appear to improve the outcomes of children who experienced child sexual abuse, these interventions need to be delivered by well-trained practitioners and knowledgeable professionals. Forensically Sensitive Therapy (FST) is perhaps the only available promising practice program, specifically designed to be used with victims when criminal and civil court cases are actively pending. While a great deal of progress has been made in understanding and treating child sexual abuse, much of this work must be considered preliminary due to the limited research, methodological challenges, and limited sample sizes. It is far less clear what interventions are effective at the larger environmental system level to prevent and reduce the prevalence and incidence of child sexual abuse. Significant challenges remain both in implementing

what we already know and in further developing programs for children and their families.

As with all domains of interpersonal violence, much more work is needed in developing strategies for early intervention and prevention of child sexual abuse. Professionals and researchers need to look to other areas for possible solutions such as the early childhood literature, which may contribute to important understanding of human development and the design of innovative early interventions. Not to be forgotten is the enhancement of parent-child relationships, which appears to act as one of the more important factors in protecting children from child sexual abuse. Caring and supportive adults remain critical to child development across the lifespan and may be a key process in creating resilient developmental pathways into adulthood. Finally, there is an urgent need to bridge the gap between research and practice. Frontline providers, particularly forensic specialists, child protection workers, and clinicians should be provided adequate education and training to competently perform investigations, assessment and evidence-based interventions as they emerge.

Summary of Evidence-Based Practice Points

In conclusion, we offer the following evidence based practice points to assist in forensic assessment and intervention:

1. Child sexual abuse is more prevalent among the general population than is reflected in child protection and crime statistics.
2. As few as 2 to 5 percent of children make erroneous or false allegations of sexual abuse.
3. More often than not, nonoffending parents are completely unaware of the abuse and, upon leaning that their child is being abused, take action to protect and support their children.
4. Disclosure of child sexual abuse is typically delayed, often well into adulthood.
5. Disclosure is a process, which sometimes includes recantations and retractions of abuse allegations, influenced by the child's attributions of blame and feelings of support and validation from others.
6. Children may experience secondary traumatization by systems interventions, including

multiple investigative interviews, medical examinations, testifying in the presence of the offender, and removal from their primary caregiver.

7. Investigation of child sexual abuse allegations is more effective when a multidisciplinary team approach is implemented. The MDT model reduces multiple interviews of the child, improves decision-making and communication among professionals, and often results in more successful prosecution of the offender.

8. Specialized forensic interview strategies, forensic evaluation protocols, and forensic medical examinations are designed to reduce iatrogenic impact, while also producing more consistent, reliable evidence used to prosecute offenders.

9. Empirically based, abuse-specific measures combined with clinical assessment strategies should be utilized in assessing the child victim, nonoffending parent, family and other social/environmental factors.

10. Cognitive-behavioral interventions demonstrate efficacy in reducing PTSD symptoms, depression, social problems, and other negative effects of child sexual abuse.

11. Families affected by sexual abuse often experience a number of other social problems, including domestic violence, substance abuse, poverty, marital problems, poor communication and poor boundaries. Intervention should address these issues, in conjunction with clinical abuse-specific treatment of the child.

12. Intervention and treatment in child sexual abuse requires specialized knowledge and skills. Professionals interested in this field should receive ongoing education and training to most effectively meet the child victim's and family's needs.

REFERENCES

Adams-Tucker, C. (1982). Proximate effects of sexual abuse in childhood: A report of 28 children. *American Journal of Psychiatry, 139*(10), 1252–1256.

Alaggia, R. (2004). Many ways of telling: Expanding conceptualizations of child sexual abuse disclosure. *Child Abuse & Neglect, 28*, 1213–1227.

American Academy of Pediatrics Committee in Child Abuse and Neglect. (1999). Guidelines for evaluation of sexual abuse of children: Subject review. *Pediatrics, 103*, 186–191.

Allard-Dansereau, C., Hebert, M., Tremblay, C., & Bernard-Bonnin, A. C. (2001). Children's response to the medical visit for allegations of sexual abuse: Maternal perceptions and predicting variables. *Child Abuse Review, 10*, 210–222.

Bensley, L., Ruggles, D., Wynkoop-Simmons, K., Harris, C., Williams, K. et al. (2004). General population norms about child abuse and neglect and associations with childhood experiences. *Child Abuse & Neglect, 28*, 1321–1337.

Berliner, L., & Conte, J. J. (1995). The effects of disclosure and intervention on sexually abused children. *Child Abuse & Neglect, 19*, 371–384.

Bolen, R. (2001). *Child Sexual Abuse: Its scope and our failure.* New York: Kluwer Academic.

Boney-McCoy, S., & Finkelhor, D. (1995). Prior victimization: A risk factor for child sexual abuse for PTSD-related symptomatology among sexually abused youth. *Child Abuse & Neglect, 19*(12), 1401–1421.

Brennan, M., & Brennan, R. E. (1988). *Strange language: Child victims under cross examination* (3rd ed.). Wagga Wagga, NSW, Australia: Riverina Murray Institute of Higher Education.

Briere, J. (1996). *Trauma Symptom Checklist for Children (TSCC) professional manual.* Odessa, FL: Psychological Assessment Resources, Inc.

Briere, J., Johnson, K., Bissada, A., Damon, L., Crouch, J. et al. (2001). The Trauma Symptom Checklist for Young Children (TSCYC): Reliability and association with abuse exposure in a multisite study. *Child Abuse & Neglect, 25*, 1001–1014.

Briere, J., & Elliot, D. (2003). Prevalence and psychological sequelae of self-reported childhood physical and sexual abuse in a general population sample of men and women. *Child Abuse and Neglect, 27*, 1205–1222.

Briere, J., & Runtz, M. (1993). Childhood sexual abuse: Long-term sequelae and implications for psychological assessment. *Journal of Interpersonal Violence, 8*, 312–330.

Brilleslijper-Kater, S. N., Friedrich, W. N., & Corwin, D. L. (2004). Sexual knowledge and emotional reaction as indicators of sexual abuse in young children: Theory and research challenges. *Child Abuse & Neglect, 28*, 1007–1017.

Campis, L. B., Hebden-Curtis, J., & Demaso, D. R. (1993). Developmental differences in detection and disclosure of sexual abuse. *Journal of the American Academy of Child Psychiatry, 32*, 920–925.

Chaffin, M., & Schultz, S. K. (2001). Psychometric evaluation of the Children's Impact of Traumatic Events Scale Revised. *Child Abuse & Neglect, 25*, 401–411.

Cicchetti, D. (2004). An odyssey of discovery: Lessons learned through three decades of research on child maltreatment. *American Psychologist,* 731–741.

Classen, C., Palesh, O., & Aggarwal, R. (2005). Sexual revictimization: A review of the empirical literature. *Trauma, Violence & Abuse, 6*(2), 103–129.

Cohen, J., Deblinger, E., Mannarino, A., & Steer, R. (2004). A multisite, randomized controlled trial for children with sexual abuse – related PTSD symptoms. *Journal of the American Academy of Child and Adolescent Psychiatry, 43*(4), 393–402.

Cohen, J. A,. & Mannarino, A. P. (2000). Predictors of treatment outcome in sexually abused children. *Child Abuse & Neglect, 24*(7), 983–994.

Cohen, J. A., Mannarino, A. P., & Knudsen, K. (2005). Treating sexually abused children: 1 year follow up of a randomized clinical trial. *Child Abuse & Neglect, 29,* 135–145.

Cole, P., & Putnam, F. (1992). Effect of incest on self and social functioning: A developmental psychopathology perspective. *Journal of Consulting and Clinical Psychology, 60,* 174–184.

Corcoran, J. (2004). Treatment outcome research with nonoffending parents of sexually abused children: A critical review. *Journal of Child Sexual Abuse, 13*(2), 59–84.

Coulborn-Faller, K., & Henry, J. (2000). Child sexual abuse: A case study in community collaboration. *Child Abuse & Neglect, 21,* 215–1225.

Cross, T. P., Finkelhor, D., & Ormrod, R. (2005). Police involvement in child protective services investigations: Literature review and secondary data analysis. *Child Maltreatment, 10,* 224–244.

Crouch, J. L., Smith, D. W., Ezzell, C. E., & Saunders (1999). Measuring reactions to sexual trauma among children: Comparing the Children's Impact of Traumatic Events Scale and the Trauma Symptom Checklist for Children. *Child Maltreatment, 4,* 255–263.

Deblinger, E., Hathaway, C. R., Lippmann, J., & Steer, R. (1993). Psychosocial characteristics and correlates of symptom distress in nonoffending mothers of sexually abused children. *Journal of Interpersonal Violence, 8*(2), 155–168.

Deblinger, E., Lippmann, J., & Steer, R. (1996). Sexually abused children suffering from posttraumatic stress symptoms: Initial treatment outcome findings. *Child Maltreatment, 1,* 310–321.

Deblinger, E., Stauffer, L., & Steer, R. (2001). Comparative efficacies of supportive and cognitive behavioral group therapies for young children who have been sexually abused and their nonoffending mothers. *Child Maltreatment, 6*(4), 332–343.

Deblinger, E., Steer, R., & Lippmann, J. (1999). Two-year follow-up study of cognitive-behavioral therapy for sexually abused children suffering posttraumatic stress symptoms. *Child Abuse & Neglect, 23,* 1371–1378.

Demarest-Tingus, K., Heger, A. H, Foy, D. W., & Leskin, G. A. (1996). Factors associated with entry into therapy in children evaluated for sexual abuse. *Child Abuse & Neglect, 20,* 63–38.

DiLillo, D. (2001). Interpersonal functioning among women reporting a history of childhood sexual abuse: Empirical findings and methodological issues. *Clinical Psychology Review, 21,* 553–576.

Elliot, A., & Carnes, C. (2001). Reactions of nonoffending parents to the sexual abuse of their child: A review of the literature. *Child Maltreatment, 6*(4), 314–331.

Everson, M., Hunter, W., Runyon, D., & Edelsohn, G. (1989). Maternal support following disclosure of incest. *America Journal of Orthopychiatry, 59*(2), 197–207.

Faller, K.C. (1988). The myth of the "collusive mother." *Journal of Interpersonal Violence, 3*(2), 190–196.

Finkelhor, D. (1984). *Child sexual abuse: New theory and research.* New York: Free Press.

Finkelhor, D. (1994a). Current information on the scope and nature of child sexual abuse. *The Future of Children, 4,* 31–53.

Finkelhor, D. (1994b). The international epidemiology of child sexual abuse. *Child Abuse and Neglect, 18,* 409–417.

Finkelhor, D. (1995). The victimization of children: A developmental perspective. *American Journal of Orthopsychiatry, 65,* 177–193.

Finkelhor, D., & Browne, A. (1985). The traumatic impact of child sexual abuse: A conceptualization. *American Journal of Orthopsychiatry, 55,* 530–541.

Finkelhor, D. & Kendall-Tackett, K. (1997). A developmental perspective on the childhood impact of crime, abuse, and violent victimization. In D. Cicchetti & S. Toth (eds.), *Rochester symposium on developmental psychopathology (Vol. 8): Developmental perspectives on trauma: Theory, research, and intervention.* Rochester, NY: University of Rochester Press.

Finkelhor, D., Ormrod, R., Turner, H., & Hamby, S. (2005). The victimization of children and youth: A comprehensive, national survey. *Child Maltreatment, 10,* 5–25.

Friedrich, W. (1998). Behavioral manifestations of child sexual abuse. *Child Abuse and Neglect, 22,* 523–531.

Friedrich, W., Fisher, J. L, Dittner, C. A, Acton, R., Berliner, L. et al. (2001). Child sexual behavior inventory: Normative, psychiatric, and sexual abuse comparisons. *Child Maltreatment, 6,* 37–49.

Ghetti, S., Alexander, K.W., & Goodman, G. (2002). Legal involvement in child sexual abuse: Consequences and interventions. *International Journal of Law and Psychiatry, 25,* 235–251.

Giovannoni, J., & Becerra, R. (1979). *Defining child abuse.* New York: Free Press.

Goodman, G., Quas, J., Bulkley, J., & Shapiro, C. (1999). Innovations for child witnesses: A national survey. *Psychology, Public Policy, and Law, 5,* 255–281.

Goodman, G., Taub, E. P., Jones, D. P. H., England, P., Port, L. K., Rudy, L. et al. (1992). Testifying in criminal court. *Monographs of the Society for Research in Child Development, 57.*

Goodman-Brown, T. B., Edelstein, R. S., Goodman, G. S., Jones, D. P. H., & Gordon, D. S. (2003). Why children tell: A model of children's disclosure of sexual abuse. *Child Abuse & Neglect, 27,* 525–540.

Hartman, C., & Burgess, A. (1989). Sexual abuse of children: Causes and consequences. In D. Cicchetti & V. Carlson (Eds.), *Child maltreatment: Theory and research on the causes and consequences of child abuse and neglect* (pp. 95–128). New York: Cambridge University Press.

Haugaard, J. (2000). The challenge of defining child sexual abuse. *American Psychologist, 55,* 1036–1039.

Henry, J. (1997). System intervention trauma to child sexual abuse victims following disclosure. *Journal of Interpersonal Violence, 12,* 499–512.

Heriot, J. (1996). Maternal protectiveness following the disclosure of intrafamilial child sexual abuse. *Journal of Interpersonal Violence, 11*(2), 181–194.

Hunter, W. M., Wanda, Coulter, M. L., Runyan, D., & Everson, M.D. (1990). Determinants of placement for sexually abused children. *Child Abuse & Neglect, 14,* 407–417.

Hutchison, E. (1994). Child maltreatment: Can it be defined? In R. Barth, J. Berrick & N. Gilbert (Eds.), *Child welfare research review* (pp. 5–15). New York: Garland.

Illinois Department of Social Services. (1985). *Child abuse and neglect investigation decisions handbook.* Springfield, IL: Author.

Institute for the Advancement of Social Work Research. (2003). Social work contributions to public health. Bridging research and practice in preventing violence. Lessons from child maltreatment and domestic violence. Retrieved October 2003 from http://www.IASWRESEARCH.ORG.

Jones, L. M., Cross, T. P., Walsh, W. A., & Simone, M. (2005). Criminal investigations of child abuse: The research behind "best practices." *Trauma, Violence & Abuse, 6*(3), 254–268.

Kazdin, A. E., & Weisz, J. R. (1998). Identifying and developing empirically supported child and adolescent treatments. *Journal of Consulting & Clinical Psychology, 66,* 19–36.

Kendall-Tackett, K., Williams, L. M., & Finkelhor, D. (1993). Impact of sexual abuse on children: A review and synthesis of recent empirical studies. *Psychological Bulletin, 113,* 164–180.

Kolko, J., & Strong, E. (1997). Multidisciplinary team approaches to the investigation and resolution of child abuse and neglect: A national survey. *Child Maltreatment, 2,* 61–72.

Korbin, J. (1994). Sociocultural factors in child maltreatment. In G. B. Melton & F. D. Barry (Eds.), *Protecting children from abuse and neglect. Foundations for a New National Strategy.* (pp. 182–223). New York: Guilford Press.

Korbin, J., Coulton, C., Lindstrom-Ufuti, H., & Spilsbury, J. (2000). Neighborhood views on the definition and etiology of child maltreatment. *Child Abuse & Neglect, 24,* 1509–1527.

Lindsey, D.(1994). *The welfare of children.* New York: Oxford Press.

London, K., Bruck, M., Ceci, S., & Shuman, D. W. (2005). Disclosure of child sexual abuse: What does the research tell us about the ways that children tell? *Psychology, Public Policy & Law, 11,* 194–226.

Lovett, B. (2004). Child sexual abuse disclosure: Maternal response and other variables impacting the victim. *Child and Adolescent Social Work Journal, 21*(4), 355–371.

Manion, I. G., McIntyre, J., Firestone. P., & Ligezinska, M. et al. (1996). *Child Abuse & Neglect, 20,* 1095–1109.

Mannarino, A. P., & Cohen, J. A. (2001). Treating sexually abused children and their families: Identifying and avoiding professional role conflicts. *Trauma, Violence & Abuse, 2,* 331–342.

Morrison, N., & Clavenna-Valleroy, J. (1998). Perceptions of maternal support as related to self-concept and self-report of depression in sexually abused female adolescents. *Journal of Child Sexual Abuse, 7*(1), 23–36.

National Child Advocacy Center (2005). Forensically sensitive therapy. Retrieved on September 20, 2005 from: http://www.nationalcac.org/professionals/model/sensitive_therapy.html.

Newman, B. S., Dannenfelser, P. L., & Pendelton, D. (2005). Child abuse investigations: Reasons for using child advocacy centers and suggestions for improvement. *Child and Adolescent Social Work Journal, 22,* 165–181.

Oates, R. K., Jones, D. P. H., Denson, D., Sirotnak, A., Gary, N. et al. (2000). Erroneous complaints about child sexual abuse. *Child Abuse & Neglect, 24,* 149–157.

Orbach, Y., Hershkowitz, I., Lamb, M. E., Sternberg, K. J., Esplin, P. et al. (2000). Assessing the value of structuring protocols for forensic interviews of alleged child abuse victims. *Child Abuse & Neglect, 24,* 733–752.

Pence, D., & Wilson, C. (1994). *Team investigation of child sexual abuse: An uneasy alliance.* Thousand Oaks, CA: Sage.

Putnam, F. Ten year research update review: Child sexual abuse. *Journal of the American Academy of Child Psychiatry, 42,* 269–278.

Rind, B., Tromonovitch, P., & Bauserman, R. (1998). A meta-analytic examination of assumed properties of child sexual abuse using college samples. *Psychological Bulletin, 124,* 22–53.

Saunders, B. E., Berliner, L., & Hanson, R. F. (Eds.). (2004). *Child physical and sexual abuse: Guidelines for treatment (Revised report: April 26, 2004).* Charleston, SC: National Crime Victims Research and Treatment Center.

Sas, L., Wolfe, D., & Gowdey, K. (1996). Children and the courts in Canada. *Criminal Justice and Behavior, 23,* 338–357.

Saywitz, K., Mannarino, A., Berliner, L., & Cohen, J. (2000). Treatment for sexually abused children. *American Psychologist, 55*(9), 1040–1049.

State of Michigan Governor's Task Force on Children's Justice and Family Independence Agency. (1999). *Forensic interviewing protocol.* Washington, D.C.: National Clearinghouse on Child Abuse and Neglect Information.

Strand, V. C., Sarmiento, T. L., & Pasquale, L. E. (2005). Assessment and screening tools for trauma in children and adolescents: A review. *Trauma, Violence & Abuse, 6,* 55–78.

Summit, R. (1983). The child sexual abuse accommodation syndrome. *Child Abuse & Neglect, 7,* 177–193.

Swanston, H., Plunkett, A., O'Toole, B., Shrimpton, S., Parkinson, P., & Oates, K. (2003). Nine years after child sexual abuse. *Child Abuse & Neglect, 27,* 967–984.

Tedesco, J., & Schnell, S. (1987). Children's reactions to child sexual abuse investigation and litigation. *Child Abuse and Neglect, 11,* 267–272.

Thomlison, B. (2004). Child maltreatment: A risk and protective factor perspective. In M. W. Fraser (Ed.), *Risk and resilience in childhood: An ecological perspective* (2nd ed.). (pp. 89–133). Washington, D.C.: NASW Press.

Trickett, P., & Putnam, F. (1998). Developmental consequences of child sexual abuse. In P. Trickett & C. Schellenbach (Eds.), *Violence against children in the family and the community* (pp. 39–56). Washington, D.C.: American Psychological Association.

Trickett, P., & Putnam, F. (1993). Impact of child sexual abuse on females: Toward a developmental, psychobiological integration. *Psychological Science, 4,* 81–87.

U.S. Department of Health and Human Services (1993). *Child sexual abuse: Intervention and treatment issues.* Washington, D.C.: U.S. Department of Health and Human Services, Administration for Children and Families.

U.S. Department of Health and Human Services, Administration on Children, Youth and Families. (2005). *Child maltreatment 2003.* Washington, D.C.: U.S. Government Printing Office.

U.S. Department of Justice (1997). *Law enforcement response to child abuse.* Washington, D.C.: U.S. Department of Justice, Office of Juvenile Justice and Delinquency Prevention.

U.S. Department of Justice (2000). *Juvenile offenders and victims: 1999 National Report.* Washington, D.C.: U.S. Department of Justice, Office of Juvenile Justice and Delinquency Prevention.

Whitcomb, D. (2003). Legal interventions for child victims. *Journal of Traumatic Stress, 16,* 149–157.

Wolfe, D. A., & McGee, R. M. (1991). Assessment of emotional status among maltreated children. In R. H. Starr & D. A. Wolfe (Eds.), *The effects of child abuse and neglect: Issues and research.* New York: Guilford Press.

Wolfe, V. V., Gentile, C., Michienzi, T., Sas, L., & Wolfe, D. A. (1991). The Children's Impact of Traumatic Events Scale: A measure of post-sexual abuse PTSD symptoms. *Behavioral Assessment, 13,* 159–383.

RESOURCE GUIDE FOR PRACTITIONERS

The following websites are helpful resources in searching for evidence-based practice in the forensic and social services. This list is in no way exhaustive but is meant to serve as a guide.

Government-Sponsored Sites

ADMINISTRATION FOR CHILDREN AND FAMILIES: NATIONAL CLEARINGHOUSE ON CHILD ABUSE AND NEGLECT – GATEWAYS TO INFORMATION: PROTECTING CHILDREN AND PROTECTING FAMILIES *(http://www.nccanch.acf.hhs.gov).* This website is a service of the Children's Bureau, Administration for Children and Families, U.S. Department of Health and Human Services. It provides practical, timely, and essential information on programs, research, legislation, and statistics related to the safety, permanency, and well-being of children and families.

OFFICE OF JUVENILE JUSTICE DELINQUENCY PREVENTION (OJJDP) MODEL PROGRAMS GUIDE *(http://www.ojjdp.gov).* This website profiles more than 175 prevention and intervention programs that can be searched by program category, target population, risk and protective factors, effectiveness rating, and other parameters.

NATIONAL CRIMINAL JUSTICE REFERENCE SERVICE LIBRARY (NCJRS) *(http://www.ojjdp.gov/publications/ncjrslibrary.html* and *http://www.ncjrs.org).* Administered through OJJDP, this website offers justice and substance abuse information to support research, policy, and program development worldwide. The abstracts database provides criminal and substance abuse information, in addition to information related to juvenile justice. The database contains summaries of more than 170,000 publications.

SUBSTANCE ABUSE AND MENTAL HEALTH SERVICES ADMINISTRATION (SAMHSA) AND CENTER FOR SUBSTANCE ABUSE PREVENTION (CSAP): MODEL PROGRAMS AND NATIONAL REGISTRY OF EFFECTIVE PROGRAMS *(http://www.samhsa.gov* and *http://modelprograms.samhsa.gov)*. This website provides information about substance abuse and mental health programs tested in communities, schools, social service organizations, and workplaces in the United States. Nominated programs are reviewed by research teams who rate the programs primarily on methodological quality but also consider other factors such as theoretical development and community involvement. Programs are rated in increasing order of quality as either promising, effective, or model.

Nonprofit Organizations, Research Groups and Other Helpful Sites

AMERICAN ACADEMY OF CHILD AND ADOLESCENT PSYCHIATRY *(http://www.aacap.org)*. This site provides information on the treatment developmental, behavioral, and mental disorders in children and adolescents, current research, and practice guidelines.

AMERICAN PROFESSIONAL SOCIETY ON THE ABUSE OF CHILDREN (APSAC) *(http://www.apsac.org)*. This national nonprofit organization focuses on meeting the needs of professionals engaged in all aspects of services for maltreated children and their families. APSAC promotes research and publishes evidence-based guidelines in assessment, interviewing, and protection of victims of child sexual abuse.

AMERICAN PROSECUTORS RESEARCH INSTITUTE *(http://www.ndaa.org/apri)*. This is a nonprofit research and program development resource and national clearinghouse for information on the prosecutorial function; committed to providing interdisciplinary responses to the complex problems of criminal justice. Provides training in forensic interviewing protocol, *Finding Words*.

ASSOCIATION FOR THE TREATMENT OF SEXUAL ABUSERS (ATSA) *(www.atsa.com)*. This is a nonprofit,

interdisciplinary organization founded to foster research, facilitate information exchange, further professional education and provide for the advancement of professional standards and practices in the field of sex offender evaluation and treatment; Focused specifically on the prevention of sexual abuse through effective management of sex offenders.

CAMPBELL CRIME AND JUSTICE COORDINATING GROUP *(http://www.aic.gov.au/campbellcj)*. Hosted by the Australian Institute of Criminology, this group is an international network that prepares, updates and disseminates systematic reviews of high-quality research conducted worldwide, on effective methods to reduce crime and delinquency or improve justice.

NATIONAL CENTER ON SEXUAL BEHAVIOR OF YOUTH *(http://www.ncsby.org)*. National training and technical assistance center developed by the Office of Juvenile Justice and Delinquency Prevention and the Center on Child Abuse and Neglect, University of Oklahoma Health Sciences Center. NCSBY is designed to provide states with information and support through national training and technical assistance in the management of children with sexual behavior problems and adolescent sex offenders.

NATIONAL CHILDREN'S ADVOCACY CENTER (NCAC) *(http://www.nationalcac.org)*. The NCAC is a national nonprofit organization that provides training, prevention, intervention and treatment services to fight child abuse and neglect; promotes professional education, research, and the development of child advocacy centers nationwide; publishes best practices and intervention protocols in cases of child sexual abuse.

NATIONAL CHILD TRAUMATIC STRESS NETWORK (NCTSN) *(http://www.nctsn.org)*. Treatment centers from all over the U.S. have come together to form a new coalition, currently comprised of 54 centers. Its purpose is to improve the quality, effectiveness, provision, and availability of therapeutic services delivered to all children and adolescents experiencing traumatic events. The Network develops and disseminates effective, evidence-based treatments; collect data for systematic study; and help to educate professionals and the public about the effects of trauma on children.

RAPE, ABUSE AND INCEST NATIONAL NETWORK (RAINN) *(http://www.rainn.org)*. National organization which created and operates the National Sexual Assault Hotline at 1.800.656.HOPE; educates the public about sexual assault; and leads national efforts to improve services to victims.

SAFER SOCIETY FOUNDATION *(http://www.safersociety.org)*. National nonprofit agency providing research, advocacy, and referral services in the prevention and treatment of sexual abuse.

SOCIETY OF CHILD AND ADOLESCENT PSYCHOLOGY & NETWORK ON YOUTH MENTAL HEALTH *(http://www.effectivechildtherapy.com)*. This site provides up-to-date information about evidence-based mental health practice for children and adolescents. Treatments listed here have been evaluated scientifically for efficacy and are updated as new treatment research is completed.

STOP IT NOW! *(http://www.stopitnow.com)*. National nonprofit agency employs a public health approach to preventing and intervening in child sexual abuse; it promotes public policy, public education, and research programs; and it also established the first helpline (1-888-PREVENT) available for individuals and families to call for support and access to resources.

Chapter 18

Battered Women: Prevalence, Warning Signs, Assessment Issues, and Intervention

Albert R. Roberts and Beverly J. Roberts

Christy, a 24-year-old college graduate who now manages a restaurant, was physically abused and stalked by a former boyfriend when she was 18, during her freshman year at college. Christy reported that she still has nightmares from time-to-time in which a current boyfriend (after the batterer) became violent towards her. She wonders if the nightmares and lethargy will ever permanently go away. (Christy's traumatic experience and her quickly and permanently breaking up with her first abusive boyfriend was facilitated by a trusting relationship with her parents, the usefulness of a police report and restraining order, and her therapy sessions with a clinical social worker.)

Pamela, a 29-year-old school teacher with two young children and a devout Roman Catholic, initially thought the emotional and physical abuse from her husband was due to the enormous stress associated with his being a medical student. Pamela convinced herself that the abuse would end as soon as her husband completed his residency and had his own medical practice. (Pamela's physical abuse lasted for several years after her husband was established as a respected physician. The turning point was the sound advice she received from her priest. As the duration and frequency of abusive incidents increased, Pamela would try to cope by praying and going to church almost every day.) Finally, she confided in both her priest and her mother. Pamela's priest urged her to take her children and leave her husband. Pamela also took her mother's advice and joined a support group at the local battered women's shelter which is sponsored by Catholic Charities. Pamela was able to leave her husband, move back to her parents' home with her children, and file for divorce (Roberts & Roberts, 2005, pp. 3–4 & 52).

These two case illustrations illustrate some of the outcomes, sleep disturbances, cognitions and rationalizations, and turning points for battered women.

Violence against women, also known as intimate partner violence, is unpredictable, harmful, and life-threatening, and much more prevalent then many people realize. Intimate partner abuse is one of the most harmful, traumatic, and life-threatening social work and public health problems in American society. Intimate partner abuse continues to be the single greatest health threat to American women between the ages of 15 and 50. More women sustain injuries as a result of intimate partner abuse than from the combined total of muggings and accidents.

- Every 9 seconds in the United States, a woman is assaulted and battered.
- Each year, 8.7 million women are victims of intimate partner violence.
- Over 90 percent of the victims of domestic violence are women.
- Every day, four women are murdered by boyfriends, husbands, and former intimate partners.
- Domestic violence is the number one cause of emergency room visits by women.
- Women are most likely to be killed when attempting to leave the abuser.
- The number one cause of women's injuries is abuse at home.

• Approximately one in every four women in America has been physically assaulted and/or raped by their intimate partners at some time in their life (Roberts & Roberts, 2005, p. 4).

The most accurate statistics on the lifetime prevalence of intimate partner violence comes from the National Violence Against Women Survey conducted by Professors Patricia Tjaden and Nancy Thoennes with grants from the National Institute of Justice and the Centers for Disease Control and Prevention (CDC). This study was based on telephone interviews with a nationally representative sample (N=16,000) of 8,000 men and 8,000 women, and indicated that 25 percent of the women and 7.6 percent of the men stated that they had been physically battered and/or raped by a spouse, cohabiting partner, or date during their lifetime. These national figures document the high prevalence and consequences of intimate partner abuse. However, in actuality some women are at much greater risk of becoming victims of intimate partner violence than other groups of women. Women at the highest risk of encountering violence from dates and steady boyfriends are high school and college students.

Zero tolerance for any type of intimate partner abuse or violence is critically important. In fact, in a dating, cohabiting, or marital relationship, there is never an excuse, justification or rationalization that allows a man (or adolescent boy) to hit a woman (or an adolescent girl). The professional literature on domestic violence is replete with citations of the horrendous problems that ensue when women have become involved in long-term relationships in which they are assaulted on a frequent basis. The author's research and practice goal is to educate social workers as well as young women and their families and friends regarding the full spectrum of violent relationships. Thus, we ultimately want to help to transmit the latest information such as the fact that there is a very likely progression, over time, from the initial first incident of being knocked down, pushed, or kicked to becoming the victim of severe beatings later on (Roberts & Roberts, 2005).

One 21-year-old woman who has solid benefits from her good therapeutic relationship with a clinical social worker (following her having been punched by a boyfriend when she was 17) now makes it a practice to tell all men she starts to date that she has a *zero*

tolerance for violence in her dating relationships. She explains that she was slapped and punched three times by her first boyfriend, and she will not allow herself to go through that type of disrespect and trauma again. In other words, no more three strikes and you're out. One abusive incident is more than enough. Thus far, her boyfriends have been sensitive to her previous victimization, and she has not been abused again. But her attitude is that, "I need to set forth these boundaries right up front, on the very first date, to reinforce to every guy I date that this isn't going to happen to me ever again. And if, in the future, I meet a guy who is put-off by my dating ground-rules, then good riddance to him!" (Roberts & Roberts, 2005, p. 6).

DOMESTIC VIOLENCE WARNING SIGNS AND ISSUES

1. Some women in dating and marital relationships think they are madly in love and as a result are willing to overlook, deny potential danger, and minimize *all* of the male's faults – including being slapped or punched occasionally when he is drunk or upset about what is happening at school or on his job. Typically, minimization involves cognitions and recollections such as I only had a small bruise on my face, and it is no big deal since my stepfather broke my mother's nose and jaw when I was a teenager. Another example would be: "I only had to go to the emergency room once for five stitches in the past four years."

2. Some women are so overly forgiving, kindhearted, or gullible that – even though immediately after being slapped or punched they were numb and in shock, and determined to break up with their abusive partner – they quickly relented when the boyfriend made profuse apologies, promised that it would never happen again, and brought them flowers and other expensive gifts.

3. Blaming themselves, also known as blaming the victim, is another all too common occurrence. These women seem to feel guilty, and believe that they did something to provoke the boyfriend's anger like forgetting to bring home a six-pack of beer or his favorite vodka and, as a result, he was justified in lashing out violently. All couples disagree and even argue from time to time. But some women have the faulty thinking that if they behave "perfectly" and

don't do anything to make the boyfriend upset, then he won't ever hit them again, and, conversely, if he does become violent, then she is at fault for causing him to become so angry.

4. The intergenerational cycle of domestic violence can also be a factor. For example, some women have been raised in a home where violence was commonplace, and they witnessed their father or stepfather beating their mother. In addition, during their childhood some women were abused physically or sexually by parents, step-parents, siblings, or other relatives. For many of these women, being victimized by a boyfriend or partner becomes part of the pattern of violence that has shaped their childhood. These women will benefit greatly from therapy provided by a psychologist or social worker with expertise in this type of problem.

ASSESSMENT

There are different methods of assessing and measuring both domestic violence, and the mental health consequences of woman battering. Several studies demonstrate that severity and duration of abuse, trauma and crisis symptoms, anxiety, depression, sleep disturbances, lack of social support, inadequate coping skills, low self-esteem, and family stressors are "good" indicators for someone in the helping profession to look for when attempting to detect or identify victims. In fact, Jackson, Petretic-Jackson, and Witte (2002) stressed that assessment protocols should be developed to assess PTSD, depression, trauma, alcohol abuse, and attitudes among domestic violence and sexual assault victims. They developed a seven-step process to follow when interviewing with victims:

1. examine the nature and circumstances of the assault
2. postassault interaction with professionals and social support
3. victim initial reaction (symptoms that are physical, cognitive, emotional, mental)
4. Current status (coping as well as the above mentioned)
5. Course of psychology symptoms and psychological history (i.e., suicide attempts)
6. Attributions – how do they feel they are doing?
7. Future Orientation-short-term plans

Assessment can also be done in the emergency room. Roberts and Roberts (2002) note that ER staff should be immediately involved in discussions with the patient and taking her "history." They should attempt to determine the availability of supportive relatives and assist with making referrals. ER intervention in the past was seen as an invasion of privacy. In addition, requesting staff to "get involved" was seen as an added burden to ER staff, which was already overworked. Today, views have changed somewhat. Often staff are responsive, supportive, and offer referrals to emergency shelters and crisis counselors, but they must do so consistently and convincingly (Roberts & Roberts, 2002).

Although the Women's Movement has assisted victims of domestic violence and continues to do so, these efforts are limited in that the provision of services is *reactive*. That is, service providers intervene when women (or others on their behalf) request assistance (Abbott & Williamson, 1999). Their study confirms previous research that has indicated that health care professionals receive little, if any, training/education in domestic violence. In their study, just over 16 percent received some domestic violence training (58% of health visitors, 10% of general practitioners, 10.5% of practice nurses, and 15% of midwives). However, the training was very limited, mainly half- or one-day workshops. Virtually all respondents said they were not adequately trained and 86 percent said they had inadequate knowledge of available services (Abbott & Williamson, 1999).

The American College of Obstetricians and Gynecologists has suggested a four-part program for physicians-education, the provision of materials that keep them up to date on resources, campaigning for the provision of adequate services, and working to raise public awareness (Jones, 1993). Findings suggest that health care professionals do not see domestic violence as an issue where they can play a major role. They are not screening for it or supporting and empowering women. In addition, assessment is not routine (McGrath, Bettacchi, Duffy, Peipert, Becke, & St. Angelo, 1997). Most primary care physicians do not inquire at annual visits about abuse. In fact, one study found that only 6 percent of women were asked personal questions about their safety (Hamberger, Saunders, & Houg, 1992).

To assist in assessment, a *proactive* stance must be taken. According to the American Medical Association, all female patients entering emergency rooms, surgery,

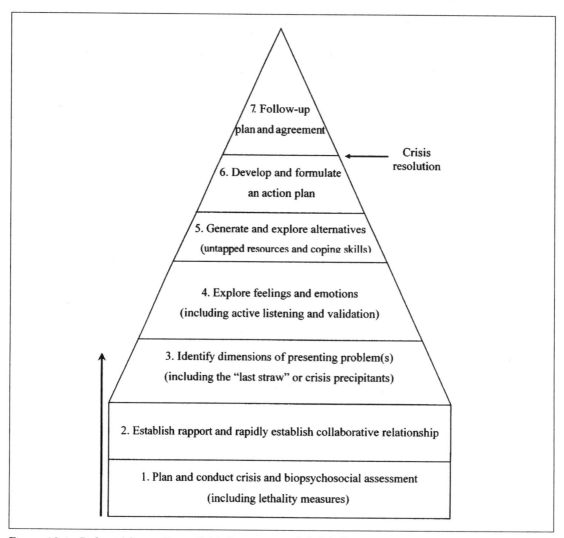

Figure 18-1. Roberts' Seven Stage Crisis Intervention Model. Source: Copyright © Albert R. Roberts, 1991. Reprinted by permission of the author.

primary care facilities, pediatric, prenatal, and mental health facilities should be screened for domestic violence. The goal should be to assess all women entering the health care system and screening for domestic violence, *even for those without a history of abuse*. This effort at *primary prevention* can remove the precipitating causes of abuse (Boes & McDermott, 2002).

SAFETY PLANNING

Our research and other studies have documented the elevated risk of severe and life-threatening injuries to survivors when they begin to permanently leave their abusive partner. We recommend that women in abusive relationships proceed with caution and be alert to the overt as well as the subtle cues and warning signs of danger and an escalation of violence. Woman trapped in battering and coercive relationships should plan ahead and utilize a strategic safety plan. We now illustrate how one of the women in our study used a safety plan.

Sally, a 25-year-old administrative assistant with one small five-year-old child, had been repeatedly abused by her husband, Carl, during a four-year-period. As a result of the repetitive abuse and her own lack of self-esteem, Sally has experienced an inability to concentrate, anxiety, nightmares, and depression. The turning point for Sally occurs when Carl comes home drunk from his job as a construction worker, and during his violent rage he breaks her jaw. Soon after he passes out in a drunken stupor, Sally takes her daughter and drives to the hospital emergency room for treatment. Sally finally decides that she must leave the batterer, and she starts to implement the safety plan she had been given during a previous phone contact with a domestic violence hotline.

Four weeks earlier, following Carl's previous drunken attack on her, he had promised that he would stop drinking and go to Alcoholics Anonymous (AA) meetings. Sally had decided that she would give Carl one last chance to stay sober, since his violence always erupted when he had been drinking. However, Sally also knew that in the past Carl had told her that the drinking would stop, but within a few weeks, he had returned to his old ways of stopping off at the bar on his way home from work. This time, Sally had prepared the following Safety Plan (Roberts & Roberts, 2005).

1. Sally leaves the house with her purse and her daughter, and drives to the emergency room. While en route to the hospital, she calls her best friend, Judy, from her cell phone and asks her to meet them at the hospital. Sally asks Judy to bring all of the emergency items that Judy had been keeping for her, such as two small suitcases with clothing, and a few toys for her daughter, the daughter's birth certificate, marriage license, and extra cash. At the emergency room (ER), the social worker takes photographs of Sally's injuries, emergency medical treatment is provided, and the hospital contacts the police and a battered women's shelter. Sally also signs release forms so that the police, county prosecutor, and/or her attorney can obtain medical records relatively quickly. When Sally is medically cleared to leave the ER, the domestic violence advocate from the battered women's shelter accompanies her and the little girl to the police station to get a copy of the temporary restraining order. After leaving the police station, Sally and her daughter are housed at a shelter for battered women.

For obvious reasons, the locations of most battered women's shelters are highly confidential and extensive efforts are made to prevent batterers from learning the location.

The following are responses from one of our earlier national surveys, which describe the ways in which shelters for battered women react to domestic violence crises such as Sally's:

The House of Ruth in Alabama would immediately give the client food and other physical necessities. Upon entering the shelter, she is asked if she would prefer talking about her ordeal or getting some sleep and talking the next day. The complete intake would be handled the next day, after the client has had a chance to rest. When the client is ready, the staff would explain the options and the consequences of her choices. The staff help the client to recognize her own feelings, support her decisions, provide advocacy, and assist her in obtaining her goals.

The Domestic Violence Shelter in Oregon: Women who have been abused and their children are welcomed and are offered food, blankets, and a room to sleep. The next day the staff have a one-on-one meeting to finish the paperwork and let the client debrief. It is important to tell her she is brave and strong to have left the batterer. The shelter staff listen to her story without judging her. Let her tell her story in her own words as many times as she needs to. If she wants it, give her information on the cycle of violence; tell her she's not crazy; give her information on resources, and offer to help her get through barriers to services.

The Family Crisis Center of Baltimore County, Maryland, conducts a crisis intake in which they assess the nature and intensity of the crisis. They provide shelter for up to 31 days. The shelter provides counseling and makes referrals to appropriate agencies, including Legal Aid. This shelter utilizes these techniques in order to empower the client: (1) Take slow steps. (2) Make client aware of the judicial system. (3) Encourage her to look at all options. (4) Set up regular counseling sessions while at the crisis shelter. (5) Encourage client to design with staff members emergency plans in case she decides to return to the abuser after leaving the shelter. The philosophy is that the shelter staff cannot make anyone do anything that she is not ready to do.

Horizon House Shelter for Women in Pennsylvania: In addition to the above mentioned focus on the abused woman, this shelter provided information on ways that they would provide assistance to the children: The staff inquire about possible injuries to the children. They work to reassure the children about being in a strange place, e.g., involve the children in selecting their bed, toys, etc. and showing them the play area and for school-age children, and the classroom where individual and group instruction takes place.

Unity House in upstate New York: In addition to the services that the other shelters provide, Unity House transports the abused women with mental health problems to the local community mental health clinic where clinical social workers responsive to survivors of domestic violence provide individual treatment. Unity House also helps the women to find an attorney who is knowledgeable and experienced about domestic violence to explore custody, visitation, and divorce provisions that will protect the woman and her children. It is extremely important for attorneys to understand the dynamics of domestic violence, how to assess lethality and severity, how to present evidence of domestic violence to the court, and to advocate for reasonable financial support and custody of the children.

Every individual in an abusive dating, cohabiting, or marital relationship (as well as those who recently ended an abusive relationship) should create a personalized safety plan. It is important to plan ahead so that when the woman makes the decision to leave the abusive partner, she does it as safely and expeditiously as possible. All too often the man's anger and violent outbursts escalate when the wife/girlfriend tries to leave the abusive relationship, file for divorce, or show signs of independence. Since the abusive male may then become desperate and more volatile, it is critically important for the woman to develop a safety plan ready for quick mobilization.

Once a violent incident has occurred in the relationship, the battering is highly likely to reoccur. The research study discussed in this book demonstrates that the longer a woman stays in an abusive relationship, the greater the likelihood that she will experience more severe and more frequent physical abuse. The escalation of violence takes place even when the man apologizes profusely and promises to change in the aftermath of the battering incident. In addition, the batterer frequently tries to isolate the woman from her former close friends and relatives, making it more difficult for her to turn to those friends and relatives for help when she decides to leave the relationship.

Step-by-Step Safety Plan and Survival Kit

There are a number of planning strategies and actions that an abused woman can put in place so that she and/or her children do not have to be battered again.

Contemplation, Planning, and Preparation:

- Make a mental image of *all* escape routes including front, back, and side exit doors, first floor windows, garage exits, elevators, stairwells, and/or fire escapes in case you need to leave your apartment or house quickly.
- Become aware of the precursors and warning signs of an imminent attack such as drug and alcohol abuse; increased verbal abuse; anger, rage, and terroristic threats; recent breakup, separation, or divorce due to domestic violence, major depression, or other mental illnesses; abuse of pets; suicidal or homicidal threats; and/or punching the wall, throwing objects, or destroying furniture
- Keep your purse and an extra set of car keys ready and accessible for a quick exit, if necessary. Decide ahead of time whether your means of transportation will be car (in which case you should have car keys, registration, and certificate of title), taxi, bus, or train and make sure you have credit cards or cash to pay for transportation, food, and housing if necessary. If you are fearful of keeping these emergency items in your regular purse (or in an old purse), then consider hiding them in your house (as long as they are easy to get to in an emergency), outside your house or with a trusted friend or neighbor. Prepare your children by teaching them how to dial 911 in case of another assault.
- Select a safe and secure place to go to such as the home of a trusted and non-judgmental friend or relative, or a motel, or an emergency shelter for battered women. The "safe place" should be one where the abuser will not be able to find you. Therefore, even if you are very friendly with the neighbor next door, that residence is not good as a long-term "safe place" because it is probably the first place the batterer would search for

you. (However, the neighbor's home may be helpful in an emergency, as a place to wait for a few minutes while the police arrive.)

- In case you need emergency transportation to escape from the batterer, have the phone numbers of the following resources easily accessible: police 911, domestic violence detective division, a victim assistance program, a battered women's shelter, and a crisis intervention hotline.
- Select a code word to use with your children, neighbors, or close relatives when you need them to call the police for you.
- If you have an Order of Protection (temporary or permanent restraining order), keep it with you at all times. Notify all close friends, neighbors, relatives, co-workers, and clergy of the protective order. Make a duplicate copy of the Order of Protection and give it to a friend or relative for safekeeping, in the event that the batterer finds and destroys the original.
- If you work in a different county or city from where you live, give a copy of the order of protection to the police department nearest to where you work.
- In case you escape to another city or county, there usually is a county registry of protection orders through which all police departments can telephone to verify or get a copy of the Order of Protection.
- If you have an Order of Protection and you hear or suspect that the batterer is outside your door or window, or, if you are away from home and he is lurking in your vicinity, immediately call police dispatch 911 for help.

During a Violent Incident:

- If the abusive partner starts to yell at, or threaten you, try to get to a room that is near the front or back door (not the bathroom or kitchen because of potential weapons such as razors and knives in these rooms).
- If possible, carry a small cell phone, which is kept in your pocket at all times, not in a purse. If he is attacking you and you are able to be out of his sight for a brief time, use the cell phone to call 911 police emergency. Some communities have a program that provides *free* cellular phones for battered women to use to contact the police.

These phones are preprogrammed to 911 and can be used *only* to call the police. Usually, a woman would not be able to receive this type of cell phone unless she has an active Order of Protection. For further information on the availability of free cellular phones, contact your *local police department* or the Toll-Free *National Domestic Violence Hotline at 1-800-799-SAFE (7233)* or the *National Coalition Against Domestic Violence at (303) 839-1852.*

- Whenever you feel you are in imminent danger or after an assault has begun, try to leave as quickly as you can and use your cell phone, or go to a public place to call the police, a 24-hour domestic violence or crisis intervention hotline, or a battered women's shelter for help. An alternative is to go to a friend or relative's house or apartment and call for help from there.
- Use your code word so your children or next door neighbor can call 911. An alternate method is having a whistle or ADT electronic pendant alarm. This type of pendant alarm is available in more than 200 cities across the United States. The woman wears this pendant around her neck, and if she is in danger from the batterer, she activates it by pushing the button on the pendant; it sends a silent alarm to ADT, which, in turn, notifies the police to respond immediately.
- If you are injured, even if the injuries appear to be relatively minor, go to your physician's office, a clinic, or hospital emergency room. Tell the nurse or doctor what happened and ask them to photograph your injuries for the records. Also, tell them that you want to sign a waiver/release form so that the county prosecutor or your private attorney can obtain copies of the medical records relatively quickly when necessary.
- If possible, save evidence including torn or bloody clothing, photographs of your injuries and/or destruction of property. Be sure to get a copy of the police report and investigation, and names and addresses of any witnesses (e.g., neighbors).
- Talk to someone about your options. Depending upon whether you live in a large city or small town there are always advocates to assist and support you in whatever decisions you make; for example, domestic violence advocates at the local battered women's shelter, victim advocates

at the prosecutor's victim/witness assistance program, police-based crisis counselors or peer advocates, hospital emergency room social workers or nurses, counselors at the local women's center that specialize in providing services to domestic violence and sexual assault victims.

Survival Kit

Have copies of the following important documents in a safe place (e.g., a bank safe deposit box — if it is in your own name, *not* jointly registered) or leave copies with a trusted friend or relative. If you decide to keep these items in a bank safe deposit box, select a secure and accessible place to keep the key. In some relationships, the man is so domineering and controlling that he keeps all of the important household documents locked away where his wife cannot get to them. If you cannot get access to some of the items listed below, that is okay. But it is essential that you keep track of your personal papers, such as your birth certificate, driver's license, and Social Security card (Roberts & Roberts, 2005).

- your birth certificate,
- your Social Security card,
- your driver's license,
- credit cards and ATM cards,
- your children's birth certificate(s),
- a prepaid long distance calling card,
- a picture of your injuries from an earlier abusive incident (I.D. to serve court papers),
- your house deed, apartment lease, rental agreement or mortgage bill,
- your income tax forms from last year,
- your passport or green card,
- your children's school records,
- your pay stubs or unemployment insurance booklet,
- any disability award letter, court support letter, court statement of unpaid child support,
- your insurance papers,
- medical records for all family members.

CONCLUSION

If you have the time to activate a plan to leave the abuser, have a suitcase ready which contains essential clothing, medication and prescriptions, a checkbook, and cash. Include toiletries such as deodorant, toothpaste, and toothbrushes. Other important items are valuable jewelry, family pictures and keepsakes, address books, your children's favorite toys, and books. If possible, remove from the home any items that have special meaning for you or your children, including the family pet. Some of these items can be stored with a friend or relative. The reason for removal of items that have special meaning (e.g., a gift from your grandmother) is the possibility that when the batterer learns you have left, he may vent his anger on household objects that he knows were valuable to you. *However, if your decision to leave is made hastily — due to a particularly violent attack — the most important action is to protect yourself (and your children) by leaving the abuser as quickly as possible.* If you seek assistance from the police and/or a shelter for battered women, they will help you to retrieve your essential belongings later. Among your documents should be any legal papers such as separation agreements, divorce papers, custody papers and/or restraining orders, as well as any papers that document joint ownership.

In Chapter 25 of the *New Jersey Criminal and Vehicle Handbook* (2C Code), there are specific rules for police officers to follow regarding the development of training courses on domestic violence. In 2C;25-20 the development of a training course and the curriculum are discussed, and changes effective 6/17/2001 are italicized. According to these rules, the Attorney General is responsible for ensuring that all law enforcement officers attend initial training within 90 days of appointment and annual in-service training of at least four hours. (Before 6/17/2001 the training was required biannually). In addition, the Administrative Office of the Courts is responsible for developing and approving the training courses and the curriculum on the handling, investigation, and response procedures concerning allegations of domestic violence. This training course is to be reviewed at least every two years, and modified by the AOC as necessary. Judges and judicial personnel must attend initial training within 90 days of their appointment and annual in-service training.

According to 2C:25-20 (3):

> The Division of Criminal Justice and the Administrative Office of the Courts shall provide that all training on the handling of domestic violence matters shall include information concerning the impact of domestic

violence on society, the dynamics of domestic violence, that statutory and case law concerning domestic violence, the necessary elements of a protection order, policies and procedures as promulgated or ordered by the Attorney General or the Supreme Court, and the use of available community resources, support services, available sanctions and treatment options. Law enforcement agencies shall: (1) establish domestic crisis teams or participate in established domestic crisis teams, and (2) shall train individual officer in methods of dealing with domestic violence and neglect and abuse of the elderly and disabled. The teams may include social workers, clergy or other persons trained in counseling, crisis intervention or in the treatment of domestic violence and neglect and abuse of the elderly and disabled victims (Courtesy of New Jersey State Police, 2000).

Although it is difficult to establish PTSD prior to a lethal incident, mental health professionals should learn to identify the typical characteristics of a battered woman experiencing symptoms, and diagnosis it as soon as possible. In order to do so, victims of domestic violence must go to health care providers for assistance. Thus, police, prosecutors, and judges need to be aware of programs for these women, and stress that victims utilize these services. Mental health professionals need more training, members of the criminal justice system need to be more aware of the plight of a battered woman, and victims of domestic violence need to know of the resources available to them by getting the proper medical attention before, during and after the domestic violence relationship has ceased.

REFERENCES

Abbott, P., & Williamson, E. (1999). Women, health and domestic violence. *Journal of Gender Studies, 8*(1): 83–102.

Aguilar, R. L., & Nightingale, N. N. (1994). The impact of specific battering experiences on the self-esteem of abused women. *Journal of Family Violence, 9*, 35–45.

American Psychiatric Association. (2000). Diagnostic and statistical manual of mental disorders: DSM-IV-TR (updated 4th ed.). Washington, D.C.: American Psychiatric Association.

Appel, A. E., & Holden, G. W. (1998). The co-occurrence of spouse and physical child abuse: A review and appraisal. *Journal of Family Psychology, 12*(4):578–599.

Astin, M. C., Lawrence, K. J., & Foy, D. W. (1993). Posttraumatic stress disorder among battered women: Risk and resiliency factors. *Violence and Victims, 8*, 17–28.

Astin, M. C., Ogland-Hand, S., Coleman, E. M. , & Foy, D. W. (1995). Posttraumatic stress disorder and child abuse among battered women: Comparison with martially distressed women. *Journal of Consulting and Clinical Psychology, 63*, 308–312.

Boes, M., & McDermott, V. (2002). Helping battered women. In Albert R. Roberts (Ed.), *Handbook of domestic violence intervention strategies*. New York: Oxford University Press.

Campbell, J. C., Kub, J., Belknap, R. A., & Templin, T. (1997). Predictors of depression in battered women. *Violence Against Women, 3*, 276–293.

Campbell, J. C., & Soeken, K. L., (1999). Women's responses to battering over time: An analysis of change. *Journal of Interpersonal Violence, 14*(1), 21–33.

Cascardi, M., & O'Leary, K. D. (1992). Depressive symptomology, self-esteem, and self-blame in battered women. *Journal of Family Violence, 7*, 249–259.

Dobobitz, H., Black, M. M., Kerr, M. A., Hussey, J. M., & Newberger, E. H. (2001). Type and timing of mothers; victimization: Effects of mothers and children. *Pediatrics, 107*(4), 728–735.

Follingstad, D. R., Brennan, A. F., House, E. S., Polek, D. S., & Rutledge, L. L. (1991). Factors moderating physical and psychological symptoms of battered women. *Journal of Family Violence, 6*, 81–95.

Gelles, R. J., & Harrop, J. W. (1989). Violence, battering, and psychological distress among women. *Journal of Interpersonal Violence, 4*, 400–420.

Gleason, W. J. (1993). Mental disorders in battered women: An empirical study. *Violence and Victims, 8*, 53–68.

Golding, J. M. (1999). Intimate partner violence as a risk factor for mental disorders: A meta-analysis. *Journal of Family Violence, 14*(2), 99–132.

Gormezy, N. (1983). Stressors of childhood. In N. Gormezy & M. Ritter (eds.), *Stress, coping and development in children* (pp. 43–84). New York: Mc Graw-Hill.

Haj-Yahia, M. M. (2000). Implications of wife abuse and battering for self-esteem, depression, and anxiety as revealed by the second Palestinian National Survey on Violence Against Women. *Journal of Family Issues, 21*(4), 435–463.

Hamberger, L. K., Saunders, D. G., & Houg, J. (1992). Prevention of domestic violence in community practice and rate of physician inquiry. *Family Medicine, 24*, 283–287.

Hattendorf, J., Otten, A. J., & Lomax, R. G. (1999). Type and severity of abuse and post traumatic stress disorder symptoms reported by women who kill abusive partners. *Violence Against Women, 5*(3):292–312.

Housekamp, B. M., & Foy, D. W. (1991). The assessment of posttraumatic stress disorder in battered women. *Journal of Interpersonal Violence, 6*, 367–375.

Jackson, T. L., Petretic-Jackson, P. A., & Witte, T. H. (2002). Mental health assessment tools and techniques for Working with battered women (pp. 278–297). In Albert R. Roberts (Ed.), *Handbook of domestic violence intervention strategies.* New York: Oxford University Press.

Jones, L, Hughes, M., & Unterstaller, U. (2001). PTSD in victims of domestic violence. *Trauma, Violence, & Abuse, 2*(2): 99–119.

Jones, R. (1993). Ending the cycle. *The Black Bag, 5*(3): 6–8.

Kemp, A., Rawlings, E. I., & Green, B. L. (1991). Post-traumatic stress disorder (PTSD) in battered women: A shelter sample. *Journal of Traumatic Stress, 4*, 137–148.

Kruttschnitt, C., & Dornfeld, M., (1992). Will they tell? Assessing preadolescents' reports of family violence. *Journal of Research in Crime and Delinquency, 29*(2): 136–147.

Martin, J.P. (2002). McGreevey seeks plan to counter rise in New Jersey crime. *The Newark Star Ledger,* Sept 22, 2002, p 1, 4.

McGrath, M. E., Bettacchi, A., Duffy, S. J., Peipert, J., Becke, B. M., & St. Angelo, L. (1997). Violence against women: Provider barriers to intervention in emergency departments. *Academy of Emergency Medicine, 4*, 297–300.

Merton, P., & Mohr, P. B. (2000). Incidence and Correlates of PTSD in Australian victims of domestic violence. *Journal of Family Violence, 15*(4):419–421.

O'Keefe, M. (1998). Posttraumatic stress disorder among incarcerated battered women who killed their abusers and those incarcerated for other offenses. *Journal of Traumatic Stress, 11*, 71–85.

Perrin, M. S., Van Hasselt, V. B., Basilio, L., & Hersen, M. (1996). Assessing the effects of violence on women in battering relationships with the Keane MMPI-PTSD Scale. *Journal of Traumatic Stress, 9*, 805–816.

Petretic-Jackson, P. A., Witte, T. H., & Jackson, T. L. (2002). Battered women treatment goals and treatment planning in A.R. Roberts (Ed.), *Handbook of domestic violence intervention strategies.* New York: Oxford University Press.

Robertiello, G. M. *Urban versus suburban victims of domestic violence.* (unpublished Final Report). Paper presented at the Academy of Criminal Justice Sciences Annual Conference, March, 2002).

Robertiello, G. M. (2003). Victim perceptions of the utility of domestic violence arrests and temporary restraining orders: A qualitative study. In A.R. Roberts (Ed.), *Critical issues in crime and justice,* (2nd ed.). Newbury Park, CA: Sage.

Roberts, A. R. (1996). Battered women who kill: A com-para-tive study of incarcerated participants with a community sample of battered women. *Journal of Family Violence, 11*, 291–304.

Roberts, A. R. (2002). (Ed.) *Handbook of domestic violence intervention strategies.* New York: Oxford University Press.

Roberts, A. R., & Schenkman Roberts, B. (2002). A comprehensive model for crisis intervention with battered women and their children. In A.R. Roberts (Ed.), *Handbook of domestic violence intervention strategies.* New York: Oxford University Press.

Roberts, A. R., & Schenkman-Roberts, B. (2005). *Ending intimate abuse: Practical guidance and survival strategies.* New York: Oxford University Press.

Roberts, G. L., Williams, G. M., Lawrence, J. M., & Raphael, B. (1998). How does domestic violence affect women's mental health? *Australian Women's Health, 28*, 117–129.

Rosen, D. (1999, March). *The impact of violence on the lives of teenage mothers.* Paper presented at the Annual Conference for the Council for Social Work Education, San Francisco.

Rossman, R. R. (1998). Descartes' error and PTSD. In G. W. Holden, R. Geffner, & E. N. Jouriles (Eds.), *Children exposed to marital violence* (223–256). Washington, D.C.: American Psychological Association.

Silvern, L., Karly, J., Waelde, L., Hodges, W. F., Starek, J., Heidt, E., & Min, K. (1995). Retrospective reports of parental partners abuse: Trauma symptoms and self-esteem among college students. *Journal of Family Violence, 10*(2), 177–202.

Simmons, R. L., Wu, C., Johnson, C., & Conger, R. D. (1995). A Test of various perspectives on the intergenerational transmission of domestic violence. *Criminology, 33*(1):141–171.

Stark, E., & Flitcraft, A. (1996). *Women at risk domestic violence and women's health.* London: Sage.

Uniform Crime Reports. (2000). *Crime in New Jersey.* Trenton, NJ: State of New Jersey, Division of State Police.

Vaz, K. M. (1995). *Black women in America.* Thousand Oaks, CA: Sage.

Vitanza, S., Vogel, L. C. M., & Marshall, L. L. (1995). Distress and symptoms of posttraumatic stress disorder in abused women. *Violence and Victims, 10*, 23–24.

Weissman, M., & Klerman, G. (1992). Depression: Current understanding and changing trends. *Annual Review of Public Health, 13*, 319–339.

Weissman, M., Bland, R., Canino, G, Faravelli, C., Greenwald, S., Hwu, H., Joyce, R., Karam, E., Lee, C., Lellouch, J., Lepine, J., Newman. S., Oakle-Browne, M., Rubio-Stipec, M., Wells, J., Wickramaratne, P., Wittchen, H., & Yeh, E. (1997). The cross-national epidemiology of panic disorder. *Archives of General Psychiatry, 54*, 305–309.

Widom, C. S. and Maxfield, M. G. (2001). *An update on the "cycle of violence."* Washington, D.C.: NIJ. U.S. Department of Justice.

www.census.gov

www.ncptsd.org

www.psych.org

www.surgeongeneral.gov

Chapter 19

Social Work and Survivor Assistance

Arlene Bowers Andrews

INTRODUCTION

Victimization may be the most common problem addressed by social workers, regardless of their specialization or employment. Of course, social workers see crime survivors when they work in programs that specialize in survivor services, but they also see them in all other settings, such as nursing homes, mental health and addictions treatment programs, schools, correctional facilities, and the host of other practice settings. Every competent social worker should be prepared to respond when any client discloses victimization. This chapter provides an overview of the basic knowledge that a social worker needs with regard to victimization and survivor services and directs the reader to additional resources for skills development. Topics include magnitude of the problem, a conceptual framework for social work action, evolving standards for effective practice, and resources for further study.

The term *survivor* is used here to refer to any person who has lived through a victimizing experience because it reflects the intrinsic strength and power of the person who is forced to adapt after a victimizing experience. This terminology deviates somewhat from the prevalent use of the terms *crime victim* and *victim services*, which are products of the criminal justice system, where victims are often treated as helpless. A social work approach to victimization assumes a more empowering approach. Here the term *victim* will be reserved for those who died as a result of the crime (except when referring to specific aspects of or direct quotations from criminal justice systems information). *Direct* survivors are those who personally experienced the victimization, including those who lost a loved one to death by victimization. *Indirect* survivors are those who share the suffering and losses because of their relationships to direct survivors or victims.

The focus here is social work responses to survivors of crime, which includes acts that could result in criminal charges against an offender, whether charges are brought or not. People are also victimized through noncriminal events such as disaster, accidents, disease, or population exploitation, but the human intent in a criminal act creates a psychological and social context that precipitates particular psychosocial effects in the survivor. The social worker's role is to prevent and address these effects.

MAGNITUDE OF THE PROBLEM

Victimization is far too common. Actual rates are difficult to determine because multiple methods are used to asses and report crime incidence and victimization rates (Kilpatrick & Acierno, 2003). A synopsis of recent statistical reports about various criminal victimization rates illustrates the enormous magnitude of this problem.

In 2003, U.S. residents age 12 or older experienced approximately 24 million crimes, of which 77 percent were property crimes and 22 percent crimes of violence (U.S. Dept. of Justice, 2005a). When victimization data is examined over multiyear periods, the conclusion is that 99 percent of Americans will be victimized, some only by minor property crimes, at some point in their lives (U.S. Dept. of Justice, 1987). For many the crime is serious: about 9.3 percent of the U.S. population has lost a relative or close friend to murder or substance-related vehicular homicide (Amick-McMullan et al., 1991).

Major disparities in victimization rates exist among population groups (U.S. Dept. of Justice, 2005b). In 2003, by race/ethnicity, for every 1,000 persons in each racial group, 29 blacks, 22 whites, and 16 persons of other races experienced a violent crime. Between 1992–2001, American Indians suffered violence at rates twice as often as blacks, 2.5 times more than whites, and 4.5 times more than Asians (Perry, 2004). By gender, except for rape/sexual assault, males had higher rates than females for other violent crimes. By socioeconomic status, people with an annual income under $7,500 were robbed and assaulted at significantly higher rates than people in households earning more.

Victimization particularly affects people of all ages who depend on others for their care. In the U.S. in 2003, people referred 2.9 million cases of child abuse and neglect to child protective services (CPS). Of these, evidence existed to verify that 906,000 children needed protection (U.S. DHHS, 2004a). For at least 1,400 children, help did not arrive in time and they died (U.S. DHHS, 2004b). In 2000 police investigated over 2,900 incidents of child pornography (Finkelhor & Ormrod, 2004).

Frail older people are also particularly vulnerable. Between 1 and 2 million Americans age 65 or older have been injured, exploited, or otherwise mistreated by someone on whom they depended for care or protection (Bonnie & Wallace, 2002). And studies have shown that people with development disabilities have a four to 10 times higher risk of becoming crime victims than persons without disabilities (Milberger et al., 2002).

Hate crimes target some groups. Across the U.S. during 2003, law enforcement reported 9,091 victims of bias crimes, of which 45 percent were for reasons of race, 16 percent for religion, 16 percent for sexual orientation, 15 percent for ethnicity-national origin, and 0.1 percent for disability (FBI, 2004).

Crimes against women are not officially recognized as hate crimes, though many would argue they are motivated by misogyny. In the U.S., 14.8 percent of women are survivors of rape at some point during their lifetimes (Tjaden & Thoennes, 2000). Amnesty International (2001) summarizes the global plight of crimes targeted at women as follows:

Every day in the United States, an average of four women are murdered by their husbands or boyfriends; a woman is raped every 6 minutes; a woman is battered every 15 seconds. In North Africa, 6,000 women are genitally mutilated each day. This year, more than 15,000 women will be sold into sexual slavery in China. Two hundred women in Bangladesh will be horribly disfigured when their spurned husbands or suitors burn them with acid. More than 7,000 women in India will be murdered by their families and in-laws in disputes over dowries. In every armed conflict investigated by Amnesty International in 1999 and 2000, the torture of women was reported, most often in the form of sexual violence.

The U.S. State Department's fifth annual *Trafficking in Persons Report* (2005) states that 600,000 to 800,000 people are trafficked across international borders each year, many others are trafficked within their own countries, and four in five survivors are women and half are children.

One in 12 women and one in 45 men will be stalked in their lifetimes (Tjaden & Thoennes, 1998). Stalking often precedes murder for women: 76 percent of femicide victims and 85 percent of attempted femicide victims had been stalked by their intimate partners in the year prior to their murder (McFarlane et al., 1999). Stalking may lead to assaults at the workplace. The U.S. Department of Labor (2004) reported 639 of 8,786 deaths at the job were due to homicide.

There's more. Social workers have been killed or attacked on the job. People get killed or injured by drunken drivers. Some lose their retirement pensions to fraudulent investment schemes. Others suffer diseases and injury induced by corporate criminal negligence leading to environmental toxicity or workplace dangers. Children get exposed to gang violence and school bullies. They watch their parents get battered, even killed. Teens shoot one another. Family members disappear or die due to organized crime wars or political disputes. Travelers get abducted or robbed. People accused of crimes get abused, as the world witnessed through photos at the Abu Ghraib prison in Iraq, and people convicted of crime face high risks of victimization while imprisoned.

Crime victimization is a global problem. The *International Crime Victim Survey* (1997) found that more than a third of urban dwellers in the world do not feel safe in their own neighborhoods and that no more than 10 percent of crime survivors, including those in the U.S., received help from a specialized victim assistance agency within their country. Survivors of crimes in an international context, such as when a citizen of one country is victimized in another or parents abduct noncustodial children and take them abroad, have special needs that are beginning to be addressed by agreements across countries (National Victim Assistance Academy, 2002).

People of all nationalities suffer terrorist attacks perpetrated by international political networks, special interest extremist groups, or lone eccentrics. In the past decade, Americans have died or been injured at the hands of terrorists in Afghanistan, Atlanta, Iraq, Madrid, London, New York City, Saudi Arabia, Somalia, Yemen, and many other places.

Contrary to popular media images, the world is not cleanly divided between perpetrators and victims, evil and good. Studies of perpetrator populations reveal most have been victimized themselves (Herrenkohl, Mason, & Kosterman, 2004; Lipsey & Derzon, 1998; Smith & Thornberry, 1995; Widom & Ames, 1994) and are at high risk of future victimization. The relationships are complex.

The litany of horrors goes on and on. The data above describe the victimizing acts, not their effects. For each act, the survivor may suffer psychological, social, physical, economic, and other losses (Amick-McMullan et al., 1991; Kilpatrick & Acierno, 2003). Although many survivors show remarkable resilience, a rather massive literature documents the association of particular victimizing acts with specific effects in large numbers of survivors. Stress responses following assault tend to be higher for women than men, young adults than older adults, and African Americans than whites (Norris, 1992). Social workers tend to be involved in treating such mental health effects as depression, anxiety, phobia, aggression, post-traumatic stress disorder (PTSD), panic disorder, dissociative disorder, chronic stress syndromes, substance abuse, social withdrawal, behavioral problems in children, and work and relational problems in adults.

Cohen, Miller and Rossman (1994) review approaches to calculating the financial cost of victimization, noting costs include direct costs to survivors such as property loss, medical and mental health care expenses, and lost income from disrupted employment as well as indirect costs such as increased insurance premiums and lost business due to fear of crime. Society incurs costs in the form of law enforcement, prosecution, defense, judiciary, corrections, shelter and other protective resources, victim assistance, and other substantial responses (Clark, Biddle, & Martin, 2002). Rational and irrational fear of victimization inhibits development of harmonious communities (Warr, 1994).

Such a massive problem requires intensive, universal action.

CONCEPTUAL FRAMEWORK FOR SOCIAL WORK ACTION

Social work with crime survivors starts with grounding in values, ecological context, and a continuum of care ranging from preventive to recovery interventions.

Value Base: Human Rights, Civil Rights

Social justice is the overarching social work ethical principle that pertains to survivors. The concept of justice can be interpreted in many ways though most people would say that after a shattering experience, justice has to do with making things right and whole again. Survivors generally seek the following: safety or protection from the offenders, restoration of a psychological sense of safety, a chance to tell their stories of the victimization and its consequences from their own perspectives and truly be heard, answers to questions about the crime, financial reparations for harms incurred and loss of work, and full accountability by the offenders (Kelly & Erez, 1997; Underwood, 2003). Survivors rely on many segments of their communities to help them attain justice, including nonprofit organizations that focus on survivor services, health and mental health systems, employers, personal networks, civil courts, and others, although some of their most significant interactions are with the various sectors of the criminal justice system.

Driven by ideology of compassion and respect for survivors, most states have passed legislation to assure certain victims' rights (NVCAN, 2005) within the criminal justice system, including rights to information, to assistance, to be heard, to attend trials and hearings, to protection from intimidation and harm, and to financial compensation. Such victims' rights are essentially civil rights pertaining to the relationship of individuals to governments. All personnel in these systems are supposed to be trained to respond to victim needs and rights. Many organizations and offices within the criminal justice system have designated victim specialists to support survivors as they exercise their rights.

The United Nations' *Declaration of Basic Principles of Justice for Victims of Crime and Abuse of Power* encourages governments to address not only survivors of criminal acts but also persons who, ". . . individually or collectively, have suffered harm, including physical or mental injury, emotional suffering, economic loss or substantial impairment of their fundamental rights, through acts or omissions that do not yet constitute violations of national criminal laws but of internationally recognized norms relating to human rights" (1989, Part B, 18).

The principles further encourage governments to incorporate into national law norms prescribing abuses of power and provide remedies such as resolution, compensation, and necessary material, medical, psychological, and social assistance. Under such principles, for example, undocumented immigrants who have restricted civil rights would have victim rights simply because they have human worth and dignity. And mutilation of women, though not illegal in certain jurisdictions, would be a violation of human rights norms.

Victim Services Network (VSN) (1999) has developed a code of ethics for providers of services to crime survivors. The code, while covering conduct included in the NASW *Code of Ethics*, also addressing such matters as informing clients of their rights, avoiding attribution of blame, and acting to promote crime prevention. Given that many survivor services providers are paraprofessional, having ethical principles to guide conduct is crucial.

Ecological Context

Each crime and each survivor is unique. Crime victimization evolves from a complex etiology based in the social environment (Andrews, 1992). Forces in individuals, family and social networks, communities, and society promote and maintain victimization and must be targeted for change in order to reduce victimization rates. Likewise, forces in this ecological context promote social competencies and the availability and quality of protection and coping assistance for survivors. Strengthening these prosocial forces reduces victimization risks and the long-term damage that can result from the aftermath of victimization.

The following case illustrates the individual nature of survivor responses. Each survivor was exposed to the same victimizing event, but her response was unique.

Shaundra, Teresa, and Elsa, high school students, stayed at school until after dusk. Walking home together, they were confronted by a gang of young men from a nearby neighborhood who taunted them, pursued them when they ran, and forced them into an alley in an isolated area. One by one, the girls were raped and then left, bruised and bleeding. Each made her way home.

Shaundra, always emotionally expressive, collapsed in her mother's arms and told exactly what happened. Her mother called 911 and EMTs arrived to take Shaundra to the hospital, where a sexual assault crisis team tended her physical and mental health needs. Shaundra talked about her emotional devastation and received supportive counseling for two years after the assault. Her mother worked with crime victim advocates in the prosecutor's office to assure that the perpetrators were caught and prosecuted. Shaundra graduated from high school and started college as planned.

After the assault, Teresa begged Shaundra and Elsa not to tell about what happened. She knew she was already in trouble with her parents for being out after dark. Her parents, who were undocumented immigrants, feared any exposure to law enforcement officials. Teresa, typically self-sufficient, blamed herself for what happened and worked hard to pretend nothing happened. When the word got out anyway, Teresa's parent sent her to live with relatives in another city and refused participation in the prosecution. At her new home, Teresa was despondent and starting failing school. She tried attaching to several boyfriends. Within a year she was pregnant and had dropped out of school.

Elsa told her mother what happened right away. They drove to the hospital and participated in the sexual assault protocol and, later, the prosecution. Elsa, who rarely cried or expressed extreme emotions, went to a counseling session but insisted she was okay. She had trouble sleeping, though, and told no one that she was buying sleeping pills, to which she became addicted. Elsa, always quiet, became stoic, even hostile in most of her interactions with peers. She continued her education but was known as a loner. Meanwhile Elsa's brother secretly organized and executed several retaliative gang attacks.

These cases illustrate the significance of individual previctimization coping patterns and family support in survivors' responses to victimization. Other factors in the social environment also influence survivors. At the social network level, people spend considerable time in small groups such as friendship networks, classes, and work teams. These groups are directly affected when one of their members is victimized, as was Elsa's brother's gang. The intentional support group is a primary intervention with survivors, particularly in response to violence against women. Understanding individual, family, and small group dynamics and knowing how to facilitate preventive and healing interventions for survivors at each level is a core role for social workers.

At the macro-level, social workers also have roles to play in promoting organizational, community, policy, and cultural responses to victimization. At the organizational level, social workers can apply their skill at developing and managing organizational structure and processes to prevent "secondary victimization," which occurs when the very organizations that are supposed to be helpful cause additional harm, as when child protective service agencies propose to take children from battered women. They can advocate for more effective responses when organizations fail to support survivors. They can promote workplace policies that support crime survivors, such as time off for court attendance, and train staff in faith-based and other organizations to provide comfort and resources.

At the community level, coordinated planning and action, sometimes accomplished through comprehensive community initiatives, can promote more effective responses from the diverse sectors that are critical to crime prevention and survivor services, including law enforcement, emergency services, health care, mental health care, child and vulnerable adult protective services, schools, housing, and other formal systems. Social workers can also help to develop informal networks for emotional, material, and informational support in communities. Many communities have unique cultural characteristics and require survivor supports that are adapted to their particular needs. Sometimes entire communities, such as the network of people affected by a school shooting, need intervention.

At the broadest level of the environment, social workers are involved in efforts to change societal attitudes of tolerance for violence and blaming victims. They have pushed hard to promote local, state, and federal policies (including legislation, administrative rule-making, and judicial decisions) that support survivors. The past three decades have produced massive reform in policies, though much remains to be done to assure policies are implemented as intended, without unanticipated harmful consequences.

Victimization Process and Social Work Responses

Within this ecological context, victimization occurs as a dynamic process that can be influenced by intentional social work interventions, summarized in Figure 19-1. A brief overview of the victimization process follows, then the remainder of the chapter is organized according to survivor services system responses, with emphasis on evidence-based practices.

In an ideal world, personal, community, and societal competencies and resources would prevent the risk of victimization. People would resolve conflict peaceably, share mutual support, tolerate differences, participate actively in their communities, and assure equitable distribution of resources. Many of the factors that create the offender's propensity for crime would be contained. Primary prevention aims to build communities and individual lives with such assets.

Certain factors, known as risk and precipitating factors, tend to precede victimizing acts. Risk factors, which may be causal or not, are conditions known to be associated with increased probability that victimization will occur. From a population perspective, certain groups, typically those least able to protect themselves, are more at risk of victimization than others (e.g., people with disabilities, with smaller stature, in low-income groups). Certain life conditions, such as family instability or homelessness, are associated with higher risks. Secondary prevention targets the risk factors for change so that the probability of victimization is reduced.

Precipitating factors are those that immediately precede the victimizing act in time and space. Even if a perpetrator has the propensity for committing a crime and a vulnerable victim is near, certain situational factors increase the probability that the victimization will actually occur. For example, the probability of sexual assaults in the case above may have been reduced if no alley was accessible, neighbors were outside, law enforcement officers were patrolling, or

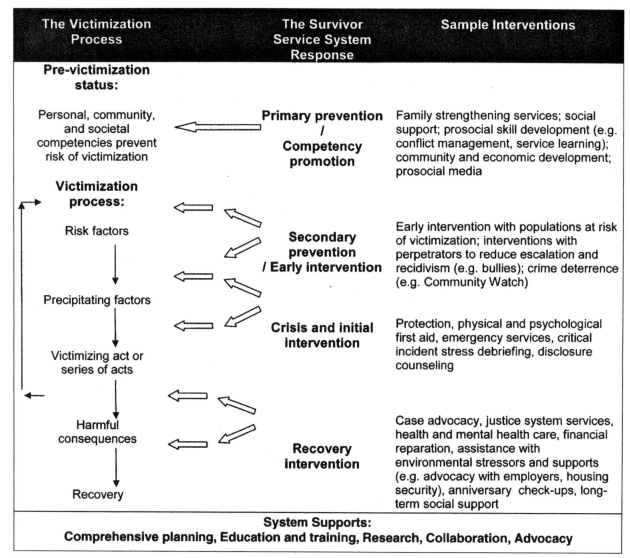

Figure 19-1. The victimization process and social work response.

emergency call buttons were at hand. Secondary prevention also aims to eliminate precipitating factors.

When victimization occurs, it may take many forms. For example, some acts are singular, sudden, and severe. Others take place chronically, leaving survivors under perpetual threat of injury, as in cases of hostages, family violence, or neglect of dependent family members. Help comes in the form of crisis intervention when victimizations become known. In some cases, the victimizing experience is not disclosed until long after the threat has passed. In any case, crisis or initial intervention aims to assure

safety and reduce the likelihood of lasting or escalating harm.

After the emergency phase, interventions are therapeutic and supportive, designed to remediate the harms and reduce further deterioration. By addressing consequences, social workers help survivors begin the process of recovery, which may take a lifetime. During recovery, the survivor feels a sense of normalcy and works to cope adaptively. The victimization is not forgotten but is integrated into the survivor's life.

A key challenge is developing delivery systems that assure all survivors have access to culturally competent assistance when they need it, at any point in the victimization process. This requires infusion of preventive, risk reduction, crisis intervention, and recovery services throughout societal institutions.

EVIDENCE-BASED PRACTICE

The remainder of this chapter highlights evidence-based practices to prevent and treat victimization. The list below is not exhaustive of all promising practices that are currently being demonstrated, but emphasizes controlled research studies or expert consensus that confirm certain practices are effective. In general, far more studies have described survivors, offenders, and the etiology of particular victimizing acts than have examined what works to effectively and sustainably reduce crime or promote survivor recovery. This review focuses on invention studies and draws from multiple disciplines because social workers are likely to find themselves in interdisciplinary contexts when they work in the field of survivor services.

One overarching principle that applies to services at any level is the requirement of cultural competence on the part of the practitioner. Social workers must be aware of their own cultural limitations and open to understanding other cultures. For example, ethnicity may affect symptomology, as demonstrated by studies that show African American and Hispanic children have more severe and extended emotional and behavioral problems following sexual abuse (Sanders-Phillips et al., 1995). It may also affect helpseeking, given that historically oppressed groups may fear law enforcement organizations. Social workers should be prepared to facilitate interpretation for people with communication barriers such as deafness or limited English-speaking capacity. Though presenting the range of skills required to assure cultural competence is beyond the scope of this chapter, those skills are intrinsic to adopting the practices discussed here.

Another overarching principle is that survivor services should be provided at the community level through a seamless system of high quality caregiving programs. These programs would address emotional, psychological, financial, and physical support to crime survivors. This requires cooperation across societal sectors (e.g., public, nonprofit, business, faith-based), governmental levels (federal, state, local), and service systems (criminal justice, victim services, health and mental health, child welfare, education, and others).

Primary Prevention

Primary prevention can include actions designed to influence individual behavior, such as teaching children prosocial skills so that they never become perpetrators, though it most often targets an entire population by changing societal structures and social norms. A key premise in primary prevention is that responsibility for stopping the crime is placed on the potential offender, not the potential victim. Thus many of these interventions aim to reach the potential offender population before they start to show risk symptoms.

Full Democratic Participation and Human Rights

Social workers can contribute their knowledge and skill with regard to community organization and policy development for advancement of broad social movements to promote human rights and development, which will prevent victimization. Population groups that have more substantial social, economic, and political capital are less likely to suffer victimization. For example, across the globe, postconflict survivors of civil war and political conflict embrace the rise of democracy and promotion of equitably distributed resources as a means to prevent victimization (Moser & McIlwine, 2000a, 2000b). This requires that the ruling powers make room for historically oppressed groups in political, economic, and social arenas and support their full participation. In countries where women suffered atrocities during political and civil wars, women have organized to assert their participation in rebuilding civil society, with mixed results because institutional sexism is so difficult to reform. Still, significant progress has been documented in places such as Afghanistan (Shelby, 2005), Peru (Cordero, 2001), and Northern Ireland (Cockburn, 1998). These groups are pushing for sustainable infrastructures that minimize the probability of future exploitive and oppressive political, economic, and social systems. UNIFEM, the United Nations' women's fund, fosters women's empowerment and equality and aspires to end violence against women globally.

Prosocial Media

Interpersonal violence rates vary from one country to another, with the United States consistently rising to the top (Wilhem, 2004). Many theories have been offered to explain the cultural differences. Some suggest that the ubiquitous presence of mass media and the excessive appetite that the U. S. population has for violent imagery is a contributing factor. Research suggests that media violence may not be the primary cause of violence, but it seems to be a contributing factor, and it particularly promotes a climate of tolerance that reduces political and collective will to act to stop it (Donnerstein & Linz, 1998; Berry, Gray, & Donnerstein, 1999). Carll (2003) found that tolerance for violence against women is so widespread that news reports minimize coverage when compared to reporting of crimes against men. Several meta-analytic reviews suggest that violent imagery in television, film and video, and computer games leads to aggressive and fearful behavior in children, though the results for older youth and adults are less clear (Browne & Hamilton-Giachritsis, 2005). Pornography does not seem to have a major role for sex offenders while they are committing their crime with the exception that some pedophiles use pornography to "groom" their child victims (Langevin & Curnoe, 2004; Nemes, 1992).

These studies suggest that interventions to reduce exposure to violent imagery, such as the American Psychological Association's (2005) call for measures to restrict children's exposure to violent media, may contribute to reduced aggression.

Family and Community Strengthening

The Perry Preschool Project (Schweinhart & Weikart, 1998), which has followed children well into adulthood, found that impoverished preschool children who participated in high quality child development programs were significantly less likely to commit crimes than children who did not have the benefit of such programs. Available, affordable, high quality child care is a frontline defense against victimization. Similarly, high quality schools that can respond to the unique learning needs of each child and promote the child's sense of competence tend to produce fewer offenders (Wilson, Lipsey, & Derzon, 2003).

Offenders are disproportionately likely to come from family and community environments where caregivers struggle to obtain basic supports such as income, food, housing, utilities, child care, health care, transportation, and other fundamentals (Tienda & Wilson, 2002). Inequitable distribution of resources and high concentrations of poverty tend to be associated with higher levels of social disorganization and higher victimization rates (van Wilsem, 2004) Many of their homes have absent fathers. Around the world, programs that target the reduction of poverty and its associated harms are regarded as crime prevention initiatives.

Comprehensive Community Initiatives

Given that victimization tends to be concentrated in particular geographic areas, prevention efforts have focused on organizing communities to promote social norms of intolerance for aggression and promotion of civic participation, interorganizational collaboration, youth development, school climate improvement, and a host of other activities that strengthen the social, economic, and political infrastructure of the area (Dusenbury et al., 1997; Hawkins, Van Horn, & Arthur, 2004; Hawkins, Catalano, & Arthur, 2002). Many of these initiatives incorporate positive youth development as a major component so that young people have the opportunity to exercise genuine responsibility for their communities and direct their energies in prosocial rather than antisocial directions (Catalano, Berglund, & Ryan, 2004; Herrenkohl, Hill, & Chung, 2003).

Secondary Prevention/Early Intervention

Secondary prevention targets identified at-risk populations, typically those engaging in minor antisocial acts, to reduce escalation or recidivism. Victimization can be prevented through prosocial skills training delivered at family homes, in schools, or in correctional facilities and by targeted environmental design and law enforcement protective measures at high-risk places (United Nations International Centre for Prevention of Crime, 1999).

Sherman et al. (1998) reviewed controlled research about crime prevention and concluded that substantially more research is needed, but credible evidence does exist that these programs work or show promise based on early studies:

- Comprehensive collaboratives that involve families, schools, labor markets, places, police, and criminal justice systems and are focused in geographic areas with high concentrations of serious juvenile crime;
- Volunteer mentoring of 10- to 14-year-olds by Big Brothers/Big Sisters is promising for the reduction of substance abuse, but not delinquency;
- Parent training for families with troublesome preadolescents;
- Placed-based strategies such as cameras, cash control, guards, fences, lighting, and other devices;
- Police actions such as extra surveillance at high crime "hot spots," police units focused on serious repeat offenders, proactive enforcement of drunk driving laws, and arrests of employed suspects for misdemeanor domestic violence;
- For serious offenders: prison-based therapeutic community treatment of drug-involved offenders, incapacitation of high-rate serious repeat offenders, and structured rehabilitation programs focused on individual risk factors;
- Employment programs aimed at older male ex-offenders no longer under court supervision.

Sherman and his colleagues reported that these programs do not seem to work:

- Police action such as increased random patrols of entire beats, more rapid response time to 911 calls, neighborhood watch, arrests of some juveniles for minor offenses, arrests of unemployed suspects for domestic assault, arrest crackdowns at drug markets, gun buyback programs, and community policing programs with no clear focus on crime risk factors.

Social Skills Training for Offenders and At-risk Populations

For years efforts have been made to reduce victimization by teaching potential offenders, those in populations with traits associated with high risk of criminal offending, to use prosocial rather than antisocial skills. Cognitive-behavioral (CB) approaches to skills development for young adolescents who show antisocial tendencies indicates consistent positive effects in reducing likelihood of criminal activity (Armstrong, 1991; Welsh & Farrington, 2005). Multi-systemic therapy (MST) effectively mobilizes family, school, peers, and community resources to deter at-risk youth from perpetrating (Henggeler et al., 1998). Programs that aim to change behavior but do not include counseling, such as the once-popular program "Scared Straight" that aims to induce fear of incarceration, has had no effect on at-risk populations and may actually increase crime by participants (Petrosino, Turpin-Petrosino, & Finckenauer, 2000).

With regard to convicted offenders, cognitive behavioral therapy, when used with fidelity to the model intervention and with high quality, tends to produce lower recidivism rates (Lipsey & Wilson, 1998). Unfortunately, when model programs are replicated in routine practice, the quality is often reduced and the effects diminish likewise. Research about boot camps concludes the camps generally have no effect although if they include a counseling component the effects are slightly higher (Flash, 2003). Specific treatments for offenders while in prison, such as drug abuse treatment and sex offender treatment, seem to have some, though limited, effects on recidivism (Welsh & Farrington, 2005).

Security Measures

Jan van Dijk, deputy director of the United Nations Interregional Crime and Justice Research Institute (2004), observes that across the world, people have observed that, "Opportunity makes the thief." Thus many risk reduction programs accept that some people have a propensity for crime and promote action to deter their acting on the propensity.

The most ubiquitous programs mobilize people to look for signs of suspicious activity and notify authorities. For at least two decades, every reader who has traveled through an airport has been recruited to participate in efforts to deter terrorists through audio messages that encourage travelers to report any unattended or suspicious packages. Other efforts that promote environmental designs such as street lighting seem to have a positive effect on reducing crime, as does increasing police surveillance through community policing (Sherman et al., 1998; Welsh & Farrington, 2005).

Dispute Resolution

Community-based dispute resolution programs are helpful in cases where two parties feel offended by one another. These cases can escalate to conflict and commission of serious crimes without effective resolution. Alternative dispute resolution (ADR) has particularly been embraced by large organizations to promote harmonious resolution of worksite. The U.S. Postal Service, after widely publicized workplace violence, embraced ADR and is conducting a multi-year to describe the elements of the process that work effectively (Bingham & Pitts, 2002). ADR is widely used in divorce and other family conflicts (Wissler, 2004).

Substance Abuse Prevention

Two-thirds of violent offenders admit they used alcohol or drugs at the time of the crime, so effective programs to prevent and treat substance abuse are likely to also reduce victimization. The propensity for violence may still be there, but the disinhibiting effects of the chemical will be reduced, and the rate of victimization will go down. This genre of actions includes deterrence of driving under the influence, so laws that require bartenders to report patrons who should not drive should also reduce victimization.

Crisis and Initial Intervention

Victimization may throw a survivor into a state of crisis manifest as bizarre behavior, irrational thinking, intense emotions, physical problems such as gastrointestinal or sleep disruptions, or interpersonal problems (Andrews, 1992). These are normal human reactions to abnormal circumstances. They typically subside as the threat of further victimization recedes, although continued presence of these symptoms over six weeks or more may be indications that mental health problems are emerging. Survivor service specialists have consensus that several interventions are necessary to reduce the risk that survivors will suffer further harm or develop extended problems (Cohen, Berliner, & Mannarino, 2003).

First Responses

Protection. First and foremost, when a survivor calls for help or reveals victimization, the worker conducts an assessment of safety and medical needs to determine injuries or imminent danger. Steps should be taken to determine risk to the survivor or others, contact protective authorities, provide shelter and sustenance, contact supportive family or others, protect privacy, and arrange a short-term course of action for safety.

Psychological First Aid. Victimization strips survivors of perceived control over their lives, which must be restored as soon as possible. A "Points of Consensus Document" regarding Early Psychological Intervention (EPI) has been jointly developed by the National Organization for Victim Assistance, American Red Cross, International Critical Incident Stress Foundation, and the Salvation Army (NOVA, 2005). The points emphasize the value of EPI, that it is no substitute for therapy, it is one part of a continuum of emergency responses, providers should have specialized training, and organizations providing EPI have a duty to collaborate with one another. The essence of EPI is to help the survivors express their feelings and perceptions, attain information to help them understand that their condition is not unusual, achieve a sense of connectedness, and receive information about how to get additional psychological help. The EPI provider screens for people with serious symptoms that require more intensive intervention. Psychological first responders should assess the survivor's ability to learn, which may be impaired by traumatic impact on memory and comprehension.

Normalcy. Workers should encourage survivors, even while still in distress, to exercise as much control as possible, including expressing their own needs (even if they seem irrational) and making decisions. Assistants should facilitate a return to typical daily routines as soon as possible because this will also help the survivor gain a sense of order and control.

Psychoeducation. Second-level crisis intervention (after safety & first aid needs are met) typically includes explaining the possible psychological and social effects of victimization, symptoms to monitor, where to go for help, developmentally appropriate tips for managing stress and promoting a sense of security, information about the criminal justice system, and other relevant information. Research indicates this may not stop the onset of serious mental health problems, but it will promote helpseeking so that symptoms can be treated (Bisson, McFarlane, & Rose, 2000).

Spiritual Counseling. Soon after victimization, survivors begin to reflect on the spiritual meaning of the event, using their own spiritual frame of reference. First responders should be prepared to help survivors as they express their spirituality and link them to spiritual advisers.

Victim Assistance

Thousands of organizations offer volunteer and professional assistance to survivors as they navigate the criminal justice system and their daily lives in the aftermath of victimization (United Nations, 1999). One group estimates that over 10,000 programs serve crime survivors in the U.S., but only a small fraction of survivors actually get services (Blomberg, Waldo, & Chester, 2002). Victim assistants can be found with police departments, prosecutor's offices, correctional facilities, parole programs, emergency rooms, specialized nonprofit organizations, and a host of other sponsors. Victim assistants may specialize in certain forms of crime such as sexual assault, crimes against children, criminal driving offenses, internet crimes, landmines, federal crimes, international crimes, torture, crimes against particular populations such as gays and lesbians, school-based crimes, and many other specialized fields.

The National Organization for Victim Assistance (NOVA) promotes high standards of service and coordination of care for survivors in the aftermath of victimization (Young, 1997), including coordinating a credentialing program. The role of the victim assistant is generally to provide flexible social support, information about many aspects of the postvictimization process, particularly with regard to psychosocial effects and the criminal justice system, referral for entitlements and services, assistance in completing forms or handling logistics, companionship and transportation when in contact with various organizations, advocacy to assure that the survivors' voice and needs are heard and addressed, protection of privacy, particularly from media intrusion (Young, 2001). Victim assistants offer a listening ear, provide extensive information and education, support the survivor in establishing a healthy routine (nutrition, rest, exercise, humor), facilitate social integration to prevent isolation, and link to professional individual or group therapy to support the survivor as re-exposure events occur. The victim assistant also serves as advocate to minimize the risk of secondary victimization as survivors confront slow compensation processes, harsh criminal justice system, insensitive remarks of friends or untrained clergy, The process of assistance must be done with keen sensitivity and compassion and careful discernment of each survivor's unique needs and readiness for particular types of information or support.

Victim assistants can be critical links to recovery services. After the initially seeking help during the crisis stage, many survivors enter an emotional numbing and denial stage. During this phase, they may become disconnected from helping resources so that later, if intrusive images and acutely anxious emotions recur, as they often do, the survivor is confused and isolated. Specialists in victim assistance will offer check-ups to survivors during the crisis stage, so that they can reach out and identify problems as they may emerge later.

Death Notification and Grief Therapy

Few jobs require as much skill and emotional stamina as notifying families that a loved has been killed. Law enforcement agencies generally have this challenging responsibility though effective practice guidelines support that a trained grief counselor accompany an officer to deliver the message in person (Byers, 2002; Kaul, 2001).

Mandatory Arrest

This controversial procedure, which involves required arrest of the perpetrator subsequent to a domestic violence call, seems to deter recidivism among perpetrators who are less dangerous but has no effect on those who are more violent (Glicken & Sechrest, 2003).

Shelter

The prevalent availability of shelters for women and children provides a temporary safe haven, but their effect on reducing the prevalence of violence or recidivism has not been studied. One study by Wolf-Smith and LaRossa (1992) suggested that shelters influenced women's perceptions of the abuser but did not change the abuser's aggressive behavior.

Assessing Victimization and Its Effects

The specific nature of the crime and its effects on a survivor can be difficult to determine. Precise diagnosis is critical from two perspectives: (a) the criminal justice system, which seeks to determine guilt of the perpetrator and needs evidence about the victimizing act and harm to the survivor; and (b) the recovery support system, which seeks to effectively support the survivor and treat the physical and psychological injuries and other losses. These systems may be in conflict with one another, as when a survivor prefers privacy within the recovery support system and the criminal justice system insists on disclosure for evidentiary purposes.

Social workers in mental health are often called upon to assess the psychosocial impact of crime on a survivor for purposes of treatment and evidence in court to demonstrate the severity of the crime. The essence of effective forensic practice is excellent mental health assessment skills. Numerous tools exist to facilitate reliable and competent assessment (Bentley, 2001; Harris, 2006; Roberts & Brownell, 1999), though the adversarial nature of the legal process has plunged mental health professionals into controversy over the scientific validity of certain assessment findings. Significant debate still exists about battered women's syndrome, a constellation of past-traumatic responses that have been used to acquit or commute the sentences of women who kill their batterers (Walker, 1984; 1992), and recovered memory, a documented amnesiatic process that particularly occurs in cases of childhood sexual abuse, though survivor statements can be induced by coaching, thus producing false memories (Freyd, 1998; van der Kolk, Hopper, & Osterman, 2001). Meticulous procedures should be followed to gain a reliable assessment for evidentiary or treatment purposes (AACAP, 1998).

Assessing child sexual assault can be a particularly challenging process. Palmer and Edmunds (2003) offer a two-part model procedure that would produce evidence that could meet clear and convincing standards and beyond a reasonable doubt standards. The model involves gathering information in three clusters: (1) presenting symptoms (problems), (2) sexual specificity (child's knowledge and behavior relative to developmental stage), and (3) child's report (how the child relates what happened and content of the communication). This information is supplemented by the physical examination and other evidence (e.g., witness corroboration). The assessor carefully integrates the findings from each cluster to make a determination of what is likely to have occurred. The

Children's Alliance (2005) is a network of accredited forensic centers that promote sound interdisciplinary child abuse assessment and treatment. Professional networks (some are included in Figure 19-2) also promote competent practice for particular types of victimization.

Recovery Support

Experts caution against a "cookie cutter" approach to the diverse survivor community. Assistance should be tailored to the unique needs of the survivors.

Victim-Witness Assistance in the Criminal Justice Process

The criminal justice process can take a long time, typically years, before resolution. Survivors have told stories of disrespect, lack of compassion, misinformation, exclusion, and general injustice as they followed apprehension and prosecution of the offender. Sophisticated victim assistance programs aim to prevent these harms. For example, the U.S. and Scottish governments cooperated in developing a range of supports for more than 600 surviving loved ones of the 270 victims who died in the terrorist bombing of Pan Am Flight 103 over Scotland in 1988 (National Victim Assistance Academy, 2002). Assistance included a dedicated phone line accessible toll-free from the 16 countries where survivors live, secure website, case briefings, staff to facilitate on-site assistance during the trial in the Netherlands in 2000, four remote closed circuit television sites for viewing the trial, mental health counseling, and other support.

Providers who specialize in victim assistance and advocacy must take care to facilitate the empowerment of the survivor, which requires considerable skill. Advocates have been known to disempower the people they aim to support (McDermott & Garofalo, 2004).

Victim impact statements (VIS) are written or oral information about how the crime affected the victims and survivors. Typically entered during the sentencing phase of an offender's trial, the VIS allows the survivors to participate in the process while providing valuable information of relevance to sentencing. Research indicates that survivors highly value the opportunity to make a victim impact statement (National Center for Victims of Crime, 1996).

Mental Health Treatment

Crime survivors are at risk of several mental disorders, particularly posttraumatic stress disorder (PTSD), depression, anxiety, and substance abuse (Foa & Rothbaum, 1998). Studies of mental health service utilization by crime survivors indicate that a majority do not receive services, though utilization rates vary by gender (women are more likely to get help), type crime (sexual assault survivors are most likely to get help), and diagnosis (those with PTSD are most likely to seek help) (Berliner & New, 1999; Hembree & Foa, 2003).

Overarching principles include assuring the survivor's full participation in all treatment decisions, because the need to regain control is paramount. Treatment providers should anticipate mistrust and avoidance and convey confidence in the treatment approach (Foa, Keane, & Friedman, 2000). They must consistently convey nonjudgmental attitudes even when horrific events are described and should take care to focus on the survivor's strengths and effective coping. A variety of treatment modalities has been provided to survivors, but only a few have been carefully studied to determine their effectiveness.

Cognitive-behavioral treatment (CBT). Studies of CBT demonstrate more consistent and larger effects than many other interventions. CBT essentially involves coaching survivors to examine thoughts and beliefs about situations seen as threatening and supporting their reinterpretation so that their associated anxiety gets reduced (Rothbaum, Meadows, Resick, & Foy, 2000). CBT is particularly effective in treating PTSD with sustained results when combined with exposure therapy, a process that involves systematically re-exposing the survivor to images or memories that evoke the traumatic experience with support to reinterpret the meaning of the events (Hembree & Foa, 2003; Cook, Schnurr, & Foa, 2004; Feeny, Foa, & Treadwell, 2004; Foa & Meadows, 1997). With children, CBT has been shown to be more effective that nondirective play therapy, supportive counseling, and community treatment (Cohen, Berliner, & Mannarino, 2003; Deblinger, Lippman, & Steer, 1996; Kolko, 1996). Given that CBT is relatively brief and goal-directed, it may be particularly appropriate for cultural groups, including African Americans and Latino/a populations, who are known to prefer such approaches (Paniaguia, 1994).

Stress reduction therapy has also produced beneficial results for some survivors. Hembree & Foa, 2003). Sustained high stress levels can lead to deterioration of mental health. The problem is exacerbated by the phenomenon that higher stress levels are associated with higher avoidance and denial, which makes help-seeking less likely. Stress management intervention may be helpful in promoting initial engagement of the survivor in treatment, though it does not seem to produce the effect on symptoms that CBT and exposure therapies have done (Hembree & Foa, 2003). Few studies of stress reduction have been conducted on populations other than female sexual assault survivors.

Pharmocological treatments have also been found to be effective for survivors who develop mental disorders (Friedman, Davidson, Mellman, & Southwick, 2000).

A promising practice, Eye Movement Desensitization and Reprocessing (EMDR), which involves a therapist eliciting rapid eye movements in the survivor while the survivor recalls and, with support, reframes the memories, has been studied with mixed results indicating no or only modest effects (Lohr, Tolin, & Lilienfeld, 1998).

Support groups and mutual support networks are popular among survivors but remarkably little research has been done to assess their effects.

Treatment of Violence and Exploitation within Family Systems

When survivors are victimized by family members, not strangers or acquaintances, recovery involves special needs. This discussion will address child abuse and domestic violence.

Treating Children. Tragically, children are harmed within their own family systems or by people outside the system. In either case, close involvement of their caregivers is essential to their recovery. In a review of treatments for child crime survivors, Cohen, Berliner, and Mannarino (2003) observe that "we do not presently have enough research to predict accurately which children need treatment or which interventions will be most beneficial to individual children" (p. 176). They offer guidelines for intervention based on knowledge to date, including: (1) routinely assess child victims for emotional or behavioral difficulties; (2) screen for distress in primary care and school settings; (3) children who show symptoms should be referred for treatment; (4) treatment should have specific, individualized goals; (5) treatment should involve parents; (6) aspects of trauma-focused CBT should be incorporated into treatment; (7) children with depression, anxiety, behavioral symptoms, or comorbid disorders should receive treatment from providers specifically trained in effective practices for those problems; (8) children should not receive treatment unless they have symptoms; and 9) use of pharmacologic agents with children should be managed only by physicians specifically trained in their use with victimized children.

With regard to very young children, Moore, Armsden, and Gogerty (1998) followed abused children randomly assigned to a preschool therapeutic milieu and found long-term positive effects.

Intimate Partner Violence (IPV) Perpetrator Treatment. When adult survivors are connected to perpetrators by commitment or shared parenting, simply escaping from or leaving the perpetrator may not be a realistic option. Additionally, perpetrators are at risk of simply finding another victim if one relationship ends, so providers have struggled to develop effective treatments to stop the violence, though research has been rather inadequate thus far. Psychoeducational groups have been demonstrated to be effective under certain conditions, with certain perpetrators. Cattaneo and Goodman's (2005) review of interventions to treat intimate partner violence, which included evaluations of batterer treatment, court remedies, and victim assistance, found no consistent findings among the diverse studies to date, but they did detect trends that warrant further study. Their review suggests that, at the individual level, the perpetrator's stake in conformity predicts less reabuse after intervention, as does higher socioeconomic status, whereas ethnicity, age, family history, and beliefs about abuse do not influence change. At the interpersonal level, history of habitual abuse indicates reabuse after intervention. Survivors and offenders report reabuse differently, raising concerns about how outcomes are measured. The authors encourage future intervention studies that take these factors into consideration.

Widely used, the groups vary considerably but generally aim to change the moral perspectives of the perpetrators by promoting empathy for their victims and reducing their propensity for power and control (Dutton & Edelson, 1986). Ascertaining effectiveness

has been complicated by the fact that in many communities, courts order men to attend the groups, which means many are there for diverse reasons and may be poorly motivated to change. Drop-out rates are high and many men are loathe to share genuine feelings or opinions in group settings. And the groups have few resources to follow or mentor men to promote genuine behavior change toward nonviolence.

Victim Compensation

Survivors incur financial losses that can be at least partially restored through two major avenues: victim compensation funds, which are public funds to which certain survivors are entitled, and restitution, which involves direct payment from the convicted offender.

Victim Compensation. A national study of the efficiency and effectiveness of state Victims of Crime Act compensation programs receiving federal funds (Newmark, Bonderman, Smith, & Liner, 2003) found that the programs did effectively facilitate survivors' compensation claims processes though further work was needed to expedite the process through automation, assure underserved populations were reached, and promote smoother collaboration between victim assistance and victim compensation programs.

Restitution. State public policy across the country holds a convicted offender responsible for the crime by promoting court orders for financial payment of restitution from the offender to the survivor. Unfortunately, the process of collecting restitution has been ineffective. One study showed only 23 percent of restitution was paid (U.S. Dept. of Justice, 2002).

Restorative Justice

Restorative justice advocates have pursued alternatives to retributive justice (van Dijk, 2004). In the U.S., the criminal justice system is currently driven by an aim to seek punishment of the offender and to deter further offending by incapacitating the offender through incarceration. Restorative justice advocates, many of whom are survivor specialists, observe the traditional criminal justice system often disappoints and retraumatizes survivors. They also recognize that high rates of incarceration may provide short-term relief but create more harm than good in the long run, because punishment alone does not reduce recidivism, promotes denial by offenders and thus fails to hold them fully accountable, brings mixed justice to survivors, polarizes communities, and generates exorbitant costs that must be borne by survivors and other innocent people.

Several promising practices, particularly those that involve survivor-offender communication in cases of nonviolent crimes, are emerging with regard to restorative justice though considerably more research is needed (Strang, 2002; Welsh & Farrington, 2005). Some have been attempted with violent crimes also, including a model of responding to sex crimes that is survivor-driven and aims to hold the offender more explicitly accountable while meeting the clearly identified needs of the survivor (Koss, Bachar, Hopkins, & Carison, 2004). Surveys of survivor perspectives on restorative justice indicate that they have hesitations, but are open to participating (Curtis-Fawley & Daly, 2005; Herman, 2005).

The most substantial move toward restorative justice in cases of violent crime has occurred through the worldwide truth and reconciliation (T&R) movement (International Reconciliation Coalition, 2005). Reconciliation occurs when people acknowledge prior harms they have done, work to undo the harms to the extent possible, recognize their differences and commonalities, and agree to live in peace with one another. Survivors of crimes committed during political oppression and civil turmoil have been given the opportunity to speak out about their experiences through processes sponsored by their governments, nonprofits, or faith-based groups. Offenders can publicly confess their guilt. Lykes, Blanche, and Hamber (2003) summarize the concerns of survivors, noting survivors of politically aided crimes often have experienced horrific acts such as rape and mutilation and have lost murdered or disappeared family members. Across the world, hundreds of thousands of survivors have told their stories, emphasizing that they were guilty of nothing and suffered indescribable agony and the deaths of their loved ones had no dignity. Over and over, they express bewilderment about why the perpetrator(s) would do such a thing and outrage that they would. Nonfinite grief and post-traumatic stress disorder are rampant.

Research indicates that survivors respond in multiple ways to truth commissions. Many feel a duty to make a record of the harm, contribute to the fact-finding, and disclose the perpetrators, but the process of reliving painful memories can be devastating,

particularly eliciting acute posttraumatic symptoms (Byrne, 2004).) Alfred Allen (2000), an Australian psychologist, reviewed the South African Truth and Reconciliation process from the survivor's perspectives and found that, though political leaders hailed the process as a major success, the process did not usually lead to healing. Rather, it revealed many mental health needs that were inadequately met. In South Africa, victim responses were affected by the fact that perpetrators who fully disclosed their crimes were offered the opportunity to apply for amnesty and many received it. The goal was to integrate the perpetrators back into the community so that the nation could begin to build cohesive community and move beyond polarization. As global efforts to reduce crime and promote harmony advance, efforts must aim to develop processes that more adequately meet survivor needs.

The essential nature of victimization is that the survivor is stripped of personal control by the offender. Survivors are understandably reluctant to participate in reconciliation, particularly within current environments and societal structures that promote retribution and separatism. Thus when survivors are interested in reconciliation, the process must be carefully facilitated to encourage victims to exercise as much personal control as possible, e.g., by making decisions about whether to participate, when and where, through what forms of communication, and with whom. In addition, reconciliation is hard for a survivor to contemplate if the memories and pain are still vivid. For example, a study of postgenocide Rwandans found that victims who met PTSD symptom criteria were less likely like to have positive attitudes toward the Rwandan national trials, belief in community, or interdependence with other ethnic groups (Pham, Weinstein, & Longman, 2004).

Empathy for the offender is a central element of reconciliation (McCullough, Worthington, & Rachel, 1997). Public confessions and sincere apologies seem to be critical for instigating an empathic response from survivors (Weiner, Graham, Peter, & Zmuidinas, 1991). Some survivors, after offenders' apology and disclosure of truth, feel moved to forgive, but that is entirely an individual choice. Forgiveness essentially is a conscious decision to let go of bitterness and vengeance (Enright & North, 1998). Forgiving does not mean the victim forgets, condones, or excuses the crime, releases the offender from accountability, or is ready for reconciliation or trust (Exline, Worthington, Hill, & McCullough, 2003). Victims who forgive typically still support imposition of significant negative consequence on the offender, but forgiveness is more likely to precede mercy and acceptance of a less harsh consequence than when retribution is sought.

Through reconciliation, offenders have an opportunity to better understand the harm they caused and the victims' needs and how they can live for the long term in a way that prevents such harm from happening again. Victims have an opportunity to release some of the anger, overcome some confusion, and accept the humanity of the offender. They can move forward in daily life with less burden and more hope for the future.

Vicarious Traumatization

Working with survivors is "heartbreaking, gut-wrenching" work, as many specialists will say. It can also be exhilarating as social workers accompany survivors along the path of personal control, healing, recovery, and thriving, even with scars from their wounds. Workers are at risk of vicarious traumatization and thus should be adept at stress management and know when stress effects are becoming unmanageable (Figley, 2003; Stamm, 1999). Most humans need relaxation, recreation, social support, healthy diet, and capacity to separate work from personal needs.

Workers need supportive work environments, too. Critical Incident Stress Management (CSIM) is a widely used procedure for workers who have been exposed to death, violence, threats, and chronic extreme stress (Mitchell, 2003). The process involves preincident training, crisis intervention, and closure sessions. At the point of crisis, group debriefings among employees enable survivor expressions of concern and identify those who need further assistance. Individual and family support are offered as needed. Though only a few controlled studies have been done about CISM, with mixed results, some show promise, as did a study of a psychiatric facility where fifteen staff left each year due to patient assaults (Flannery, 1999). After CISM, one per year left.

CONCLUSION

Victimization, a tragically pervasive human condition, can be effectively prevented and, when it does occur, its harmful effects can be moderated by effective initial and sustained support. Confronting victimization and its effects requires universal collective and political will to eliminate tolerance for oppression and promote positive social behaviors. Wherever social workers practice, they have opportunities to prevent, reduce risks, offer crisis and disclosure support, and promote wholesome recovery. The social work ecological perspective gives social workers the capacity to analyze survivor needs at the societal, community, organizational, group, family, and individual levels.

Considerably more research is needed to determine what works most effectively to prevent and treat victimization. Practitioners and social work researchers have contributed to the emerging body of knowledge about such effective interventions as human rights enforcement, prosocial skills development, crisis intervention, cognitive-behavioral therapies, support groups, assistance in the criminal justice process, and the host of other interventions that reduce the propensity some people have to commit crimes and increase the survivor's capacity to thrive even with the scars of their experiences. Social workers are fundamentally trained to support survivor assets as they manage parallel interventions that target mental and physical healing, criminal justice, and financial restoration.

RESOURCES

To equitably and competently reach any survivor, survivor service systems must be adequately developed and sustained at the local level. Hundreds of specialized survivor service resources exist to promote high quality responses and system development. The major organizations are listed here.

Amnesty International USA
www.amnestyusa.org/about/

Center for Restorative Justice and
Peacemaking
www.che.umn.edu/rjp/

Communities Against Violence
Network
www.cavnet2.org/

Federal Bureau of Investigation Office
of Victim Services
www.fbi.gov/hq/cid/victimassist/fbireso
urces/resources.htm

Institute on Victim Studies
www.washburn.edu/ce/jcvvs/

International Campaign to Ban
Landmines (ICBL), Working Group on
Victim Assistance
www.icbl.org/lm/

International Centre for Missing and
Exploited Children
www.icmec.org/

International Critical Incident Stress
Foundation
www.icisf.org/

International Fellowship of
Reconciliation
www.ifor.org

International Reconciliation Coalition
www.reconcile.org/logo.htm

International Rescue Committee:
Refugee Relief, Respect, Renewal
www.theirc.org/

International Society for Traumatic
Stress Studies
www.istss.org/

International Victimology Website
www.victimology.nl/rechts.htm

Lambda Gay / Lesbian / Bisexual /
Transgender Community Services
www.qrd.org/qrd/www/orgs/avproject/

Mothers Against Drunk Drivers
www.madd.org/home/

Murder Victim Families for
Reconciliation
www.mvfr.org/

National Association of Crime Victim
Compensation Boards
www.nacvcb.org/

National Association of Victims of
Crime Act (VOCA) Assistance
Administrators
www.navaa.org/

National Center for Children Exposed
to Violence
www.nccev.org/

National Center for Missing and
Exploited Children
www.ncmec.org

National Center for Victims of Crime
www.ncvc.org/ncvc/Main.aspx

National Center on Domestic and
Sexual Violence
www.ncdsv.org/ncd_about.html

National Center on Elder Abuse
www.elderabusecenter.org/

National Coalition Against Domestic
Violence (grassroots advocacy)
www.ncadv.org/

National Criminal Justice Reference
Service – Victims page
www.ncjrs.gov/

National Network to End Domestic
Violence (state domestic violence
coalitions)
www.nnedv.org/

National Network to End Violence Against
Immigrant Women
www.immigrantwomennetwork.org

National Organization for Parents of
Murdered Children
www.pomc.com/

National Organization for Victim
Assistance (NOVA)
www.trynova.org/

National Sexual Violence Resource
Center
www.nsvrc.org/

National Victim Assistance Academy
www.nvaa.org/about/index.html

Terrorism and International Victim
Assistance Services Division
U. S. Dept of Justice
www.ojp.usdoj/ovc/welcove/tivu.html

United Nations Crime and Justice
Information Network
www.uncjin.org/

U. S. Attorney General Guidelines for
Victim and Witness Assistance (federal
crimes)
www.usdoj.gov/olp/final.pdf

U. S. Dept. of Justice Office for Victims of
Crime
www.ojp.usdoj.gov/ovc/

U. S. Dept. of Justice Office on Violence
Against Women
www.ojp.usdoj.gov/vawo/about.htm

Victim Assistance Online (international
network)
www.vaonline.org/

Victim Offender Mediation Association
www.voma.org/

World Society of Victimology
www.world-society-victimology.de/

Figure 19-2. Major survivor services organizations.

REFERENCES

Allen, A. (2000). Truth and reconciliation: A psycholegal perspective. *Ethnicity and Health, 5*(3–4), 191–204.

American Academy of Child and Adolescent Psychiatry (AACAP). (1998). Practice parameters for the assessment and treatment of posttraumatic stress disorder in children and adolescents. *Journal of the American Academy of Child and Adolescent Psychiatry, 37*(10, Suppl.), 4–26.

American Psychological Association. (2005). *Resolution on violence in video games and interactive media.* http://www.apa.org/releases/resoulutiononvideoviolence.pdf

Amick-McMullan, A., Kilpatrick, D. G., & Resnick, H. S. (1991). Homicide as a risk factor for PTSD among surviving family members. *Behavior Modification, 15*(4), 545–559.

Amnesty International. (2001). *Broken bodies, shattered minds: Torture and ill treatment of women.* http://www.amnestyusa.org/stopviolence/factsheets/violence.html Downloaded Sept. 7, 2005.

Andrews, A. B. (1992). *Victimization and survivor services.* New York: Springer.

Armstrong, T. L. (Ed.). (1991). *Intensive interventions with high-risk youths: Promising approaches in juvenile probation and parole.* New York: Criminal Justice Press.

Bentley, K. J. (2001). *Social work practice in mental health: Contemporary roles, tasks, and techniques.* New York: Wadsworth.

Berliner, L., & New, M. (1999). The impact of health care reform: A survey of victim and offender treatment providers. *Sexual Abuse: Journal of Research and Treatment, 11*(1), 5–16.

Berry, M., Gray, T., & Donnerstein, E. (1999). Cutting film violence: Effects on perceptions, enjoyment, and arousal. *Journal of Social Psychology, 139*(5), 567–582.

Bingham, L. B., & Pitts, D. W. (2002). Highlights of mediation at work: Studies of the National REDRESS® evaluation project. *Negotiation Journal, 18*(2), 135–146.

Bisson, J. I., McFarlane, A., & Rose, S. (2000). Psychological debriefing. In E. Foa, T. Keane & M. Friedman (Eds.), *Effective treatments for PTSD: Practice guidelines from the International Society for Traumatic Stress Studies* (pp.317–319). New York: Guilford.

Blomberg, T. G., Waldo, G. P., & Chester, D. (2002). Assessment of the program implementation of comprehensive victim services in a one-stop location. *International Review of Victimology, 9*(2), 149–174.

Bonnie, R. J., & Wallace, R. B. (2002). *Elder mistreatment: Abuse, neglect, and exploitation in an aging America.* Washington, D.C.: National Academies Press.

Browne, K. D., & Hamilton-Giachritsis, C. (2005). The influence of violent media on children and adolescents: A public-health approach. *Lancet, 365,* 702–710.

Byers, B. D. (2002). Death notification: The theory and practice of delivering bad news. In J. E. Hendricks & B. D. Byers (Eds.), *Crisis intervention in criminal justice/social service* (3rd ed., pp. 326–360). Springfield, IL: Charles C Thomas.

Byrne, C. C. (2004). Benefit or burden: Victims' reflections on TRC participation. *Peace & Conflict: Journal of Peace Psychology, 10*(3),237–256.

Carll, E. K. (2003). News portrayal of violence and women: Implications for public policy. *American Behavioral Scientist, 46*(12), 1601–1610.

Catalano, R. F., Berglund, M. L., & Ryan, J. A. M. (2004). Positive youth development in the United States: Research findings on evaluations of positive youth development programs. *Annals of the American Academy of Political & Social Science, 591,* 98–124.

Cattaneo, L. B., & Goodman, L. A. (2005). Risk factors for reabuse in intimate partner violence. *Trauma, Violence, & Abuse, 6*(2), 141–175.

Clark, K.A.., Biddle, A. K., & Martin, S. L (2002). A cost-benefit analysis of the Violence Against Women Act of 1994. *Violence Against Women, 8*(4), 417–428.

Cockburn, C. (1998). *The space between us: Negotiating gender and national identities in conflict.* New York: Zed Books.

Cohen, J. A., Berliner, L., & Mannarino, A. P. (2003). Psychosocial and pharmacological interventions for child crime victims. *Journal of Traumatic Stress, 16*(2), 175–186.

Cohen, M. A., Miller, T. R., & Rossman, S. B. (1994). The costs and consequences of violent behavior in the United States. In A. J. Reiss & J. A. Roth (Eds.), *Understanding and preventing violence: Consequences and control* (vol. 4) (pp. 67–166) . Washington, D.C.: National Academy Press.

Cook, J. M., Schnurr, P. P., & Foa, E. B. (2004). Bridging the gap between posttraumatic stress disorder research and clinical practice: The example of exposure therapy. *Psychotherapy: Theory, Research, Practice, Training, 41*(4), 374–387.

Cordero, I. C. (2001). Social organizations: From victims to actors in peace building. In C. O. N. Moser & F. C. Clark (Eds.), *Victims, perpetrators, or actors? Gender, armed conflict, and political violence* (pp.151–163). New York: St. Martin's Press.

Curtis-Fawley, S., & Daly, K. (2005). Gendered violence and restorative justice. *Violence Against Women, 11*(5), 603–638.

Deblinger, E., Lippman, J., & Steer, R. (1996). Sexually abused children suffering posttraumatic stress symptoms: Initial treatment outcome findings. *Child Maltreatment, 1,* 310–321.

Donnerstein, E., & Linz, D. (1998) Mass media, sexual violence, and male viewers. In M. E. Odem & J. Clay-Warner (Eds.), *Confronting rape and sexual assault* (pp. 181–198). Wilmington, DE: SR Books.

Dusenbury, L., Falco, M., Lake, A., Brannigan, R., & Bosworth, K. (1997). Nine critical elements of promising violence prevention programs. *Journal of School Health, 67*(10), 409–415.

Dutton, D. G., & Edelson, J. L. (1986). The outcome for court mandated treatment for wife assault: A quasi-experimental evaluation. *Violence and Victims, 1*(86), 163–175.

Enright, R.D. & North, J. (Eds.) (1998). *Exploring forgiveness.* Madison, WI: University of Wisconsin.

Exline, J.J., Worthington, E.L., Hill, P., & McCullough, M.E. 2003. Forgiveness and justice: A research agenda for social and personality psychology. *Personality and Social Psychology Review, 7*(4), 337–344.

Federal Bureau of Investigation. (Nov. 2004). *Hate crime statistics 2003.* Washington D.C.: U. S. Department of Justice.

Feeny, N. C., Foa, E. B., & Treadwell, K. R. H. (2004). Posttraumatic stress disorder in youth: A critical review of the cognitive and behavioral treatment outcome literature. *Professional Psychology: Research & Practice, 35*(5), 466–476.

Figley, C. R. (Ed.). (2003). *Treating compassion fatigue.* New York: Brunner-Routledge.

Finkelhor, D., & Ormrod, R. (Dec. 2004). Child pornography: Patterns from NIBRS. *Juvenile Justice Bulletin.* Washington D.C.: Office of Juvenile Justice and Delinquency Prevention. NCJ 204911.

Flannery, R. B. (1999). Critical incident stress management and the assaulted staff action program. *International Journal of Emergency Mental Health, 2,* 103–108.

Flash, K. (2003). Treatment strategies for juvenile delinquency: Alternative solutions. *Child & Adolescent Social Work Journal, 20*(6), 509–527.

Foa, E., Keane, T., & Friedman, M. (Eds.). (2000). *Effective treatments for PTSD: Practice guidelines from the International Society for Traumatic Stress Studies.* New York: Guilford.

Foa, E. B., & Meadows, E. A. (1997). Psychosocial treatments for posttraumatic stress disorder: A critical review. *Annual Review of Psychology, 48,* 449–480.

Foa, E. B., & Rothbaum, B. O. (1998). *Treating the trauma of rape.* New York: Guilford.

Freyd, J. J. (1998). Science in the memory debate. *Ethics & Behavior, 8*(2), 101–113.

Friedman, M. J., Davidson, J. R. T., Mellman, T. A., & Southwick, S. M. (2000). Pharmacotherapy. In E. Foa, T. Keane, & M. Friedman (Eds.), *Effective treatments for PTSD: Practice guidelines from the International Society for Traumatic Stress Studies* (pp.84–105). New York: Guilford.

Glicken, M. D., & Sechrest, D. K. (2004). *The role of the helping professions in treating the victims and perpetrators of violence.* Boston: Pearson Education, Inc.

Harris, C. J. (2006). The forensic examination of post-traumatic stress disorder. *Journal of Aggression, Maltreatment & Trauma, 12*(1–2), 83–102

Hawkins, J. D., Catalano, R. F., & Arthur, M. W. (2002). Promoting science-based prevention in communities. *Addictive Behaviors, 27*(6), 951–976.

Hawkins, J. D., Van Horn, M. L., & Arthur, M. W. (2004). Community variation in risk and protective factors and substance use outcomes. *Prevention Science, 5*(4), 213–220.

Hembree, E. A., & Foa, E. B. (2003). Interventions for trauma-related emotional disturbances in adult victims of crime. *Journal of Traumatic Stress, 16*(2), 187–199.

Henggeler, S. W., Schoenwald, S. K., Borduin, C. M., Rowland, M. D., & Cunningham, P. B. (1998). *Multisystemic treatment of antisocial behavior in children and adolescents: Treatment manual for practitioners.* New York: Guilford.

Herman, J. (2005). Justice form the victim's perspective. *Violence Against Women, 11*(5), 571–602.

Herrenkohl, T. I., Hill, K. G., & Chung, I. (2003). Protective factors against serious violent behavior in adolescence: A prospective study of aggressive children. *Social Work Research, 27*(3), 179–191.

Herrenkohl, T. I., Mason, W. A., & Kosterman, R. (2004). Pathways from physical childhood abuse to partner violence in young adulthood. *Violence & Victims, 19*(2), 123–136.

International Reconciliation Coalition. (2005). www.reconcile.org/logo.htm.

Kaul, R. E. (2001). Coordinating the death notification process: The roles of the emergency room social worker and physician following a sudden death. *Brief Treatment & Crisis Intervention, 1*(2), 101–114.

Kelly, D. P., & Erez, E. (1997). Victim participation in the criminal justice system. In R. C. Davis, A. J. Lurigo & W. G. Skogan (Eds.), *Victims of crime* (2nd ed., pp. 231–244). Thousand Oaks, CA: Sage.

Kilpatrick, D. G., & Acierno, R. (2003). Mental health needs of crime victims: Epidemiology and outcomes. *Journal of Traumatic Stress, 16*(2), 119–132.

Kolko, D. J. (1996). Individual cognitive behavioral therapy and family therapy for physically abused children and their offending parents: A comparison of clinical outcomes. *Child Maltreatment, 1,* 322–342.

Koss, M. P., Bachar, K. J., Hopkins, C. Q., & Carison, C. (2004). Expanding a community's justice response to sex crimes through advocacy, prosecutorial, and public health collaboration: Introducing the RESTORE program. *Journal of Interpersonal Violence, 19*(12), 1435–1463.

Langevin, R., & Curnoe, S. (2004). The use of pornography during the commission of sexual offenses. *International Journal of Offender Therapy & Comparative Criminology, 48*(5), 572–586.

Lipsey, M. W., & Derzon, J. H. (1998). Predictors of violent or serious delinquency in adolescence and early adulthood: A synthesis of longitudinal research. In R. Loeber & D. P. Farrington (Eds.), *Serious & violent juvenile offenders: Risk factors and successful interventions* (pp. 86–105). Thousand Oaks, CA: Sage.

Lipsey, M. W., & Wilson, D. B. (1998). Effective intervention for serious juvenile offenders: A synthesis of research. In R. Loeber & D. Farrington (Eds.), *Serious and violent juvenile offenders: Risk factors and successful interventions* (pp. 313–395). Thousand Oaks, CA: Sage.

Lohr, J. M., Tolin, D. F., & Lilienfeld, S. O. (1998). Efficacy of eye movement desensitization and preprocessing: Implications for behavioral therapy. *Behavior Therapy, 29*, 123–156.

Lykes, M. B., Blanche, M. T., & Hamber, B. (2003). Narrating survival and change in Guatemala and South Africa: The politics of representation and a liberatory community psychology. *American Journal of Community Psychology, 31*(1–2), 79–90.

McCullough, M. E., Worthington, E. L., & Rachel, K. C.. (1997). Interpersonal forgiving in close relationships. *Journal of Personality and Social Psychology, 73*, 321–336.

McDermott, M. J., & Garofalo, J. (2004). When advocacy for domestic violence victims backfires: Types and sources of victim disempowerment. *Violence Against Women, 10*(11), 1245–1266.

McFarlane, J. M., Campbell, J.C., Wilt, S., Sachs, C. J., Ulrich, Y., & Xu, X. (1999). Stalking and intimate partner femicide. *Homicide Studies, 3*(4), 300–316. .

Milberger, S., LeRoy, B., Martin, A., Israel, N., Potter, L., & Patchak-Schuster, P. (2002). *Michigan study on women with physical disabilities, Final report.* Washington, D.C.: National Institute of Justice.

Mitchell, J. T. (2003). *Crisis intervention & CISM: A research summary.* Ellicott City, MD: International Critical Incident Stress Foundation. www.icisf.org. Download Sept. 26, 2005.

Moore, E., Armsden, G., & Gogerty, P. L. (1998). A twelve-year follow-up study of maltreatment at-risk children who received early therapeutic childcare. *Child Maltreatment, 3*, 3–16.

Moser, C. O. N., & McIwaine, C. (2000a). *Urban poor perceptions of violence and exclusion in Colombia.* Washington, D.C.: World Bank.

Moser, C. O. N., & McIwaine, C. (2000a). *Violence in a post-conflict context: Urban poor perceptions from Guatemala.* Washington, D.C.: World Bank.

National Center for Victims of Crime. (1996). *Statutory and constitutional protection of victims' rights: Implementation and impact on crime victims, Final Report.* Arlington, VA. Table C-9.

National Children's Alliance. (2005). Homepage. http://www.nca-online.org/welcome.html.

National Organization for Victim Assistance. (May 2005). *Early psychological intervention (EPI) points of consensus document.* http://www.trynova.org/crft/epi. Downloaded Sept. 8, 2005.

National Victim Assistance Academy. (2002). *International issues in victim assistance* (Chap 22, Sec 7). http://www.ojp.usdoj.gov/ovc/assist/nvaa2002/chapter22_7.html.

Nemes, I. (1992). The relationship between pornography and sex crimes. *Journal of Psychiatry & Law, 20*(4), 459–481.

Newmark, L., Bonderman, J., Smith, B., & Liner, B. (2003). *National evaluation of state Victims of Crime Act assistance and compensation programs: Trends and strategies of the future.* Washington, D.C.: Urban Institute.

Norris, F. H. (1992). Epidemiology of trauma: Frequency and impact of different potentially traumatic event on different demographic events. *Journal of Consulting and Clinical Psychology, 60*, 409–418.

Palmer, N. D., & Edmunds, C. N. (2003). Victims of sexual abuse and assault: Adults and children. In T. L. Underwood & C. Edmunds (Eds.), *Victim assistance: Exploring individual practice, organizational policy, and societal responses* (pp. 138–175). New York: Springer.

Paniaguia, F. (1994). *Assessing and treating culturally diverse clients: A practical guide.* Thousand Oaks, CA: Sage.

Perry, S. W. (Dec 2004). *American Indians and crime: A BJS statistical profile, 1992–2002.* NCJ 203097. Washington, D.C.: US Bureau of Justice Statistics.

Petrosino, A., Turpin-Petrosino, C., & Finckenauer, J. O. (2000). Well meaning programs can have harmful effects: Lessons from experiments of programs such as Scared Straight. *Crime and Delinquency, 46*, 354–379.

Pham, P. N., Weinstein, H. M., & Longman, T. (2004). Trauma and PTSD symptoms in Rwanda: Implications for attitudes toward justice and reconciliation. *JAMA: Journal of the American Medical Association, 292*,(5), 602–612.

Roberts, A. R. & Brownell, P. (1999). A century of forensic social work: Bridging the past to the present. *Social Work, 44*(4), 359–369.

Rothbaum, B. O., Meadows, E. A., Resick, P., & Foy, D. W. (2000). Cognitive-behavioral therapy. In E. Foa, T. Keane & M. Friedman (Eds.), *Effective treatments for PTSD: Practice guidelines from the International Society for Traumatic Stress Studies* (pp.320–325). New York: Guilford.

Sanders-Phillips, K., Moisan, P., Wadlington, S., Morgan, S., & English, K. (1995). Ethnic differences in psychological functioning among Black and Latino sexually abused girls. *Child Abuse and Neglect, 19*, 691–706.

Smith, C., & Thornberry, T. P. (1995). The relationship between childhood maltreatment and adolescent involvement in delinquency. *Criminology, 33*, 451–481.

Schweinhart, L. J., & Weikart, D. P. (1998). High/Scope Perry Preschool Program effects at age twenty-seven. In J. Crane (Ed.), *Social programs that work* (pp.148–162). New York: Russell Sage Foundation.

Shelby, D. (2005). *Afghan women compete for seats in national, provincial legislatures. International Information Programs,* U.S. Dept. of State. http://usinfo.state.gov/sa/Archive/2005/Aug/26-201799.html.

Sherman, L. W., Gottfredson, D., MacKenzie, D., Eck, J., Reuter, P., & Bushway, S. (1998). *Preventing crime: What works, what doesn't, what's promising: A report to the United States Congress.* Washington, D.C.; National Institute of Justice.

Stamm, B. H. (1999). *Secondary traumatic stress: Self-care issues for clinicians, researchers & educators* (2nd ed.). Towson, MD: Sidran Press.

Strang, H. (2002). *Repair or revenge: Victims and restorative justice.* Oxford, UK: Oxford University Press.

Tienda, M., & Wilson, W. J. (2002). Youth crime, community development, and social justice. In R. White (Ed.), *Youth in cities: A cross-national perspective* (pp. 138–164). New York: Cambridge University Press.

Tjaden, P. & Thoennes, N. (1998). *Stalking in America: Findings from the National Violence Against Women Survey.* Washington, D.C.; U.S. Dept. of Justice, NCJ 169592.

Tjaden, P., & Thoennes, N. (2000). *Full report of the prevalence, incidence, and consequences of violence against women: Findings from the National Violence Against Women Survey.* Washington, D.C.: U.S. Dept. of Justice.

Underwood, T. L. (2003). The justice system and victims. In T. L. Underwood & C. Edmunds (Eds.), *Victim assistance: Exploring individual practice, organizational policy, and societal responses* (pp. 124–137). New York: Springer.

United Nations Office for Drug Control and Crime Prevention, Centre for International Crime Prevention. (1999). *Handbook on justice for victims.* New York: Author.

U.S. Dept. of Justice, Bureau of Justice Statistics. (1987). *Lifetime likelihood of victimization. Technical Report.* NCJ-104274. Washington, D.C.: U.S. Government Printing Office.

U.S. Dept. of Justice, Bureau of Justice Statistics. (2005a) *Criminal victimization.* http://www.ojp.usdoj.gov/bjs/cvictgen.htm. Downloaded Sept. 7, 2005.

U.S. Dept. of Justice, Bureau of Justice Statistics. (2005b). *Victim characteristics.* http://www.ojp.usdoj.gov/bjs/cvict_v.htm#race. Downloaded Sept. 7, 2005.

U.S. Dept. of Justice, Office for Victims of Crime. (2002). *Restitution: Making it work. Legal Series Bulletin #5.* NCJ 189193. Washington, D.C.: U.S. Government Printing Office.

U.S. Department of Health and Human Services, Children's Bureau. (2004a). *Child maltreatment 2002.* Washington, D.C.: U.S. Government Printing Office. http://www.acf.hhs.gov/programs/cb/publications/cm03/summary.htm. Downloaded Aug. 29, 2005.

U.S. Department of Health and Human Services, Children's Bureau. (2004b). *Child abuse and neglect fatalities: Statistics and interventions.* Washington, D.C.: National Clearinghouse on Child Abuse and Neglect Information. http://nccanch.acf.hhs.gov/pubs/factsheets/fatality.cfm.

U.S. Department of Labor, Occupational Safety & Health Administration. (2004). *Bureau of labor statistics census of fatal occupational injuries (CFOI), 2004.* http://www.osha.gov/SLTC/workplaceviolence/, Sept. 7, 2005.

U.S. Dept. of State. (2005). *The Victims of Trafficking and Violence Protection Act of 2000: The 2005 trafficking in persons report.* http://www.state.gov/g/tip/rls/tiprpt/2005/.

United Nations' Declaration of Basic Principles of Justice for Victims of Crime and Abuse of Power. http://www.unhchr.ch/html/menu3/b/h_comp49.htm. International Crime Victim Survey. (1997). Homepage. http://ruljis.leidenuniv.nl/group/jfcr/www/icvs/.

van der Kolk, B. A., Hopper, J. W., & Osterman, J. E. (2001). Exploring the nature of traumatic memory: Combining clinical knowledge with laboratory methods. *Journal of Aggression, Maltreatment, & Trauma, 4,* 9–31; and Freyd, J. F., & DePrince, A. P. (Eds.). *Trauma and Cognitive Science* (pp. 9–31). Binghamton, NY: Haworth Press.

van Dijk, J. (2004). Crime prevention in a globalized world: Foundations, setbacks, and challenges. Presentation at the opening session of the Conference on Sustainable Prevention Policies and Practices. Paris, Dec. 1, 2004.

Van Wilsem, J. (2004). Criminal victimization in cross-national perspective: An analysis of rates of theft, violence, and vandalism across 27 countries. *European Journal of Criminology, 1*(1), 89–109.

Victim Services Network. (1999). *Code of professional ethics for victim service providers.* Rev. 8/99. http://www.vs2000.org/denver/en/tech_asst_training/model/code.html. Downloaded Sep. 25, 2005.

Walker, L. (1984). *The battered woman syndrome.* New York: Springer.

Walker, L. (1992). Battered women and self defense. *Notre Dame Journal of Law, Ethics, and Public Policy, 6*(2), 321–334.

Warr, M. (1994). Public perceptions and reactions to violent offending and victimization. In A. J. Reiss & J. A. Roth (Eds.), *Understanding and preventing violence: Consequences and control* (vol. 4) (pp. 1–66). Washington, D.C.: National Academy Press.

Weiner, B., Graham, S., Peter, O., & Zmuidinas, M. (1991). Public confessions and forgiveness. *Journal of Personality, 59*, 218–312.

Welsh, B. C., & Farrington, D. P. (2005). Evidence-based crime prevention: Conclusions and direction for a safer society. *Canadian Journal of Criminology and Crime Prevention, 47*(2), 337–354.

Widom, C. S., & Ames, M. A. (1994). Criminal consequences of childhood sexual victimization. *Child Abuse and Neglect, 18*, 303–318.

Wilson, S. J., Lipsey, M. W., & Derzon, J. H. (2003). The effects of school-based intervention programs on aggressive behavior: A meta-analysis. *Journal of Consulting & Clinical Psychology, 71*(1), 136–149.

Wissler, R. L. (2004). The effectiveness of court-connected dispute resolution in civil cases. *Conflict Resolution Quarterly, 22*(1–2), 55–88.

Wolf-Smith, J. H., & LaRossa, L. (1992). After he hits her. *Family Relations, 41*, 324–329.

Young, M. A. (1997). Victim rights and services: A modern saga. In R. C. Davis, A. J. Lurigo & W. G. Skogan (Eds.), *Victims of crime* (2nd ed., pp. 194–210). Thousand Oaks, CA: Sage.

Young, M. A. (2001). *Victim assistance: Frontiers and fundamentals.* Washington, D.C.: National Organization for Victim Assistance.

Chapter 20

Social Work's Role with Domestic Violence: Women and the Criminal Justice System

Sophia F. Dziegielewski and Marcia Swartz

Case Example

Susie and her boyfriend had been together for ten years. During that time she had been beaten severely and treated on several different occasions in the local hospital emergency room. Much of the abuse between the couple was reported to be mutual; however, Susie's boyfriend was never hospitalized for her return attacks. On several occasions, Susie had called police to intervene, and when they arrived after being dispatched to the domestic violence scene, Susie generally refused to press charges. Susie stated that at one time in the past, she had begun to press charges but soon dropped them after her boyfriend called from jail, telling her he loved her and begging her forgiveness. The police were getting dispatched to the scene so often that they referred to Susie and her boyfriend by their first names.

Susie tried to leave her boyfriend several times, but he always tracked her down and persuaded her to return. Susie's family was well aware of the abuse that often transpired. After awhile, both Susie's mother and sister refused to accept her calls asking for help. Susie often called them when she was fighting with her boyfriend, stating that she needed them to provide an "understanding ear or a safe place to stay." Her family was frustrated because no matter what they tried to do, Susie always seemed to return to the abusive situation. Also, whenever Susie came by, her boyfriend would threaten Susie and her family, and Susie's mother felt that Susie's father's health was not strong enough to handle all of the repeated stress.

Based on a referral from her employer, Susie confided in the counselor that she felt lost and abandoned. During the second session, Susie told the social worker that she wanted to kill her boyfriend. When asked how she would do it, Susie immediately broke down and cried and stated that she would probably be better off killing herself. The event that precipitated Susie's crisis was the fight that they had during the previous night. Susie's boyfriend insisted that she climb up a ladder and help him paint the house. Susie refused because she was four months pregnant and afraid of heights. Her refusal to climb the ladder resulted in her being hit with the ladder across her back.

Based on the information Susie provided, the social worker was able to make the following assessment: (1) Susie was being beaten on a regular basis; (2) she feared for her life and was threatening to take the life of another; (3) Susie had alienated her family and had no support system available to assist her; and (4) she was threatening to take her own life. The social worker felt that immediate intervention was essential in helping Susie to adjust to her current situation without violence to self or others. The first thing the social worker tried to do was to explore the possibilities of inpatient admission. Since the client had no medical insurance and none of the local facilities stated that they had an empty bed, an alternate plan was formed.

The social worker helped the client gain admission to the local shelter for abused women. The shelter personnel were notified of Susie's possible desire to end her life and a suicide watch was implemented. Intensive individual and group counseling resources were made available. With the help and support of the social worker, an order of protection was filed. Susie decided to press charges and asked if the social worker would help her to state her case to an attorney; the social worker agreed. Susie did press charges this time and her boyfriend was sentenced to two years in prison with the possibility of parole in six months. After helping Susie to regain the recognition and assistance of her family, Susie moved to another city and stayed with her aunt. Prior to her leaving, Susie had started making plans to give up her child for adoption.

In this case, the role of the social worker was twofold. First, the client was provided with a safe environment where she was helped to deal with her crisis. Fortunately, the social worker, as well as the shelter counselors were able to provide counseling and supportive services. Secondly, the client was provided with the help and assistance needed to create and carry out a plan of action which linked the client with the legal system. It is clear that women who have been abused by their spouses and/or significant others will need supportive services. In addition to this, however, the help and assistance of the legal institutions in this country will also be needed. These women need to know the following: (1) that legal services are available to them; (2) that supportive services such as that provided by a social worker are available; and (3) that the combined use of these services will result in assistance, eventually resolving the situation. This makes the role of the social work professional crucial. Whether working within the criminal justice system itself or outside the system in an ancillary agency, the social worker can have significant impact in assisting the survivor of domestic abuse.

DOMESTIC VIOLENCE

In recent months considerable attention has been paid to the fact that our society is considered "violent." The media speaks of violence, and more and more cases of women who have violently retaliated against their abusers are being reported. Over the last fifteen years the phrase domestic violence and the subsequent assessment, intervention and treatment

of this phenomena has clearly gained wide acceptance and recognition.

Toward a Definition of Domestic Violence

In order to discuss domestic violence, we need a broad yet simultaneously clear definition of violence. Unfortunately, such a definition does not exist. Definitions of violence range from "the use of physical force by one person against another" (Siegler, 1989) to "pushing, slapping, punching, kicking, knifing, shooting, or the throwing of objects at another person" (Gelles, 1987, p. 20).

Most individuals agree that abuse incorporates any behavior which harms the target, including psychological, emotional, and nonviolent sexual abuse (Siegler, 1989). However, consensus on the definition and description of what constitutes abuse seems to still lag behind.

Incidence

Wife battering is defined as any physical act of violence directed at a woman by her intimate male partner (Edelson, 1991). It is the single most common cause of injury to women and is likely to be the least reported crime in relation to the actual rate of its occurrence (McShane, 1979). Several studies of battered women indicate that less than 1 percent of all domestic violence cases are reported to police, and of those reported, less than half result in charges being pressed against the abuser (Siegler, 1989). Further, it is estimated that one out of every two women will be abused at some point in their lives (Statman, 1990).

Estimates indicate that approximately 12 million women are abused by their partners each year (Mancoske, Standifer, & Cauley, 1994). As many as one-half of the couples living in the United States are estimated to have experienced violence in an intimate relationship (Gelles, 1979). Finklehor et al. (1988) relates that 12 percent of the spouses they surveyed stated that they had experienced a violent incident with their mate in the last year, and 28 percent reported experiencing violence throughout the course of the marriage (Finklehor et al., 1988). Approximately 20 percent of female visits to the emergency room are the result of battering; and, more generally in the case of assault (i.e., domestic violence, date rape, etc.), 70 percent of all admissions are accounted for (Statman, 1990). With the increased incidence of abuse being addressed in the emergency room, many states have now allowed the police to arrest a batterer without a warrant when evidence is present of an injury serious enough to require emergency medical care (Statman, 1990).

Each year 2,000 to 4,000 women are beaten to death, and more than half the women in the United States have at some point been abused by their partners (Liutkus, 1994). Various studies indicate that anywhere between one-third and one-half of all women who have been murdered in the United States have been killed by a boyfriend, spouse or ex-mate (Schneider, 1994; Litsky, 1994; Stark et al., 1979), whereas 10 percent of the males murdered in America have been killed by a female partner acting in self-defense (Statman, 1990).

Laws in regard to domestic violence vary from state to state and often differ between towns and cities within the same state (Statman, 1993); however, as of 1990, only three states have mandatory reporting laws regarding the battering of women (Gelles & Cornell, 1990).

CHARACTERISTICS OF ABUSERS
AND THE ABUSED

In reporting the characteristics of the survivors of abuse there are two concerns to be addressed. First, we must be careful not to "blame the victim" for the abuse. Both the society at large and the abuser may attempt to use this information to blame the victim. For example, societal contempt was clear in the case of Hedda Nussbaum who made the cover of *Newsweek* in 1988. Her face and body had been beaten by her live-in boyfriend, Joel Steinberg, who was charged with murdering the couple's illegally adopted six-year-old daughter. The abuse within this couple was documented back to March 1978 and ended in November 1987 when Hedda asked her boyfriend for permission to telephone for help for their abused child. Unfortunately, the child was already dead from the beating she had received at the time of her phone call. In the aftermath many individuals blamed Hedda for her failure to save the child, and Judy Mann from the *Washington Post* was quoted as saying she found it "sickening" that "collusion between state and its key witness to use victimization as

an excuse for the most reprehensible behavior" (Jones, 1994: 175). Many individuals did not believe that the beatings that Hedda received, and the fear that had developed as a result of the abuse she sustained, pushed her beyond the capability of intervening for the life of her daughter, nonetheless her own.

It is also important to realize that if certain characteristics of women at risk of spousal abuse are identified, these characteristics may be used by those who batter to justify their violent behavior. Many social workers who work with batterers report the frequency with which male batterers charge that they were provoked to violence (Edleson & Tolman, 1992; Pence, 1989). Although claims that "she drove me to it" are often made to justify abusive behavior, the most recent research suggests that this is not typically the case (Ganley, 1989). Many professionals believe that these claims are more likely to reflect the abuser's denial of responsibility for his actions and must be challenged and overcome in order to progress in treatment (Edleson & Tolman, 1992).

The second issue to be remembered when discussing characteristics of the survivors of abuse is that this can also lead to the tendency of the battered women to blame themselves for the abuse, to have illusions of being able to control the abusers behavior, and to feel greater shame at having allowed themselves to be abused (Dziegielewski & Resnick, 1996). This examination is not meant to answer the question "What did I do to deserve the abuse" but rather to identify women at risk for abuse and to explore the psychological sequela of abuse.

Despite small sample sizes, several studies indicate that women who are battered have experienced childhood family violence, witnessed parental abuse, and were often abused as children (Star et al., 1979; Siegler, 1989; Gelles & Cornell, 1990; Tolman & Bennett, 1990). The battered woman typically is presented as: (1) suffering from low self-esteem, (2) lacking in self-confidence, (3) has the tendency to withdraw from situational stress in marriage, (4) experiences increased feelings of depression, hopelessness and frustration, and (5) is more prone to drug abuse, alcohol abuse and drug alcohol dependency, suicide attempts and successful suicidal and homicidal behavior (Liutkus, 1994).

Numerous reasons have been postulated as to why women choose to stay in violent relationships. Some of these reasons include: the battered woman's belief that their spouse will reform; they encounter self-doubt about the ability to manage alone; divorce may be stigmatizing and being left "alone" may be frightening; a fear of the unknown and what would happen to them if they left; poor employment options; the fear of homelessness (50% of the homeless women in this country are fleeing from domestic violence) (Mullins, 1994), as well as difficulty finding adequate day-care services for their children (Dziegielewski & Resnick, 1996; Dziegielewski, Resnick & Krause, 1996; Gelles & Cornell, 1990). It has been speculated, however, that the greatest deterrent is the fear that they would endure economic hardship outside of the relationship and that they could not manage adequate care for their children due to decreased financial support.

This fear of financial hardship is very real. Throughout time a woman's responsibility for home and children placed her in a less advantageous position as a wage earner. This resultant economic dependence of women can serve to preserve abusive situations and decrease the opportunity for leaving them. This feminization of poverty is evidenced when marital separation leads to a 73 percent drop in a woman's standard of living within the first year. Nearly 70 percent of child support payments are not made regularly, and consistent alimony payments are rarely forthcoming even after being awarded (Davidson & Jenkins, 1989). Economic subservience alone can provide ample explanation for why women stay in abusive relationships. These social and economic factors clearly support the need for therapeutic intervention that is progressive and takes into account the need for protection, prevention and economic support.

To further understand the dynamic characteristics of the abused and the abuser, high correlations between substance abuse and domestic violence have been established (Liutkus, 1994; Siegler, 1989; Tolman & Bennett, 1990; Stith et al., 1990). It is important to note here that spouse abuse is very often mutual. Both husbands and wives have been found to display repetitive, violent interactions; however, the consequences resulting from male physical violence are more profound (Siegler, 1989; Stith et al., 1990).

There is a substantial amount of data to draw upon when reaching conclusions regarding men in abusive relationships (Finkelhor et al., 1988). Abusers are more likely to accept the subordinate status of a woman as a social norm and more commonly believe violent behaviors are socially acceptable (Stith et al., 1990). Abusive males adhere to traditional stereotypic gender/sex roles and support the use of violence to maintain power and control in the family (Petretic-Jackson & Jackson, 1996).

Battering men display decreased self-esteem, diminished assertiveness, a low sense of self-efficacy, and have frequently been exposed to childhood family violence (Tolman, 1990). They are especially prone towards feelings of helplessness, powerlessness, and inadequacy. Batterers are often pathologically jealous, prone to addictions, and demonstrate passive, dependent and antisocial behaviors (Gelles & Cornell, 1990). Histories of sexual aggressiveness and violence towards others, poor impulse control, isolation and poor development of relationship skills are common traits of batterers (Finklehor et al., 1988). Educational levels, levels of occupation, and income are customarily low. In fact, unemployment or underemployment increases the likelihood of battering (Siegler, 1989; Gelles & Cornell, 1990). The woman's pregnancy is also a factor that increases the rate of male battering (Siegler, 1989; Rizk, 1988). Further, it has been indicated that 37 percent of pregnant women seeking obstetrical care report battering in their relationships (Liutkus, 1994).

A HISTORICAL PERSPECTIVE

Victimization of women is not new. Historically, women have been characterized as subordinate to men. Numerous theological teachings (Judeo-Christian as well as Moslem) instruct that women must submit to men. Roman law defined the status of women as absolutely subject to the wishes and desires of their husbands, and women were equated with other personal possessions of men (Siegler, 1989). Throughout history, paternal transmission of wealth and inheritance has been common, and even women's property was controlled by her husband after marriage. Under English Common Law, a woman had no legal existence apart from the relationship with her spouse. Men were legally responsible for the behavior of their wives and were expected to keep their women under control. For example, if a woman was raped, her father or husband could claim compensation from the perpetrator (Siegler, 1989).

In 1883, the state of Maryland outlawed wife abuse after acknowledging that violence against women was assault. In 1910, 35 states followed this lead and also adopted the view that the battering of women is equivalent to assault (Siegler, 1989). Ironically, the women's suffrage movement decreased the focus on the battering of women, as women sought to have increased political power. A woman could not legally refuse her spouse conjugal rights until the 1970s when some states adopted the concept of marital rape as legally recognized.

The advent of the feminist movement greatly altered the perception and understanding of violence perpetrated upon women. The prevailing psychoanalytic view which asserted that battered women were masochistic and gained sexual excitation from beatings was challenged (Costantino, 1981; Gelles & Harrop, 1989) and questions were raised regarding the legitimacy of labeling abused women pathological. Earlier studies which had identified the characteristics of battered women were challenged, particularly because of the small uncontrolled research samples that had been used. Finklehor et al. (1988) claimed that research failed to substantiate characteristics common to battered women, and also failed to substantiate male characteristics as predictors of their abusive behavior. A great deal could be learned by viewing the characteristics of the abuser; however, this was seldom the direction taken to understand the abuse phenomena.

Recent theories of violence towards women expound the view that battering is rooted in patriarchal society (Srinivasan & Davis, 1991). The imbalances of power between men and women leave women vulnerable to abuse. This redefinition of the problem as a social issue invalidates theories of individual pathology. Sociological perspectives investigate domestic violence in the context of social stress, learned violent response, and cycles of perpetuated family violence (Gutierrez, 1987). Feminist perspectives identify battering as a means of obtaining social control and maintaining social oppression (Gutierrez, 1987). Actually, it wasn't until the feminist movement of the 1970s that the battering of women became a problem that required attention and address (Siegler, 1990).

SURVIVORS OF ABUSE AND THE CRIMINAL JUSTICE SYSTEM

In understanding the relationship between the survivors of abuse and the legal system, Parker (1985),

as presented in Siegler (1989), identified three major themes that need to be considered. The first is the *ideology of privacy* where an individual's home is viewed as a private place. Here the acts that occur are considered sacred to the family and what is committed in the privacy of one's own home should be either ignored or overlooked by the public according to this ideology. As long as the couple continues to stay together in the same house, the husband cannot be ordered to change his behavior or to equitably distribute family resources (Siegler, 1989). Many judges will not evict a man from his home because they believe the old adage that "a man's home is his castle" and in evicting him from his home he would in turn become homeless (Mullins, 1994).

The second area discussed in Siegler (1989) is the *gap between what is written law and contemporary practice.* Throughout time the justice system has traditionally been unwilling to intercede and/or intrude in family matters. The survivor of abuse has often felt helpless to persuade police and the courts to intervene with actions designed to control their husbands; while in turn, police have often been frustrated by women who refuse to press charges when incidents occur. The reason's a woman refuses to press charges may vary, but it is clear that greater education of the dynamics of abusive relationships are needed for all involved.

The third area involves the *complexity and lack of integration of existing legal remedies.* Generally, the laws that exist are complex, contradictory, and at times unenforceable. Many times, laws regarding property, divorce, custody, financial obligations, and criminal culpability are difficult to enforce because often they are viewed as separate acts. Although, in domestic violence many of these acts overlap, they are viewed separately and therefore overlooked. Although new domestic violence statutes have reduced this confusion and have increased integration in the jurisdictions in which they have been adopted, a legal representative is still essential for successful negotiation of the system (Siegler, 1989).

Use of legal remedies have been limited in jurisdictions that have not implemented reform. Violation of the civil code are considered criminal offenses. All states have laws that address some form of assault and/or battery, disturbing the peace, disorderly conduct, trespassing and malicious mischief statutes. However, it is difficult to secure initiation of prosecution when the woman is the sole witness and the fine remains small and the probability of the charges being dismissed cannot be overruled.

Although new domestic violence statutes have reduced this confusion and have increased integration in the jurisdictions in which they have been adopted, a legal representative is still recommended for successful negotiation of the system (Siegler, 1989).

Police discretion used to be the most essential part of police work. Today, however, in regard to domestic violence, this is changing and police are now required to process charges. The degree of proarrest policies for batterers continues to evolve but research studies on the short-term effects of batterers remains questionable (Roberts, 1996b). Frisch and Caruso (1996) warn however that even the most complete legal plan to address the battered woman's needs becomes obsolete when those tasked with carrying out policy have no power in enforcing it.

THE ROLE OF THE SOCIAL WORKER

Mullarkey (1988) stated five areas in which the social worker can assist the prosecutor and provide aid to the domestic violence survivor. First, the social worker can help by *providing more information* about the type of abuse, the history of abuse and the circumstances and repercussions resulting from the abuse. Mandatory arrest policies and warrantless arrests can help, but they do not address the entire problem (Roberts, 1996b). Therefore, the role of the social worker in working with the legal representative in providing additional information, which may also include the psychosocial factors surrounding the abuse, becomes influential. After gathering this additional information, the social worker can help the legal system by helping to predict the most dangerous cases, screen survivors for treatment, and help to evaluate and predict potential treatment outcomes (Saunders, 1992). Since the needs of the battered women can be so varied and often require legal, social service, and psychological services, the role of the social worker in providing this information in an integrated way becomes essential. A well-documented community-wide approach, coordinated by the social worker, can help to provide the community-wide support needed to join the efforts of mental health, social service, judicial, and law enforcement

agencies in assisting the battered woman (Roberts, 1996b).

The second type of assistance a social worker can provide is *education*. Social workers have an obligation to educate, and to be educated by, system participants such as police telephone operators and dispatchers, police persons, prosecutors, judges, and those directly involved, such as survivors, the abusers, and family and support system members. They need to be aware of proarrest and mandatory arrest policies and what that involves, as well as the potential of electronic monitoring as part of a coordinated community effort (Roberts, 1996b).

Social workers need to help in the provision of immediate types of education and training for police telephone operators, dispatchers and police officers. The police operators and dispatchers are the first to receive the call for help, and the police person is generally the first to arrive on the scene. This education and training should include police telephone training for screening, assessment, referrals and linkages to immediate social services, basic techniques of police safety, personnel availability, dispute management and crisis intervention techniques, conflict mediation, as well as the ability to provide referral links with the social service worker (Fusco, 1989). It is important for this educative training to stress the importance of viewing the social worker, the police telephone operator and the police officer as an intervention team; and as partners, each deserves the respect, support, cooperation and feedback of the other. Further, the role of the social worker is crucial in reminding those involved in the "intervention team" of the rights of the individual, the obligations to ensure equality of access, the event of sex-role stereotyping, the social and emotion effects of discrimination upon victims, the dynamics of victimization, and other relevant psychosocial factors that need to be considered (Martin, 1988).

Roberts (1996c) believes that in addition to training front line workers, attention to education and training also needs to be provided for court clerks, case managers, legal advocates, and judges.

Many times, those trained in the legal system focus on the conviction as the primary measure for the accomplishment of justice. The feelings and pain caused by the abuser to the female survivor, her children and/or her family support system may be overlooked. The role of the social worker is important not only to educate those in the legal system of the dynamics and issues that surround the abusive situation but also to serve as a "gatekeeper" for addressing the psychosocial aspects that have occurred regardless of the legal outcome that results.

The third role that the social worker can assume in this situation is to serve as a *safe individual* with whom the survivor can develop trust and feel comfortable. As part of the dynamics that surround the abusive relationship, many of these women are isolated from family and friends and have been taught to avoid and fear contact from others outside the abusive relationship. Many times they must face conflicting feelings from within as well as the desire to escape the entire situation. With the prospect of conviction, these individuals must face the defendant and others who may threaten retaliation if the abuser faces conviction and possible incarceration. Anticipation about the outcome of the legal process may leave the survivor to feel a mixture of relief and guilt. These contradictory emotions may make the survivor hamper her own testimony and appear to others as an unreliable witness. To perform and represent herself in the best possible stance, the survivor needs to feel supported in this process. Many times, the prosecutor is rushed and cannot provide the rapport building that is needed to get the survivor to trust him/her; therefore, the role of the social worker becomes critical in providing a bridge between the legal representation and the survivor. Furthermore, the social worker must also strive to not only address but improve policies and procedures that affect survivors building continued and deserving trust on the part of the survivor (Martin, 1988).

The fourth role the social worker needs to embrace is that of *advocate*. This role has always been critical for social work professionals, and within the legal system, advocating for the survivor through all stage of the criminal process is essential. Social work professionals have the right to serve as advocates for the survivor, even before an arrest is made or while a case is pending trial or in the appellate stage (Mullarkey, 1988). The role of the survivor's advocate (aka victim's advocate) is essential to assist the client to empower herself to act as her own representative whenever possible (Martin, 1988). When this is not possible, the social work professional can speak with the permission of the client when she is either too distraught or incapacitated by the fear of retribution. Many states now permit the survivor or the survivor's advocate to address the judge at sentencing (Mullarkey, 1988).

In order, however, for the social worker to be successful as an advocate for the domestically abused woman, s/he must know and understand two major areas. The first area is the complexities that can result within the legal system. Therefore, the social worker needs to make her/himself aware of the variety of system components that are involved. These components of the legal system include law enforcement procedures, prosecution and correction possibilities. The second area is advocation with family members and the support system that the client will need to return. There are many myths and beliefs that are ingrained in our society (Roberts, 1996a). Survivors of abuse will be forced to address and confront these myths that are often subscribed to by family and friends. The role of the social worker becomes essential in advocating not only for the client but to ensure that her support system is made aware of the difficulties the client has encountered. The social worker can assist the survivor by (1) letting individuals in the support system know the strengths of the survivor and (2) the reason it is necessary for her to leave the abusive relationship, and (3) why she should formally put an end to abuse and initiate legally sanctioned punishment for the abuser.

The fifth area in which Mullarkey (1988) stated that the social worker can assist the prosecutor and provide aid to the domestic violence survivor was in the role of the *expert witness*. Here, the social worker can provide professional information to promote and clarify the understanding of the survivor's behavior (Saunders, 1992, Martin, 1988). Although many social workers welcome the opportunity to assist the client, they may also remain unsure of their role in the protection of their client's legal rights. The counseling sessions and written notes may reflect information that the social worker does not want to share for fear that disclosure of the material might harm the case of the survivor. For example, many times the survivor is angry at the abuser and voices this anger in an attempt to emotionally distance herself from the abuser. Therefore, the social worker should take careful notes and realize that these notes could be subpoenaed into a court of law. "The constitutional guarantee to confront accusers provided by the Sixth Amendment can be interpreted by any competent court to override any privacy statute or shield law" (Mullarkey, 1988:49).

Without a court order, social workers are not required to speak to defendants, attorneys or investigators outside of the courtroom. Mullarkey (1988) recommends that when social workers are summoned to the courtroom, they should take into account: (1) the importance of appearing and remaining professional and non-partisan; (2) that all questions should be answered directly and fully; (3) if a question is unclear, immediately ask for clarification; (4) the importance of going over possible questions with prosecutor before testifying; and (5) that every note, professional conversation and report prepared by a social worker is potentially discoverable by the defendant and/or his legal representation.

CONCLUSIONS

The role of the social worker in the criminal justice system remains essential. Women who become survivors of abuse need the services and protection that law enforcement can provide. In turn, survivors also need to be treated with dignity and respect. The role of the social worker is crucial in providing the following services to the survivors of abuse: (1) in *providing more information* about the type of abuse, the history of abuse and the circumstances and repercussions resulting from the abuse; (2) providing education to and be educated by system participants such as police telephone operators and dispatchers, police persons, prosecutors, judges and those directly involved such as the survivors, the abusers and family and support system members; (3) to assume the role of a *safe individual* with whom the survivor can develop trust and feel comfortable; (4) to advocate for the survivor through all stages of the criminal process; and (5) the social worker can assist the prosecutor and provide aid to the domestic violence survivor in the role of the *expert witness*.

Social workers and the legal representatives need to formulate a team approach. In using this model, legal representatives need to be trained to view domestic assault situations as appropriate and routine, requiring police intervention. In this type of intervention legal representatives and social workers will join together and work together, each serving an integral role on the intervention team.

Counseling, social service assistance and protection must be carefully linked together and available to the abuse survivor on a 24-hour basis (Roberts, 1996b). Morning or next-day referrals are a poor substitute for the immediate response that is needed in the crisis situation. Social work professionals need to be available to directly work with police and to be able to quickly provide the psychosocial intervention needed.

FUTURE DIRECTIONS

The criminal justice system should be an effective force in decreasing violence against women. Unfortunately, our society and our laws continue to view the battered woman as largely responsible for the abuse and violence she endures and have failed to provide sufficient support. Both short-term emergency support and long-term support services are needed (Davis, Hagen & Early, 1994). Further, it is crucial that initiation into the support services for battered women be done on a 24-hour basis and in conjunction with the domestic violence call. This would allow the social worker to start intervention services at the crisis scene or as soon after the incident as possible. Our current system of referral "after the fact" is not meeting the needs of many of the survivors of abuse.

The domestic violence shelter can offer an "immediate" safe place for women who wish to escape an abusive situation. Unfortunately, however, existing shelters are often too few and too far in between. There are few shelters convenient to women in rural areas, and to establish an emergency shelter for battered women in the city still requires overcoming a number of obstacles. Prior to getting approval for the facility, a review of property disposition by community boards and city planners is the requirement in many cities. However, this requirement creates the potential for not only breaching the confidentiality of the women and children who depend on the emergency shelter for services but also risks the safety of these women and children. In addition, many community residents object to having emergency shelters in their own neighborhoods because they believe it will be disruptive to the neighborhood (Mullins, 1994).

The development and establishment of an emergency shelter is costly and time consuming, and most organizations usually lack the skills, resources and time to oversee such an extensive project. Surveys show that up to 31 percent of all emergency shelters for battered women are entirely dependent upon government funding. The remaining 69 percent rely on government funding for over half of their operating expenses (Mullins, 1994). Because shelters are limited to emergency short-term relief, long-term solutions to the problem of housing still need to be addressed. The result of the decrease in federal government's funding to housing assistance programs during the past 15 years has only served to undermine the ability of low-income individuals and families to find affordable housing. The difficulty for battered women and their children in locating adequate long-term housing is further complicated when their unique concerns about the safety must be factored into their plans (Mullins, 1994).

We must establish programs and policies that recognize the severity of domestic violence, as well as develop long-term solutions to address the need for emergency housing and financial support systems. One such change in this direction is the 1994 Violence Against Women Act. The 1994 Violence Against Women Act (VAWA) is a comprehensive federal response to the problems of domestic violence that directs the focus of domestic violence away from blaming the woman for the abuse she suffers. The purpose of VAWA is to create domestic violence preventative policies. The VAWA treats domestic violence as a major law enforcement priority and provides for improved services to victims of domestic violence. Title II of the bill, the Safe Homes Act, will increase federal funding for battered women's shelters and related programs. It also establishes a new federal crime statute for spouse abuse committed during interstate travel (Roberts, 1996a).

By creating emergency and long-term solutions for battered women's housing and survival needs, VAWA represents an important step in the government's commitment to prevent domestic violence. Until recently, our society and legal system has viewed the preservation of the family as paramount. Fortunately, this is changing. We must break from our history of preserving the family at the expense of protecting the women from abuse.

Because social workers practice in a broad spectrum of the public and private sectors, they have enormous potential for impacting on the problem of violence against women (Martin, 1988). If the social work profession is truly interested in helping battered women, the profession must demand and advocate for changes in our laws and legal system that prevent domestic violence. Social workers clearly recognize the importance of counseling and supportive services; however, to plan for the future, they must never lose sight of the importance of advocacy for social policy change in assisting the survivors of domestic violence. Only by clearly understanding and outlining the role of the social worker, in conjunction with our legal counterparts, can social work make inroads towards ending violence against women (Litsky, 1994; Roberts, 1996b).

REFERENCES

Davis, L., Hagen, J., & Early, T. (1994). Social services for battered women: Are they adequate, accessible, and appropriate? *39*(6), 695–704.

Davidson, B. P., & Jenkins, P. J. (1989). Class diversity in shelter life. *Social Work, 34*(6), 491–95.

Dziegielewski, S. F., Resnick, C., & Krause, N. (1996). Shelter based crisis intervention with abused women. In A. Roberts (Ed.), *Helping battered women: New perspectives* (pp. 151–171). New York: Oxford University Press.

Dziegielewski, S. F., & Resnick, C. (1996). Crisis intervention in the shelter setting. In A. R. Roberts (Ed.), *Crisis management and brief treatment* (pp. 123–141). Chicago: Nelson Hall.

Edleson, J. L. (1991, June). Note on history: Social worker's intervention in woman abuse: 1907–1945. *Social Service Review,* June, 304–13.

Edleson, J. L. (1992). *Intervention with men who batter: An ecological approach.* Newbury Park, CA: Sage.

Finkelhor, D. (1988). *Stopping family violence.* London: Sage.

Frisch, L. A., & Caruso, J. M. (1996). In A. R. Roberts (Ed.), *Helping battered women* (pp. 102–131). New York: Oxford University Press.

Fusco, L. J. (1989). Integrating systems: Police, courts and assaulted women. In B. Pressman, G. Cameron & M. Rothery (Eds.), *Interviewing with assaulted women; Current theory, research and practice* (pp. 125–135).

Ganley, A. L. (1989). Integrating feminist and social learning analyses of aggression: Creating multiple models for intervention with men who batter. In P. L. Caesar & L. K. Hamberger (Eds.), *Treating men who batter.* New York: Springer.

Gelles, R. J. (1979). Violence in the American family. *Journal of Social Issues, 35*(1), 15–39.

Gelles, R. J. (1987). *The violent home*. London: Sage.

Gelles, R. J., & Harrop, J. W. (1989). Violence, battering, and psychological distress among women. *Journal of Interpersonal Violence, 4*(4), December, 400–420.

Gelles, R. J., & Cornell, C. P. (1990). *Intimate violence in families*. London: Sage.

Gutierrez, L. M. (1987). Social work theories and practice with battered women; A conflict-of-values analysis. *Affilia*, Summer, 36–52.

Jones, A. (1994). *Next time she'll be dead: Battering and how to stop it*. Boston: Beacon Press.

Litsky, M. (1994). Reforming the criminal justice system can decrease violence against women. In B. Leone, B. Szumski, K. de Koster, K. Swisher, C. Wekesser & W. Barbour (Eds.), *Violence against women*. San Diego, CA: Greenhaven Press.

Liutkus, J. F. (1994, April). Wife assault: An issue for women's health. *Internal Medicine*, 41–53.

Mancoske, R. J., Standifer, D., & Cauley, C. (1994). The effectiveness of brief counseling services for battered women. *Research on Social Work Practice, 4*(1), January, 53–63.

Martin, M. (1988). A social worker's response. In N. Hutchings (Ed.), *The violent family: Victimization of women, children, and elders*. New York: Human Sciences Press.

McShane, C. (1979). Community services for battered women. *Social Work, 24*(1), 34–39.

Mullarkey, E. (1988). The legal system for victims of violence. In N. Hutchings (Ed.), *The violent family: Victimization of women, children, and elders* (pp. 43–52).

Mullins, G. P. (1994). The battered woman and homelessness. *Journal of Law and Policy, 3*(1), 237–255.

Pence, E. (1989). Batterer programs: Shifting from community collusion to community confrontation. In P. L. Caesar & L. K. Hamberger (Eds.), *Treating men who batter*. New York: Springer.

Petretic-Jackson, P. A., & Jackson, T. (1996). Mental health interventions with battered women. In A. Roberts (Ed.), *Helping battered women: New perspectives* (pp. 188–221). New York: Oxford University Press.

Rizk, M. (1988, April). Domestic violence during pregnancy. *Proceedings family violence: Public health social work's role in prevention* (pp. 19–31). Bureau of Maternal and Child Health, Department of Health and Human Services, Pittsburgh, PA.

Roberts, A. R. (1996a). Introduction: Myths and realities regarding battered women. In A. Roberts (Ed.), *Helping battered women: New perspectives and remedies* (pp. 3–12). New York: Oxford University Press.

Roberts, A. R. (1996b). Police response to battered women: Past, present and future. In A. Roberts (Ed.), *Helping battered women: New perspectives and remedies* (pp. 85–95). New York: Oxford University Press.

Roberts, A. R. (1996c). Court responses to battered women. In A. Roberts (Ed.), *Helping battered women: New perspectives and remedies* (pp. 96–101). New York: Oxford University Press.

Saunders, D. G. (1992). Woman battering. In R. T. Ammerman & M. Hersen (Eds.), *Assessment of family violence; A clinical and legal source book*. New York: John Wiley and Sons.

Schneider, E. M. (1994). Society's belief in family privacy contributes to domestic violence. In B. Leone, B. Szumski, K. de Koster, K. Swisher, C. Wekesser & W. Barbour (Eds.), *Violence against women*. San Diego, CA: Greenhaven Press.

Siegler, R. T. (1989). *Domestic violence in context: An assessment of community attitudes*. Lexington, MA: D.C. Heath.

Srinivasan, M., & Davis, L. V. (1991). A shelter: An organization like any other? *Affilia, 6*(1), Spring, 38–57.

Star, B., Clark, C. G., Goetz, K. M. & O'Malia, L. (1979). Psychological aspects of wife beating. *Social Casework, 60*(8), 479–87.

Stark, E., Flitcraft, W., & Frazier, W. (1979). Medicine and patriarchal violence: The social construction of a "private" event. *International Journal of Health Services, 9*(3), 461–493.

Statman, J. B. (1990). *The battered woman's survival guide: Breaking the cycle*. Dallas, TX: Taylor.

Stith, S. M., Williams, M. B., & Rosen, K. (1990). *Violence hits home: Comprehensive treatment approaches to domestic violence*. New York: Springer.

Tolman, R. M. & Bennett, L. W. (1990). A review of quantitative research on men who batter. *Journal of Interpersonal Violence, 5*(1), March, 87–118.

Chapter **21**

The Role of Social Work in Victim/Witness Assistance Programs

Albert R. Roberts

INTRODUCTION

Twenty five years ago, victims' rights advocates and victim service and victim/witness assistance programs were rarely available in communities throughout the United States. Now, in 2006, there are over ten thousand victim/witness assistance programs, battered women's shelters, rape crisis programs, and support groups for survivors of violent crimes nationwide. The victims' movement has grown remarkably during the past two decades. The proliferation of programs is a direct result of the federal Victims of Crime Act (VOCA) funding, state and county general revenue grants, VAWA I, II, and III, and earmarking a percentage of state penalty assessments and/or fines levied on criminal offenders.

In cities and counties throughout the United States, victims of crime are receiving help from victim service and witness assistance programs. Whether people are victimized in a small town with a population of 17,000 such as Black River Falls, Wisconsin, or in major metropolitan areas such as Atlanta, New York City or San Francisco, services from a victim/witness assistance program are available to them (Roberts, 1995).

SCOPE OF THE PROBLEM

There has been a growing awareness among social work leaders, police administrators and prosecutors alike of the alarming prevalence of violent crimes and the rights of crime victims. Based on recent data from the National Crime Survey (NCS), the Federal Bureau of Investigations (2004) *Uniform Crime Reports* (UCR), aggregate estimates indicate that one violent crime occurs every 22 seconds, one aggrevated assult every 34.8 seconds, one robbery every 1.2 minutes, one forible rape every 5.8 minutes, and one murder every 32.9 minutes, somewhere in the U.S. Each year, millions of crime victims are physically, emotionally, and/or financially damaged by perpetrators of violent crime. In the aftermath of a violent crime, victims often have to cope with physical pain, psychological trauma, financial loss, and court proceedings which all too frequently seem impersonal and confusing. Many victims and witnesses have their first contact with the criminal justice system as a result of being victimized. This first meeting can be frightening and confusing. During the past fifteen years, a growing number of counties and cities have developed victim service and witness assistance programs, victim compensation programs, and specialized domestic violence programs to reduce the impact that violent crime has upon the lives of victims and witnesses.

BRIEF HISTORICAL BACKGROUND

For decades the interest of victims and witnesses were ignored by the courts. Until the mid-1970s correctional reformers and noted authors were revered as founders and international experts in criminology and penology. Millions of dollars were spent in the 1950s and 1960s on rehabilitation programs aimed at changing convicted felons into law-abiding citizens. Millions of dollars were also spent by the courts on processing and protecting the best interests of defendants. In sharp contrast to the offender, crime victims had to wait in the halls of dreary courtrooms while the defendant sometimes threatened or intimidated them. Separate waiting rooms for witnesses and/or their children were practically nonexistent. While extensive correctional treatment, educational and social services programs were available to convicted offenders (Roberts, 1971, 1974), the victim and their family who were often shattered by the victimization were given no services (McDonald, 1976).

By the mid-1970s when the first victim/witness assistance and rape crisis programs were initiated, the pendulum began to shift toward providing critically needed services for innocent crime victims and fewer rehabilitation programs for convicted felons (Roberts, 1992). The changed focus was related to how the crime victim was treated throughout the criminal justice system, from the initial contact with a police officer or detective to the testimony in court. Historically, too many crime victims had been victimized twice: first during the actual crime and then, again, when insensitive and unresponsive police and prosecutors ignored their calls or requests for assistance, and/or subjected them to harsh, repeated and victim-blaming questions (McDonald, 1976).

The crime victims' movement has come a long way in the past thirty years. Between fiscal years 1973 and 1975 the Law Enforcement Assistance Administration (LEAA) spent several million dollars for victim/witness assistance demonstration projects. During the early 1970s a growing number of prosecutors' offices in populated cities and counties throughout the United States became computerized. For the first time, several systematic victim studies were conducted. These studies indicated that "after the victim had decided to report the crime but before the problem of continuances and delays had begun to operate, many crime cases were lost because witnesses did not want to cooperate" (McDonald, 1976, p. 29).

The research documenting witness non-cooperation, and the insensitive and apathetic treatment of victims and witnesses by court staff, led to the federal LEAA funding of eighteen victim and victim/witness assistance programs. Ten of these programs were prosecutor-based witness assistance programs, four were victim assistance programs under the direction of a non-profit social service agency, a county probation department, and a police department. The remaining four programs focused on providing advocacy and

crisis intervention to victims of rape or child abuse.

In the early 1980s, with the demise of LEAA, federal grants to victim assistance programs declined. Existing programs tried to make up for the loss of LEAA seed grants by requesting county or city general revenue funding. At first, some local government sources were unwilling to allocate sufficient funds. However, between 1981 and 1985, 28 states enacted legislation to fund both established and new programs to aid victims and witnesses. The trend among state legislatures has been to raise the funds for these programs by earmarking a percentage of penalty assessments and/or fines on criminal offenders to these programs. Nineteen of the twenty-eight states fund victim/witness assistance programs through penalty assessments and fines, while the remaining nine states fund victim assistance through general state revenues (Roberts, 1990).

Since the passage of the landmark Victims of Crime Act (VOCA) of 1984, responsive federal, state and county agencies have allocated over $650 million throughout the nation to aid crime victims. A large portion of these funds come from fines and offender penalty assessments on convicted felons. Unfortunately, several states are rapidly losing ground in the collection of restitution and penalty assessments. The author predicts that those states with responsive legislators and highly organized victim compensation and restitution or corrections boards will hire the necessary number of accountants, fiscal monitors, and computer-literate administrators necessary for maintaining 90 percent or higher collection of fees (Roberts, 1995).

COMPARING VICTIM SERVICE AND VICTIM/WITNESS ASSISTANCE PROGRAMS

Victim/witness assistance programs are usually located either within the local county prosecutor's suite of offices, the county courthouse, or across the street from the court building. These programs are designed to encourage witness cooperation in the filing of criminal charges as well as testifying in court. In general, these programs include a witness notification and case monitoring system in which staff keep witnesses advised of indictment, continuances, and postponements; specific trial and hearing dates; negotiated pleas, and trial outcomes. In addition, many of these programs provide secure and comfortable reception rooms for witnesses waiting to testify in court, transportation services, and court escort in the form of accompanying the witness to court and remaining with the individual in order to explain and interpret the court proceedings. Typically, these programs also prepare and distribute court-orientation pamphlets about the adjudication process on topics such as "Crime Victims' Bill of Rights," "Witness Guidelines for Courtroom Testimony," "What You Should Know about Your Criminal Court and Court Process," and "Information Guide for Crime Victims" (Roberts, 1992).

According to the author's national organizational survey of victim service and witness assistance programs, slightly under one-third of these programs reported having some form of child care for the children of victims and witnesses while the parents testified in court. Providing responsible and structured child care for a parent while they are testifying in court can provide an important service (Roberts, 1990). Unfortunately, most criminal justice agencies are very different than social work agencies, in that they do not usually realize that victims' and witnesses' children are affected by their parents' emotional reactions, losses, physical injuries and disruptions due to being a victim of a crime. Victim/witness assistance programs should be concerned with the special needs of children not only because many parent witnesses will not be able to testify if they cannot find child care during a traumatizing court ordeal, but because it is the humane thing to do. An added benefit is that some children may have witnessed the crime and noticed additional identifying characteristics of the perpetrator (Roberts, 1995).

The overriding objectives of victim/witness assistance programs and units are to assist witnesses in overcoming the anxiety and trauma associated with testifying in court, while encouraging witness cooperation in the prosecution of criminal cases. The primary objectives in these programs are as follows:

1. Providing victims and witnesses with the message that their cooperation is essential to crime control efforts and successful criminal prosecution.
2. Informing victims and witnesses of their rights to receive dignified and compassionate treatment by criminal justice authorities.
3. Providing information to witnesses on court

process, the scheduling off the case, the trial, and the disposition.
4. Providing orientation to court and tips on how best to accurately recall the crime scene and testify (Roberts, 1990).

Victim service or crisis intervention programs for crime victims do not seem to be as common as victim/witness assistance programs. This type of program is usually lodged in a police department, sheriff's office, hospital, probation department, or not-for-profit social service agency. Typically, these programs attempt to intervene within the first 24 hours after the victimization. They provide a comprehensive range of essential services for crime victims, including responding to the crime scene; crisis counseling; help in completing victim compensation applications; emergency financial assistance and food vouchers to local supermarkets; transportation to court, the local battered women's shelter, the hospital, or the victim assistance program office; repairing or replacing broken locks and windows; assistance in replacing lost documents (e.g., birth certificates, marriage licenses, wills); and referrals to community mental health centers and social service agencies for extended counseling and short-term psychotherapy.

The primary objectives of victim service programs include providing early and timely intervention and aid to crime victims through 24-hour mobile response teams; crisis intervention at the crime scene, the hospital or local battered women's shelter; emergency lock repairs; assistance in completing victim compensation award applications; helping the victim complete forms for replacing lost documents; and referral to the prosecutor's domestic violence and sexual assault intake unit as well as community mental health centers.

What Types of Individuals Are Served by Victim/Witness Assistance Programs?

This type of program serves witnesses who pursue prosecution for the following types of criminal cases:
- aggravated murder
- murder
- voluntary manslaughter
- involuntary manslaughter
- aggravated vehicular homicide, felonious vehicular homicide

- felonious assault
- domestic violence
- child sexual abuse
- kidnapping
- abduction
- extortion
- rape
- felonious sexual penetration
- aggravated robbery
- robbery
- aggravated burglary
- burglary

What Types of Individuals Are Served by Victim Service and Crisis Intervention Programs?

Typically, these programs provide services to all victims of violent and property-related crimes. Certain types of victims have special needs, and as a result many of these victim-oriented programs have also begun to provide outreach services to the following, particularly vulnerable crime victims: the elderly, minorities (especially Hispanics, Asians, African-Americans, and native Americans), battered women, and sexually assaulted children.

The impact of crime is often severe for the elderly, non-English-speaking minorities and battered women. The elderly crime victim often has no bank account (or limited savings) from which they can withdraw funds in an emergency. Unless they receive emergency funds or food vouchers from a local victim assistance program, they often have to wait a month for their next social security check. They are also more likely to need hospital care. Physical conditions associated with aging, such as osteoporosis and frailty, can mean that elderly victims who are hurt take longer to heal and are more likely to need hospital care (Roberts, 1990). Social worker Judith Moore, coordinator of the Indianapolis Police Department Victim Assistance Unit, recently reported to the author that her unit tries to help several thousand elderly victims of burglary each year. "With only five full-time staff, we just don't have the manpower to help all the elderly/senior burglary victims." Due to cultural barriers, Hispanic and Asian women are reluctant to report domestic violence and sexual assault offenses or ask for victim assistance because reporting male offenders would seriously break cultural mores. These female victims also seem to have more intense fears of retaliation than other women. A study of 105 battered women in New Jersey, conducted by Roberts and Bonilla-Santiago, found that the overwhelming majority of Hispanic batterers used knives on their victims. Many of these women had their faces slashed and were threatened with death if they were not totally obedient (Roberts, 1992).

Battered women are frequently in critical need of crisis intervention and emergency shelter. These crime victims often turn to their local city or county law enforcement agency when confronted with the life-threatening danger posed by domestic violence. Police-based crisis intervention units in Houston, Texas; Tucson, Arizona; and San Diego, California recently reported that a large number of their crisis callers are battered women. A crisis team (always working in pairs) responds to the crime scene and provides crisis counseling, advocacy, transportation to and from medical centers and shelters, and referrals to mental health and social service agencies. The growing plight of battered women is evidenced by the increased development of emergency shelters from seven in 1974 to over 1,250 in 1995 (Roberts, 1996).

LEGISLATION, FUNDING, AND STABILITY

During the past two decades, the organizational stability as well as the number of victim/witness assistance centers and programs have varied. Most victim/witness assistance programs are developed by county and city prosecutors. Most of these prosecutor-based programs have received federal VOCA pass-through grants from their respective state attorney general's office or state VOCA coordinator on an annual basis. These programs seem to be the most well-established and stable with regard to their funding. In sharp contrast, some of the police-based and hospital-based victim assistance programs go out of business in three to five years. These temporary victim assistance programs are initiated through federal or state start-up grants (seed money), and either no monetary match or only a 10 percent match from the county or municipality budget. Unfortunately, without a sustained monetary commitment from the mayor, city council, hospital president or CEO, or police chief, these programs are bound to fail.

With adequate funding, victim assistance and rape crisis programs flourish and meet the needs of thousands of violent crime victims annually. A growing number of large medical centers and police departments have well-established programs – e.g., Beth Israel Hospital (Boston), Mt. Sinai Hospital (New York City), Santa Monica Hospital (California), Dallas Police Department (Texas), Rochester Police Department (New York), and Seattle Police Department (Washington).

The largest growth in the number of programs came about during the period from 1984–1991. For example, in the Commonwealth of Massachusetts, annual revenues surged in the beginning from $137,058 in FY 1984 to $2,286,512 in FY 1985. During the next seven fiscal years, victims witness revenues steadily increased from $2.2 million in FY 85 to $7.9 in FY 91. This represents a major increase of over 250 percent in the seven-year period. However, revenues to the victim fund dropped by 25 percent between fiscal years 1991 and 1993. On the federal level, the funding of victim services, domestic violence and witness assistance programs has also steadily increased from an allocation of more than $68 million in fiscal year 1985 to $115 million in FY 1991 (Roberts, 1995).

STAFFING PATTERNS

Victim/witness assistance programs are located throughout the United States. They are similar in a number of ways, particularly in the size and responsibility of their staff. According to the senior author's national organizational survey, three-fourths of the programs were staffed by five or fewer full-time employees. Approximately ten percent indicated that they had medium-sized staffs of eleven or more full-time employees. Only 3 percent were large programs with 24 or more full-time staff. The predominant staffing pattern consisted of a victim/witness program director/coordinator, two victim advocates/counselors, a secretary, and a data-entry person. The program coordinator reported directed to the county prosecutor, the chief counsel to the prosecutor, or a deputy prosecutor responsible for all sex crimes (e.g., sexual assault and domestic violence cases). The primary responsibility of the victim advocates/counselors is the provision of services to witnesses, particularly wit-

nesses to violent crimes where a person has been charged with one or more criminal offenses. Victim/witness advocates are responsible for accompanying the witness to the pre-filing hearing, preliminary hearing, deposition hearing, and/or the trial in order to ensure that each witness is treated fairly and compassionately by the attorneys, court clerk, and the magistrate. In addition, it is important for the coordinator or victim advocates to accompany the victim/witness to all official appointments related to the filing and processing of the criminal court cases. For example, if the victim/witness has been sexually assaulted, the victim advocate will either accompany or meet the victim at the hospital or medical facility to make sure that the victim's rights are protected.

Many programs rely on volunteer assistance to provide needed services. More than half (52%) of the respondents to Roberts's (1990) national survey reported that they utilized volunteers. While approximately one-third of the programs used one to four volunteers, almost half of the programs had eleven or more volunteers. Programs with smaller paid staff had a tendency to rely heavily on volunteers. Volunteer participation enabled programs to provide services to victims and witnesses in small communities such as Xenia, Ohio (population 130,000, four full-time staff, 14 volunteers), Greensboro, North Carolina (population 360,000, 2 full-time staff, 12 volunteers). The programs in highly populated cities had a small number of volunteers relative to their paid staff. For example, Pittsburgh, Pennsylvania with a population of over 1.5 million has a victim/witness assistance program with 14 full-time paid staff and 15–18 volunteers.

With regard to the educational background of staff, over 90 percent of the employees of victim/witness assistance programs have a bachelor's degree; of that group only 28 percent have a graduate degree. Usually the graduate degree is a masters in social work (M.S.W.), or a masters in sociology, counseling, or criminal justice. The professional degrees earned by the coordinators/directors of victim/witness assistance programs varies. Most of them have master's degrees in counseling, education, criminal justice, psychology, or social work. One-third have M.S.W. degrees, and most of these program coordinators have completed courses in social welfare policy, planning and management, administration, and crisis intervention and brief treatment (Roberts, 1990).

One of the best ways to prepare for a career in

victim services and victim assistance is to complete a block field placement at a comprehensive victim/witness assistance program. Most graduate schools of social work offer opportunities for their M.S.W. students to bridge theory and practice at a placement in a prosecutor-based victim assistance program, a sexual assault intervention center, a battered women's shelter, or at a crisis intervention unit. Graduate programs in social work are unique because of the emphasis on fieldwork, regular supervision of beginning social workers, and weekly case consultations.

REFERENCES

Bureau of Justice Statistics. (1992). *Criminal victimization in the United States, 1991.* Washington, D.C.: U.S. Government Printing Office.

Cronin, R. C., & Bourque, B. (1981). *National Evaluation Program Phase I Report: Assessment of victim witness assistance progects.* Washington, D.C.: U.S. Department of Justice.

Federal Bureau of Investigation (FBI) (2004). *Crime in the United States-2003: Uniform Crime Reports.* Washington, D.C.: U.S. Department of Justice. Government Printing office.

Gandy, J. T. (1983). Social work and victim assistance programs. In A. R. Roberts (Ed.), *Social work in juvenile and criminal justice settings.* Springfield, IL: Charles C Thomas.

McDonald, W. F. (Ed.). (1976). *Criminal justice and the victim.* Beverly Hills, CA: Sage.

Roberts, A. R. (1971). *Sourcebook on prison education: Past, present and future.* Springfield, IL: Charles C Thomas.

Roberts, A. R. (1974). *Correctional treatment of the offender.* Springfield, IL: Charles C Thomas.

Roberts, A. R. (1990). *Helping crime victims: Research, policy and practice.* Newbury Park, CA; Sage.

Roberts, A. R. (1992). Victim/witness programs: Questions and answers. *FBI Law Enforcement Bulletin, 61*(12), 12–16.

Roberts, A. R. (1995). Victim services and victim/witness assistance programs. In R. L. Edwards & J. Hopps (Eds.), *Encyclopedia of social work* (pp. 2440–2444). Washington, D.C.: NASW.

Roberts, A. R. (1996). Myths, realities and policy reforms for battered women. In A. R. Roberts (Ed.), *Helping battered women: New perspectives and remedies* (pp. 3–15). New York: Oxford University Press.

Smith, M. J. (1990). *Program evaluation in human services.* New York: Springer.

Section V

Probation, Parole, and Court Settings

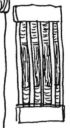

Chapter 22

Therapeutic Jurisprudence in Social Work and Criminal Justice

Carrie J. Petrucci

The collaboration and multidisciplinary trends of the early twenty-first century have continued to involve social workers in legal settings. Specialized courts, combination social work and legal clinical services, court advocates, and MSW/JD's are just a few of the opportunities for social workers to practice in various capacities with others in law (Golick & Lessem, 2004; Voyvodic & Medcalf, 2004; Wright, 2005). The field of social work also has much common ground with the topic of this chapter: therapeutic jurisprudence. Developed by law professors David Wexler and Bruce Winick, therapeutic jurisprudence focuses on the law as a social force in people's lives. This chapter will explain the basic tenets of therapeutic jurisprudence, review current social science and legal research that has explored therapeutic jurisprudence in social work and criminal justice, discuss common themes across therapeutic jurisprudence and social work, and suggest future directions. The aim of the chapter is to familiarize social work students and practitioners with what therapeutic jurisprudence is, the opportunities and debates that it presents, and how it can be utilized to improve social work and legal practice.

WHAT IS THERAPEUTIC JURISPRUDENCE?

Therapeutic jurisprudence considers how the law impacts people's health and well-being (Slobogin, 1995). Law is seen as a social force that can influence attitudes and behavior. Therapeutic jurisprudence seeks to enhance "therapeutic effects," or whatever might be considered positive consequences for those involved in law, over "antitherapeutic effects," or whatever might be considered harmful or negative consequences. Simultaneously, however, due process issues (protection of individual rights) must also be considered alongside of therapeutic and antitherapeutic consequences. A nonadversarial approach is not specifically implied. Thus, therapeutic jurisprudence is not a radical reform theory. Rather, it attempts to make change from within the legal system by asking questions related to health and well-being alongside standard due process questions. Therapeutic jurisprudence does not dictate which therapeutic or anti-therapeutic effects or due process considerations ought to take precedence; it merely suggests that all effects be explicitly stated and considered (Schopp, 1998). Moreover, change does not necessarily assume legislative action on how a law is written, although this can be pursued. Rather, change can incorporate how law is carried out in informal as well as formal legal practice that may not require formal policy changes. Stated another way, therapeutic jurisprudence asks how *legal actors, legal rules*, and *legal procedures* can be utilized to enhance therapeutic effects of law, and decrease antitherapeutic effects, without displacing due process (see Figure 22-1) (Wexler, 1990; 1995; Wexler & Winick, 1991; 1996; Winick, 1997; 2000).

By definition, therapeutic jurisprudence is an interdisciplinary approach that seeks to integrate research-based strategies from the social and behavioral sciences into legal practice. In this way, it is very much in line with the current research-based or evidence-based practice approaches in social work (Kirk & Reid, 2000). A therapeutic jurisprudence approach posits that legal practice can be enhanced by bringing the best and most appropriate strategies of other disciplines into the legal arena. In essence, effectiveness

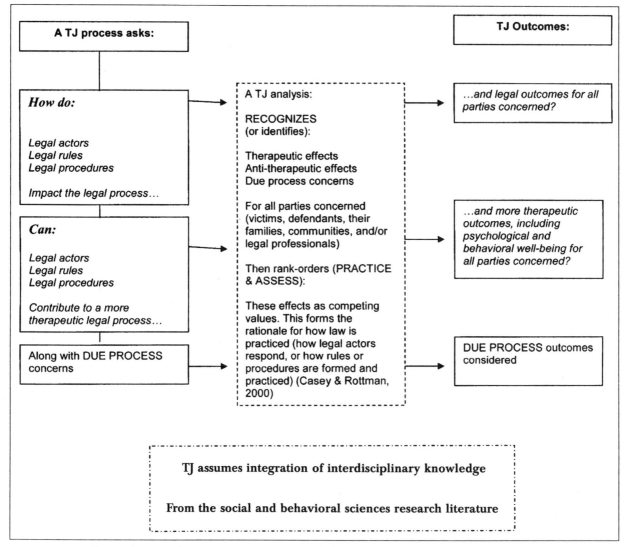

Figure 22-1. A therapeutic jurisprudence (TJ) perspective in practice and research.

of the legal system is the implicit goal, with effectiveness defined as achieving therapeutic impacts for those coming into contact with the legal system alongside of due process. David Wexler (2000) provides an example of this in his discussion of a cognitive-behavioral approach to relapse prevention plans for youth offenders. Cognitive-behavioral approaches have received considerable support in the research literature (McGuire, 2004) as has the notion of relapse prevention (Wexler, 1999). Wexler suggests that with the assistance of a probation officer or social worker, a youth would be responsible for developing

his own relapse prevention plan. This plan would include identification of the thinking patterns that got the youth into trouble, stating how he would change these thinking patterns, and coming up with a plan of what he will do when he encounters similar high-risk situations. Therapeutic jurisprudence encourages integration of these kinds of empirically tested strategies to enhance therapeutic effects.

Therapeutic jurisprudence emerged in the 1980s out of mental health law. This area of law focused on the legal issues of people with mental health issues, such as the right to refuse treatment or involuntary hospitalization. Cofounders David Wexler and Bruce Winick sought to expand considerations in the legal process beyond a focus on due process to incorporate psychological and behavioral effects (Wexler & Winick, 1991). In the last 25 years, therapeutic jurisprudence has expanded into multiple areas including: criminal law, corrections, probation, lawyering, judging, and family law (Slate et al., 2004; Stolle, Wexler, & Winick, 2000; Wexler & Winick, 1996; Winick & Wexler, 2003).

Another way of characterizing therapeutic jurisprudence identifies three levels of legal interaction to enhance therapeutic outcomes: the *individual*, the *procedural*, and the *policy level* (Rottman & Casey, 1999). At the *individual level*, the role of *legal actors* is emphasized, and the impact it may have on defendants, victims, and their families. A judge's role may be considerably different under the therapeutic jurisprudence (or "TJ") perspective. Judges are encouraged to look for "psychojudicial soft spots," or interactions that could lead to undue distress or anxiety for defendants and victims that could then contribute to antitherapeutic or unhealthy outcomes (Fritzler & Simon, 2000; Rottman & Casey, 1999; Wexler, 1998). For example, domestic violence offenders often deny or minimize their behavior through cognitive distortions such as blaming the victim, or viewing the violence and harm as unimportant (Simon, 1995; Winick, 2000). A judge utilizing TJ would consider these psychological patterns, and what effect they may have for the offender. It could be the judge's role to assist the offender to break through the denial by what the judge says or how she says it.

This example can be expanded to the *procedural level* (which can include *legal rules* and *legal procedures*). A TJ judge may not allow a domestic violence offender to plead "no contest" if it was believed or shown in research that this plea contributes to the defendant's denial of responsibility for the incident. If the defendant is allowed to avoid taking responsibility for his actions, then this feeds into his denial and minimization of the domestic violence incident, and could result in ongoing occurrences of domestic violence, putting the victim at risk. If an offender denies responsibility through a "no contest" plea, he may also be less likely to participate fully in court-ordered treatment (Rottman & Casey, 1999; Simon, 1995; Wexler, 1993; Winick, 2000).

At the *policy level*, similar considerations of therapeutic and antitherapeutic consequences would take place. For example, a TJ approach to mandatory arrest as a policy for domestic violence offenders would consider what is known about mandatory arrest based on existing research, and how the health and well-being of those concerned have been impacted. Issues of due process would also be considered. The therapeutic and antitherapeutic consequences for all parties would be made explicit to serve as a rationale for the proposed policy. However, therapeutic jurisprudence in and of itself does not dictate the policy direction to be taken. It merely lays out the framework with which to analyze the situation. For example, Dennis Sacuzzo (1999) uses therapeutic jurisprudence to argue for mandatory arrest, Linda Mills (1999) utilizes it to argue against it, and Bruce Winick (2000) suggests a compromise solution.

In summary, therapeutic jurisprudence emphasizes both the process and outcomes of the legal system. It considers how the practice of law, through its legal actors, rules, and procedures, can act as a social force that impacts the well-being of those in the legal system. Therapeutic jurisprudence seeks to minimize iatrogenic, or negative, effects of the legal process. The people considered can include victims, defendants, their families, communities, as well as the professionals involved in the legal system. What therapeutic jurisprudence brings to the legal system that was not previously at the forefront is considering law from the perspective of the competing values that result from recognizing the therapeutic and antitherapeutic consequences and due process concerns for all those touched by the law (Slobogin, 1995).

THE RELATIONSHIP BETWEEN THERAPEUTIC JURISPRUDENCE AND OTHER PERSPECTIVES

Therapeutic jurisprudence shares common ground with many current perspectives in law, including preventive law, restorative justice, and procedural justice. Legal scholar Susan Daicoff (2000) has tied several legal perspectives together under one umbrella concept that she calls the "comprehensive law movement." She identifies 10 vectors of the comprehensive law movement: therapeutic jurisprudence, preventive law, therapeutic jurisprudence/preventive law, restorative justice, procedural justice, facilitative mediation, transformative mediation, collaborative mediation, holistic law, and creative problem-solving. Each of these has two things in common. First, psychological well-being is considered from the standpoint of individuals, relationships and communities. Second, each vector considers a larger view than the traditionally narrow scope of the law. The 10 vectors can be split into two groups based on their functionality: theoretical lenses and concrete processes. Preventive law, in which the lawyer works with her client on a proactive basis to avoid foreseeable problems, is an example of a concrete process or mechanism. Therapeutic jurisprudence, restorative justice, and procedural justice are examples of the lenses through which practice can be evaluated. Daicoff (2000) suggests that therapeutic jurisprudence is positioned to be the overarching perspective of the comprehensive law movement due to its ability to capture multiple perspectives.

THERAPEUTIC JURISPRUDENCE, SPECIALIZED COURTS AND PROBLEM-SOLVING COURTS

The emergence of therapeutic jurisprudence and specialized courts occurred simultaneously in the 1980s and 1990s (Casey & Rottman, 2000). Given the commonalities, it is not surprising then that these two movements converged to some degree, first with drug courts (Hora, 2002; Hora, Schma, & Rosenthal, 1999), then with domestic violence courts (Keilitz, 2000; Petrucci, 2002; Simon, 1995), and most recently, with teen courts (Weisz, Lott, & Thai, 2002; Shiff & Wexler, 1996; Wexler, 2000) and mental health courts (Lurigio, Watson, Luchins, & Hanrahan, 2001). This is not to say that all specialized courts practice therapeutic jurisprudence, or that therapeutic jurisprudence is exclusively practiced in specialized courts. Some specialized courts knowingly utilize therapeutic jurisprudence, others do so without naming it, and others do not ascribe to it at all (Hora, Schma, & Rosenthal, 1999).

Looking at specialized courts generally, Casey and Rottman (2000) suggest a three-step process to integrating a therapeutic jurisprudence perspective into court practice:

1. *Recognition:* this step "requires courts and judges to acknowledge their role in producing therapeutic or anti-therapeutic consequences" (p. 451) as an unavoidable aspect of being in that role.
2. *Practice:* this step "involves systematically exploring where and when problems (i.e. psychojudicial soft spots) arise and how they can best be addressed" (p. 451) by the judge. Psychojudicial softspots are based on the notion of "psycholegal softspots," which are ways in which lawyers can anticipate how legal interventions or procedures may impact the client's psychological well-being (Wexler, 1998). Psychojudicial softspots refer to the same process but with a judge rather than a lawyer. Psycholegal/psychojudicial soft spots are the action point at which therapeutic consequences for a defendant or victim's psychological well-being are pursued.
3. *Assessment:* Practice strategies should be constantly assessed for effectiveness, preferably based on research. Practice strategies should also be evaluated based on "their consistency with other legal values" (p. 452) to assess whether therapeutic outcomes converge with justice outcomes.

Three general guidelines for utilizing therapeutic jurisprudence in court environments are also suggested (Casey & Rottman, 2000). First, whatever therapeutic consequences that are pursued should not conflict with accepted standards of practice. As previously discussed, therapeutic jurisprudence is not a radical reform theory and does not displace due process. Second, current social science theory and research should be incorporated, with decisions made based on systematic inquiry rather than anecdote. This refers to therapeutic jurisprudence actively pursuing empirical testing. Third, therapeutic jurisprudence does not assume a paternalistic approach; each case needs to be considered individually, and when paternalistic behaviors seem warranted, they can be pursued, but when they are not, then they should not (Casey & Rottman, 2000).

One point that is debated and largely misunderstood that is related to both therapeutic jurisprudence and specialized courts is resistance to the idea that specialized courts and therapeutic jurisprudence each have the capacity to administer punishment *and* rehabilitation. Critics and supporters alike of therapeutic jurisprudence often assume that the term "therapeutic" means a singular focus on rehabilitation, to the exclusion of any focus on punishment (Berman & Feinblatt, 2005; Davis, 2003; Fischer, 2003). This is a misinterpretation of the definition and intent of therapeutic jurisprudence. Therapeutic jurisprudence does not assume that punishment is an inherently "antitherapeutic effect;" deterrence theory reminds us that with appropriate swiftness, severity, and certainty, punishment is assumed to be effective in deterring future crime (Walker, 1991). It could be argued then, that appropriately applied, punishment may indeed be "therapeutic" to: the offender, who is deterred from committing a future offense; the victim, who remains safe from that offender; the community, who may also benefit by general deterrence, or not committing the offense based on observing the punishment of the offender. At the same time, punishment may also be considered anti-therapeutic. Clearly, not everyone will agree with this characterization of punishment. However, it is important to note that what is "therapeutic" or "antitherapeutic" is not predetermined or set by therapeutic jurisprudence; it is determined by the researcher or the practitioner in their particular context (Wexler, 1993; Winick, 1997). On a similar note, court researchers Casey and Rottman (2000) state that therapeutic jurisprudence can maintain a dual emphasis on both "rights and care perspectives." Thus, this approach can focus on appropriate legal issues of due process towards individual rights, in a manner that utilizes an ethic-of-care approach (Madden & Wayne, 2003).

Problem-solving courts have their own set of established elements that may or may not include a therapeutic jurisprudence approach. Five key elements of problem-solving courts have been identified (Berman & Feinblatt, 2005):

1. *A tailored approach to justice:* the judicial resources match the need in terms of expertise and caseload.
2. *Creative partnerships:* collaborative partnerships with community agencies are actively sought out as needed.
3. *Informed decision-making:* information beyond the basic facts of the case is sought by judges and attorneys, including the psychosocial information

on the offender, and general information on substance abuse or domestic violence.
4. *Accountability:* judicial monitoring is utilized to assure offender accountability through compliance.
5. *A focus on results:* Data is sought to measure effectiveness of court performance.

Not everyone would agree that therapeutic jurisprudence and problem-solving courts go hand-in-hand. This is largely due to problem-solving courts not always incorporating a "therapeutic dimension," as well as political factors that see the idea of "therapeutic" as a "political liability." The authors conclude that there can be cross-over between problem-solving courts and therapeutic jurisprudence, but that the relationship is more complex (Berman & Feinblatt, 2005).

How might we see judges or lawyers practicing therapeutic jurisprudence in specialized courts? A judge or attorney practicing therapeutic jurisprudence attempts to reach defendants and victims in a way that will contribute to a healthy experience and a healthy outcome in the court. Thus, *demeanor and interaction* as it relates to offender compliance is emphasized. The typically dispassionate demeanor of judges and attorneys is called into question if it does not contribute to healthy outcomes. Taking on a more sensitive and empathic approach is advocated (Fritzler & Simon, 2000). How attorneys ask questions of witnesses can also be conducted in a respectful and clear manner, enhancing the willingness of the witness (Carson, 2003). As a means to solicit the defendant's "buy-in" to issues around protective orders or child visitation, behavioral contracting is another common TJ tool, borrowed from the mental health literature. A judge works with the defendant to come up with a plan that is not only consistent with any court orders, but also workable and meaningful for defendants (Wexler, 1993; Wexler & Winick, 1991).

A judge practicing TJ would consider not only the facts of the case, but also the *broader issues* surrounding the violence, substance abuse, or mental illness affecting the family (Karan et al., 1999). Interactions at the individual level with defendants and victims would be structured to reduce the iatrogenic or harmful effects the court process may have on defendants and victims. This would most often manifest itself in judicial demeanor and communication. A TJ judge might take on a more problem-solving and involved approach, rather than the typically bureaucratic or formal demeanor (Ptacek, 1999). A TJ judge might communicate more directly with defendants to counter a defendant's cognitive distortions concerning her behavior. At the procedural level, type of plea, aggressive prosecution, close monitoring of sentence compliance, and consequences for failure to comply are all carried out with the overall goal of reducing future instances of violence by focusing on the health and well-being of defendants and victims (Rottman & Casey, 1999).

In the case of domestic violence courts, the policy goals of punishment, deterrence, and rehabilitation suggest an unusual merging of deterrence and rehabilitation as theoretical frameworks at work in domestic violence courts. In fact, the absence of any strong theory behind past approaches to domestic violence, including mandatory arrest and batterer's counseling, has been a source of criticism (Chalk & King, 1998; Tsai, 2000). The specialized domestic violence court originally developed without any particular theoretical framework (Rottman, 2000) until they were linked by some with therapeutic jurisprudence (Hora, et al., 1999; Keilitz, 2000; Rottman & Casey, 1999; Rottman, 2000; Simon, 1995; Steketee, Levey, & Keilitz, 2000; Tsai, 2000).

Domestic violence courts can be easily supported by TJ's emphasis on health and well-being for those involved in the legal setting (Fritzler & Simon, 2000). An example might be a domestic violence court's emphasis on taking cases seriously to enhance victim safety and offender accountability. As previously discussed, "no contest" pleas may not be permitted. In addition to the plea process, several procedural aspects reflect the TJ emphasis on health and improved outcomes for the parties involved in a domestic violence court. Lenient prosecuting strategies that minimize the gravity of the violence that occurred are avoided, such as use of diversion, because they can have deleterious effects on victims, and may contribute to a defendant's belief that he did not do anything wrong (Simon, 1995). Close monitoring of the defendant's compliance with sentence requirements reinforces the seriousness of the violence. Sanctions for a defendant's failure to comply further reinforces the message that the incident that occurred has importance to the court, and thus should have importance to the defendant (Simon, 1995).

CURRENT RESEARCH

The published literature on therapeutic jurisprudence can be broadly assigned into two categories: (a) legal analyses, usually in the form of law reviews; and (b) social/behavioral science research. In the legal analyses, therapeutic jurisprudence is utilized as a framework to analyze legal rules, legal procedures, and the role of legal actors. Competing values are considered from a therapeutic and antitherapeutic perspective, leading to proposals for how rules, procedures, or legal actors might be changed to accommodate a more therapeutic process and reduce harmful effects. This is a rich literature in multiple areas of law including: adult guardianship (O'Sullivan, 2000); domestic violence felony trials (Hartley, 2003); rehabilitation in criminal law (Birgden, 2004; McGuire, 2003; 2004; Ward & Eccleston, 2004); sex offender legislation (Edwards & Hensley, 2001; Granlund, 2005; Peebles, 1999); neonaticide (Schwartz & Isser, 2001); infant maltreatment (Lederman & Osofsky, 2004); children with disabilities (Cichon, 2004); and substance-abusing unmarried fathers (McMahon & Giannini, 2003). Often the concerns of oppressed populations are considered, such as maltreated children, domestic violence victims, and the mentally ill. However, this work is beyond the scope of this chapter as it focuses more specifically on the development of law. The therapeutic jurisprudence website keeps an ongoing list of this growing body of work (http://therapeuticjurisprudence.org).

Here the focus will be on the existing social and behavioral science research on therapeutic jurisprudence. A list of studies is presented in Table 22-1. An effort was made to locate studies that listed "therapeutic jurisprudence" in the abstract in multiple databases (Criminal Justice Abstracts, Lexis-Nexis Academic, MEDLINE, PAIS, PsychInfo, Social Services Abstract, and Social Work Abstracts), but it should be noted it is likely that some studies were likely missed. The variety of databases containing studies is a testament to the interdisciplinary nature of therapeutic jurisprudence research.

Table 22-1 presents the sample characteristics and type of data collection method for the therapeutic jurisprudence studies. As noted earlier, the vast majority of studies (11 or 55%) focused on the perceptions of clients or consumers of the legal system, including

Table 22-1
CHARACTERISTICS OF STUDIES OF THERAPEUTIC JURISPRUDENCE

Study	*Sample Studied*	*Quanitative/Qualitative*
Anderson, Levine, Sharma, Ferreti, Steinberg & Wallach, 1996	Therapists and child protective services workers	Qualitative
Chase & Hora, 2000	Judges	Quantitative
Ferencz & Maguire, 2000	Mental health patients and mental health professionals	Qualitative
Greer, O'Regan & Traverso, 1996	Mentally ill adults appearing for a commitment hearing	Quantitative
Herinckx, Swart, Ama, Dolezal & King, 2005	Misdemeanant mental health court participants with severe and persistent mental illness	Quantitative
Hill & Thomson, 1999	General public	Quantitative and qualitative
Holmberg & Christianson, 2002	Men convicted of murder and sexual offenders	Quantitative
Kamin & Rachlinski, 1996	College undergraduates	Quantitative and qualitative
O'Hare, 1996	Voluntary and involuntary outpatient mental health clients	Quantitative
Petrucci, 2002	Domestic violence court offenders and the judge	Qualitative
Petrucci & Quinlan, unpublished manuscript	Judges	Quantitative and qualitative
Pike & Murphy	19 parents in the Columbus Pilot Project in family court	Qualitative
Poythress & Brodsky, 1996	Hospital staff	Quantitative and qualitative
Roe & Ronen, 2003	Hospitalized psychiatric patients	Qualitative
Senjo & Leip, 2001	Drug court participants	Quantitative and qualitative
Shuman, Hamilton & Daley, 1996	Jurors	Quantitative
Susman, 1996	Mentally ill institutionalized adult patients	Quantitative
Weisz, Lott & Thai, 2002	Teen court defendants and their parents	Quantitative
Winkel, Wohlfarth & Blaauw, 2004	Adult victims of crime	Quantitative
Zito, Vitrai & Craig, 1966	Acute and chronic adult patients in psychiatric facility	Quantitative and qualitative

mentally ill patients in either residential or outpatient treatment services, men convicted of murder or sexual offenses, parents in family court, drug court participants, teen court participants and their parents, and victims of crime. Two more studies included the perspectives of both consumers of the legal system (domestic violence offenders and mental health patients) as well as professionals (judges and mental health professionals). Four studies focused exclusively on professionals including therapists, judges, and hospital staff. The three remaining studies sampled jurors, the general public, and college students. It is evident then that the therapeutic jurisprudence literature often includes the perspectives of vulnerable populations, most notably, the mentally ill. The largest percentage of studies utilized quantitative methods (45%), followed by studies that utilized both quantitative and qualitative (30%). Qualitative studies made up the smallest category (25%).

Two studies used qualitative or mixed methods strategies to identify the key elements of therapeutic jurisprudence in judicial practice. Petrucci's (2002) ethnographic study in a domestic violence court in which the judge utilized therapeutic jurisprudence identified a shared respect process between the judge and domestic violence offenders during the one year of judicial monitoring. Specific components in this process were identified, and included how the judge and defendant spoke to one another, body language of each, specific types of statements that the judge and defendant made, and a judicial role that is genuine, caring, consistent, and firm. A later study (Petrucci & Quinlan, unpublished manuscript) builds on this work and utilized a concept mapping approach with a group of judges to further delineate the key elements of judicial practice from a therapeutic jurisprudence perspective.

Several studies tested an aspect of the therapeutic jurisprudence process. These studies have produced a combination of findings that support a therapeutic jurisprudence process or produced mixed findings. Some of the studies with positive findings for the therapeutic jurisprudence process are discussed first. Chase and Hora (2000) compared judicial satisfaction among drug court judges that utilized therapeutic jurisprudence with family court judges that utilized a traditional approach. Based on a convenience sample of 194 judges, they found that the drug court judges were more likely to have a positive attitude toward litigants and had a more positive attitude about their judicial assignment. The two groups of judges did not differ on their perceived role to help litigants to solve problems, but drug court judges were more likely to perceive their court as helpful and to see improvements in litigant behavior. Senjo and Leip (2001) analyzed a random sample of drug court participants to determine what factors predicted behavior change. Their findings confirmed that supportive court monitoring comments from the judge predicted increases in offender behavior change as measured by the ratio of clean urinalysis tests over the total urinalysis tests taken. At the same time, an increase in the adversarial court monitoring approach was associated with negative offender behavior change. Holmberg and Christianson (2002) found that offenders who perceived that they were respected in the police interview were more likely to admit their crime, while in police interviews characterized by dominance, offenders were more likely to deny their crime. Each of these studies confirms the notion that positive or therapeutic effects are related to what would be generally construed as a healthy outcome.

On the other hand, some studies have shown mixed findings. In their study of a teen court, Weisz, Lott, and Thai (2002) found that teen court defendants actually became more alienated after participation in teen court compared to before. Teens' attitudes towards authority were unchanged. Recidivism was lower than general diversion programs and comparable to other teen courts, which could be considered positive. No beneficial impacts were identified, except that teens and parents scored high on their satisfaction surveys. No measure or observation of the therapeutic jurisprudence process itself was made in this study. The authors hypothesize that there may have been benefits that were not captured in the quantitative data collection methods. Another study also had mixed findings. In a secondary data analysis of 368 misdemeanant participants in a mental health court (Herinckx et al., 2005), the overall crime rate was reduced in a 12-month follow-up, which was clearly a positive finding. However, the amount of mental health services was not associated with future arrest.

Study findings often included aspects of psychological well-being on behalf of the sampled population, and a discussion of therapeutic or harmful effects.

Roe and Ronen (2003) identified "troublesome aspects" and "helpful aspects" of psychiatric hospitalization for patients. They recommended that decision-makers consider these aspects in their decision-making when assessing hospitalization needs of patients. In a study of jurors (Shuman, Hamilton, & Daley, 1996), negative health effects including symptoms of posttraumatic stress disorder and depression were measured among jurors who attended traumatic trials (involving violent crimes) compared to those who attended non-traumatic trials (involving nonviolent crimes). Post-traumatic stress disorder was not found in either group, but depression was indicated in 12 percent of the jurors who served in traumatic trials. Two studies focused on procedural justice, which analyzed perceived fairness from the perspective of mentally ill patients (Greer, O'Regan & Traverso, 1996; Susman, 1996). In both studies, patients' valued fairness in the process. Susman's (1996) study found that perceived fairness predicted patient satisfaction, regardless of the outcome of their civil commitment hearings.

Clearly, more research is needed before the effectiveness of the therapeutic jurisprudence framework can be declared. This research presents an overview of the types of inquiries that have been pursued, populations studied, and the potential for practice and policy recommendations.

COMMON GROUND BETWEEN SOCIAL WORK AND THERAPEUTIC JURISPRUDENCE

The discussions in this chapter have illustrated that there is much common ground between social work practice/research and a therapeutic jurisprudence perspective in law. Common areas are listed below.

1. Both consider *multiple perspectives* at the individual and family or micro-level, to the larger macro or policy level, as well as the interactions between these levels (Wexler, 1995), similar to the systems approach in social work.
2. Each supports a *process and outcome focus,* and advocates an understanding of the links between the two in order to improve legal practice (Madden & Wayne, 2003).

3. Both operate in an environment of *competing values* and interests that must be determined on a case-by-case basis (Slobogin, 1995). The needs of various parties must be weighed against each other to come to a decision on how these competing values are ultimately handled and what the consequences might be.
4. Both include an emphasis on *social justice* by considering the needs of those typically not given voice (Madden & Wayne, 2003), such as involuntary commitments for adults with mental health issues (Perlin, 2000). In the case of therapeutic jurisprudence, this emphasis on social justice is often not explicitly stated, but is implicit in its pursuit to increase health and well-being on behalf of vulnerable populations and decrease harmful effects.
5. In research, both support *quantitative and qualitative* approaches (Gilgun & Abrams, 2002; Petrucci, Winick, & Wexler, 2003). In this way, not only is the process explicated in more detail, but the nuances of the competing values that contribute to the outcomes can also be brought out more clearly.

Social work and law experts Robert Madden and Raymie Wayne (2003) point out six roles familiar to social work that are particularly useful when utilizing therapeutic jurisprudence as an organizing framework in legal settings:

1. Social workers can use the role of *mediator* when trying to reach consensus with others, for example, on competing values.
2. The *educator* role can be utilized to share information with lawyers and judges on psychosocial, cultural or environmental factors that impact legal clients with which legal professionals may not be as familiar.
3. Social workers are *members of an interprofessional team* in a therapeutic jurisprudence approach, with lawyers, judges, law enforcement, other treatment professionals, clients, and community members. This is because the needs of the client "transcend the expertise of any one profession" (p. 341). Social workers are accustomed to utilizing strategies and frameworks from an interdisciplinary perspective. The emphasis on communication and cross-cultural

training in the social work curriculum provides an additional advantage to working in what could be considered the foreign culture of the legal system (Madden & Wayne, 2003).

4. Social workers also assume the role of *advocate* on behalf of their clients in the legal setting in a therapeutic jurisprudence framework. Lawyers assume this role too, but there are differences in how these two roles are pursued resulting in different consequences for clients.

5. Social workers assume the role of *researcher* or *research broker.* As researchers, social workers evaluate legal practice. As research brokers, social workers introduce research-based techniques into the legal setting, as well as outcome studies that document therapeutic and anti-therapeutic effects of legal practice.

6. Finally, social workers may fill the role of *policy-makers* as they contribute to program design or design entire programs, document outcomes that are utilized in future legislative initiatives, or give voice to vulnerable populations who were previously unheard (Madden & Wayne, 2003).

Madden and Wayne (2003) also point out that social workers are uniquely prepared to address five identified "dilemmas" of therapeutic jurisprudence because the dilemmas are also common to the social work profession (Madden & Wayne, 2003; Slobogin, 1995). These dilemmas include: (a) the *identity dilemma:* this dilemma notes that therapeutic jurisprudence is very much like other perspectives and theories, so what makes it unique? Social work's interdisciplinary knowledge base and approach has been similarly criticized (Kirk & Reid, 2002); (b) the *lack of a clear definition of what is "therapeutic":* the originators of therapeutic jurisprudence have purposefully left this definition vague so that practitioners and researchers can make this determination in each setting, but some scholars have struggled with this (Melton, 1994; Wexler, 1993). Social work has also struggled with how to conceptualize therapeutic outcomes in research; (c) *empirical indeterminism:* the inability to adequately provide a research base to a therapeutic jurisprudence approach; this is due in large part to the familiar shortcomings of social science and behavioral research; (d) *the rule of law:* therapeutic jurisprudence could result in individualized

approaches to law and a deterioration of *the rule of law.* How does one implement the law fairly and equitably across defendants with a similar criminal charge but different contexts? and (e) *difficulty in balancing competing values:* this arises when a particular legal procedure is helpful to one party and harmful to another, creating the need to choose or prioritize competing needs. Madden and Wayne (2003) point out that each of these areas is familiar terrain in social work.

FUTURE RESEARCH OF THERAPEUTIC JURISPRUDENCE AND SOCIAL WORK PRACTICE

Therapeutic jurisprudence has brought an invitation to social and behavioral science researchers to consider researching legal practice (Casey & Rottman, 2000; Petrucci, Winick, & Wexler, 2003). Interdisciplinary collaboratives between social work and law schools are prime settings to explore the practice of therapeutic jurisprudence and social work and to test it further. Just as social work is participating in an evidence-based approach in its therapeutic interventions (Kirk & Reid, 2000), practice utilizing the tenets of therapeutic jurisprudence must also be empirically tested. The call for research-based practice is needed to establish what works and what does not in our legal system interventions. Social workers are uniquely positioned to make a contribution to practice and knowledge in this area.

REFERENCES

Anderson, E., Levine, M., Anupama, S., Ferretti, L., Steinberg, K., & Wallach, L. (1996). Coercive uses of mandatory reporting in therapeutic relationships. In D. B. Wexler & B. J. Winick (Eds.), *Law in a therapeutic key: Developments in therapeutic jurisprudence* (pp. 895–905). Durham, NC: Carolina Academic Press.

Berman, G., & Feinblatt, J. (2005). *Good courts: The case for problem-solving justice.* New York: The New Press.

Birgden, A., & Ward, T. (2003). Jurisprudential considerations: Pragmatic psychology through a therapeutic jurisprudence lens: psycholegal soft spots in the criminal justice system. *Psychology, Public Policy and Law 9,* 334–357.

Birgden, A. (2004). Therapeutic jurisprudence and responsivity: Finding the will and the way in offender rehabilitation. *Psychology, Crime & Law 10,* 3, 283–295.

Carson, D. (2003). Therapeutic jurisprudence and adversarial injustice: Questioning limits. *Western Criminology Review 4*, 2, 34–43.

Casey, P., & Rottman, D. B. (2000). Therapeutic jurisprudence in the courts. *Behavioral Sciences and the Law, 18*, 445–457.

Cichon, D. E. (2004). Encouraging a culture of caring for children with disabilities. *Journal of Legal Medicine, 25*, 39–62.

Chalk, R., & King, P. A. (Eds.) (1998). *Violence in families: Assessing preventions and treatment programs.* Washington, D.C.: National Academic Press.

Daicoff, S. (2000). The role of therapeutic jurisprudence within the comprehensive law movement. In D. P. Stolle, D. B. Wexler & B. J. Winick (Eds.), *Practicing therapeutic jurisprudence: Law as a helping profession* (pp. 465–492). Durham, NC: Carolina Academic Press.

Davis, W. N. (2003). Special problems for specialty courts. *ABA Journal February 2003*, 32–37.

Edwards, W., & Hensley, C. (2001). Restructuring sex offender sentencing: A therapeutic jurisprudence approach to the criminal justice process. *International Journal of Offender Therapy and Comparative Criminology, 45*, 6, 646–662.

Fischer, B. (2003). 'Doing good with a vengeance': A critical assessment of the practices, effects and implications of drug treatment courts in North America. *Criminal Justice, 3*, 3, 227–248.

Fishman, D. B. (2004). Commentary: Integrative themes: Prospects for developing a "psycholegal lexis." *Psychology, Public Policy and Law, 10*, 178–199.

Fritzler, R. B., & Simon, L. M. J. (2000). Creating a domestic violence court: Combat in the trenches. *Court Review, 37*, 1, 28–39.

Gilgun, J. F., & Abrams, L. S. (2002). The nature and usefulness of qualitative social work research. *Qualitative Social Work, 1*, 1, 39–55.

Golick, T., & Lessem, J. (2004). A law and social work clinical program for the elderly and disabled: Past and future challenges. *Washington University Journal of Law & Policy, 14*, 183–208.

Granlund, K. (2005). Student article: Does societal input lead to successful sex offender legislation? *Law and Psychology Review, 29*, 197–209.

Greer, A., O'Regan, M., & Traverso, A. (1996). Therapeutic jurisprudence and patients' perceptions of procedural due process of civil commitment hearings. In D. B. Wexler & B. J. Winick (Eds.), *Law in a therapeutic key: Developments in therapeutic jurisprudence* (pp. 923–933). Durham, NC: Carolina Academic Press.

Hartley, C. C. (2003). A therapeutic jurisprudence approach to the trial process in domestic violence felony trials. *Violence Against Women, 9*, 4, 410–437.

Herinckx, H., Swart, S. C., Ama, S. M., Dolezal, C. D., & King, S. (2005). Rearrest and linkage to mental health services among clients of the Clark County Mental Health Court Program. *Psychiatric Services, 56*, 7, 853–857.

Holmberg, U., & Christianson, S.A. (2002). Murderers' and sexual offenders' experiences of police interviews and their inclination to admit or deny crimes. *Behavioral Sciences & the Law, 20*, 31–45.

Hora, P. F. (2002). A dozen years of drug treatment courts: Uncovering our theoretical foundation and the construction of a mainstream paradigm. *Substance Use & Misuse, 37*, 12/13, 1469–1488.

Hora, P. F., Schma, W., & Rosenthal, J. T. A. (1999). Therapeutic jurisprudence and the drug court movement: Revolutionizing the criminal justice system's response to drug abuse and crime in America. *Notre Dame Law Review, 74*, 439–5556.

Kamin, K. A., & Rachlinski, J. J. (1996). Ex Post ↑ Ex Ante: Determining Liability in Hindsight. In D. B. Wexler & B. J. Winick (Eds.), *Law in a therapeutic key: Developments in therapeutic jurisprudence* (pp. 979–994). Durham, NC: Carolina Academic Press.

Karan, A., Keilitz, S., & Denaro, S. (1999). Domestic violence courts: What are they and how should we manage them? *Juvenile and Family Court Journal, 75–86.

Keilitz, S. (2000). *Specialization of domestic violence case management in the courts: A national survey.* National Center for State Courts.

Kirk, S. A., & Reid, W. J. (2002). *Science and social work: A critical appraisal.* New York: Columbia University Press.

Lederman, C. S., & Osofsky, J. D. (2004). Multiple cases with a policy and program focus: Infant mental health interventions in juvenile court: Ameliorating the effects of maltreatment and deprivation. *Psychology, Public Policy and Law, 10*, 162–176.

Lurigio, A. J., Watson, A., Luchins, D. J., & Hanrahan, P. (2001). Therapeutic jurisprudence in action: Specialized courts for the mentally ill. *Judicature, 84*, 4, 184–189.

Madden, R. G., & Wayne, R. H. (2003). Social work and the law: A therapeutic jurisprudence perspective. *Social Work, 48*, 3, 338–347.

McGuire, J. (2003). Maintaining change: Converging legal and psychological initiatives in a therapeutic jurisprudence framework. *Western Criminology Review, 4*, 2, 108–123.

McGuire, J. (2004). Commentary: Promising answers and the next generation of questions. *Psychology, Crime & Law, 10*, 3, 335–345.

McMahon, T. J., & Giannini, F. D. (2003). Special issue: Separated and unmarried fathers and the courts: Substance-abusing fathers in family court: Moving from popular stereotypes to therapeutic jurisprudence. *Family Court Review, 41*, 337.

Melton, G. (1994). Therapy through law. *Contemporary Psychology, 39*, 215–216.

Mills, L. G. (1999). Killing her softly: Intimate abuse and the violence of state intervention. *Harvard Law Review, 113*, 550–587.

O'Hare, T. (1996). Court-ordered versus voluntary clients: Problem differences and readiness for change. *Social Work, 41*, 4, 417–204.

O'Sullivan, J. L. (2000). Therapeutic alternatives to adult guardianship. *Journal of Mental Health and Aging, 6*, 2, 159–172.

Peebles, J. E. (1999). Therapeutic jurisprudence and the sentencing of sexual offenders in Canada. *International Journal of Offender Therapy and Comparative Criminology, 43*, 3, 275–290.

Perlin, M. (2000). *The hidden prejudice: Mental disability on trial.* Washington, D.C.: American Psychological Association.

Petrucci, C. J. (2002). Respect as a component in the judge-defendant interaction in a specialized domestic violence court that utilizes therapeutic jurisprudence. *Criminal Law Bulletin, 38*, 263–295.

Petrucci, C. J., & Quinlan, K. (unpublished manuscript). *Bridging the research-practice gap: Concept mapping as a mixed methods strategy in practice-based research and evaluation.*

Petrucci, C. J., Winick, B. J., & Wexler, D. B. (2003). Therapeutic jurisprudence: An invitation to social scientists. In D. Carson & R. Bull (Eds.), *Handbook of psychology in legal contexts* (2nd ed., pp. 579–601). West Sussex, England: John Wiley & Sons.

Poythress, N. G., & Brodsky, S. L. (1996). In the wake of a negligent release law suit: An investigation of professional consequences and institutional impact on a state psychiatric hospital. In D. B. Wexler & B. J. Winick (Eds.), *Law in a therapeutic key: Developments in therapeutic jurisprudence* (pp. 875–893). Durham, NC: Carolina Academic Press.

Pike, L. T., & Murphy, P. T. (2004). The Columbus Pilot in the Family Court of Western Australia: What the parents said. *Journal of Family Studies, 10*, 2, 239–251.

Ptacek, J. (1999). *Battered women in the courtroom: The power of judicial responses.* Boston, MA: Northeastern University Press.

Roe, D., & Ronen, Y. (2003). Hospitalization as experienced by the psychiatric patient: A therapeutic jurisprudence perspective. *Law and Psychiatry, 26*, 317–332.

Rottman, D. B., & Casey, P. (1999). Therapeutic jurisprudence and the emergence of problem-solving courts. *NIJ Journal,* July, 12–19.

Sacuzzo, D. P. (1999). How should the police respond to domestic violence? A therapeutic jurisprudence analysis of mandatory arrest. *Santa Clara Law Review, 39*, 765–787.

Schopp, R. F. (1998). Therapeutic jurisprudence forum: Integrating restorative justice and therapeutic jurisprudence. *Revista Juridica Universidad de Puerto Rico, 67*, 665–669.

Schwartz, L. L., & Isser, N. K. (2001). Neonaticide: An appropriate application for therapeutic jurisprudence? *Behavioral Sciences and the Law, 19*, 703–718.

Senjo, S., & Leip, L. A. (2001). Testing therapeutic jurisprudence theory: An empirical assessment of the drug court. *Western Criminology Review, 3*, 1 [Online].

Shiff, A., & Wexler, D. B. (1996). Teen court: A therapeutic jurisprudence perspective. *Criminal Law Bulletin, 32*, 342–357.

Shuman, D. W., Hamilton, J. A., & Daley, C. E. (1996). The health effects of jury service. In D. B. Wexler & B. J. Winick (Eds.), *Law in a therapeutic key: Developments in therapeutic jurisprudence* (pp. 949–977). Durham, NC: Carolina Academic Press.

Simon, L. M. J. (1995). A therapeutic jurisprudence approach to the legal processing of domestic violence cases. *Psychology, Public Policy and Law, 1*, 1, 43–79.

Slate, R. N., Feldman, R., Roskes, E., & Baerga, M. (2004). Training federal probation officers as mental health specialists. *Federal Probation, 68*, 3, 9–15.

Slobogin, C. (1995). Therapeutic jurisprudence: Five dilemmas to ponder. *Psychology, Public Policy, and Law, 1*, 193–219.

Steketee, M. W., Levey, L. S., & Keilitz, S. L. (2000). *Implementing an integrated domestic violence court: Systematic change in the District of Columbia.* State Justice Institute.

Stolle, D. P., Wexler, D. B., & Winick, B. J. (2000). *Practicing therapeutic jurisprudence: Law as a helping profession.* Durham, NC: Carolina Academic Press.

Susman, J. (1996). Resolving hospital conflicts: A study on therapeutic jurisprudence. In D. B. Wexler & B. J. Winick (Eds.), *Law in a therapeutic key: Developments in therapeutic jurisprudence* (pp. 907–922). Durham, NC: Carolina Academic Press.

Tsai, B. (2000). Note: The trend toward specialized domestic violence courts: Improvements on an effective innovation. *Fordham Law Review, 68*, 1285–1327.

Voyvodic, R., & Medcalf, M. (2004). Advancing social justice through an interdisciplinary approach to clinical legal education: The case of legal assistance of Windsor. *Washington University Journal of Law & Policy, 14*, 101–132.

Walker, N. (1991). *Why punish? Theories of punishment reassessed.* New York: Oxford University Press.

Ward, T., & Eccleston, L. (2004). Risk, responsivity, and the treatment of offenders: Introduction to the special issue. *Psychology, Crime & Law, 10*, 3, 223–227.

Weisz, V., Lott, R. C., & Thai, N. D. (2002). A teen court evaluation with a therapeutic jurisprudence perspective. *Behavioral Sciences and the Law, 20*, 381–392.

Wexler, D. B. (1990). *Therapeutic jurisprudence: The law as a therapeutic agent.* Durham, NC: Carolina Academic Press.

Wexler, D. B. (1993). New directions in therapeutic jurisprudence: Breaking the bounds of conventional mental health law scholarship. *New York Law School Journal of Human Rights, 10,* 759–776.

Wexler, D. B. (1995). Reflections on the scope of therapeutic jurisprudence. *Psychology, Public Policy and Law, 1,* 220–236.

Wexler, D. B. (1998). Therapeutic jurisprudence forum: Practicing therapeutic jurisprudence: Psycholegal soft spots and strategies. *Revista Juridica Universidad de Puerto Rico, 67,* 317–342.

Wexler, D. B. (1999). Relapse prevention planning principles for criminal law practice. *Psychology, Public Policy & Law, 5,* 1028–1033.

Wexler, D. B., & Winick, B. J. (1991). *Essays in therapeutic jurisprudence.* Durham, NC: Carolina Academic Press.

Wexler, D. B., & Winick, B. J. (1996). *Law in a therapeutic key: Developments in therapeutic jurisprudence.* Durham, NC: Carolina Academic Press.

Winick, B. J. (1997). The jurisprudence of therapeutic jurisprudence. *Psychology, Public Policy and Law, 3,* 1, 184–206.

Winick, B. J. (2000). Applying the law therapeutically in domestic violence cases. *University of Missouri-Kansas City Law Review, 69,* 1, 33–91.

Winick, B. J., & Wexler, D. B. (2003). *Judging in a therapeutic key: Therapeutic jurisprudence and the courts.* Durham, NC: Carolina Academic Press.

Winkel, F. W., Wohlfarth, T., & Blaauw, E. (2004). Police referral to victim support: The predictive and diagnostic value of the Risk (10) Screening Instrument. *Crisis, 25,* 3, 118–127.

Wright, J. L. (2005). Therapeutic jurisprudence in an interpersonal practice at the University of St. Thomas Interprofessional Center for Counseling and Legal Services. *St. Thomas Law Review, 17,* 501–512.

Zito, J., Vitrai, J., & Craig, T. J (1996). Toward a therapeutic jurisprudence analysis of medication refusal in the court review model. In D. B. Wexler & B. J. Winick (Eds.), *Law in a therapeutic key: Developments in therapeutic jurisprudence* (pp. 935–947). Durham, NC: Carolina Academic Press.

Chapter 23

Administration in Probation and Parole

Frank B. Raymond III and Johnny M. Jones

INTRODUCTION

The United States continues to experience profound increases in the number of offenders entering the criminal justice system. In 1974, around the time the first edition of this chapter was written, 1,819,000 or 1.3 percent of all U.S. residents had been incarcerated at least once during their lifetime (Bonczar, 2003). By 1991, around the introduction of the second edition of this chapter, 3,470,000 or 1.8 percent of U.S. residents had been incarcerated. And as of 2001, 5,618,000 or 2.7 percent of U.S. residents had been incarcerated at least once in their lifetimes. Bonczar also notes that if prison rates continue unchanged, 6.6 percent of U.S. residents born in 2001 will be incarcerated during their lifetime. The probation and parole numbers have increased similarly over the same period of time. As of the end of the 2003 year, a record 4,848,575 adult men and women were being supervised on probation or parole in the U.S., up from 3,757,252 in 1995 (Glaze & Palla, 2004). As predicted by authorities cited in previous editions of the chapter (e.g., Austin & McVey, 1988; DiIulio, 1991), the criminal justice population has continued to expand dramatically, creating heavy demands on prisons and probation and parole authorities. It also seems apparent that the end of growth trends and overcrowding of the corrections system is nowhere in sight.

Probation and parole systems are faced with a difficult challenge of providing effective services to their rapidly growing clientele. These systems must be well-designed, incorporating the latest knowledge of programs and services that are known to be effective. They must be well-staffed by probation and parole officers who, through the education and experience, have acquired the knowledge and skills necessary to provide effective services. At the center of these organizations, responsible for developing and managing effective programs and supervising the staff who work in these programs, are the administrators of probation and parole agencies. In order for these agencies to meet the challenges of the future successfully, they must be managed by persons who are specially qualified through training and experience to serve in these roles.

Administrators of probation and parole agencies come from a variety of backgrounds. Their education and practice experience cover a wide range. In recent years, however, increasing emphasis has been placed on recruitment of administrators who have graduate training in social sciences, with a concentration in management. Social work has proven to be one of the best equipped disciplines to provide this kind of educational experience. Accordingly, a number of probation and parole departments now give priority to hiring administrators who have graduate training in social work.

Social work education is especially effective in preparing students for management in probation and parole agencies for several reasons. First, graduate study of social work provides one with a broad understanding of the field of social services rather than a focus on one narrow component. Such a perspective is important for a probation or parole administrator who must be concerned with relating the agency appropriately to a wide variety of other systems — employment agencies, counseling services, welfare departments, educational institutions, volunteer organizations, and so on. Second, master's degree programs in social work are longer than most other graduate degree programs in human services and usually require two years of full-time study beyond the B.A. degree. Moreover, this extensive experience generally includes four semesters of field work, whereas other types of degree programs may require little or no field work. This field experience, a hallmark of social work education, is particularly important in enabling students to go beyond the acquisition of knowledge and develop skills in applying this knowledge in real-life situations. A third advantage of graduate study in social work in preparing probation and parole administrators is its humanistic orientation. While it is granted that other disciplines, such as business administration or public administration, may teach many of the same management theories as social work, they do so from a different philosophic orientation. Social work education stresses values and emphasizes that service to clients should be planned, organized, and delivered with a humanitarian objective. Thus, for example, while the administrator with a social work background and the administrator with a business administration background may be equally trained in techniques of cost-benefit analysis, philosophic differences may influence the ways in which they would define benefits and, consequently, make programmatic decisions.

Graduate programs in social work have increasingly offered specializations and concentrations. In fact, the Council on Social Work Education (CSWE) has listed 13 separate concentrations for master's level education (Lenon, 2004). This trend has resulted partly from the tremendous growth of bachelor's degree programs in social work and the consequent need for more advanced training at the graduate level. CSWE recently reported there were 293 Baccalaureate and 112 joint M.S.W./Baccalaureate accredited programs (Lenon, 2004). Opportunities to specialize in administration and/or concentrate in corrections are now widely available in graduate social work programs. More than ever, M.S.W. programs are equipped to educate students specifically for practice as probation and parole administrators.

It should be emphasized, however, that neither social work nor any other academic discipline concerned with preparing probation and parole administrators utilizes a distinct body of knowledge concerned with probation and parole agency management. Such a body of knowledge does not exist. Historically, in fact, little discussion has appeared in the corrections or social work literature regarding administrative practices in probation and parole. While certain aspects of the administrator's role have been addressed, such as caseload management and personnel supervision, a thorough body of knowledge has not yet been developed in this field. It is interesting that there is such a paucity of literature on this subject, given the importance of the administrator's job.

There are several possible reasons why so little discussion has appeared in the literature regarding management techniques in probation and parole. First, the wide variation in the organizational structure of probation and parole offices makes it particularly difficult to develop managerial principles that would be universally applicable. Furthermore, since the legal basis for agency structure varies from jurisdiction to jurisdiction, there is limited opportunity to develop organizational configurations around principles of organizational theory. Instead, management principles must be adapted to existing structures. Second, the traditional structure of probation and parole offices relative to legal systems has caused administrators to feel they have little opportunity to develop policies concerning the operation of their organizations. Rather, they often see their role as that of implementing policies and procedures that have been determined legislatively or judicially. Third, the lack of literature regarding administration in probation and parole may be attributable to the fact that many probation agencies are relatively small and fractionalized, resulting in reliance by administrators on management strategies and techniques borrowed from social work or other disciplines or developed through personal experience.

It is unfortunate that a systematic body of literature regarding administrative practices in probation and parole has not yet been developed. Probation and parole agencies, like other components of the correctional system, have been criticized throughout the years for inability to demonstrate effectiveness in rehabilitating offenders (Amos & Newman, 1975; Byrne, Lurigio, & Petersilio, 1992; Finckenaure, 1982; Lipton, Martinson, & Wilkes, 1975; Petersilio, 1998; Smith & Berlin, 1976). If administrators of probation and parole agencies are to modify their programs in order to achieve greater effectiveness and efficiency, they need a thorough understanding of managerial principles. Certainly there are factors related to agency success that may be beyond the control of administrators, such as the decisions to grant, deny, or revoke probation, or the length of the probation period. However, there are many aspects of agency operation for which administrators have considerable responsibility and authority, and they are accountable for the agency's performance relative to these areas. In order to make appropriate decisions in those areas where they have managerial discretion and thus enhance agency effectiveness, administrators need to be knowledgeable of organizational and management theory.

Many probation and parole administrators have learned management theory in disciplines such as social work, business administration, public administration, social psychology, and political science. Theoretical perspectives acquired in these disciplines have been applied by administrators in different ways as they have attempted to relate them to their individual organizations and particular needs. Since this approach does not result in a unique theory of management that can be uniformly applied to probation and parole administration, it may be challenged by those who desire simple answers and pure models. Indeed in earlier years, a number of organizational theorists sought to develop management theories that prescribe *the best* ways of managing organizations (Taylor, 1947). However, contemporary trends among organizational theorists continue towards contingency, or situational, approaches to management. That is, rather than advocating the one best way of managing an organization, these writers contend that management theory should develop knowledge of fundamental relationships and basic techniques that can be applied to a given practical problem for the purpose of achieving the best possible results for *that* situation (DuBrin, 2006; Koontz & O'Donnell, 1986; Weinbach, 2003).

The following pages of this chapter will reflect a contingency perspective on management theory. Given this perspective, the social worker's role as administrator of a probation or parole agency will be discussed in terms of operational functions. That is, management theory will be presented regarding the five basic functions of all managers – planning, organizing, staffing, directing and leading, and controlling. This operational perspective assumes that the fundamentals of management are universal and apply in all kinds of enterprises, including probation and parole agencies.

The five managerial functions can best be understood when illustrated by example. Thus, a case involving a probation and parole agency will be presented below, and this situation will be dealt with throughout the chapter in terms of application of the five functions of management.

Case Example: The Situation

During the past year, the Lowman County Probation and Parole Agency has received a great deal of public criticism. This criticism, which was triggered by several notorious crimes involving parolees, became focused on the overall ineffectiveness of the agency as measured by recidivism rates. The administrator resigned under pressure of the adverse publicity and Mark Donaldson was hired to replace him.

Mark received his MSW degree from the local university and for the past five years had served as assistant director of a community-based social services program. Upon arriving at the Lowman County Probation and Parole Agency, he found the program in a state of turmoil. In his first meetings with his twenty-one member professional staff, Mark discovered that there was a diversity of opinions as to whether the agency was supposed to function as a control entity or as a treatment program. Staff who had been with the agency for most of its existence tended to operate as control agents, while newer staff (those who had been employed for two years or less) generally tended to be more treatment oriented. The previous administrator had utilized a philosophy of letting each staff member function as s/he thought best, using any style of client supervision. Those who functioned as controllers complained to Mark that staff who focused on treatment spent too much time with their clients with little results. Those staff who were treatment oriented charged that the controllers were ineffective in changing client behavior and, therefore, did little to reduce the high recidivism rate.

After the investigation of the personnel records, Mark determined that the newer staff had been hired from among the graduates of the university's six-year-old BSW program, while older staff had a variety of backgrounds in terms of education and experience. Further, no staff had received any training after initial orientation. An annual evaluation sheet was completed for each staff member, but all agents received "good" to "excellent" ratings each year.

There were no intermediate supervisors in the agency. Meetings between the previous administrator and staff had been held infrequently and consisted of the administrator's report of new policies received from the central office. The policy manual was a hodgepodge of central office directives stuffed into a folder in the administrator's office.

A file on caseload assignments revealed that these were made by the administrator's secretary who used a random assignment method. Agents' last names were alphabetically listed and a running tally was kept of cases assigned. When a new case came in form the court or the parole board, it was given to the next agent named on the list, even though other agents may have conducted previous presentence investigations or parole investigations on that case.

PLANNING

In creating within the probation and parole office an environment for the effective performance of personnel, the first essential task of the administrator is to see that purposes and objectives, and methods of attaining them, are clearly understood. If the probation or parole agency is to be effective, agents and other staff must know what they are expected to accomplish. This is the function of planning, which is the most basic of all the managerial functions. Simply stated, planning is deciding in advance what to do, how to do it, when to do it, and who is to do it.

Since the probation and parole administrator's other functions of organizing, staffing, directing and leading, and controlling are designed to support the accomplishment of the agency's objectives, planning logically precedes the execution of all other managerial functions. In other words, planning must occur in order for the administrator to be able to establish the objectives of the agency, create the kind of organization that can best attain these objectives, decide the type of personnel that are needed, determine how these personnel are to be directed and led, and define the kinds of control to be applied to ensure that objectives will be achieved.

Like managers of other social agencies, probation and parole administrators often feel that their potential for planning is severely restricted, given the constraints within which they must operate. These constraints include factors such as the legal structure of the organization; staff size; caseloads whose size cannot be predetermined or controlled; and increased demands placed on the probation system by the implementation of intermediate sanctions such as intensive supervised probation, house arrests, shock incarceration, community service, boot camps, electronic monitoring, and day fines (Harris, Petersen, & Rapoza, 2001; Petersilia, 1998; Sluder, Sapp, & Langston, 1994). However, the manager of any organization is faced with constraints, although they may be of a different nature, and these constraints do not preclude successful planning. Given the constraints that may affect planning, the administrator can still exercise a wide range of choices in developing plans. For example, even though the geographic boundaries of the agency may be established, the administrator may have flexibility in determining the most feasible location of local offices. Or, although it may not be possible to control caseload size or staff size, caseload management techniques that will enhance the efficiency of the probation agents can be planned. Finally, while conditions of probation and parole may be set by the court or parole board, alternative ways of supervising clients and ensuring compliance with these conditions may be planned.

If planning is to be effective, the administrator must recognize that there are many different types of plans that are appropriate for the probation or parole agency. Since a plan encompasses any course of future action, plans are varied. They are often classified in the literature as purposes or missions, objectives, strategies, policies, rules, procedures, programs, and budgets (DuBrin, 2006; Weinbach, 2003). These various types of plans are interrelated. The degree of the probation or parole administrator's involvement in each of these areas of planning will vary relative to agency structure and one's position within the organizational chain of command.

In order for planning to be successful, the administrator should involve probation agents and other staff in the planning process. As a result of this involvement, employees have a clearer knowledge of what is expected of them, and they gave a higher commitment to carrying out plans and achieving objectives that resulted from decisions they helped make (Allen Eskridge, Latessa, & Vito, 1985; Clean & Latessa, 1993; Harris, Clean, & Baird, 1989; Raymond, 1974; Slate, Wells, & Johnson, 2003). For example, by participating in the development of a mission statement, probation agents are forced to clarify their philosophy regarding the perennial issue of treatment versus control. As another example, in helping to decide the types of treatment programs to be used in the agency, probation and parole agents may have to examine new and different alternatives and evaluate the efficacy of traditional approaches. As a final example, if agents participate in defining treatment objectives and establishing how the attainment of these will be measured, it will be necessary for them to differentiate between administrative and operational definitions of "success," which will undoubtedly benefit them in evaluating their own supervisory efforts. Thus, while final responsibility for planning must rest with the administrator of the probation or parole agency, many benefits, including stress and burnout reduction, can be realized from including staff in the decision-making process (Slate, Wells, & Johnson, 2003).

All planning is ultimately aimed at the attainment of the agency's mission and objectives. Indeed, unless objectives are clearly established during the planning process, there will be no way that the administrator can subsequently evaluate the results of a program and determine whether or not planning was successful (the control function of management). As early as 30 years ago the National Advisory Commission on Corrections emphasized that in order for a probation agency to be effective it must develop a goal-oriented service delivery system and specify measurable objectives based on priorities and needs assessment (National Advisory Commission on Criminal Justice Standards and Goals, 1973). Historically, however, probation and parole systems have lacked a consistent mission to anchor their objectives (Breed, 1984; Conrad, 1985; Holt, 1998; McAnany, 1984; Petersilia, 1985). Since everything that an agency hopes to accomplish flows from its mission and objectives, the lack of such a clear-cut mission in probation and parole has resulted in role descriptions of officers that range from control (Barkdull, 1976) to case management (Whitehead, 1984) to offender rehabilitation (Gendreau & Paparozzi, 1993; Shicor, 1992).

Because of the importance of having a definite mission and establishing clear and measurable objectives in the planning process, administrators of social service agencies in general and correctional managers in particular continue to give attention to lessons learned from programs of managing by objectives or results (McConkie, 1975; Weinbach, 2003). One of these approaches, Management by Objectives, is a systematic approach to managerial problem-solving and decision-making. It is a process whereby managers and subordinates engage in the process of identifying organizational goals and objectives and structuring the agency's operation around these goals and objectives. The process focuses attention on solving problems and attaining results rather than on activities that lead to those results. The basic concern is setting measurable objectives and providing avenues for achieving them. Thus, Management by Objectives entails a highly formalized, systematic approach to planning, involving administrators and other personnel. Because of its many advantages, this system of management has been incorporated, to various degrees, by many correctional agencies, including probation and parole departments.

Case Example: Planning Function

In the previously cited problem situation at the Lowman County Probation and Parole Agency, Mark Donaldson determined that the first need of the program was to facilitate the development of a management plan. He believed the agency must be concerned with both control and treatment in order to be of benefit to the clients and the community. Expanding on the statutory mandate for the agency, Mark wrote a statement of purpose (or mission) that encompassed these two functions. He then established a task force to develop the actual goals and objectives based on the purpose/mission statement. In selecting the task force, which he chaired, Mark was careful to include representatives from each of the two philosophical persuasions.

The task force was divided into three subcommittees and instructed to develop appropriate goals relating to designated areas within the agency's purpose, measurable objectives for each goal, and a reasonable timeframe to test out the attainment of each objective. One subcommittee was assigned responsibility of developing plans relative to pre-sentence investigations and parole investigations. A second subcommittee was to develop plans regarding supervision of probationers and parolees. A third subcommittee had the responsibility of making plans relative to agency policy, staff management, and community relations. Each subcommittee was given two weeks to prepare its initial draft.

At the next meeting, the proposals were presented. After a great deal of discussion, the task force completed an overall plan that was basically agreeable to all members. The draft plan was then distributed to the entire staff for additional comments and suggestions. After further revisions, the final plan was prepared. Goals included, for example, "to create a community advisory board," and "to reduce the recidivism rate by 5 percent during the next 12 months." An example of an objective included was "to prepare complete pre-sentence investigation reports on all cases within two weeks after assignment." A staff meeting was held, during which Mark and the task force members fully explained the plan and answered questions about it.

It was explained to the agents that they would be expected to develop individual objectives relating to their work. These objectives would be based upon and supportive of the goals and objectives of the agency. For instance, an agent developed as one of his objectives the following: "to offer group counseling sessions during one evening each week for clients whose circumstances preclude daytime meetings." It was explained to agents that part of their annual evaluation would be based on how well they achieved their objectives.

It was decided to test the new plan for a six-month period. At the end of that time, the rate of success in attaining individual and organizational objectives would be determined. The task force would then compile the results, make revisions as needed, and develop a one year plan using the six month plan as a basis.

ORGANIZING

The second major function of the administrator of a probation and parole agency is organizing. Simply stated, organizing means creating a structure by establishing relationships among people, work, and physical resources. The purpose of organizing is to provide a framework for staff activities in order to integrate those activities and direct them toward a shared focus (Weinbach, 2003).

An important question related to organizing in probation and parole administration is whether probation services should be centralized or decentralized – a common concern of social agencies. Generally, the organizational structure of the probation service of a given jurisdiction is outlined by statute. However, detailed structure and procedures may be determined by administrative regulation, in which case the administrator can have considerable authority in determining the extent to which services within the jurisdiction will be centralized or decentralized.

Corrections literature presents arguments supporting both centralization and decentralization. The most frequently cited arguments in favor of centralization are that a centrally administered system is more free of local political considerations; it can develop uniform policies and procedures, leading to a greater likelihood that the same level of services will be provided to all clients; it contributes to greater efficiency in the disposition of resources; and it has greater potential to develop innovative programs, demonstration projects, and correctional research. On the other hand, arguments supporting decentralized arrangements include: local probation or parole programs can generally develop better support from local citizens and agencies, local units can be more flexible and less bound by bureaucratic rigidity, and probation agents working for a local unit are more likely to be thoroughly familiar with the local community (Killinger, Kerper, & Cromwell, 1976).

While the probation and parole administrator's authority to determine the degree of centralization/decentralization may be limited by statute, there are other means of organizing that may be employed; for example, the administrator may develop departments or divisions based on function. Departmentalization by function means the grouping of activities on the basis of similarity of skills required or on basis of a common purpose (DuBrin, 2006). This is perhaps the most common type of departmentalization among all types of organizations, including social work agencies. When probation and parole agencies are organized around groupings of tasks and activities into relatively discrete functions, this usually involves assignment of agents to either investigation or supervision functions. This type of functional specialization in probation and parole has the advantages of enhancing the development of expertise, facilitating supervisory control of performance, and eliminating neglect of one function in favor of the other. On the other hand, it may be argued that such specialization results in unequal workloads with consequent morale problems, and that probation agents who handle both investigation and supervision will have a greater knowledge base and repertoire of skills than those who specialize.

The administrator of a probation or parole agency may also organize the department based upon case load assignment of probationers or parolees. Five major caseload assignment models have been utilized historically (Carter & Wilkins, 1976). First, the conventional model utilizes the random assignment of probationers to available probation officers. Second, with the numbers game model, the object is to balance numerically all of the caseloads within the agency. Third, the conventional model with geographic consideration restricts caseloads to clients living in specific geographic areas. Fourth, the single factor specialized model assigns probationers to caseloads on the basis of a single shared characteristic, such as drug abuse, mental deficiency, or type of offense. Fifth, the vertical model is based on classification by a combination of characteristics. Each of these models has advantages and disadvantages, and too little research has been done to conclude which caseload management strategy is more effective or efficient. The administrator must consider the unique needs and circumstances of the probation and parole agency in determining the caseload assignment model that will be most appropriate.

The chief administrator of a probation and parole agency will likely have subordinate administrators, such as supervisors or agents in charge, unless the agency is particularly small. In developing an organizational structure with several administrative positions, the chief administrator of a probation or parole agency should keep in mind several important principles of organizing. First, the line of authority from the chief administrator to every subordinate position should be clear, if effective communication and responsible decision making are to occur. Second, subordinate administrators should be delegated adequate

authority to enable them to do their job. Third, it should be made clear that subordinates are responsible to their superiors and that the superiors cannot escape responsibility for the organization activities of their subordinates. Fourth, insofar as possible, each individual should have a reporting relationship to a single superior in order to avoid a problem of conflict in instructions and to enhance the feeling of personal responsibility for results. Fifth, subordinate administrators with authority to make certain decisions should be required to make these decisions and not be allowed to refer them upward in the agency structure (Clegg, 1970; Koontz et al., 1986). When these principles are followed, the job of every administrator in a probation and parole agency becomes easier and the operation of the agency becomes more effective.

Case Example: Organizing Function

Mark Donaldson recognized he had two primary problems in the organization of his agency. The first was the absence of intermediate supervisors to help assume some of the responsibility for overseeing staff functions and responding to problems. He was particularly aware of the potential for staff resentment of his interference in their daily schedules since he was the new administrator who had already begun changing a system in which staff had become comfortable, if not satisfied. He also believed his time could be better spent in activities other than direct supervision. Since he had developed a close working relationship with the staff members who composed the planning task force and had been favorably impressed with their ability to communicate and reach compromises for the benefit of the agency, he asked these people to serve as the personnel committee to recommend persons to serve as intermediate supervisors. Based on their recommendations, Mark promoted four agents to supervisory positions. Each intermediate supervisor was assigned five to seven staff members to direct.

Mark's second organizing problem pertained to the assignment of caseloads. The arbitrary random assignment that had been used caused agents to spend valuable time traveling from one end of the county to the other. Given this system, agents were unable to develop a thorough knowledge of a community or establish a relationship with any particular neighborhood. Furthermore, this method of case assignment ignored the fact that individual agents were more skilled in working with certain kinds of problems than others. To address this problem, Mark met with his intermediate supervisors and developed a new organizational plan. The county was divided into four separate regions, and each officer was assigned cases in one region only. Furthermore, each supervisor was responsible for supervision of agents in a single region. Additionally, several officers who appeared to have exceptional skills in working with youthful offenders were assigned caseloads comprised predominantly of this type of client. Every effort was made to equalize caseloads among agents, although it was recognized this could not be completely accomplished.

STAFFING

The third function of the administrator of a probation or parole agency is staffing, which has to do with selection, appraisal, and development of personnel to fill the roles designed into the organizational structure of the agency. The ultimate success of the agency is largely dependent upon the manner in which the administrator carries out these three elements of staffing.

There is great discrepancy among jurisdictions as to the preservice educational requirements for probation and parole officers, more than for most social agencies. Requirements set by statute or by administrative regulation vary from high school or less to graduate degrees plus prior experience. Over 30 years ago the standards set by the American Bar Association (1970) and the National Advisory Commission (1973) called for a minimum educational requirement of a bachelor's degree for probation agents. The American Bar Association also suggested the need for postgraduate study and recommended uniform state standards for all probation officers. The American Correctional Association (1977) has also stressed the value of undergraduate and graduate degrees. Furthermore, it is generally accepted by criminal justice planners, administrators, and educators that a university graduate is more capable and competent as a probation or parole officer (Anderson,

Mangels, & Dyson, 2003; Carter & Wilkins, 1976; Echaore-McDavid, 2000; Newman, 1971). Some writers (for example, see Smith & Berlin, 1976, p. 35) have asserted that a master's degree in social work offers the best preparation for work in probation and parole settings. It should be noted, however, that there is little empirical research to demonstrate what type of preservice training is most effective in enhancing the overall performance of probation and parole officers. More research needs to be done in this area.

In the selection of probation and parole officers, a number of merit systems and agencies use some form of written examinations. Some systems require the utilization of mass-produced employment tests. Because of problems entailed when such tests are used in the selection process, every effort should be made by the administrator to conduct personal evaluations of potential staff. Usually the administrator of the probation or parole agency participates in some phase of the selection process. If a subordinate administrator is to serve as immediate supervisor of the individual being selected, however, this supervisor should also participate in the selection process.

The staffing function also includes the provision of in-service training, and there are two types. The first type, orientation training, should be provided as soon as possible after the employee is hired. This training for the probation or parole agent generally includes a combination of classroom and on-the-job training. In training new employees, it is advantageous for probation and parole agencies to make greater use of technological aids such as videos, professional films, and computer-based training. Developments in technology in recent years have made it possible to provide a great deal of education and training through interactive computer applications, whereby the learner is able to master the subject matter at his or her own pace (Raymond & Pike, 1997; Raymond 2005). Furthermore, an increasing amount of training is now available to probation and parole personnel through the Internet (Yarcheck, Gavazzi, & Dascoli, 2003). Regardless of the type of the orientation training offered, it is essential that it cover five important areas: the goals of the agency, the policies of the agency, the organizational structure, the objective that the agent being trained is to accomplish, and the roles to be performed by the agent.

The second type of in-service training is developmental training. This type of training tends to concentrate on the development of specialized treatment modalities or case supervision skills. In probation and parole agencies, this training is usually conducted by the immediate supervisor. Several methods may be used. First, if several people are to be trained and the training involves dissemination of concepts and details for the first time, the lecture may be the most effective method. Second, when the training is concerned with common problems experienced by agents, such as how to deal with certain types of clients, the group conference may be the most appropriate method. Third, simulation and role playing are effective methods of helping agents develop treatment skills. Fourth, individual conferences involving personal instruction and guidance are helpful in enabling the agent to develop knowledge and skills through solving real-life problems. Fifth, in those probation or parole agencies having specialized tasks, such as investigation and supervision, job rotation may be used to enable the agent to learn more about the agency's overall structure and functioning (Eckles et al., 1989).

The third element of staffing is appraisal, which is a formal rating of how well the employee has handled job duties during a given period of time. Performance appraisals have three purposes: to determine the agent's job competence, assess his/her need for further training and development, and help determine compensation and promotion decisions. Given these purposes, performance appraisal should be regarded as an ongoing process. That is, although the formal evaluation must be completed at prescribed intervals, the administrator should let the agent know how s/he is performing on a day-to-day basis through supervisory conferences. In this manner, the results of the formal evaluation entail no surprises.

The type of evaluation often used in probation and parole agencies, as in most social agencies, it the "trait appraisal." Trait-rating evaluation systems generally include several items related to personal characteristics such as leadership, industry, or judgment, as well as several work oriented characteristics such as job knowledge, casework skills, or performance of tasks on time. Sole reliance on this type of evaluation is highly problematic in that the items are very subjective, the criteria are nebulous, the items may have little to do with the probation agent's actual performance,

and, because of the foregoing problems, administrators often tend to rate employees too positively. However, failure to include some trait evaluation may overlook such important employee characteristics as honesty, loyalty, and creativity (DuBrin, 2006; Koontz et al., 1986).

A relatively new development in management thought is the use of multirater systems, such as "360-degree feedback" where a sampling of several workers evaluate individual job performance (DuBrin, 2006, p. 321). This form of evaluation allows for input of perspectives from subordinates, peers, and superiors in the evaluation of performance, which may provide a better picture of both individual strengths and areas of needed improvement. Probation and parole administrators may benefit from sharing power in the evaluation process. Besides, when one person points out an area needing improvement, it may be easier to dismiss than when several give the same feedback. On the other hand, probation and parole administrators need to open themselves up to feedback in this type of system as well.

Perhaps the best tool for probation and parole officers to use in appraising agents and other employees would include a system of evaluating performance in terms of the individual's accomplishment of verifiable objectives. As noted earlier, clear objectives should be established for the agency and specific objectives should be defined for each employee based on the agency's objectives. These objectives should be made clear to the agent during the orientation phase, work should be structured around these, and the performance appraisal should be in terms of the agent's attainment of these objectives (Cohn, 1987). In establishing specific objectives for the probation agent, the administrator should involve the agent in the process. This involvement not only helps the agent understand what is expected but also serves as a motivating factor. The development of individual objectives is clearly illustrated in the Management by Objectives system, although such objectives can be developed when other systems of management are used (McConkie, 1975; Weinbach, 2003).

Case Example: Staffing Function

In reviewing his staffing policies and determining needs, Mark found that a bachelor's degree in "criminal justice or a human services field" had been a requirement of the central office for six years. All members of the current staff met this requirement, but their backgrounds varied and included the fields of criminal justice, social work, sociology, psychology, education, and religion. Their previous employment had included law enforcement, teaching, social work in public agencies, and the ministry. Several agents had been hired upon graduation from a BSW program and had no previous experience.

Given this variety of backgrounds, Mark felt it would be helpful for the staff to consider the philosophical issue on which they seemed to be in greatest disagreement – the control/treatment dilemma. He decided an in-service training program was needed for this purpose. He set up four one-day sessions and brought in consultants from the academic setting to guide the sessions. In addition to leading discussions on these issues, the consultants employed role playing, small group simulations, and values clarification exercises to help the agents examine their beliefs, values, and practice orientations.

After these initial sessions, Mark held monthly follow-up sessions. These were more informal and focused on particular problem situations of clients served by the agency. Mark or one of the immediate supervisors led these sessions. Based on the material used in the initial and follow-up sessions, Mark developed an initial orientation and training program to be used for future training of new agents.

After their appointment, the intermediate supervisors were sent to a three-day training session on the fundamentals of staff supervision. This session was sponsored by the state central office. A supervisor orientation manual was also developed by the intermediate supervisors for future use.

Staff evaluation became Mark's next area of concern. Because of state policy, he had to continue using the evaluation forms already available, but he made changes in the procedure. Mark instituted an additional evaluation system whereby each agent was rated according to his achievement of specific objectives that he helped set. These individual objectives, it will be recalled, related to the goals and objectives that were developed for the agency. The intermediate supervisors were given the task of evaluating the agents under

their direction. Since the supervisors met with their agents on a regular basis, the completion of periodic evaluation forms simply formalized what each supervisor and individual agent already knew about the agent's job performance. In addition, Mark asked his intermediate supervisors to seek evaluations from each of their subordinates and provide a self-evaluation for discussion in his evaluation of their performance.

DIRECTING AND LEADING

The fourth function of administrators of probation and parole agencies is that of directing and leading the agency employees. Directing and leading are the interpersonal aspects of managing by which employees are helped to understand and contribute effectively and efficiently to the attainment of the agency objectives. This function has to do with establishing the proper relationship with employees, communicating effectively with them, supervising them appropriately, motivating them, and helping them work towards the achievement of the agency's objectives. Administrators with graduate training in social work generally have a good grasp of this function.

It is probable that the administrator of a probation and parole agency will relate to employees on the basis of his/her assumptions about human nature and behavior. In a classic work, Douglas McGregor (1960) identified two opposite orientations of administrators based on their assumptions about human beings. Theory X managers assume that people have an inherent dislike for work; they must be coerced, controlled, directed, and threatened to get them to pursue organizational goals; and the average person prefers to be directed, wishes to avoid responsibility, has little ambition, and wants security above all. Historically most probation agencies have operated according to these suppositions; for example, the emphasis on maintaining tight schedules, the importance of documentation of one's work, and the insistence on conforming to agency regulations are evidences of a Theory X orientation (Sigurdson, McEachern, & Carter, 1973).

It has been emphasized, however, that the administrator of a probation or parole agency should strive for a Theory Y approach to management (Sigurdson et al., 1973). According to McGregor (1960), an administrator with a Theory Y orientation assumes that physical and mental work is as natural as play or rest; people are self-directed and will strive to achieve objectives to which they are committed; people not only accept but seek responsibility; and most people have high degrees of imagination, ingenuity, and creativity which they will use to solve organizational problems if given the opportunity. The administrator with this orientation will seek to maximize human growth and development and will do so by creating an organizational environment in which individuals realize that they can achieve their own goals by directing their efforts toward the achievement of the organizational goals. A number of writers have suggested that in a model probation department a Theory Y orientation to management should prevail. As in any administrative position, open communication should occur at all levels, the administrator should involve staff in decision making insofar as possible, individuals should be involved in setting their work objectives and in evaluating their effectiveness, and a client orientation rather than a bureaucratic orientation should be encouraged (Chavaria, 1994; Janes, 1993; Sigurdson et al., 1973).

There has been substantial research in social work and other disciplines to support the relationship between the administrator's supervisory style and the response on the part of the persons supervised. It has been well documented (e.g., Austin, 1981; Odiorne, 1970) that an autocratic style of leadership results in poor morale and, generally, inefficient work among employees. Furthermore, the *laissez-faire*-type leadership tends to produce frustration among employees, poor commitment to organizational goals, and poor quality work. The democratic style of leadership, on the other hand, typically results in more effective and efficient work performance and greater job satisfaction among employees. While these findings generally apply to most organizations, the administrator of a probation or parole agency should realize that different situations call for different types of leadership. For example, it may be necessary for the administrator to assume more of an autocratic style in supervising some agents, whereas other agents may function better under a *laissez-faire*-type of leadership. Furthermore, a situation in which a large number of presentence reports must be completed in a short period of time may call for a rather autocratic style on the part of the administrator.

In carrying out the function of directing and leading, the administrator of a probation and parole agency needs to give attention to those factors that produce the greatest motivation among employees. In his seminal research on employee motivation, Herzberg (1968) made a distinction between two types of factors. The first group of factors, called "maintenance" or "hygiene" factors, includes such things as agency policy and administration, supervision, working conditions, interpersonal relations, salary, status, and job security. Herzberg found that the presence of these factors will not motivate people in an organization; yet they must be present or dissatisfaction will arise. The second group of factors, called "motivators," all relate to job content and include such things as achievement, recognition, challenging work, advancement, and growth on the job. Their existence will yield feelings of satisfaction, and they are, therefore, real motivators.

Since probation and parole agencies are public organizations, the administrator may have little control over some of the "maintenance" factors (Herzberg, 1968). However, through the appropriate leadership style, s/he can see to it that many of the true "motivators" are present in the agency. For example, the administrator can recognize the accomplishments and achievements of probation agents or other staff, or job rotation can be used in agencies having specialized functions in order to present agents with the challenge of learning new tasks (DuBrin, 2006; Kettner, 2002; Mills, 1990; Weinbach, 2003). Finally, giving the probation agent increased responsibility as a result of demonstrated competence can be a successful technique for motivating (DuBrin, 2006; Kettner, 2002; Smith & Berlin, 1976; Weinbach, 2003).

Case Example: Directing and Leading Function

Mark approached his leadership role with a goal of obtaining maximum staff input in decision making. He had involved staff in the beginning during the development of the agency's goals and objectives, its policy manual, and its organizational structure because he believed staff would be more supportive of any plan that they had helped create. He continued this practice by submitting drafts of major intra-agency policies to his supervisors and instructing them to review these with all agents for comments prior to finalization.

Mark held weekly meetings with his supervisors to discuss progress and problems. These supervisors then met with their staff members to report on the administrative meeting. Mark met with the total staff once a month.

Mark also saw the value in providing staff with opportunities to associate with their peers from other agencies. He believed such meetings stimulated ideas about how others in the field dealt with problems and made improvements in agencies. Furthermore, the break in the routine could help reduce tensions created by the job. Within budgetary limitations, he tried to create as many opportunities as possible for supervisors and agents to attend conferences and other workshops. He tried to ensure that all agents were provided these opportunities for continuing education.

Another technique Mark implemented within a few months after coming to the agency proved to be particularly useful in motivating staff. He initiated agent-led seminars on a bimonthly basis. Agents selected to conduct the seminars were chosen on the basis of demonstrated excellence in a particular area such as report writing or working with drug abusers. This approach not only stimulated other agents to revise their own methods and develop new skills, but it also served as a reward of recognition for those who excelled in a given area.

CONTROLLING

The final function of probation and parole administrators is that of controlling, which is the measurement and correction of the performance of activities by subordinates in order to make sure that the agency's objectives and the plans devised to attain them are being accomplished. In order for this function to be performed, it is necessary that the probation or parole agency have clearly stated objectives and a data system that can measure the effectiveness of various probation service components (Cohn, 1997). Unfortunately, these two prerequisites have traditionally been absent in probation and parole departments, as is true for most social service organizations.

Several events have occurred historically, however, that have caused probation and parole administrators to give more serious attention to the function of control. First, the growth of the criminal justice system in general over the past three decades (Bonczar, 2003; DiIulio, 1991; Glaze & Palla, 2004) and the consequent operational problems have caused public attention to be focused upon the structure and functioning of the system's components, including probation and parole services. Second, the continued general emphasis on accountability of all public agencies has created public scrutiny of probation and parole agencies (Cohn, 1991). Third, the lack of demonstrated success of all components of the criminal justice system has caused administrators to look for more effective and efficient treatment programs and better means of measuring effectiveness and efficiency (DiIulio, 1991; Petersilia, 1999). Finally, the growing utilization of information technology has facilitated the establishment of management information systems in all areas of human services, including probation and parole, and such systems make control more feasible. That is, these management information systems enable the administrator to gather client information in order to monitor, evaluate, and ultimately improve client services (Fein, 1974; Hoshino & McDonald, 1975; Raymond, 1981; Soma, 1994; Young, 1974).

In order for the administrator of a probation or parole agency to carry out the control function, it is necessary that the agency's objectives are clearly identified. These objectives should be as specific and quantitative (and hence measurable and verifiable) as is possible. Thus, it is not adequate for the agency to express objectives in terms such as "to rehabilitate individuals who are placed on parole." Instead, objectives must be stated in terms such as "to reduce by 10 percent the number of parolees returned to confinement within the next twelve months." As stated earlier in this chapter, the planning function of the administrator should involve the development of objectives such as these.

In performing the control function, the administrator of a probation or parole agency must have sufficient flexibility to develop an organizational structure that has the greatest potential for achieving the stated objectives of the agency. That is, the administrator should be able to create the necessary work units, develop appropriate policies and procedures, and design and implement programs aimed at the achievement of the agency's objectives. As stated earlier in this chapter, this effort comprises the organizing function of the administrator. Unfortunately, factors such as staff size, caseload size, and legal mandates occasionally militate against the creation of an organization that can fulfill the agency's objectives in an optimum manner. Nonetheless, operating within these constraints, the administrator must seek to achieve maximum agency effectiveness and efficiency through designing the program structure and continually modifying it as needed based on feedback concerned with the degree of achievement of agency objectives.

Finally, then, in order for the control function to be carried out, the administrator of the probation and parole agency must design some type of information system that can provide accurate, detailed data that can be rapidly procured and is specifically related to decision-making requirements, planning requirements, and measurement of agency objectives. There are two basic models for information systems for social agencies: administrative management information systems and caseload management systems. Administrative management information systems serve three functions: to control and coordinate employee behavior, provide information for long-term planning, and provide information to external groups. Systems of this type have the capability of generating point in time reports, period in time reports, and notification reports that are automatically initiated by conditions that vary from previously established standards (Coffey, 1974). Caseload management information systems utilize information for decision making at the level of service delivery. The functions of this type of information system are to control client behavior, provide information for individual agent planning, and provide information for management use.

The probation and parole administrator can utilize a comprehensive information system in order to determine what the agency is doing that is effective for selective offenders, ascertain what the agency is doing that is not effective for selective offenders, and identify areas in which changes might be made to increase the overall performance of the agency. It is possible through computer technology to construct a mathematical model of a probation agency. Such a model can be used to analyze a variety of program possibilities and conduct "experiments" where real-life experimentation is not feasible (Austin, 1981; Raymond, 1978; Sigurdson et al., 1973). Computer technology also makes it possible to conduct cost/benefit analyses to evaluate existing program components in terms of efficiency or the relative costs involved in achieving program objectives through alternative approaches (Nelson, 1975; Raymond, 1981). During recent years, computers have been increasingly used by social agencies for numerous purposes, including program evaluation (Moriarty & Carter, 1998).

In addition to the monitoring of programs and program components to ensure agency effectiveness, the control function of administrators includes the ongoing assessment of the performance of individual staff members. At this level, also, effectiveness is measured in terms of the attainment of stated objectives (Jacques, 1989). If the probation or parole administrator has established with each probation agent clear and measurable individual objectives that grow out of and support the agency and program objectives, the evaluation of each individual's effectiveness will be a part of the total system evaluation (Cohn, 1987). Consequently, during the process of performance appraisal the probation agents can see clearly how their roles fit into the overall agency structure and how their performance contributes to the general success of the agency.

Case Example: Controlling Function

The weekly meetings between Mark and his supervisory staff were spent in part on reporting and assessing each unit's progress on agency objectives and discussing problems therein. In addition, Mark met with individual units as needed to address problems and explore alternatives.

Supervisory reports generally included a statistical breakdown of number of clients contacted, categories of services provided, and hours spent per client during the week. These data were compiled and submitted to the central office on a quarterly basis and analyzed by Mark and the supervisors in relation to the goals and objectives that had been established for the agency. For example, at the end of six months, Mark reviewed the report on staff hours and realized most agents were having to work a good deal of overtime to complete all of their presentence investigations.

This was partially due to their attempts to meet the objective of preparing complete presentence investigation reports on all referrals within two weeks. Given the fact that each agent was preparing an average of four presentence reports each week, it became obvious that the objective was unrealistic. Accordingly, it was decided that rather than preparing complete presentence reports on all cases, partial reports would be developed for appropriate clients based on certain criteria. This plan proved to be more effective.

After a six-month period, it was also determined that supervisors and their agents were spending relatively too much time discussing individual cases. A decision was made to initiate client staffings as a means of dealing with client problem situations in a way that could be educational for all agents. Each supervisor began to meet with the agents under his supervision twice monthly. During staffings, agents would review selected cases relative to plans of action developed by the agent, tasks undertaken with the client, and problems encountered. In addition to being an effective means of problem solving and staff development, this process also helped Mark and the supervisors assess the ability of the agents.

Case Example: Conclusion

At the end of the first 12 months, Mark and his staff had sufficient data to develop a five-year plan and document to the central office the need for additional staff to conduct the work of the agency. The recidivism rate had been lowered by 3 percent and public criticism of the agency had virtually ceased. The community advisory board had proven to be particularly helpful in achieving "good press" for the agency, developing job placement sources for clients, and securing the assistance of civic and religious groups when needed. Mark had lost five staff members during the year – two obtained other jobs, one returned to school, and two left due to dissatisfaction with the changes. The operation appeared to be running smoothly, and a positive working atmosphere prevailed. While Mark had not achieved all he had hoped and a number of problems still existed, his sound management practices had obviously produced many positive results.

CONCLUSION

This chapter has considered the role of the probation or parole administrator from an operational perspective. That is, attention has been focused on the major managerial functions performed by probation and parole administrators. These functions include planning, organizing, staffing, directing and leading, and controlling.

These five managerial functions are performed by administrators at all levels in probation and parole agencies, just as they are carried out by administrators at various levels in any type of social agency or other agency. The degree to which each function is performed by probation and parole administrators may vary, of course, from one managerial level to another. Furthermore, the degree to which these functions are carried out may vary from agency to agency. Regardless of the statutory, judicial, or other conditions affecting the operation of the probation and parole agency, however, agency administrators inevitably perform all these functions.

It is obvious that the five managerial functions discussed in this chapter are interrelated. Sound planning, including establishment of clear objectives, is necessary in order for the probation and parole administrator to know what kind of organization is necessary to achieve the objectives. The establishment of objectives and the development of an organizational structure helps the administrator know what kind of people will have to be hired, what type of training they will need, and how they will be evaluated. The probation or parole agency's objectives, the organizational structure, and the people hired will affect the kind of leadership and direction provided by the administrator. Standards of control can be established only after measurable objectives have been planned, and the administrator can keep the agency goal-directed through changes in the organizational structure, changes in personnel, and changes in methods of leadership and directing.

It is understandable that the managerial functions performed by the probation and parole administrator would intermesh in this manner. The tasks of the administrator of a social agency are never discrete, and any actions in one area of work inevitably affect other areas. Thus, the administrator does not typically perform the functions of planning, organizing, staffing, directing and leading, and controlling in a sequential fashion. Rather, these functions are carried out simultaneously in the day-to-day work of the administrator. A sound knowledge of these managerial functions and an awareness of how they interrelate will enhance the administrator's performance of the challenging job of managing a probation or parole agency.

Although the philosophy undergirding probation and parole has changed from time to time, resulting in different approaches to practice, the dual emphasis on reform and control has always been present (Purkiss, Kifer, Hemmens, & Burton, 2003) and will likely continue for many years. Sluder, Sapp, and Langston (1994), after reviewing the philosophies that have guided probation historically, concluded that future probation systems would be based primarily on rehabilitation goals, and secondarily upon control goals. While offender reform strategies should be the guiding force of probation and parole in the future, control themes will continue to be an important part of probation and parole work. Administrators of probation and parole agencies must develop mission statements, goals, objectives, and programs which reflect both ideologies.

Future administrators of probation and parole agencies must develop and manage programs that are part of a larger system of alternatives to incarceration. In recent years, a number of intermediate sanctions have been introduced to the probation system, including intensive supervised probation, house arrest, shock incarceration, boot camps, community service, restitution, and day fines (DeJong & Franzeen, 1993; Petersilia, 1998). Such alternatives may be part of a coherent system of graduated penalties such as Morris and Tonry (1990) described in their seminal work. According to a number of writers (Byrne & Brewster, 1993; Byrne, Lurigio, & Petersilia, 1992; Palmer, 1992; Wilson, Bouffard, & Mackenzie, 2005), those programs which focus primarily on offender rehabilitation are effective, whereas those that are more surveillance oriented are generally ineffective. The future administrator must be knowledgeable of such programs and their efficacy, and must be able to design probation and parole services that make appropriate use of these alternatives.

As the probation and parole population continues to grow, administrators' roles in recruiting, training, supervising, leading, and consequently, retaining personnel will become more complex and challenging.

Administrators of probation and parole agencies will be responsible for overseeing the work of larger and larger staffs. In recruiting these staffs, administrators must hire probation and parole officers who represent diversity, including women and persons of color. This should be done not just to meet affirmative action goals, but to ensure the presence of staff that is optimally effective in dealing with an increasingly diverse population. The knowledge and skills needed by probation and parole staff will require personnel with appropriate education and experience to prepare them for the demands and challenges of these positions. Personnel of this caliber must be led by administrators who can inspire them, motivate them, and guide them to carry out their jobs with commitment and enthusiasm.

The role of the administrator of a probation and parole agency has always been difficult and demanding, and it will likely become even more so in the future. It will remain, however, a fulfilling and rewarding role – especially for those who are able to employ sound management principles in administering probation and parole agencies.

REFERENCES

Allen, H. E., Eskridge, C., Latessa, E., & Vito, G. (1985). *Probation and parole in America.* New York: Free Press.

American Bar Association (1970). *Standards relating to probation.* New York: American Bar Association, Project on Standards for Criminal Justice.

American Correction Association (1977). *Manual of standards for adult probation and parole field services.* College Park, MD: American Correctional Association.

Amos, W. E., & Newman, C. L. (1975). *Parole.* New York: Federal Legal Publications, Inc.

Anderson, J. F., Mangels, N. J., & Dyson, L. (2003). *Criminal justice and criminology: A career guide to local, state, federal, and academic positions.* Maryland: University Press of America, Inc.

Austin, J., & McVey, A. D. (1988). *The NCCD prison population forecast: The growing imprisonment of America.* San Francisco: National Council on Crime and Delinquency.

Austin, M. J. (1981). *Supervisory management for the human services.* Englewood Cliffs, NJ: Prentice-Hall.

Barkdull, W. (1976). Probation: Call it control and mean it. *Federal Probation, 53*(2), 49–60.

Bonczar, T. P. (2003). Prevalence of imprisonment in the U.S. population, 1974–2001. *Bureau of Justice Statistics: Special Report.* Washington, D.C.: U.S. Department of

Justice, Bureau of Justice Statistics. Retrieved August, 22nd 2005 from http://www.ojp.usdoj.gov/bjs/abstract/piusp01.htm.

Breed, A. (1984). Foreword. In P. McAnany, D. Thompson & D. Fogel (Eds.), *Probation and justice: Reconsideration of mission.* Cambridge, MA: Oelgeschlager, Gunn, & Hain.

Byrne, J., Lurigio, A., & Petersilia, J. (1992). *Smart sentencing: The emergence of intermediate sanctions.* Newbury Park, CA: Sage.

Byrne, J., & Brewster, M. (1993). Choosing the future of American correction: Punishment or reform? *Federal Probation, 57*(4), 3–9.

Carter, R. M., & Wilkins, L. T. (Eds.) (1976). Caseloads: Some conceptual models. *Probation and parole* (2nd ed.). New York: John Wiley & Sons.

Chavaria, F. R. (1994). Building synergy in probation. *Federal Probation, 58*(3), 18–22.

Clear, T. R., & Latessa, E. J. (1993). Probation officers' roles in intensive supervision: Surveillance versus treatment. *Justice Quarterly, 10*(1), 67–88.

Clegg, R. K. (1990). *Probation and parole.* Springfield, IL: Charles C Thomas.

Coffey, A. R. (1974). *Administration of criminal justice.* Englewood Cliffs, NJ: Prentice-Hall.

Cohn, A. W. (1987). The failure of correctional management-the potential for reversal. *Federal Probation, 51*(4), 3–7.

Cohn, A. W. (1991). The failure of correctional management-reviewed: Present and future dimensions. *Federal Probation, 55*(2), 12–16.

Conrad, J. P. (1985). The penal dilemma and its emerging solution. *Crime & Delinquency, 31,* 411–422.

DeJong, W., & Franzeen, S. (1993). On the role of intermediate sanctions in correctional reform: The views of criminal justice professionals. *Journal of Criminal Justice, 16*(1), 47–73.

DiIulio, J. I. (1991). *No escape: The future of American corrections.* New York: Basic Books.

DuBrin, A. J. (2006). *Essentials of management* (7th ed.). New York: Thomson/South Western.

Echaore-McDavid, S. (2000). *Career opportunities in law enforcement, security, and protective services.* New York: Facts on File, Inc.

Eckles, R. W., Carmichael, R. L., & Sarchet, B. R. (1989). *Essentials of management for first-line supervision* (2nd ed.). New York: John Wiley & Sons.

Fein, E. (1974). A data system for an agency. *Social Casework, 20*(1).

Gendreau, P., & Paparozzi, M. (1993). Does "punishing smarter" work? An assessment of the new generation of alternative sanctions in probation. *Forum on Correction Research, 5*(3), 33–38.

Glaze, L. E., & Palla, S. (2004). Probation and parole in the United States, 2003. *Bureau of Justice Statistics: Bulletin.* Washington, D.C.: U.S. Department of Justice, Bureau of Justice Statistics. Retrieved August, 22nd 2005 from http://www.ojp.usdoj.gov/bjs/abstract/ppus03.htm.

Harris, P. M., Clean, T. R., & Baird, S. C. (1989). Have community services officers changed their attitudes toward their work? *Justice Quarterly, 6*(2), 233–246.

Harris, P. M., Petersen, R. D., & Rapoza, S. (2001). Between probation and revocation: A study of intermediate sanctions decision-making. *Journal of Criminal Justice, 29,* 307–318.

Herzberg, F. (1968). One more time: How do you motivate employees? *Harvard Business Review, 46*(1).

Holt, N. (1998). The current state of parole in America. In J. Petersilia (Ed.), *Community corrections: Probation, parole, and intermediate sanctions.* New York: Oxford University Press.

Hoshino, G., & McDonald, T. P. (1975). Agencies in the computer age. *Social Work, 20*(1).

Kettner, P. M. (2002). *Achieving excellence in the management of human service organizations.* Boston: Allyn & Bacon.

Killinger, G. C., Kerper, H. B., & Cromwell, P. F., Jr. (1976). *Probation and parole in the criminal justice system.* St. Paul, MN: West.

Koontz, H., O'Donnell, C., & Weirich, H. (1986). *Essentials of management* (4th ed.). New York: McGraw-Hill.

Lenon, T. M. (2004). *Statistics on social work education in the United States: 2002.* Alexandria, VA: Council on Social Work Education.

Lipton, D., Martinson, R., & Wilks, J. (1975). *The effectiveness of correctional treatment: A survey of treatment evaluation studies.* New York: Praeger.

McAnany, P. (1984). Mission and justice: Clarifying probation's legal context. In P. McAnany, D. Thomson, & D. Fogel (Eds.), *Probation and justice: Reconsideration of mission.* Cambridge, MA: Oelgeschlager, Gunn, and Hain.

McConkie, M. L. (1975). *Management by objectives: A corrections perspective.* Washington, D.C.: U.S. Government Printing Office.

McGregor, D. (1960). *The human side of enterprise.* New York: McGraw-Hill.

Mills, D. K. (1990). Career issues for probation officers. *Federal Probation, 57*(4), 28–33.

Moriarty, L.J., Carter, D.L. (1998). *Criminal justice technology in the 21st century.* Springfield, IL: Charles C Thomas.

Morris, N., & Tonry, M. (1990). *Between prison and probation: Intermediate punishments in a rational sentencing system.* New York: Oxford University Press.

National Advisory Commission on Criminal Justice Standards and Goals. (1973). *Corrections.* Washington, D.C.: U.S. Government Printing Office.

Nelson, C. W. (1975). Cost-benefit analysis and alternatives to incarceration. *Federal Probation, 39,* p. 43.

Newman, C. L. (1971). *Personnel practices in adult parole systems.* Springfield, IL: Charles C Thomas.

Odiorne, G. S. (1970). *Training by objectives.* London: Macmillan.

Palmer, T. (1992). *The re-emergence of correctional intervention.* Newbury Park, CA: Sage.

Petersilia, J. (1985). Community Supervision: Trends and critical issues. *Crime and Delinquency, 31,* 411–422.

Petersilia, J. (Ed.) (1998). *Community corrections: Probation, parole, and intermediate sanctions.* New York: Oxford University Press.

Petersilia, J. (1999). A decade of experimenting with intermediate sanctions: What have we learned? *Justice Research and Policy, 1*(1), 9–23.

Purkiss, M., Kifer, M., Hemmens, C., & Burton, V. S. (2003). Probation officer functions – a statutory analysis. *Federal Probation, 67*(1), 12–23.

Raymond, F. B. (1981). Program evaluation. In R. M. Grinnell, Jr. (Ed.). *Social work research and evaluation.* Itasca, IL: F. E. Peacock.

Raymond, F. B. (1978). The cybernetic model as a means to accountability: An agency example. *Arete, 5*(1), 23–35.

Raymond, F. B. (1974). To punish or to treat. *Social Work, 19*(3), 305–311.

Raymond, F. B. (2006). The history of continuing education in social work and the evolution of distance education modalities. In P. Abels (Ed.), *Distance education in social work.* New York: Springer.

Raymond, F. B., & Pike, C. K. (1997). Social work education: Electronic technologies. In R. L. Edwards et al.

(Eds.), *Encyclopedia of social work: 1997 supplement* (19th ed., pp. 281–299. Washington, D.C.: NASW Press.

Shicor, D. (1992). Following the penological pendulum: The survival of rehabilitation. *Federal Probation, 56,* 305–311.

Sigurdson, H. R., McEachern, A. W., & Carter, R. M. (1973). Administrative innovation in probation services: A design for increasing effectiveness. *Crime and Delinquency, 19*(3), 353–366.

Slate, R. N., Wells, T. L., & Johnson, W. W. (2003). Opening the manager's door: State probation officer stress and perceptions of participation in workplace decision making. *Crime & Delinquency, 49*(4), 519–541.

Sluder, R. D., Sapp, A. D., & Langston, D. C. (1994). Guiding philosophies for probation in the 21st century. *Federal Probation, 58*(3), 3–10.

Smith, A. B., & Berlin, L. (1976). *Introduction to probation and parole.* St. Paul, MN: West.

Soma, J. (1994). Group reporting – A sensible way to manage high caseloads. *Federal Probation, 58*(3), 26–28.

Taylor, F. (1947). *Scientific management.* New York: Harper & Brothers.

Wilson, D. B., Bouffard, L. A., & Mackenzie, D. L. (2005). A quantitative review of structured, goal-oriented, cognitive-behavioral programs for offenders. *Criminal Justice and Behavior, 32*(2), 172–204.

Weinbach, R. W. (2003). *The social worker as manager* (4th ed.). Boston: Allyn & Bacon.

Yarchek, C. M., Gavazzi, S. M., & Dascoli, K. (2003). Internet training for juvenile justice professionals. *Federal Probation, 67*(3), 54–60.

Chapter 24

Doing Justice for Mental Illness and Society: Federal Probation and Pretrial Services Officers as Mental Health Specialists

Risdon N. Slate, Erik Roskes, Richard Feldman, and Migdalia Baerga

At the beginning of this century, approximately 6.6 million people were on probation, in jail or prison, or on parole in the United States. Of this population, over two million were incarcerated in the nation's jails and prisons (Bureau of Justice Statistics, 2003A). In fact, the number of those incarcerated in the United States has quadrupled since 1980 (Bureau of Justice Statistics, 2003B).

It is estimated that roughly 5 percent of Americans in society have a serious mental illness, and Americans with mental illnesses are significantly overrepresented in the criminal justice system (Council of State Governments et al., 2002). Mental health problems are notably common among correctional populations, including community corrections populations. However, it is difficult to obtain meaningful data on the prevalence of mental illness among correctional populations (Pinta, 2000; Clear et al., 1993). A variety of efforts have been made to attempt to understand the rates of mental illness among different correctional populations, the role of mental illness in propelling individuals into the correctional system, and the importance of collaboration between mental health and correctional professionals in managing persons with mental illness.

An estimated 16 percent of inmates in jails and prisons, or 284,000 individuals, reported suffering from mental health problems or having been admitted to a hospital for mental health reasons (Ditton,

1999). This finding, while subject to criticism because it relied primarily on the self-report of the correctional populations surveyed, fairly closely reflected previous research findings (for instance, see Steadman et al., 1987; Teplin, 1990; Teplin et al., 1996; Pinta, 1999). Statistics such as these fuel the concern, noted by Petersilia (1999), that the majority of these persons with mental illness who are currently incarcerated will return to the community under some type of supervised release.

The prevalence of mental illness among the community corrections population is less well studied. However, about 16 percent of probationers, or approximately 548,000 individuals, are estimated to have mental health needs (Ditton, 1999). According to Lurigio (2001), no studies have measured the number of parolees with serious mental illnesses in the United States, but he estimates that 5 to 10 percent of those on parole have serious mental illnesses. This discrepancy between the percentage of persons with mental illness who are incarcerated or on probation (about 16 percent) versus those on parole (5–10%) may stem in part directly from those individuals' mental illness. Many mentally ill people in correctional environments may not receive adequate or optimal treatment and may therefore be unable to comply with institutional rules and regulations. The symptoms they display may thus prolong their incarceration and reduce the likelihood of their receiving parole.

Reprinted with permission from *Federal Probation*, December, 2003.

Despite these large numbers, the criminal justice system appears ill equipped to meet the special needs of persons with mental illness who are incarcerated or on custodial release in the community. For example, only 15 percent of probation departments nationally acknowledge operating a special program for mentally ill probationers (Lurigio, 2000). Likewise, Lurigio (2001) indicates that most parole agents lack the exposure and foundation to handle those who are mentally ill under their supervision. A national survey reflects that fewer than 25 percent of parole administrators report operating specialized programs for mentally ill clients; Camp and Camp (1997) found no parole agencies that reported providing any specialized mental health services for offenders with mental illness.

CRIMINALIZING MENTAL ILLNESS

A number of rationales have been offered to explain the criminalization of the mentally ill. Deinstitutionalization – the release of persons with mental illness from state hospitals under the erroneous assumption that adequate treatment programs would be put in place in the community to serve this population – is one common explanation for the criminalization of the mentally ill (Kalinich, Embert, & Senese, 1991; Winfree & Wooldredge, 1991). Primarily because of a lack of funding, community treatment programs generally never emerged (Jerrell & Komisaruk, 1991; Sargeant, 1992; Torrey, 1995). The deinstitutionalization movement has shifted more than 400,000 people, from 500,000 persons in 1960 being housed in state hospitals to fewer than 60,000 patients being housed in such public hospitals today (Sharfstein, 2000). Note, however, that a recent study of inmates with mental illness found that only about half of them had ever been in a psychiatric hospital at all (Fisher et al. 2002). The authors compared this to findings from the National Comorbidity Survey (which can be accessed at http://www.icpsr.umich.edu:8080/SAMHDA-STUDY/06693.xml) that about 18 percent of a similar control group had been hospitalized. Thus, those in jail were three times as likely to have been hospitalized. The implication of this study is that access to inpatient care may not be the issue at all. However, it is possible that *at the time of the incident leading to arrest*, lack of access to inpatient care may result in an individual being detained in the correctional setting. Hogan (2000), the Director of Mental Health for Ohio and the chair of President Bush's New Freedom Commission on Mental Health, cautions that to suggest that deinstitutionalization alone is responsible for the criminalization of the mentally ill is an oversimplification and may mistakenly imply that somehow reinstitutionalization is the proper solution.

Some suggest that managed-care companies sometimes invoke penalties against primary care providers and frontline mental health service providers who make too many referrals to psychiatrists (Miller, 1997), and Stone (1997) maintains that fewer persons with mental illness would wind up in jail if they had adequate insurance coverage. Similarly, "medication reimbursement caps, capitation, restricted formularies, preferred pharmacy networks, co-payment plans, 'economic credentialing,' and the use of nonmedical professionals to screen mentally disordered patients" (Miller, 1997: 1207–1208) have been identified as impediments to adequate treatment for persons with mental illness. In an era of managed care, some psychiatrists face conflicting responsibilities to the patient and to the payer, and patient care may suffer as a result (Miller, 1997).

Three strikes laws have also likely contributed to institutionalizing the mentally ill within the criminal justice system as well, in part because those with mental illness may, when the illness is not effectively treated, be less able to follow the rule of law. They may thus be more vulnerable to long-term incarceration for minor crimes than are those without mental illness. Other explanations for the criminalization of the mentally ill are offered by Goldkamp and Irons-Guynn (2000) and include the growing homeless population, co-occurring disorders (whereby mental illness often coexists with a substance abuse problem), law enforcement crackdowns as part of the war on drugs, and police focus on quality of life and ordinance violations.

Some law enforcement officers refer to locking up persons with mental illness as mercy bookings, believing that at least shelter, food, and safety will be provided for those in need while detained (Sargeant, 1992). Unfortunately, the treatment for their illness encountered in jails is often nonexistent or woefully inadequate (Butterfield, 1998; Kerle, 1998). According to Walsh and Bricourt (1997), over 20 percent of jails offer no formal access to treatment for the mentally ill, and Kerle (1998), in a study of more than 3,000 jails nationwide, found only 35 with mental health treatment models worth replicating. As for treatment of the mentally ill, Ditton (1999) in a self-report survey found approximately 60 percent of state and federal prison inmates and 41 percent of jail inmates/detainees indicating that they had received some sort of mental health service.

Whatever the reasons, the criminal justice system has become the social service system of last resort. "With 3,500 and 2,800 mentally ill inmates respectively, the Los Angeles County Jail and New York Rikers Island Jail are currently the two largest psychiatric inpatient treatment facilities in the country" (Sharfstein, 2001:3).

PROBATION OFFICERS AS RESOURCE BROKERS

Even an inmate fortunate enough to receive some semblance of mental health treatment while incarcerated will find that discharge planning, particularly from jails, is often nonexistent (Steadman & Veysey, 1997). This deficiency can result in persons with mental illness being released into the community with no medication, follow-up appointments or any assurance of contact with the mental health treatment community (Osher, Steadman, & Barr, 2003). Mental health courts have been one mechanism for enlisting probation officers to assist in establishing this vital link of mental health treatment upon release from custody into the community (Slate, 2003). Griffin et al. (2002) have found that such courts rely upon probation officers, community treatment providers or mental health court staff, or on teams made up of both probation and mental health treatment personnel, for monitoring and assisting in linkage to community services. Probation officers have played integral roles in status hearings before the court (Lurigio & Swartz, 2000; Petrila, Poythress, McGaha, & Boothroyd, 2001) and can serve as resource brokers or boundary spanners in navigating and linking clients to mental health treatment, housing, benefits, and vocational/employment opportunities (McCampbell, 2001; Steadman et al., 2001). Probation officers also play a pivotal role in providing the court with a comprehensive history of the client's background when a presentence or prerelease investigation is ordered.

Unfortunately, unless symptoms of mental illness are overtly obvious at the time of offense or manifest themselves at sentencing, such specialized attention from the criminal justice system rarely is available to the person with mental illness who encounters the criminal justice system. As noted by Veysey (1994), probation officers typically do not have the background and experience to deal with persons with mental illness effectively. However, specialized programs are emerging, with an influx of more resources and better training for probation officers. With these fiscal, training, and personnel resources, mental health treatment can be mandated as a condition of release (Lurigio & Swartz, 2000; Roskes & Feldman, 1999; Roskes & Feldman, 2000). For example, specialized programs have emerged for probationers with mental illness in the Cook County Adult Probation Office in Chicago (see Lurigio & Swartz, 2000), for parolees under the supervision of five outpatient clinics and a conditional release project within the California Department of Corrections (Lurigio, 2001) and for those under probation, parole, supervised release, or conditional release supervision with the U.S. Probation Office in Baltimore (Lurigio, 2001; Roskes & Feldman, 1999, 2000). Broward County, Florida, which established the nation's first mental health court for misdemeanants (Slate, 2000), has now implemented 32 hours of specialized training for probation officers who supervise in the community felons who are mentally ill (E. Miller, personal communication, May 12, 2003).

Assertive community treatment (ACT) is also a team approach to care that can provide coordinated treatment and supervision options to individuals with mental illness who encounter the criminal justice system. ACT models include psychiatrists, substance abuse specialists, housing procurement specialists, rehabilitation and vocational counselors, clinicians, nurses, and peer counselors who offer necessary services and assist in monitoring the client in jail if necessary (Lurigio & Swartz, 2000; Allness & Knoedler, 1999; Kondo, 2000; Edgar, 2001). These practitioners follow the client into the community to assist in psychosocial rehabilitation and facilitate community living, with the goal of eliminating or reducing institutionalizations (Allness & Knoedler, 1999). Although recipients of ACT services typically receive such services voluntarily, probation officers have at times ended up as members of ACT teams because of court-ordered conditional releases (Sheppard, Freitas, & Hurley, 2002; Herbert, Conklin, & Keaton, 2002).

RECIDIVISM

Probation officers sometimes feel torn between the conflicting roles of law enforcement agent and social worker, and this can be particularly true when called upon to supervise persons with mental illness in the community. There is some research focusing on the criminal recidivism of the mentally ill offender. Participation in mental health treatment for those under conditional release in the community has been found to be correlated with a lower risk of incarceration for technical violations; however, those who were revoked for a technical violation have been found to be six times more likely to have been the recipients of intensive supervision (Solomon et al., 2002). While these researchers noted that the jail system being studied had a comprehensive mental health treatment system in place that made it easier to reincarcerate violators, they indicated that results appear mixed on whether intensive case management services lessen the risk of imprisonment. The researchers concluded that: "providing services that emphasize monitoring tends to increase the risk of incarceration for technical violations of criminal justice sanctions. However, any participation in treatment and motivation to participate in treatment appears to reduce the risk of incarceration" (2002:50).

A recent study (Harris & Koepsell, 1998) found that a group of mentally ill offenders had an equivalent recidivism rate when compared to a matched control group of nonmentally ill offenders. However, the same group has reported that the introduction of pre- and postrelease interagency coordination significantly reduced the recidivism risk in a pilot group (Harris et al., 1998). Another study recently reported that the introduction of case management services led to a significant decrease in the recidivism rate of mentally ill offenders (Ventura et al., 1998), and previous research has demonstrated that judicially monitored treatment resulted in good outcomes during a one-year follow-up phase (Lamb et al., 1996). Taken together, this work indicates that the mentally ill of-

fender has a high likelihood of having ongoing contact with the criminal justice and correctional systems, and there are clinical interventions that may be able to positively affect the recidivism rate.

PROBATION OFFICERS AS PART OF THE DISCHARGE PLANNING PROCESS

Of all services provided to inmates, discharge planning for persons with mental illness being released from jails has been found to be least likely to be offered (Steadman & Veysey, 1997). Recently, *Brad H. v. City of New York* (1999), which was the first class action suit ever initiated for mentally ill jail or prison inmates, resulted in the New York City jail system being ordered to arrange discharge planning services for mentally ill inmates being released into the community (Barr, 2003, complaint is available at www.urbanjustice.org/litigation/PDFs/Brad HComplaint.pdf; settlement document is available at www.urbanjustice.org/litigation/PDFs/BradSettlementMHP.pdf). Osher, Steadman, and Barr (2003) maintain that probation officers can be cross-trained with mental health professionals and work hand-in-hand with clinicians in supervising those with mental illness released into the community, relying on graduated sanctions that rise to include hospitalization instead of incarceration.

THERAPEUTIC JURISPRUDENCE

Therapeutic jurisprudence has been described as an assessment of how "substantive rules, legal procedures and the roles of lawyers and judges produce therapeutic or antitherapeutic consequences" (Wexler & Winick, 1991: 981). It is argued that lawyers engaged in the adversarial process of law have a tendency to ignore the long-range consequences of their decisions for both their clients and society (Finkleman & Grisso, 1994; Miller, 1997).

The traditional criminal justice system tends to look backward finding fault and assessing blame, carrying out a punishment upon someone for perpetrating a criminal act, without much, if any, consideration of the consequences of the imposition of the penalty on the perpetrator or society. . . . Decisions within the therapeutic jurisprudence framework are made with consideration of future ramifications for individuals, relationships and society long after a person's contact with the criminal justice system has ceased (Slate, 2003:15).

Probation officers are strategically located within the criminal justice system to assist with dispensing therapeutic jurisprudence, and their actions can benefit not only those under their supervision but society as well. Armed with carefully crafted conditional and supervised release plans, appropriate monitoring, adequate resources, and proper training, probation officers can function as therapeutic jurisprudence change agents, helping people change their lives for the better. The remainder of this chapter will focus on how the Federal Probation and Pretrial Services System is grappling with effectively supervising persons with mental illness on their caseloads.

FEDERAL PROBATION AND PRETRIAL SERVICES DATA

As of September 30, 2002, a total of 34,880 cases were receiving pretrial supervision from United States Pretrial Services, and a total of 108,792 cases were under the supervision of the United States Probation office (Administrative Office of the U.S. Courts [data on file], 2003, February 25). These latter cases include individuals on probation, on parole, and on supervised or conditional release.

Of the cases on supervision, 14 percent (n=4,720) of those on pretrial release and 18 percent (n=19,731) of those on probation (this category refers to those on parole and supervised or conditional release as well) had a special condition for mental health treatment (Administrative Office of the U.S. Courts, 2003, February 25). Of these cases, 31 percent (n=1,454) of those on pretrial release and 47 percent (n=9,340) of those on probation supervision received contracted services. Congress appropriates funds for the federal judiciary annually. The funding pays for employee salaries as well as a myriad of programs for defendants and offenders [including mental health treatment] (Administrative Office of the U.S. Courts, *Court and Community,* January 2003). Certainly, those not receiving contracted services may be rendered assistance from Medicaid, Medicare, the Veterans Administration, private insurance carriers, and/or via free or sliding fee community-based

programs. The total mental health expenditures for contracted services for fiscal year 2002, according to the Administrative Office of the U.S. Courts (2003, February 25), was $10,731,324 or an average of $994 per contracted case.

Data is not available for the clinical or legal breakdown of individuals under the jurisdiction of U.S. Probation or Pretrial Services on a national basis. Roskes and Feldman (1999) published a pilot study examining some of this information. They found that their shared cases primarily had psychotic illnesses: 44 percent (7 of 16) were diagnosed with schizophrenia and 50 percent (8 of 16) with severe mood disorders, including major depression and bipolar disorder. In addition, 94 percent (15/16) of the cases had co-occurring substance abuse or dependence. Finally, 44 percent (7/16) were also diagnosed with a personality disorder, six (38 percent) of whom met criteria for antisocial personality disorder. Each of these co-morbidities is relevant for both treatment and supervision agencies, as they make both treatment and supervision much more complicated and make collaboration all the more relevant.

Roskes and Feldman (1999) also examined the crimes that had been committed by their cases. Bank robbery was the most common index offense, occurring in 44 percent (7/16) of the cases. One (6 percent) of the index offenses was a serious personal crime (kidnapping, rape, assault with intent to murder). One of the individuals convicted of bank robbery subsequently killed a correctional officer while incarcerated. Another 44 percent of the index offenses were a variety of property crimes.

MENTAL HEALTH SPECIALISTS

Some officers within the federal probation and pretrial services system have been classified as mental health specialists (Administrative Office of the U.S. Courts, 2003, January). As with probation officers who serve as substance abuse specialists (Torres & Latta, 2000), agency philosophy can have a significant impact on the style of supervision rendered by mental health specialists and whether or not someone is designated as a mental health specialist in a particular district.

Typically these mental health specialists have a solid foundation in mental health education, and in a number of instances they are licensed/certified clinical social workers, counselors, or psychologists (Administrative Office of the U.S. Courts, 2003, January). While there is no standardized national mental health training program currently in effect, officers are routinely exposed to and participate in local, regional, or national specialized mental health and/or substance abuse treatment conferences (such as regional or circuit trainings, annual district trainings, and specialized training sponsored by the Federal Judicial Center (FJC) and/or the Administrative Office of the U.S. Courts via the Federal Judicial Television Network [FJTN]). Included among the topics covered during such training sessions are discussions of mental health, substance abuse, domestic violence, dual disorders and assessment, and treatment and supervision of sex offenders. For instance, in May of 1999, the Administrative Office of the U.S. Courts hosted a national mental health and substance abuse conference, at which the former U.S. Surgeon General, David Satcher, served as the keynote speaker. Because of specialized training opportunities such as this one, mental health specialists or line officers working with mental health cases are adept at recognizing the signs and symptoms of mental illness and can coordinate required services in the community, often using contractual agreements (Administrative Office of the U.S. Courts, 2003, January). Often, the U.S. District Court or the U.S. Parole Commission orders a defendant and/or offender to participate in a mental health evaluation and/or treatment. In these cases, mental health specialists often serve as contractual brokers to ensure such services as counseling (individual, group, or family), psychological/psychiatric testing and assessment, medication, transit to and from mental health treatment, and even money for food and clothing in emergencies (Administrative Office of the U.S. Courts, 2003, January). These officers also play an integral role by being keenly aware of issues related to noncompliance with court-ordered conditions of release and are equipped to monitor problems that require a proactive response.

DISCUSSION

The finding that 14 percent of individuals on pretrial release and 18 percent of offenders on probation,

parole, supervised or conditional release in the federal system have mental health conditions is remarkably consistent with existing research indicating prevalence rates of mental illness in correctional populations. This provides some reassurance that the evaluators recommending such conditions and the judges imposing these conditions are (in a statistical sense, at least) imposing the most appropriate special conditions to foster strategies not only aimed at stabilizing mental health symptoms that may present a danger to a defendant/offender, the officer, and/or other third parties, but also to maximize the individual's potential for living and functioning effectively in the community. At the most basic level, therefore, the needs of the population are being met. Clearly, more research is needed in this important area. Nonetheless, the state of our science suggests that these interventions can be helpful, and are common sense as well.

In our experience, it is clear that several attitudes and skills are required for the most effective community-based treatment of the offender with mental illness. First and foremost, all should recognize that this collaboration can increase the likelihood of a successful community reintegration for an offender with mental illness. Many clinicians and supervising personnel are unaware of the body of research demonstrating that clinical interventions can help mentally ill offenders successfully re-enter the community.

Next, all involved must be willing to view each other as important team members in the management of these individuals. This willingness does not necessarily come easily, and in many instances we have experienced that one party is for some reason unable to develop a working relationship with another party in the management team. It is all too easy to find mental health providers who are unwilling to work with individuals who have legal entanglements; conversely, many probation agents and officers, particularly those with large caseloads, find themselves unable to deal with the complexities of the person with mental illness and prefer not to maintain them on their caseloads. Thus, to effectively manage mental health cases, particularly chronic and/or severely mentally ill individuals, a strong case can be established to ensure that officers with specialized mental health duties be allowed to carry significantly smaller caseloads than the average officer. Officers working with mental health cases (particularly severe or chronic mentally ill individuals) more often than not make intensive field (community) contacts, and maintain active collateral contacts with treatment providers, local law enforcement officials, and family/community support systems. Additionally, they are responsible for ongoing assessment of third-party risk issues, treatment referrals and/or proactively fostering strategies to address uncooperative behaviors (such as noncompliance with court-ordered conditions).

These relationships work best if a team approach is developed that makes use of each team member's strengths and skills. Ideally, these should complement one another, to minimize the likelihood of someone falling through cracks in the safety net. Thus, in establishing a collaborative partnership, we envision the roles of the probation officer (primarily public safety in orientation) and of the clinical providers (primarily concerned with psychiatric well-being of the individual client) as part of a "whole picture" rather than as competing with each other.

A final crucial factor is the ability to speak and understand each other's language (Roskes & Feldman, 1999). The jargons of the criminal justice and mental health systems are sophisticated codes that allow practitioners to easily communicate but often keep nonpractitioners in the dark. Our experience together has convinced us that the ability to communicate and respect each other's roles is a key to the successful treatment of the defendant and/or offender with mental illness.

Examples of collaborative models offering comprehensive services to mentally ill offenders in the community can be found in Milwaukee, Wisconsin, and Multnomah County, Oregon (see Roskes et al., 1999). However, there are numerous barriers to the development of such collaborative models. Managers of probation offices and other supervising agencies do not always understand the prevalence of behavioral disorders and the added layers of complexity presented by these cases; therefore, the need for specialized services for such individuals is not always clear to the managers of these agencies. Given the minimal understanding that many agencies have about the role of mental illness in the genesis of criminal behaviors, supervising agents are unable to effectively manage these cases. For instance, the ability of an individual with mental illness to adhere to even standard conditions of supervision may be far inferior to that of the average case. Given

such lack of understanding, it is not surprising that managers of probation offices seldom encourage (or pay for) the development of specialized expertise in the area of mental illness. Instead, they may conclude that people with mental illness are doomed to a high level of recidivism and therefore fail to invest the required time and energy in maintaining such cases in the community.

Mental health providers also have a reluctance to work with patients who are under the jurisdiction of the criminal justice system. Most providers of care have a very limited understanding of the role of the supervising agency in the management of a case in the community. The supervisory agent's preference for maintaining cases safely in the community is poorly understood by the average mental health professional. In addition, mental health providers are (rightly or wrongly) afraid of clients who are involved in the legal system. At times, the referred client may not meet the so-called "target population requirements" or "medical necessity criteria" of the Medicaid or other payment system. Thus, providers have concerns about who is responsible for payment for services. While the federal probation system can pay for at least some services, this is not generally the case for state supervising agencies. Finally, providers may be concerned with liability issues surrounding the care of this population. Thus, rather than learning how fruitful it can be to work in a collaborative fashion with supervising agencies, many mental health providers simply refuse to accept these cases.

CONCLUSION

It has been the experience of the authors that collaborations such as these can work and can greatly benefit the clients involved in the collaboration, enhancing their community adjustment in a way that less integrated service cannot. Several such cases are described in the literature (see Roskes et al., 1999), and we have seen a number of other such cases. Such collaborations take work to maintain, as with all relationships. It is not clear that we are able to justify such work in a "bottom-line"-oriented fashion. Rather, we focus on the mission of the probation officer to help offenders transition back into their communities as participating citizens. For the offender with mental illness, competent and collaborative mental health care is a part of that mission. What better way for probation and pretrial services officers to aid in this process than by assisting persons with mental illness to become responsible for their actions to the ultimate benefit of all?

REFERENCES

Administrative Office of U.S. Courts. (2003, February 25). Office of Probation and Pretrial Services. Washington, D.C.

Administrative Office of the U.S. Courts. (2003, January). *Mental health treatment.* Court & Community. Office of Probation and Pretrial Services. Washington, D.C.

Allness, D. J., & Knoedler, W. H. (1999). *The PACT Model of Community-based treatment for persons with severe and persistent mental illnesses: A manual for PACT start-up.* Arlington, VA: National Alliance for the Mentally Ill.

Barr, H. (2003). Transinstitutionalization in the courts: Brad H. v. City of New York and the fight for discharge planning for people with psychiatric disabilities leaving Rikers Island. *Crime & Delinquency, 49*(1), 97–123.

Brad H. v. City of New York. (1999). Supreme Court of the State of New York, County of New York, Index No. 117882/99), (IAS Part 23). Retrieved from http://www.urbanjustice.org.

Bureau of Justice Statistics. (2003A). *Corrections Statistics.* Washington, D.C.: U.S. Department of Justice, Bureau of Justice Statistics. Retrieved May 22, 2003, from the World Wide Web: http://www.ojp.usdoj.gov/bjs/correct.htm.

Bureau of Justice Statistics. (2003B). *Number of sentenced inmates incarcerated under state and federal jurisdiction per 100,000, 1980–2001. Correctional populations in the United States, 1997 and Prisoners 2001.* Washington, D.C.: U.S. Department of Justice, Bureau of Justice Statistics. Retrieved May 22, 2003, from the World Wide Web: http://www.ojp.usdoj.gov/bjs/glance/incrt.htm.

Butterfield, F. (1998, March 5). Prisons replace hospitals for the nation's mentally ill. *The New York Times,* pp. IA, 18A.

Camp, C., &Camp, G. (1997). *The corrections yearbook.* South Salem, NY: Criminal Justice Institute.

Clear, T. R., Byrne, J. M., & Dvoskin, J. A. (1993). The transition from being an inmate: Discharge planning, parole, and community based services for mentally ill offenders. In H.J. Steadman & J. J. Cocozza (Eds.), *Mental illness in America's prisons* (pp. 131–158). Seattle, WA: The National Coalition for the Mentally Ill in the Criminal Justice System.

Council of State Governments, Police Executive Research Forum, Pretrial Services Resource Center, Association of State Correctional Administrators, Bazelon Center for Mental Health Law, and the Center for Behavioral Health, Justice, and Public Policy. (2002). *Criminal Justice/Mental Health Consensus Project.* New York: Council of State Governments.

Ditton, P. M. (1999). *Mental health and treatment of inmates and probationers.* Washington, D.C.: U.S. Department of Justice, Bureau of Justice Statistics.

Edgar, E. (2001 Fall). *Assertive community treatment provides jail diversion.* NAMI Advocate, 28.

Finkelman, D., & Grisso, T. (1994). Therapeutic jurisprudence: From idea to application. *New England Journal on Criminal and Civil Confinement, 20,* 243–257.

Fisher, W. H., Packer, I. K., Banks, S. M., Smith, D.,Simon, L. J., & Roy-Bujnowski, K. (2002) Self-Reported lifetime psychiatric hospitalization histories of jail detainees with mental disorders: Comparison with a non-incarcerated national sample. *Journal of Behavioral Health Services and Research, 29,* 458–465.

Goldkamp, J. S., & Irons-Guynn, C. (2000). *Emerging judicial strategies for the mentally ill in the criminal caseload: Mental health courts in Fort Lauderdale, Seattle, San Bernardino, and Anchorage.* Washington, D.C.: U.S. Department of Justice, Office of Justice Programs, Bureau of Justice Assistance.

Griffin, P. A., Steadman, H. J., & Petrila, J. (2002). The use of criminal charges and sanctions in mental health courts. *Psychiatric Services, 53,* 1285–1289.

Harris V., & Koepsell, T. D. (1998). Rearrest among mentally ill offenders. *Journal of the American Academy of Psychiatry and the Law, 26*(3), 393–402.

Harris V., Trupin, E., & Wood, P. (1998, October 24). *Mentally ill offenders and community transitions.* Paper presented at the 29th Annual Meeting of the American Academy of Psychiatry and the Law, New Orleans.

Herbert, A., Conklin, R., & Keaton, S. (2002, October 30). *Breaking the cycle of recidivism through effective case management.* Paper presented at the National GAINS Center Conference, San Francisco.

Hogan, M. F. (2000, September, 21). Testimony before the subcommittee on Crime of the Committee on the Judiciary, U.S. House of Representatives. Retrieved May 18, 2002 from the World Wide Web: http://www.house.gov/judiciary/hoga0921.htm.

Jerrell, J. M., & Komisaruk, R. (1991). Public policy issues in the delivery of mental health services in a jail setting. In J. A. Thompson & G. L. Mays, (Eds.), *American jails: Public policy issues* (pp. 100–115). Chicago: Nelson-Hall.

Kalinich, D., Embert, P., & Senese, J. (1991). Mental health services for jail inmates: Imprecise standards, traditional philosophies, and the need for change. In J. A. Thompson & G. L. Mays (Eds.), *American jails: Public policy issues* (pp. 79–99). Chicago: Nelson-Hall.

Kerle, K. E. (1998). *American jails: Looking to the future,* Boston: Butterworth-Heinemann.

Kondo, L. L. (2000). Therapeutic jurisprudence: Issues, analysis and applications: Advocacy of the establishment of mental health specialty courts in the provision of therapeutic justice for mentally ill offenders. *Seattle University Law Review, 24,* 373–464.

Lamb, H. R., Weinberger, L. E., & Reston-Parham, C. (1996). Court intervention to address the mental health needs of mentally ill offenders. *Psychiatric Services, 47*(3), 275–281.

Lurigio, A. J. (2001). Effective services for parolees with mental illnesses. *Crime & Delinquency, 47*(3), 446–461.

Lurigio, A. J., & Swartz, J. A. (2000). Changing the contours of the criminal justice system to meet the needs of persons with serious mental illness. In J. Horney (Ed.), *Policies, processes, and decisions of the criminal justice system* (pp. 45–108). Washington D.C.: U.S. Department of Justice, National Institute of Justice.

McCampbell, S. W. (2001). Mental health courts: What sheriffs need to know. *Sheriff, 53*(2), 40–43.

Miller, E. (2003, May 12). Advocacy Advisory meeting. Orlando, Florida.

Miller, R. D. (1997). Symposium on coercion: An interdisciplinary examination of coercion, exploitation, and the law: III. Coerced confinement and treatment: The continuum of coercion: Constitutional and clinical considerations in the treatment of mentally disordered persons. *Denver University Law Review, 74,* 1169–1214.

Osher, F., Steadman, H. J., & Barr, H. (2003). A best practice approach to community reentry from jails for inmates with co-occurring disorders: The APIC mode. *Crime & Delinquency, 49*(1), 79–96.

Petersilia, J. M. (1999). Parole and prisoner reentry in the United States. In M. Tonry & J. M. Petersilia (Eds.), *Prisons* (pp. 479–529). Chicago: University of Chicago Press.

Petrila, J., Poythress, N. G., McGaha, A., & Boothroyd, R. A. (2001). Preliminary observations from an evaluation of the Broward County mental health court. *Court Review, 37,* 14–22.

Pinta, E. R. (1999). The prevalence of serious mental disorders among U.S. prisoners. *Correctional Mental Health Report, 1,* 34, 44–47.

Pinta, E. R. (2000). Prison mental disorder rates – What do they mean? *Correctional Mental Health Report* (1) 81, 91–92.

Roskes, E., Feldman, R., Arrington, S., & Leisher, M. (1999). A model program for the treatment of mentally ill offenders in the community. *Community Mental Health Journal, 35,* 461–472.

Roskes, E., & Feldman, R. (1999). A collaborative community-based treatment program for offenders with mental illness. *Psychiatric Services, 50,* 1614–1619.

Roskes, E., & Feldman, R. (2000). Treater or monitor? Collaboration between mental health providers and probation officers. *Correctional Mental Health Report, 1,* 69–70.

Sargeant, G. (1992, December). Back to bedlam: Mentally ill often jailed without charges. *Trial,* pp. 96–98.

Sharfstein, S. S. (2001). The case for caring coercion. *Catalyst, 3*(4), 1–2.

Sharfstein, S. S. (2000, September, 21). *Testimony before the Subcommittee on Crime of the Committee on the Judiciary, U.S. House of Representatives.* Retrieved May 17, 2003 from the World Wide Web: http://www.house.gov/dudiciary/shar0921.htm.

Sheppard, R., Freitas, F., & Hurley, K. (2002, October 28). *Assertive community treatment and the mentally ill offender.* Paper presented at the National GAINS Center Conference, San Francisco.

Slate, R. N. (2003). From the jailhouse to Capitol Hill: Impacting mental health court legislation and defining what constitutes a mental health court. *Crime & Delinquency, 49*(1), 6–29.

Slate, R. N. (2000). Courts for mentally ill offenders: Necessity or abdication of responsibility. In G.L. Mays & P.R. Gregware (Eds.), *Courts and Justice* (2nd ed., pp. 432–450). Prospect Heights, IL: Waveland Press.

Solomon, P., Draine, J., & Marcus, S. C. (2002). Predicting incarceration of clients of a psychiatric probation and parole service. *Psychiatric Services, 53*(1), 50–56.

Steadman, H. J., Davidson, S., & Brown, C. (2001). Mental health courts: Their promise and unanswered questions. *Psychiatric Services, 52*(4), 457–458.

Steadman, H. J., Faasiak, S., Dvoskin, J., & Holohean, E. J. (1987). A survey of mental disability among state prison inmates. *Hospital and Community Psychiatry, 38,* 1086–1090.

Steadman, H. J., & Veysey, B. (1997, January). *Providing services for jail inmates with mental disorders.* (Research in brief.) Washington, D.C.: National Institute of Justice.

Stone, T. H. (1997). Therapeutic implications of incarceration for persons with severe mental disorders: Searching for rational health policy. *American Journal of Criminal Law, 24,* 283–358.

Teplin, L. A. (1990). The prevalence of severe mental disorder among male urban jail detainees: Comparison with the Epidemiologic Catchment Area Study. *American Journal of Public Health, 80,* 663–669.

Teplin, L. A., Abram, K. M., & McClelland, G. M. (1996). Prevalence of psychiatric disorders among incarcerated women. *Archives of General Psychiatry, 53,* 505–512.

Torres, S., & Latta, R. M. (2000). Selecting the substance abuse specialist. *Federal Probation, 64*(1), 46–50.

Torrey, E. F. (1995). Jails and prisons – America's new mental hospitals. *American Journal of Public Health, 85*(12), 1611–1613.

Ventura, L. A., Cassel, C. A., Jacoby, J. E., & Huang, B. (1998). Case management and recidivism of mentally ill persons released from jail. *Psychiatric Services, 49*(10), 1330–1337.

Veysey, B. (1994). Challenges for the future. In topics in community corrections (pp. 3–10). Longmont, CO: U.S. Department of Justice, National Institute of Corrections.

Walsh, J., & Bricourt, J. (1997, July-August). Services for persons with mental illness in jail: Implications for family involvement. *Families in Society: The Journal of Contemporary Human Services*, pp. 420–428.

Wexler, D. B., & Winick, B. J. (1991). Therapeutic jurisprudence as a new approach to mental health law policy analysis and research. *University of Miami Law Review, 45*, 979–1004.

Winfree, L. T., & Wooldredge, J. D. (1991). Exploring suicides and deaths by natural causes in America's large jails: A panel study of institutional change, 1978 and 1983. In J.A. Thompson & G.L. Mays (Eds.), *American jails: Public policy issues* (pp. 63–78). Chicago: Nelson-Hall.

Chapter 25

Motivational Interviewing for Probation Staff: Increasing the Readiness to Change[1]

Michael D. Clark

Motivational Interviewing makes a lot of sense to me – I mean, it seems to be a lot like banking. We've got to make a deposit before we can expect to make a withdrawal. (Training participant, 2005)

This chapter focuses on increasing motivation with "involuntary clients," also known as mandated offenders placed under probation supervision by court orders. Motivational Interviewing (Miller & Rollnick, 1991) is an approach that was first developed and applied in the field of addictions but has broadened and become a favored approach for use with numerous populations across a variety of settings (Burke, Arkowitz, & Dunn, 2002). In our own field of criminal justice, evidence-based practice as outlined by criminologists and social workers has recommended that justice staff be responsive to motivational issues with offenders (Andrews & Bonta, 2003; Roberts & Yeager, 2004). This chapter attempts to lend substance to that recommendation with suggestions for direct practice application.

Probation staff clamor for "how to's" and seek knowledge as they work hard to manage high volume caseloads. But patience is necessary as Motivational Interviewing (MI) is not just a collection of techniques to apply *on* an offender. Raising motivation levels and increasing an offender's readiness to change requires a certain "climate," – a helpful attitude and a supportive approach that one would take *with* an offender. This climate becomes grist for developing a helping relationship – and it is imperative that this relationship occur between agent and probationer if enduring change is to occur. This chapter will examine this type of climate across the criminal justice field (the macro-perspective), within probation departments (the mezzo-perspective) and into the individual pairing of any officer and offender (the micro-perspective).

ACROSS THE CRIMINAL JUSTICE FIELD (MACRO): WHAT BUSINESS ARE WE IN?

Duncan, Miller, and Sparks (2004), promoting outcome-informed efforts, recall a landmark article by Theodore Levitt, a Harvard business professor. Levitt (1975) recounted the rise of the railroad industry throughout much of the 1800s and into the next century. The railroad industry vaulted to tremendous success as it laid track from city to city, crisscrossing and connecting our continent. Millions of dollars were pocketed by those laying the track and building this nation's rail infrastructure. The pace of life quickened and demand rose for speedy travel.

However, as the first baby-boomers began to leave their nests in the1960s, the railroads were in trouble – actually in serious decline. Why? Railroad executives would answer that it was due to the need for speedier transportation and faster communication that was being filled in other ways (i.e., cars, trucking industry, telecommunications, etc.). That reasoning made no sense to Levitt. To this business professor, it begged a question. Duncan, Miller, and Sparks (2002: 80) note the irony:

[1]. Reprinted with the permission of the publisher from *Federal Probation*, 2005, 69(2).

The railroad industry, Levitt (1975) argued, was not in trouble 'because the need was being filled by others . . . but because it was *not* filled by the railroads themselves' (p. 19). Why did the industry not diversify when it had the chance? Because, as it turns out, railroad executives had come to believe they were in the *train* rather than the *transportation* business.

Due to this limiting conception, trucking and air-freight industries prospered while locomotive engines fell into disrepair, parked on rusted tracks in the back of neglected railroad yards. The railroad industry had come to believe they were in the railroad business instead of the transportation business.

It would seem that probation, as a criminal justice entity, is much like the railroad industry of our past century – for it has come to believe that it is in the *probation business* rather than the *behavior change business*. Our field seems primarily concerned with the process of probation – insuring adequate supervision, compliance to probation orders, and the completion of mounds of attendant paperwork. Process takes center stage rather than a principal focus on strategies and techniques that will encourage positive behavior change (outcomes).

The problem lies in the mindset that pervades the probation and parole field that allows outcomes to take a back seat to process. Consider a recent lament by a deputy director who manages a fairly large community corrections division. Engaged in a discussion regarding the "business of probation" during a recent training session, he offered his state's "probation officer of the year award" as an example. This annual contest awards much more than a certificate or a new wristwatch – the prize is a week-long vacation in the Caribbean! As can be imagined, staff keep a constant eye on their efforts and work hard to win the prize. However, this deputy director noted the field is so process-oriented that whatever agent might win this trip would do so because of timely paperwork completion, more face-to-face meetings than required, comprehensive report writing, and punctual court appearances. Yet if outcomes were considered, this same officer, enjoying the sun and waves from a relaxing beach-side cabaña, might be embarrassed to know his/her caseload detailed a 30 percent absconding rate or a 60 percent recidivism rate. Sadly, this situation is not one-of-a-kind. Another state's "officer of the year" award is even easier to determine; it is awarded to the staff member who has the highest rate for collection of *court fees*. Process is king. The business of probation occupies the limelight.

For those who might bristle at this implication, a quick inventory is telling: If your department requires new-agent training, how much of this orientation curriculum involves motivational enhancement training or strategies/techniques to encourage positive behavior change? Consider any continuing education training recently conducted by your department. More often than not, training titles would have included phrases such as, "Managing the . . .," "Supervising the . . .," "Officer Safety," "Computer Training," "Risk Assessment" or the ubiquitous phrase, "How To Deal With The . . . (sex offender, dually-diagnosed, hostile client, etc.)." This is not to imply these training topics as unimportant, but rather to point out the sheer absence of any tactical curiosity regarding positive behavior change. Whether training topics or articles in professional journals, both appear pertinent to probation services – not behavior change. The business of probation proliferates. Managing trumps motivating. Supervision obscures relationships. Intimidation overshadows encouragement. Compliance remains in ascendancy. Wither change.

Looking to our past may help us to understand the present, allowing us to examine why we find ourselves in this current state. It would seem we were born into a correctional world that had always known tension between the ideals of punishment and treatment. Our field seems unable to extricate itself from a seemingly hypnotic-hold of a "tough-as-nails" approach. To try to understand how the probation field became mesmerized is to appreciate two swings of the crime control pendulum that have occurred over the last 50 years. Psychological and sociological theories of criminal behavior gained prominence in the 1940s and helped the principle of rehabilitation of offenders (offender treatment) to flourish throughout the 1950s and 1960s (Gendreau & Ross, 1987). However, evidence to support the treatment paradigm did not keep pace by tracking outcomes and building supportive evidence, so the pendulum swing of correctional policy started to move back to the punishment and "just desserts" approach. Rehabilitation lost favor by the late 1970s and began to recede during the 1980s.

One swing followed another as the ideal of punishment lost ground. Clive Hollin (2000) notes, "If the 1980s saw the fall of the rehabilitation ideal, then the early 1990s witnessed a spectacular resurrection . . . (this) resurrection of treatment can be directly traced to the impact of a string of meta-analytic studies of the effects of offender treatment published towards the end of the 1980s and into the 1990s." The predominance of punishment had not demonstrated effectiveness, and in many instances, was shown to increase recidivism. With the advent of the 1990s, supervision and treatment has enjoyed more certainty of success (Andrew & Bonta, 2003; Bernfield et al., 2001).

With the current pendulum swing back to treatment, there is a call for motivational enhancement of offenders. With the rise of evidence-based practice, Andrews et al. (1990) details "three principles of effective intervention" that include: (1) risk assessment, (2) targeting criminogenic needs, and (3) responsivity. The rubric of "responsivity" is defined as an effort that will "Insure that individuals are suited to the treatment intervention. Be responsive to temperament, learning style, *motivation*, culture and gender of offenders undergoing treatment when assigning and delivering programs" (emphasis added — pp. 374–375).

How, then, is probation staff to be responsive to motivational issues and work to enhance offender readiness to change, when a good portion of our criminal justice culture (macro) remains stuck in an adversarial "get-tough" atmosphere? Anthropology may offer an explanation. Steven Pinker, in his 1997 landmark book, *How the Mind Works*, notes that there are parts of our current human brain and body that once served a survival purpose in our primordial cave-dwelling past — yet today these same body parts — no longer serve any real function. These anthropological remnants become an appropriate analogy for the "tough-as-nails" stance that many embrace within our probation field. What "worked" for the sole emphasis on punishment and penalty (stopping negative behavior), continues only as an obstacle for increasing motivation and assisting change (starting positive behavior).

A SECOND PENDULUM SWING?

We've witnessed the pendulum swing between the punishment and treatment camps in our field, yet could there actually be *two* pendulums? I propose

there are two, one that is research-based and another that is practice-based. The research pendulum swings in the foreground, set in motion by criminologists who suggest what course-of-action will reduce crime. However, I believe there is a second pendulum, with a swing moving in the background, moving much slower and shadowing the first. This pendulum swing involves the atmosphere and attitudes of those who work within the probation field. This chapter calls attention to this "practice pendulum," that is created by – but not always in sync with – the research pendulum. To understand this second pendulum is to understand that our field seems shackled by a lag-effect; out-of-date attitudes held by many in the field who seek not only compliance from offenders but dominance and primacy over them as well. This holdover from the "just desserts"/punishment era remains alive, suppressing behavior change as it limits an offender's involvement to passive and submissive roles. The brain is dead, but the body continues.

An example of how shackled our field has become can be seen in a recent discussion I had with a training participant following a Motivational Interviewing session. The probation agent approached my podium at the conclusion of a session:

Agent: Interesting training session, but now you've got me thinking.
MC: What's on your mind?
Agent: Well, I'm thinking that I should probably shake hands with my probationers.
MC: You don't?
Agent: No. I was hired out of the prison. There's a "no touch" policy inside facilities. We (staff) can't touch, they (inmates) can't touch. Nothing's allowed, not even hand-shaking.
MC: But . . . (pause) you're working probation now, you're not working in the prison any longer.
Agent: Yea. That's why this training's got me thinking. I mean, yesterday I was walking a new case to the lobby door and he stuck out his hand to shake with me. I got a little angry and said, "I don't shake hands!" "When you get dismissed, maybe then I'll shake your hand."
MC: Wow. Pretty hard to make the kinds of connections we've been talking about in this training session if you won't even shake hands.
Agent: Yea. That's what's got me thinking.
MC: Must be hard to make the transition over

from prison. But, hey, don't be too hard on your-self. How long have you been in this job (com-munity-based probation)?

Agent: Four years.

Four years! I was left speechless. I understood – at that moment – that I had been wrong to assume even the most basic conditions of a helping relationship might be in place across our field. Allow me to draw and analogy to this agent's response. This interchange could well be akin to hiking many miles into a barren desert only to cross paths with someone who was sweltering in a thick winter jacket. Incredulous, you might ask, why one would wear such bizarre attire in the blazing heat of the day? You would be shocked to hear the insensible answer, "Four years ago I use to hike in the cold northern latitudes!"

The Center for Strength-Based Strategies began an inquiry to assess other probation departments only to find this practice of refusing to shake an of-fered hand is not uncommon. A basic respectful act such as returning an overture to shake hands can be denied. Have we lost our way – such that this "busi-ness of probation" has become an enterprise so bel-ligerent to behavior change? There two facts about those we work with; that offenders are (1) human, and (2) humans who have committed a crime. It is of grave concern that some officer attitudes and behav-iors might seem contentious to the first of these two immutable facts.

WITHIN PROBATION DEPARTMENTS (MEZZO): THE OBSTACLE OF THE "EITHER/OR"

Despite such obstacles, what about this recent pendulum swing that has brought our field back to a focus on treatment? What is this business of behavior change? How does change occur? And more impor-tantly to our field, how can department policy and a probation officer's efforts increase an offender's readiness to change? These questions can guide our departments toward a fundamental change in both attitude and objectives.

Change is a process that often takes time. It can occur by sudden insight or dramatic shifts (i.e., epiphanies, "wake up calls") but the vast majority of change occurs slowly and incrementally. The Stages

of Change theory (Prochaska & DiClemente, 1983) has even mapped out these incremental steps, lend-ing support to the idea that change is a "process" rather than a point-in-time event. When working with probationers new to our system (or those re-turning) who may pose harm to themselves or others, initial objectives must begin with offender stabiliza-tion. Those who are out-of-control must be brought into control, hence compliance becomes an all-im-portant first step in offender supervision. If we did not, we would be neglecting our primary mission of social control at the community's peril.

It's time to expose a form of "either/or" concep-tualization by probation staff that ends up as a stum-bling block for improved outcomes. This block is analogous to brewing tea. To enjoy a cup of tea, it's not hot water *or* tea leaves, rather it's hot water *and* tea leaves, the key combination that allows the brew to be served. However, there are those that would strip this sensibility from our own field of probation. Their concrete thinking would have us believe in a limiting contrast; that we either secure compliance *or* increase the readiness to change, that one either im-poses sanctions *or* establishes a helping relationship. As a fish might ask, "what water?" This contrast is so pervasive it is seldom noticed or examined. Motiva-tional Interviewing contends that objectives of con-trol and motivation can exist side-by-side. This "both/and" inclusiveness will be sketched-out later in this chapter.

Those who show little respect to offenders and adopt an adversarial style are only successful in im-posing (once again) another type of unproductive either/or contrast: Either one is tough or soft. A tough, unyielding approach could be characterized as "hold-ing the line." Those who take a tough approach justify their harsh attitudes and abrasive conduct towards of-fenders believing this hardened stance is the only true option. To do otherwise would constitute a soft ap-proach which is merely "wanting to be liked" or "trying to be friends." While heavy-handed advocates may not achieve acceptable levels of success with their adver-sarial approach, they feel a relief that (at least) they will never be accused of acting indulgent or pandering to the offender. It has long been a reaction in our field to blame the offender when change does not occur (Clark, 1995). Rather than examine our own efforts, a lack of improvement is explained away as more ev-idence of the intractable nature of probationers.

Why is a tough approach tolerated in our field? How can it be purged? Our field needs to dissuade the "us vs. them" mindset as it becomes a hindrance to all – hampering the officer/probationer relationship, department objectives, offender improvement and ultimately the safety of our communities. Space prohibits a review of the multitude of studies (Miller & Rollnick, 2002; Hubble, Duncan, & Miller, 1999) that find a confrontational counseling style limits effectiveness. One such review (Miller, Benefield, & Tonnigan, 1993) is telling. This study found that a directive-confrontational counselor style produced twice the resistance, and only half as many "positive" client behaviors as did a supportive, client-centered approach. The researchers concluded that *the more staff confronted, the more the clients drank at twelve-month follow up.* Problems are compounded as a confrontational style not only pushes success away, but can make matters worse.

It would seem that those who swagger and take delight in adopting a "tough" approach do so without knowledge of this large body of research regarding counselor style. It is at this juncture that many probation staff claim, "We're not counselors! – our job is to enforce the orders of the court." This claim only serves to disappoint and underscore that our field remains fixated on the business of probation – not the business of behavior change.

This brings to mind staff who do not adopt this abrasive style but must work around those who do. These staff witness the insensitive attitudes and disrespectful treatment of offenders and become reactive to it. However, much like a crowd that shrinks back in a bully's presence, these same department colleagues and supervisors fall silent and fail to challenge this callous conduct. In a recent discussion with a deputy chief of a large probation department, this manager bemoaned that his department was rife with those who refused to shake hands with probationers – yet justified this beleaguered tolerance as proof that he was *progressive* in allowing diversity of officer styles(!)

It is understandable why many are reluctant to confront. The defense used by the tough crowd is as insidious as it is absolute. "Tough-as-nails" staff again evoke an either/or contrast. They contend that to challenge their insensitive behavior could only come from someone who was "soft" – and staff thought to be soft lack authority and substance. This incredulous mindset shields them from criticism and any

subsequent self-evaluation. Shielded because anyone who might call their behavior into question would be thought to lack credibility *for the sole reason that they disfavor heavy-handed ways!* The criticism, or the person who might raise it, would be dismissed – a priori – as lacking integrity.

I am reminded of a probation supervisor who tried to confront a staff member who was known for intimidation tactics and would brag in back-office chatter about his ill-treatment of probationers. When the supervisor tried to contend that his use of intimidation was both unethical and ineffective, the officer confounded the interchange by a numbing use of the either/or contrast. The officer retorted, "So, what you're saying is that I should molly-coddle them (probationers)?" "No," the supervisor answered, "but you can't use the stick all the time, there are times to use the carrot as well." The officer retorted sarcastically, "so, I'm supposed to be their friend, right?" "No," again replied the supervisor, "but I speak of basic respect." "Respect?" cried the officer, "respect *these* people after what they've done?" "Look," the supervisor pleaded, "it's just not effective to constantly go after them." The officer rejoined with a rhetorical question, "So, you're telling me that hugging them is more effective?" After several go-rounds the exasperated supervisor finally stated, "I guess what I'm trying to say is that you just need to be a little more 'touchy-feely' with those you supervise." The probation officer finished the exchange with the mocking statement, "That's right! When I *touch* them, I want them to *feel* it!" Frustrated by the close-mindedness, the supervisor withdrew.

A clarification is necessary. MI considers "confrontation to be the goal, not the counselor style." That is, the goal of all helping is to create a "self-confrontation" that prompts offenders to "see and accept an uncomfortable reality" (Miller & Rollnick, 1991, p. 13). This awareness, of coming face-to-face with a disquieting image of oneself, is often a prerequisite for intentional change. However, one would not try to impose this awareness by forcing it upon someone through a confrontational *style.* To do so often makes matters worse. Multiple research studies (Rollnick, Mason, & Butler, 1999; Tomlin & Richardson, 2004) repeatedly demonstrate that a harsh, coercive style often prompts a "paradoxical response" – the more one is directive and presses, the more the other person backs away. Rather than evoking change, it causes an offender to become more entrenched in the problem, arguing and defending his/her current negative behavior. Probation agents are familiar with this "backing away." It can take active or passive forms, gearing up with the strong emotionality of arguing and tense opposition, or alternately, by shutting down through the absence of emotions, as with passive-aggressive silence – a "Who cares?" dismissal.

FINDING THE MIDDLE GROUND

To understand and further behavior change is to understand the interpersonal climate between officer and probationer that encourages change. Motivational enhancement steers clear of both the hard and a soft approach. The "hard' approach is overly-directive and places offenders in passive, recipient roles. A "soft" approach correspondingly places the officer in a role that is too passive. A soft approach is also vulnerable to a condition characterized as "professional dangerousness" (Turnell & Edwards, 1999) where an officer, in attempting to keep a hard-won relationship at all costs, refuses to bring violations to the court's attention when they should ("I won't tell this time – but don't do it again"). Here the officer has swung too far to the opposite extreme and is not directive enough. The hope and belief that the officer can build an alliance and work together with an offender to make things better is not the same as ignoring violations. Believing that offenders are worth doing business with is not at all the same thing as adopting the easiest way of doing business with them.

It would seem neither side wins this debate as both approaches reduce offender outcomes – each for a different reason.[1] An emerging motivational approach finds middle ground by those who understand the "both/and" inclusion. With Motivational Interviewing as utilized by probation staff, officers are taught to cooperate with the offender, not the criminal behavior. Probation staff can examine how to impose sanctions *and* build helpful relationships, and with training, agents can build the skills to supervise for compliance *and* increase the offender's readiness for change.

This is not new to our field. Start your own single-subject research by asking any probation supervisor to offer a frank (but discreet) evaluation of his/her department staff he/she supervises. Many supervisors can easily walk down department hallways – and with candor – point to the offices of agents who have the abilities to build helpful alliances with offenders without compromising probation orders. These staff seem to understand that compliance and behavior change are not mutually exclusive efforts. What are the traits and skills that make these agents so different? With an eye to effective relationships that are so essential for encouraging change, why are not more probation departments hiring with these inclusive (therapeutic) abilities as criteria for employment?

As noted, there is an abundance of research citing how a confrontational approach repels those we work with and becomes an obstacle for change. Probation departments must speed-up this "practice pendulum swing" by finding their voice; labeling the "tough" approach for what it is – an obstacle. Departments must become empowered to establish a climate that will both ensure compliance and foster hoped-for behavior change.

INTO THE INDIVIDUAL PAIRING OF OFFICER AND OFFENDER (MICRO): A HELPFUL MIX

I am unrepentantly optimistic as movements are occurring both outside our field and within our own ranks – all to help the second pendulum swing of officer attitudes to keep pace. There are efforts underway that sketch a helpful mix for how to "hold the line" with offenders, while at the same time encouraging positive behavior change in probation work

---

1. This is similar to Bazemore and Terry's (1997) treatise on viewing offenders in a dichotomy as either villains or victims. Those adopting a "tough" approach may well be influenced by the villain view while those adopting a "soft" approach may do so if they view offenders through only a victim lens. A villain lens would reduce outcomes as villains "don't care" and "don't want to change." A victim lens would hold progress back since as victims, they're not responsible and since they didn't cause the trouble, they shouldn't be involved in the resolution. These authors suggest adopting a third view (or lens). Since offenders will come to us as villains or victims, we need to move beyond these limiting views to see offenders with a third lens – as capable and as a resource in the process of change. This "third lens" as proposed by Bazemore & Terry corresponds with a motivational approach (middle ground) that lies between the extremes of "tough" and "soft."

(Clark, 1997; Mann et al., 2002).

A further contribution involves a critical look at the power attributed to a probation agent and how that power is used. I have argued elsewhere (Clark, 2001) and repeat my contention that a therapeutic relationship in probation work can be established through (1) perspective, (2) role-taking by the officer, and (3) skillful negotiations with the probationer.

1. Perspective

To utilize MI, probation staff must adopt a "lens" or a way of viewing the offender that is consistent with the Strengths Perspective (Clark, 1997, 1998). The Strengths Perspective in the justice field is first and foremost a belief in the offenders' ability to change. Although it would be naïve and disingenuous to deny the reality of the harm inflicted by those we work with, Saleebey (1992) cautions:

> If there are genuinely evil people, beyond grace and hope, it is best not to make that assumption about any individual first . . . even if we are to work with someone whose actions are beyond our capacity to understand and accept, we must ask ourselves if they have useful skills and behaviors, even motivations and aspirations that can be tapped in the service of change and to a less-destructive way of life? (p. 238)

This Strengths perspective embraces the science of "getting up." For the previous 40 years, criminal justice has focused on the science and classification of "falling down" as evidenced by our sole focus on deficits, disorders, and failure.[2] The Strengths perspective pays attentions to what strengths, resources, and assets probationers might turn to as they attempt to manage and overcome their troubles. Any probation officer could easily bemoan, "But so many offenders don't care to overcome, they don't believe change is important – they don't seem ready or willing to change."

2. Role-taking

There is great power attached to a court. When used appropriately, it can help to change the trajectory of someone's life, bringing health and improvements that radiate throughout a family (and across the larger community). But when this power is abused or misapplied, the trauma and pain that results can continue long after court documents yellow with age. Who wields this power that holds such potential for benefit or harm? A helpful motivational perspective answers, "Not the officer!" The locus of power is actually centered in the judicial bench rather than to any individual officer. To bring this power home to roost with the officer is not only incorrect but can limit or stifle the very relationship that becomes the conveyor of positive behavior change. Take for example a short passage included in a chapter entitled, "Ethical Considerations" found within the latest edition of Miller and Rollnick's text on Motivational Interviewing (2002: 166): ". . . consider a counselor who works with offenders on parole and probation and who has the power *at any time* to revoke that status and order incarceration" (emphasis added). Although this excerpt speaks to the power of "counselors" who work with offenders, it could be argued that the power attributed to the supervising probation officer would be even greater. However, accurately stated, no officer is truly vested with the power to jail an offender, apply new consequences, or to increase consequences by personal decision or whim. This is not a case of "splitting hairs" with a play on words. An agent must petition the court. The court then works to substantiate the alleged violations of probation in a formal hearing and *it is the court* that determines guilt or innocence and imposes additional sanctions where appropriate.

There is no intent to disparage those who may not understand the judicial process, only to point out how pervasive this misperception has become across our culture. The statement that the probation officer ". . . has the power at any time to revoke that status and order incarceration . . ." demonstrates something akin to an unfounded "urban legend" that gains credibility only through the endless retelling. Legend becomes fact. This mistaken attribution of power is not only limiting for the motivational-inclined officer, but an

---

2. A good example of this sole focus is evidenced by our fields skewed use of "risk" factors. The terms "Risk and Protective factors" came from resiliency research, started in the 1950s. Risk and protective factors were thought to be indivisible, much like the natural pairing of two eyes or two ears – they came as a pair, inseparable from each other yet complimentary to each other. One could not speak of risk factors without noting protective factors as well. However, as evidenced in our field, "risk factors" came to the forefront and now exclusively dominates while "protective factors" are seldom mentioned – much less assessed and integrated in probation plans.

incorrect understanding of probation jurisprudence.

I do not gloss over personal abuses of power, or even systemic bias that prompts disrespectful treatment of offenders. Officers can (and do) illegitimately grasp at this power base ("I'll lock you up!") or consistently intimidate as a personal style, heaping abuse dissolutely on offenders. However, abuses of power are not specific to probation agents and can occur within any helping endeavor. Abuses may well crop up with greater frequency in the criminal justice field, yet I would assert that this becomes an ex post facto argument for the greater expansion, rather than preclusion, of Motivational Interviewing within our ranks.

3. *Skillful Negotiation*

Misperceptions are understandable and easy to overlook when proffered from outside the criminal justice field but far more troublesome when furthered by criminologists within the field. Consider this short treatise from criminal justice academician Robert Mills (1980: 46)

> The distinguishing feature of corrections that differentiates it from other helping professions is the large amount of socially sanctioned authority, both actual and delegated, carried by the corrections official . . .The officer must learn to become comfortable with his authority, and to use it with restraint in the service of the officer and client's objectives.
>
> The reaction of some inexperienced officers is to banish the "big stick," and go hide it in the judge's chambers or in the warden's office. Such officers seem to believe that social casework and counseling can proceed in corrections in the same basis as in an outpatient clinic, that their "good guy in the white hat" image is somehow tarnished by the possession of so much power over their clients. Officers who conduct investigations and counseling while denying their own authority are usually perceived as being weak, and are subject to easy manipulation by their clients.

With all due respect, my suggestion is that officers do exactly what Mills cautions against! Motivational Interviewing, as utilized within the field of probation, is determined not to personally assume the "big stick." It furthers an officer's ability to influence change when they place the "stick" with the judge, their supervisor, or even to use "agency policy" as a convenient catch-all. Motivationally-inclined officers lament to the probationer who might be considering a violation of probation orders, "You can certainly ignore that order (refuse to obey, avoid this mandate), but my (supervisor, judge, responsibilities, policy, position) will force me assess a consequence. It's your choice, but is there anything we can do to help you avoid those consequences?" Many find that *not* exerting force as this juncture improves the likelihood that a decision for compliance will eventually overtake the emotions of the moment.

This role-taking becomes not a "weakness" as purported by Mills, but rather a strength. When using MI with mandated clients, I am mindful of the distinction of "power versus force." Force, for all it's bluster can often make a situation worse, compelling an offender to exert themselves where skillful negotiation could well de-escalate the situation. MI-inclined officers choose power over force to increase readiness to change and improve outcomes by establishing "fit" with a probationer ("How can we come together on this?"), than with the use of adversarial *force* from the "me vs. you" nexus of dominance (you have no choice, you *will* do this!).[3] I believe the ability to create and maintain a helping relationship – so essential to the spirit of Motivational Interviewing – can only be realized by placing the "big stick" with others.

Miller and Rollnick (2002: 173–174) detailed a helpful example of this skillful negotiation with probationers. It begins with an honest explanation of the duality of an officer's roles: certainly to supervise and report compliance to probation orders but also to act as a helper and lend assistance:

> I have two different roles here, and it is sometimes tricky for me to put them together. One of them is as a representative of the court, to ensure that you keep the

---

3. This contrast of power vs. force, so pertinent to which type of influence should be applied by probation staff can also be found as a book title by David Hawkins (2002) *Power vs. Force: The Hidden Determinants of Human Behavior*. In this book Hawkins states, "Whereas power always results in a win-win solution, force produces win-lose situations . . . the way to finesse a (solution) is to seek the answer which will make all sides happy and still be practical. . . . Successful solutions are based on the powerful principle that resolution occurs not by attacking the negative, but by fostering the positive." Hawkins concludes, "Only the childish proceed from the assumption that human behavior can be explained in black and white terms. (pps. 138–139) I would contend the "either/or" conception is similar to the "black and white terms" as noted by Hawkins.

conditions of probation that the judge sets for you, and I have to honor this role. The other is to be your counselor, to help you make changes in your life that we agree would be beneficial. There are also likely to be some areas we'll discover, where I am hoping to see a change that you're not sure you want to make. What I hope is that by talking together here (when you report), we can resolve some of those differences and are able to find areas of change we can agree on. I'm sure I'll be asking you to consider some changes that right now don't sound very good to you, and that's normal. We'll keep exploring those issues during our time together, and see if we can come to some agreement. How does that sound to you?

Should compliance become an issue, the officer negotiates "How do we (you, significant others and myself) keep them (the judge, the court, agency policy) off your back?"

In training, I find staff new to Motivational Interviewing have a hard time negotiating these dual roles. Concrete thinking of either/or tends to dominate. "I either supervise or seek compliance (applying sanctions for failure to comply) or I practice Motivational Interviewing and try to motivate and establish a therapeutic alliance." It's not "tea leaves *or* water," it's a good-enough blend that creates the brew. Helping staff to adopt a both/and conception is central to the business of behavior change.

Our field's ambivalence regarding intimidation and heavy confrontation must be systemically addressed. There is a tiresome practice of privately judging this behavior as reprehensible – yet publicly we say nothing. If behavior change is truly paramount, then intimidation and heavy-handed treatment is inappropriate and must be openly denounced across our field and within our departments. Only then will we stop the false dichotomy of "tough/soft" which continues to drain our field of its effectiveness. Only then will probation departments be populated with staff that can enforce orders and increase the readiness to change. Only then will a true decision be made as to whether we're in the business of probation or whether we're in the business of changing behavior.

POSTSCRIPT

Ward and Brown (2004) note a probation officer's attitudes towards an offender will emanate from their conception of the nature and value of probationers as human beings – and to what extent engaging in harmful actions diminishes that value. There is a question that looms for all probation departments who may want to embrace a change in focus – is an offender entitled to be treated with basic respect for no other reason than they hold intrinsic value as a person? This issue is not as straightforward as it might seem. Some officers feel the need to act out society's anger towards those they are assigned to, believing anything less would condone their wrongdoing. Motivated, one might suspect, by the idea that at least they've "done something" by conveying their disgust for illegal behaviors. It would not be far-fetched to assume that if the process of arrest, court appearances, and conviction did not instill a sense of shame or deviance, then any disgust shown by a supervising officer could be pointless. Viets, Walker, and Miller (2002) note, "People do not respond warmly to being shamed, coerced, berated, or deprived of choice. There is little evidence for the belief that "if you can make them feel *bad* enough, they will change" (emphasis in original). Confrontation and disrespectful behavior pushes change further away. These behaviors are staff-focused (engaged in to make the probation officer feel better) rather than changed-focused (creating a climate that will assist change).

With overwhelming research in hand that a confrontational style inhibits outcomes, it would seem that allowing the voice of those who say the world is flat to coexist with those who know it to be round, brings assurance and honor to no one. Will our field intervene? Will departments continue to allow a hostile, confrontational style to be tolerated as an acceptable way of "doing business?"

For those who conceptualize our "business" of probation as the sole mission of enforcing the courts orders, the debilitating answer is "yes." Turnell and Edwards (1999) caution, "Very few people will listen to or allow themselves to be influenced by someone who seems unresponsive to them and is simply forcing them to conform." Externally-imposed compliance is the least enduring type of change with negative behavior returning once the coercive force is withdrawn. Could the sole focus on compliance and the ensuing "business of probation" actually create more "business" – via the revolving door of repeat offenders?

It is appealing to excuse our field any goals

beyond the status quo of compliance. The higher ambition to increase an offender's readiness to change could be considered an ideal – an idyllic notion that becomes impossible to reach due to issues of time constraints and practicality. Research (Clark, 2004) notes that there is a wide disparity of caseload numbers, which allows some staff the luxury of over 30 (plus) minutes for an offender "check-in" while some are afforded only seven minutes (on average) to gather information. Just how practical can embracing a motivational style be when one considers such short time frames? Students of behavior change would call attention to the depressing fact that pushing change aside does not take long – an officer can easily *decrease the likelihood of offender change* – choking hoped-for goals all in brief office visits.

To borrow a phrase from quantum physics, there is an "alternate universe" emerging within our field. Progressive departments are importing training to teach officers the strategies and techniques for increasing the likelihood of change, even in constrained and limited time frames. "Making the most" of what one has conveys the relevancy of Motivational Interviewing for probation staff.

Acknowledgment

Per Federal monograph #109, the United States Probation & Parole Services-Western Michigan District undertook an extensive Strength-based and Motivational Interviewing initiative (2005). This author wishes to thank and extend his appreciation to this Western Michigan district as this training initiative lent both insights and impetus for this chapter.

REFERENCES

Andrews, D. A., & Bonta, J. (2003). *The psychology of criminal conduct* (3rd ed.). Cincinnati, OH: Anderson

Andrews, D. A., Zinger, I., Hoge, R. D., Bonta, J., Gendreau, P., Cullen, F. T., (August, 1990). *Does correctional treatment work? A clinically relevant and psychological in-*formed meta-analysis" criminology.

Bazemore, G., & Terry, C. (1997). Developing delinquent youth: A reintegrative model for rehabilitation and a new role for the juvenile justice system. *Child Welfare*, 665–716.

Bernfield, G. A., Farrington, D. P., & Leschied, A. W. (2001). *Offender rehabilitation in practice: Implementing and evaluating effective programs.* New York: John Wiley & Sons.

Burke, B. L., Arkowitz, H., & Dunn, C. (2002). The efficacy of motivational interviewing and its adaptations: What we know so far. In W. Miller & S. Rollnick (Eds.), *Motivational interviewing: Preparing people for change* (2nd ed.). New York: Guilford Press.

Clark, M. D. (Spring, 1995). The problem with problem solving: A critical review. *Journal for Juvenile Justice and Detention Service.*

Clark, M. D. (April, 1997). Strength based practice: A new paradigm. *Corrections Today*, 201–202.

Clark, M. D. (June, 1998). Strength based practice: The ABCs of working with adolescents who don't want to work with you. *Federal Probation Quarterly*, 46–53.

Clark, M. D. (June, 2001). Influencing positive behavior change: Increasing the tehrapeutic approach of juvenile courts. *Federal Probation Quarterly*, 18–27.

Clark, M. D. (Jaunary, 2004). Unpublished research. Qualitative polling of probation depeartments-community corrections divisions across twelve states 1999–2003.

Duncan, B., Miller, S., & Sparks, J. (2004). *The heroic client: A revolutionary way to improve effectiveness through client-directed, outcome-informed therapy.* San Francisco: Jossey-Bass.

Gendreau, P., & Ross, R. R. (September, 1987). Revivification of rehabilitation: Evidence from the 1980's. *Justice Quarterly*, 349–407.

Hawkins, D. R. (2002). *Power vs. force: The hidden determinants of human behavior.* Sedona, AZ: Veritas Publishing.

Hollin, C. (2001). *Handbook of offender assessment and treatment.* New York: John Wiley & Sons.

Hubble, M., Duncan, B., & Miller, S. (1999). *The heart and soul of change: What works in therapy.* Washington, D.C.: American Psychological Association.

Levitt, T. (September-October, 1975). Marketing myopia. *Harvard Business Review*, 19-31.

Mann, R. E., Ginsburg, J. I. D., & Weekes, J. R. (2002). Motivational interviewing with offenders." In M. McMurran (Ed.), *Motivating offenders to change: A guide to enhancing engagement in therapy.* New York: John Wiley & Sons.

Miller, W. R., & Rollnick, S. (1991) *Motivational interviewing: Preparing people for change.* New York: Guilford Press.

Miller, W. R. & Rollnick, S. (2002). *Motivational interviewing: Preparing people for change* (2nd ed.). New York: Guilford Press.

Miller, W. R., Benefield, R. G., & Tonnigan, J. S. (1993). Enhancing motivation for change in problem drinking: A controlled comparison of two therapists styles *Journal of Consulting and Clinical Psychology*, 455–461.

Mills, R. (1980). *Offender assessment: A casebook in corrections.* Cincinnati: Anderson.

Pinker, S. (1997). *How the mind works.* New York: Norton.

Prochaska, J. O., & DiClemente, C. C. (1983). Stages and processes of self-change in smoking: Toward an integrative model of change. *Journal of Consulting and Clinical Psychology*, 390–395.

Roberts, A. R., & Yeager, K. R. (2004). *Evidence-based practice manual: Research and outcome measures in health and human services.* New York: Oxford University Press.

Rollnick, S., Mason, P., & Butler, C. (1999). *Health behavior change: A guide for practitioners.*

Saleebey, D. (2002). *The strengths perspective in social work practice* (3rd ed.). New York: Longman.

Tomlin, K. M., & Richardson, H. (2004). *Motivational interviewing and stages of change: Integrating best practices for substance abuse professionals.*

Turnell, A., & Edwards, S. (1999). *Signs of safety: A solution and safety oriented approach to child protection casework.* New York: WW Norton.

Viets, V. L., Walker, D., & Miller, W. R. (2002). What is motivation to change: A scientific analysis. In M. McMurran (Ed.), *Motivating offenders to change: A guide to enhancing engagement in therapy.* NY: John Wiley & Sons.

Ward, T., & Brown, M. (2004). The good lives model and conceptual issues in offender rehabilitation. *Psychology, Crime and Law, 10*(3), 243–247.

Adult Corrections: Institutional and Community-Based Forensic Work

Chapter 26

Preparing Social Workers for Practice in Correctional Institutions

André Ivanoff, Nancy J. Smyth, and Catherine N. Dulmus

Globally, more than 8.75 million individuals are incarcerated, with almost two million of these individuals incarcerated in the United States. With 686 per 100,000 of the U.S. national population incarcerated in 2001, the United States has the distinction of having the highest prison population rate in the world (Walmsley, 2003). This distinction has resulted in corrections becoming a U.S. growth industry (Roberts & Brownell, 1999) as the total number of adult federal, state, and private correctional facilities increased 14 percent from 1995–2000 (U.S. Department of Justice, 2003). This does not account for the more than 134,000 youth residing in some 3000 correction facilities in the United States (Sickmund, 2004).

In addition to the social dysfunction that resulted in incarceration, adult and youth inmates present with multiple bio-psycho-social needs. Over 60 percent of youth in the juvenile justice system have behavioral, mental or emotional disorders and are in need of treatment (Lieter, 1993). Almost 40 percent of adult inmates are mentally ill (Ditton, 1999), with suicide accounting for over 6 percent of inmate deaths (U.S. Department of Justice, 2003). HIV/AIDS is also a concern, with over 23,000 adult inmates identified as HIV positive. According to Dr. Albert Roberts (personal communication, November 18, 2005), the most prevalent physical health problems in state prisons throughout the United States are cancer, hepatitis-C, cardiovascular disease, liver disease, diabetes, and lung disease. In addition to mental and physical illnesses (including substance abuse), multiple other issues present themselves related to things such as lack of employment skills, educational deficits, and family needs. Certainly, incarcerated individuals would benefit from forensic social work services.

Though the emphasis in criminal justice continues to be dominated by a punitive rather than rehabilitative-oriented treatment of the offender, the pendulum does appear to be slowly swinging back. Evidence of this includes major funding from different states to provide mental health treatment for incarcerated offenders, as well as the recent U.S. Supreme Court decision holding that, in light of evolving standards of decency, it is unconstitutional to execute the mentally retarded (Stone, 2002). If the pendulum continues to swing towards rehabilitation and humane treatment, more roles for social work will present themselves in corrections.

Barker (1995) defines forensic social work as, "the practice specialty in social work that focuses on the law and educating law professionals about social welfare issues and social workers about the legal aspects of their objectives" (p. 140). This definition incorporates the practice of social work in family violence and the courts, juvenile justice and adult corrections, and law enforcement (Roberts, 1997). Building on Barker's definition, Roberts, Springer, & Brownell, in Chapter 1, operationally define forensic social work as, "policies, practices, legal issues, and social work roles with juvenile and adult offenders as well as victims of crimes."

While the field of corrections includes services across a variety of settings, for the purposes of this chapter, we limit our discussion to forensic social work services in residential correctional settings. Residential institutions include jails, juvenile and adult detention centers, and prisons. We chose to focus on residential settings because they account for a significant and growing segment of the population involved in corrections. Individuals placed in these settings, whether referred to as "detainees," "inmates," "residents," or "offenders" (if convicted) are particularly at risk of continuing social dysfunction due to their isolation from the larger community. Certainly though, parole, probation, and rapidly increasing community sentencing options such as house arrest and electronic monitoring are also important correctional methods (see Chapter 14 by McNeece and colleagues) which would benefit from forensic social work.

Though in recent years social work has begun to respond to the challenge of meeting the needs of incarcerated individuals (Roberts & Brownell, 1999), an uneasy relationship and decreasing professional attention between social work and criminal justice continues. This disconnect may be attributed to several factors, including:

1. Criminal justice is authoritarian which is diametrically opposed to social work values such as client self determination and a strength-based approach.
2. Role strain related to role inconsistency, training incongruity, and interprofessional status tensions (Needleman & Needleman, 1997).
3. An essential conflict between the philosophies of criminal justice settings and mental health treatment (Brennan, Gedric, Jacoby, Tardy, & Tyson, 1986; Neddleman, 1997).
4. A small, but growing number of criminal justice and forensic social work courses and field experiences provided in schools of social work (Roberts & Brownell, 1999).

These issues warrant careful scrutiny and each should be addressed in developing recruitment programs and curricula. However, in addition to these issues, there is a lack of basic familiarity with the day-to-day operations of correctional institutions that contributes to social workers' lack of receptivity and preparedness for work there. Our focus here is on this latter, more circumscribed issue: how can social workers prepare for work in correctional institutions? We begin by examining the institutional environment and the practitioner's role in this environment. Next, we identify specific areas of training that should be addressed to prepare for work in correctional institutions. We conclude by recommending specific preparation methods.

THE ECOLOGY OF CORRECTIONAL SETTINGS

Charles entered jail at age 18 following two juvenile arrests and a conviction for criminal possession of a controlled substance. He was sentenced to 10 months in the county correctional facility. Upon meeting with the social worker, Charles indicated that he was motivated to avoid "the life," particularly because he had very recently become a father and wanted to play a positive role in his son's life. With the assistance of social work intervention, Charles completed his GED, obtained a competitive, highly prized work assignment as an orderly in the jail infirmary, and maintained contact with his son's mother. After release, he immediately entered a drug rehabilitation program and was afterwards accepted into a vocational training program for ex-offenders.

Ronald was a 56-year-old white, married engineer who was arrested and sentenced to five to eight years in the state prison for sexually abusing several pre-teenage boys. Following his incarceration at the state reception center, he was withdrawn and fearful, at times visibly agitated. Following the intake social worker's assessment, he was immediately placed on suicide watch and moved to a dormitory. Given the status of his offense, it was also recommended that his sentence be served in a protective custody unit, a recommendation followed by correctional administration.

Correctional institutions are characterized by four different philosophies: retribution, deterrence, incapacitation, and rehabilitation or treatment. Realistically, most systems use a mixture of these philosophies. The majority of these philosophies focus on punishment rather than rehabilitation, consistent with current public sentiment. This is in direct contrast to the value social work places on treatment and on the capacity of individuals to change their behavior through counseling, education, and involvement in adaptive activity. Social work's major historical contributions to criminal justice involve the demonstration of this rehabilitative model. This philosophical difference creates potential for conflict. Choosing a goal of cooperative coexistence and mutually productive outcomes demands that social workers clearly understand how these philosophies are operationalized.

A liberal representation of present-day correctional institutions might describe their functions as twofold: to punish the offender and to protect members of the community from further victimization. The second function is to rehabilitate offenders through participation in programmatic activities designed to modify their behavior upon re-entry to the community. The relative emphasis on either of these functions has important implications for institutional services.

However, neither punishment nor rehabilitation is the primary concern of correctional staff when it comes to the day-to-day operation of the institution. The overriding concerns are the safety and security of personnel and inmates. Therefore, the rehabilitative or punitive value of activities for an inmate is not of highest importance and may even be regarded as irrelevant. Activities, whether punitive denial of privilege or rehabilitative programming, are generally viewed favorably by correctional staff because they provide greater safety and security. Busy inmates tend to create fewer problems than idle inmates.

Opportunities for forensic social work practice in institutions take two general forms: supportive and linkage. Supportive function practice is provided in the adjunctive fields of mental health and substance abuse, vocational rehabilitation, and education, and it is generally limited to the particular function involved. Generally, social workers attached to the mental health unit in a prison work exclusively with mental health issues, while social workers attached to the substance abuse unit are concerned with addictions treatment. However, the organization of these supportive services varies from state to state and facility to facility, and in some settings, it is not unheard of that supportive function personnel may be asked to assume some form of security duties on some occasions (Weinberger & Sreenivasan, 1994).

The second function of forensic social work practice in correctional institutions is that of advocacy, brokerage, and linkage between incarcerated individuals and their communities. Practitioners in this role often are able to influence the acquisition of services for families of inmates in the community and for the residents themselves within the institution. In addition, social workers often play critical roles in decisions made about residents' lives within the institution. The social worker's input may influence decisions regarding a resident's transfer within and between facilities as well as decisions made by parole boards and in competency hearings.

As an example, Moritza was a 32-year-old Latina mother of three who was HIV-positive; her husband was a former intravenous drug user. She was serving a six-month sentence for possession of crack cocaine. Prior to this incarceration, Mortiza had not discussed her illness from an active problem-solving perspective. Social work staff arranged access to appropriate health and supportive services in the jail, including a support group for HIV positive mothers of young children. With the social worker's assistance and while still in jail, Moritza contacted community agencies providing housing assistance, services for HIV-positive women, and a women's prison aftercare program. She obtained information about these services and was later interviewed and accepted into a drug treatment program. At her release, Moritza's plan included immediate, intensive, outpatient drug treatment; temporary housing at her mother's; and weekly supervised visits with her children.

Forensic social work offers an array of opportunities as well as administrative, institutional, and clinical challenges. While each correctional system and facility has unique characteristics, there also are common themes across correctional institutions that set them apart from typical practice settings.

KNOWLEDGE AND SKILLS NEEDED FOR PRACTICE IN CORRECTIONAL SETTINGS

Correctional Politics

The current correctional philosophies described above focus more on punishment than on rehabilitation. This difference in priorities, if not understood, can create conflict. Although all practitioners should understand the philosophy and culture of their agencies, in correctional settings, this understanding is directly related to the safety and security of the individual practitioner, other staff, and the inmates. As staff of the correctional institution, social workers may be regarded as agents of social control. Although some may find this an uncomfortable image, the reality is that social workers do function in authoritative and arguably coercive roles in corrections. This, however, does not separate practitioners in correctional settings from those in child welfare, or many health and mental health, settings.

While severely disadvantaged life circumstances characterize most incarcerated individuals, social workers who understand the dynamics of human development without excusing abusive or criminal behavior may be most effective in working with this population. What does this mean? Holding individuals accountable for their behavior has the highest likelihood of moving them toward changing future behavior. The use of authority can be effective in preventing further criminality, as it has the potential to create a personal crisis for the offender that may force a review of attitudes and behavior (Nevers et al., 1990).

Simultaneously, the practitioner also should acknowledge and respond to the real environmental and emotional crises that can be created by incarceration. For example, the first 24 hours of incarceration is widely recognized as a period of high suicide risk, particularly for first-time offenders (Hayes, 2001). Social workers who are not formally part of the correctional department, i.e., those working for health or mental health agencies under contract to corrections, may also build alliances with offenders more readily and may even advocate on their behalf within the criminal justice system. In some cases, social workers may be in the best position to identify important diagnostic issues such as coexisting substance abuse and major mental disorders and to advocate for effective management of these dual disorders through tailored correctional programming, housing, or both.

In order to maximize their effectiveness, practitioners must analyze the organizational politics of a correctional institution at both the macro- and micro-level. The natural disjunctures between law enforcement, health care, and rehabilitative programming can result in unavoidable daily tensions and misunderstandings as personnel interact and carry out daily tasks. Although the complexities of intra-agency politics demand careful study over time, basic information can be helpful in framing practitioners' initial experiences.

First, a thorough description of the basic organizational hierarchy is important, noting divisions between rehabilitative or program and correctional staff. Knowledge of the relative power of particular staff positions and organizational subdivisions within the institution can be useful. In many facilities, higher-level administrative positions tend to be filled by correctional staff, with program and rehabilitative staff occupying less powerful positions, except within

their exclusive domains. Those correctional institutions run by wardens (superintendents) or deputy wardens who have been promoted from rehabilitative positions will probably accord more influence and prestige to rehabilitative and program staff than those settings that have promoted only correctional staff. The correctional staff and administration are always the ultimate authority; however, security reigns supreme in areas of physical security or in any type of crisis. Wherever the practitioner's formal sanction is lodged in the organization, and whatever role or position the social worker may fill, correctional administrators are ultimately in control of the physical environment. A hard-learned lesson from several years ago when we were trying to obtain access to inmates for an assessment study, the words of a state corrections administrator live on in our memories: "Remember, WE have the keys!"

The social worker's position within the organization deserves close examination. Social workers employed by guest agencies will wield less direct influence within the overall institution than will those employed by the primary setting. Nelson and Berger (1988) offer four models under which offenders receive mental health treatment. These models, which may help clarify role possibilities, are distinguished by the type of setting in which they occur (mental health or corrections) and how the mental health and security services are administered (by primary agency or by a guest" or secondary agency). For example, mental health services in a correctional setting may be delivered in one of two ways: (1) settings where both mental health and security services are provided by the corrections department; or (2) settings where mental health services are provided by a separately administered department of mental health while security needs are administered by corrections. Administration of such mental health services follows similar patterns: (1) where both mental health and security services are provided by the department of mental health (e.g., a forensic unit within a mental health facility; or (2) where mental health services are provided by the mental health department and the security needs are administered by department of corrections (Nelson & Berger, 1988). The argument for placing mental health services under the administration of corrections is that it provides access to more resources and decreases problems (Weinberger & Sreenivasan, 1994). Social workers practice within each of these different models but enjoy differential control and professional status.

Finally, it is also important to observe the relative position of the agency within the community. In some areas, correctional facilities are well-regarded by their surrounding communities and provide an important source of employment to the local economy. In other areas, facilities are perceived with fear or distaste, and inmate labor or work-release programs may be perceived as a threat to local unions or workers. All of this affects how facility personnel view their work, the others they work with, the programs, and the residents of the facility.

Correctional Security

Security is of paramount concern in corrections. Because this is not the case in most social work practice settings, social workers need to understand that security regulations in criminal justice settings are rarely arbitrary. They are designed to maintain order and to reduce the threat of danger and violence to staff and inmates. Except in special punishment situations, the rules are generally not intended to denigrate or ridicule the individual inmate. Granted, selected and biased implementation of the rules does occur and may involve ridicule and physical violence toward inmates, particularly when correctional staff themselves feel threatened or challenged by lack of security.

Security is the most visible symbol of the traditional prison and is palpably present upon entering. Symbolic and real examples of security include wearing visible identification at all times, search of one's possessions, hand stamps, invisible ink, heavy doors, straight lines of inmates walking down halls accompanied by closely scanning correctional officers, the count, nightsticks, riot gear, mace, punishment areas, lockdown, and bathrooms with no doors.

These symbols of curtailed freedom may cause a visceral response to the environment. If a social worker enters a correctional institution unfamiliar with its purpose and with the high levels of structure necessary for the safety of the residents as well as for staff, security may be misinterpreted as a draconian, nonsensical infringement of reasonable freedom. Detention facilities, for example, which house individuals who have not yet been convicted, often display high levels of security, as the potential for violence among detainees varies widely.

Prior to beginning work in a correctional setting, social workers should be informed what constitutes contraband in the particular facility where they will be working, as this varies based on facility design and security level. It is also helpful if the reasons why items are designated as contraband are explained to new practitioners, e.g., chewing gum because it can be put in locks to prevent them from closing securely. What is labeled as contraband varies widely, from weapons, nail files, and electronic equipment to newspapers, oral contraceptives, and "DMX" or "Buster Rhymes" on compact disc. Staff are commonly prohibited from responding to resident requests to bring items into the facility for them and from giving residents even seemingly innocuous items, such as pencils and pens. Further, taking anything out of the facility for a resident, e.g., a letter to be mailed, a message to a family member or friend, is also a security breach. As a general rule, it is a good idea to bring in only what is needed, to avoid embarrassment and possible security violations.

Safety is the first goal of security procedures in correctional facilities. While correctional officers are responsible for protecting civilians in facilities, their ability to do so depends heavily on civilian awareness and practice of personal safety and security procedures. More subtly, it also means demonstrating the knowledge of these rules and procedures through one's behavior.

Confidentiality is a high priority in correctional settings, not only for clinical and ethical reasons, but because it is closely related to security. Within prison culture, information is exchanged and used as currency. A misspoken comment made in passing might be overheard by a correctional officer who casually repeats it where residents can overhear. If this information can be used to hurt, make someone vulnerable to coercion, or gain something of value, prison norms suggest that it will be used. Information carelessly passed on can prove harmful or even deadly. However, security concerns also raise questions about making exceptions to confidentiality. The ethical "duty to protect" (VandeCreek & Knapp, 1993) becomes an ethical obligation to protect the larger community within the institution, suggesting that appropriate exceptions to confidentiality should be defined more broadly than they might be in practice outside the institution (Severson, 1994). For example, Severson (1994) raises questions about the ethical obligation to notify security personnel when an inmate discloses possession of contraband that poses a serious risk to the inmate community.

RELATIONSHIPS WITH OTHER CORRECTIONAL STAFF

In addition to security and confidentiality, there are direct factors in relationships with correctional officers that affect the ability to function effectively in a correctional setting. Professional staff should always be cordial to correctional officers, uniformed and civilian. While it is not uncommon for beginning social workers to initially feel resentment or lack of trust toward correctional staff, for their part, correctional staff tend to regard new social workers as simply more work for them, e.g., additional not-prison-smart people to protect.

The ability to get along with correctional staff can mean the difference between clinical success and failure. This is because, in many institutions, clinical staff are reliant on correctional officers to escort inmates to them as well as to return them to their cells or dorms in timely fashion. This escort function is also often necessary if practitioners should need to meet with an inmate in a housing are a (e.g., a punitive segregation unit) or conduct a group or housing unit (e.g., a mental observation unit). Not all facilities require correctional officer escorts for professional staff; however, if required, their disinterest or disinclination to take a long walk to collect someone from a far housing unit can prevent clinical work from taking place. A relationship based on respect for the correctional officer's often difficult role can be facilitating. In fairness, officers are not totally responsible for facility movement. There are often security or administrative procedures that may slow down activity and work; however, the correctional officer is the best source of information about the causes and resolutions of such slowdowns.

The functions, concerns, policies, and programmatic problems of a correctional staff member are markedly different than those of a social worker. Although not a part of social work's professional ethos, in a correctional setting, the social worker should learn to understand and tolerate being ignored and perhaps even spoken to harshly while remaining calm, not responding in kind, and not assuming this behavior is personally directed.

During the first weeks in the institution, social workers are particularly aware of the interactions between residents and correctional staff. Social workers should be encouraged to explore all questionable or troubling interactions as soon as possible with their supervisor before discussing them with peers, with other staff, or with the involved resident or correctional staff member. Inaccurate perceptions can be corrected and the context and complexity of these relationships examined. Also, if exploitation or abuse of residents is occurring, the social worker needs the support and action of the supervisor to effectively intervene.

Ethnicity and Gender Issues in Correctional Settings

The majority of residents in urban detention or correctional facilities and in state prisons are men and women of color, primarily African-American and Hispanic. In some settings, e.g., maximum security prisons located in rural settings, this is coupled with high numbers of white, mostly male, correctional officers and professional staff. While the proportions may vary somewhat, these racial, ethnic, and gender overrepresentations create issues and tensions for correctional staff, professionals and residents of all groups. In larger facilities, issues of sexual orientation and homophobia add to the tension. Given the gender segregation that characterizes correctional facilities, there is often a great deal of same-sex, i.e., homosexual, sexual activity among residents. However, many of the individuals engaging in these activities may not identify their primary sexual orientation as gay or lesbian. Some residents may find that their sexual behavior elicits questioning of their sexual orientation.

Social workers should be encouraged to explore and discuss their reactions to these imbalances, initially as they affect safety and security, then politically and philosophically. For clinical practitioners, the impact and interaction of environment with authority, gender, race, and sexual orientation should be explored in depth, focusing on particular clients. For practitioners in supervisory positions, issues related to race and gender may come into play among employees. Male staff within correctional institutions often are resistant to having women work in correctional facilities, particularly in security functions (Fry

& Glase, 1987), and homophobia may affect interaction with openly gay staff.

In a more typical agency setting, social workers are ideally trained to recognize norms and differences toward the goal of assessment within the cultural context. This is imperative for practice in correctional settings. It is doubly difficult to understand resident behavior and concerns without some knowledge of the culture of their racial and ethnic groups; beyond this, however, knowledge of the subculture and experience of incarceration is required, particularly in its impact on identity and self-concept (cf., Sykes 1965 for a good discussion of this). Both the prison subculture and the impact of incarceration are likely outside the experience of most practitioners who enter work in correctional settings. The helping relationship is also strongly affected by the correctional environment and culture. In a correctional setting, all those who come in contact with an offender are in authoritative and potentially coercive positions. This adds a dimension that may be difficult to interpret for those inexperienced in criminal justice or forensic social work, compounded by the ethnic and gender differences that may also strongly affect the helping relationship.

Among social workers who identify with offenders based on ethnic, racial, or other disadvantaged group membership, the conflict can be even more pronounced, or may make the practitioner's position of authority less comfortable, with the social worker feeling as though she or he is really the only one who truly cares about trying to help a disadvantaged resident. Practitioners may have difficulty regarding themselves as part of the agency or with limits and professional boundaries. These can have serious implications for safety and security and may also prevent the practitioner from using the most effective change methods to facilitate change and accomplish goals.

ETHICS AND PROFESSIONAL RESPONSIBILITY FOR PRACTICE IN CORRECTIONAL SETTINGS

Ethical Conflicts

Much has been written about the ethical conflicts associated with psychological practice in criminal justice and correctional settings, but less in social work. In addition to philosophical conflict with the limited

mission of the correctional institution, difference is also rooted in the conflicting roles that some professional staff may be asked to perform. For example, clinical practitioners may find themselves in a disciplinary hearing where they are expected to advocate for the interests of the entire correctional community, interests that may be opposed to those of particular individuals served by the practitioner. Weinberger and Sreenivasan (1994) note that there are some circumstances where correctional administrators might request a practitioner evaluate an inmate without informed consent. Finally, under unusual circumstances, e.g., an emergency, inadequate staffing, etc., practitioners may be asked to perform security functions, a task that could compromise residents' perceptions of the practitioner as a credible and confidential therapeutic resource (Weinberger & Sreenivasan, 1994). Conflicts such as these have led some to advocate the development of detailed professional practice standards to guide practitioners in correctional settings in resolving these ethical conflicts. In the absence of such standards, Severson (1994) suggests that social workers inform inmates of their responsibilities to the individual and the institution, and then carefully document the provision of informed consent. Additionally, she suggests that practitioners can work to clarify their roles with administrators, as well as educate policymakers about the implications of these role conflicts on long-term job effectiveness.

Personal Models of Practice and Research-based Practice

Once the social worker has begun practice in the correctional setting, information about practice should be, as much as possible, systematically organized into a model of practice. The development and use of personal practice models in social work practice is described by Mullen (1983). Personal practice models are explicit conceptual schemes that express an individual practitioner's view of practice and give more systematic direction to work with specific clients. Motivated by pragmatic interests, such models provide summary generalizations and practice guidelines that provide direction to practice. The generalizations explain the practitioner's understanding of the dimensions of practice, and the practice guidelines offer prescriptive practice principles that are synthesized from the generalizations (Mullen, 1983).

Ethical practice is also evidence-based practice. This means that practitioners should select, whenever possible, intervention methods that are supported by empirical evidence over those that are not supported by research evidence (Gambrill, 1999). While many types of social work intervention do not have data to support them, such research evidence is rapidly accumulating in many practice settings, including corrections. One such example is the suicide screening and risk assessment instrument developed by Cox, McCarty, Landsberg, and Paravati (1988). Designed in response to the high rates of suicide in local jail and detention facilities across New York State, the instrument is a simple 17-item checklist, derived from both clinical and research sources. It takes about 10 minutes to administer. In the six years this screening instrument has been in use, the rate of suicide in local jails and detention facilities in New York state has significantly decreased (Cox & Morchauser, 1993). Another example is the recently published special issue of the *Journal of Evidence-Based Social Work*, guest edited by Rapp-Paglicci (2005), that focused exclusively on juvenile offenders and mental illness. These resources and others will assist the forensic social worker in evidence-based practice.

Practice Evaluation

A final point under this topic of ethics and professional responsibility concerns practice accountability. Practitioners in correctional settings have the same obligation to their clients as those in an unrestricted environment: to determine whether the service provided moved the client in the direction of stated goals.

BEFORE BEGINNING PRACTICE IN CORRECTIONAL SETTINGS

1. Obtain a general orientation to practice in criminal justice or correctional practice. In our experience, talking with other individuals working in correctional agencies prior to beginning work is a worthwhile use of time. Asking basic questions about the issues described above and allowing time for questions can allay anxieties and make expectations somewhat more realistic (Sheafor & Jenkins, 1982). Recently hired psychologists at the Federal Bureau

of Prisons are required to attend and successfully complete a three-week training program entitled, "Introduction to Correctional Techniques" (Federal Bureau of Prisons, 1986). The program was designed to teach basic correctional concepts and tasks, including inmate discipline, self-defense, use of firearms, and searching for contraband. While this program was accompanied by the expectation that psychologists will engage in custody-oriented activities, often a clear ethical conflict, new staff were as well prepared as correctional staff to face prison conduct (Clingempeel, Mulvey, & Peppucci, 1980).

2. *Focus on general information and preparation.* Anxieties about beginning a job in a correctional institution may be expressed in a multitude of small but worrisome questions that can be answered during a first orientation contact or with a supervisor, ranging from appropriate dress to concern about security lapses. An orientation packet that outlines this information (and is mailed out to a new employee) can go a long way toward easing the anxiety that accompanies a new job in such an alien setting. Shortly after being hired, a new worker learns how and where to sit in an interview room with a resident, how to end a session when uncomfortable, and how to identify behavioral signs of building rage and potential violence. No one truly expects the new employee to arrive on site knowing how these procedures are handled in a specific facility.

Acknowledge and allow initial anxieties and concerns. It is normal to be anxious about beginning work in a new setting; when that setting is a correctional facility, one's own concerns may be heightened by well-meaning friends and family expressing concern about your safety. "How close are the correctional officers?" "Is there a panic button under your foot?" In reality, these concerns serve a function as they heighten vigilance and monitoring, important in learning about this setting. Over time, a desensitization occurs and the initially startling sounds, sights, and experiences become a part of the everyday montage.

3. *Reading as preparation.* Readings on inmate culture and the impact of incarceration can help practitioners understand the cultural context of correctional facilities. These should be read with the understanding that each institution is unique, so such readings are considered an exposure to the general milieu and experience of incarceration and not as a guide to the specific dynamics of an individual

institution. A list of suggested books is given at the end of this chapter.

4. Consider wise and planful use of supervision. Practitioners who are new to correctional settings may be intimidated by the setting and initially act quite dependent on their supervisors (Norton, 1990). Such practitioners may need particular assistance in the following areas: (1) identifying skills that may not easily transfer to this setting without some modification, such as empathy, unconditional regard, and exploring unconscious impulses; (2) maintaining boundaries between self and client, in particular, how to avoid manipulation; and (3) identifying intervention methods that are more likely to be effective with this population (Norton, 1990). Opportunities for cofacilitation of groups and individual sessions are particularly valuable in helping practitioners make the transition to this setting.

Once social workers move beyond the initial adjustment to work in a correctional setting, a second important supervisory task involves helping practitioners achieve a balanced perspective about the clients' capacity for change. There is a danger that practitioners will become quickly discouraged, feeling that the possibilities of change are too small in this challenging population (Norton, 1990). As supervision progresses, more detailed content related to correctional social work is naturally provided concerning issues such as the role the social worker plays in parole hearings, misconduct reviews, and practice and intervention in specialty areas of the prison (e.g., protective custody, mental observation units, and segregated punitive housing) (Norton, 1990). Supervision also can assist with managing the stress of working in an environment with "walls and . . . razor wire" (Norton, 1990, p. 18).

CONCLUSIONS

The need for social workers in correctional settings increases as we incarcerate ever-growing numbers of offenders. The increasing incidence of severe and terminal physical illness, mental disorder, developmental delay, and severe substance abuse problems among those incarcerated makes this need even more pressing. Practice in correctional settings can provide rich and challenging clinical experience and professional opportunities for social workers prepared

to enter these institutions. Presently, however, few schools of social work offer academic coursework or an organized fieldwork curriculum on practice in correctional settings. Consequently, emerging social workers and faculty alike are likely unfamiliar and may be uncomfortable with choosing or promoting correctional employment. Our experience suggest that planned and thoughtful preparation for the realities and exigencies of these settings can positively affect social workers' understanding, expectations, and ability to carry out effective practice in these settings.

REFERENCES

Barker, R. L. (1995). *The social work dictionary.* Washington, D.C.: NASW Press.

Brennan, T. P. , Gedric, A.E., Jacoby, S. E., Tardy, M. J., & Tyson, K. B. (1986). Forensic social work: Practice and vision. *Social Work, 67*(6), 340–350.

Clingempeel, W. G., Mulvey, E., & Peppucci, N. D. (1980). A national study of ethical dilemmas of psychologists in the criminal justice system. In J. Monahan (Ed.), *Who is the client?* (pp. 126–153). Washington, D.C.: American Psychological Association Press.

Cox, J. F., McCarty, D. W., Landsberg, G., & Paravati, M. P. (1988). A model for crisis intervention services within local jails. *International Journal of Law and Psychiatry, 11*(4), 391–407.

Cox, J. F., & Morchauser, P. (1993). Community forensic initiatives in New York State. *Innovations in Research in Clinical Service, Community Support and Rehabilitation, 2,* 29–38.

Ditton, P. M. (1999). *Mental health and treatment of inmates and probationers: Bureau of Justice Statistics special report.* Washington, D.C.: U.S. Department of Justice.

Federal Bureau of Prisons. (1986). *Introduction to correctional techniques.* Washington, D.C.: U.S. Department of Justice.

Gambrill, E. (1999). Evidenced-based practice: An alternative to authority-based practice. *Families in Society, 80* (4), 341–350.

Hayes, L. M. (2001). Jail suicide risk despite denial (or: When actions speak louder than words): 21st column in a series. *The Journal of Crisis Intervention and Suicide Prevention, 22*(1), 7–9.

Lieter, V. (1993). Special analysis of data from the OJJDP Conditions of Confinement Study. Washington, D.C.: Office of Juvenile Justice and Delinquency Prevention.

Mullen, E. J. (1983). Personal practice models. In A. Rosenblatt & D. Waldfogel (Eds.), *Handbook of clinical social work.* San Francisco: Jossey-Bass.

Needleman, C. (1997). Conflicting philosophies of juvenile justice. In A. R. Roberts (Ed.), *Social work in juvenile and criminal justice settings* (2nd. ed., pp. 215–223). Springfield, IL: Charles C Thomas.

Needleman, C., & Needleman, M. L. (1997). Social work with juvenile offenders. In A. R. Roberts (Ed.), *Social work in juvenile and criminal justice settings* (2nd. ed., pp. 224–248). Springfield, IL: Charles C Thomas.

Nelson, S. H., & Berger, V. F. (1988). Current issues in state mental health forensic programs. *Bulletin of the American Academy of Psychiatry and Law, 16*, 67–75.

Nevers, D., Piliavin, I., Schneck, D., & Henderson, M. (March, 1990). *Criminal justice and social work education: Lost opportunity for the profession and the client.* Paper presented at the Council on Social Work Education's Annual Program Meeting, Reno, Nevada.

Norton, S. C. (1990). Supervision needs of correctional mental health counselors. *Journal of Addictions and Offender Counseling, 1*, 13–19.

Rapp-Paglicci, L. A. (Ed.). (2005). Juvenile offenders and mental illness. Special issue: *Journal of Evidence-Based Social Work, 2*(3/4).

Roberts, A. (1997). The history and role of social work in law enforcement. In A.R. Roberts (Ed.), *Social work in juvenile and criminal justice settings* (2nd. ed., pp. 105–115). Springfield, IL: Charles C Thomas.

Roberts, A., & Brownell, P. (1999). Century of forensic social work: Bridging the past to the present. *Social Work, 44*(4), 359–369.

Severson, M. (1994). Adapting social work values to the corrections environment. *Social Work, 39*, 451–456.

Sheafor, B. W., & Jenkins, L. E. (1982). *Quality field instruction in social work: Program development and maintenance.* New York: Longman.

Sickman, M. (2004). *Census of juveniles in residential placement report.* Washington, D.C.: National Center for Juvenile Justice.

Stone, A. A. (2002). Supreme Court decision raises new ethical questions for psychiatry. *Psychiatric Times, 29*(9). Retrieved online: www.psychiatrictimes.com/p020901b. html.

Sykes, G. M. (1965). *The society of captives: A study of a maximum security prison.* Princeton, NJ: Princeton University Press.

Umbreit. M. S. (1993). Crime victims and offenders in mediation: An emerging area of social work practice. *Social Work, 38*, 69–73.

U.S. Department of Justice. (2003). *Census of State and Correctional Facilities, 2000.* Washington, D.C.: Office of Justice Programs.

VandeCreek, L., & Knapp, S. (1993). *Tarasoff and beyond: Legal and clinical considerations in the treatment of life-endangering patients* (2nd ed.). Sarasota, FL: Professional Resource Press.

Walmsley, R. (2003). Global incarceration and prison trends. *Forum on Crime and Society, 3*(1/2), 65–78.

Weinberger, L. E., & Sreenivasan, S. (1994). Ethical and professional conflicts in correctional psychology. Professional psychology: *Research and practice, 25*, 161–167.

PREPARING FOR PRACTICE IN CORRECTIONAL SETTINGS

Suggested Readings

Giallombardo, R. (1966). *Society of women: A study of a womens' prison.* NY: John Wiley & Sons. Qualitative research on a women's prison and inmate culture of "family" and "kinship" relationships. Although this is out of print you can often track down used copies.

Harris, J. (1988). *They always call us ladies: Stories from prison.* NY: Charles Scribner's Sons. Jean Harris's account of her experience in a women's prison. She includes a history of Bedford Hills prison, the stories of some other inmates, and her experiences caring for the children of inmates.

Ivanoff, A., Blythe, B. J. & Tripodi, T. (1994). *Involuntary clients in social work practice: A research-based approach.* Hawthorne, NY: Aldine de Gruyter.

Irwin, J. (1970). *The felon.* Los Angeles, CA: University of California Press. Qualitative research on a large sample of male inmates that covers the experience of imprisonment, doing time, re-entry to society and the parole experience. Also see Irwin, J. (1985). *The jail: Managing the underclass in American society* (Berkeley: University of California Press) and Irwin, J., & Austin, J. (1993). *It's about time: America's imprisonment binge* (Belmont, CA: Wadsworth).

Manocchio, A. J., & Dunn, J. (1970). *The time game: Two views of prison.* Beverly Hills, CA: Sage Publications. Two contrasting accounts, that of a male and his counselor, of an inmate's incarceration and of life and work in prison.

Pollock-Byrne, J. M. (1990). *Women, prison, and crime.* Pacific Grove, CA: Brooks/Cole. Excellent overview of female criminality, prisonization and contrast between female and male facilities. Well documented and an interesting, easy read.

Rooney, R. H. (1992). *Strategies for work with involuntary clients.* New York: Columbia University Press.

Sykes, G. M. (1985). *The society of captives: A study of a maximum security prison.* Princeton, NJ: Princeton University Press. A classic study of the pains of imprisonment and roles in the male inmate culture.

Chapter 27

Female Offenders and the Criminal Justice System

Patricia Brownell, Keva M. Miller and Martha L. Raimon

INTRODUCTION

Forensic social workers who serve women in prison must possess a comprehensive understanding of the complicated and multifaceted issues women offenders face within the criminal justice system. In addition, forensic social workers need to acquire knowledge about state and federal policies that affect sentencing and child welfare issues; the psychological and emotional implications of imprisonment; and programs and services geared toward helping incarcerated women and their families cope during the incarceration period. A broad and specialized knowledge base enables forensic social workers to address difficulties women encounter upon entry in the criminal justice system, while in the correctional system, and the process of reentry into society.

This conceptualization reflects the operational definition of the policy and practice realms of forensic social work with juvenile and adult offenders (Roberts & Brownell, 1999). As Barker (1995) notes, "forensic social work is the practice specialty that focuses on the law and educating law professionals about social welfare issues and social workers about the legal aspects of their objectives" (p. 140). Forensic social work has its roots in nineteenth century charity work: Jane Addams, founder of Hull House, served as the first woman president of the National Conference of Charities and Corrections, which was formed in 1897 (Roberts & Brownell, 1999).

In this chapter, attention is given to issues such as domestic violence, substance abuse, and entitlements for female offenders' families. Emphasis is placed on reentry as it relates to reconnecting with children, other family members, and successful reintegration into the community. Moreover, suggestions concerning issues that forensic social workers should consider when in search of evidence-based interventions are provided. These include direct service provision, collaborative efforts with interdisciplinary teams, and advocacy on behalf of female offenders and their families.

SCOPE OF THE PROBLEM

There is a paucity of research and practice literature on the consequences prison has on women and their families. In recent years, however, there has been a concerted effort to learn more about female offenders and associated issues that affect them while they are incarcerated and once released. This increased interest in female offenders can be attributed to the changes in prison demographics. Women historically have represented a small portion of the United States incarcerated population. In 1970, approximately 5,635 women were in federal and state prisons. However, this trend is rapidly changing as women are the fastest growing population in the correctional system (Seifert & Pimlott, 2001). Since 1986, the rate of female incarceration has increased by 400 percent. According to a recent government report, in 2004, the number of incarcerated women in federal and state prisons increased by 4 percent from the year 2003, which was more than double the 1.8 percent increase in the men's prison population (U.S. Department of Justice, 2005). Currently it is estimated that 90,000 to 100,000 women are in federal and state prison across the country (Enders et al., 2005; Ruiz, 2002).

It is well documented that minorities are disproportionately represented in the prison population. Women of color, particularly African American and Latina women, make up a disproportionate share of women sentenced to prison in this country. Approximately two-thirds of women offenders confined in jails and prisons are minority – black, Hispanic, and races other than white. While the rate of incarceration of women has increased 400 percent since 1986, it has increased 800 percent in the same time period for African American women. Nearly half of the women in prison have never been married, yet seven in 10 women under correctional supervision have children under the age of 18. Although the majority of women involved in the criminal justice system have at least a high school education, they have generally had difficulty within educational systems prior to incarceration. Only about one in four women in state prison reported that they had been employed full time prior to their arrest. Many incarcerated women lived in impoverished communities and about 30 percent reported receiving public assistance prior to their arrest (Greenfeld & Snell, 1999). Women offenders in prison are, on average, older than men by almost three years. An estimated 62 percent of violent female offenders had a prior relationship with their victims such as a marriage, prior marriage, some form of intimate relationship, or friendship. Of victims murdered by women offenders, almost 44 percent were spouses, former spouses, and nonmarital intimates (Greenfeld & Snell, 1999).

Several issues have contributed to the burgeoning number of women entering the correctional system and the changing demographics of the female incarcerated population. In the early 1980s, the concern for public safety and overall discontentment with the United States' correctional system became highly publicized (Gartner & Kruttschnitt, 2004). Ideologies and theories concerning crime and how to punish criminal offenders spurred a tough stance on crime. Efforts to rehabilitate offenders were replaced with punitive alternatives such as longer prison terms, automatic life sentences for a third felony conviction, and abolishment of federal parole. These issues, among many others, affect the way forensic social workers provide services to this population.

LITERATURE REVIEW

How women enter the criminal justice system has implications for their sentencing; whether they are sentenced to an alternative to incarceration (ATI) program that incorporates treatment either in the

community or a treatment facility, or to jail or prison; and their reentry to the community postincarceration. For forensic social workers, understanding the pathways by which women enter the criminal justice system, as well as incarceration and reentry issues for female offenders, are critical to effective service delivery for them and their families.

Pathways to Prison for Women Offenders

Pathways to prison for female offenders are affected by legislative policies, programmatic alternatives, and sociodemographic characteristics. Following is a discussion of legislative policies, as well as social problems like substance abuse and domestic violence related homicides and other felony crimes committed by battered women against their perpetrators, all of which create differential pathways to incarceration of women offenders.

Legislative Policies that Affect Female Offenders in the Criminal Justice System

Federal and state policies such as the Federal Sentencing Reform Act of 1984, the Adoption and Safe Families Act of 1997, and the Personal Responsibility and Work Opportunity Reconciliation Act of 1996, title I, Temporary Assistance for Needy Families, (P. L. 104–193), have had a significant impact on female offenders and their families. These policies, along with a public outcry for tougher sentencing, have changed the ways in which female offenders are sentenced and have placed profound burdens on children and their caregivers.

FEDERAL GUIDELINES AND SENTENCING. The Sentencing Reform Act of 1984 was enacted to increase uniformity and proportionality in federal judicial sentencing while maintaining general deterrence, incapacitation, and rehabilitation among offenders (United States Sentencing Commission, 1991). Prior to its passage, there was concern that unwarranted sentencing disparities occurred among federal court judges. Many believed that the sentencing disparities were either the result of intentional or unconscious biases against minority offenders. Individuals from impoverished minority communities were said to receive consistently longer prison sentences. Imposing sentences based on race, class, and gender are the clearest forms of unwarranted disparity and discrimination (Hofer et al., 1999). The law requires that variations in sentences be limited to the seriousness of the crime and the danger the defendant poses to society.

The Act attempted to rectify sentence discrepancies through maximum and mandatory minimum sentencing guidelines. The sentencing criteria were based on the nature and seriousness of the crime, the statutory purposes for sentencing, and relevant defendant characteristics such as prior convictions and level of remorse demonstrated (United States Sentencing Commission, 2004). A system of downward departure was implemented to permit judges to *depart* from the sentencing guidelines if there were "significant and extenuating circumstances" presented in the case. The implementation of federal guidelines appeared to be a well-intentioned and laudable goal among policy makers. However, the unintended consequences of sentence reform did not become apparent until several years after the guidelines were put into practice.

Gabrielle S. is a Hispanic 32-year-old single mother of three daughters, ages eleven, five, and three years old. Her youngest daughter, who has a developmental disability, requires supervision around the clock. Three years ago, Gabrielle was arrested for distribution of three grams of cocaine. One year later, she pled guilty to distribution of cocaine and faced 16 to 20 months of incarceration according to the Federal Sentencing Guidelines. Gabrielle's estranged mother refused to allow Gabrielle's children to live with her during Gabrielle's incarceration. Gabrielle does not have other relatives to care for her children. The presiding judge over Gabrielle's case noted that she had no prior record, was attempting to improve her family's quality of life by attending college courses, was holding a part-time job, and was her children's primary caregiver. The judge decided to take all of these circumstances into consideration and granted Gabrielle a downward departure from the Federal Guidelines' applicable sentencing range. Gabrielle was sentenced to five years probation and fined $10,000. The state appealed the downward departure, citing that "family responsibilities" were irrelevant and did not reflect extraordinary circumstances sufficient to invoke a downward departure. The court ruled in favor of

the state on the basis that custodial issues are not grounds for a downward departure. Further, the court found that the children would be appropriately placed in the care of child protective services.

CONSEQUENCES OF THE FEDERAL GUIDELINES. By most accounts, the federal sentencing created a system of disarray. After the implementation of the guidelines, many criminal justice experts, including federal judges, began to oppose mandatory sentencing and advocate for the removal of the rigid guidelines. They argued that the Act curtailed the federal judges' discretion and gave undue power to prosecuting attorneys. The increase in the women's prison population occurred during the years of mandatory sentencing. Despite Congress' effort to end racial disparity through sentencing guidelines, the federal guidelines appeared to create further inequalities and discrimination (Bushway & Piehl, 2001). Women of color in particular were increasingly being sentenced to long mandatory minimum sentences. The Sentencing Commission (1991) reported that their review of the data indicated that the guidelines had not been successful in preventing disparate applications of mandatory minimum sentences. The Commission found that minorities were less likely to benefit from a downward departure and escape mandatory minimum sentences.

Women often commit low-level drug-related offenses, which under the guidelines carried severe mandatory minimum sentences regardless of their level of culpability. Many women are required to serve the entirety of their sentence as a consequence of Congress abolishing parole and decreasing the maximum sentence reduction for good behavior. Women offenders usually have less leverage to plea bargain than men because they are generally unable to provide prosecutors with significant information about higher level drug offenders (American Civil Liberties Union, 2005). Consequently, most women have less ability than men to satisfactorily plea bargain for a reduced sentence. Under the federal guidelines the judges had virtually no discretion to consider a parent's family responsibilities. Instead, the guidelines required that judges take a gender-neutral stance in imposing sentences.

NEW ERA IN FEDERAL SENTENCING. In January, 2005, the United States Supreme Court struck down the 20-year policy in mandatory federal sentencing in a narrow five to four decision (Families Against Mandatory Minimums, 2005). The decision allows judges to use the guidelines as advisory. Under the new advisory federal guidelines there is greater opportunity for defense attorneys to present their client's mitigating circumstances that may help defendants receive proportional and fair sentencing (American Civil Liberties Union, 2005). Although the guidelines are currently advisory, many are cautiously optimistic that the new policy will effectively combat crime and provide an unbiased approach to punishment. There is concern that the flexibility in sentencing will create untenable inconsistencies in sentencing across jurisdictions. The implications of the Supreme Court's decision to allow greater judicial discretion are uncertain. There are women still serving time under the old sentencing framework, and the new guidelines do not affect these sentences.

Incarcerated Women Substance Abusers

Karen B. is a 28-year-old African American woman detained in a municipal jail on a misdemeanor charge. Because of a history of multiple arrests, Karen is likely to be sentenced to a maximum of nine months in jail. She has a history of prostitution and heroin addiction dating from early adolescence. Karen's mother was also a prostitute and brought men home with her. Karen recalls that when she was as young as five years old, she and her older sister were instructed on numerous occasions to steal from the customers while her mother worked. Karen dropped out of school and began abusing drugs and prostituting by 12 years old.

Karen began using heroin with the father of her third child. Her youngest child tested positive for the drug as a newborn three months ago. Her four children were removed as a result of a neglect petition filed by the state. Once Karen lost custody of her children, her public assistance case was closed, and she began to prostitute more frequently to support her drug habit. In the past five years, she has been hospitalized three times for beatings from clients and her boyfriend/pimp, and she has several scars on her body. Karen has no vocational skills, no permanent address, and does not know the status of her children in foster care or with what agency they have been placed. She expresses

fear about continuing her present life once released from prison and interest in a drug rehabilitation program. She also talks about trying to contact her children but does not know how to go about doing this. Overall, she expresses pessimism about her future and does not believe that there are options available to her for changing her life.

Substance abuse is a growing problem among women prisoners and drug-related crimes in particular contributed to the rise in the female prison population. Between 1986 and 2000, the number of women incarcerated for offenses involving drugs has risen by 888 percent (American Civil Liberties Union, 2005). In 1989 more than one in three women inmates was jailed for drug-related offenses, up from one in eight in 1983. As of 1993, 34 percent of women in jail were serving time for drug offenses (National Women's Law Center, 1993). Currently about half of women offenders in state prisons reported using drugs, alcohol, or both at the time of their arrest, and drug use was reported more than alcohol use (Greenfeld & Snell, 1999).

Incarcerated Battered Women Who Killed their Perpetrators

Bureau of Justice Statistics reports as well as other studies (Daly & Wilson, 1988) found that in the majority of partner homicides committed by women, the women perpetrators have been battered prior to the homicide event. Researchers like Browne (1987) found that women who killed their partners had experienced a greater frequency of violence and sexual assaults in their relationships, sustained more injuries, and received more death threats than women who received services for domestic violence but did not kill their batterers. Posttraumatic stress disorder was found to be prevalent in a sample of women incarcerated for killing their partners, as compared with a sample of women incarcerated for other reasons (O'Keefe, 1998).

Special Populations

Domestic Violence and History of Child Abuse

Carol J. is a 20-year-old-Caucasian-woman and single mother of an eight month old son. She admits that her biggest mistake was becoming involved with her boyfriend. He was only two years her senior but had an extensive juvenile record and one four-year stay in state prison for cocaine possession. Carol's boyfriend was emotionally and physically abusive, constantly threatening to harm her and her son. The night of her arrest, Carol was the driver of the "getaway" car for her boyfriend and his two friends after they burglarized two homes. Carol had no prior criminal record, held a stable job as an administrative assistant, and was a victim of domestic violence. Regardless, she was sentenced to seven years in state prison for participating in the burglary. Since Carol's sentencing three months ago, her son has been shuffled among relatives' homes. She lost custody of her son when she became incarcerated. Relatives are willing to assume responsibility for him to prevent a nonrelative foster care placement and would like for Carol to have the opportunity to care for him once she returns. The county public child welfare office cannot authorize financial assistance to caregiving relatives because the child is not in a formal kinship foster care placement. Carol's family is unable to provide adequate financial support for her son and is fearful that they may have to seek formal services kinship care arrangements.

In addition to the problems of poverty, substance abuse and communicable diseases presented by women inmates, they also often have a history of childhood or adult abuse, perpetrated by a family member or significant other. According to research by the National Women's Law Center (1993), 41 percent of women in prison and 44 percent of women in jail had either been physically or sexually assaulted at some point during their lifetime prior to incarceration. A later government report indicated that approximately 60 percent of all women prisoners were abused at least once in their lives (Greenfeld & Snell, 1999). Researchers estimate that the number of female victims of domestic violence incarcerated for killing their batters ranges from 800 to 2,000 (National Clearinghouse for the Defense of Battered Women, 1992). However, women who commit violent crimes against a domestic partner often have no prior criminal record, pose little further danger to society,

and are less likely to recidivate than other offenders (Women in Prison Project, 2004).

Older Women Offenders

As the number of women in prison has increased, the number of older incarcerated women has increased as well (Reviere & Young, 2004). In addition, while still relatively small, the number of elderly prisoners (55 years and older) has significantly increased and women are the fastest growing subset of the prison population (Women in Prison Project, 2005). While more research is needed on older women prisoners (Kerbs, 2000), some information is available based on small studies. In one study by Kratcoski and Babb (1990), twice as many older women compared with older men stated that they never had visitors.

While Kratcoski and Babb found that older female offenders lacked support systems both within and outside prison, and experienced a stronger sense of isolation than older men, they also found that older incarcerated women were twice as likely to report diseases like heart, lung, and degenerative diseases. This supports other findings of geriatric inmates that they experienced difficulties with activities of daily living (ADLs) and experienced one or more chronic health conditions, with older women prisoners reporting more health concerns (Legal Services for Prisoners with Children, n.d.). Pierson (2001) notes that older women prisoners may suffer from poor nutrition as prison food may not take into consideration their special nutritional needs, resulting in chronic diseases such as heart disease, high blood pressure, diabetes, osteoporosis, and atherosclerosis.

Pregnant and Parenting Incarcerated Women

Many incarcerated women are either mothers or expecting mothers. Sixty-four percent of mothers in state prisons and 84 percent in federal prisons reported living with their children prior to incarceration (Women In Prison Project, 2004). Approximately 25 percent of women entering prison are either pregnant or delivered a child within the year of their incarceration (Seifert & Pimlott, 2001). Forensic social workers do not necessarily narrow their focus solely on the female offender, as her family system is intricately involved in her functioning during and after the incarceration period.

The Impact of Maternal Incarceration on Families

The Department of Justice's Bureau of Justice Statistics thoroughly documented the statistics on parental incarceration in a report issued in 2000 (Mumola, 2002). According to the report, most prisoners are parents of minor children. Among women in state prison, two-thirds were living with their children prior to their incarceration as compared with one half of men in state prison (Mumola, 2002). Of parents in federal prison, 55 percent of fathers and 84 percent of mothers were living with their children before their incarceration (Mumola, 2002). Most telling, approximately 80 percent of the mothers who lived with their children prior to their incarceration were single parents (Genty, 2003; Mumola, 2002).

The numbers of families affected by parental incarceration have risen dramatically in the last decade due to the increase in the numbers of women in prison. The number of children with an incarcerated mother almost doubled in that time frame, from 64,000 in 1991 to 126,000 in 1999. Race is an undeniable factor in these calculations: one out of every 14 African American children had at least one parent in prison in 1999, whereas for all children the figure was only 2 percent. African American and Hispanic children are nearly nine and three times more likely respectively to have a parent in state or federal prison than their Caucasian counterparts (Mumola, 2000).

A man's incarceration can result in mild to moderate family tensions while on average a women's incarceration can have a significant impact on a family. The impact of a women's imprisonment is of particular significance when child placement issues are a factor. Unlike male offenders, women are generally the sole caregivers of their children at some point in a child's life, if not immediately prior to incarceration. Children of incarcerated mothers are more likely than noncustodial male parents to experience the trauma of mother-child separation as a result of maternal incarceration (Poehlmann, 2005). Many children of incarcerated mothers are vulnerable to multiple ephemeral placements when their mothers are incarcerated as they are often shuttled to grandparents, other relatives, friends, or placed in the foster care system. The separation that occurs when a parent is incarcerated too often leads to a permanent and irreversible rift of an otherwise intact family system.

Challenges to family permanency when women with dependent children are incarcerated have increased in recent years as a result of new federal legislation relating to foster care placements. As the rate of incarceration of women increases, so too does the rate of dislocation of their children. Statistics, however, mask the real suffering of these families. A generation of children is at risk for experiencing trauma of unparalleled proportions: the trauma of mother-child separation as a result of maternal incarceration. The affect of this renting falls most strongly upon children, but is also felt by mothers, other caregivers, and communities.

NUMBERS OF CHILDREN AFFECTED. Notably, neither the foster care system nor the criminal justice system keeps reliable data on the number of incarcerated parents with children in foster care in this country. The Mumola Report suggests that 10 percent of mothers and 2 percent of fathers in state prison had children in foster care (Mumola, 2002). Many experts believe this number to be low, particularly because parents reporting living arrangements with kin may not be accounting for foster care status (Farmer, 2005). The Center for Children of Incarcerated Parents conducted a study in 1998 intended to measure the numbers of children with a currently incarcerated parent and the numbers of children who had ever experienced parental incarceration (Genty, 2003; Johnston, 1999). The study found that 70 percent of the children had had a parent incarcerated at some point while they were in foster care (Johnston, 1999).

TIME AND DISTANCE. Time and distance play key roles in determining the longevity of a family system when a parent, particularly a mother, is incarcerated (Genty, 2003). As is previously discussed in this chapter, the increasing severity of sentences makes it probable that children of incarcerated parents will be separated from their parents for considerable portions of their childhoods. The average time served for mothers in state prisons is four years; however, for mothers in federal prison, the average is five and one half years (Mumola, 2002). Incarceration alone would be a significant barrier to maintaining family ties, but the fact that most women's facilities are a day's journey from where their families live creates additional, often insurmountable burdens.

One obvious burden imposed by distance is the difficulty it creates for children to visit their mothers. Experts have long opined about the importance of visits to the well-being of children of incarcerated parents (Johnston, 1995). Yet, according to the Mumola report, only half of incarcerated parents in state prisons see their children (Mumola, 2002). The other 50 percent of incarcerated parents report infrequent visits or no visits from their children (Seymour, 1998). Some of this is due to lack of transportation and geographical proximity. It is difficult for caregivers to arrange visits when parents are in prisons hundreds of miles from where their children reside. Over 50 percent of state inmates and 40 percent of federal inmates live between 100 and 500 miles from their children and 43 percent of federal inmates live more than 500 miles from their children (Mumola, 2000). Prison policies, and/or the fragile relationships of caregivers to their kin in prison, and their attitudes about children's visits to prisons may also prevent visits.

Visits play a critical role in whether mothers maintain their legal rights to their children while incarcerated (Ross et al., 2004). A judge may look askance at returning a child to a mother who has not parented her child for years, even from behind bars. For a mother with a child in foster care, lack of visits is the trigger to a termination of parental rights proceeding and the permanent severing of her legal relationship with her child.

ADDRESSING THE NEED. Anecdotal evidence suggests improved outcomes for families affected by maternal incarceration when advocates facilitate communication between the incarcerated mother and outside agencies. There are a limited number of programs attempting to provide services to incarcerated mothers with children in foster care at risk of termination. Chicago Legal Advocacy for Incarcerated Mothers provides legal and educational services to mothers to help them maintain contact with their children. The Incarcerated Mothers Program (IMP) of Edwin Gould Services for Children and Families seeks to prevent foster care placement by assisting women and their children during and after the time of arrest, court, jail, sentencing, and return to the community (Fernandez, 2005). In New York, the Women's Prison Association and Home, Inc. (WPA) collaborates with Volunteers of Legal Service, Inc.

(VOLS) to assist incarcerated mothers with legal issues relating to custody and visitation. The Incarcerated Mother's Law Project (IMLP) also makes connections with other service providers for formerly incarcerated women who are attempting reunification (Women's Prison Association and Home, Inc., 2005).

Effects of Child Welfare Policies on Incarcerated Women and Their Families

In November of 1997, President Clinton signed into law (P.L. 105–89) the Adoption and Safe Families Act of 1997 (ASFA). This new law modified the Adoption Assistance and Child Welfare Act (P.L. 96–272) in significant ways and created a sea change in the practice of child welfare across the country. In the intervening years, a storm of activity has taken place with ASFA provisions as its central purpose. Foster care agencies, social workers, lawyers, family courts and litigants have had to make adjustments to practice to meet the demands of this sweeping legislation. For families involved simultaneously in the foster care and criminal justice systems, ASFA has meant coming to terms with an exceedingly high risk of the permanent loss of parental rights.

ASFA requires all families with children in foster care to negotiate a new time frame. Now, with limited exceptions, termination of parental rights proceedings must be filed if a child has been in foster care for 15 of the most recent 22 months. Given the average length of women's sentences discussed above, and the fact that many mothers lose custody of their children prior to arrest as a result of substance abuse, most incarcerated mothers with children in foster care are at extremely high risk of permanently losing rights to their children.

However, ASFA provides exceptions to an otherwise tight time frame, although states hold varying interpretations of those exceptions. The legislation provides guidelines to child welfare workers to determine what is considered "reasonable effort" to have custody remanded to the biological parent. If a child is placed with a relative, the state, through its child protective agency, may make a determination not to move toward termination. If the state can document compelling reasons why termination is *not* in the child's best interest, it is not required to proceed with the termination. In these limited instances, agencies can instead maintain status quo, modify placement decisions, or reunite the family. This is a complex and nuanced statute, not one ready made for bureaucracies to manage. Its intention, clearly stated, is that foster care agencies make calculated, meaningful case by case decisions about which families merit special status. Agencies, as part of their statutory duty to provide reunification services to families, are charged with making these critical decisions. Yet, the question arises as to whether the intensions of ASFA truly benefit children and families.

THE CHALLENGES OF ASFA. An agency worker typically does not have much information to rely upon in making a decision as to whether to terminate the rights of an incarcerated mother. Practical realities intrude: phone calls are difficult to make and return, visits are logistically difficult and sometimes impossible due to distance and the entrenched bureaucracy of corrections, services inside exist but are hard to assess. Without a lawyer to argue for services on her behalf during the period her case is not reviewed in court, a mother's ability to challenge decisions is compromised (Raimon, 2001). Foster care caseworkers hampered by caseloads may fail to form relationships with incarcerated mothers and their families the same way that they form relationships with families on the outside. When a family becomes nothing more than a case file, a caseworker cannot make meaningful assessments as to whether to file a termination petition.

Children who have parents in the correctional system and need out-of-home care face unique challenges regarding temporary and permanency planning. Criteria are particularly difficult to adhere to if individuals are serving long prison sentences. Society tends to have a bias against children reuniting with their imprisoned parents. This bias is clearly reflected in the ASFA legislation such that there are few specific guidelines to meet the criteria of making reasonable efforts for imprisoned parents (Smith, 2000). Even if a parent is released from prison within a year of his/her arrest and/or incarceration, he/she may not have gone through the necessary rehabilitative process required by either the correctional and/or child welfare systems.

Financial Implications of Female Incarceration

Many women who enter the criminal justice system are single parents and the sole provider for their

families prior to their incarceration (Reed & Reed, 1997). Thus, there is a foreboding economic impact on the family left behind. Even in situations where the woman is struggling to meet her family's needs, the change in family composition is economically devastating. When women go to prison, there is a high probability that their children are vulnerable to being placed in relatives' homes where there already exist economic strain (Miller, in press). The new addition increases the financial strain to overburdened families that often encounter barriers to the receipt of public assistance such as Temporary Assistance for Needy Families (Young & Smith, 2000).

ADDRESSING THE NEED. Temporary Assistance to Needy Families or TANF (P. L. 104–193, Title I), the income assistance block grant for indigent families with dependent children, is available for children of incarcerated parents who are living with relatives in informal care giving situations. These children may be eligible for child-only cash grants and Medicaid, even though the relative caregivers are not TANF eligible themselves. While county Department of Social Services (DSS) employees may not be familiar with the state regulations that define eligibility for child-only TANF cases, relatives caring for children of incarcerated parents may apply for and obtain benefits for these children. There are no federal time limits on TANF benefits for child-only cases (Mullen, 2000).

Reentry Issues for Women Transitioning from Prison to the Community

When the Personal Responsibility and Work Reconciliation Act of 1996 (P. L. 104–193) was enacted in 1996, title I (Temporary Assistance to Needy Families) included Section 115. This placed a lifetime ban on TANF and food stamp benefits for otherwise eligible indigent parents of dependent children if they had been convicted of a drug-related felony. The federal provision allowed states the choice to opt out of or modify the ban on TANF applicants with histories of drug-related felonies when they passed state welfare reform acts. To date, 34 states and the District of Columbia have eliminated or modified this ban. However, over 92,000 women are currently affected by the ban and 135,000 children are at risk of losing family stability due to reduced family income. Of the seven states that implemented the ban in part or full, women of color represent the majority of women subject to the law (Allard, 2002).

PRACTICAL INFORMATION

Recommendations for Finding Treatments

Clinical social work, including counseling models that reflect an empowerment orientation, have been proposed as appropriate interventions for incarcerated female offenders. According to van Wormer (2001), motivational interviewing (also see chapter 25) and narrative therapy can be effectively incorporated into a five-stage, empowerment counseling model that includes dialogue, development of awareness and future goals, motivational and feeling work, cognitive therapeutic approaches and anxiety, and anger and stress management techniques. These techniques could be useful in helping women adapt to incarceration and effectively reintegrate into their families and communities once they are released. The techniques learned from these therapeutic approaches can be used to address underlying issues that contributed to a woman's incarceration.

As suggested in a recent American Civil Liberty Union report, issues such as addiction to controlled substances, the trauma associated with domestic violence, and mental illness are linked to drug crimes perpetrated by female offenders (American Civil Liberties Union, 2005). The ACLU report recommends that individuals working with female offenders take a close look at the underlying causes of women's involvement in drug-related crimes. A forensic social worker's role may be to help a female offender explore emotional and other related issues that are inextricably connected to the offense. Exploration and resolution of these issues are crucial to help prevent recidivism. Consideration to potential underlying causes for a woman's incarceration may include:

- addiction to substances;
- psychological impairment;
- domestic violence;
- trauma associated with childhood physical, emotional, or sexual abuse;
- low self-esteem; and
- poverty and related issues.

Another important task for the forensic social worker to consider when working with female offenders is to determine to what extent the selected treatments have demonstrated empirical support for effectiveness in practice settings. As the forensic social worker surveys literature and examines treatment manuals, she must determine whether the interventions she is considering are appropriate to the population for which she is providing services. For example, a treatment addressing issues related to drug and alcohol dependence may have demonstrated effectiveness; however, under closer investigation, the social worker may realize that outcome studies are limited to Caucasian women. Consequently, the chosen treatment may not be one of the most effective among the female African American and/or Latina offender population. In addition to examining the empirical evidence, a forensic social worker must consider whether the intervention addresses the real needs of the female offender.

CSAT (Kassebaum, 1999) provides recommendations for tailoring treatment for female offenders, with the aim to provide the most effective service delivery system possible (see Table 27-1).

Recommendations for Working Systemically with Incarcerated Women, their Children, and Caregivers

An interdisciplinary approach to practice includes social workers who provide services within a criminal justice setting. Appropriate intervention plans are twofold to address both issues of mother-child bonding, and expectations and preparation of reentry into the family system and society.

Many prison-based programs focus on visits alone. There is a lack of attention to the entire family system. Decisions surrounding visits should be based on a thorough understanding of the dynamics of the parent and children's right to visits. Additionally, the needs of the caregiver should be taken into account. Caregivers are often neglected in the visiting process and they are at times confused as to how to handle the emotional fall-out children experience prior to and proceeding visits. Caregivers are often left without supports themselves to handle their own emotional struggles related to a family member's incarceration and the extra responsibility of caring for their children. The goal of an integrative and comprehensive approach is to provide services that include briefing

Table 27-1
TEN RECOMMENDATIONS FOR TAILORING TREATMENT
FOR FEMALE OFFENDERS

1. **Each woman should receive a thorough assessment of her needs that is female-specific and culturally relevant**. Very few instruments exist that are specific for women or even women-focused. The important issue is to be aware that the assessment needs to be comprehensive and to include domains that are particularly relevant to women. Appropriate instruments, as woman-focused as possible, should be used to obtain a complete criminal history; medical history; history of substance abuse; physical, emotional, and sexual abuse history; psychological history; and educational level.

2. **While a woman is incarcerated, a treatment team should do an in-depth assessment to identify the range of her medical, substance abuse, criminal justice, and psychosocial problems and develop an individualized treatment plan**. That plan should address all the needs identified in the assessment, including homelessness. Treatment services should begin in the institution.

3. **Each woman should be tested for HIV/AIDS and be provided with pre- and posttest counseling** as appropriate to State law, regulations, and administrative guidelines. In prison and jail programs for women, HIV testing should be available. The women need to be educated about HIV and encouraged to undergo HIV/AIDS testing. Counseling should be provided for all women tested for HIV/AIDS.

4. **Medical care should be provided for the woman through formal arrangements with community-based health care facilities**. This care should include screening and treatment for infectious diseases, including sexually transmitted diseases and hepatitis, and immunizations. It should also include obstetrical and gynecological care, including prenatal obstetrical services for pregnant clients.

5. **Substance abuse education and counseling, psychological counseling (where appropriate), and other women-specific and culturally appropriate therapeutic activities should be provided throughout the continuum of care**. Services should be offered in the context of family and other interpersonal relationships, including individual, group, and family counseling. Counseling based on individualized treatment plans should be provided for women who have experienced physical, sexual, psychological, and emotional abuse and trauma. Counseling based on individualized treatment plans should also be provided for relapse prevention.

6. **Family planning counseling should be provided**. This needs to include information on prenatal care, birth control options, adoption, and education on perinatal transmission of HIV.

7. **Training in parenting skills should directly involve the mother-child dyad and, whenever possible, involve other family members**. Women in treatment should be permitted and encouraged to participate in programs for their children, such as Head Start and Parent and Child Centers that incorporate parent participation.

8. **Interagency agreements should be developed with relevant child welfare agencies** to address the needs of the children whose mothers are in local correctional facilities and to help make possible regular visits from children to the mothers who do not have custody of their children.

9. **Formal linkages should be established with community providers for provision of all necessary services**. The services should include basic needs of food, clothing, housing, finances; assistance in legal matters, family planning, and vocational/educational needs; transportation; health care; mental health services; and support services.

10. **Specialized services should be provided for the children of female offenders**. Children and other family members should be included in all levels of the services delivery network —in the continuum of prevention, treatment, and recovery. The program should provide therapeutic child care and child development services, including supervision of children while their mothers are engaged in treatment and other rehabilitative activities in the community.

Source: Kassebaum, P. A. (1999). *Substance abuse treatment for women offenders: Guide to promising practices* (DHHS Publication No. (SMA) 99-3303). Rockville, MD: U. S. Department of Health and Human Services, Substance Abuse and Mental Health Services Administration, Center for Substance Abuse Treatment.

the incarcerated mother and caregiver; preparing children for visits; helping facilitate visits; and debriefing mothers, caregivers, and children at the conclusion of the visits.

Prepping Tasks:
- *Prepare children for visits* – discuss any feelings, concerns, or expectations for the visit with their mother.
- *Prepare mother for visits* – discuss any feelings, concerns, or expectations of child's reactions to the meeting and explore mother's goals for the visit.
- *Prepare caregivers for visits* – discuss the potential reactions children may have after meeting with their mothers and explore what are normal emotional and behavioral reactions the children may exhibit at the conclusion of the visit.

Visiting Tasks:
- *Facilitate mother-child interactions*
- *Ensure concurrent facilitation of caregiver support groups*

Postvisit Processing Tasks:
- *Processing for the child* – debrief and explore emotional reactions to visits with their mother.
- *Processing for the mother* – debrief and explore emotional reactions to the visits with her children and reviewing what went well during the visit and what could have been improved upon for future visits.
- *Processing for the caregiver* – explore concerns about the child's reaction to the visit and explore preparedness for handling potential fall-out from the visits.

On-going services geared toward helping mother and children cope with the separation and aid in effective mother-child interactions must be readily available. These groups primarily focus on mother and children's groups that meet separately.

Additional Counseling for Individuals and/or Groups:
- Children support groups
- Incarcerated mothers support groups
- Incarcerated mother child development training
- Parent-child interaction training

Secondly, it is important that there be extensive planning with child welfare workers to prepare mother, caregiver, and child for reentry. New custodial arrangements

need to be discussed and organized among the forensic social worker, child welfare worker, and most importantly, the incarcerated mother.

Collaborative interdisciplinary services include:
- Identifying and fully explaining family law issues, including possible legal referrals
- Discussing children's functioning within the foster care system
- Reviewing issues regarding termination of parental rights
- Identifying referrals that may help women reenter family systems and the community

As a standard procedure, social workers should keep a log of client-worker interactions to systematically identify issues that emerge and how they are to be addressed. On a larger systemic level, forensic social workers should meet periodically with criminal justice and child welfare stakeholders to identify issues surrounding interdisciplinary collaboration and the perceived benefits, limitations, and effective strategies to address shared obstacles.

Operational programs like the Children of Incarcerated Parents (CHIPP), developed by New York City's Administration for Children's Service (NYC Administration for Children Services, 2005) assist incarcerated parents in understanding their rights and provide them with tools to act on those rights. These materials, disseminated to incarcerated mothers, remind them that they have the right to:

- know the reason her child is in foster care;
- identify family or others to explore as resources to care for children during her incarceration;
- be assigned an attorney to represent her in any Family Court proceeding involving foster care;
- know the name of her child's caseworker, her supervisor, and the name and address of the foster care agency;
- be kept informed of steps needed to reunite with her child;
- be provided with necessary reunification services;
- participate in her child's service plan and to receive a copy of the plan;
- be notified in advance of the date of the service plan meeting and participate in the meeting; and
- visit with her child in the absence of a court order to the contrary and participate in her child's visiting plan.

An incarcerated mother also requires assistance in keeping track of any contact she may have had with a caseworker or agency responsible for the care of her child. This is particularly important in the context of the Adoption and Safe Families Act. Tools can be developed that facilitate the documentation of vital information (NYC Administration of Children's Services, 2005). Tools may include information such as:

- Phone number called
- Date of call
- Name of person/agency called
- Message left
- Date of scheduled visit
- Date of actual visit or reason for missed visit
- Letter sent to whom, the date, and address
- Response date
- Name of person who responded.

CLINICAL OR LEGAL ISSUES

Forensic social workers working with mothers in prison and upon their release often work in isolation of the legal issues that they confront, even when those issues overlap family and community. Lawyers working with women in prison typically work without the benefit of social work expertise. This disconnect, so prevalent in other areas of the law, compounds an incarcerated mother's barriers to successful reintegration into society. A fundamental shift in practice would incorporate social workers into a mother's legal strategy. Social workers are uniquely qualified to address the social service issues that are raised in nearly every case having to do with an incarcerated parent, such as:

- What programs are appropriate for this parent?
- Is she in need of different or different quality services?
- Has each child received sufficient support during the separation?
- Is family counseling needed? When?
- Is reunification well timed or should it be completed on a different time frame?

Lawyers are ill-suited to answer these questions, yet by default, they are often in the untenable position of doing so without sufficient expertise. However, the social worker, for her part, must be prepared to address these issues and many more within a legal context. She must take into account every prevailing factor possible. For example, the forensic social worker must understand that the ramifications of waiting too long to move a child home may result in the termination of parental rights (TPR) proceeding. Additionally, referring a mother to a preventive service program may, due to mandatory reporting, risk a subsequent removal. The optimal situation is a collaborative response, comprised of social worker and lawyer, who, over time, craft a legal and social work strategy. This strategy should be governed by the client's expressed needs, which allows everyone to make the most meaningful decisions possible. This model is only beginning to be utilized as a means of maximizing best practices from each discipline.

DESCRIPTION OF INTERVENTIONS

Promoting Mother-Child Bonds

While visits between children and their incarcerated mothers have been identified as important in maintaining family bonds, one survey reported that 54 percent of mothers in state prisons stated they had never been visited by their children (San Francisco Partnership for Incarcerated Parents, 2003). The Children with Incarcerated Parents (CHIPP), operated by the New York City Administration for Children's Services, provides opportunities for foster care children to visit mothers who are incarcerated at Riker's Island jail. Social workers employed by the program provide counseling services to the children and their mothers (Gunn, 2004).

Training for custodial relatives of children with incarcerated parents is suggested as an intervention strategy by research on attachment relationships (Poehlmann, 2005). Children were found to adjust better to maternal incarceration when they were told about the incarceration in open and age-appropriate ways. While families may experience discomfort in discussing this with children, the confusion children experience when not told about their mothers' situation in a way they can understand may hinder their ability to integrate this experience emotionally and result in long-term relational impairments with their mothers and others.

Female offenders and their children also fare better when there is regular communication and face-to-face contact. Positive mother-child attachment is crucial for connection and essential for parents to assume their role in helping children deal with the daily issues they encounter throughout life. Therefore, select programs across the country are geared toward facilitating that process by offering mother-child visitation programs that help enhance relationships. One example includes the Girl Scouts Beyond Bars (GSBB) which was established by Maryland's Correctional Institution for Women in 1992 (Block & Potthast, 1998). New Jersey, South Carolina, Texas, and Washington are among many other states that have replicated the enhanced GSBB program.

The GSBB program builds on attachment theoretical concepts that an affectional secure bond with a parent can further enhance emotional and behavioral development. The program provides opportunities for female offenders and their daughters to build and enhance their relationships, and encourages and facilitates visits, which have shown to decrease the stress of mother-child separation and help mothers reduce anxiety about postincarceration reunification with children. An impact assessment of the program indicated that those children who participated in the group visited their mother 64 percent, 11.6 times a year, versus children in the control group at a rate of 49 percent, 6.1 times a year. Preliminary research has shown that the program is moderately successful in increasing both mothers' and daughters' self-esteem. Mothers also feel better about their abilities to provide parental support during the incarceration period.

Reentry Programs

Innovative reentry programs in localities like New York City have focused on reuniting female offenders transitioning from jail or prison, often with a history of substance abuse, with their children and into the community. The Albert and Mildred Dreitzer Women and Children's Center is a facility that supports the reintegration of formerly incarcerated women with substance abuse problems into the community through both transitional and permanent housing combined with substance abuse treatment, counseling, and child-focused programs like Early Head Start. The Sarah Powell Huntington House of the Women's Prison Association and Home, Inc. is a model shelter program that provides intensive case management to mothers with a goal of reunification who have been involved in the criminal justice system.

Successful reintegration of female offenders in the community and reunification with their children may depend on the availability of public benefits and entitlements like TANF, Medicaid, and food stamps. The 1996 federal welfare law (Personal Responsibility and Work Opportunity Reconciliation Act – P.L. 104–193) includes a clause barring anyone with a drug-related felony from receiving these benefits. For reentry programs to be beneficial and effective, social work advocates for incarcerated women and their children must develop coalitions with other advocacy groups to work with state legislatures to seek waivers to these provisions.

SUMMARY AND CONCLUSION

The increase in rate of incarceration for women raises significant challenges for professional social workers, lawyers, and legal advocates in recent years. Federal legislation, like the most recent sentencing laws, the Personal Responsibility and Work Opportunity Reconciliation Act, and the Adoption and Safe Families Act, provide both opportunities and limitations to family-focused interventions that benefit women in the criminal justice system and their children. As suggested in this chapter, it is critical for forensic social workers as well as the advocacy community to keep abreast of the legislative changes, both enacted and pending. Service plans and interventions must incorporate findings from current research into the social demographics of women who enter the criminal justice system. These findings must also play a more prominent role in creating effective clinical and programmatic interventions to promote successful reentry into the community and reunification with family and children.

REFERENCES

Allard, P. (2002). *Life sentences: Denying welfare benefits to women convicted of drug felonies*. Washington, D.C.: The Sentencing Project.

Barker, R. L. (1995). *The social work dictionary*. Washington, D.C.: NASW Press.

American Civil Liberties Union. (2005). *Caught in the net: The impact of drug policies on women and families*. American

Civil Liberties Union, Break the Chains: Communities of Color and the War on Drugs, and Brennan Center for Justice at New York University, New York, NY.

Block, K. J., & Potthast, M. J. (1998). Girl scouts behind bars: Facilitating parent-child contact in correctional settings. *Child Welfare, 77*(5), 561–578.

Browne, A. (1987). *When battered women kill.* New York: Macmillan.

Bushway, S. D., & Piehl, A. M. (2001). Judging judicial discretion: Legal factors and racial discrimination in sentencing. *Law and Society Review, 35*(4), 733–764.

Daly, M., & Wilson, M. (1988). *Homicide.* New York: Aldine de Gruyter.

Danzy, N., & Jackson, S. M. (1997). Family preservation and support services: A missed opportunity for kinship care. *Child Welfare, 76,* 31–44.

Enders, S. R., Paterniti, D. A., & Meyers, F. J. (2005). An approach to develop effective health care decision making for women in prison. *Journal of Palliative Medicine, 8*(2), 432–439.

Families Against Mandatory Minimums. (2005). *Understanding Booker and Fanfan: Federal sentencing guidelines are advisory but mandatory minimum sentences still stand.* Retrieved October 28, 2005, from http://www.famm.org/index2.htm.

Farmer, A. (2005). Mothers in prison losing all parental rights. *Women's eNews,* June 21, 2005.

Fernandez, L. (2005). *The forgotten children.* New York: NASW. Retrieved October 28, 2005, from http://www.nycnasw.org/TheForgottenChildren.htm.

Gartner, R., & Kruttschnitt, C. (2004). A brief history of doing time: The California institution for women in the 1960s and the 1990s. *Law & Society Review, 38*(2), 267–304.

Genty, P. M. (2003). Damage to family relationships as a collateral consequence of parental incarceration. *Fordham Urban Law Journal, 30,* 1671–1672.

Gunn, A. (2004). Separation of incarcerated mother from child: The impact on childhood development and the call for greater clinical and policy interventions. *Advocates' Forum,* 52–62.

Hofer, P. J., Blackwell, K. R., & Ruback, R. B. (1999). The effect of the federal sentencing guidelines on inter-judge sentencing disparity. *Journal of Criminal Law & Criminology, 90*(1), 239–322.

Johnston, D. (1999). Children of criminal offenders and foster care. *Family and Corrections Network Report,* October, 1999.

Johnston, D. (1995). Effects of parental incarceration. In K. Gabel & D. Johnston (Eds.), *Children of incarcerated parents* (pp. 59–88). New York: Lexington Books.

Kassebaum, P. A. (1999). *Substance abuse treatment for women offenders: Guide to promising practices* (DHHS Publication No. (SMA) 99–3303). Rockville, MD: U.S. Department of Health and Human Services, Substance Abuse and Mental Health Services Administration, Center for Substance Abuse Treatment.

Kerbs, J. J. (2000). The older prisoner: Social, psychological, and medical considerations. In M. B. Rothman, B. D. Dunlop & P. Entzel, (Eds.), *Elders, crime, and the criminal justice system: Myths, perceptions, and reality in the 21st century.* New York: Springer.

Kratcoski, P. C., & Babb, S. (1990). Adjustment of older inmates: An analysis of institutional structure and gender. *Journal of Contemporary Criminal Justice, 6*(4), 264–281.

Legal Services for Prisoners with Children. (n.d.). *Elderly prisoner health care campaign.* Retrieved October 10, 2005. from http://www.prisonerswithchildren.org/news/elderprisoners.html.

Miller, K. M. (in press). Risk and resilience among African American children of incarcerated parents. *Journal of Human Behavior in the Social Environment, 13*(1/2).

Mullen, F. (2000). Grandparents and welfare reform. In C. B. Coz (Ed.), *To grandmother's house we go and stay: Perspectives on custodial grandparents* (pp. 113–131). New York: Springer.

Mumola, C. J. (2000). *Bureau of Justice Statistics bulletin: Incarcerated parents and their children.* Washington, D.C.: U.S. Department of Justice.

Mumola, C. (2002). *Special report: Incarcerated parents and their children.* Washington, D.C.: U.S. Department of Justice, Bureau of Justice Statistics.

New York City Administration for Children's Services. (2005). *Out of sight, not out of mind: Important information for incarcerated parents whose children are in foster care.* New York: Administration for Children's Services, New York.

O'Keefe, M. (1998). Posttraumatic stress disorder among incarcerated battered women: A comparison of battered women who killed their abuser and those incarcerated for other offenses. *Journal of Traumatic Stress, 11*(1), 71–85.

Palladia: Programs/Residential Treatment the Albert and Mildren Dreitzer Women+Children's Center. Retrieved September 29, 2005 from http://www.palladiainc.org.

Pierson, C. (2001). *Legal corner: Growing old in prison – what will it mean?* California Coalition for Women Prisoners: The Fire Inside, 17. Retrieved October 10, 2005 from http://www.womenprisoners.org/fire/ooo212.html.

Poehlmann, J. (2005). Representations of attachment relationships in children of incarcerated mothers. *Child Development, 76*(3), 679–696.

Raimon, M. L. (2001). Barriers to achieving justice for incarcerated parents. *Fordham Law Review, 70,* 243.

Reed, D. F., & Reed, E. L. (1997). Children of incarcerated parents. *Social Justice, 24*(3), 152–170.

Reviere, R., & Young, V. D. (2004). Aging behind bars: Health care for older female inmates. *Journal of Women and Aging, 16*(1/2), 55–69.

Roberts, A. R., & Brownell, P. (1999). A century of forensic social work: Bridging the past to the present. *Social Work, 44*(4), 359–369.

Ross, T. (2004). *Hard data on hard times: An empirical analysis of maternal incarceration, foster care, and incarceration.* New York: Vera Institute of Justice.

Ruiz, D. S. (2002). The increase incarcerations among women and its impact on grandmother caregivers: Some racial considerations – statistical data included. *Journal of Sociology and Social Welfare, 29*(3), 179–198.

San Francisco Partnership for Incarcerated Parents. (2003). *Children of incarcerated parents: A Bill of Rights.* Stockton, CA: Friends Outside.

Seifert, K., & Pimlott, S. (2001). Improving pregnancy outcome during imprisonment: A model residential care program. *Social Work, 46*(2), 125–134.

Seymour, C. B. (1998). Children with parents in prison: Child welfare policy, program, and practice issues. *Child Welfare, 77*(5), 460–493.

Simmons, C. W. (2000). *Children of incarcerated parents.* California Bureau Research Reports. Retrieved October 25, 2003 from http://www.fcnetwork.org/reading/simmons.html.

Smith, G. T. (2000). The adoption and safe families act of 1997: Its impact on prisoner mothers and their children. *Women, Girls, & Criminal Justice, 1*(1).

Greenfeld, L. A., & Snell, T. L. (1999). *Women offenders.* Washington, D.C.: U.S. Department of Justice, Bureau of Justice Statistics, NCJ 175688

United States Department of Justice. (2005). *Prison statistics.* Washington, D.C.: Bureau of Justice Statistics Retrieved October 25, 2005, from http://www.ojp.usdoj.gov/bjs/prisons.htm.

United States Sentencing Commission. (1991). *Special report to the Congress: Mandatory minimum penalties in the federal criminal justice system.*

United States Sentencing Commission. (2004). *Guidelines manual.* Washington D.C.: Office of Publishing and Public Affairs. Retrieved August 11, 2005 from http://www.ussc.gov/2004guid/gl2004.pdf.

van Wormer, K. (2001). *Counseling female offenders and victims: A strengths-restorative approach.* New York: Springer.

Women in Prison Project. (2004). *Coalition for women in prison: Proposal for reform.*

Women in Prison Project. (2005). *Why focus on incarcerated women?* Retrieved October 10, 2005, from http://www.correctionalassociation.org.

Women's Prison Association. (2005). *Family support services.* Retrieved October 25, 2005, from http://www.wpaonline.org/services/support.htm.

Young, D. S., & Smith, C. J. (2000). When moms are incarcerated: The needs of children, mothers, and caregivers. *The Journal of Contemporary Human Services, 81*(2), 130–141.

RELEVANT RESOURCES FOR PRACTITIONERS

1. Women's Prison Association – helps women with reentry needs and discharge planning, www.wpaonline. org.
2. Volunteers of Legal Services (VOLS) – provides pro bono civil legal services to incarcerated women in the New York City area, www.volsprobono.org/.
3. Chicago Legal Advocacy for Incarcerated Mothers (CLAIM) – offers legal and educational services to help maintain bonds between incarcerated mothers and their children. CLAIM also advocates for programs and policies that are advantageous for incarcerated women, www.claim-il.org.
4. American Civil Liberties Union (ACLU) – The Brennan Center for Justice Report is a resource that addresses the multiple issues women in prison encounter. There is a specific focus on drug policies and how they impact women's sentencing and incarceration terms, www.fairlaws4families.org.
5. Edwin Gould Services for Children and Families – www.egscf.org.
6. American Association of Retired Persons (AARP) – AARP has a special section on their website dedicated to supporting grandparents who are raising their grandchildren, www.aarp.org/families/grandparents/.
7. Video of Troop 1500. Their mothers may be convicted thieves, murderers, and drug dealers, but the girls of Troop 1500 want to be doctors, social workers, and marine biologists. Meeting once a month at Hilltop Prison in Gatesville, Texas, this innovative Girl Scout program brings daughters together with their inmate mothers, offering them a chance to rebuild their broken relationships. Intimately involved with the troop for several years, the directors took their cameras far beyond meetings to explore the painful context of broken families. Powerful insight comes from interviews shot by the girls themselves, which reveal their conflicted feelings of anger and joy, abandonment and intimacy as well as the deep influence their mothers still have on the girls. Troop 1500 poignantly reveals how an inspired yet controversial effort by the 90+ year old Girl Scouts Organization is working to help these at-risk young girls deal with their unique circumstances and break the cycle of crime within families, http://www. mobilusmedia.com/.

Chapter **28**

Social Work within a Maximum Security Setting

David Showalter and Marian Hunsinger

Residents of our penitentiaries are individuals who most often come from low socioeconomic backgrounds. They are usually poorly educated, many times not having completed high school. There is a disproportionately high number of inmates from minority groups such as blacks, Chicanos, and Indians. Many times, they are unskilled and have little or no hope of obtaining adequate employment. Many come from broken homes, while a significant proportion were abused as children. Most inmates have a relatively low self-concept and many emotional problems. The majority have probably abused drugs or alcohol consistently. Generally, inmates have little trust or respect for their fellow human beings. They usually possess poor social and communication skills. In essence, our prisons are full of people extremely short on resources and long on problems.

Working within the walls of a prison challenges the staff with a very tough double bind. On one hand, the employee is forced to work in a negative and restrictive environment. On the other hand, the employee is forced to work with clients with severe problems who are in the institution against their will. The worker must face overwhelming problems with very few resources available to improve the environment or to provide alternatives to their clients. Working in an environment under constant conflict with strong forces pulling in opposite directions, the worker is faced with the difficult task of maintaining his or her own emotional stability. Failure to handle the stress in a positive manner will result in a burnout for the worker. The worker then would become one more negative factor in an already negative situation. The authors contend that social work is an excellent profession to effectively cope with the various problems and stress of working in a prison. First, social workers are trained to study the effects of environment. The well-trained social worker can then develop a realistic plan for changing the environment or help the client develop more effective skills to cope with the environment. Second, the social worker is trained to analyze the individual and make an assessment of the behavior and attitudes creating problems. The social worker, through clinical treatment, helps the client recognize his or her problems and develop a more effective pattern of behavior and attitudes. Third, the social worker is trained to develop a high level of self-awareness. This is extremely important in being able to cope with the problems and stress of working in a prison. The social worker should have an advantage over most professions in recognizing his or her own stress when it reaches a high level. The worker also has the knowledge and training to be able to choose a positive method to cope with the stress and tension. The result can be an individual effectively functioning under high stress while members of other professions are burning out.

In recommending social workers as employees for prisons, the authors would like to point out that we have in mind individuals trained at an accredited school of social work. The authors feel that a bachelor of social work is the minimum amount of formal training necessary to meet the advantages we have outlined for social workers. There is no way to ensure that individuals without the formal degree will have had access to the knowledge and skills necessary for functioning effectively in a prison. Working within a prison is a challenge that social workers need to look at more seriously. It could possibly open up a new field of employment for social workers at a time when many positions are being cut. A real challenge is provided for individual social workers who appreciate the rewards of successfully meeting a challenge. Within this chapter the authors hope to provide information that will help the reader understand the role and function a social worker can fill in a prison setting. We also hope to identify some of the special problems facing social workers within the correctional institution. Perhaps this information will enable some social workers to make the decision to seek employment in a prison setting.

SOCIAL WORKER AS THERAPIST

Perhaps one of the most important and, at the same time, toughest roles a social worker can fill is that of therapist. As pointed out in other parts of this chapter, the issues of confidentiality and a security role provide tough double binds for the social worker. This makes the role of therapist even more difficult. Both of these issues affect the trust that the inmate is willing to offer the therapist. If the inmate believes the social worker will break the confidentiality bond or if the inmate perceives that the social worker is acting in a strong security role, the inmate will refuse to trust the social worker. Thus, one of the very essential elements of the therapeutic relationship is lost from the very beginning.

One of the most important foundations of social work is the idea of client self-determination. The concepts involve the idea that the more an individual can accomplish for himself, the more confident an individual will become in his own abilities to handle problems and responsibility. The concept also involves recognition of the right of an individual to decide his own fate.

Incarceration within a prison provides barriers to an inmate being able to use self-determination. The inmate is allowed very little responsibility. Instead, the whole environment is one that encourages dependency. The reason for this is obvious. It is essential that order and control be maintained within a prison so that escapes and people being hurt are kept to a minimum. There are many rules and regulation that govern the inmate's daily life. He is told when to eat, when to lock up, etc. Jobs are assigned to him that usually do not keep him busy and do not involve much skill. There are usually very few activities and recreation from which he can choose. In short, being

in prison takes away the individual's right to decide many things and offers few choices for those decisions that are allowed.

A second major barrier to client self-determination is the inmate himself. A large number of inmates are very angry individuals who tend to blame families, friends, society, police, courts, and prison officials for their problems. Many of the reasons for their anger are legitimate such as abuse as a child, discrimination because of minority status, miscarriage of justice, lack of educational or employment opportunities, etc. However, there are many instances in which the problems are magnified out of proportion or are nonexistent. In any case, it is very scary for these inmates to be presented with the idea that they are responsible for their decisions and actions. It is much easier to focus blame and responsibility elsewhere besides self. This gets in the way of the individual's growth and development. In fact, it is highly likely that until an inmate is willing to accept responsibility for his actions and decisions, he will be unable to adjust successfully to society.

Following a policy of client self-determination is essential if a social worker is to function effectively. The client must come to understand that even within the rigid confines of a prison he can determine some of the direction for his life. Since the inmate may very well blame others for his actions and situation, it is likely to be very difficult. Learning to make choices about his life in prison can help him understand that a person can usually make choices concerning his life if he is willing. This is an important step for the client. He can learn to gain control over his life by accepting responsibility for himself. The social worker will have to be creative and imaginative to help the client find ways to follow a course of self-determination. However, if the social worker is willing to look, he or she will be able to find several issues over which the client can have control. The key is to make sure that the issues are realistic, within the bounds of prison rules, and within the capacity of the client. Most importantly, the issues must have value for the client. The following is a case example in which a social worker helps an inmate develop a new perspective. The power of the new perspective enables the client to improve his personal relationships and helps him to develop a sense of self-responsibility.

The inmate in this case is a short black man who is thirty years of age. Presently this man is serving his second term in a maximum security prison. His present sentence is five years for robbery. He had earned his living while in society by pimping. His women friends would support him by selling their sexual favors or by getting a job and giving him their paycheck. The inmate will be referred to hereafter as Sam.

Sam sought help from the social worker because he was bitter, resentful, and fearful of the direction his life had taken so far. He tended to blame his father and the criminal justice system for the problems he had in life. The immediate crisis that prompted him to seek help was the fact that one of his girlfriends had just given birth to his first child. Parenthood struck him hard. He started seriously thinking about marrying the woman, we will call her Nancy, and settling down to raise a family. From his perspective, the problem was that Nancy wanted little to do with him. She visited only a few times and usually did not answer his letters. She had been one of the women who had supported him by working and prostitution. It was quite evident from her behavior since his incarceration that she had ambivalent feelings about him at best. Counseling during the first few months focused on trying to help him resolve the relationship. During this period of time, other important facts came to light. Sam was extremely tired of his life-style and of having to serve time in prison. As he put it, "I am getting older and there is no retirement plan for people with my life-style. Either people die young in my life-style, spend most of their lives in prison, or end up friendless and penniless." Another important piece of information was that he held women in contempt. He viewed them as robots that he could get to do anything he wanted. He bragged that he chose his girlfriends young and trained them to think and act as he desired. He states that he did not believe they could think on their own. He had no respect for them as people.

After a couple of months, it became very clear that the relationship with Nancy would not work out. She refused to visit, write, or come in for a counseling session. During this period of time, the social worker had attempted to help Sam realize his attitude toward women and behavior toward Nancy had probably helped create her unwillingness to get back under his control once she had escaped as a result of his incarceration. Sam resisted this idea very strongly.

During a counseling session Sam asked the social worker, a male, what a woman's perspective on his problem might be. The social worker suggested that Sam might be able to discuss the problem with a female social worker on staff. Sam's immediate reaction was one of surprise and fear. He made it very clear that in no way did he want to talk with the female social worker directly. The male social worker confronted him about his fear. After a considerable amount of confrontation mixed with encouragement and support, Sam was able to admit that he was scared of women who were not under his control. Sam admitted that he had never felt accepted by women and was afraid of rejection. He had solved his problem in several ways. First, he was the first to reject a woman before she had a chance to reject him. Second, he only chose to be around women with very low self-esteem and who were very dependent upon their men. Third, he became involved with his girlfriends when they were young and taught them to be dependent on him. Sam admitted being too scared to even talk with a woman if she was independent and self-assured. The social worker pointed out that this perspective of women was unhealthy, which by now Sam was able to admit. Sam informed the social worker that one of the reasons he wanted to maintain his relationship with Nancy was because she was somewhat more independent than the others, for which he respected her. This is probably the reason she was able to maintain her distance once she was able to establish it. Soon thereafter, Sam was able to decide that he wanted to change the way he thought about women and related to them. He set a goal for himself to be able to think of women and treat them with respect.

Sam has made very positive progress toward this goal through therapy. He is now able to carry on a normal conversation with self-assured women. He no longer encourages women to send him money, nor does he lead them on with promises of a permanent relationship when he gets out of prison. Instead, he asks women to write or visit as friends and clearly lets them know the only thing he can offer or wants is friendship. This behavior is new for Sam but has been very rewarding. He feels more self-confident and does not fear rejection as much. He hopes that upon his release he will be able to establish a relationship with a woman independent enough to be a partner for him instead of his being the dominant one.

This particular issue has been an important turning point for Sam. It helped him realize that even while in prison he can determine what direction some of the important issues of his life will take. Sam has made several positive changes. He is trying to develop good work habits, something he never had. Sam is now the inmate leader of a small group of prisoners who are seeking ways to improve their lives with the aid of an outside social worker. Finally, Sam is developing a positive attitude toward life. He is learning that he can control his own destiny even while in prison if he is willing to take responsibility for himself and make what positive choices are available to him.

From their training and experience, social workers understand the importance of environment and significant others in the life of their clients. This knowledge can be very useful in a penitentiary. The inmate's family is very important to him because it is the only thing of value in his life. It represents his hopes for the future. Since the family is so important to the inmate, it can be used as a lure to help encourage the inmate to seek treatment. Unfortunately, for many reasons, family counseling is not widely practiced in prisons. This problem is discussed in an article entitled "Marital and Family Counseling in Prison" in the May 1980 issue of the journal *Social Work* (Showalter & Jones, 1980).

Social workers employed within a prison could have a positive influence on this problem. They could use their knowledge to encourage prison administrators to pursue a policy of supporting marriage and family counseling. In the California Corrections System, Norman Holt and Donald Miller found strong evidence that family support helped inmates do their time with fewer rule violations and increased changes for successful completion of parole (Holt & Miller, 1972). There certainly are indications that such a policy could be of benefit to the inmate and to the prison.

Following is a case example of how a social worker successfully used marriage and family counseling within a prison. Names are fictitious.

Ralph is a twenty-six-year-old white male serving a long sentence for murder. His father had served time in prison when he was young. Ralph is married with three young children. He had served time before on drug charges.

Ralph approached the social worker for help when he found his wife had gone on a vacation to another state with his uncle. He was afraid of sexual involvement and was thinking seriously of divorcing his wife. The social worker suggested that he get his wife to come in for a counseling session. Ralph agreed and was able to convince Kathy, his wife, to come in. The first couple of sessions were exploratory in nature, and several serious problems were identified. First, Kathy had been very dependent on Ralph when he was free and let him make all of the decisions. Now that he was locked up, she resented him trying to control her life by demanding she stay home all the time and care for the kids. She denied doing anything wrong by taking a vacation. Second, Ralph had a strong need to retain his control over Kathy and his children. He was unable to express trust for her. Third, Ralph's mother was creating problems for Kathy, interfering with the way she raised the children. Ralph supported his mother over Kathy. Fourth, Adam, the oldest child at eight, was starting to demonstrate behavior problems and refused to obey Kathy. Fifth, Ralph had gotten Kathy into legal trouble by having her bring drugs to him when he was in jail. She was on probation. Counseling sessions were set up and continued over several months. There was significant success but also a rather dramatic failure. One of the approaches used by the social worker was to help Kathy develop a more positive self-image. The social worker used assertiveness training to help Kathy learn to stand up to Ralph for her rights. There was a failure in that against her better judgment she let Ralph persuade her to smuggle money into him during visits. She got caught and the marriage counseling sessions had to be stopped as a result.

However, there were a number of successes as a result of these counseling sessions. First, Ralph decided not to pursue a divorce. Second, Ralph learned not to try to exercise so much control over Kathy's life. He learned to trust her to go out and have fun. Third, Kathy did learn to speak up to Ralph about her rights on many important issues even though she failed on the one. Fourth, Ralph learned to support Kathy when his mother began to interfere. Fifth, Ralph was able to explain to Adam why he was in jail and help his son recognize that he was still loved. Both Ralph and Kathy were able to recognize Adam's problems as being serious, and Kathy took him to a private therapist. Ralph learned not to put so many financial demands on Kathy, since she was struggling to support the family. Seventh, Kathy learned to start looking for new interests for herself. Presently, she is going to school to study to be a nurse. Finally, Ralph was able to adjust to serving his time better. He is creating fewer problems for the prison administration because he is more content.

Minority groups are vastly overrepresented in our prisons by population. There is a far higher percentage of them in prison population than in society. Each minority group has a somewhat different culture, customs, and values than the general society, sometimes including a language difference, as is the case with many Hispanics. There is strong evidence that their overrepresentation in prison is partly due to these differences. The minority inmates must try to cope with a system designed to meet the minimum needs of a white Anglo-Saxon group. On the other hand, prison administrators must try to make their system flexible and endeavor to meet some of the needs of the minority population without adequate funds or resources. There are many harsh double binds for both groups.

The social worker can be useful in this situation, as he or she is taught to be sensitive to the various minority group members' needs. First, the worker can provide emotional support for his or her minority clients and treat their values and beliefs with respect. Second, the worker can help his or her clients rationally explore what legitimate avenues there are to pursue their customs and values. Third, the social worker can work toward helping the overworked prison administration to be more sensitive to the various minority groups' needs. Many times, the administrator may be insensitive unknowingly or unintentionally.

STRENGTHENING SUPPORT SYSTEMS

Acceptable social support systems are often a weak area in the life of an inmate. Family and marital relationships may be tenuous. Trust or confidence in social service agencies can be nonexistent. Their use of friends as a support system has often been in a negative direction. Even their criminal support system, i.e., "inmates stick together" or "honor among thieves," is proved over and over again to be unreliable. Thus, the social worker needs to work with the inmate to strengthen the support he does have and develop support in other areas he has never used.

Marital relationships can be one of the best support systems an inmate has going for himself. However, many factors of incarceration work at weakening this bond. The greatest assistance toward strengthening this tie will come from the treatment staff. One such program developed at Kansas State Penitentiary is called "A Marriage Workshop." Approximately fourteen hours of a single weekend are devoted to individual couple and small group work with inmates and their spouses. Specific time is given to learning and evaluating good communication skills. emphasis is placed on problem-solving techniques and the opportunity for each couple to pick a specific problem and work through it in the presence of a therapist.

A committed effort is necessary to sustain a healthy relationship. Some couples try to ignore the fact that incarceration makes a change in their relationship. New problems have developed because of the separation. The inmate, for the most part, has no chance to provide financial support. Old problems have possibly intensified. If trusting each other was a problem in the past, this new arrangement will exploit that condition. If the wife was too dependent, it is a rude jolt to now be in charge, and if she was independent, circumstances will force her to capitalize on that quality. If these matters are not dealt with, the partnership will deteriorate to an empty shell and divorce will probably result. This is a common occurrence for a number of inmates. For those who continue their marriage, it is useful to consider the changes brought on by incarceration before they get paroled and are overwhelmed by them on their release.

One couple who participated in the workshop had a special problem. Ted was arrested the same day Sue had their only baby. Consequently, he had never lived at home anytime in the four years of the child's life. Ted would soon be eligible for parole and back living with the family. Special attention had to be given to the possible problems that might arise. Normal conflicts in family building were discussed as well as some signs and situations to be alert for as needing professional help. This opportunity for preparation gave the transition a better chance to succeed.

Sometimes the support most needed is the support to let a relationship end. An inmate, George, tried on two occasions, months apart, to set up weekly marriage counseling sessions for himself and his wife.

Both times the wife offered a few weak excuses why she could not make it to the sessions. The therapist was able to help George admit that the relationship was over, even though that was not the way he wanted it to be. While an inmate is incarcerated, his family is often seen as the most important thing to him and it is hard to relinquish that. George resisted handling his feelings of loss in a positive way. The therapist pointed out to him how damaging his anger and resentment could be, but he chose not to participate in individual counseling.

The normal support system of friends is often overlooked by inmates. The people they chose to believe or trust in the past have often had a negative influence on their life. Some decided they did not want any friends, as a means of avoiding being hurt in life. If they had a history of being abused as children, it is hard to open up to the idea that there is support that can come from people. Sometimes the social worker can use friends as a tool in therapy. Jim was an inmate who had successfully completed counseling. By mutual agreement, he sat in on a session with Bill who was having a hard time seeing the social worker as someone who wanted to help him instead of making his time harder. Jim and Bill had known each other on the street. Bill would listen to Jim and sought him out as a friend in prison. Likewise, when inmates work on the same job and develop a friendship, they can help each other in therapy by giving feedback on progress they see daily. Also, fellow group members can turn into friends. During therapy, an inmate can take a good look at the people he chose as friends in the past and discover some of the reasons why.

Another reason for friends as a support system was noted in an article written by Fred for the Lifer's Club magazine. Fred, halfway through for a parole eligibility on his life sentence, wrote:

> Any effort to develop friends, and constructive acquaintances, allows us to strengthen our ability to coexist with different types of individuals, (regardless of "where"), and also helps us to understand and cope with individualized attitudes and life cycles. These "prison formed" friendships are sometimes used for escape from physical attacks, i.e., the more "friends" an inmate has, the less likely he is to be physically abused, for fear of retribution from that inmate's friends. This is a very real faction of prison life, and "prison friendships," to be considered.

. . . friendships among inmates many times tend to be more closely knit, more open and honest, in the emotional sense, there are, in reality, no "secrets" about one's personal life in prison. Everyone knows, (or can easily find out if he so desires), where another inmate lives, where he works, whether or not he is interested in sports and what kind, whether or not he gambles, if he is an aggressive person; a multitude of personal facts are evident to all. Considering that these and many other subjects are openly known about other inmates – when one strikes up a friendship on the inside – personal high-lights of another's behavior and/or life style is apparent.

Most inmates distrust social service agencies. Even when they knew things were falling apart for themselves on the streets, they did not ask for help that might have prevented their incarceration. Either pride or distrust contributed to them missing out on available help. The social worker can do many things to change this for the future. Simple explanations of some known agencies help the inmate know some types of assistance is available. Assertiveness will teach an inmate how to ask with a good chance of receiving aid. Often, the inmate has now learned the value of therapy and will seek it on the streets to insure he maintains his freedom. If nothing else, the social worker has modeled what social services can do if given the opportunity.

ADVOCACY AND MOBILIZING RESOURCES

One of the key functions of a social worker is that of advocate. Sometimes his or her clients are trapped within a situation where they are unable to effectively speak for themselves. At these times social workers have stepped into the role of advocate and promoted their client's case.

In many instances the client is without adequate resources to meet his needs. The resources may be unavailable or the client may lack the influence that would enable him to obtain the services or material that he needs. In these cases, social workers have traditionally intervened for their clients to mobilize whatever resources were available. The social work intervention then enables the client to obtain services that will enable him to cope more effectively with his problems and start to make changes.

Within a prison setting, the inmates are without official power or influence. There is a very real scarcity of resources available for prisoners. The social work skills of advocacy and mobilization of resources can be essential for helping a client cope within a prison. Without social work intervention, the inmate may find himself in a powerless position without being able to find an effective way to cope. The social worker's intervention may provide the inmate with some hope for the future. Following is a case example of a social worker using such skills for inmates in a helpless position. The names are fictitious.

Don was a 28-year-old black man serving a mandatory 15-year sentence for murder. He was attacked by another inmate with a knife over a misunderstanding between the two of them. As a result of the attack, Don was completely paralyzed from the neck down. He had no feeling or movement in any of his limbs or the trunk of his body. Don was kept in the infirmary of the prison. He was fed by hand by the infirmary staff. His body waste was removed on a regular basis, and he was given daily sponge baths. Before the attack, Don was known as a self-reliant person who was happy and friendly. He was well liked by both inmates and staff. After the attack, he became very angry, withdrawn, bitter, and resentful. No matter how much attention the staff was able to pay him or what they did for him, Don continued to withdraw into himself.

Julia, one of the staff social workers, became aware of his situation after several weeks had passed. She went to the infirmary to talk with him, trying to find ways to be of help. He was very bitter and frightened about having to spend the rest of his life paralyzed and dependent upon others for his needs. He was deeply concerned that he still had five years to serve on his sentence with no chance for parole before then. He complained that he was developing bedsores because the staff did not have enough time to turn him over often enough. He also felt that his body waste was not being removed often enough. The most severe problem was simply that nobody was working with him to help him start learning how to cope with his feelings of being paralyzed.

Julia decided to work with Don to see how she could help improve his situation. First, she assured him that she would visit him regularly to let him discuss his feelings. She set up a schedule to visit with him three times a week for a half hour. Second, she talked with the infirmary to see if Don could be turned over more often and his body waste picked up more regularly. The infirmary was simply unable to make such a commitment because of staff and time shortages, although they were quite concerned about Don. Julia then approached several inmates who had been Don's friends before the attack. Don had ignored their attempts to be friendly since the attack. When Julia asked for their help, they were happy to volunteer.

She then asked the deputy director of the institution if the inmates could be allowed to work with Don. The deputy director approved the idea. Julia next discussed with Don the idea of letting his friends help him and convinced him to try it. A regular schedule was set up for Don's friends to visit with him, remove his body waste, turn him over, exercise his limbs, and feed him. This arrangement proved to be highly satisfactory. Don's physical needs received more than adequate attention. Don was able to start discussing his feelings with people that he felt cared. Over the months, he became less frightened and angry. He started learning to develop a more healthy and positive attitude toward himself.

After Julia had mobilized resources for Don, in this instance a number of friends to provide a support network for him, she turned to the more difficult issue of advocacy. She felt there would be no useful purpose for Don to spend another five years in his present position. The only possibility for early release would be a pardon from the governor. This is a very difficult process. Very few pardons are granted, and the process takes a lengthy amount of time. She contacted the governor's office and discussed the case with the pardon attorney. He encouraged her to pursue the case but told her the road would be difficult.

Julia spent six full months working on obtaining the pardon. The details are too complex to list here, but a summary of the accomplishments could help enlighten the reader on what a social worker can accomplish when determined. Julia had a full medical evaluation completed on Don by outside medical experts to provide proof of his total disability. She contacted his family and worked with them on forming a realistic plan to cope with Don if he were released. She contacted a nursing home and obtained their agreement to accept Don as a patient for several months. She acquired the agreement of a physical therapist to work with Don to try to rehabilitate his limbs to some degree. She contacted the vocational rehabilitation services and they agreed to pay for the nursing home and physical therapy.

Midway through this process, it was discovered that a detainer had been placed on Don from another state for a crime 10-years-old. The effect of the detainer would be that if Don received a pardon, he would be transferred to the new state to face charges there. This development was highly discouraging. Julia contacted the state and asked them to withdraw their detainer. The new state was reluctant to do so. The result was several weeks of negotiations in which Julia finally convinced the other state to withdraw their detainer. She accomplished this by first convincing them Don really was paralyzed and, second, pointing out that they would have to assume financial responsibility for him if they insisted upon keeping the detainer on him.

Don finally received a pardon and was released through the hard work of Julia. She was able to get him physical and emotional help while he was incarcerated. She was able to obtain a pardon through a very difficult and lengthy negotiations process. She enabled the family to develop realistic plans for his release, which included services from a nursing home and a physical therapist. Through her efforts, a detainer was removed that would have made the whole effort worthless. Finally, she was able to help Don start to come to grips with the fact that he was paralyzed for life. This was probably her biggest accomplishment, as Don was deeply withdrawn into himself when she first started working with him. This case illustrates very clearly the positive work a social worker can accomplish by applying knowledge and skills. Through the use of advocacy and mobilization of resources, Julia was able to manage a positive outcome for a case that seemed totally hopeless. A social worker was able to successfully manage this case when all other correction officials had given up hope.

SECURITY ROLE AND CONFIDENTIALITY

Security is the primary purpose of a penitentiary. This is a fact that a social worker employed within a prison setting must learn to cope with. The social worker must come to grips with the fact that security will get first consideration over treatment at all times out of necessity. Little can be accomplished by constantly fighting this concept. Much can be done if the social worker will adopt the idea of treatment being in a working relationship with security. The social worker needs to be security minded for his own safety and the appropriate operation of the institution.

One of the benefits of social workers to the operation of a penitentiary is that they can create and implement programs that may reduce some security problems. Most inmates need to learn good communication skills they can use in dealing with other inmates and civilian and security staff. Assertiveness training is an example of a program that can be helpful in teaching effective communication. Guards also can be taught this method of dealing with inmates to improve their interactions with these individuals. Inappropriate ways of handling anger cause many problems within the penitentiary. Learning how to handle feelings in a positive manner can make a difference in how inmates respond to anger and frustration. Drug and alcohol abuse is another common source of security problems. Many methods of counseling can be effective in helping inmates learn to reduce stress and tension and not need a chemical crutch. In this manner, social workers can make a significant contribution in the area of security. Programs that teach inmates to communicate effectively and cope with their feelings contribute to security because it helps reduce stress and tension.

These contributions of the social worker to the security force will be of an indirect nature. There must be a clear understanding on both sides that the treatment staff will not be a spy network for security use. Occasionally, the social worker will provide information to security, but that should not be a regular occurrence. The guard force may find out the same information that the social worker knows, but seldom should the source of that information be the social worker.

Basically, one of the requirements of any employee in a prison is to be an extension of the security force. In whatever capacity they have, caution and good sense is necessary for the reasonable functioning overall of the institution. The social worker must see that inmates do not misuse programs. If marriage counseling sessions are used for the spouse to smuggle in contraband to the inmate, those sessions must stop. The social worker can reinforce the essential premise of the institution that the inmate is responsible for his actions and that he is responsible for the consequences of his actions. During a marriage workshop, as described above, the social worker must be alert that it is not used as just extra visiting time or for unauthorized physical contact. In developing innovative programs, the security risks and needs should be openly dealt with. It is unrealistic to feel that nothing can happen, since the project is treatment oriented. The social worker can role model that reasonable rules can be followed and beneficial results obtained. Too often, inmates have a distorted view of rules and their value. This is another opportunity for the social worker to use the inmate's present situation as a teaching tool.

Confidentiality is an equally important factor that needs special emphasis in a penitentiary setting. Most inmates by nature do not trust authority or official people, and the social worker usually fits that definition. Consequently, the worker must make a special effort to establish trust and prove that confidentiality is possible and honored. As sometimes happens in relationships, there will be testing to see if the social worker backs up his or her word. That should be expected and handled with consideration.

The inmate has a right to expect that he can say things in confidence as a client and not be penalized. This helps build the clinical relationship that must be based on trust, openness, and honesty. For many, they are not used to admitting anything, thinking that will protect them. Consequently, the honesty demanded in therapy is frightening. It takes time to build up the trust level. Once offenders learn the liberating experience of honestly confronting themselves, therapy sessions may resemble a confessional and should be treated similarly.

Under certain circumstances, the security role of the social worker will require that the confidentiality bond be broken. Any information regarding an inmate planning to harm himself or another inmate or attempting to escape would be dealt with from a different point of view. The appropriate people must be notified, even though the information was gained in confidence. Here a social worker walks a tightrope between treatment and security. As an example, an inmate had been in therapy for several months. During a session, Tom mentioned that he had heard other inmates asking around the mess hall for contribution of packs of cigarettes to have a certain staff member killed. Although Tom admitted he did not like this staff member, he did not feel he should be killed. Tom was told by the social worker that this information would be passed on to the proper people but he would not be named as the source. If it became important for his name to be given, the social worker would discuss with Tom the reasons why that was necessary before proceeding to give Tom's name. Tom accepted this procedure and the therapeutic relationship continued.

As with most situations in life, there will be circumstances that do not fit neatly into categories of how to be handled. How does the social worker respond to an inmate saying, "I was so made at one inmate the other day I got a knife and was going to go find him, but decided not to do it?" Basically, the worker must make a judgment, depending upon the therapy session and how much, if any, danger still exists. There is no simple answer to how this should be handled. Professional skill and reasoning will be the best guidance.

CONCLUSION

Social work within a prison is an area that has not received much attention from the profession or social workers as individuals. There is an overwhelming amount of problems within a prison that demand effective methods of coping. The problems produce great amounts of stress and tension for the individual who is employed in such an environment. Coping with the problems and stress requires a professional who is successfully able to cope with the kinds of people in such an institution. Social work certainly provides the training, knowledge, and skill for such an undertaking.

The work provides a real challenge to the individual who enjoys accomplishing worthwhile objectives under difficult conditions. It is by no means impossible, as a large number of individuals from many professions successfully work in such an environment. The satisfaction from accomplishing a difficult objective in a prison environment is very great.

The individual has to learn to keep his or her expectations realistic. There certainly is no lack of realistic challenge for an individual. The creative individual who is willing to spend time and energy working on a problem will find solutions that can be rewarding to both the worker and his or her clients.

The authors encourage social workers to consider a prison when thinking about a place of employment. The social worker will find a working environment full of challenges that has great potential for achieving professional growth and development. On the other hand, prisons will gain the benefit of the expertise of the social worker. It can be a rewarding experience both ways.

REFERENCES

Bartollas, C. (1975). Sisyphus in a juvenile institution. *Social Work, 20*(5), 364–368.

Brown, B. S. (1967). The casework role in a penal setting. *Journal of Criminal Law, Criminology, and Police Science, 58*(2), 919–996.

Handler, E. (1975). Social work and corrections. Comments on an uneasy partnership. *Criminology, 13*(3), 240–254.

Holt, N., & Miller, D. (1972). Explorations in inmate-family relationships. California Department of Corrections, Research Report #46.

Holtman, P. (1979). The prison social worker. *Process, 58*(6), 159–165.

Kelling, G. (1968). Caught in a crossfire —Corrections and the dilemmas of social workers. *Crime and Delinquency, 14*(1), 26–30.

Showalter, D., & Jones, C. W. (1980). Marital and family counseling in prisons. *Social Work, 25*(3), 224–228.

Stafvaltz, Z. (1978). The social worker in prison with special reference to two projects. *Staffälligenhilfe, 27*(4), 217–221.

The prison social worker. (1979). *Process, 58*(4), entire issue.

Chapter 29

Correctional Social Work with Criminal Offenders and Their Children

Denise Johnston

INTRODUCTION

In 2004, there were more than 1.3 million parents in U.S. jails and prisons (Center for Children of Incarcerated Parents, 2005). These parents have more than 2.7 million dependent children. Their numbers have been increasing for 30 years and have become the focus of increasing professional, public, and governmental attention. Nevertheless, greater interest in parents involved in the criminal justice system and their children has not produced a corresponding body of accessible information that can be used by practitioners working in correctional settings. The following review attempts to collect and report empirical data on this population by succeeding stages of the justice process.

> Drugs and crime are like a bad dream and, no matter what anyone says, most of us eventually wake up. It's just a matter of time. But you and I been to jail and we know that time hurts . . . it hurts our children most of all.
>
> A formerly incarcerated mother
> From "StreetReady" (Phase ReEntry Program, 1991)

PARENTAL CRIME

Imprisoned parents have a different criminal offense profile than other prisoners (Mumola, 2000), suggesting that they may commit different patterns of crime as well. Parents in state and federal prisons are more likely than other prisoners to be convicted of drug crimes (23.9% vs 16.7%) and are less likely than other prisoners to be convicted of violent crimes (43.9% vs 51.1%).

PARENTAL ARREST

There is no reliable data on the number or percentage of persons who commit crimes and are subsequently arrested. Arrest rates reflect not only criminal activity, but also changes in criminal statutes, crime detection, and policing trends. The rates of arrests for all classes of offenses have remained stable or slightly decreased since 1998 (FBI, 2005).

Charges at Parental Arrest

Crimes are separated by law into *felonies* and *misdemeanors*. Most states define felonies as crimes punishable (1) by death or imprisonment in a state or federal prison, or (2) by death or imprisonment in any setting for more than one year. Misdemeanors are defined as all other crimes. However, recent changes in sentencing statutes and the overcrowding of correctional facilities have led to the breakdown of these distinctions in correctional practice. There is no information available about the arrest offenses of parents involved in the criminal justice system.

Parental Arrest and Gender

The overwhelming majority of crimes and arrests occurs among males. Male and female arrest patterns also differ. A greater proportion of males than females are arrested for violent offenses (particularly homicide, assaults, and robbery), some property offenses (including burglary and motor vehicle theft), and public order offenses (particularly DWI/DUI). A greater proportion of females than males are arrested for fraud, larceny/theft, all drug charges, and some public order offenses (U.S. Department of Justice [USDJ], 1992). These gender-related differences probably apply to arrested parents.

Parental Arrest and Criminal Justice Status

Although most incarcerated parents had no criminal justice status (i.e., probation, parole) at the time of arrest, the large majority had prior convictions and/or incarcerations (Mumola, 2000). More than one-third (34.7%) of mothers incarcerated in state prisons were first-time offenders with no criminal justice history at the time of their arrest, while more than half (55.6%) were on probation or parole for a prior offense. Similarly, about 22 percent of fathers incarcerated in state prisons had no criminal justice history when arrested but 47.8 percent were on probation or parole. From 32 percent (mothers) to 45 percent (fathers) had three or more prior sentences to probation and/or incarceration.

Parental Drug Use and Arrest

More than half of all imprisoned parents used drugs in the month prior to their arrest, with about a third using drugs at the time of their arrest (Mumola, 2000). These figures may not apply to criminal offenders who are arrested but not sentenced to imprisonment. In every category, imprisoned mothers reported higher rates of drug use than imprisoned fathers, including committing their offenses in order to get money to buy drugs (32.2% vs 18.5%); these figures are consistent with recent data on jailed persons (Karberg & James, 2005). The proportions were reversed for alcohol use, with fathers more likely than mothers to have a history of alcohol dependence and committing their current crime under the influence of alcohol.

> When my mother was arrested, it was the worst day of my life.
>
> Alex, 13 years
> From "I Know How You Feel . . ."
> (Prison MATCH, 1985)

Children and Parental Arrest

There were approximately 14 million arrests in the U.S. in 2004; the Center for Children of Incarcerated Parents (2005) has estimated that these include approximately 6.5 million arrests of fathers of dependent children and 2.25 million arrests of mothers of dependent children. It is important to note than arrested and incarcerated populations differ significantly. Arrested persons are younger, more likely to be white and are charged with less serious offenses than persons who are eventually incarcerated. Arrestees include persons who will not be charged, adjudicated, or convicted, as well as persons who will be cited or detained briefly and then released to the community before adjudication and conviction, and persons who will be convicted but not sentenced to incarceration. Therefore, parental arrest presents different child-related issues than parental incarceration.

About 20 percent of prisoners' children have witnessed parental arrest (Johnston, 1991; Silbaugh, cited in Nolan, 2003). The witnessing of parental arrest may be traumatizing for children, particularly when it results in the loss of a primary caregiver and/or the child's placement or home. There is some evidence that children who have witnessed parental arrest will develop a different pattern of legal socialization (including hostility to law enforcement and a lower likelihood of calling upon the police when endangered) than other children (Stanton, 1980). One of the potential outcomes of parental arrest is the placement of children in the child welfare system.

There is no research on paternal arrest. Research on maternal arrest has been extremely limited and primarily related to foster care issues. The Vera Institute (Ehrensaft, Khashu, Ross, & Wamsley, 2003) found that very few children are removed from the custody of their mothers as the result of maternal arrest on criminal charges; only 0.5–1.7 percent of women offenders with children in foster care had those children removed from their custody at the time they were arrested. In fact, children were most likely to have been placed in foster care within the year *prior* to maternal arrest in these families.

Interventions for children at the time of parental arrest are rare. Most jurisdictions have no formal policies for management of children present at parental arrests. The most comprehensive existing models grew out of efforts to assist child victims of violence and trauma, such as the New Haven Child Development Community Policing Program, or children endangered by methamphetamine production, such as California's Drug Endangered Children

Program. While there have been suggestions that child welfare agency screening should be routine at the time of parental arrest (California Assembly Bill 2315), this does not happen in the great majority of jurisdictions; social welfare considerations in evaluating this approach include identification of the appropriate agency for making placement decisions at the time of parental arrest, if any; screening procedures for potential caregivers; and the funding of these services for the millions of parental arrests that occur each year.

Outcomes of Parental Arrests

Following arrest, parents and other offenders may be given a citation to appear in court and be released, temporarily detained before release on bail or personal recognizance, detained throughout adjudication because they cannot pay their bail, or detained without bail. The presence of children in the offender's home and/or the parent's role in childcare may be considered in determining eligibility for release on personal recognizance (i.e., a promise to return to court for adjudication). Preventive detention (detention without bail) occurs when the very serious nature of a crime, or the offender's history, suggests that she/he is dangerous and/or may fail to appear at trial if released. Probation and parole violators are also detained without bail.

Social Work Tasks at Parental Arrest

Currently, there is no generally-accepted role for social workers at the time of parental arrest. The potential role of child welfare workers at the time of parental arrest is in dispute (Nolan, 2003).

Although most children of criminal offenders are not present when their parents are arrested, several jurisdictions have developed services related to parental arrest (Bloom, 1995; Nolan, 2003). Most of these services are trauma-focused and provide crisis-intervention services through law enforcement collaborations with mental health agencies. Other programs focus on child welfare and involve collaborations between law enforcement, child protective services agencies, prosecutors, pediatric health care providers, and/or child shelters. Development of services for children of arrested parents is an appropriate social work activity.

Considerations for social welfare services at the time of parental arrest are (1) the safety of the children, at the arrest site and immediately following the arrest, including consideration of the potentially traumatic effects of witnessing a parent being arrested; (2) arrangement of child placements by the parent, or by appropriate authorities in situations where parents do not designate a caregiver or where a designated caregiver is unavailable; and (3) removal of the children from the current parent/caregiver's care and/or custody, in situations where children are victims or participants in the crime, where the parent/caregiver has harmed or endangered the child, and/or where the child is already under jurisdiction of the Juvenile Court.

PARENTS UNDER CORRECTIONAL SUPERVISION IN LOCKED FACILITIES

Approximately half of all arrested persons, or about one-third of people convicted of a crime, are sentenced to incarceration. Parents sentenced to incarceration are sent to jails or to prisons. Jails have historically housed persons awaiting trial and persons sentenced for misdemeanor crimes. Prisons have historically housed persons sentenced for felony crimes to more than one year of incarceration. However, these traditional distinctions have broken down as recent changes in sentencing laws and correctional practice have resulted in greater numbers of persons with misdemeanor crimes serving prison sentences and greater numbers of felons serving sentences in jail of less than one year. In addition, for logistical reasons like overcrowding, some states are forced to house state prisoners in local jails. It is also important to note that persons charged with federal crimes are detained in separate federal detention centers and serve sentences to incarceration in federal prisons which may be located outside of their home state.

JAILED PARENTS

According to the U.S. Bureau of Justice Statistics (Harrison & Beck, 2005), there were more than 700,000 persons in jail on any day in 2004; approximately 12.3 percent of these prisoners were female and that proportion has increased each year since

1995. Most jailed persons are people of color. Nationally, less than 40 percent of jailed persons have been convicted; among convicted jailed persons, about three-quarters will serve their sentences in jail (James, 2004). The rest are being detained while awaiting trial. Most jailed persons are held in the 50 largest jails in the U.S.; the Los Angeles, California, and New York, New York jail systems together hold almost 5 percent of all jailed persons in the U.S. The mean jail sentence is 23 months and the mean time to be served in jail is 10 months; both have increased substantially over the past decade (James, 2004).

Jailed persons of both sexes are likely to have been raised apart from one parent (56.4%); they are also likely (46.3%) to have a family member who has been incarcerated, with the rate of family member incarceration being highest for black women (USDJ, 1991). Jailed persons are also more likely to have experienced parental substance abuse (20%) and physical or sexual abuse as children (18.2%). Higher numbers of jailed women have been physically (44.9%) or sexually (35.9%) abused compared to jailed men (James, 2004).

James (2004) found that almost half of all jailed persons were on probation or parole when arrested and about four in 10 had previous sentences to probation and/or incarceration. Only 27 percent had no prior convictions; this means that about one in four arrested people are active criminal offenders who are not included in official criminal justice agency counts. Estimates of the numbers of children of criminal offenders should include children of this group, as well as children of prisoners, parolees, and probationers.

Parents account for about 60 percent of jailed males and 70 percent of jailed females (Center for Children of Incarcerated Parents, 2005).

Jailed Fathers

There is very little research on fathers in jail. One of the few studies that included jailed fathers (Walker, 2003) surveyed 66 men in an urban, northeastern county jail. About 42 percent of the men's children lived with them prior to arrest and the majority of those had lived with both their fathers and biological mothers. Prior to paternal incarceration, only 13 percent of the men's children had lived with their fathers for their entire lives while 21 percent had been completely estranged from their fathers. The report contained no demographic information about the jailed fathers studied.

> If he had been thinking of us kids, he wouldn't have done what he did.
>
> Louisa, 11 years
> Daughter of an incarcerated father

> I was (sitting in jail) thinking about my kids, and it was hard. See, I know how to do time, I just don't know how to do feelings.
>
> Jesse, Incarcerated father
> From the videotape "Children of Incarcerated Parents"

Jailed Mothers

Most women in jail are mothers. They come from troubled families with histories of substance abuse, physical and sexual victimization, criminal activity, and mental illness (Hairston, 1990; James, 2004; Johnston, 1991). They typically began using drugs in early adolescence and had their first pregnancies as teenagers. The majority have had multiple arrests prior to their current incarceration; their current arrests for property and drug offenses are most commonly related to substance dependency. The majority of jailed mothers face multiple problems at reentry (Johnston, 1991). While their early reentry problems are related to subsistence needs, family relationship problems increase with the length of time since release. Postrelease drug and alcohol use are significant; about one in three women experience this problem in the week after release, but one month later over half report substance abuse or dependency.

Pregnant women comprise about 6 to 10 percent of women entering jail. The prenatal lives of their infants are characterized by high levels of tobacco exposure (Barkauskas, Low, & Pimlott, 2002), stress (Shelton, Armstrong, & Cochran,1983; Fogel, 1993; Hufft, 1992), maternal emotional distress and psychological risk factors (Fogel & Belyea, 2001; Wismont, 2000), and maternal victimization by violence (Sable, Fieberg, Martin, & Kupper, 1999). Early studies found high rates of spontaneous abortion, premature birth, and perinatal morbidity and mortality among the infants of women offenders (McCall, Casteel, & Shaw, 1985; Stauber, Weingart, & Koubenec, 1984), but more recent research suggests that perinatal outcomes in the jail are similar to those of matched controls in the community (Mertens, 2001).

Children of Jailed Parents

There has been almost no empirical research on children of jailed parents. Virtually all studies touching on this topic have involved surveys or interviews of jailed parents (see Hairston, 1990; Henriques, 1982; Johnston, 1991; Walker, 2003); and while a few have included some data collection through interviews or focus groups with children of jailed parents (Walker, 2003), only one has actually included more structured, objective methods of collecting empirical data from or on the children themselves (Stanton, 1980). Similarly, few have attempted to examine a representative sample of the children of jailed parents; for example, only one researcher has included the children of jailed fathers (Walker, 2003). The limited size of the study populations and lack of scientific rigor in study design – significantly including the absence of randomly selected study samples – makes it difficult to generalize from the data collected in the available reports.

In spite of the weakness of the available data, it is possible to draw some conclusions about the children of jailed parents from what is known about the parents' experience. Both federal (USDJ, 1992) and other (Johnston, 1991) data suggest that a substantial number of jailed persons cycle in and out of jail without going on to prison, and that many jailed persons are arrested frequently without being detained or sentenced to incarceration. These offenders have had disrupted childhoods and have substantial histories of trauma; they are typically involved in substance abuse or dependency and many are mentally ill. The implications of these conditions for the children of parents who are jailed but do not go on to prison are grave; the high level of need and the requirement for multiple, costly, and coordinated services often defeat service providers, and the high level of mobility of the index client – the jailed parent – in the community makes sustained services and follow-up extremely difficult. Finally, unlike most parents released from prison, jailed mothers and fathers often return to the community without the correctional supervision (i.e., probation, parole) that can serve as a brake on drug use and offending, as well as a source of linkages to community resources and supports.

Social Work Tasks in the Jail

On any given day, about 30 percent of jailed persons will be detainees awaiting trial (James, 2004); it is likely that this proportion also applies to jailed parents. Detained persons have multiple needs that might be met by social work practitioners, beginning with the need for crisis intervention. Arrested persons also need basic information about the adjudication process (attorney name and telephone number; the specifics of their criminal charges; the availability and amount of their bail; the address of the court, so family members can attend hearings); the need for liaison with criminal justice entities (including their probation or parole officers, their attorneys, a bail bondsperson), and the need to locate and/or make contact with their families. Both detained and sentenced persons may have need of assistance with referrals to medical, social, and other services, as well as to placements in counseling, drug treatment programs, and job-related services. These needs typically go unmet or are addressed by community service agency providers, rather than by social workers.

The majority of jailed persons have been convicted of a criminal charge and are either serving their sentences to incarceration in jail or awaiting transportation to prison. Some jailed parents in this category will need logistical assistance in a variety of areas, as they make arrangements to be away from home and family for longer periods. For example, while most jailed parents have arranged temporary placements for their children at the time of arrest, a significant minority will need assistance with long-term child placements. Parents with children in the foster care system may need assistance in communicating with child welfare workers, their Dependency Court attorneys, or the Juvenile Dependency Court; this is especially important for parents of children whose entry into foster care immediately preceded or was the result of parental arrest. Where the social worker determines it is appropriate, she/he may advocate for parent-child reunification and or specific child placements with the Child Protective Services or with the Dependency Court.

Social workers may also provide assistance to the family members of jailed parents. Relatives of jailed parents often need information about the parent's location and mailing address; the criminal justice status of the parent; jail visitation; and the parent's attorney, probation officer, or parole officer. They may also need assistance in accessing community resources and with child custody/placement matters.

IMPRISONED PARENTS

The first comprehensive, large-scale study of imprisoned parents by a governmental agency was conducted by the U.S. Department of Justice, Bureau of Justice Statistics in 1999 (Mumola, 2000). Unless otherwise indicated, the data reported in this section was developed by that seminal study.

In 1999, U.S. state and federal prisons held a total of 721,500 parents who had about 1.5 million minor children; at that time, parents comprised 55 percent of all state and 63 percent of all federal prisoners. States with the largest numbers of incarcerated parents include Texas, California, New York, and Florida (Harrison & Beck, 2005). From 1991 to 1999, the number of parents in state prisons increased by 55 percent, while the number of parents in federal prisons more than doubled.

Increases in prison populations during the past two decades have been the result of (1) increasing sentence lengths, due to changes in sentencing statutes; and (2) increased rates of court commitments to state prisons, particularly for women convicted of drug charges (USDJ, 1991). Increased court commitments for nonviolent and drug crimes are particularly important for women offenders who are mothers, since most have been convicted of crimes in these categories.

> My worst prison is being separated from my children.
>
> An incarcerated mother (Prison MATCH, 1987)

Characteristics of Imprisoned Parents

Most (93%) imprisoned parents are fathers, although women prisoners are more likely than male prisoners to have minor children. Like the larger group of prisoners, imprisoned parents are disproportionately persons of color. The racial and ethnic distribution of imprisoned parents generally reflects that of the larger population of prisoners. However, while blacks (44%) and Hispanics (19%) are overrepresented among the general prison population and imprisoned parents at about the same rate, whites are underrepresented in both groups, comprising 35 percent of the general prison population but only 29 percent of imprisoned parents.

The median age of imprisoned parents is about 32 years, slightly younger than prisoners who are not parents. More than half of imprisoned parents have been married; about 23 percent of parents incarcerated in state prisons and 36 percent of those incarcerated in federal prisons are currently married.

All prisoners have low levels of educational attainment, with less than half completing high school; however, parents incarcerated in federal prisons are more likely than those in state prisons (25% vs 13%) to have attended college. Most (70.9%) imprisoned parents report being employed prior to their current incarceration and report having had a higher rate of employment than prisoners who were not parents (64.8%). In both parent and nonparent groups, prisoners report receiving preincarceration income from wages (about 67%), illegal activities (about 28%), and family or friends. About 15 percent of parents incarcerated in state prisons received welfare, Social Security or other entitlement income, while less than 1 percent of all imprisoned parents received child support or alimony. Preincarceration income was less than $2,000 per month for 77 percent of mothers and 78 percent of fathers incarcerated in state prisons.

Like other prisoners, both imprisoned mothers and imprisoned fathers have histories of interrupted care in childhood, parent-child separations, placement in foster care at a higher than average rate, childhood trauma, mental illness, and substance abuse/dependency (Beck, Gilliard, Greenfield, Harlow et al., 1993; Task Force on the Female Offender, 1990). The most recent federal data suggests than the majority of imprisoned parents have a substantial involvement in drugs and that drug use among imprisoned parents is more common than among nonparents who are prisoners. About 85 percent of parents incarcerated in state prisons have ever used drugs, with more than half (58.1%) reporting use in the month before incarceration and one-third (33.6%) reporting use of drugs at the time they committed their current offense. Mothers in state prison reported much more substantial histories of drug use than fathers, and were more likely to have committed their current offense under the influence of drugs (39% vs 20%), committed their offense to get money for drugs (32% vs 18%), or used drugs intravenously (29% vs 19%).

Imprisoned parents are less likely than incarcerated nonparents to be identified as mentally ill. Among nonparent prisoners, 18.7 percent were reported to be mentally ill, compared to 14.1 percent of imprisoned parents. Gender was a factor in mental illness among incarcerated parents, with imprisoned mothers in state and federal prisons reporting indications of mental illness at almost twice the rate of imprisoned fathers.

About 20 percent of mothers incarcerated in state prisons, compared to 8.5 percent of fathers, were homeless in the year prior to incarceration. Among federal prisoners, the homelessness was much less common – about 3.7 percent among imprisoned fathers and 5 percent among imprisoned mothers.

Parent Criminal Justice History and Status

Most incarcerated parents in both the state (77.2%) and federal (62.5%) prison systems had a history of previous criminal convictions. Among parents in state prisons, slightly less than half were on probation (23.7%) or parole (24.8%) when arrested for their current offense, compared to 12.7 percent and 14.2 percent, respectively, of parents in federal prisons. While from one-fifth to one-third had no previous history of probation or incarceration, over 77 percent of parents in state prisons and more than 62 percent of parents in federal prisons had served a previous sentence to probation or incarceration. Parents in state prisons were slightly more likely than nonparent prisoners to have served a prior sentence.

Overall, state and federal prisoners have different offense histories, with state prisoners being more likely to have been convicted of violent offenses and federal prisoners more likely to have been convicted of drug offenses. Among both state and federal prisoners, however, parents have a different offense pattern than nonparents. Violent crimes, for example, are significantly less common among parents (43.9%) than among nonparents (51.1%) in state prison, while drug offenses are significantly more common (23.9% vs 16.7%). Property and public order offense rates are similar among parent and nonparent prisoners.

However, imprisoned mothers and fathers are typically incarcerated for different types of offenses. Imprisonment for violent offenses were far more common among incarcerated fathers (45%) than mothers (26%), while mothers were more likely than fathers to be serving sentences for drug offenses (35% vs 23%) and fraud (11% vs 2%).

Sentences of Imprisoned Parents

Parents in prison are also serving sentences of different lengths, based upon gender. While the average sentence length of all parents in state prisons is 146 months, the mean sentence length for fathers is 150 months versus a mean sentence length of 94 months for mothers. In the federal prison system, fathers are serving mean sentences of 124 months, compared to mean sentences of 83 months among mothers. It is important to remember, however, that sentence length does not reflect the actual time served by prisoners. Among fathers imprisoned in state correctional facilities, the estimated mean time to be served is 82 months, compared to 49 months for mothers; in the federal prison system, the estimated mean time to be served is 105 months for fathers and 66 months for mothers. The difference in sentence length between state and federal prisons (including the shorter sentences but longer mean time to be served in federal settings) reflects the different sentencing and conditional release statutes for state and federal crimes.

Prisoners as Parents

Imprisoned parents share some strong commonalities. Both mothers and fathers in prison are incarcerated at a great distance from their children's homes, with the mean distance being over 100 miles for more than 62 percent of state and 84 percent of federal prisoners (Mumola, 2000); the lower rate of female incarcerations means that there are fewer women's prisons in any given state, so that women are likely to be imprisoned at a greater distance from their children's homes than males. Also, the great majority of both male and female prisoners are likely to have minor children residing with single and/or elderly female caregivers (Johnston, 1995).

Historically, incarcerated mothers and fathers have received different amounts of attention and scrutiny, have been provided with different types and levels of services, and have been considered to function very differently as parents. There has been very little research on or services for incarcerated men as fathers, and male prisoners have traditionally been perceived as less interested and involved in their children's lives than incarcerated mothers. At the same time, mothers in prison have been perceived as the primary caregivers of, and their incarceration as a traumatic separation from their children. Neither of these views is completely correct.

> My father was a career criminal and frequently incarcerated. As I grew up, I would see him from time to time. These times with my father often included tests to see how I would handle new experiences. I believed these tests helped him with his own pain, knowing he would not always be there for me. He wanted to make sure I could handle things for myself through everything that would be coming at me through life. These experiences were his way of telling me that I should get used to fending for myself . . . My experience with my son differs dramatically. My father knew he wouldn't be there and tried to prepare me for that. I didn't do this with my son because I thought I would always be there for him and I was not. I was arrested when he was young and have been incarcerated for almost ten years.
>
> An imprisoned father (Johnston & Carlin, 1996)

Imprisoned Fathers as Parents

There were about 668,000 fathers of 1.3 million minor children in U.S. state and federal prisons in 1999 (Mumola, 2000); less than half of these men lived with any of their children prior to their incarceration. Imprisoned fathers typically have 2.05 minor children (Center for Children of Incarcerated Parents, 2005) each and have had these children by different mothers (Hairston, 1989). Their family networks are complex; typically, imprisoned fathers do not maintain an on-going relationship with any of their children's biological mothers, although almost all of their children live with these mothers during the father's incarceration. Approximately one in 10 of their children live with the children's grandparents (Hairston, 1995; Mumola, 2000), and very small numbers live in other placements.

At least partly due to the lack of relationship with their children's mothers, imprisoned fathers have less contact with their minor children than imprisoned mothers. More than 20 percent of imprisoned fathers have no contact of any kind with their children during

incarceration, compared to less than 12 percent of imprisoned mothers. Among fathers in state prisons, almost half (42%) have telephone contact and 21 percent have visits with their children at least once a month. Fathers in federal prison have more contact with their children, with 72 percent having at least monthly telephone contact and 23 percent having at least monthly visits.

Imprisoned fathers often have a limited fund of knowledge about their children's lives and limited involvement with their children (Hairston, 1989). In the absence of substantial contact and communication with their children, these fathers nevertheless express concerns about their parent-child relationships, the lack of child guidance and supervision, and the possibility that they might be replaced in their children's lives or forgotten.

While imprisoned fathers are less likely than imprisoned mothers (1.8% vs 9.6%) to have children in foster care, they commonly have child custody problems (Carlin, 2000). Many of these problems are not under the jurisdiction of either the Juvenile Dependency or Family Courts, leaving imprisoned fathers without the benefit of court-ordered legal representation and related social services as they attempt to locate, communicate with, and/or obtain access to their children.

Almost every facet of paternal incarceration remains unexplored; for example, there is virtually no empirical research on the emotional and relational aspects of the imprisonment of fathers. Carlin (2001) has likened the challenge of establishing meaningful father-child attachments after a father has spent years in prison to an "emotional ravine," describing the reluctance of fathers to open up emotionally to their children and the obstacles presented by the anger that children experience toward absentee fathers. The extent to which formerly imprisoned fathers and their children experience reunion has not been the subject of research and is essentially unknown.

Imprisoned Mothers as Parents

National and other large-scale studies of female prisoners have long determined that about 70 to 80 percent are mothers with an average of 2.4 dependent children each (Baunach, 1979; Bloom & Steinhart, 1993; Hunter, 1980; McGowan & Blumenthal, 1978; Mumola, 2000; Zalba, 1964), Approximately 6 percent of women entering prison each year are pregnant; most of these deliver during their term of incarceration (Beck et al., 1993).

Prior to their current incarceration, about two-thirds of imprisoned mothers lived with at least one of their dependent children, less than one in six lived in a two-parent household, and about one in three lived alone with their children (Mumola, 2000). Imprisoned mothers typically have had their children by different fathers (Johnston, 2001). Their family networks are less complex than those of imprisoned fathers, largely because their children do not remain for long in their fathers' care or custody. Most imprisoned mothers have their children in the care of a grandparent, usually the mother's own mother (Johnston, 1995a; Mumola, 2000). Approximately one in four have at least one minor child who resides with that child's biological father, and a similar proportion resides with other relatives (Mumola, 2000).

Imprisoned mothers have been found to have appropriate parental attitudes, beliefs, and concerns when compared to their matched peers in the community (LeFlore & Holston, 1990). Their effectiveness as parents is primarily limited by behavioral issues, including specifically substance abuse and addiction.

Like imprisoned fathers, imprisoned mothers have limited contact with their minor children (Mumola, 2000). Although almost 90 percent of imprisoned mothers have some type of contact with their children during incarceration, only 53.6 percent of mothers in state prisons have monthly telephone contact with their children, and only 23.8 percent have at least monthly visits. Mothers in federal prison have more contact with their children, with 81.1 percent having at least monthly telephone contact and 19.5 percent having at least monthly visits. These figures should be interpreted in light of the greater distances at which mothers are incarcerated from their home communities.

Imprisoned mothers have a more limited fund of knowledge about and involvement in their children's lives than has previously been assumed by advocates and researchers, based upon child living arrangements prior to maternal incarceration. Johnston (2001) studied women prisoners in residential mother-child correctional programs and found that more than half reported they had not lived with any of their children immediately prior to incarceration.

Most of the mothers who were living with one or more of their children prior to incarceration were living with an allo-parent (co-caregiver) or were living with their own parent who cared for both the mother and her children. Additionally, more than 20 percent of the mothers studied had never parented any of their children. These figures are consistent with studies of children of criminal offenders done in the community (Johnston, 2003).

> JB's son remained in her care but was placed under Child Protective Services [CPS] supervision after a positive neonatal drug test. When the baby was 3 months old, JB was arrested for receiving stolen property and sentenced to serve 2 years in prison. The infant was placed in foster care with an unrelated couple interested in adoption. JB communicated regularly with her CPS worker and completed all her reunification requirements in prison. However, the baby was never brought to visit, even though the foster parents lived close to the prison and visits had been ordered by the court. When JB complained to the CPS worker, the worker told her foster parents cannot be forced to bring a child to a prison to visit. After 15 months, the social worker recommended the infant be adopted, due to JB's lack of contact with him.
>
> (Johnston, 1995d)

Among criminal offender populations, imprisoned mothers experience the greatest difficulty in retaining legal custody of their children, largely due to their high level of involvement in the foster care system. About one in ten mothers in prison has a child in foster care, compared to less than 2 percent of imprisoned fathers (Mumola, 2000). Prisoners of both genders are adversely affected by the terms of the Adoptions and Safe Families Act of 1997, which mandates reduced state timelines for the provision of family reunification services and rapid establishment of permanent child placements, particularly for younger children (Genty, 2003). However, imprisoned mothers are more likely than male prisoners to (1) be identified in child custody proceedings; (2) be drug-involved, and particularly drug-dependent, making achievement of family reunification requirements more difficult; (3) have children by a criminal and/or incarcerated partner, making placement with the other biological parent impossible; and (4) have family members involved in the criminal justice system, reducing the likelihood of kinship placements for their children.

Children of Imprisoned Parents

There have also been no large-scale studies of children of state and/or federal prisoners. A series of small research projects on limited numbers of children were done during the past 40 years (Fritsch & Burkhart, 1980; Sack et al., 1977; Zalba, 1964), but none of these studies involved direct examination of the children. Most larger studies that have investigated children of prisoners have obtained data through interviews with incarcerated parents or the children's caregivers (Applied Behavioral Health Policy, 2004; Bloom & Steinhart, 1993; McGowan & Blumenthal, 1978).

In the landmark federal study of incarcerated parents conducted in 1999, Mumola (2000) found that 2.1 percent of all U.S. children had a parent in state or federal prison. Race is a significant predictor of parental incarceration, with 7.0 percent of black children having an imprisoned parent, compared to 2.6 percent of Hispanic children and 0.8 percent of white children. The same study found that children of U.S. prisoners have an average age of eight years; the majority are under 10 years of age, including 2.1 percent who are infants, 20.4 percent who are toddlers and young children, and 35.1 percent who are between five and nine years of age.

The federal study examined children's placements prior to and during parental imprisonment by parent. However, while earlier and smaller studies had similar findings, some also examined living arrangements by child, producing different data. For example, while the federal study found that about 60 percent of imprisoned mothers lived with their children prior to incarceration, other studies have found that from 40 to 74 percent of the children of women prisoners were living with their mothers prior to maternal arrest (Baunach, 1979; Bloom & Steinhart, 1993; McGowan & Blumenthal, 1978; Zalba, 1964). Similar data is not available for the children of imprisoned fathers. However, an early study compared child living arrangements prior to maternal incarceration with the number of times the mother had been incarcerated and concluded that each successive incarceration substantially reduces a mother's chance of living with her children again (McGowan & Blumenthal, 1978).

Similarly, federal researchers examined parent-child contact by parent. While the frequency with which imprisoned parents make and receive telephone calls and visits with their children is known, the rate at which children of prisoners speak by telephone or visit with their parents is not known.

Children of imprisoned parents most often live with their biological mothers or maternal grandmothers; these two categories account for the living arrangements of more than 90 percent of all prisoners' children (Johnston, 1995b; Mumola, 2000). Even half a century ago, children of prisoners typically lived apart from at least one of their siblings (Zalba, 1964), and several studies over the interval since that time have established that a significant number of these children also experience multiple caregivers (Catan, 1991) and/or placements (Baunach, 1979; Johnston, 1991 & 1992; Zalba, 1964), a phenomenon associated with increased emotional difficulties and school problems (Johnston, 1991).

Virtually all studies of prisoners' families and children that have examined child living conditions have found them to be poor (Johnston, 1992; Prison Visitation Project, 1993; Schneller, 1978). Researchers found the children to have low per capita income and high-density, poor quality housing. Significantly, studies found that while conditions in the areas of housing, food, and clothing were the same or worse for children during paternal imprisonment when compared to the period before the father's arrest (Schneller, 1978), financial conditions did not improve with the release and/or return to the family of imprisoned parents (Johnston, 1992).

Additional information relating to children of prisoners can be found in studies of undifferentiated groups of children of criminal offenders. The Center for Children of Incarcerated Parents has produced a small body of research conducted on children of parents who have been incarcerated at some time during the children's lives (Johnston, 1991, 1992, 1993, 1996, 2001, 2003). About one in four of these children had a currently incarcerated parent at the time they were studied. This research found that significant proportions of the children – including 39.5 percent of the children of male offenders and 19.3 percent of the children of female offenders – had never lived with their offender parents, compared to 9.3 percent of randomly-selected public school children who had never lived with their fathers and 0.7 percent who had never lived with their mothers (Johnston, 2001). It identified three factors that distinguish children of criminal offenders from their neighborhood peers, including an inadequate quality of care largely due to poverty, a lack of family support and the experience of childhood trauma (Johnston, 1992). Studying randomly-selected public school children, the Center also found that parental incarceration significantly impacted the rate at which children and parents reside together, with about 50 percent of the children of formerly incarcerated mothers residing with their mothers and only about 13 percent of the children of formerly incarcerated fathers residing with those fathers (Johnston, 2003).

> My incarceration denied my son those things that every child should have and experience from parents: protection, caregiving, bonding, emotional support. Because I was not there for him, I think he simply put aside his needs and resigned himself to the notion that they would not be met until I would one day return. Being the son of a criminal offender myself, I know these feelings he has experienced, and I could see them in him. I could see him put his needs deeper and deeper from the surface while he acted out the hurt and pain he felt in his everyday life.
>
> An imprisoned father (Johnston & Carlin, 1996)

Children of criminal offenders have been of interest to society primarily as a result of their high risk of juvenile and adult offending (Glueck & Glueck, 1950; McCord & McCord, 1959; Robins, West & Herjanic, 1975; Federal Register, 2001). There are no studies that have actually measured the rate at which these children become involved in the criminal justice system themselves, but the Center for Children of Incarcerated Parents (2004) has recently estimated that rate to be 30–50 percent of the male children of adult offenders.

Parent-Child Programs in the Prison

Parent-child programming in correctional settings is essentially limited to services that increase parent-child contact and communication. The large proportion of prisoners' children who have never lived with and/or are estranged from their incarcerated parents, and the relatively small proportion of children who visit imprisoned parents frequently, make other prison-based services involving children unreasonable.

> A mother reported that she had visited with her 7 year old daughter through a glass visiting window on Saturday. On Sunday, she telephoned her daughter who asked, "Mommy, are you dead?" The mother responded that of course she was not dead, hadn't the girl just seen at their visit? "I know, Mommy," the daughter said, "but that was like TV and I wasn't sure if you were real."
>
> (Johnston, 1995b)

While special parent-child visitation programs were first developed in significant numbers in the 1970's and 1980's (Cannings, 1990), children have always been able to participate in regular prison visiting. It has often been assumed that the correctional environment is harmful to visiting children, based upon the typical behavioral reactions – such as hyperactivity, aggression and withdrawal – seen in children following prison visits. However, objective examination of the behavioral outcomes of parent/child prison visiting found that there were no sustained negative effects of visitation. While reactive behaviors before, during, and after visits were extremely common, these behaviors were developmentally appropriate and lasted less than 2 days in the great majority of children studied (Johnston, 1995c).

Jail and prison nurseries (Gabel & Girard, 1995) have been subject to similar criticisms. Most prison nurseries which existed in the U.S. prior to 1970 have been closed. The infant outcomes for residents of newer nurseries established over the past two decades have not yet been formally evaluated. However, in Great Britain, which maintained nurseries in four of its five women's prisons at the time, Catan (1991) has examined the effects of the prison nursery program on child development. She compared children born in prison and reared for up to 18 months in prison nurseries with children born in prison and released to care on the outside. There were no sustained or significant developmental effects on infants who had lived temporarily in a prison nursery.

From a limited body of literature, it appears that the effects of the correctional environment on infants who reside in the jail or prison nursery, and on infants and children who visit jails and prisons, are negligible. In accordance with what is known about children's abilities and development, the emotional environment created by the parent and the children's outside caregivers appears to be a far more significant influence on children who participate in these correctional programs.

Social Work Tasks with Imprisoned Parents

Criminal offenders need to resolve several critical developmental issues in order to function appropriately and effectively as parents to their minor children; this work may or may not take place in the prison. However, parents who are prisoners also face critical situational issues that must be addressed during incarceration. Social workers may be of assistance to imprisoned parents and their children in both areas.

Parental Identity, Empowerment, and Authority

Developing or maintaining a healthy, cohesive sense of identity is a challenge faced by all criminal offenders. Virtually all repeat offenders have had the types of relational, familial, and social experiences in childhood that prevent full achievement of that critical developmental task in adolescence (Johnston, forthcoming). Before they reach adulthood, most engaged in patterns of maladaptive, antisocial behavior (Johnston, 1995b) and many have become parents (Arizona Behavior Johnston, 1991; Hairston, 1989; Johnston, 1991) or otherwise prematurely assumed adult roles, further reducing the likelihood that they will achieve this developmental milestone in an age-appropriate way.

At the same time, like all other prisoners, parents are disempowered by incarceration. However, unlike other prisoners, imprisoned mothers and fathers are also disempowered as parents and stripped of parental authority in significant ways. The simplest manifestations of this disempowerment – such as having to ask for permission to get up to use the bathroom during visits, while their children may move about the visiting room freely – can have profound effects on prisoners' children and the parent-child relationship.

Social workers can help prisoners explore their own childhood development and their developmental needs as parents through a variety of mechanisms. They can provide, or arrange for the provision of parenting and child development classes; support groups for incarcerated parents; parent counseling and psychotherapy; and developmentally-appropriate parent-child activities. They can also provide education and information for prison staff that will foster correctional practices that help prisoners maintain a sense of empowerment and authority as parents. Finally, social workers can advocate for systemic or institutional correctional policies that are developmentally responsive to the needs of imprisoned parents and their children.

Early Parent-Child Separations and Their Sequelae

Parental incarceration is rarely the cause of the first separation experienced by criminal offenders and their children (Ehrensaft et al., 2003; Johnston, 2001 & 2003). It is highly likely that the same factors that lead to early parent-child separations also lead to parental incarcerations and are related to the outcomes seen in children of prisoners. Because large scale studies strongly suggest that each succeeding incarceration reduces the likelihood that prisoners and their children will reunify after the parent is released (McGowan & Blumenthal, 1978; Zalba, 1964), it is critically important that the issues – such as posttraumatic states, mental illness and substance dependency – underlying these linked phenomena be addressed prior to, during, and after parental incarcerations in order to break intergenerational cycles of dysfunction.

Social workers in correctional settings have the opportunity to help incarcerated parents address both the issues underlying early parent-child separations and the outcomes of these separations, from full parent-child estrangement, to lack of a substantial parent-child relationship, to lack of parent-child contact and communication. Social workers can insure that parents who wish to explore underlying issues have related reading materials, educational opportunities, and therapeutic services available to them in the prison. They can help develop and implement or support existing prison-based drug treatment and mental health services for prisoners, and link prisoners who are being released to similar services in the community; this is a particularly important activity, since recent research suggests that participation in postrelease, residential drug treatment can significantly reduce recidivism (Messina, 2005). They can create or support services that assist incarcerated parents to locate children from whom they are estranged, and "reconnection" services that bring together prisoners and their children who do not currently have active relationships.

Maintaining the Parent-Child Relationship

When the National Council on Crime and Delinquency (Bloom & Steinhart, 1993) reprised the landmark "Why Punish the Children?" study (McGowan & Blumenthal, 1978) in 1992, it found that mother-child prison visitation had declined from 92 percent in 1978 to less than 50 percent in 1992. This is of great concern, since continuing contact between parent and child is perhaps the most significant predictor of family reunification following parental incarceration.

Although the worrisome decline in the ability of most incarcerated parents to maintain contact with their children is largely due to the lack of relationship and contact between these parents and children prior to incarceration, three logistical obstacles challenge the parent-child relationship for even those families that lived together under one roof prior to parental incarceration. These include (1) restriction of prison telephone privileges to mutually exclusive systems of collect calls, which burden the children's caregivers, or prisoner telephone credits, which limit calling by indigent prisoners; (2) location of the majority of prison facilities in rural and outlying areas not affordably or otherwise accessible to the children of prisoners, most of whom reside in cities; and (3) lack of financial and worker support from the child welfare system for visitation between incarcerated parents and their children in foster care.

> SH was completing an 18 month sentence to incarceration when she requested assistance (from the Center for Children of Incarcerated Parents) in contesting a CPS recommendation of adoption for her 16 month infant in foster care. (A Center advocate) pulled together a team consisting of SH's Juvenile Court attorney, her correctional social worker, her parole planning officer and a residential drug treatment program director . . . to contest the CPS recommendation. . . . In spite of strenuous opposition from CPS, and following numerous hearings, reunification services were reinstated and SH's infant came to live with her at the treatment program after her release. One year later, SH completed treatment and parole. Two years later, the CPS case was closed and full custody of the child was returned to SH.
>
> (Johnston, 1995d)

Social workers in correctional settings can offer substantial assistance to imprisoned parents and their children in this area. They can (1) advocate within their correctional system for adoption of a telephone system that does not exploit callers or call recipients, and for the availability of free telephone calls for indigent prisoners; (2) advocate for the classification or reclassification of individual prisoners to correctional facilities that are more accessible to their children and children's caregivers and/or facilitate the placement of pregnant and parenting mothers in alternative, community-based correctional settings where they may serve their time with their children (Johnston & Michalak, 2002); (3) advocate for the release of individual prisoners to work furlough and other community-based facilities that will increase their accessibility to their children; and (4) participate actively in the child welfare cases of incarcerated parents, encouraging the courts to order and enforce orders to parent-child visitation for prisoners and their children in foster care.

PARENTS AFTER IMPRISONMENT

Approximately 366,620 fathers and 31,700 mothers were released from state and federal prisons in 2003, the last year for which data is available (Harrison & Beck, 2005).

Parental Reentry

All former prisoners face multiple barriers to reintegration into society (Travis, Cincotta & Solomon, 2003). Recent federal and local legislation, as well as public agency guidelines, have increased the possibility that the formerly incarcerated will be unable to find housing and financial support. While these circumstances increase the difficulty of successful reentry for all former prisoners, they have grave implications for formerly incarcerated parents and their families.

The Urban Institute (Travis, Cincotta, & Solomon, 2003) identified difficulty in finding employment as one of the critical reentry issues for former prisoners who are parents. In addition to lack of education and job skills, they face statutory barriers to employment in certain professions and reluctance on the part of employers to hire them. Broad categories of employment that are often closed to ex-offenders include childcare, nursing, pharmacy, banking, mortgage and loan, teaching, and public transportation. Virtually all studies have found low levels of postincarceration employment among former prisoners (Griswold & Pearson, 2005; La Vigne, Visher, & Castro, 2004; Nelson, Deess, & Allen, 1999), low level wages for those who do find employment (La Vigne, Visher, & Castro, 2004) and ineffective employment preparation and training programs for former prisoners (Griswold & Pearson, 2005).

Without employment, many former prisoners must fall back on public assistance. However, the Personal Responsibility and Work Opportunity Reconciliation Act, enacted in 1996, permanently barred those with a drug-related felony conviction from receiving federal cash assistance and food stamps during their lifetime. While states may modify the law through affirmative legislation stating specifically that drug felons are to be eligible for benefits, only nine states had opted out of the ban and only 18 had modified it in the first five years after it was enacted (Jacobs, 2001). The federal welfare law also prohibits states from providing Temporary Assistance for Needy Families (TANF), Supplemental Security Income, housing, and food stamps to individuals who are "violating a condition of probation or parole," and all TANF recipients are subject to a five-year limit on the length of time they can receive benefits over the course of their lives. These circumstances decrease the likelihood that former prisoners who are unemployed will be able to live with and/or support their children.

While there are some large scale programs designed to assist former offenders on welfare with job training and financial support, many of these programs have serious limitations. The California Cal-Works Program (Reardon, DeMartini, & Klardon, 2004), for example, provides income, job training and childcare for offenders on probation who are receiving public assistance but excludes persons with felony convictions, rendering the program unavailable to virtually all parents leaving prison.

Of equal concern is the inability of formerly incarcerated parents to acquire housing, one of the core requirements for regaining the custody of a child in foster care. Currently, a history of drug convictions bars parents from living in federally funded public housing (Jacobs, 2001). Some jurisdictions have also implemented criminal record checks for people applying for Section 8 (subsidized housing) certificates. These policies are particularly burdensome in urban areas where housing availability is severely limited and undoubtedly contribute to the high rate of homelessness among former prisoners.

Finally, former prisoners are often faced with the need to pay a child support debt that accrued prior to and during their term of incarceration. Parents with child support obligations have been found to enter prison with an average of more than $10,000 owed, while the average child support debt accumulated during imprisonment has been found to be in the range of $5,000–$6,000 (Griswold & Pearson, 2005). Not surprisingly, the proportion of parents who pay child support following release from prison is about the same as the proportion who pay support prior to being incarcerated. A review of child support programs for prisoners in four states found that while employment is the key to child support payment for former prisoners, employment and earnings are extremely low among that group of parents and increasing sanctions for these parents without improving their employment status and earnings has no effect on payments (Griswold & Pearson, 2005).

> When I got out, I didn't have anyplace to go. My mom was drinking and my sister don't talk to me, so I ended up going back with this woman I used to be with, even though she's got a cocaine problem and is tricking a little bit. She wouldn't help me get to the parole or the clinic and I couldn't get my meds and after a few days, I just gave up and started doing it all, too.
>
> ("StreetReady," Phase ReEntry Programs, 1991)

The situation of parents reentering society from prison is grim. Unable to find work at a living wage, disqualified from housing and income assistance, yet faced with the demand for child support payments and/or the need to attain a social and economic status that allows them to regain custody of their children, formerly incarcerated parents – like other former prisoners –are positioned by their circumstances to reoffend.

Parental Recidivism

Recidivism is the rate at which formerly convicted offenders return to crime. The last national report on recidivism was based on data collected on U.S. prisoners released in 1994; 67.5 percent of all former state and federal prisoners were rearrested for a felony or serious misdemeanor charge within three years.

Women's rates had increased significantly from 1983, when 51.9 percent of women recidivated (USDJ, 1989). Among prisoners released in 1994, 68.4 percent of formerly incarcerated men were rearrested within three years, compared to 57.6 percent of formerly incarcerated women (Langan & Levin, 2002).

Recidivism has steadily increased since the 1960s and 1970s, when general recidivism rates were 10–35 percent and parole revocation/reincarceration rates were about 25 percent (Hindelang et al., 1979). Most recidivist offenders are rearrested during the first year of the three year postrelease period (Langan & Levin, 2002). Recidivism is related to offense patterns, with high rates of rearrest for most property crimes and drug offenses. While there is no information on the recidivism rates of formerly incarcerated parents, their offense patterns (higher rates of convictions for property and drug crimes) suggest that they may be rearrested more often than their more violent, non-parent peers.

Parent-Child Reunification

There has been no substantive research on the rate at which imprisoned mothers and fathers reunify with their children following incarceration. Given that more than 40 percent of the children of parents who have been incarcerated have never lived with those parents (Johnston, 2003), the low rates at which parents lived with their children immediately prior to incarceration (Mumola, 2000), the low rates at which imprisoned parents and their children have substantial contact during parental incarceration (Bloom & Steinhart, 1993; Mumola, 2000), the fact that parents in prison have had their children by multiple partners (Hairston, 1989; Johnston, 2001), and the separate placement and custody statuses of the children of the same imprisoned parent (Johnston, 1995a), it is clear that a majority of these parents and children will not live together following the parent's release from prison.

However, Johnston's study (2003) of randomly-selected public school children who had experienced parental incarceration suggests that women offenders and their children are far more likely to be living together at some point following maternal incarceration (50% of the children) than male offenders and their children (13% of the children). One reason may be that children are most often raised by their biological mothers and male offenders, with children by different mothers, are unlikely to be able to reside with all of their children under one roof at any time, including after release from incarceration, while this is more possible for formerly incarcerated mothers. Another explanation may be that male offenders serve longer sentences to incarceration, which are likely to have a greater negative impact on parent-child relationships.

Johnston's findings support those of a study by Hunter (1980) of women parolees in Michigan. Hunter found that after release about half of the mothers had reunified with all of their children, while about 84 percent had reunified with at least one child. The mother's age at the time of her first child's birth and the living arrangements of mother and children prior to incarceration were predictors of full reunification, with younger mothers and those who had not lived with their children prior to incarceration having the lowest rates of post-release reunification.

Parent-child reunification issues are complex and often center around issues of power and authority within family relationships (Johnston, 1995a). Conflicts between the parent, the child and the child's caregiver prior to and during incarceration can have a profound effect on family dynamics during the immediate postrelease period. Prerelease planning, including documentation of parent-caregiver-child agreements allow incarcerated parents, older children, and the children's caregivers to negotiate the terms of child care during parental incarceration, reducing potential family conflicts after the parent's release (Center for Children of Incarcerated Parents, 1994).

ISSUES IN CORRECTIONAL SOCIAL WORK FOR THE PRACTITIONER

As described, criminal offenders have multiple issues and multiple service needs at every point in the justice process, from before the time of parental arrest to after an incarcerated parent's release from correctional custody. Criminal offenders are also the quintessential "resistant" clients (Harris, 1971); their high rates of reoffending, rearrest, reconviction, and reincarceration are often experienced by service providers as "service failures." Similarly, the children and families of criminal offenders have an even broader range of needs and are logistically difficult to serve for practitioners based inside the criminal justice system. Finally, the various environments in which this group of clients is found – from their violent, high crime communities to the courts to the jails to the prisons – are usually unsupportive, harsh and even traumatizing for workers. The many challenges of working with these populations contribute to the high incidence of compassion fatigue (Figley, 1995) among correctional workers. Indeed, secondary traumatization (which occurs when workers develop symptoms of traumatization from working with traumatized populations) is a substantial risk for all correctional workers.

At the same time, work with any group of children and families, but especially (high risk) populations like families of criminal offenders, is likely to elicit a variety of unconscious reactions among practitioners, all of whom have child and family issues of their own. Maintaining appropriate practice boundaries, and remaining empathetic and hopeful in the face of these clients' negative characteristics, can begin to seem impossible.

There are several approaches that correctional social workers can take to address these risks and reduce the possibility that their work will become psychologically damaging. The Center for Children of Incarcerated Parents has developed a list of recommendations for human services providers in correctional settings; these include:

Recommendation 1: Practitioners should be carefully screened and trained to minimize the risk of compassion fatigue and secondary traumatization. Exclusionary criteria should include a history of unresolved personal trauma.

Recommendation 2: Practitioners should receive an extended period of initial program-specific training with screening components that include observation of practitioner-client interactions, followed by substantial training on a regular, ongoing basis.

Recommendation 3: Practitioners should participate regularly in individual, reflective supervision as well as biweekly or monthly process groups that address the effects of the work on themselves and their colleagues.

Recommendation 4: Practitioners should regularly engage in respite activities.

Recommendation 5: Practitioners should be provided with or should create a substantial pool of referral and placement resources in order to avoid becoming overwhelmed by their inability to fill clients' multiple unmet needs.

Recommendation 6: Practitioners should carry a varied caseload and attempt to vary their immediate working environments within locked correctional settings.

Social work with criminal offenders and their families is difficult, demanding, and often unsuccessful by community standards. However, practitioners can improve the lives of these parents and their children by becoming familiar with empirical data on the population; linking them with services in and outside of locked correctional facilities; providing them with educational, family support, and therapeutic services; and helping correctional institutions and workers to recognize and begin to address issues of parental identity and empowerment, parent-child separation, and maintenance of the parent-child relationship through every stage of the justice process.

REFERENCES

Applied Behavioral Health Policy. (2004). *An epidemiological study of the prevalence and needs of children of incarcerated parents within the state of Arizona.* Tucson, AZ: University of Arizona.

Barkauskas, V. H., Low, L. K., & Pimlott, S. (2002). Health outcomes of incarcerated pregnant women & their infants in a community-based program. *Journal of Midwifery & Women's Health, 47*(5).

Baunauch, P. J. (1979, November). *Mothering from behind prison walls.* Paper presented at the meeting of the American Society of Criminology, Philadelphia, Pennsylvania.

Beck, A., Gilliard, D., Greenfield, L., Harlow, D., Hester, T., Jankowski, L., Snell, T., Stephan, J. & Morton, D. (1993). *Survey of state prisoners.* NCJ-136949. Washington, D.C.: Bureau of Justice Statistics.

Beck, A., & Shipley, B. E. (1989). *Recidivism of prisoners released in 1983.* NCJ-116261. Washington, D.C.: Bureau of Justice Statistics.

Bloom, B. (1995). Public policy & the children of incarcerated parents. In K. Gabel & D. Johnston (Eds.), *Children of incarcerated parents.* New York: Lexington Books.

Bloom, B., & Steinhart, D. (1993). *Why punish the children: A reappraisal of the children of incarcerated mothers in America.*

San Francisco: National Council on Crime & Delinquency.

Cannings, K. (1990). *Bridging the gap: Programs and services to facilitate contact between inmate parents and their children.* Ottawa, Canada: Ministry of the Solicitor General.

Carlin, M. (2000). Asserting parental rights from prison. *Family & Corrections Network Report, 22*:1–3.

Catan, L. (1992). Infants with mothers in prison. In R. Shaw (Ed.), *Prisoners' children* (pp. 13–28). London: Routledge.

Center for Children of Incarcerated Parents. (1994). *Family contracts package.* Pasadena, CA: Pacific Oaks Center for Children of Incarcerated Parents.

Center for Children of Incarcerated Parents. (2005). *Data sheet 3A: How many are there?* Eagle Rock, CA: Authors.

Crawford, J. (1990). *The female offender: What does the future hold?* Arlington, VA: American Correctional Association.

Fritsch, T. A., & Burkhead, J. D. (1982). Behavioral reactions of children to parental absence due to imprisonment. *Family Relations, 30*:83–88.

Ehrensaft, M., Khashu, A., Ross, T., & Wamsley, M. (2003). *Patterns of criminal conviction and incarceration among mothers of children in foster care in New York City.* New York: Vera Institute of Criminal Justice.

Federal Bureau of Investigation. (2005). www.fbi.gov/ucr/cius_02/htm/web/arrested/04-NC.html.

Figley, C. (1995). *Compassion fatigue: Secondary traumatic stress disorders in those who treat the traumatized.* New York: Brunner/Mazel.

Fogel, C. (1993). Pregnant inmates: Risk factors and pregnancy outcomes. *Journal of Obstetric, Gynecologic & Neonatal Nursing, 22*(1):33–39.

Fogel, C., & Belyea, M. (2001). Psychological risk factors in pregnant inmates. *Maternal Child Nursing Journal, 26*:10–16.

Gabel, K., & Johnston, D. (Eds.) (1995). *Children of incarcerated parents.* New York: Lexington Books.

Gabel, K., & Girard, K. (1995). Long-term care nurseries in prisons. In K. Gabel & D. Johnston (Eds.), *Children of incarcerated parents.* New York: Lexington Books.

Garcia, S. (1992). Drug addiction and mother/child welfare: Rights, laws and discretionary decisionmaking. *Journal of Legal Medicine, 13*:129–203.

Genty, P. (2003). Damage to family relationships as a collateral consequence of parental incarceration. *Fordham Urban Law Journal, 30*:1671–1678.

Greenfield, L. A., & Snell, T. L. (1999). *Women offenders.* Publication No. NCJ 175688. Washington, D.C.: Bureau of Justice Statistics.

Griswold, E. A., & Pearson, J. (2005). Turning offenders into responsible parents and child support payers. *Family Court Review, 43*(3):358–371.

Hairston, C. F. (1989). Men in prison: Family characteristics and family views. *Journal of Offender Counseling, Services and Rehabilitation, 14*(1):23–30.

Hairston, C. F. (1990). Mothers in jail: Parent-child separation and jail visitation. *Affilia, 6*(2).

Harrison, P. M., & Beck, A. J. (2004). *Prisoners in 2003.* Publication No. NCJ 205335. Washington, D.C.: Bureau of Justice Statistics.

Harris, G. (1987). *The resistant client.* Lanham, MD: American Correctional Association.

Harrison, P. M., & Beck, A. J. (2005). *Prison and jail inmates at midyear, 2004.* Publication No. NCJ 208801. Washington, D.C.: Bureau of Justice Statistics.

Henriques, Z. (1982). *Imprisoned mothers and their children.* Washington, D.C.: University Press of America.

Hindelang, M. et al. (1979). *Sourcebook of criminal justice statistics.* Washington, D.C.: U.S. Government Printing Office.

Hirsch, A. E., Dietrich, S. M., Landau, R., Schneider, P.D., Ackelsberg, I., Bernstein-Baker, J. et al. (2002). *Every door closed: Barriers facing parents with criminal records.* Washington, D.C.: Center for Law and Social Policy and Community Legal Services.

Hoffman, K. S. (1983). Women offenders and social work practice. In A. R. Roberts (Ed.), *Social work in juvenile and criminal justice settings.* Springfield, Illinois: Charles C Thomas.

Hufft, A. G. (1992). Psychosocial adaptation to pregnancy in prison. *Journal of Psychosocial Nursing, 30*:19–22.

Hunter, S. M. (1980, September). *Life after prison: Women and their children.* Paper presented at the American Society of Criminology, San Francisco, California.

Jacobs, A. (2001). Give'em a fighting chance: Women offenders re-enter society. *Criminal Justice 16*(1):44.

James, D. J. (2004). *Profile of jail inmates, 2002.* Publication No. NCJ 201932. Washington, D.C.: Bureau of Justice Statistics.

Johnston, D. (1991). *Report No. 21: Jailed mothers.* Pasadena, CA: Pacific Oaks Center for Children of Incarcerated Parents.

Johnston, D. (1992). *Children of offenders.* Pasadena, CA: Pacific Oaks Center for Children of Incarcerated Parents.

Johnston, D. (1995a). Care and placement of prisoners' children. In K. Gabel & D. Johnston (Eds.), *Children of incarcerated parents.* New York: Lexington Books.

Johnston, D. (1995b). Effects of parental incarceration. In K. Gabel & D. Johnston (Eds.), *Children of incarcerated parents.* New York: Lexington Books.

Johnston, D. (1995c). Parent/child visitation in the jail or prison. In K. Gabel & D. Johnston (Eds.), *Children of incarcerated parents.* New York: Lexington Books.

Johnston, D. (1995d). The child custody issues of women prisoners. *Prison Journal, 75*(2):222–239.

Johnston, D. (2001). *Incarceration of women and effects on parenting.* Paper presented at the Institute for Policy Studies Conference, The Effects of Incarceration on Children and Families, May 5.

Johnston, D. (2003). What works for children of prisoners. In V.L. Gadsden, (Ed.), *Heading home: Offender reintegration into the family.* Lanham, MD: American Correctional Association.

Johnston, D., & Carlin, M. (1996). Enduring trauma in the lives of children of criminal offenders. *Progress: Family Systems Research and Therapy, 5*:9–36.

Johnston, D., & Michalak, E. (2002). CCIP Research Report No. 26: *Mother-child correctional programs in the United States.* Eagle Rock, CA: Center for Children of Incarcerated Parents.

Karberg, J. C., & James, D.J. (2005). *Substance dependence, abuse and treatment of jail inmates, 2002.* Publication No. NCJ 209588. Washington, D.C.: Bureau of Justice Statistics.

Langan P. A., & Levin, D. J. (2002). *Recidivism of prisoners released in 1994.* Publication No. NCJ 193427. Washington, D.C.: Bureau of Justice Statistics.

LaVigne, N. G., Visher, C., & Castro, J. (2004). *Chicago prisoners? Experiences returning home.* Washington, D.C.: Urban Institute.

LeFlore, L., & Holston, M. A. (1990). Perceived importance of parenting behaviors as reported by inmate mothers: An exploratory study. *Journal of Offender Counseling, Services and Rehabilitation, 14*(1):5–21.

McCall, C., Casteel, J., & Shaw, N. (1985). *Pregnancy in prison: A needs assessment of prenatal outcomes in three California penal institutions.* Oakland, CA: Prison MATCH.

McGowan, B., & Blumenthal, K. (1978). *Why punish the children?* New York: Children's Defense Fund.

Mertens, D. J. (2001). Pregnancy outcomes of inmates in a large county jail setting. *Public Health Nursing, 18*(1):45–53.

Messina, N. (2005). *Correlates of recidivism among men and women parolees from prison-based substance abuse programs.* Presented at the Second Workshop of the Committee on Ethical Considerations for Revisions to DHHS Regulations on Protection of Prisoners Involved in Research, Institute of Medicine of the National Academies, San Francisco (July 18).

Mumola, C. (2000). *Incarcerated parents and their children.* Publication No. NCJ 182335. Washington, D.C.: Bureau of Justice Statistics.

Nelson, M., Deess, P., & Allen, C. (1999). *The first month out: Post-incarceration experiences in New York City.* New York: The Vera Institute.

Nolan, C. (2003). *Children of arrested parents.* Berkeley, CA: California Research Bureau.

Phase ReEntry Programs. (1991). *StreetReady.* Pasadena, CA: The Pacific Oaks Center for Children of Incarcerated Parents.

Prison MATCH. (1984). *I know how you feel . . . because this happened to me.* San Francisco: Authors.

Prison Visitation Project. (1993). *Needs assessment of children whose parents are incarcerated.* Richmond, VA: Department of Mental Health, Mental Retardation and Substance Abuse Services.

Reardon, E., DeMartini, C., & Klerman, J (2003). *Results from the First California Health & Social Services Survey.* Santa Monica, CA: The Rand Corporation.

Sable, M. R., Finberg, J. R.,, Martin, S. L., & Kuper, L. L. (1999). Violent victimization experiences of pregnant prisoners. *American Journal of Orthopsychiatry, 69*(3): 392–397.

Sack, W. H., Seidler, J., & Thomas, S. (1976). Children of imprisoned parents: A psychosocial exploration. *American Journal of Orthopsychiatry, 46*(4):618–628.

Schneller, D.P. (1978). *The prisoner's family.* San Francisco: R&E Research Associates.

Shelton, B., Armstrong, F., & Cochran, S. (1983). Childbearing while incarcerated. *Maternal-Child Nursing, 8*(1):23–24.

Shuter, J., Bell, D., Graham, D., Holbrook, K. A., & Bellin, E. Y. (1998). Rates of and risk factors for trichomoniasis among pregnant inmates in New York City. *Sexually Transmitted Disease, 25*(6):308–309.

Stauber, M., Weingart, B., & Koubenc, J. (1984). Pregnancy, labor & postpartum in women prisoners. *Geburtshilfe Frauenheilkd, 44*(11):731–737.

Stanton, A. (1980). *When mothers go to jail.* Lexington, Massachusetts: Lexington Books.

Sutton, L. P. (1975). *Criminal sentencing: An empirical analysis of variations imposed in federal district courts.* Unpublished doctoral dissertation, State University of New York, Albany, New York.

Travis, J., Cincotta, E. M., & Solomon, A. (2003). *Families left behind: The hidden costs of incarceration and reentry.* Washington, D.C.: Urban Institute.

United States Department of Justice. (1991). *Women in prison.* NCJ-127991. Washington, D.C.: Bureau of justice Statistics.

United States Department of Justice. (1992), *Women in jail, 1989.* NCJ-134732. Washington, D.C.: Bureau of Justice Statistics.

Walker, C. (2005). *Where are the children of prisoners?* Paper presented at the 2005 National Conference of the Child Welfare League of America, Washington, D.C. (March 8).

Wismont, J. M. (2000). The lived pregnancy experience of women in prison. *Journal of Midwifery and Women's Health, 45*(4):292–300.

Zalba, S. (1964). *Women prisoners and their families.* Sacramento, CA: Department of Social Welfare and Department of Corrections.

Chapter 30

Strengthening Families as Natural Support Systems for Offenders[1]

Susan Hoffman Fishman and Albert S. Alissi

Service programs in the field of corrections traditionally focus their efforts on rehabilitating, controlling, or otherwise "treating" the individual offender, while little systematic attention is given to spouses, parents, children, relatives, and other significantly related individuals whose well-being is often placed in jeopardy as a result of the offender's incarceration. Although the offender in prison is provided with food, clothing, shelter, some opportunity for job training, and other types of physical and emotional support, the family, specifically the woman, he has left behind has had to deal with all their needs alone. Not only must the woman establish a new life, care for her children, and withstand the type of social criticism that can occur as a result of the crime committed by her loved one but she must also learn to cope with the unfamiliar and often frightening court and prison systems in order to maintain meaningful contact with the offender (Schwartz & Weintraub, 1974).

It has been documented that inmates who do maintain family ties while in prison have a better chance of remaining out of prison after their release. Drawing from a study of 412 prisoners of a minimum security facility in California, Holt and Miller (1972) concluded that there was a strong and consistently positive relationship between parole success and the maintenance of strong family ties during imprisonment. The study suggests that family members, as a natural support group for offenders, have a tremendous potential for assisting in the reintegration of the offender to community life.

Since family members themselves, however, are under new pressures and face new financial and emotional burdens during the separation process, they are usually not in a position to serve in an effective helping capacity until they stabilize their own lives and adapt to the "crisis" situation brought on by their loved one's incarceration.

Judith Weintraub and Mary Schwartz recognized and documented the need and importance of prompt assistance for families of offenders (Schwartz & Weintraub, 1974; Weintraub, 1976). It is these individuals who must be helped to sustain themselves and maintain stable relationships during separation so that the family unit can offer an offender the support and security he will need upon his release. Although specialized assistance to prisoners' families can be essential to the well-being of the family members themselves and their corresponding ability to assist in the reintegration process of the offender, recognition of the unique needs of these families and appropriate services are not available through existing social service agencies. And even though existing literature on families of offenders clearly indicates the specific needs of this special group, it presents little guidance on concrete, practical service programs that can effectively address such needs (Bakker et al., 1978; Schneller, 1975; Zemans & Cavan, 1958; Wilmer et al., 1966; Morris, 1967; Fridman & Esselstyn, 1965; Fenlon, 1972).

The purpose of this chapter is to describe an innovative pilot program in Connecticut that was designed to meet the special needs of offenders' families and has been formally evaluated as being highly successful in accomplishing that task.

Women in Crisis is a private, non-profit program that utilizes trained volunteers to support and assist women from the Greater Hartford area whose

---

1. From *Federal Probation*, 1979, 43(3) pp. 16–21. Reprinted with the permission of the publisher.

husbands, boyfriends, or sons have been sentenced to prison for the first time. Women in Crisis was implemented in March of 1977.[2] During the planning stages of the project, the Advisory Board of Women in Crisis developed several basic, underlying concepts and premises upon which the program itself now operates: (1) the use of volunteers as service providers, (2) the relationship as the primary tool of the volunteer, and (3) advocacy as a role of the volunteer.

THE USE OF VOLUNTEERS AS SERVICE PROVIDERS

The first decision reached by the planners of Women in Crisis was an overwhelming commitment to the use of trained women volunteers as the primary service providers to clients. The Board and staff reached this decision after carefully documenting available research and observing the experiences of numerous women whose men were sent to prison. They realized that women whose men are sentenced to prison experience what is usually termed as a "crisis" in their lives, a short-term situational disturbance. Except in unusual circumstances, they are not pathologically damaged (Schwartz & Weintraub, 1974). Based on this information, the Board concluded that most women could adjust to the abrupt and distressing change in their life-styles with the help of an informed, sensitive individual (volunteer).

In September 1978, a study of the first eight months of the program's operation was completed under the supervision of the University of Connecticut School of Social Work (Women in Crisis Program Evaluation, 1978). The researcher drew a total population sample including all clients and volunteers engaged in the Women in Crisis Program from March 1, 1977 through October 31, 1977. Interview schedules and questionnaires were developed, pretested in the field, and administered. Clients and volunteers were contacted using all available information on record at the Women in Crisis office. In all, twenty-two out of a total possible sample of forty clients were administered a personal interview; sixteen were unable to be contacted, and two refused to be interviewed. In addition, fourteen of the fifteen volunteers who had provided the services to the clients in the sample were identified and interviewed. The interview procedure was standardized and systematically applied to clients and volunteers alike. The study offered evidence that those volunteers who had been recruited from the community, trained by the program, and assigned to assist families of offenders had been highly successful in their roles and offered invaluable services to their clients. In addition, statements made by volunteers, clients, and representatives from the community agencies connected with the program stressed several important reasons why volunteers can and should be major service-givers for the Women in Crisis Program. All of these factors have universal implications:

1. Volunteers as helpers are not seen by potential clients as professional "do-gooders" or as part of any system connected with their recent experiences, but rather as concerned people addressing basic human needs.

2. Volunteers as private citizens, taxpayers, and community participants have a vested interest in the functioning of the correctional process. Their involvement in this process not only serves as a means of monitoring the system but can also serve as a tool for its improvement. One fine example of volunteers as pacemakers for change has occurred over the past year-and-a-half at Superior Court in Hartford. Volunteers from Women in Crisis are present in court each sentencing day to approach and assist families immediately after an offender is sentenced and taken away. When the program initially began this service, court officials were suspicious of the volunteers and seemed indifferent to the needs of families in the court setting. For months, however, they have observed the positive effects resulting from information and support provided to families in court, and as a result, the sensitivity level of these court personnel has changed dramatically. Prosecutors, public defenders, and sheriffs are now personally escorting families to Women in Crisis volunteers for assistance and are openly acknowledging an understanding of the stress being experienced by the families.

3. As a result of their participation in the program, volunteers receive personal satisfactions and

---

2. Much of the early leadership in developing the program came from Margaret Worthington, a retired social worker, who conceived of the program in 1975 and served as the first president of the Women in Crisis board of directors.

opportunities for education and growth. All volunteers are required to complete the intensive Women in Crisis training program before assignment is made. Training consists of four classroom sessions, each three hours in length. Topics include an introduction to the criminal justice system, values clarification, interpersonal skills, crisis intervention, the culture of poverty, and a description of resources in the community. In addition to the classroom sessions, volunteers are also provided with orientations to Correctional Institutions and Superior Court. Periodic in-service training sessions are held throughout the year in order to provide detailed information on specialized topics of interest to Women in Crisis volunteers.

This growth and increased awareness of volunteers, in turn, affects the attitudes of others in the community with whom they come in contact. Women in Crisis volunteers interviewed for the program study highlighted some additional benefits gained through their involvement with the program. Half of the women interviewed observed an increase in their own sensitivity to the problems and strengths of others; approximately one-third of the volunteers felt that their communication skills became more highly developed; and one-third emphasized the satisfaction they received from making new acquaintances and coming to know women from different social and economic backgrounds.

4. The participation of volunteers as the primary service providers to families of offenders is economically feasible for the program itself in a time when costs of services continue to increase.

RELATIONSHIP AS THE PRIMARY TOOL OF THE VOLUNTEER

A second major concept, which was substantiated by the data in the evaluation study of the program, identified the informal, personal, and nonprofessional relationship between the volunteer and her client as the most important factor in the client's adjustment to her new life. At certain times, particularly on sentencing day, on the first visit to the institution, and during the first few weeks of adjustment, the "woman in crisis" was in crucial need of the human, practical, and uncomplicated assistance that was offered by an objective, informal volunteer.

Sentencing Day. Regardless of the nature of the crime committed by an offender and the likelihood that the offense would necessitate his incarceration, most families are not prepared for the possibility that the man will, in fact, be going to prison for an indefinite length of time and, as a result, display symptoms of shock, panic, or emotional turmoil in court when sentencing does occur. Therefore, Women in Crisis was structured in such a way that volunteers, under the supervision of a court liaison staff person, would be available in court each sentencing day to provide immediate information on court procedures and prison rules as well as practical guidance and emotional support. The evaluation study substantiated the assumption that Women in Crisis clients would need and respond positively to informed, well-meaning volunteers in court, regardless of differences in race or social background.

Eighty-nine percent of those clients interviewed felt that it was important for them to have had someone in court to assist them on sentencing day and the vast majority of clients stated that the race of their volunteer made no difference to them. The type of human support that volunteers provide each week can best be understood by examining the specific experiences of Mrs. S. and her volunteer, Jan.

Mrs. S., a woman in her fifties, is a widow with five sons. Her eldest son was in court to be sentenced for a sexual offense. Mrs. S. spoke in open court to the judge. She told him how she had tried to help her son and how difficult it had been for her. Jan approached Mrs. S. after the judge had sentenced the young man, explained who she was, and asked if she could be of any assistance to her. Mrs. S. and Jan sat down together in the hallway, whereupon Mrs. S. put her head on Jan's shoulder and wept. She then expressed her feelings of frustration and shame in speaking before the judge. Jan assured her that her comments had made a great impact on the court. After talking with Jan for another fifteen minutes, Mrs. S. told Jan that "just as I thought I didn't have anyone to turn to, you were there to help me."

First Visit. The first visit by a woman to her loved one in prison is usually a very difficult experience. There are a great many specific regulations and a precise visiting procedure outlined by the institution that can be overwhelming to a family member who is unaccustomed to expressing feelings in such a structured environment. The location of the prison itself can often present an unsurmountable problem to a family without access to private transportation.[3]

The ability of a family member to acquire the appropriate information and support necessary to overcome these practical and emotional obstacles can determine her feelings towards subsequent visits. For this reason, the initial advisory board and staff of Women in Crisis felt that it was imperative for a volunteer, as part of her job responsibilities, to accompany a woman on her first visit to the prison. The volunteer would, in no way, be part of the actual visit itself but would be available to guide the woman through the procedure and discuss her reactions to it before and after the visit itself. In addition, by offering private transportation during weekday hours, the volunteers would be providing the "woman in crisis" with the opportunity to visit for the first time under less crowded conditions and for a longer period of time.

The evaluation study of Women in Crisis supported the program's commitment to the use of volunteers as helpers on the first visit. Over half of the clients interviewed experienced fear and nervousness before their first visit to the institution. Two-thirds of the clients interviewed indicated that they talked with their volunteers about their feelings prior to the first visit. Over 85 percent of the clients who were accompanied by their volunteers on their first visit said they relied heavily on the volunteer's presence. When asked whether it was helpful to have had a volunteer go with them on the first visit, 93 percent of the clients responded positively. Only those clients who were already familiar with the procedure felt that the volunteer's assistance was not imperative. It would seem, therefore, from this data that the presence of a caring, objective person at this critical time in the family's adjustment process is very helpful. One volunteer described a client's first visit and her own role as an important helper:

> When I met Dee for the first time, I was amazed that she seemed so calm and so much in control of herself. Until we went up to the prison together for that first visit, I wasn't sure what I could offer her. We talked

quietly during the drive to Somers, but as we approached the parking lot of the prison, I noticed that her expression suddenly changed. We walked together to the metal detector and into the first waiting area. At this point, Dee completely broke down, refused to go any further and insisted that she would never come to this awful place again. I sat with her as she cried and quietly encouraged her to go into the visiting room, since her husband was probably just as nervous and anxious to see her as she was. After what seemed like hours, she did finally go in. Later she told me that she would never have done so if it had not been for me.

It should be mentioned at this point that Women in Crisis volunteers are instructed to accompany a client *only* on this first critical visit. The program does not want the volunteer to spend her time simply as a chauffeur. Nor does it feel that it is helpful for the "woman in crisis" to develop a dependency on the volunteer for transportation over a long period of time. Clients are, therefore, encouraged to develop their own resources. Since many clients mentioned during the evaluation interviews that the institution was frightening for them only until they became familiar with the visiting routine, it is apparent that continued volunteer support on additional visits is unnecessary.

The Six- to Eight-Week Adjustment Period. In addition to the critical support that a volunteer provides to her client at the specific points of crisis on sentencing day and on the first visit, a volunteer is also available as a resource on a continuing, intensive basis for the six- to eight-week period, which usually reflects the average critical adjustment time for a woman whose loved one has recently been incarcerated. Periodic follow-up can continue until the point when the man is released from the institution if the family desires support. Clients interviewed indicated that of all the types of assistance provided by the volunteers during this adjustment period it was the most helpful to have been able to relate on a human level to another person, to have "someone to talk to." The following letter, which one client wrote to her volunteer, describes the impact that their relationship had on her life:

---

3. Somers Correctional Institution in Somers, Connecticut, is the primary intake prison for adult male felons in Connecticut and, like many prisons throughout the country, is located in an area of the state that is not on any preestablished, major passenger routes. Until April of 1978, when Women in Crisis successfully advocated on behalf of its clients for increased public bus service to Somers, there was only one bus per week, which traveled from Hartford, the major urban area serviced by the program. This bus traveled only on the weekend when visiting hours are shorter and when the visiting room is the most congested. There is, however, no regular public transportation from other areas of Connecticut to Somers.

Dear Meg:

I wrote you this letter to know how you field. I wish that when you recive this letter you are in good condition of health.

Mrs. Meg, I wish you have a good luck in your summer vacation, I meet you because you was a wonder-women, who I was the pleasure to know. I would never forget the day I know you because you bring me your friendly when I was alone.

Have a great summer vacation with all of your families. Stay as nice as you are. I will always remember you.

Sincerely,

Your friend, Maria

ADVOCACY AS A ROLE OF THE VOLUNTEER

Although the initial Board of Women in Crisis considered the emotional support and assistance provided to a family member by a volunteer to be of critical importance, it also recognized additional concerns of clients that could not be addressed through emotional support alone. Families in turmoil need accurate information in order to make rational decisions about their future. They need to identify and establish contact with the appropriate personnel at the institution so that their concerns and fears about their loved ones can be expressed and addressed. They may need practical, professional services or crisis intervention to alleviate ongoing emergency situations. Many families facing problems so soon after the offender's incarceration feel helpless and overwhelmed. For this reason, the planners of Women in Crisis concluded that it would be important for well trained, informed volunteers, as part of their job assignment, to assume a role of advocacy on behalf of their clients. They, as vocal representatives of an established organization, could serve as liaisons and investigators to gather and interpret necessary information and steer clients towards appropriate, existing services. They could also intervene on issues relating to the prison if the client had a justifiable complaint and received no satisfactory response to it.

Since March 1977 when the program began operation, volunteers have assumed advocacy roles in specific cases. Various types of services that volunteers have provided and the results of their intervention are summarized below:

An agitated mother called her volunteer because her son had been writing to her and complaining that he was being heavily drugged at the prison. Since the mother was unable to clarify the situation, the volunteer called the institution as a representative of Women in Crisis and established, to the mother's relief, that the inmate was not being medicated.

In her conversations with a young family member, one volunteer discovered that, as of mid-October, the woman had not enrolled her children in school. The woman was embarrassed that the youngsters did not have proper clothing to wear to school. The volunteer suggested to the woman that they visit a local clothing bank together. When the woman acquired sufficient clothing for her children, she and the volunteer went to the school and registered her children in classes.

A volunteer whose client was being evicted from her apartment spent countless hours with her as the woman searched for suitable living quarters for herself and her small children.

A volunteer whose client was lonely and isolated in a suburban town arranged for a scholarship to a class at the local YWCA for the woman so that she could meet and be with other women during the day.

An offender contacted the agency for help in reestablishing a relationship with his three and one-half-year-old son who was living with his former wife's parents. The parents had never responded to any of the offender's letters to them. A volunteer wrote a letter to the in-laws informing them of the man's desire to see his son upon his release from prison. When the in-laws responded to the letter, the volunteer was able to reassure them about the man's intentions and his awareness of the difficulties such a visit might cause. The in-laws were appreciative of the support offered by the volunteer and agreed to one initial visit between the child and his father. Subsequent visits ensued.

ADDITIONAL SERVICES

Although Women in Crisis was established to address the needs of offenders' families during the critical period immediately following the man's sentencing and initial incarceration, the program has begun to develop services at other key points in time when family members are equally in need of vital assistance. Judith Weintraub, in her article, "The Delivery of Services to Families of Offenders" (1976), identifies arrest and arraignment and pre- and postrelease as additionally turbulent and bewildering periods of crisis for families of offenders. The experiences of Women in Crisis over the past two years have substantiated her observations.

When loved ones cannot raise bail and must remain incarcerated for varying lengths of time prior to sentencing, families face practical, emotional, and financial burdens as a result of the man's abrupt absence from the home. Vital information on court and jail procedures is as confusing and difficult to obtain as it is once the man is sentenced. Family members whose men have served their time and are preparing to reenter community life have adjusted to new roles and taken on new responsibilities during the man's absence. Their expectations may not be consistent with those of the offender whose life in prison has been so vastly different from their daily existence on the street. Common goals and realistic plans must be established between the man and his family so that the offender may experience a smooth transition between prison and community life.

Women in Crisis volunteers have begun to provide support services to families of felony offenders who remain incarcerated prior to sentencing. These family members (whose loved ones are classified as "transfers") receive the same type of services provided by the agency to families of sentenced offenders. Counselors and other personnel at the correctional facility, private attorneys, public defenders, and bondsmen refer "transfer" families in need to the agency on a regular basis.

Within the "Return to Community" component, a family counselor is available to assist an offender and his family establish realistic goals and facilitate effective communication among family members. The family counselor is in the process of determining methods for utilizing trained volunteers within this new project.

Women in Crisis also runs "personal growth classes" and group activities for family members of offenders. These sessions not only provide the opportunity for women to gather socially but also allow them to discuss common problems and learn new skills that may be valuable to them as they adjust to new lives on their own. Some of the topics that have been addressed in the past include single person parenting, money management, and interpersonal communication.

SUMMARY

Existing literature is limited in that it hypothesizes on the various means for meeting needs of offenders'

families but does not present concrete programs and methods for dealing with these specific needs. Women in Crisis authenticates a method of providing services that has major advantages. In the first place, it is practical and can be offered with limited financial resources because it utilizes trained women volunteers as primary service providers. In addition, it provides the opportunity for volunteers, as representatives of their communities, to serve in a positive way and contribute to the adjustment process of offenders' families. Not only do these volunteers realize personal rewards and satisfactions but they also offer an effective, straight-forward form of assistance that is viewed as genuine by family members "in crisis." To the extent that families are assisted in dealing with crises, there is every reason to believe that they can be strengthened to become a major source of support in furthering the rehabilitation of the offender as well.

REFERENCES

Bakker, L. J., Morris, B. A., & Janus, L. M. (1978). Hidden victims of crime. *Social Work 23*:2.

Brodsky, S. (1975). *Families and friends of men in prison*. Lexington, MA: D.C. Heath & Co.

Fenlon, St. M. (1972). An innovative project for wives of prisoners. *FCI Treatment Notes, 3*:2.

Friedman, S., & Esselstyn, T. C. (1965). The adjustment of children of jail inmates. *Federal Probation, 29*:4.

Holt, N., & Miller, D. (1972). *Explorations in inmate family relationships*. Research Division, California Department of Correction Report Number 46, Sacramento, CA.

Morris, P. (1967). Fathers in prison. *British Journal of Criminology, 7*.

Schafer, N. E. (1978). Prison visiting: A background for change. *Federal Probation, 42*:3.

Schneller, D. (1975). Some social and psychological effects on the families of negro prisoners. *American Journal of Correction, 37*:1.

Schwartz, M., & Weintraub, J. (1974). The prisoner's wife: A study in crisis. *Federal Probation, 38*:4.

Wilmer, H. A., Marks, I., & Pogue, E. (1966). Group treatment of prisoners and their families. *Mental Hygiene, 50*.

Weintraub, J. (1976). The delivery of services to families of prisoners. *Federal Probation, 40*:4.

Women in Crisis Program Evaluation: March 1, 1977–October 31, 1977. (Hartford, CT: Women in Crisis) 1978. Unpublished document.

Zemans, E., & Cavan, R. (1958). Marital relationships of prisoners. *Journal of Criminal Law, Criminology and Police Science, 47*:1.

Chapter **31**

When Prisoners Return to the Community: Political, Economic, and Social Consequences

Joan Petersilia

In 1999, state prisons admitted about 591,000 prisoners and released almost the same number – about 538,000. If federal prisoners and those released from secure juvenile facilities are included, nearly 600,000 inmates arrive on the doorsteps of communities throughout the country each year. Virtually no systematic, comprehensive attention has been paid by policymakers to dealing with people after they are released, an issue that has been termed "prisoner reentry." Failure to do so may well backfire, and the crime reduction gains made in recent years erode, unless we consider the cumulative impact of tens of thousands of returning felons on families, children, and communities. In particular, failure to pay attention to parole services is unfortunate, since most inmates, at the point of release, have an initial strong desire to succeed.

Of course, inmates have always been released from prison, and officials have long struggled with how to help them succeed. But the current situation is different. The numbers dwarf anything in our history, the needs of parolees are more serious, and the corrections system retains few rehabilitation programs. A number of unfortunate collateral consequences are likely, including increases in child abuse, family violence, the spread of infectious diseases, homelessness, and community disorganization. And with 1.3 million prisoners, many more people have real-life knowledge of the prison experience. Being incarcerated is becoming almost a normal experience for people in some communities. This phenomenon may affect the socialization of young people, the ability of prison

sentences to scare and deter, and the future trajectory of crime rates and crime victimization.

PAROLE IN THE U.S. – MANAGING MORE PEOPLE, MANAGING THEM LESS WELL

Changes in sentencing practices, coupled with a decrease in availability of rehabilitation programs, have placed new demands on the parole system. Support and funding have declined, resulting in dangerously high caseloads. Parolees sometimes abscond from supervision, often without consequence. Not surprisingly, most parolees fail to lead law-abiding lives and are rearrested.

DETERMINATE SENTENCING MEANS AUTOMATIC RELEASE

Parole in the United States has changed dramatically since the mid-1970s, when most inmates served open-ended, indeterminate prison terms – 10 years to life, for example – and a parole board, usually appointed by the governor, had wide discretion to release inmates or keep them behind bars. In principle, offenders were paroled only if they were rehabilitated and had ties to the community – such as a family or a job. This made release from prison a privilege to be earned. If inmates violated parole, they could be returned to prison to serve the balance of their term – a strong incentive not to commit crimes.

Reprinted with permission from *Federal Probation*, June, 2001, Vol. 65, Issue 1, p. 3.

Today, indeterminate sentencing and discretionary release have been replaced in 14 states with determinate sentencing and automatic release (Tonry, 1999). Offenders receive fixed terms at the time of their initial sentencing and are automatically released at the end of their prison term, usually with credits for good time. For example, in California, where more than 125,000 prisoners are released each year, no parole board asks whether the inmate is ready for release, since he or she must be released once the prisoner has served the determinate term imposed by the court. Most California offenders are then subject to a one-year term of parole supervision. A parolee must generally be released to the county where he last resided before going to prison. Since offenders overwhelmingly come from poor, culturally isolated, inner-city neighborhoods, that is where they return.

Indeterminate sentencing was abolished because of its discretionary quality. Studies showed that wide disparities resulted when the characteristics of the crime and the offender were taken into account, and were influenced by the offender's race, socioeconomic characteristics, and place of conviction. But most corrections officials believe that some ability to individualize is necessary, since it provides a way to take account of changes in behavior that occur after the offender was incarcerated. Imprisonment can cause psychological breakdown, depression, or mental illness, or reveal previously unrecognized personal problems, and the parole board can adjust release dates accordingly.

MOST PAROLEES HAVE UNMET NEEDS

State and federal incarceration rates quadrupled between 1980–1996, and the U.S. prison population now exceeds 1.3 million persons. Sentences for drug offending are the major reason for increases in admissions – accounting for approximately 45 percent of the growth. Aggravated assault and sexual assault are also major contributors to growth (Blumstein & Beck, 1999).

State and federal government have allocated increasing shares of their budgets to building and operating prisons. California, for example, with the largest prison-building program, has built 21 prisons since the mid-1980s, and its corrections budget grew from 2 percent of the state general fund in 1981–1982 to nearly 8 percent in 2000–2001. Similar patterns exist

nationwide, and prison spending was the fastest growing budget item in nearly every state in the 1990s. Increased dollars have funded operating costs for more prisons, but not more rehabilitation programs. Fewer programs, and a lack of incentives for inmates to participate in them, mean that fewer inmates leave prison having participated in programs to address work, education, and substance use deficiencies. In-prison substance abuse programs are expanding, but programs are often minimal and many inmates do little more than serve time before they are released. The Office of National Drug Control Policy reported that 70–85 percent of state prison inmates need substance abuse treatment; however, just 13 percent receive any kind of treatment in prison (McCaffrey, 1998).

These reductions come at a time when inmates need more help, not less. Many have long histories of crime and substance use, are gang members, and lack marketable skills. Deinstitutionalization has also led to a greater number of mentally ill people being admitted to prisons and jails. A recent survey revealed that nearly one in five U.S. prisoners reports having a mental illness (Ditton 1999). Psychologists warn that overcrowded and larger "super max" prisons can cause serious psychological problems, since prisoners in such institutions spend many hours in solitary or segregated housing, and those who study prison coping have found that greater time in isolation results in depression and heightened anxiety (Liebling, 1999).

Gangs have become major factors in many prisons, with implications for in-prison and postprison behavior. Racial tensions in prison mean that inmates tend to be more preoccupied with finding a safe niche than with long-term self-improvement. Gang conflicts started (or continued) in prison get settled after release: "There is an awful lot of potential rage coming out of prison to haunt our future" (Abramsky, 1999).

PAROLEE SUPERVISION REPLACES SERVICES

Upon release, 80 percent of parolees are assigned to a parole officer. The remaining 20 percent – including some of the most serious – will "max out" (e.g., not have received any credits for good time) and will receive no supervision. The offenders least willing to engage in rehabilitative programs are often not subject to parole supervision and services. About 100,000 parolees (about 1 in 5) left prison in 1998 with no postcustody supervision.

Parole officers are charged with enforcing conditions of release, including finding and maintaining employment, no drug use, and not associating with known criminals. The number of parole agents has not kept pace with the increased caseloads. In the 1970s, one agent ordinarily was assigned 45 parolees; today, caseloads of 70 are common – far higher than the 35 to 50 considered ideal. Eighty percent of all U.S. parolees are supervised on "regular" rather than intensive caseloads, which means less than two 15-minute face-to-face contacts per month (Petersilia 1999). Supervision costs about $2,200 per parolee, per year, compared to about $22,000 per year, per prisoner. Those arrangements do not permit much monitoring, and the *Los Angeles Times* recently reported that parole agents in California have lost track of about one-fourth of the 127,000 parolees they were supposed to supervise in 1999 (Associated Press 1999). Nationally, about 9 percent of all parolees have absconded (Bonczar, 1999).

MOST PAROLEES RETURN TO PRISON

Persons released from prison face a multitude of difficulties. They remain largely uneducated, unskilled, and usually without solid family support systems – to which are added the burdens of a prison record. Not surprisingly, most parolees fail, and rather quickly – rearrests are most common in the first six months after release.

Fully two-thirds of all those released on parole will be rearrested within three years. Parole failures now constitute a growing proportion of all new prison admissions. In 1980, parole violators constituted 18 percent of all admissions, but recent years have seen a steady increase to the point where they constituted 35 percent of all new admissions in 1997 (Beck & Mumola, 1999).

THE COLLATERAL CONSEQUENCES OF PAROLE RELEASE

Recycling parolees in and out of families and communities has unfortunate effects on community cohesion, employment and economic well-being, democratic participation, family stabilization and childhood development, mental and physical health, and homelessness (Hagan & Dinovitzer, 1999).

Community Cohesion and Social Disintegration

The social characteristics of neighborhoods – particularly poverty, ethnic composition, and residential instability – influence crime. There are "tipping points," beyond which communities are no longer able to exert positive influences on the behavior of residents. Norms start to change, disorder and incivilities increase, out-migration follows, and crime and violence increase (Wilson, 1987).

Elijah Anderson vividly illustrates the breakdown of social cohesion in socially disorganized communities. Moral authority increasingly is vested in "street-smart" young men for whom drugs and crime are a way of life. Attitudes, behaviors, and lessons learned in prison are transmitted into the free society. Anderson concludes that as "family caretakers and role models disappear or decline in influence, and as unemployment and poverty become more persistent, the community, particularly its children, becomes vulnerable to a variety of social ills, including crime, drugs, family disorganization, generalized demoralization and unemployment" (Anderson, 1990, p. 4).

Prison gangs have growing influence in inner-city communities. Joan Moore notes that most California prisons are violent and dangerous places, and new inmates search for protection and connections. Many find both in gangs. Inevitably, gang loyalties are exported to the neighborhoods. The revolving prison door strengthens street gang ties. One researcher commented, "In California . . . frankly I don't think the gangs would continue existing as they are without the prison scene" (Moore, 1996, p. 73). Moore also found that state-raised youth, whose adolescence involved recurring trips to California juvenile detention facilities, were the most committed to the most crime-oriented gangs. She warns that as more youth are incarcerated, earlier in their criminal career, larger numbers of youths will come out of prison with hostile attitudes and will exert strong negative influences on neighborhoods.

Rose, Clear, and Scully (1999) explored the direct effects of offenders going to prison from Tallahassee,

Florida, and returning to their home community after one year in prison. Rather than reducing crime (i.e., through the deterrent or rehabilitative effects of prison), releasing offenders into the community in 1996 resulted in increases in crime in 1997, after other factors taken into even were account. One explanation is individualistic, that offenders "make up for lost time" and resume their criminal careers with renewed energy. But Rose et al. offer another explanation that focuses on the destabilizing effect of releasing large numbers of parolees on the communities' ability to influence its members. They argue that "coerced mobility" (i.e., forced removal from a community), like voluntary mobility, is a type of people-churning that inhibits integration and promotes isolation and anonymity – factors associated with increased crime.

Work and Economic Well-Being

The majority of inmates leave prison with no savings, no immediate entitlement to unemployment benefits, and few employment prospects. One year after release, as many as 60 percent of former inmates are not employed in the regular labor market, and there is increasing reluctance among employers to hire ex-offenders. A survey in five major U.S. cities found that 65 percent of all employers said they would not knowingly hire an ex-offender (regardless of the offense), and between 30 and 40 percent had checked the criminal records of their most recent employees (Holzer, 1996). Unemployment is closely related to drug and alcohol abuse. Losing a job can lead to substance abuse, which in turn is related to child and family violence.

The "get-tough" movement of the 1980s increased employment restrictions on parolees. In California, for example, parolees are barred from law, real estate, medicine, nursing, physical therapy, and education. In Colorado, the jobs of dentist, engineer, nurse, pharmacist, physician, and real estate agent are closed to convicted felons. Their criminal record may also preclude them from retaining parental rights, be grounds for divorce, and bar them from jury service.

Simon (1993) notes that these disabilities are inherently contradictory. The U.S. spends millions of dollars to "rehabilitate" offenders, convincing them that they need to obtain legitimate employment, and then frustrates whatever was accomplished by barring

them from many kinds of employment and its rewards. Moreover, the loss of a solid industrial base, which has traditionally supplied jobs within poorer inner-city communities, has left urban parolees with few opportunities.

The underemployment of ex-felons has broader economic implications. One reason America's unemployment statistics look so good compared with those of other industrial democracies is that 1.6 million mainly low-skilled workers – precisely the group unlikely to find work in a high-tech economy – have been incarcerated, and are thus not considered part of the labor force (Western & Becket, 1999). If they were included, U.S. unemployment rates would be 2 percent higher. Recycling ex-offenders back into the job market with reduced job prospects will have the effect of increasing unemployment rates in the long run.

Family Stabilization and Childhood Development

Women are about 7 percent of the U.S. prison population, but their incarceration rates are increasing faster than those for men. About 80 percent of U.S. female inmates are mothers with, on average, two dependent children; two-thirds of their children are under 10 (Snell, 1994). More than half of incarcerated men are parents of children under 18 years of age. Altogether, more than 1.5 million children have parents in U.S. prisons, and the number will increase as the proportion of female inmates increases.

We know little about the effects of a parent's incarceration on childhood development, but it is likely to be significant. When mothers are incarcerated, their children are usually cared for by grandparents or other relatives or placed in foster care. One study found that roughly half of these children do not see their mothers the entire time they are in prison (because there are fewer prisons for women, women are often incarcerated further away from their children than are men, making family visits more difficult). The vast majority of imprisoned mothers, however, expect to resume their parenting role and reside with their children after their release, although it is uncertain how many actually do (Bloom & Steinhart, 1993).

Mothers released from prison have difficulty finding services such as housing, employment, and childcare, and this causes stress for them and their children.

Children of incarcerated and released parents often suffer confusion, sadness, and social stigma, and these feelings often result in school-related difficulties, low self-esteem, aggressive behavior, and general emotional dysfunction. If the parents are negative role models, children fail to develop positive attitudes about work and responsibility. Children of incarcerated parents are five times more likely to serve time in prison than are children whose parents are not incarcerated (Beck et al., 1993).

We have no data on involvement of parolees in family violence, but it may be significant. Risk factors for child abuse and neglect include poverty, unemployment, alcohol/drug abuse, low self-esteem, and poor health of parents – common attributes of parolees. Concentrated poverty and social disorganization increase child abuse and neglect and other adjustment problems, which in turn constitute risk factors for later crime and violence.

Mental and Physical Health

Prisoners have significantly more medical and mental health problems than the general population, due to lifestyles that often include crowded or itinerant living conditions, intravenous drug use, poverty, and high rates of substance abuse. In prisons, 50-year-olds are commonly considered old, in part because the health of the average 50-year-old prisoner approximates that of average persons 10 years older in the free community. While in prison, inmates have access to state-provided health care, but upon release, most are unable easily to obtain health care and have the potential for spreading disease (particularly tuberculosis, hepatitis, and HIV) and presenting serious public health risks (McDonald, 1999).

In New York City, a major multidrug-resistant form of tuberculosis emerged in 1989, with 80 percent of cases being traced to jails and prisons. By 1991, the Rikers Island Jail had one of the highest TB rates in the nation. In Los Angeles, an outbreak of meningitis in the county jail moved into the surrounding neighborhoods.

At year-end 1996, 2.3 percent of all state and federal prison inmates were known to be infected with the human immunodeficiency virus (HIV), a rate six times higher than in the general U.S. population. The rate grows faster among prisoners than elsewhere because they live in close living quarters. Public health

experts predict that these rates will continue to escalate and eventually make their way to the streets, particularly as more drug offenders, many of whom engage in intravenous drug use, share needles, or trade sex for drugs, are incarcerated (May, 2000).

Inmates with mental illness also are increasingly being imprisoned – and being released. In 1998, 16 percent of jail or prison inmates reported either a mental condition or an overnight stay in a mental hospital (Bureau of Justice Statistics, 1999). Even when public mental health services are available, many mentally ill individuals fail to use them because they fear institutionalization, deny they are mentally ill, or distrust the mental health system.

Democratic Participation and Political Alienation

An estimated 3.9 million Americans – one in 50 adults – were in 1998 permanently unable to vote as a result of a felony conviction. Of these, 1.4 million were African American males, representing 13 percent of all black men. The numbers will certainly increase. In 1996, a young black man aged 16 had a 28.5 percent chance of spending time in prison during his life. The comparable figure for white men was 4.4 percent (Bonczar & Beck, 1997; Mauer, 1999). Denying large segments of the minority population the right to vote will likely alienate former offenders further. Disillusionment with the political process also erodes citizens' feelings of engagement and makes them less willing to participate in local activities and to exert informal social control over residents. This is important, since our most effective crime-fighting tools require community collaboration and active engagement.

Housing and Homelessness

The latest Census counts about 230,000 homeless in America. In the late 1980s an estimated quarter of them had served prison sentences. The figure is surely higher now, with many U.S. cities reporting a critical shortage of low-cost housing. California officials report that 10 percent of the state's parolees remain homeless, but in urban areas such as San Francisco and Los Angeles the rate reached 30 percent to 50 percent (Legislative Analysis Office, 1999).

Transients, panhandling, and vagrants increase citizens' fears, and that ultimately contributes to increased crime and violence. This is because neighborhood crime often worsens when law-abiding citizens are afraid to go onto streets filled with graffiti, transients, and loitering youth. Fearful citizens eventually yield control of the streets to people who are not frightened by these signs of decay, and who often are the people who created the problem in the first place. A vicious cycle begins. Wilson and Kelling illustrate this by describing how a broken window can influence crime rates. If the first broken window in a building is not repaired, people who like breaking windows may assume no one cares, and break some more. Soon, the building will have no windows. As "broken windows" spread – homelessness, prostitution, graffiti, panhandling – businesses and law-abiding citizens move away, and disorder escalates, leading to more serious crime (Wilson & Keiling, 1982).

RESPONDING TO THE PROBLEM

Government officials voice growing concern about the problem of prisoner reentry. Former Attorney General Janet Reno recently called prisoner reentry "one of the most pressing problems we face as a nation" (Reno, 2000). Former President Clinton included $60 million in his 2000–2001 federal budget for "Project Reentry," a federal program to encourage responsible fatherhood among offenders, job training for parolees, and establishment of reentry courts. Reentry courts are modeled on "drug courts," which use judges instead of corrections officers to monitor released offenders (Travis, 2000). California's former Governor Gray Davis, in a "State of the State" address, called for hiring 100 new parole officers to increase surveillance of high-risk offenders and find the 20 percent of California parolees who have absconded.

Initiatives like these may or may not prove useful, but often they are not based on thoughtful analysis and debate. It is safe to say that parole has received less research attention in recent years than any other part of the correctional system. A congressionally mandated evaluation of prevention programs included just one parole evaluation among hundreds of recent studies that were examined (Sherman et al., 1997). I have spent many years working on probation effectiveness but know of no similar body of knowledge on parole effectiveness. Without better information,

the public is unlikely to give corrections officials the political permission to invest in rehabilitation and job training programs for parolees. With better information, we might be able to persuade voters and elected officials to shift away from solely punitive crime policies and toward polities that balance incapacitation, rehabilitation, and just punishment.

Parole release also needs to be reconsidered. In 1977, 72 percent of all U.S. prisoners were released after appearing before a parole board, but that figure had declined to 28 percent by 1997, the lowest since the federal government began compiling statistics on the subject. Parole was abolished because it came to symbolize the alleged leniency of a system in which hardened criminals were "let out" early. If parole were abolished, politicians argued, then parole boards could not release offenders early, and inmates would serve longer terms. However, this has not happened. Stivers (2000) shows that, after controlling for offender and offense characteristics, inmates released in 1995 in nonparole states served seven months less, on average, than did inmates with the same characteristics released in states using discretionary parole. Similar experiences in Florida, Connecticut, and Colorado caused those states to reinstate discretionary parole after discovering that abolition resulted in shorter terms being served by most offenders.

Parole experts have been saying all along that the public is misinformed when it labels parole as lenient. To the contrary, through their exercise of discretion, parole boards can target more violent and dangerous offenders for longer periods of incarceration. When states abolish parole or reduce parole authorities' discretion, they replace a rational, controlled system of "earned" release for selected inmates with "automatic" release for nearly all inmates (Burke, 1995). Non-parole systems may sound tough, but they remove an important gate-keeping role that can protect communities and victims.

Parole boards are in a position to demand participation in drug treatment, and research shows that coerced drug treatment is as successful in achieving abstinence as is voluntary participation. Parole boards can also require an adequate plan for a job and residence in the community – and that has the added benefit of refocusing prison staff and corrections budgets on transition planning.

Parole boards can meet personally with the victim. Involving victims in parole hearings has been one of the major changes in parole in recent years. Ninety percent of parole boards now provide information to victims on the parole process, and 70 percent allow victims to be present during the parole hearing.

Perhaps most important, parole boards can reconsider the tentative release date when more information about the offense and offender has been collected, and the offender's behavior in prison has been observed. Over 90 percent of U.S. offenders receive criminal sentences as a result of pleading guilty to offenses and not as a result of a trial. Usually they plead guilty to a reduced charge. Because there is no trial, there is little opportunity to fully air the circumstances surrounding the crime or the risks presented by the criminal. The parole board can revisit the case to discover how much injury the victim really suffered, or whether a gun was involved – even though the offense to which the offender pled, by definition, indicates no weapon was involved. Burke observes: "In a system which incorporates discretionary parole, the system gets a second chance to make sure it is doing the right thing" (Burke, 1995, p. 7).

Ironically, "no-parole" systems also significantly undercut postrelease supervision. When parole boards have no ability to select who will be released, they are forced to supervise a more serious parolee population, and not one of their own choosing. Parole officers say it is impossible to assure cooperation of offenders when offenders know they will be released regardless of their willingness to comply with certain conditions (e.g., get a job). And, due to prison crowding, some states are no longer allowing parolees to be returned to prison for technical violations. Parole officers say that parole has lost its power to encourage inmates toward rehabilitation and sanction parole failures. Field supervision tends to be undervalued and, eventually, underfunded and understaffed.

No one would argue for a return to the unfettered discretion that parole boards exercised in the 1960s. That led to unwarranted disparities. Parole release decisions must be principled, and incorporate explicit standards and clue process protections. Parole guidelines, which are used in many states, can establish uniformity in parole decisions, and objectively weigh factors known to be associated with recidivism. Rather than entitle inmates to be released at the end of a fixed time period, parole guidelines specify when the offender becomes eligible for release.

We also need to rethink who should be responsible for making parole release decisions. In most states, the chair and all members of the parole board are appointed by the governor; in two-thirds of the states, there are no professional qualifications for parole board membership. While this may increase the political accountability of the parole board, it also makes it highly vulnerable to improper political pressures. In Ohio, by contrast, parole board members are appointed by the director of corrections, serve in civil service positions, and must have an extensive background in criminal justice.

CONCLUDING REMARKS

Parole supervision and release raise complicated issues and deserve more attention than they now get. Nearly 700,000 parolees are doing time on U.S. streets. Most have been released to parole systems that provide few services and impose conditions that almost guarantee parolees' failure. Monitoring systems are getting better, and public tolerance for failure is decreasing. A rising tide of parolees is back in prison, putting pressure on states to build more prisons and, in turn, taking money away from rehabilitation programs that might help offenders stay out of prison. Parolees will continue to receive fewer services to help them deal with their underlying problems, assuring that recidivism rates and returns to prison remain high – and public support for parole remains low.

This situation represents formidable challenges to policy makers. The public will not support community-based punishments until they have been shown to "work," and they won't have an opportunity to "work" without sufficient funding and research. Spending on parole services in California, for example, was cut 44 percent in 1997, causing parole caseloads nearly to double (now at a ratio of 82-to-1). When caseloads increase, services decline, and even parolees who are motivated to change have little opportunity to do so.

In 2001, the United States is likely to have two million people in jails and prisons and more people on parole than ever before. If parole revocation trends continue, more than half of those entering prison in the year 2001 will be parole failures. Given the increasing human and financial costs associated with prison – and all of the collateral consequences parolees pose to families, children, and communities – investing in effective reentry programs may be one of the best investments we make.

REFERENCES

Anderson, E. (1990). *Streetwise: Race, class, and change in an urban community.* New York: W. W. Norton & Company.

Abramsky, S. (1999). When they get out. *The Atlantic Monthly, 283*: 6: 30–36.

Associated Press. (1999). *State agencies lost track of parolees.* Santa Barbara News Press.

Beck, A., Gilliard, D, & Greenfeld, L. (1993). *Survey of state prison inmates 1991.* Washington D.C.: Bureau of Justice Statistics.

Beck, A., & Mumola, C. (1999). *Prisoners in 1998.* Washington DC: Bureau of Justice Statistics.

Bloom, B., & Steinhart, D. (1993). *Why punish the children: A reappraisal of the children of incarcerated mothers in America.* San Francisco: National Council on Crime and Delinquency.

Blumstein, A. & Beck, A. (1999). Prison growth in U.S. Prisons, 1980–1986. In M. Tonry & Petersilia, J. (Eds.), *Prisons.* Chicago: University of Chicago Press.

Bonczar, T. P., & Beck, A. J. (1997). *Lifetime likelihood of going to state or federal prison.* Washington, D.C.: Bureau of Justice Statistics.

Bonczar, T., & Glaze, L. (1999). *Probation and parole in the United States.* Washington, D.C.: Bureau of Justice Statistics.

Bureau of Justice Statistics. (1999). *Mental health and treatment of inmates and probationers.* Washington D.C.: Bureau of Justice Statistics.

Burke, P. B. (1995). *Abolishing parole: Why the emperor has no clothes.* Lexington, KY: American Probation and Parole Association.

Ditton, P. (1999). *Mental health and treatment of inmates and probationers.* Washington D.C.: Bureau of Justice Statistics.

Hagan, J., & Dinovitzer, R. (1999). Collateral consequences of imprisonment for children, communities, and prisoners. In M. Tonry & J. Petersilia (Eds.), *Prisons.* Chicago: University of Chicago Press.

Holzer, H. (1996). *What employers want: Job prospects for less-educated workers.* New York: Russell Sage.

Legislative Analysts Office. (1999). *Crosscutting issues: Judiciary and criminal justice 1999* [cited 2/8100 2000]. Available from www.lao.cca.gov/analysis.

Liebling, A. (1999). Prison suicide and prisoner coping. In M. Tonry & J. Petersilia, J. (Eds.), *Prisons.* Chicago: University of Chicago Press.

Mauer, M. (1999). *The race to incarcerate.* New York: The New Press.

May, J. P. (2000). Feeding a public health epidemic. In J. P. May (Ed.), *Building violence. How America's rush to incarcerte creates more violence.* Thousand Oaks, CA: Sage.

McCaffrey, B. (1998). *Drug treatment in the criminal justice system.* Washington, D.C.: Office of National Drug Control Policy.

McDonald, D. C. (1999). Medical care in prisons. In M. Tonry & J. Petersilla (Eds.), *Prisons.* Chicago: University of Chicago Press.

Moore, J. (1996). Bearing the burden: How incarceration weakens inner-city communities. Paper presented at The Unintended Consequences of Incarceration, at New York City.

Petersilia, J. (1999). Parole and prisoner reentry in the United States. In M. Tonry & J. Petersilia (Eds.), *Prisons.* Chicago: University of Chicago Press.

Reno, J. (2000). Remarks of the Honorable Janet Reno on Reentry Court Initiative. February 10, U.S. Department of Justice, at http://www.usdoj.gov/ag/speeches/2000.

Rose, D., Clear, T., & Scully, K. (1999). *Coercive mobility and crime: Incarceration and social disorganization.* Paper presented at American Society of Criminology meetings, Toronto, Canada.

Sherman, L., Gottfredson, D., Mackenzie, D. Eck, J., Reuter, P., & Bushway, S. (1997). *Preventing crime: What works, what doesn't, what's promising.* College Park, MD: University of Maryland Press.

Simon, J. (1993). *Poor discipline: Parole and the social control of the underclass, 1890–1990.* Chicago: University of Chicago Press.

Snell, T. L. (1994). *Women in prison.* Washington D.C.: Bureau of Justice Statistics.

Stivers, C. (2000). *Impacts of discretionary parole release on length of sentence serviced and recidivism* (unpublished manuscript). School of Social Ecology, University of California, Irvine.

Tonry, M. (1999). *Reconsidering indeterminate and structured sentencing.* Research in Brief, National Institute of Justice, U.S. Department of Justice, Washington, D.C.

Travis, J. (2000). *But they all come back: Rethinking reentry, research in brief – Sentencing & Corrections: Issues for the 21st Century.* Washington, D.C.: U.S. Department of Justice, National Institute of Justice.

Western, B., & Beckett, K. (1999). *How unregulated is the U.S. labor market? The penal system as a labor market institution.* Princeton, NJ: Princeton University Press.

Wilson, J. Q., & Kalling, G. L. (1982). Broken windows. *Atlantic Monthly* (March): 29–38.

Wilson, W. J. (1987). *The truly disadvantaged: The inner city, the underclass, and public policy.* Chicago: University of Chicago Press.

Author Index

N

X

Y

Young, M. A., 257, 268
Young, S. E., 149
Young, V. D., 355, 364

Z

Zahnow, S., 68, 73
Zalba, S., 383, 385, 387, 393
Zamberlan, C., 158, 167

Zastrow, C., 193, 201, 207
Zemans, E., 394, 399
Zhang, S. X., 174, 185
Zigler, E., 179, 185
Zimmerman, R. S., 152, 167
Zinger, I., 336
Zito, J., 293, 299
Zmuidinas, M., 261, 268

Subject Index